MW01492239

The Heirs of Vijayanagara

THE HEIRS OF VIJAYANAGARA

Court Politics in Early Modern South India

Lennart Bes

LEIDEN UNIVERSITY PRESS

Funded by the Dutch Research Council (NWO): 317-51-010

Cover illustration: Detail of a textile hanging (one of seven related panels), probably produced in south-east India around the early seventeenth century, depicting a south Indian court, Brooklyn Museum, Museum Expedition 1913-1914, Museum Collection Fund, no. 14.719.7 (courtesy Brooklyn Museum).

Cover design: Geert de Koning
Lay-out: Crius Group

ISBN 978 90 8728 371 1
e-ISBN 978 94 0060 416 2
NUR 680

The rulers ... were the following:

King Raghunatha Nayaka ruled the kingdom of Cholamandalam [Tanjavur].
The king of Tiruchirappalli [Madurai] was Muttu Virappa Nayaka.
The previous king in the kingdom of Senji was Senji Varadappa Nayaka.
The name of the king of Ikkeri was Basavappa Nayaka.
The name of the king of Mysore was Srirangadeva [sic].

All of them were kings without a crown.

— Tamil scholars in Tanjavur listing the kings who ruled the "Tamils," in response to a question posed by German Pietist missionaries in 1712

(Daniel Jeyaraj and Richard Fox Young (eds), *Hindu-Christian Epistolary Self-Disclosures: "Malabarian Correspondence" between German Pietist Missionaries and South Indian Hindus (1712–1714)* (Wiesbaden, 2013), 258-9)

LEIDEN
UNIVERSITY PRESS

With compliments,

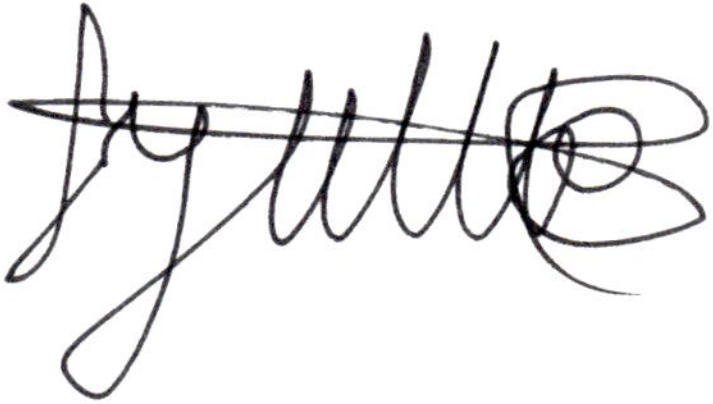

Leiden University Press

Rapenburg 73
2311 GJ Leiden
The Netherlands
Telephone: +31 71 527 1451
E-mail: info@lup.nl
Website: www.lup.nl

Contents

Acknowledgements

This book, my first monograph, is based on my doctoral dissertation, submitted to the Radboud University Nijmegen in 2018. I largely wrote it within the framework of the Eurasian Empires programme (2011-16), while based at Leiden University with the other participants in this project. Funded by the Dutch Research Council (NWO), the Eurasian Empires programme was devoted to the study of imperial dynasties, courts, and states in late medieval and early modern Asia and Europe from both comparative and connective perspectives.

The origins of my research, however, go back much further. It all started when I first wandered around south India as a backpacker and was struck by the great beauty and power embodied in the architectural remains of the region's past. Inspired and curious, I enrolled as an Indology student at Leiden University's Kern Institute, where I read the seminal work on south-east India's early modern Nayaka states by Velcheru Narayana Rao, David Shulman, and Sanjay Subrahmanyam: *Symbols of Substance* (1992). I was especially intrigued by the plea made on the book's very last pages to use the unexplored records of the Dutch East India Company (VOC) to study these kingdoms.

Ironically, although Dutch myself, I was hardly aware that these documents were important sources for Indian history. My subsequent forays into the VOC archives for my MA thesis on the Ramnad kingdom indeed showed their great relevance, especially when used together with south Indian sources. Inspired by the abovementioned plea, I have been working with these records ever since. The result is the present book, rather fittingly appearing in the series *Colonial and Global History through Dutch Sources*, which promotes historical research of non-European regions that combines local and Dutch source materials.

For getting here, I first of all wish to thank my two former supervisors, Peter Rietbergen of the Radboud University Nijmegen and Jos Gommans of Leiden University, both of whom were already involved in my research before the Eurasian Empires programme commenced. To Jos Gommans I owe my entry into academia in the first place. If it was not for his constant encouragement, constructive criticism, and generous friendship over the decades—and our various joint activities, such as the series *Dutch Sources on South Asia*—I would never have graduated, next found employment as a researcher at the Netherlands National Archives, and then obtained a doctoral degree, followed by a teaching stint at Leiden University's Institute for History. To Peter Rietbergen I am very grateful for his stimulating, calm yet warm, and highly valuable supervision. I have always greatly appreciated his insistence on putting my interests, ideas, and wishes first, despite his responsibility as my main supervisor to make me finish my dissertation within a reasonable period of time.

Further, nothing could have provided me with more inspiring, motivating, and pleasant surroundings to conduct my research than the wonderful Eurasian Empires programme. In both academic and social terms, I have strongly benefitted from the project's diverse and open-minded character. Thus, I am most thankful to its other supervisors, Jeroen Duindam and Maaike van Berkel, and its coordinators, Rebecca Wensma and later Josephine van den Bent, for their many supportive comments and good company. This also very much goes for my fellow imperial explorers in the programme: Barend Noordam, Cumhur Bekar, Elif Özgen, Hans Voeten, Kim Ragetli, Liesbeth Geevers, Marie Favereau-Doumenjou, Richard van Leeuwen, and Willem Flinterman. All of them contributed to making this an unforgettable experience, with a perfect combination of learning, leisure, and *ʿaṣabīya*.

From the scholarly world beyond my official academic setting, I would like to thank wholeheartedly Phillip Wagoner, who acted as an informal advisor. Right from the beginning of my doctoral research, his enthusiasm and knowledge of south Indian history, art, languages, and sources have been truly helpful, elevating, and reassuring. I am also sincerely grateful to Sanjay Subrahmanyam, who was already willing to answer my letters when I was still an undergraduate student (having just read *Symbols of Substance*). Over the years, his extensive and always prompt replies concerning all kinds of aspects of and sources for Indian history have been enormously beneficial and enriching.

I recall with much pleasure the numerous conversations I had with Gijs Kruijtzer, Sebastiaan Derks, and Thomas Rookmaaker, all of them historians or Indologists as well as close friends, a combination that rendered their input more personal and therefore very valuable. Moreover, I was really lucky to enjoy the privilege of regularly consulting Pauline Lunsingh Scheurleer whenever I insecurely entered the field of Indian art history, Anna Seastrand (in disguise or not) for her thoughts on a whole variety of subjects, Elaine Fisher for issues concerning Hinduism in the Nayaka states, and Herman Tieken for matters related to both Dravidian languages and Sanskrit.

Others who generously assisted me in overcoming linguistic (and other) hurdles include: Caleb Simmons, David Shulman, Elise Oosterom, Emma Flatt, Erik Gøbel, Katherine Kasdorf, Nikhil Bellarykar, and Subah Dayal, to all of whom I am most thankful. I also greatly appreciate the help of George Michell and John Fritz, spiders in the web of Vijayanagara and Nayaka studies, who put me in touch with all sorts of people, ranging from south Indian royalty to scholars in many different fields. Further, I am very grateful to the following people for allowing me to freely use their photos: Anna Dallapiccola, Clare Arni, Crispin Branfoot, Kesava Rajarajan, P.S. Ramanujam, Patrick Harrigan, and Purnima Srikrishna.

Additionally, over the course of time I mailed so many questions to other people—who usually responded with very kind and useful messages—that this study would have been much less complete had it been written in the pre-digital age. Among those I wish to thank for that, or for any other assistance, are: A. Govindankutty Menon, Abul Kalam Azad, Alicia Schrikker, Amita Kanekar, Amol Bankar, Ananya Chakravarti, André Wink, Anila Verghese, Anna Ślączka, Arjun Bali, Betty Seid, Bhaswati Bhattacharya, Bob Del Bontà, Cathleen Cummings, Christopher Chekuri, Claire Weeda, Cynthia Talbot, Daud Ali, Davesh Soneji, David Pierdominici Leão, Dirk Kolff, Dominic Goodall, Edgar Pereira, Elena Mucciarelli, Elizabeth Bridges, Genie Yoo, Gita Pai, Guido van Meersbergen, Hanna te Velde, Hemanth Thiru, Ilanit Lœwy Shacham, Indira Peterson, Ines Županov, Iris Farkhondeh, Jaap Geraerts, Janine Henry, Jason Schwartz, Mr Jayasimha of the Mythic Society, the late Jean Deloche, Jean-François Hurpré, Jennifer Howes, Jeyaseela Stephen, Jinah Kim, Joan-Pau Rubiés, Joanna Kirkpatrick, Jorge Flores, Judith Pollmann, K. Seshadri, K.S. Mathew, Kaarle Wirta, Kesavan Veluthat, Krishna Devaraya of Anegondi, Leslie Orr, Mahmood Kooria, Manjusha Kuruppath, Manu Devadevan, Margarida Borges, Marika Sardar, Marilyn Hedges, Mary Storm, Meenu Rabecca, Michael Linderman, Michael Pearson, Mrinalini Vasudevan, Nadeera Seneviratne-Rupesinghe, Nobuhiro Ota, Noelle Richardson, Pamela Price, Paolo Aranha, Patrick Olivelle, Pedro Pinto, Peter Bisschop, Pierre Moreira, Pius Malekandathil, Prithvi Datta Chandra Shobhi, Pushkar Sohoni, Remco Raben, Rosemary Crill, Roy Fischel, Samuel Ostroff, Sanne Muurling, Shelley Christine Lamare, Stephen Markel, Suchitra Balasubrahmanyan, Sukhad Keshkamat, Swarnamalya Ganesh, the late Teotonio de Souza, Tristan Mostert, Valérie Gillet, Valerie Stoker, Venkatesh Jois Keladi, Whitney Cox, Y. Subbarayalu, Y.H. Nayakwadi, and several anonymous reviewers.

Many others contributed to the warm academic environment in which I could tackle my research, in particular: Anita van Dissel, Anjana Singh, Carolien Stolte, Hugo s'Jacob, the late J.C. Heesterman, Johan & the Huizingas, Leonard Blussé, Lodewijk Wagenaar, Markus Vink, Michiel van Groesen, Murari Kumar Jha, Norifumi Daito, Olivier Hekster, Paul van der Velde, Pimmanus Wibulsilp, Sanne Ravensbergen, Suze Zijlstra, Tanja Döller and other staff members of the Radboud University Nijmegen's Faculty of Arts, and the wider Cosmopolis community at the Institute for History of Leiden University.

I am also grateful for the comments of audiences to whom I presented my research in earlier stages. Spanning the decade from 2011 to 2021, these occasions included the Eurasian Empires summer schools and concluding conference at the Universities of Leiden and Amsterdam, the Encompass conference at the University of Colombo, the Empire in Asia conference at the National University of Singapore, the Vijayanagara and Nayaka seminars on new research directions at the University of Chicago, the Indian History Congress at Thiruvananthapuram's University of Kerala, the Cross-Cultural Diplomacy workshop at the University of Warwick, the Indian Renascences Coffee Break conference at the Universität Tübingen, the Cosmopolitan Kalamkaris seminar at Delhi's National Museum Institute, the International Convention of Asia Scholars at Leiden, the Deccan Heritage Foundation webinar series, guest lectures at Kochi's Sree Sankaracharya University of Sanskrit, at Yogyakarta's Universitas Gadjah Mada, and at the Universities of Antwerp, Groningen, Nalanda, Oxford, and Tokyo, and various small-scale meetings in Leiden.

Exchanging ideas, experiences, and advice with all the people mentioned above has really turned out to be one of the great joys of academia for me. Of course, despite all this much appreciated help, the errors that are undoubtedly present in this study solely remain my responsibility. That applies to any of the ideas, assumptions, and conclusions presented here, too.

Also, I wish to show my appreciation for the helpful repositories where I consulted unpublished sources, in particular my delightful former colleagues at the Netherlands National Archives, the great staff at the British Library's Asian & African Studies reading room, and the unforgettable employees of the Tamil Nadu Archives. Moreover, I would like to mention Yde Bouma, who produced the two wonderful maps in this book, and Claire O'Halloran and Kate Delaney, who checked my English in this whole text and in parts of it, respectively.

I must further acknowledge the *Journal of Economic and Social History of the Orient*, *Leidschrift*, and *Modern Asian Studies*, journals in which earlier publications of mine have appeared, and sections of which I have used (largely in modified form) in the present work. Additionally, I am thankful to the Institut Français de Pondichéry and the École française d'Extrême-Orient (EFEO) for allowing me to use photos of the Minakshi Sundareshvara Temple in Madurai and the Narumpunadasvami Temple in Tiruppudaimarudur. I am also grateful to the Brooklyn Museum, the British Library Board, and the Marg Foundation for their permission to reproduce a south Indian textile hanging, a British map, and a photo of the Subrahmanya Shrine in Tanjavur, respectively.

Furthermore, I am both happy and sad to thank my parents Con and Loekie, who, each in their very own manner, always stimulated my interest in India and its history. Without them, I would have neither finished school, nor been introduced to Asia, nor had the chance to travel there over and over again. I dedicate this work to their memory, my mother unfortunately having passed away shortly before my doctoral scholarship started, and my father just as I finished the final draft of this book. Some credit should go to my brother Niels, too, whose occasional mildly ironic remarks on my academic pursuits kept me seeing things in perspective.

Finally, my very dear and beautiful Jinna provided more support and encouragement than one could ever hope to receive from a partner. Despite her habit—as a true medievalist—of always questioning my interpretation of historical sources, she inspired me academically as well as morally. She bore with my endless ponderings on the possible meanings of royal dress styles in south India, patiently listened to my supposedly funny stories from the Dutch East India Company records, and endured me as I moaned over the burden of describing more than ninety successions to south Indian thrones. Yet, she was also willing to read my writings, comment on both style and contents, and still make sure I stayed happy. I owe her far more than these few words can express.

Amsterdam, December 2021

List of Maps, Tables, and Illustrations

Maps

Tables

Illustrations

List of Abbreviations

AAS	Asian & African Studies department (in BL, formerly Oriental & India Office Collections, or OIOC).
AM	Additional Manuscripts (in BL/MMC).
ANRI	*Arsip Nasional Republik Indonesia* (National Archives Republic Indonesia), Jakarta.
BC	*Buitenland* collection ("foreign countries") (in ANRI).
BL	British Library, London.
DCGCC	Archives of the Dutch Central Government of Coastal Ceylon (in DNA).
DNA	Department of National Archives, Colombo.
DR	Dutch Records (in TNA).
HRB	*Hoge Regering Batavia* collection (Batavia High Government) (in NA).
MG	Mackenzie General collection (in BL/AAS).
MM	Mackenzie Miscellaneous collection (in BL/AAS).
MMC	Manuscript and Map Collections (in BL).
MT	Mackenzie Translations collection (in BL/AAS).
NA	*Nationaal Archief* (National Archives), The Hague.
OI	Orme Collection: India (in BL/AAS).
OOV	Orme Collection: O.V. (in BL/AAS).
RA	*Rigsarkivet* (State Archives), Copenhagen.
TNA	Tamil Nadu Archives, Chennai.
VOC	(Archives of the) *Verenigde Oost-Indische Compagnie* (Dutch East India Company) (in NA).

Notes on Spelling and Citation

As this study concerns at least nine dynasties in five states, it includes terms and names from several Indian languages, principally Kannada, Marathi, Persian, Sanskrit, Tamil, and Telugu. From the accompanying five to six scripts, names of people, deities, castes and other groups, buildings, and geographic locations have been transliterated without diacritical marks with the aim to both approximate correct pronunciation and follow common spelling. Thus, for example, the ruler of Ramnad is referred to with the more familiar spelling "Setupati," rather than the exact transliteration of the Tamil original, *cētupati*.

Other non-English terms unknown to a broad readership—which besides the abovementioned Indian languages derive from Dutch and Portuguese—as well as titles of Indian literary texts have been transliterated with diacritical marks when applicable and are italicised. It has however proved impossible to ascertain the correct spelling in each and every case, for instance when it is unclear to which language words belong, different versions are found in secondary literature and even in primary sources, or words occur in several languages with slight variations.

This work contains a number of extensive literal quotations and detailed summaries of primary sources. These summaries are set in a slightly smaller font than the main text, while literal quotations have the same small font and are moreover indented. In literal quotes, punctuation marks have been added, long sentences broken into shorter ones, and lengthy passages divided into paragraphs so as to improve intelligibility. Citations from Dutch texts have generally been translated as literally as English grammar and readability allow. Both in such translations and in quotes from English texts in the Mackenzie collections, original spellings of names and Indian terms have usually been retained, whether cited in full or summarised.

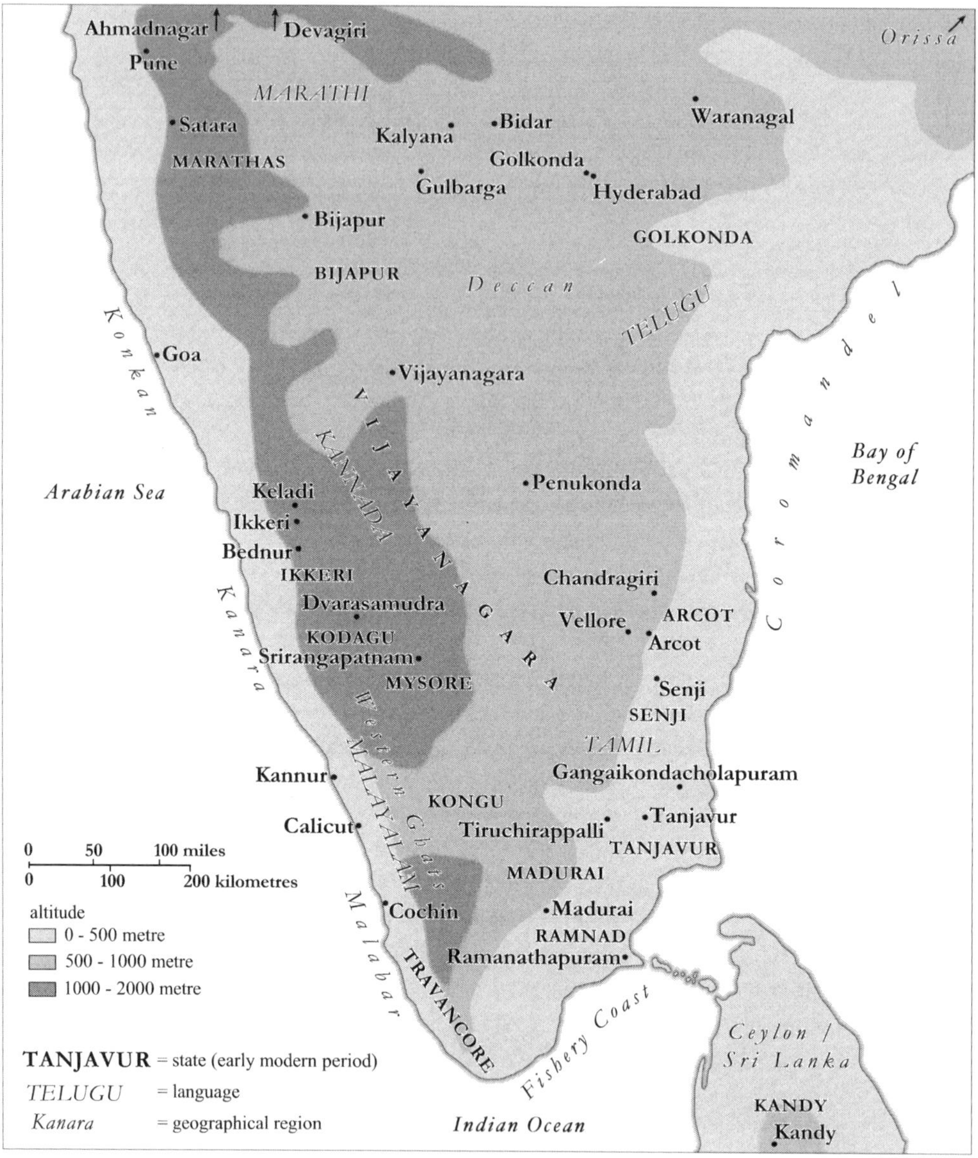

Major political centres and geographic and linguistic regions in late medieval and early modern south India.

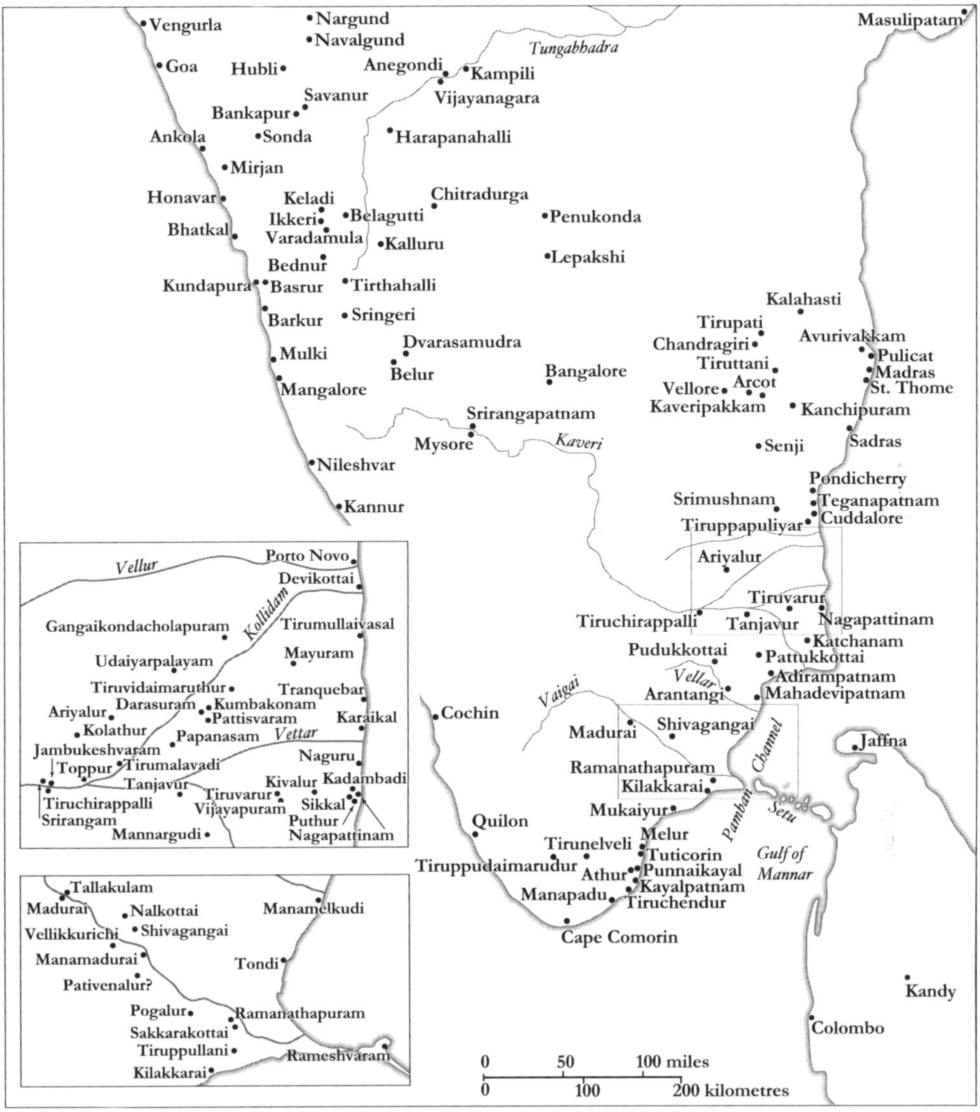

Towns, rivers, and waters in south India mentioned in this study.

Introduction

> "If Vijayanagar is now only its name and, as a kingdom, is so little remembered ..., it isn't only because it was so completely wiped out, but also because it contributed so little; it was itself a reassertion from the past ..."
>
> — V.S. Naipaul, *India: A Wounded Civilization* (1977).[1]

Thus wrote the renowned author V.S. Naipaul after his second trip to India in the mid-1970s. In these lines, he referred to the legacy of the south Indian Vijayanagara state, which existed from the fourteenth to the seventeenth centuries CE and is often considered the region's last empire.[2] After his visit to its capital—now best known as Hampi—Naipaul rather gloomily described the unusual landscape as unfriendly and declared the buildings and sculptures to have been archaic even when they were created.[3] In his view, Vijayanagara largely emulated the culture of

[1] V.S. Naipaul, *India: A Wounded Civilization* (London, 1977), 15.

[2] For discussions on Vijayanagara's imperial nature, see: Burton Stein, *Vijayanagara* (Cambridge, 1989), 27; Velcheru Narayana Rao and Sanjay Subrahmanyam, "Ideologies of State Building in Vijayanagara and Post-Vijayanagara South India: Some Reflections," in Peter Fibiger Bang and Dariusz Kołodziejczyk (eds), *Universal Empire: A Comparative Approach to Imperial Culture and Representation in Eurasian History* (Cambridge, 2012), 215-17; T.V. Mahalingam, *South Indian Polity* (Madras, 1967), 8; Jack A. Goldstone and John F. Haldon, "Ancient States, Empires, and Exploitation: Problems and Perspectives," in Ian Morris and Walter Scheidel (eds), *The Dynamics of Ancient Empires: State Power from Assyria to Byzantium* (New York, 2009); Carla M. Sinopoli and Kathleen D. Morrison, "Dimensions of Imperial Control: The Vijayanagara Capital," *American Anthropologist* (New Series) 97, 1 (1995); Carla M. Sinopoli, "From the Lion Throne: Political and Social Dynamics of the Vijayanagara Empire," *Journal of the Economic and Social History of the Orient* 43, 3 (2000); Elizabeth Jane Bridges White, "Beyond Empire: Vijayanagara Imperialism and the Emergence of the Keladi-Ikkeri Nayaka State, 1499-1763 C.E." (unpublished dissertation, University of Michigan, 2015), 19-25; P.K. Gode, "Ākāśabhairava-Kalpa, an Unknown Source of the History of Vijayanagara," in idem, *Studies in Indian Literary History*, vol. II (Bombay, 1954), 130-1. For an early seventeenth-century Flemish merchant's view, stating that Vijayanagara's ruler was considered an emperor rather than a king "in the entire East," see Jaques de Coutre, *Aziatische omzwervingen: Het levensverhaal van Jaques de Coutre, een Brugs diamanthandelaar 1591-1627*, ed. Johan Verberckmoes and Eddy Stols (Berchem, 1988), 168.

[3] In an earlier travel account—relating his first stay in India, in the early 1960s—Naipaul had been milder about the capital's remains, admiring its grand lay-out, impressive architecture, and spectacular natural surroundings. See V.S. Naipaul, *An Area of Darkness* (London, 1964), 215-16.

preceding states without adding much of its own. At its height, decay would already have set in, accelerated by the many wars this "Hindu kingdom" fought with its Muslim-ruled neighbours. And after what Naipaul regarded as an inevitable conquest by these sultanates, Vijayanagara presumably vanished entirely.[4]

But although perhaps currently not well remembered, Vijayanagara was neither completely wiped out nor did it innovate and contribute "little." During its gradual fragmentation from the sixteenth century onward, the empire gave rise to several succeeding kingdoms—reigned over by former vassals—that flourished in the following centuries. Some of them survived until the British came to dominate south India in the late eighteenth century or even beyond India's independence in 1947. These so-called Vijayanagara successor states derived their origins, legitimacy, political organisation, court culture, art, architecture, and so on, at least partially from their parental empire, rather than from the older polities mentioned by Naipaul. Indeed, Vijayanagara contributed substantially, and in many different fields, to its successors and remained a political and cultural focus point for south Indian royal courts right into the colonial period.

Those politico-cultural legacies of Vijayanagara among its heirs form the general theme of the present research. It deals with what is here termed "court politics": political culture and political developments at the royal courts of these states, covering both single events and long-term patterns. Phrased differently, this study defines court politics as activities of rulers, courtiers, and other people that affected the courts' political functioning. Thus, court politics comprise the strategies employed by various parties to preserve or enhance their power or status at court, and the reactions of others to these strategies, be they supportive or antagonistic. In particular, this work is concerned with the role of dynasties in court politics and investigates how ruling families achieved, maintained, legitimised, displayed, and finally lost their positions.

Court politics being a vast, multi-faceted subject, this research must limit itself to a selection of its aspects. It deals consecutively with dynastic foundations, successions to the throne, the power of courtiers, court protocol and insults, politico-cultural influences from Muslim-ruled states, and relations between the successor states—with a chapter devoted to each topic. To gain an optimal view of these matters, extensive bodies of local (south Indian) as well as external

[4] Naipaul, *India: A Wounded Civilization*, 14-18. Notably, it seems Naipaul did not so much stress the idea of Vijayanagara as a bulwark of Hinduism (like several historians have done) as emphasise its supposed archaic nature and lack of innovation. For some responses to Naipaul's writings on Vijayanagara, in particular its perceived Hindu character, see: Sanjay Subrahmanyam, *Is "Indian Civilization" a Myth? Fictions and Histories* (Ranikhet, 2013), 4; William Dalrymple, "'Sir Vidia Gets It Badly Wrong'," *Outlook* (15 Mar. 2004); V.K. Bawa (ed.), "Rama Raya and the Fall of the Vijayanagara Empire: V.S. Naipaul versus William Dalrymple," *Deccan Studies* II, 2 (2004).

(European) primary sources are investigated and juxtaposed, a combination that is only possible from the period under study onward.

The overall approach of this research is a systematic comparison of court politics in several Vijayanagara successor states, both among these kingdoms and with the empire itself. A comparative analysis of the courts and dynasties of Vijayanagara and its heirs has hitherto not been conducted, and this study hopes to fill that gap to some extent. Central questions are: How did these states resemble and differ from each other with regard to court politics? Did the heirs of Vijayanagara form a distinct group? How did Vijayanagara's legacies manifest themselves at the successors' courts? And in addition to what was inherited from the empire, how were court politics shaped by features that varied among the heirs—like the dynasties' origins and the kingdoms' geographic conditions—and by broader developments in the region? Further, what were the general characteristics of court politics in these states and what consequences did these have for the position of kings? And how does all this relate to previous research, not only on Vijayanagara and its successors but also on earlier south Indian courts, for which external sources are non-existent or at best very limited?

Besides "court politics," other central concepts in this work—court, dynasty, and courtier—need to be specified, the more so since these European terms do not necessarily have clear equivalents in the languages of Vijayanagara and its heirs.[5] "Court" is often defined as the spatial abode of a ruler as well as the social circle around him or her. This two-fold meaning is found both in several south Indian terms and within the European idea of courts. Words like *āsthānam*, *kolu(vu)*, and *(per)olugu* (appearing in several variations in Dravidian languages), and *sabhā* (Sanskrit) all include spatial as well as social aspects, denoting the residence and the retinue of the ruler.[6] Therefore, in this research too, "court" is used as a broad term, indicating both the royal palace complex or moving camp and all people present there, in whatever capacity. Courts are here considered to have been not strictly demarcated entities but fluid, open-ended communities partly overlapping with the rest of society.

For "dynasty," the most common south Indian word appears to have been *vaṃśam* (deriving from Sanskrit and its spelling again varying in Dravidian languages), meaning "family" or "lineage." South Indian dynastic chronicles are

[5] These include Kannada, Tamil, and Telugu, which are Dravidian languages (native to south India), and Sanskrit and Marathi, which belong to the Indo-Aryan language family (originating in north and west India).

[6] The often used term *darbār* (adopted from Persian into many Indian languages) is more specific, referring to the king's physical and spiritual presence at assemblies. Thus, it differs from the concept of "court" as used here.

regularly referred to as *vaṃśāvaḷi* and *vaṃśa carita*, "family line" or "family history." In agreement with this broad meaning, in this study dynasties comprise not just series of rulers but also their extended families, including collateral branches, in-laws, and adoptees. As shown in Chapter 2, even such distant family members could succeed to the throne. Consequently, the terms "dynasty," "royal family," and "(royal) house" are used here interchangeably.

Finally, for want of a better term, this work employs the notion of "courtier," which is somewhat problematic as it has no fixed meaning in south Indian history, let alone a clear European parallel. In accordance with the discussion of "court" above, a wide definition of "courtier" is adopted here, covering basically everyone somehow active at court—continuously or intermittently—such as officials and servants of all kinds, the entire royal family, and regular visitors from beyond the court. The term "courtier" is discussed in more detail in the introduction to Chapter 3.[7]

All aforementioned thematic chapters cover the courts of Vijayanagara itself and a selection of its heirs. Getting a grasp of the multitude of royal houses reigning over these states is something of a challenge, but this dynastic constellation can be briefly summarised as follows. Four consecutive families ruled Vijayanagara: the Sangamas, Saluvas, Tuluvas, and Aravidus. From the early sixteenth century on, under the latter two houses, several provincial chiefs appointed by the imperial court founded their own dynasties, five of which came to reign over relatively large and increasingly autonomous kingdoms while the empire disintegrated. These main successor states were Madurai, Tanjavur, Senji, and Ikkeri—all ruled by so-called Nayaka houses—and Mysore, governed by the Wodeyar dynasty. The first three of these kingdoms were located in the empire's south-eastern Tamil-speaking zone, the other two in the north-western region where Kannada was spoken.

In the course of the seventeenth century, some of Vijayanagara's heirs themselves fragmented or were taken over by other dynasties. The Ramnad kingdom, ruled by the Setupati house, gradually seceded from Madurai. Tanjavur's Nayaka rulers were replaced by the Bhonsle (or Maratha) house, which originated in western India. The other main Nayaka dynasties in the Tamil area, Senji and Madurai, and the last rulers of Vijayanagara itself, were also overthrown in the seventeenth and early eighteenth centuries. The two successor houses in the Kannada area,

[7] I thank David Shulman, Phillip Wagoner, Caleb Simmons, Nikhil Bellarykar, Gijs Kruijtzer, and Herman Tieken for discussing these Indian terms with me. See also Nicholas B. Dirks, *The Hollow Crown: Ethnohistory of an Indian Kingdom* (Cambridge, 1987), xxvii, 75. For general descriptions of these concepts, see: Jeroen Duindam, *Dynasties: A Global History of Power, 1300–1800* (Cambridge, 2016), 4, 157-9, 235-6; idem, "The Court as a Meeting Point: Cohesion, Competition, Control," in Maaike van Berkel and Jeroen Duindam (eds), *Prince, Pen, and Sword: Eurasian Perspectives* (Leiden/Boston, 2018), 37-40, especially n. 14.

Mysore's Wodeyars and Ikkeri's Nayakas, suffered the same fate in the late eighteenth century, but the former dynasty was later reinstalled by the British colonial government as a quasi-independent monarchy. During this new phase, Ramnad's Setupatis and Tanjavur's Bhonsles were also incorporated into the colonial system, as demoted land-holding chiefs and pensioned-off kings, respectively. Thus, several dynasties lasted through the British period into independent India and still enjoy an informal regal status today.

For reasons explained below, the present work is largely concerned with four kingdoms—or five dynasties—among this variety of Vijayanagara's heirs: Ikkeri, Madurai, Ramnad, and Tanjavur, the last under both the Nayakas and the Bhonsles. This research limits itself to the period before the British came to control south India, when these states still held both formal and actual power: roughly the centuries between 1500 and 1800.

After this outline of the study's main research questions, concepts, and spatial and temporal coverage, the remainder of this chapter consists of a historical survey, a discussion of primary sources, a historiographic overview, and an explanation of this work's structure.

Historical Background

As said, this research largely focuses on the period from the early sixteenth to the late eighteenth centuries, often called the "early modern" age.[8] During this time Vijayanagara reached its zenith—signalling the beginning of its disintegration—followed by the emergence, flourishing, and decline of its heirs. But this study also considers the preceding "late medieval" era, which saw the rise and fall of Vijayanagara's predecessors and the foundation and growth of the empire itself. During the whole of these two periods, together spanning the major part of the second millennium, south India witnessed a succession of empires—or at least supra-regional powers—that fragmented into smaller, regional states, which in turn were absorbed or defeated by new empires that eventually broke up, too

[8] I use the terms "early modern" and "medieval" merely as convenient temporal markers. I do not take a stand here in debates on the applicability of these concepts, as used for European history, to (south) India's history. For some discussions on this issue, see: Daud Ali, "The Idea of the Medieval in the Writing of South Asian History: Contexts, Methods and Politics," *Social History* 39, 3 (2014); Sanjay Subrahmanyam, *Penumbral Visions: Making Polities in Early Modern South India* (New Delhi, 2001), 259-65; Hermann Kulke, *History of Precolonial India: Issues and Debates*, ed. Bhairabi Prasad Sahu, trans. Parnal Chirmuley (New Delhi, 2018), 141-52. See also Jeroen Duindam, "Rulers and Elites in Global History: Introductory Observations," in Maaike van Berkel and Jeroen Duindam (eds), *Prince, Pen, and Sword: Eurasian Perspectives* (Leiden/Boston, 2018), 9-10, n. 22.

(see table 1).[9] Despite those recurrent changes, memories of vanished dynasties lived on and often became part of the legitimation practices of succeeding royal houses, which cultivated or invented ties with former imperial overlords and other erstwhile polities.[10]

In the centuries preceding Vijayanagara's beginnings, south India was initially dominated by two powerful dynasties: the Chalukyas, reigning from Kalyana (or Kalyani) in the Kannada-speaking area on the northern Deccan plateau; and the Cholas, centred at Tanjavur and Gangaikondacholapuram in the south-eastern Kaveri River delta, where Tamil was spoken. By the eleventh century, both polities had grown far beyond their homelands, holding sway over various linguistic and political areas. When from the late twelfth century onward their power waned, smaller, subordinated states rose and attained autonomy.

Thus, by the thirteenth century, south India comprised several regional successor kingdoms, each located in a largely mono-linguistic zone and ruled by a royal house of local origin. The three main dynasties that succeeded the Chalukyas were all based in the Deccan. In this plateau's south-west and east respectively, the Hoysalas at their capital Dvarasamudra ruled a region of Kannada speakers, while the Kakatiyas, based at Warangal, governed a Telugu-speaking area. In the Deccan's north-west, the Yadavas (or Sevunas) at Devagiri reigned over a zone where Marathi was spoken. In addition, much of the peninsula's Tamil-speaking south, formerly under Chola rule, was controlled by the Pandyas of Madurai.

[9] The best-known overview of south India's history is K.A. Nilakanta Sastri, *A History of South India: From Prehistoric Times to the Fall of Vijayanagar* (Madras, 1975), but it pays little attention to Vijayanagara's heirs. A recent, historiographically revised history of the region, including the empire's successors, is found in Noboru Karashima (ed.), *A Concise History of South India: Issues and Interpretations* (New Delhi, 2014). For recent histories of late medieval and early modern India, placing the south in a wider context, see: Catherine B. Asher and Cynthia Talbot, *India before Europe* (Cambridge, 2006); Richard M. Eaton, *India in the Persianate Age 1000-1765* (London, 2019). A survey of India's history that pays more attention to the south than usual is Burton Stein, *A History of India* (Oxford, 1998). For discussions of historiography treating the south as a separate region, see: Janaki Nair, "Beyond Exceptionalism: South India and the Modern Historical Imagination," *The Indian Economic and Social History Review* 43, 3 (2006); Narayana Rao and Subrahmanyam, "Ideologies of State Building," 210-11.

[10] In addition to examples elsewhere in this study, concerning Vijayanagara and its successors, see for instance: Daud Ali, "Royal Eulogy as World History: Rethinking Copper-Plate Inscriptions in Cōḻa India," in Ronald Inden, Jonathan Walters, and Daud Ali (eds), *Querying the Medieval: Texts and the History of Practices in South Asia* (Oxford, 2000), for example 189, 192-3, 199-200; Richard M. Eaton and Phillip B. Wagoner, *Power, Memory, Architecture: Contested Sites on India's Deccan Plateau, 1300-1600* (New Delhi, 2014), 14-15.

Table 1: South India's succession of dynasties, 2nd millennium CE (strongly simplified), with arrows indicating close succession ties between polities.

until 13th cent.			CHOLAS				CHALUKYAS		
						↓	↓		↓
11th-14th cent.			Pandyas			Hoysalas	Kakatiyas		Yadavas
14th century					*DELHI SULTANATE conquests*				
				↓			↓		
14th-17th cent.			VIJAYANAGARA				BAHMANIS		
	↓	↓	↓	↓	↓	↓	↓	↓	↓
16th-18th cent.	Madurai	Tanjavur	Senji	Mysore	Ikkeri	Bijapur	Golkonda	Ahmadnagar	2 more
	↓	↓							
17th-18th cent.	Ramnad		*MARATHA conquests*				*MUGHAL conquests*		
18th-20th cent.					*BRITISH conquests*				

All these regional houses looked back to earlier states to justify or strengthen their position. The successor dynasties of the Chalukya house—itself tellingly named after the powerful Chalukyas of Badami in the Kannada region (sixth to eighth centuries)—imitated phrases from Chalukya inscriptions in their own epigraphy, adopted court offices and practices from their overlords, and tried to conquer the former imperial capital Kalyana. The Pandyas, as well as the Cholas for that matter, took their names from earlier, semi-mythical dynasties based in the same areas. At least since the medieval period, the Tamil-speaking lands comprised a number of politico-cultural regions or centres, called *maṇḍalams* (circles), that harboured a succession of polities, including Tondaimandalam in the north, Cholamandalam in the centrally located Kaveri River delta, and Pandyamandalam, with the ancient southern town of Madurai.[11] Notably, the main heirs of Vijayanagara that later appeared in the Tamil zone each occupied one of these *maṇḍalams*.[12]

[11] Some recent works on dynasties and polities preceding Vijayanagara include: Eaton and Wagoner, *Power, Memory, Architecture*, chs 1-2; Cynthia Talbot, *Precolonial India in Practice: Society, Region, and Identity in Medieval Andhra* (New Delhi, 2001), chs 1-4; Daud Ali, "The Betel-Bag Bearer in Medieval South Indian History: A Study from Inscriptions," in Manu Devadevan (ed.), *Clio and Her Descendants: Essays for Kesavan Veluthat* (Delhi, 2018), 537-47; Ali, "Royal Eulogy as World History."

[12] These terms were still used in the early modern period. For some references in Dutch East India Company records, see: *Nationaal Archief*, The Hague (hereafter NA), Archives of the *Verenigde Oostindische Compagnie* (Dutch East India Company, access no. 1.04.02, hereafter VOC), no. 1055, f. 275; no. 2147, f. 4838: treaty with Senji ("Tonda Mandalan"), Mar. 1610, instructions for Dutch envoys to Tanjavur ("Chiolemandelan"), Mar. 1730. For discussions of the Tamil *maṇḍalams*, see: Burton Stein, "Circulation and the Historical Geography of Tamil Country," *The Journal of Asian Studies* XXXVII, 1 (1977), 18-26; David Ludden, "Spectres of Agrarian Territory in Southern India," *The Indian Economic and Social History Review* 39, 2-3 (2002), 243-4; Jennifer Howes, *The Courts of Pre-Colonial South*

In the late medieval kingdoms emerging on the Deccan plateau from the former Chalukya realm—the abovementioned Hoysalas, Kakatiyas, and Yadavas—the close regional ties between territory, language, and dynasty were fuelled by local warriors who often belonged to castes (*jātis*)[13] with a low ritual status in society. A number of them bore the title of *nāyaka*, a broad designation that denoted a military leader, landholder, or local notable and could be assumed by anyone.[14] These warriors developed pastoral, sparsely inhabited, dry frontier zones into sedentary farming areas and patronised both long-venerated and newly built temples. Thus, they created integrative political and commercial networks.

Their influential role exemplified the relatively egalitarian character of these societies. Most valued here were individually acquired occupational and military skills, regardless of one's ancestry and caste. This view formed a marked contrast to the classical notion that status and power were based on hereditary aristocratic credentials—like a high caste—as had long been advocated by the priestly Brahmin *varṇa*, the highest of the four main caste categories. Indeed, even the Kakatiya rulers were proud members of the Shudra *varṇa*, the lowest category, instead of the second highest Kshatriya or warrior *varṇa*, to which kings traditionally belonged.[15]

These regional states were all annihilated in the early fourteenth century, following the expansion of the militarily superior north Indian Delhi sultanate under the Khalji and Tughluq houses. Although Delhi's rule in south India turned out to be short-lived, its impact was far-reaching. Until then dominated by local, "Indic" culture and religion, the region now assimilated strong influences from the Muslim-ruled Delhi sultanate, itself shaped by practices and ideas from the

India: Material Culture and Kingship (London/New York, 2003), 186-9. See also British Library: Asian & African Studies department (formerly Oriental & India Office Collections), London (hereafter BL/AAS), Mackenzie General collection (hereafter MG), no. 1, pt. 7D: "The present Maratta Rajas who are managing the country of Tanja-Nagaram," f. 69 (possibly translated from a Tamil text, see J.S. Cotton, J.H.R.T. Charpentier, and E.H. Johnston, *Catalogue of Manuscripts in European Languages Belonging to the Library of the India Office*, vol. I, pt. II, *The Mackenzie General and Miscellaneous Collections* (London, 1992), 8-9); Mackenzie Translations collection (hereafter MT), class VII (Telugu: Northern Circars), no. 23: "Chronological account of Bijayanagar," f. 134 (translated from a "Gentoo [Hindu] book" in 1797).

[13] *Jāti*: endogamous, commensal, corporate group ranked in society on perceived level of ritual purity.

[14] For recent historiographic surveys of *nāyakas*, see for instance: Nobuhiro Ota, "A Reappraisal of Studies on *Nāyakas*," *Journal of Karnataka Studies* 5, 2 (2008); Manu V. Devadevan, *A Prehistory of Hinduism* (Warsaw/Berlin, 2016), 128-33.

[15] Talbot, *Precolonial India in Practice*, chs 1-4. For a summary, see Richard M. Eaton, *A Social History of the Deccan, 1300-1761: Eight Indian Lives* (Cambridge, 2005), 12-16.

Persian-speaking world. These were manifest in, for instance, political and social organisation, court culture, law, art, and military technology. After Delhi's conquest of the south, its sultans installed their own servants, but also native chiefs such as *nāyakas*, as landholders and commanders in the region. By 1340, however, insurgences had forced the sultanate to retreat from south India.

One of Delhi's rebellious commanders formed a powerful sultanate in the northern Deccan, ruled by the Bahmani house from its capitals at Gulbarga and Bidar. But in the late fifteenth century, the Bahmani state fragmented into five successor sultanates, including those of Bijapur, Golkonda, and Ahmadnagar. The sequence of politico-military appointments by Delhi in south India and the subsequent power vacuum after its withdrawal also provided excellent opportunities for ambitious local warriors and chiefs, like *nāyakas*. Among them were the Sangama brothers, who, after a period of military service for one or several rulers, founded a dynasty of their own in the southern Deccan. Thus arose around the 1340s the Vijayanagara state, with its headquarters at the abode of a regional Hindu deity, located in a dry and thinly populated Kannada-speaking area. Although only this capital was named Vijayanagara ("city of victory") and the Sangamas themselves called their realm Karnataka,[16] modern historiography has used the former term to refer to the empire as a whole. The new kingdom soon acquired imperial dimensions and came to encompass large parts of south India, including fertile, heavily populated coastal areas and covering several linguistic zones, most notably the Kannada-, Telugu-, and Tamil-speaking regions. These various areas harboured vastly different types of society, both sedentary (such as priests, peasants, artisans, and traders) and semi-nomadic (like herdsmen, warriors, and forest dwellers).

The Vijayanagara court also greatly extended its religious patronage, as shown both in the building of temples for pan-Indian Hindu gods in the capital and in endowments to sanctuaries and Brahmins in distant, recently annexed regions. But, although the emperors professed various and changing strands of Hinduism—reflecting efforts to forge ties with different religious power bases—their polity possessed many characteristics found in its Muslim-ruled neighbours.

16 See, for instance: Shrinivas V. Padigar, "Inscriptions of the Vijayanagara Rulers: Volumes: I to III (Kannada Inscriptions)," in Shrinivas Ritti and Y. Subbarayalu (eds), *Vijayanagara and Kṛṣṇadēvarāya* (New Delhi/Bangalore, 2010), 160-1; Vasundhara Filliozat, "Hampi – Vijayanagar," in G.S. Dikshit (ed.), *Early Vijayanagara: Studies in Its History & Culture (Proceedings of S. Srikantaya Centenary Seminar)* (Bangalore, n.d. [1988]), 183-4; Subrahmanyam, *Penumbral Visions*, 186, 229. The Dutch also used corruptions of the term Karnataka for Vijayanagara. See: NA, VOC, no. 2317, f. 329; no. 2631, ff. 407-10: final reports (*memorie van overgave*) of Coromandel Governors Adriaan Pla and Jacob Mossel, Feb. 1734, Feb. 1744; *Beknopte historie, van het Mogolsche keyzerryk en de zuydelyke aangrensende ryken* (Batavia, 1758), 1.

Unlike preceding regional kingdoms, Vijayanagara became a transregional, multi-ethno-lingual, outward-looking state, like the Bahmani sultanate and its successors. Many of the aforementioned aspects of Perso-Islamic political culture manifested themselves in Vijayanagara. This transformation was partially linked to military developments, including the need for war horses and soldiers with special skills and the incorporation of *nāyakas* into the imperial system. Over the centuries, many such warriors migrated from the Deccan to the peninsula's south—where they came to be known as *vaḍugas* or northerners—taking their languages and martial ethos with them.

With the empire's expansion came commercial and monetary changes, too, like a growing dependency on long-distance trade and revenue collection. As for the latter, fiscal management was one of several administrative and financial activities in which Brahmins had now become engaged. At courts, ports, markets, and fortresses, they served as ministers, bankers, scribes, merchants, and accountants. As for overseas trade, besides all sorts of Asian mercantile networks this involved from around 1500 the Portuguese *Estado da Índia* ("State of India") under a viceroy seated in Goa, followed about a century later by the chartered trading companies of the Dutch, the English, and the Danes, and after some further decades the French. In their wake came European missionaries, travel writers, mercenaries, artists, and private traders.

Between the late fifteenth and late sixteenth centuries, the role of military men remained decisive in Vijayanagara's politics. Imperial generalissimos usurped the throne three times, in each case leading to a new dynasty. After the rule of the Sangama and Saluva houses, Vijayanagara's power and glory are generally thought to have reached their zenith in the first half of the sixteenth century under the Tuluva dynasty. This was also the time when the empire started disintegrating. The Vijayanagara court had gradually and partially replaced a system that left rulers of subjugated regions in place as long as they acknowledged their overlord, with the practice of appointing imperial relatives, generals, and other courtiers as governors in far-flung or newly conquered territories.

This created opportunities for ambitious warriors once again. Several governors and chiefs—some commanding fertile, populous, and wealthy coastal areas far removed from the empire's dry core zone—founded dynasties of their own that grew ever more autonomous. They were allowed to maintain their increasingly regal positions in return for military, financial, and ceremonial support to the central court. Many of these houses bore the title of "Nayaka," referring to their martial origins as *nāyakas* and continuing the dominant political role of warriors from low-ranking castes in Vijayanagara and its immediate predecessors. Besides referring to a military function, the term *nāyaka* thus came to be used as a dynastic name by various newly emerging royal families: the Nayaka houses that ruled many of the Vijayanagara successor states.[17]

The empire's fragmentation accelerated when in 1565 its troops were defeated and the capital was attacked by the combined armies of the neighbouring Deccan sultanates,[18] after Vijayanagara had humiliated them militarily and diplomatically for ages. The imperial household was forced to flee south-eastward and became a court on the run of sorts, every few decades relocating between the towns Penukonda, Chandragiri, and Vellore. Now under the reign of the Aravidu house, the empire continued to shrink during the following years.[19]

By the seventeenth century, large parts of Vijayanagara's former territory were ruled by a handful of powerful dynasties that had originated from imperial governorships. Referring to the three most prominent heirs in the Tamil-speaking region, in 1675 a high official of the Dutch East India Company, Rijcklof van Goens, described this political state of affairs as follows:

> The land of Tansjaour [Tanjavur] ... has since long been a member of the Carnaticase realm [Vijayanagara], but it has always had its own sovereign [*souvereijne*] princes, named Naick [Nayaka] by them, being related to the Carnaticasen king—[as are] the Naiken of Madure [Madurai] and Singier [Senji]—in the same manner as the elector-kings of Germany to the emperor, or it may be at least compared to that ...[20]

[17] In the early modern period, the *nāyaka* title was still borne by a wide variety of people. To mention one unusual case, in 1672 at the port of Tuticorin the Dutch Admiral Hendrik Adriaan van Rheede conferred on a locally employed soldier the designation of "Neijke" in return for his services to the Dutch East India Company. See Department of National Archives, Colombo (hereafter DNA), Archives of the Dutch Central Government of Coastal Ceylon (access no. 1, hereafter DCGCC), no. 2672, ff. 15v-16: final report of Tuticorin's chief (*opperhoofd*) Laurens Pijl, Dec. 1672.

[18] For some recent, revisionist literature on the famed "Talikota" battle of 1565 and the extent of the destruction of the imperial capital, see respectively: Sanjay Subrahmanyam, *Courtly Encounters: Translating Courtliness and Violence in Early Modern Eurasia* (Cambridge (MA)/London, 2012), ch. 1; Mark T. Lycett and Kathleen D. Morrison, "The 'Fall' of Vijayanagara Reconsidered: Political Destruction and Historical Construction in South Indian History," *Journal of the Economic and Social History of the Orient* 56, 3 (2013).

[19] For some relatively recent overviews of the political history of Vijayanagara and connections with its predecessors and successors, see: Stein, *Vijayanagara*; Eaton, *A Social History of the Deccan*, chs 1-4; Talbot, *Precolonial India in Practice*, ch. 5; Eaton and Wagoner, *Power, Memory, Architecture*, chs 1, 3; Velcheru Narayana Rao, David Shulman, and Sanjay Subrahmanyam, *Symbols of Substance: Court and State in Nāyaka Period Tamilnadu* (Delhi, 1992), ch. II.

[20] NA, *Hoge Regering Batavia* collection (Batavia High Government, access no. 1.04.17, hereafter HRB), no. 542 (unpaginated, 1st document, c. halfway, section "Tansjaour"): description of Ceylon, Madurai, south Coromandel, Malabar, and Kanara by Rijcklof van Goens, Sept. 1675 (translation mine); quote also partly included in François Valentijn, *Oud en Nieuw Oost-Indiën*, vol. 5 (Dordrecht, 1726), 8th book, 233.

The comparison to Germany—more accurately the Holy Roman Empire, whose ruler was chosen by a college of royal and ecclesiastical electors—seems far-fetched and the Nayakas certainly did not officially elect Vijayanagara's emperors.[21] Yet, Van Goens' remark shows that these dynasties were considered to have grown independent for all practical purposes but continued to recognise Vijayanagara's formal supremacy. As the English put it in 1642, "… every Naique is a king in his owne country, and will attend the greate kinge [of Vijayanagara] at theire pleasure."[22]

South India had thus entered an age of regional kingdoms again, but this new political constellation differed from the regional kingdoms that had preceded the empire. The close links between dynasty, language, and territory found under the Hoysalas, Kakatiyas, Yadavas, and Pandyas no longer existed. Vast parts of the Kannada-, Telugu-, and Marathi-speaking areas were now governed by the Deccan sultans, who were of Central and West Asian descent and whose principal court languages were Persian and to a lesser extent Dakhani.[23] Local kings still held sway over the remainder of the Kannada zone, but this region was divided into a number of states. And much of the Tamil area was ruled by several *vaḍuga* houses, families with a northern, Telugu background.

It may be asked which states could actually be regarded as successors of Vijayanagara. Modern historiography has generally distinguished five kingdoms as the major offshoots of the empire: Tanjavur (or Tanjore), Madurai, and Senji (or Gingee) in the Tamil area, and Ikkeri (also called Keladi) and Mysore in the Kannada zone.[24] That these five were considered the main heirs by contemporaries, too, is suggested by historical notions in the region reported by European visitors. In 1712, when German Pietist missionaries enquired who were the rulers of the "Tamils," local scholars in Tanjavur mentioned the kings of Tanjavur, Madurai,

[21] However, in the 1640s the Jesuit Balthazar da Costa wrote that the Nayaka of Madurai, Tirumalai, declared the new (and last) Vijayanagara emperor, Sriranga III, could not be formally installed without the Nayakas' consent. See A. Saulière (ed.), "The Revolt of the Southern Nayaks" [pt. 1], *Journal of Indian History* XLII, I (1964), 97. Perhaps Van Goens' remark referred to the alleged influence of the Nayakas during the empire's last phase.

[22] William Foster (ed.), *The English Factories in India 1642–1645: A Calendar of Documents in the India Office, Westminster* (Oxford, 1913), 50; Henry Davison Love (ed.), *Vestiges of Old Madras 1640–1800, Traced from the East India Company's Records Preserved at Fort St. George and the India Office, and from Other Sources* (London, 1913), vol. I, 46.

[23] For languages in the Deccan sultanates, see Sumit Guha, "Transitions and Translations: Regional Power Vernacular Identity in the Dakhan, 1500-1800," *Comparative Studies of South Asia, Africa and the Middle East* 24, 2 (2004), 25-6.

[24] Stein, *Vijayanagara*, 130-3; Narayana Rao and Subrahmanyam, "Ideologies of State Building," 212-13.

Senji, Ikkeri, and Mysore.[25] Probably denoting the ongoing formal subordination of these monarchs to the now defunct Vijayanagara polity, the Tanjavur scholars added that these rulers were all "kings without a crown."[26] Further, in 1738 the governor of the Dutch settlements on south India's Coromandel (or eastern) Coast, Elias Guillot, wrote to his successor Jacob Mossel:

> Under the king of Carnatica [Vijayanagara] were in the past three prominent Naiks or monarchs, who paid their tribute, and at his coronation had to carry: ... the Naijk of Madure or Tritsjenapalli [Tiruchirappalli]—under whom the Theuver lord [of Ramnad] was a visiadoor [governor][27]—the spittoon, the Naijk of Singi the betel [-leaf] box,[28] and the Naik of Tansjour the fan. Apart from these Naijks, there were two other great visiadoors or generals [*veldwagters*], of Maijsjoer and Ikeri ...[29]

Regardless of this distinction made by both contemporaneous observers and current scholars, there were in fact all sorts of polities succeeding Vijayanagara in some way, and their number and shared characteristics are hard to determine. As said, Vijayanagara itself continued to exist under the Aravidu dynasty until the mid-seventeenth century, now based near the east coast in the Tamil-Telugu border zone. Having lost its glorious initial capital and much of its prestige, it had been practically reduced to a regional kingdom, although it still harboured imperial ambitions.

25 For the scholars' literal statement, see the introduction to Chapter 6.

26 Daniel Jeyaraj and Richard Fox Young (eds), *Hindu-Christian Epistolary Self-Disclosures: "Malabarian Correspondence" between German Pietist Missionaries and South Indian Hindus (1712–1714)* (Wiesbaden, 2013), 258-61.

27 The term "visiadoor" (from the Portuguese "vigiador," watcher or guard) was used by the Dutch as a generic reference to people with political or military power somehow subordinated to a higher authority. It could indicate kings who only nominally acknowledged an overlord (as in the quote above), semi-autonomous rulers of smaller principalities, local representatives of higher powers, guards, or even (foot)soldiers. See for instance: NA, VOC, no. 1231, f. 791; no. 1321, f. 881v; no. 1508, f. 172v: letters from Pulicat and Nagapattinam to Batavia, Oct. 1659, Aug. 1676, Oct. 1692; Sanjay Subrahmanyam, *Improvising Empire: Portuguese Trade and Settlement in the Bay of Bengal, 1500-1700* (Delhi, 1990), 191 (n. 9); idem, *Penumbral Visions*, 112.

28 For the court office of betel-bearer and the formalising, binding, and honouring functions of the donation of betel-leaves by kings to servants and visitors, see Ali, "The Betel-Bag Bearer."

29 NA, VOC, no. 2443, ff. 2679-80 (translation mine). See also: *Beknopte historie*, 1-2; J.E. Heeres and F.W. Stapel (eds), *Corpus diplomaticum Neerlando-Indicum: Verzameling van politieke contracten en verdere verdragen door de Nederlanders in het oosten gesloten, van privilegebrieven aan hen verleend, enz.*, vol. 1 (The Hague, 1907), 546. The latter Dutch source identifies the same five main successor states, declaring that "tributary to the Carnaticase king were the overlords of Maisoer, Jkeri, Madure, Tansjour, and Sinsij."

The seventeenth century also witnessed the emergence of various "indirect" successors of the empire. The Nayaka houses of Tanjavur and Senji were themselves succeeded by invading Maratha dynasties (belonging to the prominent Bhonsle family), after interludes of Madurai and Bijapur rule respectively. The Marathas originated from the Marathi-speaking north-west Deccan, which had never been part of Vijayanagara, and their links with the empire were therefore rather distant. Additionally, in the course of the seventeenth century, the kingdom of Ramnad in the south-east of the Tamil region seceded from Madurai, and, as its inclusion in the Dutch quote above indicates, it became an important state in its own right. In turn, Ramnad experienced several partitions itself in the decades around 1700, leading to the rise of the Pudukkottai and Shivagangai kingdoms.[30]

Besides the five main heirs of Vijayanagara and the abovementioned indirect successors, numerous other small (often still under-researched) states, with varying levels of autonomy, traced their origins and legitimacy back to the empire in various ways and to different degrees.[31] Three examples, among many, are Sonda in the Kannada region—also ruled by a Nayaka dynasty—and Ariyalur and Udaiyarpalayam in the Tamil zone. Their rulers were all powerful enough to maintain diplomatic contacts and conclude commercial treaties with the Portuguese, the Dutch, or the English.[32] Further, near the southernmost Kannada-Tamil boundary

[30] For Shivagangai, see Chapter 2 (Ramnad section). For Pudukkottai, see Dirks, *The Hollow Crown*, chs 4-6.

[31] One overview of such smaller polities is found in Henry Heras, *The Aravidu Dynasty of Vijayanagara*, vol. 1 (Madras, 1927), 172-93, 424-7, mentioning for example Yelahanka (among whose rulers was Kempe Gowda, founder of Bangalore), Belur, Chitradurga, Honavar, Bhatkal, Ullal, Gangolli, and Vellore, all but the last in the Kannada area. Other principalities in this region included Gersoppa, Barkur, Bangher, Harapanahalli, and Santebennuru. See: Sanjay Subrahmanyam, *The Political Economy of Commerce: Southern India 1500-1650* (Cambridge, 1990), 121; Devadevan, *A Prehistory of Hinduism*, 127-8. For some minor states in the central Tamil zone—for instance Ariyalur, Udaiyarpalayam, and Turaiyur—see: Lewis Moore, *A Manual of the Trichinopoly District in the Presidency of Madras* (Madras, 1878), 254-62; F.R. Hemingway, *Trichinopoly*, vol. I (Madras, 1907), 344-6, 350-3.

[32] For Ariyalur, see Chapters 1, 6 and previous note. For Udaiyarpalayam, like Ariyalur situated north-east of Tanjavur and supplying the Dutch with textiles, see previous note and: A. Vadivelu, *The Aristocracy of Southern India* (Madras, 1903), vol. II, 196-243; NA, VOC, no. 1343, ff. 65v, 91v; no. 1349, ff. 1405-7; no. 1463, ff. 173v, 215-16; no. 1617, ff. 67v-8v; no. 2631, ff. 412, 433: report on the Tanjavur lands, May 1679, letters from Nagapattinam to Batavia, from Pulicat to Gentlemen XVII, June-July 1679, Dec. 1688, June 1699, treaty with Udaiyarpalayam, 1688, final report of Jacob Mossel, Feb. 1744; *Beknopte historie*, 3. For Sonda (or Sunda), north of Ikkeri and producing pepper, see: NA, VOC, no. 1274, ff. 179v-80v; no. 2461, f. 92v: Basrur diary extract, July 1670, letter from Cochin to Batavia, Apr. 1739; Severine Silva, "The Nayaks of Soonda," *The Quarterly Journal of the Mythic Society* LXV, 2 (1974); A.R. Kulkarni, "The Chiefs of Sonda (Swādi) and the Marathas in the Seventeenth Century," in G.S. Dikshit (ed.), *Studies in Keladi History (Seminar Papers)* (Bangalore, 1981); João Melo, "Seeking Prestige and Survival: Gift-Exchange Practices between the Portuguese Estado da Índia and Asian Rulers," *Journal of the Economic*

lay the states of Kongu and Kodagu (or Coorg), the former ruled by yet another Nayaka house and the latter by a branch or close ally of Ikkeri's royal family.[33]

In the far south of the Tamil-speaking area there were several dozens of tiny polities—traditionally numbering seventy-two—whose rulers were known as Palaiyakkarars or, in its anglicised form, "Poligars." Although nominally subordinated to the Nayakas of Madurai, they regularly operated rather independently, especially after their overlords were overthrown in the 1730s. Partly originating in the Deccan and bearing the title of Nayaka, many of these houses mentioned Vijayanagara in their origin stories.[34] Some chiefs in the region where Marathi was spoken also produced texts referring to ancient ties with the empire, which served to back claims in judicial disputes. A principality in the far north-east of the Telugu area bore the very name of Vijayanagara (often spelled Vizianagaram), allegedly acquired during the reign of the empire's most celebrated monarch, Krishna(deva) Raya. And the chieftains of Belagutti in the Kannada region even declared that

and Social History of the Orient 56, 4/5 (2013), 686-8; B.S. Shastry, "The Portuguese and Immadi Sadashiva Raya of Swadi (Sonda), 1745-1764," *South Indian History Congress: Proceedings of Fifth Annual Conference* (Tirupati, 1987); Foster, *The English Factories in India 1668–1669* (Oxford, 1927), 111-12, 115-16, 268; Charles Fawcett (ed.), *The English Factories in India* (New Series, 1670-7, 1678-84), vol. I (The Western Presidency) (Oxford, 1936), 297-8, vol. III, *Bombay, Surat, and Malabar Coast* (Oxford, 1954), 403-4.

[33] For Kongu, see: C.M. Ramachandra Chettiar, "Rule of Vijayanagara over Kongu Country," in S. Krishnaswami Aiyangar *et al.* (eds), *Vijayanagara Sexcentenary Commemoration Volume* (Dharwar, 1936); T.V. Mahalingam, *Readings in South Indian History*, ed. K.S. Ramachandran (Delhi, 1977), 154; V. Rangachari, "The History of the Naik Kingdom of Madura," *The Indian Antiquary: A Journal of Oriental Research* XLIII (1914), 133-5. For Kodagu, see: B. Lewis Rice, *Mysore and Coorg: From the Inscriptions* (London, 1909), 133-6; Subrahmanyam, *Penumbral Visions*, 69-70, 76-9; "A Biographical Account of the Ancestors of the Present Rajah of Coorga," in *The Asiatic Annual Register, or, a View of the History of Hindustan, and of the Politics, Commerce and Literature of Asia, for the Year 1800* (London, 1801), section "Characters."

[34] For the Palaiyakkarars in the Tamil zone, see: K. Rajayyan, *Rise and Fall of the Poligars of Tamilnadu* (Madras, 1974); G. Revathy, *History of Tamil Nadu: The Palayams* (New Delhi, 2005); P.M. Lalitha, *Palayagars as Feudatories under the Nayaks of Madurai* (Chennai, 2009); T.V. Mahalingam (ed.), *Mackenzie Manuscripts: Summaries of the Historical Manuscripts in the Mackenzie Collection*, vol. I (Madras, 1972); Dirks, *The Hollow Crown*, chs 1-6. The last two works contain references to connections with Vijayanagara. For a published version, with English translation, of one of several texts listing these Palaiyakkarars—here 75, including the rulers of Ramnad, Pudukkottai, and Ariyalur—see S. Soundarapandian (ed.), "Palayappattu Vivaram / Estates of Polegars," *Bulletin of the Government Oriental Manuscripts Library* 28 (2001), 1-24. For other lists, see: William Taylor (ed.), *Oriental Historical Manuscripts in the Tamil Language, Translated with Annotations* (Madras, 1835), vol. II, 161-6; C.S. Srinivasachari, "The Southern Poligars and Their Place in the Political System," in D.R. Bhandarkar *et al.* (eds), *B. C. Law Volume*, pt. I (Calcutta, 1945), 246-9; idem, *Ananda Ranga Pillai: The "Pepys" of French India* (Madras, 1940), 200-5 (n. 22). The term Palaiyakkarars could refer to chieftains all over the Vijayanagara area. For examples in the Kannada and Telugu regions, see: J.C. Dua, *Palegars of South India: Forms and Contents of Their Resistance in Ceded Districts* (New Delhi, 1996), 1-2, 47-64; Subrahmanyam, *Penumbral Visions*, 72-3.

one of their sons was installed as Vijayanagara's emperor after the Aravidu ruler Tirumala had supposedly left no lawful heir to the throne.[35]

Mysore's late-eighteenth-century Muslim ruler Tipu Sultan, too, sought to connect himself to the empire, partly through presenting himself as the successor of Ikkeri's Nayakas and Mysore's Wodeyars, for instance continuing some of their religious activities.[36] As a final example, the kingdom of Kandy in central Ceylon (or Sri Lanka) might be regarded as an indirect successor state from 1739 onward, when its throne was occupied by kings professing to belong to Madurai's Nayaka family. Even though this kinship was remote, the claim served as an important justification for the royal position of what came to be called the Kandyan Nayakas.[37]

Given this wide range of kingdoms and dynasties, the question of what should be considered a heir of Vijayanagara can be answered in various ways. Any state that emerged, directly or indirectly, from the empire's disintegration or otherwise sought legitimation through some sort of association with Vijayanagara could be regarded as such. However, this study aims to focus on a selection of the larger successors that together represent as much political and socio-cultural diversity as possible. At the same time, substantial and diverse sets of primary sources should be available to research these kingdoms. As it turns out, five polities fit these criteria: Nayaka-ruled Ikkeri, Tanjavur, and Madurai, all direct heirs; Ramnad, an indirect successor; and Bhonsle-ruled Tanjavur, which because of its distant connection with Vijayanagara provides a useful counterpoint to the other kingdoms.

The Nayaka dynasties of Ikkeri, Tanjavur, and Madurai were direct heirs of Vijayanagara as their founders were installed by the empire itself. Therefore, politically and culturally, the courts of these states were closely related to that of Vijayanagara. Yet, these royal houses, and the kingdoms they governed, differed from each other, as well as from the various indirect successors and from the

[35] Sumit Guha, *History and Collective Memory in South Asia, 1200–2000* (Seattle, 2019), 113; Sri Sri Sri Raja Saheb, "The Origin of Vizayanagar in Kalinga," *Deccan History Conference (First Session)* (Hyderabad, 1945), 286-7; S. Ranganatha Rao, "The Beḷagutti Kaifiyats," *The Quarterly Journal of the Mythic Society* XXXV, 2 (1944), 69.

[36] Caleb Simmons, *Devotional Sovereignty: Kingship and Religion in India* (New York, 2020), 18, 33-4, 48-9, 58-9, 66-72.

[37] Lorna S. Dewaraja, *The Kandyan Kingdom of Sri Lanka 1707-1782* (2nd edition, Colombo, 1988), ch. II; Gananath Obeyesekere, "Between the Portuguese and the Nāyakas: The Many Faces of the Kandyan Kingdom, 1591-1765," in Zoltán Biedermann and Alan Strathern (eds), *Sri Lanka at the Crossroads of History* (London, 2017); Julius Valentijn Stein van Gollenesse, *Memoir of Julius Stein van Gollenesse, Governor of Ceylon 1743-1751, for His Successor Gerrit Joan Vreeland, 28th February, 1751*, ed. Sinnappah Arasaratnam (Colombo, 1974), 13; Joan Gideon Loten, *Memoir of Joan Gideon Loten 1752–1757*, ed. E. Reimers (Colombo, 1935), 3; W.Ph. Coolhaas *et al.* (eds), *Generale Missiven van Gouverneurs-Generaal en Raden aan Heren XVII der VOC*, vol. XI (The Hague, 2004), 423. See also Chapter 6 and the Epilogue of the present study.

imperial dynasties themselves. This was maybe most notable with respect to dynastic origins and geographic and demographic characteristics.

As for the former aspect, the Nayaka houses reigning at Madurai and Tanjavur (and Senji) rose after their founders achieved high military ranks at the Vijayanagara court and were appointed governors in areas far south of their place of origin. Consequently, the Tamil zone came to be ruled by *vaḍugas*, Telugu-speaking immigrants. In contrast, in the Kannada region, the kings of Ikkeri (and Mysore) descended from local chiefs, who were incorporated into the empire and recognised as rulers of their own realms. Besides these direct heirs, indirect successors gained power through secession—for instance the Setupatis of Ramnad, who broke off from Madurai—or by conquest, such as the Maratha Bhonsles of Tanjavur, who succeeded this kingdom's Nayaka house. Thus, some royal families had stronger local roots and therefore possibly held closer ties with individuals and groups at their courts than did houses of foreign origin, which perhaps maintained a certain distance from such parties.

The kingdoms' physical aspects also made them distinct from one another. The archives of the Dutch East India Company occasionally refer to the sizes of the various successor states. Several Dutch documents from around the mid-seventeenth century declare that Ikkeri ran along India's western Kanara and Malabar coasts from "Mirzee" (Mirjan?) near Ankola in the north, down to Nileshvar, some 50 miles south of the port of Mangalore, altogether stretching about 200 miles. Travelling to the kingdom's eastern boundaries in the interior from various points along the shore was said to take two to three-and-a-half days, which suggests distances of between approximately 40 and 80 miles.[38] The kingdom thus shared borders with Sonda, Bijapur, Mysore, and Kannur (or Cannanore, in Malabar), as well as several smaller principalities. Dutch reports of about a century later reveal that Ikkeri's then coastal strip still occupied more or less the same area, including the ports of Honavar, Bhatkal, Basrur (or Barcelore, near Kundapura), Barkur, Mulki, and Mangalore.[39] Secondary literature, based on other sources, presents a comparable

[38] Reports of Dutch diplomatic missions to Ikkeri make clear that the (largely uphill) journey from their coastal settlement at Basrur to the kingdom's capital Bednur, a distance of around 40 miles, took about two days. For an eighteenth-century Dutch description of this road—saying it was beautiful, tree-lined, clean, and safe even for foreigners sleeping with their pockets full of money—see Jacobus Canter Visscher, *Mallabaarse Brieven, behelzende eene naukeurige beschryving van de kust van Mallabaar* ... (Leeuwarden, 1743), 69.

[39] NA, VOC, no. 1224, ff. 74, 77-8v; no. 2601, ff. 169v-70: report on "Canara" (Ikkeri), July 1657, "Malabar dictionary," 1743; HRB, no. 542 (unpaginated, 1st document, c. halfway, after the section on Malabar): description of Ceylon, Madurai, south Coromandel, Malabar, and Kanara by Rijcklof van Goens, Sept. 1675; Hugo K. s'Jacob (ed.), *De Nederlanders in Kerala 1663-1701: De memories en instructies betreffende het commandement Malabar van de Verenigde Oost-Indische Compagnie* (The Hague,

demarcation of Ikkeri's territory, although it claims that parts of the kingdom's eastern limits lay over 100 miles from the shore.[40]

As for Tanjavur, Dutch records of the decades around the mid-eighteenth century state that this kingdom covered the area between the Kollidam (or Coleroon) River in the north and the lands of Ramnad and its offshoots in the south. The latter boundaries were often contested and regularly shifted, but generally seem to have run along a zone comprising the towns of Pudukkottai and Arantangi and the port of Adirampatnam on the eastern Coromandel Coast. In the west, Tanjavur neighboured on Madurai, the border lying between Tanjavur town and nearby Tiruchirappalli, one of Madurai's capitals. The Dutch wrote that Tanjavur encompassed five provinces, centred around the towns of Mannargudi, Pattukkottai, Papanasam, Kumbakonam, and Mayuram. All this considered, it must have roughly measured 50 to 70 miles both from north to south and from east to west.

The Ramnad kingdom, south of Tanjavur, was probably slightly bigger when it attained practical autonomy in the late seventeenth century, but it soon lost considerable parts of its territory when Pudukkottai and Shivagangai seceded from it. Besides, the border with Tanjavur appears to have moved southward in the first half of the eighteenth century, in the 1740s said to have reached the eastern shore at Manamelkudi. In the same period, but also in the mid-1670s for instance, Ramnad's southern littoral did not extend much further westward than the port of Kilakkarai.

Finally, Madurai, lying west of Tanjavur and Ramnad, was several times larger than those states. It stretched—still according to the Dutch—from Cape Comorin (Kanyakumari) and the major part of the Fishery Coast in the far south all the way north of the Kollidam River, where it bordered the kingdoms of Mysore, Senji, and Ariyalur, while the mountain range known as the Western Ghats marked its western limits. Although the Jesuit Bouchet claimed in the early eighteenth century that Madurai's size was similar to that of Portugal, the kingdom thus appears to have been somewhat smaller, covering about 200 miles from north to south and an average of around 60 miles from east to west. A largely similar territorial division between the major states is depicted in Dutch and British maps from the late seventeenth and mid-eighteenth centuries, respectively (see illustration 1).[41]

1976), 84, 192; Julius Valentijn Stein van Gollenesse, *Memoir on the Malabar Coast by J. V. Stein van Gollenesse ...*, ed. A.J. van der Burg (Madras, 1908), 15-16. The latter work is also available in English: A. Galletti, A.J. van der Burg, and P. Groot (eds), *The Dutch in Malabar: Being a Translation of Selections Nos. 1 and 2 with Introduction and Notes* (Madras, 1911), there see 68.

40 K.D. Swaminathan, *The Nāyakas of Ikkēri* (Madras, 1957), 2, map facing title page; K.N. Chitnis, *Keḷadi Polity* (Dharwar, 1974), xiii, 86-9; A. Sundara, *The Keḷadi Nāyakas: Architecture and Art*, vol. V, pt. 2, *The Shivappa Nayaka Palace in Shimoga* (Mysore, 1987), x.

41 NA, VOC, no. 1615B, f. 471; no. 2317, f. 329; no. 2443, ff. 2682-3, 2693-4; no. 2631, ff. 417-23: map in report of inspection tour by Ceylon Governor Gerrit de Heere, Sept.-Oct. 1699, final reports of

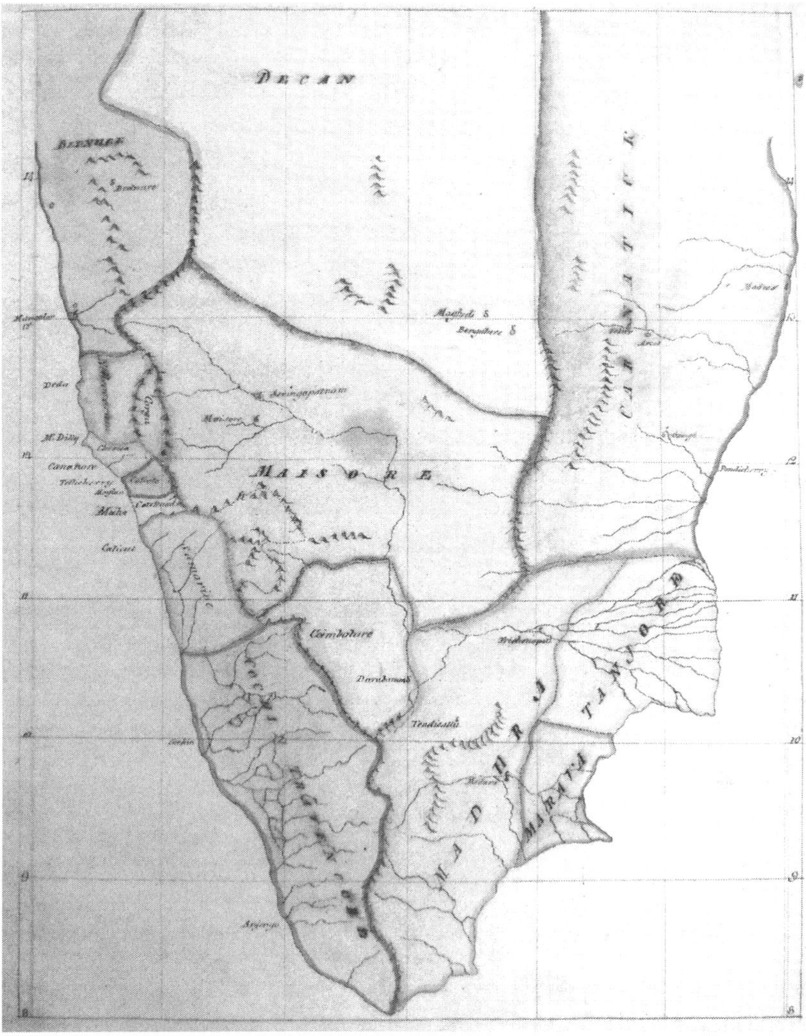

Illustration 1: "Promontory of India for the intelligence of Hyder Ally's [Haidar Ali Khan's] war, copied from Captain Kapper, reduced," British map of south India's kingdoms, including, from top-left to bottom-right, Ikkeri ("Bednure"), Mysore, Madurai, Tanjavur, and Ramnad ("Marava"), original probably c. 1760s-70s, British Library, Asian & African Studies department, Orme Collection: O.V., no. 333, sheet 6 (photo by the author, courtesy British Library Board).

In the Tamil-speaking zone too, the territorial division observed by the Dutch generally agrees with what is concluded in secondary literature.[42] In fact, the situation came quite close to traditional local notions on borders between political regions (or *maṇḍalams*) in this area. These held, for example, that the boundary between the Chola realm (Tanjavur) and the Pandya realm (Madurai, including Ramnad) was demarcated by the Vellar River, which flows into the sea right at the abovementioned town of Manamelkudi.[43] The Dutch records also suggest that although borders often moved and claims to land frequently overlapped, boundaries were still fixed in the sense that at a given moment it was usually clear where the actual control of one party ended and that of another began. These documents contain many statements that territories extended up to specific towns, rivers, capes, or mountains.[44]

With respect to the kingdoms' geographic and demographic characteristics, Tanjavur was situated in a fertile river delta that supported intensive wet-land agriculture and a dense, largely sedentary, and highly stratified population. Ramnad's demography was different, located as it was in a semi-arid region,

the Coromandel Governors Adriaan Pla, Elias Guillot, and Jacob Mossel, Feb. 1734, Sept. 1738, Feb. 1744; *Beknopte historie*, 85-6, 91-2, 95-6; HRB, no. 542 (unpaginated, 1st document, c. halfway, section "Teuverslant"): description of Ceylon, Madurai, south Coromandel, Malabar, and Kanara by Rijcklof van Goens, Sept. 1675; *Lettres édifiantes et curieuses, écrites des missions étrangères, nouvelle edition*, vol. XIII, *Mémoires des Indes* (Paris, 1781), 126; Robert Orme, *A History of the Military Transactions of the British Nation in Indostan, from the Year MDCCXLV ...*, vol. 1 (London, 1763), 112-13; Markus Vink (ed.), *Mission to Madurai: Dutch Embassies to the Nayaka Court of Madurai in the Seventeenth Century* (New Delhi, 2012), 303-4, 352; BL/AAS, Orme Collection, O.V. series (hereafter OOV), no. 333, sheet 6: "Promontory of India for the intelligence of Hyder Ally's war, copied from Captain Kapper, reduced." For reproductions of the Dutch map, see: Jos Gommans, Jeroen Bos, Gijs Kruijtzer, *et al.* (eds), *Grote Atlas van de Verenigde Oost-Indische Compagnie / Comprehensive Atlas of the Dutch United East India Company*, vol. VI, *Voor-Indië, Perzië, Arabisch Schiereiland / India, Persia, Arabian Peninsula* (Voorburg, 2010), sheet 301 (see also sheet 165, which is only accurate for Tanjavur and the coasts of Madurai and Ramnad); Vink, *Mission to Madurai*, fig. 2 (between 12-13).

[42] K.R. Subramanian, *The Maratha Rajas of Tanjore* (Madras, 1928), 79, map facing title page; Subrahmanyam, *Penumbral Visions*, 146; R. Sathyanatha Aiyar, *History of the Nayaks of Madura* (Madras, 1924), 55-7.

[43] BL/AAS, MG, no. 1, pt. 25: "The limits of the Cholla, Pandian and Charan countries," f. 187 (a translation of three Tamil verses). See also BL/AAS, MT, class VII, no. 23: "Chronological account of Bijayanagar," f. 134.

[44] In addition to the previous footnotes, see: NA, VOC, no. 1195, ff. 496-6v; no. 1351, f. 2358; no. 2400, ff. 410v-11; no. 2956, f. 1223; no. 8985, ff. 104, 117v: letters from Pulicat, Nagapattinam, and Colombo to Batavia, July 1652, Jan. 1680, June 1737, reports of missions to Mysore and Ramnad, Dec. 1680, Jan. 1681, June 1759; Lodewijk Wagenaar *et al.* (eds), *Gouverneur Van Imhoff op dienstreis in 1739 naar Cochin, Travancore en Tuticorin, en terug over Jaffna en Mannar naar Colombo (zondag 25 januari tot zaterdag 18 april)* (Zutphen, 2007), 168; Valentijn, *Oud en Nieuw Oost-Indiën*, vol. 5, 8th book, 236, 238. But see also Talbot, *Precolonial India in Practice*, 138-9; Howes, *The Courts of Pre-Colonial South India*, 174-6.

where towns were surrounded by dry wilderness and woods. It harboured a sparse populace, of which roving, independent-minded herdsmen and warrior bands formed a substantial portion. Madurai combined physical and societal elements of Tanjavur and Ramnad, the latter region being initially part of it. With its much larger size, Madurai encompassed riverine and populous lands as well as thinly inhabited wasteland and forests. Another combination was found in Ikkeri, where the successive capitals and most of its territory lay in a hilly and wooded upland area, separated by the Western Ghats from the kingdom's riverine coastal strip. This was another very fertile region.[45] According to the early eighteenth-century Dutch Pastor Jacobus Canter Visscher, Ikkeri served as "the granary of entire India [*Noorder-Indie*, "Northern Indies"]."[46]

As mentioned, the variety that these four kingdoms—and their five dynasties—together represent is one reason why they are the focus of this work. They are systematically and extensively discussed in every chapter. Occasionally, however, this study deals with other heirs of Vijayanagara when they provide illustrative

[45] For south India's geography and its impact on demography, society, and politics, see: O.H.K. Spate and A.T.A. Learmonth, *India and Pakistan: A General and Regional Geography* (3rd edition, Suffolk, 1967), 47, 669-73, 684-7, 700-3, 762-82; Talbot, *Precolonial India in Practice*, 43-7, 170; J.C. Heesterman, "Warrior, Peasant and Brahmin," *Modern Asian Studies* 29, 3 (1995); Jos Gommans, "The Silent Frontier in South Asia, c. A.D. 1100-1800," *Journal of World History* 9, 1 (1998), 2-4; Burton Stein, "Agrarian Integration in South India," in Robert Eric Frykenberg (ed.), *Land Control and Social Structure in Indian History* (Madison, 1969), 188, 206; idem, *Vijayanagara*, 15-17, 21, 24-5, 44-7; B.A. Saletore, *Social and Political Life in the Vijayanagara Empire (A.D. 1346–A.D. 1646)* (Madras, 1934), vol. I, 39-44; Subrahmanyam, *The Political Economy of Commerce*, 9-25; idem, *Penumbral Visions*, 226; David Ludden, *Peasant History in South India* (Princeton/Guildford, 1985), 81-96; Nagendra E. Rao, *Craft Production and Trade in South Kanara A.D. 1000-1763* (New Delhi, 2006), 6-10; Pamela G. Price, *Kingship and Political Practice in Colonial India* (Cambridge, 1996), 7-10; Mahalingam, *South Indian Polity*, ch. 1; Velcheru Narayana Rao, David Shulman, and Sanjay Subrahmanyam, *Textures of Time: Writing History in South India 1600-1800* (Delhi, 2001), 179; Kathleen D. Morrison, *Fields of Victory: Vijayanagara and the Course of Intensification* (Berkeley, 1995), passim, especially ch. 2; idem, "Coercion, Resistance, and Hierarchy: Local Processes and Imperial Strategies in the Vijayanagara Empire," in Susan E. Alcock *et al.* (eds), *Empires: Perspectives from Archaeology and History* (Cambridge, 2001), 258-9; Bridges White, "Beyond Empire," 100; David Shulman, "On South Indian Bandits and Kings," *The Indian Economic and Social History Review* 17, 3 (1980), 288-90, 301-6; Lennart Bes, "The Setupatis, the Dutch, and Other Bandits in Eighteenth-Century Ramnad (South India)," *Journal of the Economic and Social History of the Orient* 44, 4 (2001), 545-6, 563-6. For Dutch and Jesuit descriptions of these kingdoms' geographic and demographic features, see: NA, HRB, no. 542 (unpaginated, 1st document, c. halfway, sections "Tansjaour," "Teuverslant," and subsequent folios): description of Ceylon, Madurai, south Coromandel, Malabar, and Kanara by Rijcklof van Goens, Sept. 1675; Valentijn, *Oud en Nieuw Oost-Indiën*, vol. 5, 8th book, 233-4, 236; Vink, *Mission to Madurai*, 304-8, 352-3; *Lettres édifiantes et curieuses*, vol. X, *Mémoires des Indes* (Paris, 1781), 61, vol. XIII, 126-36; Saulière, "The Revolt of the Southern Nayaks" [pt. 1], 91; Saulier, "Madurai and Tanjore," 786.

[46] Canter Visscher, *Mallabaarse Brieven*, 68-9.

examples or noteworthy exceptions with regard to the chapters' themes. These states are primarily Mysore (in Chapters 3-6), Senji (3, 6), Shivagangai (2, 6, Epilogue), and Ariyalur (1, 6). The second reason for focusing on Ikkeri, Tanjavur, Madurai, and Ramnad is the availability of voluminous, diverse, and mostly unexplored sources for these kingdoms, described in detail in the following section.

Sources

In contrast to its medieval period, south India's early modern history can be researched with large quantities of primary sources created not only by local actors but also by external parties.[47] Both of these bodies of source materials comprise various sub-groups. Local sources include epigraphic records, literary texts, and what little remains of state administration, as well as visual materials and objects, such as works of art, architecture, archaeological findings, and coins. Among the external sources are records and maps of European mercantile powers, accounts and drawings of foreign travellers, and documents of Christian missions. Most of these categories can be further divided according to individual source creators, such as specific courts, trading companies, missionary orders, and private persons. Several of the sets of materials thus distinguished still remain unpublished and have hardly been used for research. Further, they all present their own historiographic challenges, for example with regard to accessibility, interpretation, and linguistic variety.

Therefore, any researcher of Vijayanagara's heirs must make a balanced choice from this wealth of sources. Besides all sorts of published materials, the present study chiefly uses two distinct but complementary bodies of unpublished sources, one of local origin and one of foreign provenance. Both cover all selected Vijayanagara successor states, are of considerable size, and have been little explored so far. They comprise, first, south Indian literary works found among the translated so-called Mackenzie manuscripts, and second, the archives of the Dutch East India Company. Having very different backgrounds—assorted erudite

[47] For a survey of sources for the Nayaka kingdoms in the Tamil region, see Narayana Rao, Shulman, and Subrahmanyam, *Symbols of Substance*, 334-40. For published inscriptions and literary texts, see also Stein, *Vijayanagara*, 147. For (inexhaustive) overviews for the individual kingdoms, see: Swaminathan, *The Nāyakas of Ikkēri*, 5-11; Chitnis, *Keḷadi Polity*, ch. 1; B.S. Shastry, *Goa-Kanara Portuguese Relations 1498-1763*, ed. Charles J. Borges (New Delhi, 2000), 315-20; V. Vriddhagirisan, *The Nayaks of Tanjore* (Annamalainagar, 1942), 3-8; C.K. Srinivasan, *Maratha Rule in the Carnatic* (Annamalainagar, 1944), 5-17; Sathyanatha Aiyar, *History of the Nayaks of Madura*, 33-9; K. Seshadri, "The Sētupatis of Ramnad" (unpublished dissertation, University of Madurai, 1976), 1-4; S. Kadhirvel, *A History of the Maravas, 1700-1802* (Madurai, 1977), ch. 1.

or artistic prose and poetry versus an interrelated set of business records—these two collections greatly differ in content, style, structure, purpose, and intended audience. Consequently, they provide two divergent kinds of information, which often offer context and nuance to one another. Especially when events or people are referred to in both these local and external materials—whether they confirm, complement, or contradict one another—one can compare the sources' various viewpoints and thus better appreciate their value.

As said, only for the early modern period is it possible to study pre-colonial south Indian courts and dynasties with the help of extensive sets of local as well as foreign source materials, allowing for historiographic richness and depth not possible for previous phases of the region's past. As such, the findings of the present work can have implications for the historiography of earlier Indian courts and dynasties, by necessity based solely or chiefly on local sources, providing less diverse perspectives. Thus, considering the conclusions in the following chapters, Indian court politics before the early modern period—particularly aspects like successions to the throne, the power of courtiers, court protocol, and relations between courts—may have been different from what historians have hitherto concluded.

The rest of this section is concerned with the two main sets of sources used for this research: the translated Mackenzie manuscripts and the archives of the Dutch East India Company.[48]

Literary texts produced at and around the courts and temples of Vijayanagara and its heirs were composed for cultured and polyglot audiences that included royals, courtiers, scholars, artists, priests, and visitors. The contents and styles of these works are very diverse, their structures and meanings can be complex, and they are scattered over many places. To begin with, they date from different phases in a period of nearly half a millennium: between the mid-fourteenth and early nineteenth centuries. They were written in at least five languages (from two language families), in equally as many scripts: Kannada, Marathi, Sanskrit, Tamil, and Telugu. The courts in question were all multilingual, and almost none of these languages was confined to just one kingdom.[49] Further, the texts were inscribed on dried palm leaves, carved in stone and metal, written on paper, or orally transmitted.

[48] For the use of south Indian inscriptions, works of art, and court administration, see Chapters 2 and 5.

[49] For extreme multilingualism in literary texts from Tanjavur, see: Indira Viswanathan Peterson, "Multilingual Dramas at the Tanjavur Maratha Court and Literary Cultures in Early Modern South India," *The Medieval History Journal* 14, 2 (2011); Radhika Seshan, "From Folk Culture to Court Culture: The *Kuravanji* in the Tanjore Court," *Proceedings of the Indian History Congress* 65 (2004). For linguistic variety in inscriptions of Vijayanagara and its successors, see Emmanuel Francis, "Imperial Languages

Works pertaining to courts and dynasties appeared in several forms, for instance *vaṃśāvaḷis* (family histories), *charitras* or *caritramus* (biographies, chronicles, historical tales), *kaifiyats* (local histories, town records, often reconstructed at the end of the early modern period), *bakhairs* (narratives, memoirs), and other genres.[50] Some south Indian chronicles even have come to us in versions recorded by Portuguese and Dutch merchants in the sixteenth and seventeenth centuries.[51] Still, many texts must have been lost, while those that remain are kept at different locations, in south India and elsewhere, with various degrees of accessibility. Only part of these have been published, mostly in their original language, and occasionally in English translation, in the latter case often offering just a summary or excerpts.[52]

A large body of texts, however, is available in manuscript English translations, which belong to the well-known but only partly explored Mackenzie collections. About the turn of the nineteenth century, Colonel Colin Mackenzie served as the first surveyor-general of India, appointed after the British East India Company came to control substantial parts of south India in the last decades of the eighteenth century. In the years around 1800, Mackenzie and his team of local assistants—most prominently the Brahmin Kavali brothers Venkata Borayya and Venkata Lakshmayya—acquired numerous texts in various Indian languages. Ranging from

and Public Writings in Tamil South India: A Bird's-Eye View in the Very *Longue Durée*," in Peter C. Bisschop and Elizabeth A. Cecil (eds), *Primary Sources and Asian Pasts* (Berlin/Boston, 2021), 168-77.

50 For discussions of literary genres, see: Narayana Rao, Shulman, and Subrahmanyam, *Symbols of Substance*, 334-8; idem, *Textures of Time*, 19-23, 226-8; Phillip B. Wagoner, "From Manuscript to Archive to Print: The Mackenzie Collection and Later Telugu Literary Historiography," in Thomas R. Trautman (ed.), *The Madras School of Orientalism: Producing Knowledge in Colonial South India* (Oxford, 2009), 197-8; Nicholas B. Dirks, *Castes of Mind: Colonialism and the Making of Modern India* (Princeton/Oxford, 2001), 86-9; idem, *The Hollow Crown*, 75-6; Rama Sundari Mantena, *The Origins of Modern Historiography in India: Antiquarianism and Philology, 1780-1880* (New York, 2012), 4, 125, 131, 180-1; Guha, *History and Collective Memory in South Asia*, 83-93; Nobuhiro Ota, "Bēḍa Nāyakas and Their Historical Narratives in Karnataka during the Post-Vijayanagara Period," in Noboru Karashima (ed.), *Kingship in Indian History* (New Delhi, 2004) 190 (n. 1). See also BL/AAS, MT, class VII, no. 23: "Chronological account of Bijayanagar," ff. 140v-1, for eighteenth-century descriptions of some genres.

51 See the chronicles on Vijayanagara by Fernão Nunes (c. early 1530s)—published in Portuguese in David Lopes (ed.), *Chronica dos Reis de Bisnaga: Manuscripto inedito do seculo XVI* (Lisbon, 1897), and in English in Robert Sewell, *A Forgotten Empire (Vijayanagar): A Contribution to the History of India* (London, 1900), 291-395—and on the Nayakas of Madurai by Adolph Bassingh (1677), published in Dutch and English in Vink, *Mission to Madurai*, 283-365. The Dutch original was also published in Valentijn, *Oud en Nieuw Oost-Indiën*, vol. 5, 8th book, 285-301. On request of Ceylon's Dutch Governor Jan Schreuder, Bassingh's account was updated in 1762 by G.F. Holst to include the last decades of Nayaka rule and Madurai's subsequent history. See NA, VOC, no. 3052, ff. 1896-975; no. 11306, ff. 0-155. See also Jan Schreuder, *Memoir of Jan Schreuder 1757-1762*, ed. E. Reimers (Colombo, 1946), 37.

52 For such publications, see the references in the sections dealing with the individual dynasties.

palm-leaf documents kept in palaces and temples to inscriptions and oral traditions recorded on the spot, they were collected to obtain a clearer picture of the region's political past. Including dynastic chronicles, town and temple histories, laudatory poems, royal proclamations, and the like, these texts could help the colonial administration judge the validity of claims of local rulers to titles, honours, privileges, land, real estate, revenues, etc.[53] The majority of the collected documents are still kept at various places in south India.[54]

In addition, Mackenzie's staff prepared English translations of many hundreds of texts—mostly of a political and dynastic nature, it seems—which were later shipped to London.[55] Of some of these manuscripts, original versions in Indian languages seem unavailable, because they have become lost or texts were directly recorded in English. Thus, those materials may be the only extant copies of certain works.[56] In any case, several hundred of the English-language manuscripts, translated from all abovementioned languages, pertain to the dynasties and courts of Vijayanagara and its heirs, both great and small, direct and indirect.[57] This set of texts allows a comparative study of a large number of underexplored local sources, from various linguistic backgrounds and concerning several states, within a reasonable amount of time.

Taken together, Mackenzie's manuscript translations, other materials published or summarised in English, and secondary literature discussing relevant texts, constitute a sizeable body of local sources on court politics. Still, researching these works involves several difficulties. The translations of Mackenzie's assistants are sometimes of doubtful quality, regularly containing quaint English and illegible handwriting, and should be used selectively and with caution. Moreover, part of the texts Mackenzie gathered—in their original languages as well as their English translations—were corrupted or even fabricated for the occasion. Collected by the British to determine the historical positions of south Indian kings and chiefs, these

[53] In addition to the previous and following notes, see Mantena, *The Origins of Modern Historiography in India*, 44, 60-85.

[54] Most of the texts in Indian languages collected by Mackenzie are found in the Government Oriental Manuscripts Library (GOML) at the University of Madras (Chennai).

[55] English translations were sometimes made as soon as the originals were acquired during expeditions. See BL/AAS, MT, class XII (letters and reports, from local agents collecting texts, traditions, etc.), no. 9: "Monthly memorendum & report of C.V. Lutchmia to Major C. Makinzee S.M.S. of the progress made in collection of historical materials" (1804), ff. 82v, 89, 96.

[56] For examples of possibly unique text versions, see Cotton, Charpentier, and Johnston, *Catalogue of Manuscripts in European Languages*, vol. I, pt. II, 9-10, 17, 29-32, 36-9, 52, 85-6, 400.

[57] These manuscript translations are now kept in the British Library (Asian & African Studies department), London, divided into several sub-collections. Three of these include texts concerning Vijayanagara and its successor states: Mackenzie General, Mackenzie Miscellaneous, and Mackenzie Translations.

documents were partially compiled by those rulers with an agenda to impress Company officials, to the extent that some texts came to resemble petitions. They can thus contain inflated claims with regard to descent, status, property, past events, and whatever else supported power aspirations.[58]

The question is, however, which parts of these texts may have been relevant to the colonial administration. Passages describing late-eighteenth-century political developments could certainly be of interest to British functionaries. But it seems unlikely that stories composed much earlier were largely re-invented or modified to convince the British of current political claims. The bulk of most works appears to consist of original textual sections. This particularly applies to stories in which the latest events occurred before the British gained power and to texts concerning states and dynasties already vanished by this time. The works that do include petitions to the colonial administration (usually at the end of a narrative) chiefly derive from minor chiefs, such as the Palaiyakkarars, who wielded some local power when Mackenzie collected his materials, rather than the main Vijayanagara successor states, most of which no longer existed in that period.

It has been suggested that *kaifiyats* (local histories) in particular contain sections adapted or invented with contemporary political targets in mind, as they were partly compiled at the request of the British and based on contributions by local informants. But perhaps for this very reason, the narrative accounts in some *kaifiyats* actually claim to relate historical events instead of legendary tales. Thus, part of this genre and most texts in other styles are considered original in the sense that they remained largely unadjusted when collected or contain authentic memories.[59] At any rate, even if some passages were (re)constructed at that time, these still reflect politico-cultural ideas of the royal houses these works deal with. Consequently, all these materials at least provide us with notions of dynastic self-perception.

[58] Mahalingam, *Mackenzie Manuscripts*, vol. I, xxvii; David M. Blake, "Introduction," in Cotton, Charpentier, and Johnston, *Catalogue of Manuscripts in European Languages*, vol. I, pt. II, xlvii, l-lii; Dirks, *Castes of Mind*, 30, 86, 91, 100-4; idem, *The Hollow Crown*, 76-7; idem, "Colin Mackenzie: Autobiography of an Archive," in Thomas R. Trautman (ed.), *The Madras School of Orientalism: Producing Knowledge in Colonial South India* (Oxford, 2009), 30-2, 35, 38; Rama Sundari Mantena, "The Kavali Brothers: Intellectual Life in Early Colonial Madras," in idem; Wagoner, "From Manuscript to Archive to Print," 190-1; Guha, *History and Collective Memory in South Asia*, 109-17; Simmons, *Devotional Sovereignty*, 109-14. See also Pushkar Sohoni (ed.), *The Great Inscription at Tanjore: Bhoṃsalevaṃśacaritra* (forthcoming).

[59] Wagoner, "From Manuscript to Archive to Print," 197-8; Dirks, *The Hollow Crown*, 76-8; Mantena, *The Origins of Modern Historiography in India*, ch. 4, especially 125-33, 136, 141, 149; Bhavani Raman, *Document Raj: Writing and Scribes in Early Colonial India* (Ranikhet, 2012), 59, 64, 141; Talbot, *Precolonial India in Practice*, 203; Janaki Nair, "Eighteenth-Century Passages to a *History of Mysore*," in Raziuddin Aquil and Partha Chatterjee (eds), *History in the Vernacular* (Ranikhet, 2008), 70; Subrahmanyam, *Penumbral Visions*, 206-7.

Besides authenticity, there are issues of content and context. First, many literary works include sections that might be considered imaginary rather than historical. We thus read of superhuman powers, natural miracles, magical spells, divine interventions, and so on. But although these descriptions could be labelled as historically inaccurate, they reflect traditions, beliefs, and perceptions apparently deemed essential elements of these stories. Therefore, they must not be excluded from historical analyses but regarded as relevant information.

Further, while this study concerns courts and dynasties, several texts rather pertain to areas, towns, persons, castes, temples, and so on, and therefore have a different perspective. Of course, these entities overlap and the focus of stories sometimes shifts. Tales of heroes become chronicles of dynasties, and in turn change into histories of kingdoms, towns, or regions. These varying viewpoints tie in with the question of who composed these works and for what purpose. Many texts were written or sponsored by members of royal houses, court poets, temple priests, or subordinated chiefs, and thus represent their opinions and agendas. In many other instances, the authors or patrons have not been ascertained, but such works were often produced by classes of literary men connected to the courts, including secretaries, scribes, and accountants, and known, for example, as *karaṇams* or *kaṇakkuppiḷḷais*.[60]

Still, sometimes it is not even clear when and where texts were first collected and their context is entirely obscure. In those cases, one often remains in the dark about the composers' goals and ideas. Stories about dynasties could have been produced by succeeding royal houses seeing themselves as heirs to their predecessors and glorifying them to enhance their own status. Texts linking kings to specific deities may have been compiled by monastic orders devoted to those deities with the aim of stressing their own importance. Whenever the author's background, position, or motives are unknown, one must try to work with the components of the story itself to contextualise it and attain some idea of the creator's viewpoint.

In addition to the perspectives of Indian writers and their benefactors, there are accounts of developments in Vijayanagara and its heirs produced by Europeans. These records often appear to describe how events unfolded in practice—or at least how they were observed and interpreted by Europeans—and are mostly quite

[60] Narayana Rao, Shulman, and Subrahmanyam, *Textures of Time*, 11, ch. 3; Raman, *Document Raj*, 12, 38, 59-60; Narayana Rao and Subrahmanyam, "History and Politics in the Vernacular: Reflections on Medieval and Early Modern South India," in Raziuddin Aquil and Partha Chatterjee (eds), *History in the Vernacular* (Ranikhet, 2008), 52-6, of which a slightly modified version is found in idem, "Notes on Political Thought in Medieval and Early Modern India," *Modern Asian Studies* 43, 1 (2009); there, see 201-5.

precisely dated. In fact, they are regularly the only truly contemporary sources available. Therefore, these "foreign" reports form a valuable addition to the local materials. As far as European materials are concerned, this study is largely based on the archives of the Dutch East India Company, also known under its Dutch acronym VOC.[61] For long periods in the seventeenth and eighteenth centuries, this company maintained coastal trading stations in all Vijayanagara successor states considered here, and in the area governed by the empire's final Aravidu dynasty.

The Dutch started appearing in south Indian waters around the turn of the seventeenth century.[62] Soon, they secured permission from the Nayakas of Senji and the imperial Aravidu house to set up trading posts on the south-eastern Coromandel Coast, consecutively at Teganapatnam in 1608 (followed after two years by Tiruppapuliyar) and at Pulicat in 1610.[63] Regular contacts with the other successor states commenced only several decades later.[64] In the southern Tamil zone, the VOC first settled on the shores of Tanjavur in 1644 and Madurai in 1645 when it opened factories in Tirumullaivasal and Kayalpatnam, respectively. Relations with these Nayaka courts grew closer after the Dutch conquered the

[61] Archival materials of the VOC (*Verenigde Oostindische Compagnie*, "United East-Indies Company") are stored at various repositories. Most important for Vijayanagara and its heirs are the archives of the Company directors in the Dutch Republic—especially the series of *overgekomen brieven en papieren* (OBP, letters and papers received from Asia)—kept at the National Archives in The Hague (for all states), and to a lesser extent those of the Malabar establishment (for Ikkeri), stored at the Tamil Nadu Archives in Chennai, and of the Ceylon establishment (for Madurai and Ramnad), kept at the Department of National Archives in Colombo.

[62] For general overviews of the Dutch in India, see: George Winius and Markus Vink, *The Merchant-Warrior Pacified: The VOC (The Dutch East India Co.) and Its Changing Political Economy in India* (Delhi, 1991); Jos Gommans, *The Unseen World: The Netherlands and India from 1550* (Amsterdam, 2018); Heert Terpstra, *De Nederlanders in Voor-Indië* (Amsterdam, 1947); Om Prakash, *European Commercial Enterprise in Pre-Colonial India* (Cambridge, 1998); Pieter C. Emmer and Jos J.L. Gommans, *The Dutch Overseas Empire, 1600–1800* (Cambridge, 2021), chs 3, 7-8.

[63] Heeres and Stapel, *Corpus diplomaticum Neerlando-Indicum*, vol. 1, 55, 78-81, 83-5; Pieter van Dam, *Beschryvinge van de Oostindische Compagnie*, vol. 2.2, ed. F.W. Stapel (The Hague, 1932), 225-9; Heert Terpstra, *De vestiging van de Nederlanders aan de kust van Koromandel* (Groningen, 1911), 85-158; Tapan Raychaudhuri, *Jan Company in Coromandel 1605-1690: A Study in the Interrelations of European Commerce and Traditional Economies* (The Hague, 1962), 19-21; S. Jeyaseela Stephen, "Rise and Decline of Pulicat under the Dutch East India Company (AD.1612-1690)," *The Historical Review: A Bi-Annual Journal of History and Archaeology* (New Series) X, 1-2 (2002), 2-3, 14, 20-2.

[64] The VOC maintained no relations with the Wodeyar court of Mysore, save for a brief period in the 1670s-80s. See the conclusions of Chapters 3-4, and: Lennart Bes, "Thalassophobia, Women's Power, and Diplomatic Insult at Karnataka Courts: Two Dutch Embassies to Mysore and Ikkeri in the 1680s" (unpublished paper, 2014); Binu John Mailaparambil, "The VOC and the Prospects of Trade between Cannanore and Mysore in the Late Seventeenth Century," in K.S. Mathew and J. Varkey (eds), *Winds of Spices: Essays on Portuguese Establishments in Medieval India with Special Reference to Cannanore* (Tellicherry, 2006), 211-20.

major ports of Nagapattinam (in Tanjavur) and Tuticorin (in Madurai) from the Portuguese, both in 1658.[65] In that same year, the first treaty was signed between the VOC and the Setupatis of Ramnad, where the Company established a small trading lodge at the port of Kilakkarai in 1690, after an earlier, short stay at the port of Adirampatnam from 1674.[66]

In Tanjavur, Madurai, and Vijayanagara, the main commodities purchased by the VOC comprised various types of textiles, exported to the Dutch Republic and the South-east Asian archipelago. In addition, the Gulf of Mannar off Madurai's and Ramnad's littoral was the site of regular and highly lucrative pearl fisheries—this shore was hence known as the Fishery Coast—monitored by the VOC after it had become the main maritime power in the region. Apart from commercial motivations, the Company valued a continuous presence in Ramnad for strategic reasons since that kingdom controlled one of only two sea passages of some size between the Indian mainland and Ceylon, the Pamban Channel. Although Dutch-Ramnad agreements stipulated that only the VOC was allowed to use this route, a nearby stronghold proved necessary for the Company to help enforce this agreement to at least some degree.[67]

On the western Kanara Coast, as Ikkeri's shore was called, the VOC set up a small station at the port of Basrur (near Kundapura) about 1660, following a treaty with the kingdom's Nayakas in 1657. Besides some pepper, Ikkeri provided the Dutch principally with rice, needed to feed their numerous personnel on the Malabar Coast and Ceylon further south.[68] In addition, around 1637 a more northern factory

[65] Sinnappah Arasaratnam, "The Politics of Commerce in the Coastal Kingdoms of Tamil Nad, 1650-1700," *South Asia: Journal of South Asian Studies* 1 (1971); idem, "The Dutch East India Company and the Kingdom of Madura, 1650-1700," *Tamil Culture* X, 1 (1963); Raychaudhuri, *Jan Company in Coromandel*, 56-7; Markus Vink, "Encounters on the Opposite Coast: Cross-Cultural Contacts between the Dutch East India Company and the Nayaka State of Madurai in the Seventeenth Century" (unpublished dissertation, University of Minnesota, 1999), 203-10, 240-8; K.A. Nilakanta Sastri, "Tirumala Naik, the Portuguese and the Dutch," *Indian Historical Records Commission: Proceedings of Meetings*, vol. XVI (Delhi, 1939); Heeres and Stapel, *Corpus diplomaticum Neerlando-Indicum*, vol. 1, 455-7, vol. 2 (The Hague, 1931), 123-8, 137-9, 142-9; Valentijn, *Oud en Nieuw Oost-Indiën*, vol. 5, 1st book, 3-4, 8th book, 234-5. For the VOC's initial contacts with Tanjavur's Bhonsle court, see Nikhil Bellarykar, "Conflict and Co-operation: Preliminary Explorations in VOC – Tanjavur (Maratha) Relations during 1676-1691," *Prag Samiksha* 5, 9 (2017).

[66] Bes, "The Setupatis, the Dutch, and Other Bandits," 549-51; Sinnappah Arasaratnam, "Commercial Policies of the Sethupathis of Ramanathapuram 1660-1690," in R.E. Asher (ed.), *Proceedings of the Second International Conference Seminar of Tamil Studies*, vol. 2 (Madras, 1968); Vink, *Mission to Madurai*, 429 (n. 33); Heeres and Stapel, *Corpus diplomaticum Neerlando-Indicum*, vol. 2, 113-14.

[67] See the literature mentioned in the previous footnotes. See also Sinnappah Arasaratnam, *Merchants, Companies and Commerce on the Coromandel Coast 1650-1740* (Delhi, 1986).

[68] Heeres and Stapel, *Corpus diplomaticum Neerlando-Indicum*, vol. 2, 104-13; Canter Visscher, *Mallabaarse Brieven*, 69; Bes, "Thalassophobia, Women's Power, and Diplomatic Insult"; K.G. Vasantha Madhava, "The Dutch in Coastal Karnataka 1602-1763," *The Quarterly Journal of the Mythic Society* 73, 3-4

was founded at Vengurla on the Konkan Coast, again largely for strategic purposes, situated as this town was just north of Portuguese-ruled Goa. While Vengurla initially fell under the Bijapur sultanate and was later conquered by the Maratha King Shivaji Bhonsle, it lay close to Ikkeri's territories and its resident Dutchmen maintained contacts with this kingdom until at least the late 1670s.[69]

Through all those coastal settlements, by the mid-seventeenth century the VOC had become deeply engaged with these states, regularly exchanging embassies, correspondence, and commodities with the courts. This involvement lasted until Vijayanagara's successor dynasties were dethroned—in Madurai around 1739, in Ikkeri in 1763—or came to be fully dominated by the British and the Mughal successor state of Arcot from the 1770s on, as happened in Tanjavur and Ramnad. None of the other European powers in south India (Portuguese, Danes, French, and British) maintained such continuous relations with all these dynasties during this period.[70]

Keeping a close watch on the inland courts from their factories, the Dutch generally compiled extensive accounts of local political and dynastic developments. Largely unexplored and unpublished, these records have much to add to our often limited knowledge of such events, sometimes even basic facts like the years in which incidents took place. Relevant types of documents in the VOC archives include correspondence between several Dutch settlements in south India and Ceylon, letters from those establishments to the Company's Asian headquarters in Batavia (on Java) and directors in the Dutch Republic, proceedings or minutes of Company meetings (*resoluties*), final reports or memorandums of departing VOC officials for their successors (*memories van overgave*), various papers concerning embassies exchanged between the Company and the courts, and correspondence with the kingdoms' rulers and courtiers. In the latter category, the many letters received from courts and their representatives in fact embody south Indian perspectives within this corpus of Dutch sources, albeit in translated and perhaps misinterpreted form.[71]

(1982), 2-5; B. Shreedhara Naik, "European Trade and Politics in Medieval South Canara," *Proceedings of the Indian History Congress* 69 (2008), 367-9; Rao, *Craft Production and Trade in South Kanara*, 158-61; Pius Fidelis Pinto, *History of Christians in Coastal Karnataka (1500 – 1763 A.D.)* (Mangalore, 1999), 97-103.

69 Om Prakash, "The Dutch Factory at Vengurla in the Seventeenth Century," in A.R. Kulkarni, M.A. Nayeem, and T.R. de Souza (eds), *Medieval Deccan History: Commemoration Volume in Honour of P.M. Joshi* (Bombay, 1996); Tycho Walaardt, "Peper of Portugezen: Een geschiedenis van de Hollandse factorij Vengurla in de nabijheid van Goa in de zeventiende eeuw" (unpublished MA thesis, Leiden University, 1999); Ishrat Alam, "The Dutch East-India Company Trade at Vengurla in the Seventeenth Century," *Proceedings of the Indian History Congress* 64 (2003).

70 For a survey of European settlements in South Asia during this period, see Joseph E. Schwartzberg *et al.*, *A Historical Atlas of South Asia* (New York, 1992), 50.

71 The mentioned VOC factories were part of three regional Company establishments (*kantoren*). Basrur came under the Malabar *kantoor*, headquartered in Cochin. Nagapattinam was part of the

Among all these documents, the dozens of lengthy reports and diaries of the Company's diplomatic missions contain a particular wealth of information on such subjects as relations between people at court, royal display, and court protocol. Surveying the known VOC embassies to Vijayanagara's heirs, counting only those involving Dutch envoys rather than local brokers, one finds the following minimum numbers and periods: Ikkeri, twelve (1657-1735); Tanjavur, seven (1645-1764, nearly all falling in the period of the Bhonsle dynasty); Madurai, four (1645-89); and Ramnad, thirteen (1658-1759). There were also encounters between the Dutch and monarchs during the latter's tours of their kingdoms, as happened at least twice in Ikkeri (1729-38), four times in Tanjavur (1725-41), and no fewer than nine times in Madurai (1705-31).[72] In addition, the successor states of Mysore and Senji received respectively one (1681) and about three (c. 1608-44) Dutch embassies. Finally, there were at least five VOC missions to Vijayanagara's Aravidu rulers (1610-45) and three visits by them to the Dutch (c. 1629-46).[73] Detailed reports are not available for each

Coromandel *kantoor*, seated until 1690 and after 1781 at Pulicat, and between these years at Nagapattinam itself. Tuticorin and its dependency Kilakkarai belonged to the Ceylon *kantoor*, based in Colombo. Vengurla formed a separate unit until it was put under the Surat *kantoor* in 1673 and under Malabar in 1676. For the VOC's administrative structure in South Asia and its archival organisation, see Jos Gommans, Lennart Bes, and Gijs Kruijtzer, *Dutch Sources on South Asia c. 1600-1825*, vol. 1, *Bibliography and Archival Guide to the National Archives at The Hague (The Netherlands)* (New Delhi, 2001).

72 From at least the 1690s to the 1730s, the Nayakas of Madurai made frequent inspection tours to the kingdom's southern Fishery Coast (including pilgrimage sites at Tiruchendur and Punnaikayal). See also Chapters 4-5. In addition to the sources mentioned there, see: NA, VOC, no. 1478, f. 1156; no. 2185, ff. 997-1023v; no. 8935, ff. 708-18: letter from Tuticorin to Jaffna, July 1690, (extracts of) correspondence between Tuticorin and Colombo, May-June 1721, Apr.-June 1731, and report of meeting with the Nayaka at Tuticorin, May 1731; Coolhaas *et al.*, *Generale Missiven*, vol. VI (The Hague, 1976), 445-6, vol. VII, 369, 567, vol. VIII, 19. For references to these trips in local sources, see: Rangachari, "The History of the Naik Kingdom of Madura," *Indian Antiquary* XLVI, 186; Sathyanatha Aiyar, *History of the Nayaks of Madura*, 229-30, 366 (no. 222), 368 (no. 230).

73 For lists of VOC records on some of these encounters—in the National Archives at The Hague for all courts, the Tamil Nadu Archives at Chennai for Ikkeri, and the Department of National Archives at Colombo for Madurai and Ramnad—see: Gommans, Bes, and Kruijtzer, *Dutch Sources on South Asia*, vol. 1, 194-6, 244-51, 255, 312-13; Lennart Bes and Gijs Kruijtzer, *Dutch Sources on South Asia c. 1600-1825*, vol. 3, *Archival Guide to Repositories outside The Netherlands* (New Delhi, 2015), 219, 297. For various missions in the early seventeenth century, see: the first few volumes of H.T. Colenbrander *et al.* (eds), *Dagh-register gehouden int Casteel Batavia vant passerende daer ter plaetse als over geheel Nederlandts-India anno ... [1624-82]* (Batavia/The Hague, 1887-1931); Terpstra, *De vestiging van de Nederlanders aan de kust van Koromandel*, 85-6, 118, 124, 129-32; Raychaudhuri, *Jan Company in Coromandel*, chs II-III; N. Mac Leod, *De Oost-Indische Compagnie als zeemogendheid in Azië* (Rijwijk, 1927), vols I-II. Documents of embassies to Madurai in 1668, 1677, and 1689 have been published and translated in Vink, *Mission to Madurai*. For missions to Ramnad in 1731, 1736, and 1743, see Bes, "Friendship as Long as the Sun and Moon Shine," 34-6, 47-9, 64-71. For missions to Mysore in 1681 and Ikkeri in 1684, see Bes, "Thalassophobia, Women's Power, and Diplomatic Insult." This survey does not include several

mission, however, as is the case with all embassies to Senji and Nayaka-ruled Tanjavur, and all but one to Vijayanagara.

Apart from what VOC envoys personally observed during their missions and what rulers and courtiers chose to write to the Dutch, the Company received much information from spies, interpreters, merchants, local authorities, personal contacts, gossips, and so on. While this knowledge was thus frequently acquired indirectly and no doubt filtered by VOC employees, it often comprised south Indian views on events and some of the informants in question were well-connected to court circles. Further, while Portuguese often served as the lingua franca between these parties and the VOC, several Dutchmen lived in south India for many years and used native languages to communicate.[74]

However, the VOC records often omit to say how information was gathered, or who was responsible for compiling descriptions of regional developments, and we cannot determine how knowledgeable or biased Dutch officials and their Indian informers were in individual cases. Such documents are frequently anonymous or were collectively signed by Company personnel. The abovementioned embassy reports are among the few types of VOC records that can be attributed to specific employees—in this case the envoys—and thus provide a more personal perspective. But a drawback of these accounts is that there were few or no Company servants accompanying the ambassadors who were able to verify their reports.

All this compels us to be critical of the information in the Dutch archives, the more so because it regularly differs from what local sources purport. For example, political events and relationships at court presented as harmonious in south Indian texts are often depicted as much less peaceful in Company records (see Chapters 2-3). Indeed, VOC sources generally describe the courts of the Vijayanagara successor states as characterised by constant rivalry and periodic violence. But while in those instances Dutch documents thus downright contradict local materials, in other cases the two bodies of sources rather support or complement one another, especially with regard to more cultural aspects of court politics, like protocol and royal representation (see Chapters 4-5).

embassies to Mysore under Haidar Ali Khan and Tipu Sultan (1761-99), for which see J. van Lohuizen, *The Dutch East India Company and Mysore* (The Hague, 1961) .

[74] For Dutchmen speaking Telugu, Marathi, Tamil, or Malayalam, see: NA, VOC, no. 1756, ff. 1199v, 1203; no. 2015, f. 614; no. 2147, ff. 4835v, 4840; no. 2351, f. 3999; no. 2386, f. 167; no. 2956, f. 1242: report of Madurai Nayaka's visit to Tuticorin, July 1708, reports of missions to Ramnad and Tanjavur, Apr. 1724, Nov. 1735, July 1759, Nagapattinam proceedings (*resoluties*), Mar. 1730, Oct. 1735; Valentijn, *Oud en Nieuw Oost-Indiën*, vol. 5, 8th book, 237-8; Gijs Kruijtzer, *Xenophobia in Seventeenth-Century India* (Leiden, 2009), 224; A.G. Menon, "Colonial Linguistics and the Spoken Language," *International Journal of Dravidian Linguistics* 32, 1 (2003), 80-2.

One reason that the VOC reported on regional politics in great detail was to be aware of the changing balance of power at courts, so it could approach the right people for trade concessions and other privileges. Also, Company officials needed to explain to their superiors how political events might lead to disorder, affect commerce, and lower profits. It of course happened that such officials (including ambassadors) exaggerated their accounts about supposedly arrogant rulers, cunning courtiers, and uncooperative local authorities. For example, claims by VOC employees that unreasonable behaviour of Indian parties hindered the Company's activities could actually serve to conceal mismanagement, corruption,[75] or diplomatic blunders on the part of the Dutch.

But the fact that the VOC archives comprised business administration—and documents would therefore be forwarded to other functionaries who checked and used them—means that matters could not be portrayed in too fanciful a manner. The VOC's policies with regard to the courts were based on its own documentation, and unreliable or fabricated information would soon reveal itself as such because of the Company's ongoing, intense relations with the courts. Further, if local news proved false later on, this would usually be mentioned and corrected in subsequent reports.

Still, VOC records were often prejudiced or derogatory. The Dutch greatly disliked political instability, since this hampered their trade. Thus, they habitually condemned the turmoil ensuing from local power struggles, inter-state wars, and their own disputes with the courts. They frequently attributed such developments to "effeminate," "oblivious," or "fickle" kings, and "merciless," "greedy," or "deceitful" courtiers.[76] These designations demonstrate the general inclination of the Dutch to regard Indian people as alien and inferior. Some common European stereotypes of Asia, however, like its alleged endemic violence and insatiable lust, are not really

75 In the Vijayanagara successor states, corruption under the VOC seems to have been mostly of a relatively small scale. For two rare severe cases, in Ramnad and Ikkeri respectively, see: Bes, "The Setupatis, the Dutch, and Other Bandits," 541, 571; NA, VOC, no. 1299, ff. 350-2: letter from Cochin to Gentlemen XVII, Dec. 1674.

76 For some examples (among many), see: NA, VOC, no. 1227, f. 116v; no. 1251, f. 751; no. 1268, ff. 1114v, 1115v; no. 1333, f. 111; no. 1615C, f. 643v; no. 1835, ff. 285, 288; no. 2015, ff. 598, 601; no. 2229, f. 2035; no. 2291, 509; no. 2354, ff. 1583-4; no. 2386, f. 67; no. 2925, f. 842; no. 8955, f. 244: letters from Pulicat to Ceylon, from Tuticorin to Colombo, from Nagapattinam and Colombo to Batavia, June 1658, Oct. 1678, Aug. 1713, Aug. 1732, July 1733, Feb. 1758, report of mission to Travancore, Madurai, and Ramnad, Mar.-Oct. 1665, reports of missions to Ikkeri and Ramnad, May 1668, Feb. 1699, Apr. 1724, Mar. 1735, report on Malabar, May 1732, Nagapattinam proceedings, Nov. 1735; DNA, DCGCC, no. 2704, ff. 20-20v: final report of Tuticorin's chief Johannes Ferdinandus Crijtsman, June 1757; Vink, *Mission to Madurai*, 309, 353; Valentijn, *Oud en Nieuw Oost-Indiën*, vol. 5, 8th book, 162; Sanjay Subrahmanyam, "Forcing the Doors of Heathendom: Ethnography, Violence, and the Dutch East India Company," in Charles H. Parker and Jerry H. Bentley (eds), *Between the Middle Ages and Modernity: Individual and Community in the Early Modern World* (Lanham/Plymouth, 2007), 143.

standard in the Company's archives. Not all rulers are depicted here as oriental despots terrorising their subjects and indulging in their harems, and far from every court official is portrayed as a sly king-maker plotting to eliminate his rivals.

Again, these documents were supposed to serve as trustworthy and confidential business records, not as personal travel accounts aimed at attracting a wide audience by way of sensational stories about an exoticised Asia. Overall, it appears that while VOC servants tended to use condescending terms for local groups as a whole—such as rulers, courtiers, Hindus ("heathens"), and Muslims ("Moors")—they were more nuanced when they referred to individual people, of whatever background or position. They downright despised certain Indians but sincerely respected others and even maintained relations of friendship or intimacy with some.[77]

Yet, the Dutch obviously viewed much in south India through a homemade lens, and matters related to dynasties, courts, and states are likely to have been construed and labelled on the basis of European political notions and terminology. Therefore, it is not always certain what VOC records exactly refer to when they use words such as *vorstje* ("little king"), *vrijheer* ("free lord"), *keijserrijk* ("empire"), *natie* ("nation"), and *independent*, to name a few cases. A term like "little king" may not have had the same connotations in the VOC context as it has in modern historiography on south India. This further underscores the necessity to be careful with these materials, and beware of, for instance, simplifications, misinterpretations, exaggerations, mistaken identities, or forged stories.

However, it appears that with regard to court politics in the Vijayanagara successor states, the Dutch largely strove to pursue a pragmatic, non-intervening policy. In all these kingdoms, the VOC basically remained a trading company: it certainly commanded economic and military power but it never managed or even tried to attain political control beyond a few coastal settlements, let alone dominate states. Although the Dutch obviously had their preferences for certain courtiers, pretenders to the throne, and court merchants—those considered "friends of the Company"—the VOC refrained from seriously supporting or opposing these people. Indeed, the Company's higher officials sometimes explicitly warned their subordinates not to get involved in these kingdoms' power struggles.[78] As far as can be concluded from the VOC sources, the Dutch never attempted to influence

[77] For friendships of a VOC servant in Ikkeri with a local governor and the prominent merchant Narayana Malu, see: NA, VOC, no. 1288, ff. 638-8v: letter from Cochin to Batavia, July 1672; Coolhaas *et al.*, *Generale Missiven*, vol. III (The Hague, 1968), 911. For an intimate Dutch-Indian relationship in Ramnad, see Bes, "The Setupatis, the Dutch, and Other Bandits," 571.

[78] See, for example, NA, VOC, no. 2403, ff. 1969-9v: letter from Colombo to Tuticorin, Apr. 1737. See also: NA, VOC, no. 1324, ff. 402-2v: letter from Nagapattinam to Colombo, Dec. 1677; Hendrick Becker, *Memoir of Hendrick Becker, Governor and Director of Ceylon, for His Successor, Isaac Augustyn Rumpf, 1716*, ed. Sophia Anthonisz (Colombo, 1914), 34; Arasaratnam, "The Politics of Commerce," 13.

developments at the courts, apart from occasional (and usually fruitless) requests to replace local court representatives at ports where the Company was active.[79]

Further, once political and dynastic events had passed and the new state of affairs became clear, there was little reason for the Dutch to record things differently from what they thought were the actual circumstances. The VOC had no real interest in the outcome of competition at the courts other than the wish that the people in power, on or behind the throne, would adhere to the standing trade agreements. Therefore, by and large, the Dutch adopted a practical approach, trying to cultivate relations with whoever could promote their interests.[80] Because of this combination of a relatively disinterested stance and rather direct access to information, the VOC reports on political developments in these kingdoms can be considered comparatively factual.[81]

[79] It is doubtful whether the VOC was able to interfere with political developments in these kingdoms at all. This would require large-scale inland military operations, entailing high costs without guarantee of satisfactory results. Even a Dutch attempt in 1746 to occupy the relatively small Rameshvaram island off the Ramnad coast, because of a trade conflict, became a failure. See Lennart Bes and Crispin Branfoot, "'From All Quarters of the Indian World': Hindu Kings, Dutch Merchants and the Temple at Rameshvaram" (forthcoming), and the section on Ramnad in Chapter 4.

[80] The VOC did not pursue a neutral policy in various other Asian regions, such as on India's south-western Malabar Coast and in the South-east Asian archipelago, where it was sometimes actively involved in political struggles. For overviews of relations between Asian courts and the VOC, see: Emmer and Gommans, *The Dutch Overseas Empire*, pt. III; Elsbeth Locher-Scholten and Peter Rietbergen (eds), *Hof en handel: Aziatische vorsten en de VOC 1620-1720* (Leiden, 2004); Jurrien van Goor, "Merchants as Diplomats: Embassies as an Illustration of European-Asian Relations," in idem (ed.), *Preclude to Colonialism: The Dutch in Asia* (Hilversum, 2004); idem (ed.), *Trading Companies in Asia 1600-1830* (Utrecht, 1986); Gerrit Knaap and Ger Teitler (eds), *De Verenigde Oost-Indische Compagnie tussen oorlog en diplomatie* (Leiden, 2002); Robert Ross and George D. Winius (eds), *All of One Company: The VOC in Biographical Perspective* (Utrecht, 1986); Adam Clulow and Tristan Mostert (eds), *The Dutch and English East India Companies: Diplomacy, Trade and Violence in Early Modern Asia* (Amsterdam, 2018).

[81] For Dutch or European perceptions of India and the value of Dutch primary sources for researching India's history—mostly concerning the Mughal empire—see: Manjusha Kuruppath, *Staging Asia: The Dutch East India Company and the Amsterdam Theatre, c. 1650 to 1780* (Leiden, 2016), 13-23, 33-50, 129-48; James D. Tracy, "Asian Despotism? Mughal Government as Seen from the Dutch East India Company Factory in Surat," *Journal of Early Modern History* 3, 3 (1999); Guido van Meersbergen, "Ethnography and Encounter: Dutch and English Approaches to Cross-Cultural Contact in Seventeenth-Century South Asia" (unpublished dissertation, University College London, 2015), passim, in particular ch. 1 and Conclusion; idem, "Writing East India Company History after the Cultural Turn: Interdisciplinary Perspectives on the Seventeenth-Century East India Company and Verenigde Oostindische Compagnie," *Journal for Early Modern Cultural Studies* 17, 3 (2017); Kruijtzer, *Xenophobia in Seventeenth-Century India*, 11-17; Vink, "Encounters on the Opposite Coast," 14-17; idem, *Mission to Madurai*, 35-7, 86-124; Subrahmanyam, "Forcing the Doors of Heathendom"; Jos Gommans and Jitske Kuiper, "The Surat Castle Revolutions: Myth of an Anglo-Bania Order and Dutch Neutrality, c. 1740-60," *Journal of Early Modern History* 10, 4 (2006), 384-9: Jos Gommans, "Rethinking the VOC: Two Cheers for Progress," *BMGN – Low Countries*

While the Mackenzie manuscript translations and the VOC records together appear to serve as a balanced combination of sources, exhaustive research of even this selection has proved unfeasible. Whereas all possibly relevant translated Mackenzie manuscripts have been consulted (though not all used) for this work, the vast VOC archives contain so many documents on late Vijayanagara and in particular its heirs that these cannot be studied in their entirety by a single scholar. Consequently, for the latter materials, the focus lies mostly on epochs of notable local political developments or intense Indo-Dutch interaction, which occasions usually produced extensive reports and correspondence. This research therefore generally covers periods surrounding successions to thrones, diplomatic missions, conflicts, and the like. In addition, a number of phases in between such dynamic times have also been studied in detail, so as to gain insight into court politics during quieter stages, which witnessed more stability and continuity in the kingdoms.[82]

Historiography

Scholars in fields as diverse as history, archaeology, religious studies, Indology, anthropology, and art history have written extensively about Vijayanagara, much less about its successors, and very little about these states from a comparative perspective. Works pertaining to the empire include a large number of political and dynastic histories, source publications, collections of miscellaneous papers, and monographs and articles on topics ranging from politics, warfare, and economy to architecture, literature, and religion. Moreover, this Vijayanagara library is frequently being added to.[83]

Historical Review 134, 2 (2019); Carolien Stolte, "Onbekend en onbemind: Over de 'anonimiteit' van lokale medewerkers in zeventiende-eeuws India," in Lodewijk Wagenaar (ed.), *Aan de overkant: Ontmoetingen in dienst van de VOC en WIC (1600-1800)* (Leiden, 2015); Jorge Flores, "'I Will Do as My Father Did': On Portuguese and Other European Views of Mughal Succession Crises," *e-Journal of Portuguese History* 3, 2 (2005), 10-13, 17-18. For some long-term perspectives, see: Joan-Pau Rubiés, *Travel and Ethnology in the Renaissance: South India through European Eyes, 1250-1625* (Cambridge, 2000), for example 28-34; Sanjay Subrahmanyam, *Europe's India: Words, People, Empires, 1500–1800* (Cambridge/London, 2017); idem, *Explorations in Connected History: From the Tagus to the Ganges* (New Delhi, 2005), 17-22, 43-4, 243-4; Peter Rietbergen, *Europa's India: Fascinatie en cultureel imperialisme, circa 1750-circa 2000* (Nijmegen, 2007).

[82] Besides many individual years, more or less continuous periods I have studied in detail in the VOC archives include: for Ikkeri, 1660s-80s, 1730s, 1750s; for Tanjavur, 1660s-90s, 1720s-40s; and for Ramnad, 1720s-50s. See also the overview of consulted sources at the end of this work. Dutch records on Madurai and Ramnad from the 1650s-90s are extensively analysed in Vink, "Encounters on the Opposite Coast."

[83] For overviews of Vijayanagara's historiography, see: Stein, *Vijayanagara*, 2-12, 147-51; Sanjay Subrahmanyam, "Aspects of State Formation in South India and Southeast Asia, 1500-1650," *The Indian*

While V.S. Naipaul stated that the empire is little remembered, this is even truer for its heirs, which have received a fraction of the scholarly attention paid to Vijayanagara. A few works deal with the histories of the individual dynasties, supplemented with publications concerning art, literature, and relations with European powers, among other subjects. The output of new studies concerning these kingdoms has increased in the last decades, but much research still needs to be done and large bodies of primary sources remain uncharted, including much of the Dutch materials. The dynastic historiography is outdated, having been written mostly between the 1920s and 1970s and hardly updated since then.[84] The number of works comparing the successors to one another or to its parental state, the main subject of this study, is downright small.

In consequence, historiographic debates are mostly limited to Vijayanagara and rarely concern its offshoots. Three main discussions have dominated the imperial field, which are briefly considered here. The first deals with the issue of whether Vijayanagara was a "Hindu" bulwark, deliberately constructed against invasions in the name of Islam. The empire has long been seen (and continues to be seen) by several historians as the last place where Hinduism and Indic civilisation flourished in all their purity, fiercely defended against alleged destructive pressures

Economic and Social History Review 23, 4 (1986), 357-66; idem, "Agreeing to Disagree: Burton Stein on Vijayanagara," *South Asia Research* 17, 2 (1997); idem, *Courtly Encounters*, 38-43; Anila Verghese, *Archaeology, Art and Religion: New Perspectives on Vijayanagara* (New Delhi, 2000), ch. 2; Guha, *History and Collective Memory in South Asia*, 147-52; Christopher Chekuri, "Between Family and Empire: Nayaka Strategies of Rule in Vijayanagara South India, 1400-1700" (unpublished dissertation, University of Wisconsin-Madison, 2005), ch. 1; idem, "'Fathers' and 'Sons': Inscribing Self and Empire at Vijayanagara, Fifteenth and Sixteenth Centuries," *The Medieval History Journal* 15, 1 (2012), 141-3; Narayana Rao and Subrahmanyam, "Ideologies of State Building," 213-15; Ota, "A Reappraisal of Studies on *Nāyakas*"; Aniruddha Ray, "The Rise and Fall of Vijayanagar – An Alternative Hypothesis to 'Hindu Nationalism' Thesis," *Proceedings of the Indian History Congress* 64 (2003); S. Chandrashekar, "Robert Sewell's Vijayanagara – A Critique," in Shrinivas Ritti and Y. Subbarayalu (eds), *Vijayanagara and Kṛṣṇadēvarāya* (New Delhi/Bangalore, 2010); Anila Verghese, "Introduction," in idem and Anna Libera Dallapiccola (eds), *South India under Vijayanagara: Art and Archaeology* (New Delhi, 2011), 1-5; and the two bibliographies in Anna Libera Dallapiccola and Stephanie Zingel-Avé Lallemant (eds), *Vijayanagara – City and Empire: New Currents of Research*, vol. 2 (Wiesbaden, 1985), 1-65. For historiographic surveys of the Kannada and Tamil regions, focusing on research by Indian scholars, see: Suryanath U. Kamath (ed.), "Special Number on Karnataka Historiography," *The Quarterly Journal of the Mythic Society* LXXX, 1-4 (1989); N. Subrahmanian, *Tamilian Historiography* (Madurai, 1988).

[84] For (partially outdated) overviews of the historiography of individual successor states, see: Swaminathan, *The Nāyakas of Ikkēri*, 11; Chitnis, *Keḷadi Polity*, vii-ix; Shastry, *Goa-Kanara Portuguese Relations*, 320; Vriddhagirisan, *The Nayaks of Tanjore*, 1-3; Srinivasan, *Maratha Rule in the Carnatic*, 4-5; Subrahmanyam, *Penumbral Visions*, 143-63; Sathyanatha Aiyar, *History of the Nayaks of Madura*, 29-33. For Madurai and Coromandel as well as the historiography of Euro-Indian relations, see also Vink, "Encounters on the Opposite Coast," 2-14.

from Muslim-ruled states.[85] But, as explained earlier, various recent studies argue that Vijayanagara did actually undergo and even actively looked for Perso-Islamic influences from preceding and neighbouring sultanates.[86] This new perspective does not seem to have yet been discussed by supporters of the former viewpoint. Chapter 5 of the present study investigates this borrowing from the Islamic world by the successor states.

Another dispute concerns the question whether Vijayanagara's founding dynasty came from a Kannada-speaking background and sought to associate itself with the earlier Hoysala kingdom in the western Deccan, or stemmed from a Telugu-speaking environment and looked for connections with the erstwhile Kakatiya state in the Deccan's east.[87] Although this debate was brought about by regional patriotism now somewhat vanished, links with older polities continue to be researched. In the past few decades, primary sources dating from various periods in the empire's history have been analysed for royal legitimation efforts based on assumed relations with earlier dynasties. These studies suggest that ties were also forged with houses other than the Hoysalas and Kakatiyas.[88] As discussed in Chapter 1, it appears that over the course of time rulers claimed links with several

[85] Among many other works, see: K.A. Nilakanta Sastri and N. Venkataramanayya (eds), *Further Sources of Vijayanagara History*, vol. I (Madras, 1946); Heras, *The Aravidu Dynasty of Vijayanagara*, vol. I; S. Krishnaswami Aiyangar, *South India and Her Muhammadan Invaders* (London, 1921); and, more recently, Suryanath U. Kamath, *Krishnadevaraya of Vijayanagara and His Times* (Bangalore, 2009), 1-9; Shrinivas Ritti and B.R. Gopal (eds), *Inscriptions of the Vijayanagara Rulers*, vol. I, *Inscriptions of the Rulers of the Sangama Dynasty (1336 A.D. – 1485 A.D.)*, pt. 1 (New Delhi, 2004), li-iii.

[86] See the references in the historical background section of this chapter and in Chapter 5.

[87] For studies supporting the Kannada claim, see: Henry Heras, *Beginnings of Vijayanagara History* (Bombay, 1929); Saletore, *Social and Political Life in the Vijayanagara Empire*; S. Krishnaswami Aiyangar *et al.* (eds), *Vijayanagara Sexcentenary Commemoration Volume* (Dharwar, 1936), reprinted as *Vijayanagara. History and Legacy* (New Delhi, 2000); S. Srikantaya, *Founders of Vijayanagara* (Bangalore, 1938); and also, more recently: Dikshit, *Early Vijayanagara*; idem, "The Foundation of Vijayanagar," *The Karnataka Historical Review* XXVI (1992), 1-2; Kamath, *Krishnadevaraya of Vijayanagara*, 6. For works championing the Telugu cause, see: N. Venkata Ramanayya, *Vijayanagara: Origin of the City and the Empire* (Madras, 1933); idem, *Studies in the History of the Third Dynasty of Vijayanagara* (Madras, 1935). For perhaps more impartial views, both concluding in favour of the Hoysala connection, see: Vasundhara Filliozat (ed.), *l'Épigraphie de Vijayanagar du début à 1377* (Paris, 1973); Hermann Kulke, "Mahārājas, Mahants and Historians: Reflections on the Historiography of Early Vijayanagara and Sringeri," in Anna Libera Dallapiccola and Stephanie Zingel-Avé Lallemant (eds), *Vijayanagara – City and Empire: New Currents of Research*, vol. 1 (Wiesbaden, 1985); and especially idem, *History of Precolonial India*, 106.

[88] For examples, see: Phillip B. Wagoner, "Retrieving the Chalukyan Past: The Stepped Tank in the Royal Centre," in Anila Verghese and Anna Libera Dallapiccola (eds), *South India under Vijayanagara: Art and Archaeology* (New Delhi, 2011); idem, "Harihara, Bukka, and the Sultan: The Delhi Sultanate in the Political Imagination of Vijayanagara," in David Gilmartin and Bruce B. Lawrence (eds), *Beyond Turk and Hindu: Rethinking Religious Identities in Islamic South Asia* (Gainesville, 2000); Cynthia Talbot,

earlier kingdoms, including Muslim-ruled states, to legitimise themselves in the eyes of varying audiences. Indeed, already in the 1510s the Portuguese official Tomé Pires suggested that different regional backgrounds and identities did not exclude one another in Vijayanagara, simply noting that "the king is a heathen of Kanara [Kannada area], and on the other hand he is a Kling [person from the Telugu region, or more generally Coromandel]."[89]

A third debate pertains to Vijayanagara's political structure. Over the years, scholars have used several non-Indian models to characterise the empire's organisation, with mixed results. Among other classifications, it has been described as "centralised" (a war-state with strong military control and tributary governors), "feudal" (a paramount king among petty chiefs holding fiefs), and "segmentary" (replicating political units on different levels, with a ritual sovereign centre being exemplary rather than coercive). While some theories have now been discarded, this discussion continues, for example with suggestions to consider Vijayanagara's political set-up on south Indian terms and an increasing appreciation of changes during the empire's long existence and spatial variation within its enormous realm.[90] The present study has little to contribute to these ideas, as it is concerned with political relations at the courts of the relatively small heirs rather than with imperial political structures. Nevertheless, connections of the successor dynasties with their formal overlords as well as subordinate chiefs and governors are treated in several places in this research.

As said, with regard to the central subject of the present work—a comparative survey of court politics in Vijayanagara's heirs—both the output of studies and historiographic debate have been limited so far. Apart from some general remarks

"The Story of Prataparudra: Hindu Historiography on the Deccan Frontier," in the same volume; Eaton, *A Social History of the Deccan*, ch. 4.

89 Tomé Pires, *The Suma Oriental of Tomé Pires: An Account of the East, from the Red Sea to China, Written in Malacca and India in 1512-1515 …*, ed. Armando Cortesão (London, 1944), vol. I, 64; Rubiés, *Travel and Ethnology in the Renaissance*, 207-8. "Kling" (or *keling*) was the Malay term for Indians from the Coromandel Coast and was therefore used in Melaka, where Pires wrote his work. See also: Burton Stein, *Peasant State and Society in Medieval South India* (New Delhi, 1980), 394; Velcheru Narayana Rao, "Coconut and Honey: Sanskrit and Telugu in Medieval Andhra," in idem (ed.), *Text and Tradition in South India* (Ranikhet, 2016), 152-6.

90 For the centralised, feudal, and segmentary approaches respectively, see for instance: Nilakanta Sastri, *A History of South India*; Noburu Karashima, *Towards a New Formation: South Indian Society under Vijayanagar Rule* (New Delhi, 1992); Stein, *Peasant State and Society*. For a survey of these views, see Ota, "A Reappraisal of Studies on *Nāyakas*." For alternative approaches and general overviews, see: Subrahmanyam, "Aspects of State Formation," 366-77; Morrison, "Coercion, Resistance, and Hierarchy"; Chekuri, "'Fathers' and 'Sons'"; Eaton, *A Social History of the Deccan*, 80; Narayana Rao, Shulman, and Subrahmanyam, *Symbols of Substance*, ch. II; Hermann Kulke (ed.), *The State in India 1000-1700* (Delhi, 1995).

and a few comparisons in the field of art and architecture,[91] the only studies that deal with this topic to a certain extent focus on the main Nayaka states in the Tamil region: Madurai, Tanjavur, and Senji. This body of pioneering research has appeared in the past three decades in mostly collaborative publications by a small number of scholars from various disciplinary and linguistic backgrounds.[92] They argue that Nayaka kingship in the Tamil zone was profoundly different from previous political forms, calling it "an exotic departure" from earlier south Indian kingship.[93] Developments accompanying this shift are thought to have ranged from economic changes, such as increasing commerce and monetisation, to social and cultural transformations, with growing attention to the individual and the body.

These scholars regard as typical for the Nayaka dynasties the lack of claims to high-caste status and legitimising genealogies. Nayaka kings actually prided themselves on belonging to the low-caste Shudra *varṇa* (caste category) instead of the

[91] See: Stein, *Vijayanagara*, 130-9; B. Surendra Rao, "State Formation in Mysore: The Wodeyars," in R. Champakalakshmy, Kesavan Veluthat, and T.R. Venugopalan (eds), *State and Society in Pre-Modern South India* (Thrissur, 2002), 181; George Michell, *Architecture and Art of Southern India: Vijayanagara and the Successor States* (Cambridge, 1995); Crispin Branfoot, "Imperial Memory: The Vijayanagara Legacy in the Art of the Tamil Nayakas," in Anila Verghese (ed.), *Krishnadevaraya and His Times* (Mumbai, 2013); Howes, *The Courts of Pre-Colonial South India*, ch. 2; Amita Kanekar, "Stylistic Origins and Change in the Temples of the Ikkeri Nayakas," in Anila Verghese (ed.), *Krishnadevaraya and His Times* (Mumbai, 2013).

[92] This concerns the research by Velcheru Narayana Rao, David Shulman, and Sanjay Subrahmanyam, working together in various combinations. Their studies first appeared in several articles from the late 1980s on, the earliest mostly included (partially or entirely) in the collaborative works *Symbols of Substance* (1992) and, to a lesser extent, *Textures of Time* (2001), as well as in Subrahmanyam's *Penumbral Visions* (2001). Articles in these monographs (in slightly revised versions) relevant for the present study are: Velcheru Narayana Rao and David Shulman, "History, Biography and Poetry at the Tanjavur Nāyaka Court," *Social Analysis* 25 (1989); idem, "The Powers of Parody in Nāyaka-Period Tanjavur," in Arjun Appadurai, Frank J. Korom, and Margaret A. Mills (eds), *Gender, Genre, and Power in South Asian Expressive Traditions* (Philadelphia, 1991); Sanjay Subrahmanyam and David Shulman, "The Men Who Would Be King? The Politics of Expansion in Early Seventeenth-Century Northern Tamilnadu," *Modern Asian Studies* 24, 2 (1990); David Shulman and Velcheru Narayana Rao, "Marriage-Broker for the God: The Tanjavur Nāyakas and the Maṉṉārkuṭi Temple," in Hans Bakker (ed.), *The Sacred Centre as the Focus of Political Interest* (Groningen, 1992); Sanjay Subrahmanyam, "The Politics of Fiscal Decline: A Reconsideration of Maratha Tanjavur, 1676-1799," *The Indian Economic and Social History Review* 32, 2 (1995); idem, "Reflections on State-Making and History-Making in South India," *Journal of the Economic and Social History of the Orient* XLI, 3 (1998); idem, "Recovering Babel: Polyglot Histories from the Eighteenth-Century Tamil Country," in Daud Ali (ed.), *Invoking the Past: The Uses of History in South Asia* (New Delhi, 1999); David Shulman and Sanjay Subrahmanyam, "Prince of Poets and Ports: Cītakkāti, the Maraikkāyars and Ramnad, ca. 1690-1710," in Anna Libera Dallapiccola and Stephanie Zingel-Avé Lallement (eds), *Islam and Indian Regions*, vol. 1 (Stuttgart, 1993). With the exception of the last work, this study uses the revised editions in the abovementioned monographs.

[93] Narayana Rao, Shulman, and Subrahmanyam, *Symbols of Substance*, 56.

high-ranking Kshatriya or warrior *varṇa*. At the same time, the Nayakas assumed a divine status and were presented as human incarnations of their gods. The king was no longer only submissive to the deity as the latter had become much more dependent on the former. Indeed, the king could be considered to have become god himself. As these scholars suggest, all this changed the role of Brahmins at court. Their importance as ministers, advisors, or recipients of gifts would have decreased.[94]

Also, the notion that power and authority at Indic courts generally derived from the mutual dependence between king and Brahmin, is deemed inapplicable to the Nayaka states. In brief, that notion holds that the Indian king, traditionally a Kshatriya warrior, was prone to commit violence. He therefore needed the Brahmin, belonging to the highest *varṇa*, to sanction his reign. In turn, the Brahmin relied on the king for protection and subsistence.[95] However, arguing that under the Nayaka dynasties king and deity had become one, some of the abovementioned scholars working on Vijayanagara's successors reason that the king now no longer depended on the Brahmin's sanctioning. Thus, in this new construction of south Indian kingship, Brahmins were just servants of the god-king, like everyone else.[96]

Further, according to these scholars, portable wealth, mobility unhindered by ties to specific lands, and personal, loyal linkages to higher authorities were all new elements in the founding of the Nayaka kingdoms. Another proposed notion is that these states were eternally "becoming," suggesting they never completed the full cycle of state formation, maturity, and decay, as illustrated by the Nayakas' continuous referring to their (former) Vijayanagara overlords and their general unwillingness to proclaim full sovereignty. Besides, Nayaka court culture laid great emphasis on physical enjoyment (*bhoga*), particularly of eroticism and food,

[94] Narayana Rao, Shulman, and Subrahmanyam, *Symbols of Substance*; Narayana Rao and Subrahmanyam, "Ideologies of State Building," 223-9; Velcheru Narayana Rao, "Multiple Literary Cultures in Telugu: Court, Temple, and Public," in idem (ed.), *Text and Tradition in South India* (Ranikhet, 2016), 62-3.

[95] For this notion, see for instance: Louis Dumont, *Religion/Politics and History in India: Collected Papers in Indian Sociology* (Paris/The Hague, 1970), 43-5, 63-9; J.C. Heesterman, *The Inner Conflict of Tradition: Essays in Indian Ritual, Kingship, and Society* (Chicago/London, 1985), 111-12, 125-7, 141-2, 152-6; J. Gonda, *Ancient Indian Kingship from the Religious Point of View* (Leiden, 1966), 62-7; David Shulman, *The King and the Clown in South Indian Myth and Poetry* (Princeton, 1985), chs II-III; André Wink, *Land and Sovereignty in India: Agrarian Society and Politics under the Eighteenth-Century Maratha Svarājya* (Cambridge, 1986), 17-19; Darry Dinnell, "*Sāmrājyalakṣmīpīṭhikā*: An Imperial Tantric Manual from Vijayanagara" (unpublished MA thesis, McGill University, 2011), 28-32, 100-6; Karashima, *A Concise History of South India*, 91-2.

[96] Narayana Rao and Subrahmanyam, "Ideologies of State Building," 224; Narayana Rao, "Coconut and Honey," 167. For the more classical king-Brahmin interdependence still found in Vijayanagara under Krishna Raya, see Narayana Rao, "Coconut and Honey," 154. But see also Dinnell, "*Sāmrājyalakṣmīpīṭhikā*," passim, especially ch. 3.

instead of military achievements. This focus manifested itself for instance in literature—where the king triumphed in bed rather than in war—in the performance of religious deeds—involving the feeding of Brahmin priests rather than donations of land and goods to temple deities—and in art—which portrayed the Nayakas not in refined or trim shapes but as heavier figures, often sporting protruding bellies.[97]

The studies setting forth these arguments have opened up the field and set a standard for subsequent research on the Vijayanagara successor states. But ground-breaking, wide-ranging, and inspiring though they are, these studies still leave many questions unanswered. First, the major heirs in the Kannada area, Ikkeri and Mysore (as well as smaller offshoots), remain largely unexplored from a comparative perspective. Second, the mentioned research on the successors in the Tamil zone focuses on general Nayaka concepts of kingship and literary court culture rather than on a comparison of more prosaic matters like dynastic developments and day-to-day court politics.

Our knowledge of such basics is as yet relatively limited, however, and these data have been far from systematically analysed. It might thus be said that for the history of Vijayanagara's heirs, many bones still need to be added to the flesh as it were, instead of the other way round, as is often the case with political historiography. The present study aims at doing precisely that: looking at both the Tamil and Kannada regions, it provides much new basic information on the successor courts, portraying rulers, successions, courtiers, coalitions, conflicts, diplomatic encounters, ceremonies, and so on. But it also attempts to go further than that and evaluate these matters, discussing patterns and variations, trying to explain these, and comparing the successors with one another.

The abovementioned body of research on the Tamil Nayaka kingdoms has initiated some minor debate on Vijayanagara's legacies among its heirs, revolving around the question of how much kingship in the successor states differed from that in earlier polities. In response to the suggestion that the Nayaka period signified a new phase, it has been put forward there was actually a strong ideological continuity between the Nayakas of Madurai and previous dynasties. In this view, some of the allegedly new elements, such as vertical ties with other royal houses, already existed in the Vijayanagara period. Likewise, it has been claimed that certain earlier aspects of dynastic politics, for example the emphasis on genealogical credentials, did not disappear but still played a significant role for Madurai's Nayakas.[98] Thus, such continuities, rather than striking changes, would have

[97] Narayana Rao, Shulman, and Subrahmanyam, *Symbols of Substance*; Narayana Rao and Subrahmanyam, "Ideologies of State Building," 223-9.

[98] Wagoner, "Harihara, Bukka, and the Sultan," 313-14; Crispin Branfoot, "Dynastic Genealogies, Portraiture, and the Place of the Past in Early Modern South India," *Artibus Asiae* LXXII, 2 (2012), 376;

typified Nayaka kingship—a view that the outcome of the present study largely underwrites.

Finally, the political and dynastic historiography on individual Vijayanagara successor states has so far mostly aimed at bringing together basic facts and establishing chronologies. In several such studies, historians portray kings as the most powerful figures at court, or even as absolute rulers, whose position was rarely challenged. Court politics are commonly presented as essentially static and harmonious.[99] Consequently, successions to the throne would have mostly proceeded peacefully, courtiers usually served as loyal functionaries in clearly demarcated offices, and court protocol was widely adhered to since everyone basically acknowledged their place in the court's hierarchy. Thus, on the whole, one's position, status, and power at court—including the king's—were supposedly largely fixed, both in relation to other parties and in time. As the following chapters demonstrate, this research comes to different conclusions.

Secondary literature dealing with individual heirs of Vijayanagara has generated little historiographic discussion about court politics, either in general or on the specific themes of the present research: foundation myths, successions, courtiers, court protocol, influences from the Islamic world, and mutual relations. As explained in the respective chapters, some of these subjects have hardly been analysed at all, while others have been problematised to some extent but still have produced little debate. Moreover, almost none of these themes have been treated in a comparative manner. With the exception of the Conclusion, the following chapters therefore engage in debates with existing historiography to a limited degree. Indeed, this research intends to initiate such discussions.

Given the *status quaestionis* sketched here, a systematic and comparative study of court politics in the Vijayanagara successor states may prove a significant contribution to the historiography of early modern south India. This work hopes to fill some of the current lacunae, through both its comparative approach and its selection of themes, regions, and sources.

idem, "Heroic Rulers and Devoted Servants: Performing Kingship in the Tamil Temple," in idem (ed.), *Portraiture in South Asia since the Mughals: Art, Representation and History* (London/New York, 2018), 174.

99 For some examples, see: Chitnis, *Keḷadi Polity*, 53; Swaminathan, *The Nāyakas of Ikkēri*, 163; Vriddhagirisan, *The Nayaks of Tanjore*, 168; Subramanian, *The Maratha Rajas of Tanjore*, 77; Sathyanatha Aiyar, *History of the Nayaks of Madura*, 238; M. Aseem Banu, "Polity under the Nayaks of Madurai (1529-1736)" (unpublished dissertation, Madurai Kamaraj University, 1981), 16-18, 26; Seshadri, "The Sētupatis of Ramnad," 183; and also: Venkata Ramanayya, *Studies in the History of the Third Dynasty*, 93-4; Madhao P. Patil, *Court Life under the Vijayanagar Rulers* (Delhi, 1999), 50, 58. See also Emma J. Flatt, *The Courts of the Deccan Sultanates: Living Well in the Persian Cosmopolis* (Cambridge, 2019), p. 10.

Structure

This research addresses various aspects of court politics, with a chapter devoted to each. With the exception of Chapter 6, all chapters are organised largely in the same manner. The opening sections introduce the central topic, problematising it, discussing sources and historiography (if any), and explaining the chapter's internal structure. Subsequently, the chapters' central sections focus on the various states and dynasties, always in the same order: first Vijayanagara and next, in more detail, its heirs Ikkeri, Tanjavur—under the Nayakas and the Bhonsles respectively—Madurai, and Ramnad. All these regional sections end with partial conclusions. The chapters' final sections compare the successor states with one another and with the empire and draw general conclusions. This choice for thematic chapters with regional subdivisions, rather than a fully thematic or regional structure, aims at producing both distinct descriptions of individual courts and comparative analyses of the specific research topics.

The chapters' subjects are closely related and follow from one another. Chapters 1 and 2 and the Epilogue together comprise dynastic histories, looking at the origin, all successions, and demise of each royal house, respectively. Chapters 3 and 4 adopt a less exhaustive and dynasty-centred approach and analyse the roles of courtiers and court protocol, investigating both particular events and long-term patterns. Finally, Chapters 5 and 6 zoom out spatially and consider connections between courts, respectively treating influences from Muslim-ruled polities and discussing relations of the successor states among themselves and with Vijayanagara.

More specifically, Chapter 1 concerns dynastic foundations and foundation myths. Each royal house presented stories of its origin to its subjects and other courts. Both the actual foundations and the ways these events came to be depicted over the course of time were essential elements of court politics. Thus, this chapter considers the historical beginnings of Vijayanagara and its heirs, but especially focuses on their origin myths, since these stories served to legitimise the rise to kingship. In order to compare the royal houses, this study identifies motifs that are found in all or most origin stories but manifest themselves in different forms. These include claims to exalted descent, martial skills, divine interventions, natural miracles, real or imagined links to earlier dynasties, acquisition of wealth and royal symbols, cultivation of land, and dynastic continuity.

Essential for such continuity, all dynasties faced the question of succession. Succession practices took various forms and Chapter 2 discusses this diversity by making three comparisons, which all demonstrate great differences: the discrepancy between formal succession principles and actual succession struggles; the contrast between the portrayal of successions in local texts and in European accounts; and the distinct succession practices under each dynasty. The chapter treats every succession in Vijayanagara and the selected heirs, with those after 1500 examined in detail. Our knowledge of many of these occasions has been limited so far, but European and particularly Dutch records contain extensive references to them. Thus, this chapter also presents updated chronologies and genealogies of the successor houses. As such, it takes up the call of a few decades ago for a much needed revision of the dynastic histories of the successor states.[100]

Closely linked to dynastic succession was the influence of courtiers, a term used here in its broadest sense. Chapter 3 is devoted to this diverse group, which comprised numerous contenders for power, both inside and outside the court: people holding official governmental positions, members of the dynasty's extended family, local governors and chiefs, tax-farming magnates and traders, and so on. Operating in rivalling but fluid factions, they could all play a significant role in court politics and thus share in (or take over) the ruler's power. Their influence depended on several factors, such as their formal ranks in the political system, patronage networks, family ties, personal skills, financial means, and mere luck. Based on both local and external sources, this chapter looks at the official functions at each court, traces the careers of individual courtiers, and investigates which people were in actual control. Unlike in Chapter 2, an exhaustive overview is not possible here. Therefore, this chapter considers a selection of cases that both clearly emerge from the sources and together reveal general patterns by including illustrative examples as well as notable exceptions.

The same selection criteria are followed in Chapter 4, which concerns court protocol and insult. These can be regarded as manifestations of attempts to forge, confirm, strengthen, or strain relations between parties at court. Thus, they shed more or a different light on power struggles, inter-state contacts, and diplomatic encounters. On the surface, relationships may have appeared harmonious or at least "courteous," but certain ceremonial—or the departure from it—hinted at the opposite. Humiliating ritual or breach of protocol could indicate hierarchical or discordant relations, but might also assume a life of its own and worsen contacts. This chapter first identifies on what occasions ceremonial was practised and what purposes it served. Next follow descriptions and analyses of protocol and diplomatic insult at each court, examining underlying meanings and effects on relationships. Accounts of Dutch embassies to these kingdoms and missions by the courts to VOC settlements form a major source for this chapter. While Indian texts on protocol are mostly of a normative character, Dutch reports contain numerous references to how it proceeded in practice, describing audience rituals, gift-giving, welcoming and departure ceremonies, eloquence, diplomatic humiliations, and so on. Since protocol during these cross-cultural encounters appears to have been

[100] Narayana Rao, Shulman, and Subrahmanyam, *Symbols of Substance*, xi.

largely based on south Indian customs, it is likely to be representative of local ceremonial in general.

A specific aspect of court protocol—or, more broadly, court culture—concerned influences from the Perso-Islamic world, discussed in Chapter 5. As mentioned, Vijayanagara was affected by politico-cultural ideas and practices from earlier and contemporaneous sultanate courts. This was for instance expressed in court ritual, governmental and military organisation, royal representation in art and texts, and alleged ties to Muslim dynasties. The central issue of this chapter is to what extent Vijayanagara's receptivity to the sultanates' political culture was maintained by its heirs—which mostly bordered Muslim-ruled states and became tributary to them—and how this reflected broader political developments. Aspects of Perso-Islamic influence considered here are dynastic titles, royal dress, and, to a lesser degree, the role of the archetypical sultan of Delhi in court literature. Besides literary works and Dutch records, this chapter is based on inscriptions and works of art (paintings and sculptures) commissioned by the royal houses.

Chapter 6 also treats connections between courts, but looks at the successor states' relations among themselves and with Vijayanagara. Analysing Indian and European sources, this chapter investigates both the heirs' perceptions of each other in literary texts and their multi-faceted, ambivalent coexistence in day-to-day politics. An attempt is thus made to answer the question of whether Vijayanagara's successors regarded themselves as some kind of politico-cultural collective because of their common past and ongoing close, mutual involvement.

The Conclusion reflects on the previous chapters for an overall comparison of the successor states with one another and the empire. Combining the findings in all chapters for each kingdom and considering similarities and differences, this section formulates the central conclusions of this research—pointing to the dynamic nature of these courts and the continuities with earlier periods—and juxtaposes these ideas against the existing historiography.

This study ends with an epilogue about the divergent fortunes of the imperial and successor houses after the demise of their states, or at least their power, showing that neither Vijayanagara nor its offshoots were "completely wiped out"—as V.S. Naipaul phrased it—but in fact left a legacy, traces of which survive until the present day. The chapter that now follows, however, discusses the very beginnings of these dynasties.

CHAPTER 1

Foundations and Foundation Myths

In the realm of Aunagondy lived a man called Niwary. Favoured by his king, he served as the chief of the Coonumnagur lands. In the Shaka year 1227, Niwary's domains passed to his three sons, one of whom, Ramninar, was noticed by the king for his knowledge, wisdom, and valour. The king, Ramroyl, therefore ordered Ramninar to destroy the Caler bands, who were plundering and killing travellers in Aunagondy's southern regions. Accordingly, Ramninar went south and drove all Calers across the Colada River. On his way back home, crossing the wood-apple jungle, he noticed the beautiful trees there and resolved to halt for some days.

Then, one of Ramninar's hunting dogs spotted a lizard ("mosoly") and ran to it, but the lizard jumped on the dog and bit it fiercely. Thereupon, Ramninar concluded this place was very powerful and he decided to settle down here. That night, the goddess Voopaloo Aumen appeared to him in a dream, telling him that she dwelt underground at this site. She urged him to build her a shrine, name his first son after her, and worship her, in return for various favours. Ramninar then sent for his troops, cut down the jungle, and fixed his domain's boundaries between the Colada and Valar Rivers and the villages of Aunacody and Calatoor. He erected a mud fort, populated his new town, and had his brother Bhoomaninar come over. With his other brother, Creestananinar, he travelled back to the Aunagondy king, now named Nroosinvaroyl, and informed him of all that had happened in the south. Arguing that the ancestral lands of Coonumnagur were not sufficient for his subsistence, Ramninar asked the king to install him as chief of the newly established territory.

So it happened. While his brother Creestananinar now became chief of Coonumnagur, Ramninar was granted various titles and other honours, including the use of a palanquin and the name of his household goddess, thus being called Ramvoopalamalavarayninar. He was made commander over twelve war elephants, 7,200 horse riders, and 8,000 foot soldiers. Governing his possessions as a subordinate of Coteyam Viswanitnaiq, ruler of Pondedesam, he steadily increased his power. When Ramninar was again called by the king to defeat the invading Pratoproodra, he razed the enemy's camp and snatched some of his emblems, such as the flag depicting Haunoominta. He then returned to his grateful king and received the lion-head emblem ("simalatot"), whereupon he was sent back to his new town, named Aureyaloor. He reigned over his domain for many years and was then succeeded by his brother Bhoomavoopalamalavarayninar, followed by fifteen other relatives, together ruling for 469 years.[1]

[1] BL/AAS, MT, class III (Tamil: Southern Provinces), no. 35: "Kyfeyeat of the Paulagars of Aureyaloor Paulaput," ff. 110-15. For a summary of a slightly different version, see Hemingway, *Trichinopoly*, vol.

These events, leading to the foundation of a dynasty by a certain Ramninar, are chronicled in the opening section of a text titled "Kyfeyeat of the Paulagars of Aureyaloor Paulaput." This *kaifīyat* (local history) relates the past of the Palaiyakkarars, or chiefs, of Ariyalur, a town 25 miles north of Tanjavur. As the text states in its closing lines, it was composed around 1800 CE by an eminent servant of the Ariyalur chief, and in 1821 translated from the Tamil original into English, recorded in a nine-page manuscript.[2]

Apart from what the foundation story in this *kaifīyat* has to offer, little appears to be known of the origins and early history of the Ariyalur dynasty. Some local sources claim the polity was founded in 1573 by a chief named Arasunilaiyitta Krishnappa Malavaraya. Ariyalur's rulers are said first to have been subordinates of the Nayakas of Senji and the last Aravidu emperors of Vijayanagara, before Madurai's Nayakas became their overlords in the early 1700s. The place is briefly mentioned in a few other south Indian texts, mostly as a forested area sheltering expelled occupants of the Tanjavur throne.[3]

Records of the Dutch East India Company from the late seventeenth and early eighteenth centuries occasionally deal with Ariyalur, since the Dutch concluded a treaty with its rulers for the purchase of textiles in the 1680s. These sources refer to them just as local chiefs (*visiadoors*) or as "land lords," "free lords," and "wood lords" (*lantheeren, vrijheeren, bosheeren*). All these terms imply a semi-subordinate position in the region's dynastic hierarchy—according to the Dutch initially under Madurai, then under Tanjavur, but by the mid-eighteenth century largely autonomous—while the last designation confirms the wooded (and perhaps remote) nature of Ariyalur's territory.[4] Finally, a district handbook compiled by the

I, 344-5. The summary presented here retains the original English spelling of personal and geographic names. I thank Herman Tieken for helping me make sense of some corrupted Tamil words. The meaning of "mosoly" is uncertain, but it may be a corruption of *mucali*, meaning lizard or alligator among other things. It may also derive from *mucal* or *muyal*, rabbit or hare. Considering the many hares in Indian foundation myths, the latter translation is tempting, but I have chosen for lizard, as "mosoly" seems closest to *mucali*.

[2] The text's composer and translator are respectively mentioned as "Pachanotpilla" and "Boboo Row."

[3] R.V.R. Sai Sravan, "Coinage of Madurai Nayakas – A Reappraisal," *Numismatic Digest* 42 (2018), 131; S. Krishnaswami Aiyangar (ed.), *Sources of Vijayanagar History* (Madras, 1919), 326-7; Mahalingam, *Mackenzie Manuscripts*, vol. II (Madras, 1976), 347.

[4] NA, VOC, no. 1299, f. 139; no. 1313, f. 349v; no. 1333, f. 104v; no. 1340, ff. 1346v-8; no. 1349, ff. 1407-7v; no. 1350, ff. 27-9; no. 1449, f. 311; no. 1454, ff. 937-7v, 1011, 1019-20; no. 1494, ff. 636-1110 (no. 5); no. 2631, f. 433: letters from Nagapattinam and Pulicat to Batavia and superintendent Rijcklof van Goens on Ceylon, Dec. 1674, Apr. 1675, Oct. 1678, Aug. 1688, report on the Tanjavur lands and letter from Tirumullaivasal to Nagapattinam, May 1679, correspondence and treaties with Ariyalur, June-July 1688, June 1689, final report (*memorie van overgave*) of Jacob Mossel, Feb. 1744; DNA, DCGCC, no. 3352: report on visit of

British colonial government in the late nineteenth century declares that it proved impossible to gather any reliable information on the Ariyalur rulers before the mid-eighteenth century.[5]

However, the *kaifiyat* cited above, "mythical" though some of its passages may appear, reveals many aspects of the origin of Ariyalur's ruling house—in any case aspects deemed significant enough by the dynasty to be incorporated into the family's foundation myth. Some of the story's elements are clearly linked to historical places, people, and events. The chiefs Niwary and Ramninar serve kings of a realm referred to by a term doubtlessly denoting Anegondi, a town that was part of Vijayanagara's capital region. The kings' names are obviously corruptions of Rama Raya and Narasimha Raya, names and titles borne by historical Vijayanagara rulers. As the text suggests, Ramninar is active in an area near the Kollidam (or Coleroon) River in the empire's south to subdue Kallars—a caste, notably, to which Ariyalur's historical rulers themselves belonged, according to some sources.[6]

Later, Ramninar is said to rule a piece of land that can still be easily located: it lay between the Kollidam and Vellur Rivers and was centred around the town of Ariyalur. His regional overlord, reigning over the Pandya Desam or Madurai realm, can be identified as Kotiya Vishvanatha Nayaka, founder of Madurai's Nayaka dynasty. The invading enemy whom Ramninar defeats at the king's request is most probably Prataparudra, the Gajapati ruler of Orissa. In sum, these elements of the foundation myth tell us about a chief who pacified an area in the Tamil zone (by subjugating what were possibly his fellow caste men), then ruled it as a subordinate of the Nayaka kings of Madurai, and was acknowledged by the Vijayanagara emperors. Ariyalur can thus be considered a Vijayanagara successor state in the sense that its dynasty traced its origin back to imperial recognition.

Other components of the text may seem harder to explain, but these are equally significant for understanding the dynasty's origin. To start with, the story centres around an exceptional individual, whose name is rendered as "Ramninar," perhaps a corruption of Rama Nayinar. His background is somewhat obscure, but his father occupies a politico-military position under a mighty king. Ramninar himself possesses great physical and intellectual skills and performs heroic feats in an area south of his ancestral lands. This links him to the ruling dynasty—Vijayanagara's

an Ariyalur envoy to Colombo, Nov. 1683; *Beknopte historie*, 85. For Jesuit and French references to Ariyalur's forests as a place of refuge, see respectively: A. Saulière (ed.), "The Revolt of the Southern Nayaks" [pt. 2], *Journal of Indian History* XLIV, I (1966), 175; François Martin, *India in the 17th Century (Social, Economic and Political): Memoirs of François Martin (1670-1694)*, ed. Lotika Varadarajan, vol. 1, pt. II (New Delhi, 1983), 561, 575, 587, 590, 592-7, 621, 641, 670.

5 Moore, *A Manual of the Trichinopoly District*, 254.

6 Moore, *A Manual of the Trichinopoly District*, 260. Ariyalur's rulers may also have belonged to the Palli or Vanniyan caste. See Hemingway, *Trichinopoly*, vol. I, 344.

imperial house—which rewards his military services with titles, land, troops, and honours like the use of a palanquin (sedan chair). Besides receiving political recognition, Ramninar's prowess is acknowledged by a deity, the local goddess of the future principality's site, called "Voopaloo Aumen," which probably refers to Oppilada Amman.[7] Through name-gifting and prosperity in return for worship, this deity is intimately tied to the dynasty-to-be. A natural miracle, that of prey (lizard) attacking predator (dog), further signifies the auspicious character of this spot and the status of the hero.

Ramninar subsequently establishes the new realm: he clears jungle areas, sets the borders, and has the capital populated and defended. While one of his brothers stays in the family's ancestral region, Ramninar's migration to the south has now become permanent. On other occasions, a link is forged with a local dynastic power—Madurai's Nayakas—and Ramninar acquires more royal insignia, such as emblems of a lion's head and "Haunoominta," possibly referring to the Monkey-King Hanuman. Finally, after Ramninar's long rule, the text continues with his successors, first his other brother, who has already played a role in the foundation, and then fifteen other relatives, all bearing the title of Malavaraya.[8] Thus, Ramninar's installation is shown to have become a hereditary, dynastic office. By the time the Ariyalur *kaifiyat* was compiled, this position had allegedly been held by the family for almost five centuries.[9]

Analysing this origin myth, we distinguish the following motifs: the founder's descent and status, his physical skills, political ties with other dynasties, religious recognition, auspicious natural miracles, migration, land clearance and territorial markers, acquisition of royal symbols, and the establishment of a hereditary dynasty.[10] All these elements seem to be aimed at legitimating or at least explaining the rise and present status of Ariyalur's royal house.[11] Thus, this *kaifiyat* serves

[7] See Sai Sravan, "Coinage of Madurai Nayakas," 133.

[8] The VOC also used this term for Ariyalur's chiefs, leading to corruptions like "Mallawaraijen" and "Malleweragie." See: NA, VOC, no. 1454, ff. 1019-20: correspondence and treaty with Ariyalur, June-July 1688; DNA, DCGCC, no. 3352: report on a visit of an Ariyalur envoy to Colombo, Nov. 1683.

[9] Some parts of the text are unclear to me. I have not been able to identify ancestral "Coonumnagur." Perhaps it denotes Kunnam, about six miles north of Ariyalur. The year in which these lands passed to Ramninar and his brothers—Shaka 1227 or c. 1305 CE—seems illogical. Vijayanagara was founded several decades later and it is unlikely Ariyalur's chiefs wished to link themselves to earlier dynasties at Anegondi. Another version of the text states Ariyalur's foundation took place in 1405, which appears more logical. See Hemingway, *Trichinopoly*, vol. I, 344. Further, I cannot locate the villages of "Aunacody" and "Calatoor," although the latter may refer to Kolathur, some miles west of Ariyalur.

[10] See also Talbot, *Precolonial India in Practice*, 144.

[11] For analyses of south Indian origin myths, see: Dirks, *The Hollow Crown*, 71-107; Kesavan Veluthat, *The Political Structure of Early Medieval South India* (2nd edition, Hyderabad, 2012), ch. 1, especially 48-51, 55. For Indian origin myths in general, see Pushkar Sohoni, "The Hunt for a Location:

as a useful example of south Indian foundation stories. Many of the text's motifs are also found in the origin stories of the larger and better-known Vijayanagara successor states, and of the empire itself.

This chapter is concerned with the question of how these elements manifest themselves in the origin myths of Vijayanagara's heirs. The purpose is not to thoroughly discuss the narrative of every story, the historical reliability of the texts, or the genre of foundation myths in general. Rather, the chapter aims at a comparison of motifs shared by all or most royal houses to see how these resemble or differ from one another. Foundation stories are regarded here as texts, produced by dynasties, their courtiers, and other associated parties, that relate to those dynasties' beginnings, regardless of the level of historical accuracy.

To deal with the problem of the uncertain provenance of a number of texts—making their relevance doubtful—this study concentrates on events and developments that figure relatively often in the different stories. Therefore, some of the following sections discuss composite versions of origin myths, combining those more regular motifs.[12] Such an approach can be justified in this case, as the purpose is to compare the stories' various elements, rather than to analyse each text on its own. However, attention is also paid to textual passages that deviate from the more common versions.

While historians have extensively analysed Vijayanagara's foundation myths, they have considered only some of the successors' origin stories in detail and have seldom researched them from a comparative perspective.[13] One exception concerns a comparative analysis of the myths of the main heirs in the Tamil-speaking area, the Nayakas of Madurai, Tanjavur, and Senji. According to this analysis—already discussed in the historiography section of the Introduction—the foundation stories of those dynasties show that their form of kingship strongly differed from that of Vijayanagara's royal houses.[14] However, based on a comparison of the motifs in a much wider range of myths, the present chapter concludes that this view needs further nuance since the origin stories of the various successor states varied

Narratives on the Foundation of Cities in South and Southeast Asia," *Asian Ethnology* 77, 1-2 (2018); Romila Thapar, "Origin Myths and the Early Indian Historical Tradition," in idem (ed.), *Ancient Indian Social History: Some Interpretations* (London, 1978), passim, especially 295-7, 302, 320-1; Simmons, *Devotional Sovereignty*, 18-19.

12 I have partially borrowed this approach from William J. Jackson, *Vijayanagara Voices: Exploring South Indian History and Hindu Literature* (Aldershot/Burlington, 2005), 2.

13 These studies are referred to in the subsequent sections. Comparative analyses include: Phillip B. Wagoner (ed.), *Tidings of the King: A Translation and Ethnohistorical Analysis of the* Rāyavācakamu (Honolulu, 1993), 313-14; Dirks, *The Hollow Crown*, chs 3, 6; Heras, *Beginnings of Vijayanagara History*, 9-11; Subrahmanyam, *Penumbral Visions*, ch. 6. See also the next footnote.

14 Narayana Rao, Shulman, and Subrahmanyam, *Symbols of Substance*, 38-56.

substantially among each other and at the same time all shared several elements with the empire's foundation myths.

Starting with Vijayanagara's dynasties and then turning to its heirs, the sections below first look at the actual origins of each royal house, followed by summaries of the foundation stories and overviews of the motifs found in them. In the last section, each motif is considered separately as it appears (or does not appear) in the origin myths of the different dynasties. The chapter ends with general conclusions on how all stories compare to each other.

Vijayanagara

Sangamas

Neither the empire's historical origins nor the provenance of its foundation stories is entirely clear. In fact, little is known with any certainty about the beginnings of Vijayanagara. Much of what is reasonably definite has been touched upon in the previous chapter. In brief, the early fourteenth-century expansion of the Delhi sultanate into south India and its forced withdrawal around 1340 enabled local chiefs and other military men to set up their own polities. These warriors included five sons of Sangama, a chieftain who may have served the Hoysala rulers or another local dynasty. Each operating from their own regional powerbase, the Sangama brothers together founded a state in the Kannada-speaking zone.[15]

Thus emerged Vijayanagara, with its capital on the banks of the Tungabhadra River in an arid and sparsely inhabited region. This strategically chosen spot was the abode of the local goddess Pampa, who guarded the river-crossing here and, through her marriage with Shiva's manifestation Virupaksha, was linked to the pantheon of pan-Indian Hindu gods. The site also had connections with Vishnu, the other main Hindu deity, because his incarnation Rama was believed to have visited the monkey-kingdom of Kishkinda, located at this place, as told in the *Rāmāyaṇa* epic.[16]

[15] For recent summaries of these events, see: Eaton, *India in the Persianate Age*, 80-8; Devadevan, *A Prehistory of Hinduism*, 48-51.

[16] For links between the Vijayanagara capital and the *Rāmāyaṇa*, see: John McKim Malville and John M. Fritz, "Cosmos and Kings at Vijayanagara," in Clive L.N. Ruggles and Nicholas J. Saunders (eds), *Astronomies and Cultures* (Niwot, 1993), 143-7, 154-60; Anila Verghese, "The Sacred Topography of Hampi-Vijayanagara," in idem and Anna Libera Dallapiccola (eds), *South India under Vijayanagara: Art and Archaeology* (New Delhi, 2011), 140-2; Anna Libera Dallapiccola, "Ramayana in Southern Indian Art: Themes and Variations," in idem, 182-9; Anila Verghese, "Deities, Cults and Kings at Vijayanagara," *World Archaeology* 36, 3 (2004), 421, 424, 429; idem, *Religious Traditions at Vijayanagara: As Revealed through Its Monuments* (New Delhi, 1995), ch. 4; John M. Fritz, "Vijayanagara. Authority and Meaning

Inscriptions left by the Sangama dynasty—as the Sangama brothers' descendants came to be known—and other (near-)contemporary sources seem ambiguous about the founders' political and regional background. This has given rise to a heated historiographic debate, mostly held in the 1920s and 1930s. As explained in the Introduction, the discussion concerns the question of whether the Sangama brothers had links with the Kannada area and the Hoysala dynasty, or with the Telugu zone and the Kakatiya house. In addition, Vijayanagara's later dynasties appear to have produced foundation myths that naturally concerned their own past, but also pertained to the roots of the first imperial house. Thus, certain stories about Vijayanagara's foundation by the Sangamas were probably not introduced before the empire's third dynasty, the Tuluvas. Also, some studies suggest that several later Vijayanagara rulers traced their origins back to Kalyana's Chalukya dynasty based in the northern Deccan or to the Delhi sultanate and the Kampili kingdom in the Kannada region.[17]

This coexistence of different foundation myths dating from several dynastic phases makes it hard to draw firm conclusions about Vijayanagara's actual beginnings. Instead, we consider the stories themselves. Since we are interested in the various motifs in these texts, below follows a composite and abridged version of the better-known accounts on the origins of the Sangamas and their empire.

Some stories begin by relating that Muhammad-bin-Tughluq, sultan of Delhi, had installed his nephew Baha al-Din Gushtasp as governor in one of his southern provinces. But when the sultan died, his nephew rebelled against the successor. This new sultan sent an army, upon which Baha al-Din Gushtasp sought refuge with the king of Kampili, a mountainous, isolated kingdom. Finding his palace then besieged by the sultan's overwhelming forces and valuing martial honour over a shameful capitulation, the Kampili Raja and his men resolved to fight to the death, while their women threw themselves into the flames. Delhi's troops thus caught Baha al-Din Gushtasp and flayed him alive. But five sons of a chief named Sangama, who according to inscriptions descended from the Moon,[18] were spared after they surrendered.

of a South Indian Imperial Capital," *American Anthropologist* 88, 1 (1986), 52; idem, "Was Vijayanagara a 'Cosmic City'?," in Anna Libera Dallapiccola and Stephanie Zingel-Avé Lallemant (eds), *Vijayanagara – City and Empire: New Currents of Research* (Wiesbaden, 1985), vol. 1, 265-71; Natalie Tobert, *Anegondi: Architectural Ethnography of a Royal Village* (New Delhi, 2000), 50-1.

17 Eaton, *A Social History of the Deccan*, 94-9; Wagoner, "Retrieving the Chalukyan Past"; idem, "Harihara, Bukka, and the Sultan"; idem, *Tidings of the King*, 184; Barbara Mears, "Symbols of Coins of the Vijayanagara Empire," *South Asian Studies* 24, 1 (2008), 78.

18 For Lunar and Solar royal lines, see for example: J.G. de Casparis, "Inscriptions and South Asian Dynastic Traditions," in R.J. Moore (ed.), *Traditions and Politics in South Asia* (New Delhi, 1979), 105-11; Ali, "Royal Eulogy as World History," 176-93; Thapar, "Origin Myths and the Early Indian Historical Tradition," 299-309.

As several texts go, some or all of these fierce brothers, who had defended Kampili's frontiers, were then taken captive to Delhi. There, one night, two of them, Harihara and Bukka, experienced a terrible thunderstorm. In the ensuing chaos, the prison door accidentally opened, but the brothers chose not to flee. Greatly impressed by their loyalty, the sultan released Harihara and Bukka and assigned them the task of pacifying the recently conquered southern lands, which were disrupted by plundering rebels.

Back in the south, the Sangama brothers came to govern a territory directly north of the Tungabhadra River. One of the myth's versions has it that one day, while sleeping in a forest, Harihara had a dream in which a wise man presented him with a *liṅgam*, Shiva's phallic symbol, saying it would bring him prosperity, victory, and a kingdom. On another occasion, when the brothers were hunting in the forests on the river's southern bank, close to a shrine of Virupaksha, a hare turned against the dogs that were chasing it and bit them. The great Brahmin sage Vidyaranya, meditating nearby, explained that this event demonstrated the great power of this spot, where no enemy could harm even the weak. A city and a kingdom should therefore be founded here.

In one tradition, this foundation had already been foretold to Vidyaranya by several deities and seers during a pilgrimage to Benares on the Ganga River (Varanasi on the Ganges). In yet an earlier stage, the sage tried to gain a vision of the goddess Bhuvaneshvari in order to attain wealth, but his efforts proved unsuccessful. Disappointed, Vidyaranya renounced the world and became a hermit. Only then did Bhuvaneshvari finally appear to him and grant his wish to be showered with gold from the sky to make the future kingdom prosper.

According to some texts, now that the hour to found the city had come, Vidyaranya determined the precise rituals and perfect time for the occasion. Exactly at the most auspicious moment, the sage would blow a conch shell from some distance upon which the founding ceremony was to commence. But a nearby wandering monk, announcing his begging for alms, happened to blow his own conch shell just a bit earlier. Vidyaranya's confused assistants now executed the prescribed rituals too soon, in consequence of which the city would not exist for 3,600 glorious years, but instead survive for only 360 less glorious years.[19]

[19] For an explanation of this episode, see Wagoner, *Tidings of the King*, 31-47. One text says this accident was deliberately caused by Indra, king of the gods, who did not wish to see Vijayanagara city "remain forever fortunate and victorious." The reason for this is not given. See BL/AAS, MG, no. 11, pt. 3b: "History of the kings of Beejanagur & Anagoondy," f. 15 (account compiled in 1801 by Mackenzie's assistant Borayya Kavali Venkata from enquiries made in the area of Vijayanagara city; see also Colin Mackenzie (ed.), "History of the Kings of Veejanagur, or Beejanagur, and Anagoondy, from Enquiries Made at Alputtun and Anagoondy ...," in Lawrence Dundas Campbell (ed.), *The Asiatic Annual Register, or, View of the History of Hindustan, and of the Politics, Commerce, and Literature of Asia, for the Year*

Nevertheless, the city's first king, Harihara, started constructing palaces, temples, and fortifications, moved his people there, and named the place "Vidyanagara" after the sage. After a reign of many years, he was succeeded by his brother Bukka.[20]

Additionally, some versions of the foundation myths say that the Sangama brothers served the king of Warangal (instead of Kampili) before they were taken to Delhi and that the southern rebels they subdued on the sultan's behalf were in fact the

1804 (London, 1806), section "Characters," 24-33, which appears to be a published version of this manuscript).

20 This inexhaustive summary is partly based on the composite story in Jackson, *Vijayanagara Voices*, 2-9, 14 (ns 12, 19), who in turn compiled his synthesis from several publications (see 14, n. 17). Vijayanagara's different foundation myths are dealt with in a whole body of primary sources and secondary literature. Some of the most obvious works—also used for the abridged version here—include: Nilakanta Sastri and Venkataramanayya, *Further Sources of Vijayanagara History*, vol. III, 6-15; Sewell, *A Forgotten Empire*, 16-23, 291-300; Rubiés, *Travel and Ethnology in the Renaissance*, 259-63; Heras, *Beginnings of Vijayanagara History*; Venkata Ramanayya, *Vijayanagara*; Srikantaya, *Founders of Vijayanagara*; Kulke, "Mahārājas, Mahants and Historians"; Wagoner, *Tidings of the King*, 33-50, 77-86, 165-9, 181-90; idem, "Harihara, Bukka, and the Sultan"; Nobuhiro Ota, "Who Built 'the City of Victory'? Representation of a 'Hindu' Capital in an 'Islamicate' World," in Crispin Bates and Minoru Mio (eds), *Cities in South Asia* (London/New York, 2015); Subrahmanyam, *Penumbral Visions*, 187-92; M.H. Rāma Sharma, *The History of the Vijayanagar Empire: Beginnings and Expansion (1308-1569)*, ed. M.H. Gopal, vol. I (Bombay, 1978), 10-23; Nilakanta Sastri, *A History of South India*, 233-41; Anna Libera Dallapiccola (ed.) and C.T.M. Kotraiah (trans.), *King, Court and Capital: An Anthology of Kannada Literary Sources from the Vijayanagara Period* (New Delhi, 2003), 24; Verghese, "Deities, Cults and Kings at Vijayanagara," 419-21; Sohoni, "The Hunt for a Location," 226-7; Eaton, *A Social History of the Deccan*, chs 1-2; Mahalingam, *Mackenzie Manuscripts*, vol. II, 43-4; Dinnell, "*Sāmrājyalakṣmīpīṭhikā*," 57. See also B.A. Dodamani, *Gaṅgādevī's Madhurāvijayaṁ: A Literary Study* (Delhi, 2008), 3-7, for an interesting version of which the source is unfortunately not mentioned. For the Sangamas' Lunar descent, see for example: Robert Sewell (ed.), *Lists of Inscriptions, and Sketch of the Dynasties of Southern India* (Madras, 1884), 11-14; N. Ramesan (ed.), "The Krāku Grant of Harihara II," in N. Venkataramanayya and P.V. Parabrahma Sastry (eds), *Epigraphia Āndhrica*, vol. II (Hyderabad, 1974), 74; N. Venkataramanayya (ed.), "Pedda Cheppalli Plates of Dēvarāya II," in idem (ed.), *Epigraphia Andhrica*, vol. I (Hyderabad, 1969), 33, 39; Dirks, *The Hollow Crown*, 36; BL/AAS, MG, no. 10, pt. 15: "Danaputram at Chitteldroog," f. 237 (translated from a Sanskrit copper engraving found at Chitradurga in 1800); no. 3, pt. 4c: "Hurry-Hurra Royer Vumshum," f. 131. For more Vijayanagara origin stories in the English Mackenzie manuscripts, mostly concerning the role of Vidyaranya, see: BL/AAS, MG, no. 3, pt. 1: "Sketch of the general history of the peninsula," ff. 45-6 (probably translated from a Telugu text collected in 1801 from the Brahmins "Auhobala Sastry" and "Yanam Acharee" at the town of "Paughur," perhaps Pavagada west of Penukonda; see ff. 19, 23 and Cotton, Charpentier, and Johnston, *Catalogue of Manuscripts in European Languages*, vol. I, pt. II, 29); no. 11, pt. 3b: "History of the kings of Beejanagur & Anagoondy," ff. 13-16 (see also Mackenzie, "History of the Kings of Veejanagur"); no. 40, last pt.: "History of the kings of Beejayanagurr," ff. 357-70 (translated from a Telugu text in 1797, in turn translated by Brahmins at Nellore from a Sanskrit palm-leaf text, see ff. 353-5 and Cotton, Charpentier, and Johnston, *Catalogue of Manuscripts in European Languages*, vol. I, pt. II, 400); MT, class VII, no. 23: "Chronological account of Bijayanagar," ff. 130-3.

Hoysalas. Finally, other accounts claim the Sangamas were local cowherds before Vidyaranya installed them as the rulers of Vijayanagara.[21]

As said, certain elements of these various stories perhaps date from the period of the later Tuluva dynasty. In particular the role of the sage Vidyaranya may have been introduced in the sixteenth century through forged inscriptions by the monastic order of Sringeri, in the Kannada area. The sage had been a member of this order, which thus sought to promote itself by emphasising its essential role in the empire's origins.[22] The possible late provenance of these elements makes them no less relevant for our purpose, however, as it was under the Tuluva house that the dynasties of the main successor states were installed or incorporated into the imperial political system. It is therefore likely that the foundation myths of those dynasties were related to imperial origin stories current in the Tuluva period.

Saluvas, Tuluvas, and Aravidus

Besides what can be considered the "standard" foundation myths of Vijayanagara and the Sangama dynasty, there are sources concerning the origins of the empire's second, third, and fourth dynasties: the Saluvas, Tuluvas, and Aravidus. In its relatively few inscriptions and literary texts, the short-lived Saluva house (c. 1485-1503) refers to several direct forefathers who, as military officers of the Sangamas, destroyed the armies of the sultan of Madurai and other kings, and restored the important temple of Srirangam in the Tamil region.

A Sanskrit work titled *Sāḷuvābhyudaya*, written at the Saluva court by the poet Rajanatha Dindima II, describes how the deity Narasimha (in his local manifestation Ahobilanarasimha) appears in a dream to the father of the dynasty's founder. The god, a form of Vishnu, announces his own birth in the human world as the father's son. This human Narasimha—the first Saluva ruler—performs various military feats (some in locations as far as the Himalaya mountains), worships Shiva at different temples, and honours Brahmins and scholars. He is anointed as *cakravarti* or universal emperor (literally "turner of the wheel") in Benares, while music and a shower of flowers come from heaven. Hereafter Saluva Narasimha returns to the imperial capital, laden with tribute from subordinate kings.

The *Rāmābhyudaya*, another Sanskrit poem composed under Saluva rule, even states that Saluva Narasimha's immediate ancestors included several universal kings and a goddess. Other sources mention that the Saluva family originated from

[21] For a recent discussion of Vijayanagara's foundation myths that includes these alternative versions, see Ota, "Who Built 'the City of Victory'?"

[22] Heras, *Beginnings of Vijayanagara History*, 11-35; Kulke, "Mahārājas, Mahants and Historians," 122-4; Devadevan, *A Prehistory of Hinduism*, 50-2.

the Chalukya dynasty of Kalyana and had marital alliances with the Sangama dynasty. Finally, both inscriptions and manuscripts trace the Saluva family's ancestry back to several legendary figures and eventually the Moon.[23]

The next dynasty of Vijayanagara, the Tuluvas (c. 1503-70), largely employed the same motifs to explain its origins: celestial descent, ancestors with great physical skills, links to earlier imperial houses, and connections with important temples and deities. Various poems written by or dedicated to the Tuluva rulers Krishna (or Krishnadeva) Raya and Achyuta (or Achyutadeva) Raya, such as the former's Telugu *Āmuktamālyada*, relate how their ancestors sprang from the Lunar race, defeated numerous kings and sultans all over India, and endowed Hindu shrines. Notably, the Telugu work *Manucaritramu* of the Tuluva court poet Allasani Peddana further specifies that this dynasty belonged to a more exalted Lunar family branch than the Sangamas, stressing the Tuluvas' distinct and particularly prominent status. In a somewhat contradictory manner, some inscriptions actually claim that Krishna Raya and Sadashiva Raya, the last Tuluva, descended from the Sangama house.[24]

The origin myths of the final Aravidu dynasty (c. 1570-1660s) are of a similar kind, including frequent references to military heroes and the Moon as ancestors. But the Aravidu stories appear especially keen on establishing kinship ties with the earlier imperial houses and the Chalukyas of Kalyana (whom the Saluvas claimed as ancestors too). Although the first de facto Aravidu ruler, Rama Raya, was a son-in-law

[23] Krishnaswami Aiyangar, *Sources of Vijayanagar History*, 29-32, 85-6, 90-2; P. Rama Sarma, *Saluva Dynasty of Vijayanagar* (Hyderabad, 1979), 32-49; Ewa Dębicka-Borek, "The Bravery of Sāḷuva Narasiṃha and the Grace of Narasiṃha Deity," in Tiziana Pontillo (ed.), *Indologica Taurinensia: The Journal of the International Association of Sanskrit Studies*, vol. XL (Turin, 2014); Rāma Sharma, *The History of the Vijayanagar Empire*, vol. I, 87-8; Eaton and Wagoner, *Power, Memory, Architecture*, 119 (n. 35).

[24] Krishna(deva) Raya, *Sri Krishna Deva Raya: Āmuktamālyada*, ed. Srinivas Sistla (Visakhapatnam, 2010), 140-5; Krishnaswami Aiyangar, *Sources of Vijayanagar History*, 106-8, 133, 170-6; BL/AAS, MG, no. 10, pt. 2: "Vaamashavally of Cristna-Deva-Rayaloo," ff. 41-3 (which appears to be the introductory section to the *Āmuktamālyada*, see Cotton, Charpentier, and Johnston, *Catalogue of Manuscripts in European Languages*, vol. I, pt. II, 89-91); Allasani Peddana, *The Story of Manu*, trans. Velcheru Narayana Rao and David Shulman (Cambridge (MA)/London, 2015), 18-27; Srinivas Reddy, *Raya: Krishnadevaraya of Vijayanagara* (New Delhi, 2020), 5-6; Padigar, "Inscriptions of the Vijayanagara Rulers," 162; Sewell, *List of Inscriptions*, 4-5, 12, 16, 18, 30; P.V. Parabrahma Sastry (ed.), "Polepalli Grant of Achyutarāya," in idem (ed.), *Epigraphia Āndhrica*, vol. IV (Hyderabad, 1975), 133; Eaton and Wagoner, *Power, Memory, Architecture*, 119 (n. 35). See also: Velcheru Narayana Rao, David Shulman, and Sanjay Subrahmanyam, "A New Imperial Idiom in the Sixteenth Century: Krishnadevaraya and His Political Theory of Vijayanagara," in Sheldon Pollock (ed.), *Forms of Knowledge in Early Modern Asia: Explorations in the Intellectual History of India and Tibet, 1500-1800* (Durham/London, 2011), 74; Narayana Rao and Subrahmanyam, "Ideologies of State Building," 219.

of the Tuluva emperor Krishna Raya, one text declares him to be Krishna Raya's son. Another work from the Aravidu period states that the Sangamas, Saluvas, and Tuluvas all belonged to the same "race." Yet another story from this time suggests that Krishna Raya (third dynasty) was a son of Saluva Narasimha (second dynasty), who in turn was a son of the Sangama ruler Bukka (first dynasty). Still other texts have it that Vira Narasimha (third dynasty) was a son or distant cousin of Saluva Narasimha (second dynasty), that the former's brothers Krishna Raya and Achyuta Raya were Saluva Narasimha's descendants, or that the latter was the son of Praudha, the last Sangama ruler (first dynasty). Furthermore, various inscriptions mention Tuluva and Aravidu rulers with Saluva family titles.[25] All these claims seem to reflect efforts to connect the consecutive imperial houses to each other or even present them as one continuous dynasty or *vaṃśam* (family).

As for Aravidu links with the erstwhile Chalukya dynasty and its capital Kalyana, titles of for example Rama Raya and Venkata I glorify them as descendants and emperors of the Chalukyas, and as founders, lords, kings, and conquerors of Kalyana. Aravidu court literature, such as the Telugu *Rāma rāja charitra* (probably commissioned by Rama Raya himself), also mentions Aravidu rulers as having Chalukya ancestors, maintaining the Kalyana kingdom, and being Chalukya emperors themselves.[26] Finally, after the Aravidus had shifted the imperial capital

[25] Krishnaswami Aiyangar, *Sources of Vijayanagar History*, 79-80, 102, 190, 204, 210, 216, 224; Nilakanta Sastri and Venkataramanayya, *Further Sources of Vijayanagara History*, vol. III, 70-1, 83; BL/AAS, MG, no. 3, pt. 4d: "Veera Narasinga Royer Vumsham," f. 141; no. 3, pt. 1: "Sketch of the general history of the peninsula," f. 47; no. 40, last pt.: "History of the kings of Beejayanagurr," ff. 370-2; no. 10, pt. 4a: "Account of Bisnagur," f. 65; no. 11, pt. 3a: "History of the Anagoondy Rajahs," ff. 9-10 (related in 1801 by the chief of Anegondi, probably named Timmapah and residing in Kamalapur, see: Cotton, Charpentier, and Johnston, *Catalogue of Manuscripts in European Languages*, vol. I, pt. II, 98-100; Colin Mackenzie (ed.), "History of the Anagoondy Rajahs, Taken from the Verbal Account of Timmapah, the Present Representative of that Family, at Camlapore ...," in Lawrence Dundas Campbell (ed.), *The Asiatic Annual Register, or, View of the History of Hindustan, and of the Politics, Commerce, and Literature of Asia, for the Year 1804* (London, 1806), section "Characters," 21-4, which appears to be a published version of this manuscript); no. 11, pt. 3b: "History of the kings of Beejanagur & Anagoondy," f. 17 (see also Mackenzie, "History of the Kings of Veejanagur"); no. 11, pt. 17: "Genealogy or Vanshavallee of Kistna Rayeel," 160 (collected or compiled in 1800); Robert Sewell (ed.), *The Historical Inscriptions of Southern India (Collected till 1923) and Outlines of Political History* (Madras, 1932), 241, 266; idem, *Lists of Inscriptions*, 2-3, 21; Heras, *The Aravidu Dynasty of Vijayanagara*, vol. I, 17-20; Kamath, *Krishnadevaraya of Vijayanagara*, 21, 23.

[26] Alan Butterworth and V. Venugopaul Chetty (eds), *A Collection of the Inscriptions on Copper-Plates and Stones in the Nellore District* (Madras, 1905), pt. I, 33, 41; Eaton, *A Social History of the Deccan*, 94-9; Wagoner, "Retrieving the Chalukyan Past," 130-2; Eaton and Wagoner, *Power, Memory, Architecture*, 85-116; H.H. Wilson, *The Mackenzie Collection: A Descriptive Catalogue of the Oriental Manuscripts and Other Articles Illustrative of the Literature, History, Statistics and Antiquities of the South of India; Collected by the Late Lieut. Col. Colin Mackenzie*, vol. I (Calcutta, 1828; published with

to the south of the Telugu-speaking region, inscriptions sometimes designated them as "sultan of Warangal." Thus, they now also sought to associate themselves with Warangal's Kakatiya dynasty, which had ruled the Telugu zone in the past.[27]

***

Although there are differences between the origin myths of the four imperial houses—for example with regard to descent and alleged relations with earlier dynasties—the basic elements are largely similar to each other as well as to those in Ariyalur's foundation myth, summarised in this chapter's introduction. Looking at each of these motifs, one notices that all Vijayanagara's dynastic founders are generally portrayed as being of extraordinary descent, with ancestors including the Moon and other deities, glorious past kings, and forefathers known for their heroic martial deeds. All founders themselves also excel in physical prowess, defending boundaries, subjugating sultans, or conquering kingdoms.

Each imperial house claims ties with earlier dynasties. Among these, the kings of Kampili and the sultans of Delhi seem most prominent in the stories on the Sangamas, some of which possibly emerged only under the Tuluvas and would thus actually reflect their views.[28] But, as explained, scholars have also mentioned the Hoysalas and Kakatiyas in this respect. The Saluva and Aravidu houses appear to share a focus on the Chalukyas of Kalyana. Additionally, the second, third, and fourth dynasties all link themselves to the previous imperial houses through military service and marital or blood bonds.

Connections of a religious nature range from the sage Vidyaranya and Harihara's dream of receiving Shiva's *liṅgam* to heavenly omens at Narasimha Saluva's coronation and the relationships of all founders with temples. The natural wonder of a hare attacking dogs indicates the significance of the Vijayanagara site as a place of refuge, where the weak can withstand the powerful. As for migration, whichever earlier state the Sangama founders are associated with (a combination of Kampili and Delhi or one of the Hoysala and Kakatiya kingdoms), the brothers have to cover vast distances to reach their new territory. The same applies to the Saluvas and Aravidus, considering their claim to originate in Kalyana. Besides,

vol. II in one volume at Madras, 1882), 297-9, 303; William Taylor, *Catalogue Raisonné[e] of Oriental Manuscripts in the Library of the (Late) College, Fort Saint George, [Now in Charge of the Board of Examiners] in the Government Library*, vol. III (Madras, 1862), 200-1; Krishnaswami Aiyangar, *Sources of Vijayanagar History*, 182.

[27] Talbot, *Precolonial India in Practice*, 196.

[28] For links with Kampili, see also: N. Venkata Ramanayya, *Kampili and Vijayanagara* (Madras, 1929); V.K. Bhandarkar, "Kampili Raya and the Founders of Vijayanagara," *Proceedings of the Indian History Congress* 5 (1941).

Narasimha Saluva needs to travel back and forth to Benares in north India to be anointed as emperor. The sage Vidyaranya also visits Benares, and other locations around India, before he can play his part in the empire's foundation.

The clearance of land is referred to when the Sangama brothers are said to be hunting in forests while they spot the miraculous hare at the site of their capital-to-be. Further, origin stories from different dynastic periods make clear that Harihara's regal position becomes a hereditary office when it passes to his relatives. The texts mention as his successor his brother Bukka, followed by other Sangama descendants, or trace the family line directly to kings of later imperial dynasties.

Vijayanagara's origin myths appear to be silent on the acquisition of symbols of royalty. This might be explained by the fact that the imperial houses do not claim to have been installed by another, external dynasty. One story traces the Sangamas' initial appointment to the sultan of Delhi, but by the time they found their kingdom with the assistance of the sage Vidyaranya, this earlier link has been severed. The Sangamas therefore do not receive royal symbols from any overlord, unlike Ramninar of Ariyalur who acquires emblems and other honours when he renders military service to his master.

Finally, Vijayanagara's origin stories include an aspect seemingly missing in Ariyalur's myth: the acquisition of wealth to set up a kingdom. As we are told, Vidyaranya seeks to obtain a fortune but the goddess Bhuvaneshvari he prays to does not acknowledge him. Only when he gives up his worldly desires is his wish granted, with the condition that the treasure be used to foster Vijayanagara's prosperity. A variation on this theme might be the passage about Narasimha Saluva carrying his vassals' tributes on his return to the imperial capital.

Successor States

In comparison with Vijayanagara's many different origin stories, the foundation myths of its heirs are relatively few and uniform. The following pages first consider the Nayakas of Ikkeri, based in the Kannada region. Next, moving to the Tamil zone, this survey discusses the two houses consecutively ruling Tanjavur, the Nayakas and the Bhonsles, and then turns to the Nayakas of Madurai and the Setupatis reigning over Madurai's offshoot, Ramnad.

Nayakas of Ikkeri

The circumstances of the rise of Ikkeri's Nayakas are unclear. The dynasty's earliest inscription, dating from 1506 in the name of one Chaudappa, does not refer to the Vijayanagara emperors, even though they held sway over this region. Chaudappa, an adherent of the Lingayat religious tradition (devoted to Shiva and rejecting caste discrimination), seems to have been a semi-autonomous chief wielding some authority in the area around the town of Keladi, in the hilly, wooded central Kannada zone. The dynasty's history becomes less obscure under Chaudappa's son Sadashiva Nayaka, who is thought to have reigned until the 1560s, now from the nearby town of Ikkeri. Inscriptions of the mid-sixteenth century state that Sadashiva governed several provinces on behalf of Vijayanagara's Tuluva rulers. By this time, the family's power had apparently been recognised and incorporated by the empire. Chaudappa and Sadashiva can thus together be considered as the founders of Ikkeri's Nayaka house.[29]

The dynasty's origin myths are found in several texts. Two of these have been published in their original language and are extensively discussed in secondary literature. First, the *Śivatattva ratnākara* is an encyclopaedic poem, composed in Sanskrit by Ikkeri's King Basavappa (or Basavaraja) Nayaka in the early eighteenth century, that includes a section on the dynasty's history. Second, the Kannada *Keḷadinṛpa vijayam*, allegedly written in the second half of the eighteenth century by Linganna Kavi, a descendant of an Ikkeri court poet, narrates the story of the royal house from its foundation to its fall in 1763.[30]

A third text, probably originally titled *Keḷadi arasara vaṃśāvaḷi* in Kannada, is available in a forty-six-page manuscript English translation in the Mackenzie collections. This genealogical account of Ikkeri's Nayakas also starts with the founders of the dynasty but ends a few years before its termination, at least in the English version. Its author and date of composition are unknown.[31] The abridged

[29] Swaminathan, *The Nāyakas of Ikkēri*, 12-30; Chitnis, *Keḷadi Polity*, 7-13. For the Lingayat sect, see for example Nilakanta Sastri, *A History of South India*, 435-6.

[30] Radha Krishnamurthy, *Sivatattva Ratnākara of Keladi Basavaraja: A Cultural Study* (Keladi, 1995); K.N. Chitnis, "Sivatattvaratnakara with Special Reference to Polity," *Proceedings of the Indian History Congress* 28 (1966); M. Chidananda Murthy, "*Keḷadinṛipa Vijayam* – A Historical Poem," in G.S. Dikshit (ed.), *Studies in Keladi History (Seminar Papers)* (Bangalore, 1981); B.R. Gopal, "A Note on the Genealogy of the Early Chiefs of Keḷadi," in idem; Taylor, *Catalogue Raisonné*, vol. III, 237; Swaminathan, *The Nāyakas of Ikkēri*, 6-8; Chitnis, *Keḷadi Polity*, 4-6. See also the introductions in the two volumes of Basavappa Nayaka (Basavaraja), *Śivatattva Ratnākara of Basavarāja of Keḷadi*, ed. S. Narayanaswamy Sastry and R. Rama Shastry (Mysore, 1964, 1969). For a comparison of the two texts, see K.R. Basava Raja, "Sources of the History of Minor Principalities," in S.P. Sen (ed.), *Sources of the History of India*, vol. I (Calcutta, 1988), 79-81.

[31] BL/AAS, MG, no. 6, pt. 11: "Historical account of Beedoonoor or Caladee Samstanum," ff. 61-83v. For some (very limited) background information on this text and its probable original name, see: Cotton, Charpentier, and Johnston, *Catalogue of Manuscripts in European Languages*, vol. I, pt. II, 63-4; Wilson, *The Mackenzie Collection*, vol. II, 48-9; R. Narasimhachar, "The Keladi Rajas of Ikkeri and Bednur," *Journal of the Royal Asiatic Society* (New Series) 43, 1 (1911), 188. This text possibly originated as a summary or collection of excerpts from the *Keḷadinṛpa vijayam* since it appears to overlap with

foundation story that follows (retaining the original English spelling of names) is based on this translated *Keḷadi arasara vaṃśāvaḷi*, but largely agrees with the relevant sections in the other two texts.

In the village of Caladee near Halabaidoo, in an ant hole, the god Ram-Eswur appeared as a lingam (phallic symbol). At that time, the village headman ("goud") of Caladee, Baswapah, was a pious worshipper of Eswur and a man of great wisdom. By his devout and virtuous wife Baswaka he had two sons, Choudapah and Badrapah. After their birth, Baswapah's wealth and property increased. When the sons had attained manhood, they became great warriors and subsisted on husbandry. Ram-Eswur, the tutelary god of Halabaidoo, once appeared in Choudapah's dream as a Brahmin, and explained he had incarnated in (what was now referred to as) a snake hole in the jungle of Caladee. That was proved by a black cow owned by Choudapah that went daily to the snake hole with her calf and poured her milk into it. Choudapah was further told that if he witnessed this and worshipped the lingam, he would obtain riches and affluence.

Overjoyed, Choudapah looked for the cow, observed what had been foretold, and found the lingam in the snake hole. He had the jungle cleared, built a small shrine of straw at that site, and allotted revenues for daily worship. One day, when Choudapah returned from his fields and was tired, he rested under a mango tree. His mother, alarmed by his long absence, went searching for him. She found him asleep under the tree, while a snake was rearing its crest and waving its head over him. The snake then moved away, and when Choudapah was woken up by his mother, it waved its head and signalled them to follow it into the paddy grounds. There the snake slapped the earth, urging them to dig here, and disappeared. Choudapah marked the spot and soon returned with his younger brother Badrapah. They found a great pot full of treasure in the ground and built a strong house with it.

Choudapah had a son named Sadaseva and married him to two virgins. They continued their worship of the god Caladee-Ram-Eswur and cultivated their lands. Now King Auchoota-Rayaloo of Veedyanagur heard about Choudapah and the treasure he had discovered. Thinking that a humble man should not be deprived of his good fortune, the king elevated Choudapah to a suitable rank and dignity. He sent him and his brother Badrapah a letter, palanquins, horses, and presents, and had them brought into his presence. Seated in his audience hall, the king received them graciously and enquired how they had obtained their riches. Hearing their reply, he concluded the brothers were truly devout worshippers and honoured them.

At this time, arrogant chieftains and Moorish people were causing disturbances all over the country, and the king ordered Choudapah and Badrapah to destroy or expel these people.

the sections of that work that have a more narrative character. I thank Caleb Simmons for bringing this to my notice. For a reference that possibly concerns the acquisition of the original version of either of these texts (although reported to be in Sanskrit, written in Kannada script) by Colin Mackenzie's assistants from an "astronomer," see BL/AAS, MT, class XII, no. 11: "Report of the Soobarow Marratta writer to Major C. Mackenzie" (1805), ff. 105, 111.

Accordingly, the brothers fought with them and brought several prisoners back. The king was so pleased with their valour that he granted them the eight districts of Caladee and other places, and honoured them with the conch shell ("sankoo"), the wheel ("chakrum"), other insignia, and troops. Then the brothers returned home, summoned the chiefs of their lands before them, and asked them to populate the country. Choudapah built a palace ("aramonnee") at Caladee, was acknowledged by royal order in the Shaka year 1422, and received precious offerings from the inhabitants of Caladee and Ekaree. In the latter place, he saw a hare resisting one of his dogs. Considering that this location was favoured by heaven and full of valour, he built a strong fort and a magnificent palace there. He also erected a stone temple for the god Ram-Eswur. After thirteen years Choudapah departed from this world and his son Sadaseva Naik reigned with great charity.[32]

The text continues with the military feats performed by Ikkeri's new ruler Sadashiva Nayaka ("Sadaseva Naik") for Vijayanagara's Tuluva rulers. He subjugates a number of rebels and conquers some provinces of the Deccan sultanates, such as Kalyana and Gulbarga ("Calyanum," "Calabaraga"). In return, he receives honours from the emperor, including a valuable dagger, jewels, betel-leaves (to be consumed with areca-nuts), titles, and the ring of the captured sultan of Bidar. Furthermore, Sadashiva builds temples, endows Brahmin villages, and performs other religious duties.[33]

As said, the origin myth above is only marginally different from the foundation stories in the *Śivatattva ratnākara* and *Keḷadinṛpa vijayam*. In the *Śivatattva ratnākara*, for instance, Chaudappa's boy servant is led by the cow to some bushes, where Chaudappa finds the *liṅgam* (Shiva's phallic symbol). After a dream foretelling the discovery of a treasure, Chaudappa stumbles upon it while ploughing his field. He uses this wealth to assemble a group of followers and increase his power. That attracts the attention of the Vijayanagara emperor—now Krishna Raya instead of Achyuta Raya—who grants him the title of Nayaka (V 2:27-50, 4:37-48). The *Keḷadinṛpa vijayam* adds that Chaudappa finds a sword together with the *liṅgam* and that Sadashiva Nayaka serves his namesake Sadashiva Raya, the last Tuluva emperor. Further, Chaudappa's father Basavappa is said to descend from Basaveshvara, a form of Shiva. Both texts also state that Sadashiva Nayaka's conquest of Kalyana is instructed by Vijayanagara's first Aravidu ruler, Rama Raya, in return for lands and titles.[34] Finally, according to some traditions, Chaudappa

32 BL/AAS, MG, no. 6, pt. 11: "Historical account of Beedoonoor or Caladee Samstanum," ff. 61-2, 64-5v.

33 BL/AAS, MG, no. 6, pt. 11: "Historical account of Beedoonoor or Caladee Samstanum," ff. 65v-7.

34 Krishnamurthy, *Sivatattva Ratnākara of Keladi Basavaraja*, 103-6; Swaminathan, *The Nāyakas of Ikkēri*, 12-22; Chitnis, *Keḷadi Polity*, 8-13, 52; Krishnaswami Aiyangar, *Sources of Vijayanagar History*, 194-6; Nilakanta Sastri and Venkataramanayya, *Further Sources of Vijayanagara History*, vol. III, 97-9, 189-92; Heras, *The Aravidu Dynasty of Vijayanagara*, vol. I, 177-9. For yet other (sometimes rather different) versions of the dynasty's origins and subsequent history, see: Mahalingam, *Mackenzie*

can acquire his treasure only in return for a human sacrifice. Two servants, Yadava and Murari, volunteer to be killed on the condition, as one story has it, that their names will be forever honoured by the Ikkeri Nayakas.[35]

By and large, one observes the same elements here as for Vijayanagara and Ariyalur. To start with the founders' ancestry, this is portrayed as relatively modest in two of the three texts: Chaudappa's father is probably a village headman ("goud"),[36] belonging to a family of cowherds. One text states that his father is of divine descent, but that does not necessarily conflict with his humble profession. Next, Chaudappa and his son Sadashiva possess great military skills, and besides subduing rebellious chiefs, Sadashiva even defeats some of the Deccan sultans. The texts describe in detail the strong connections with the Vijayanagara overlords, both the Tuluvas and Aravidus, who acknowledge and enhance the status of Ikkeri's rulers after their heroic services.

A link is perhaps also forged with the erstwhile Hoysala dynasty. The tutelary deity Rameshvar ("Ram-Eswur") of "Halabaidoo"—not far from Keladi ("Caladee")—appears in Chaudappa's dream announcing he has manifested himself as a *liṅgam*. "Halabaidoo" is possibly a corruption of Halebid (some hundred miles from Keladi), the name of the Hoysala capital Dvarasamudra after its destruction by Delhi's forces in the fourteenth century. The main temple there is dedicated to Shiva, while the name Rameshvar and the *liṅgam* are also associated with this god. All this might suggest that the former Hoysala tutelary deity is now attached to the nascent Ikkeri dynasty.[37] That ties in with the religious credentials of the founders,

Manuscripts, vol. II, 403; Francis Buchanan, *A Journey from Madras through the Countries of Mysore, Canara, and Malabar*, vol. III (London, 1807), 254-6; S.N. Naraharayya, "Keladi Dynasty" [pt. 1], *The Quarterly Journal of the Mythic Society* (New Series) XXI, 4 (1931), 370-3; T.C.S. Manian, "Keladi Chiefs: Their Contribution to the History of Mysore," *The Asiatic Review* (New Series) XXXIV, 120 (1938), 773-4; Ranganatha Rao, "The Beḷagutti Kaifiyats," 70; R. Shama Shastry (trans.), "Malnad Chiefs (Extract from Chronicles Compiled around 1820 A.D.)," *The Quarterly Journal of the Mythic Society* XII, I (1921), 45-50. The text in the last work may be a *kaifiyat* (local history) of the town of Sagar, located between Keladi and Ikkeri towns.

35 The sources for the story about the servants' sacrifice are not entirely clear in the secondary literature. Besides, the *Keḷadinṛpa vijayam* states Yadava Murari was a single person, a local chief who disobeyed the Vijayanagara rulers and was therefore captured by Sadashiva Nayaka. See: Chitnis, *Keḷadi Polity*, 9, 11; B. Lewis Rice, *Mysore: A Gazetteer Compiled for Government* (revised edition, Westminster, 1897), vol. II, 458; Naraharayya, "Keladi Dynasty" [pt. 1], 372; Lewis Rice, *Mysore and Coorg*, 156; Swaminathan, *The Nāyakas of Ikkēri*, 14, 26; Manian, "Keladi Chiefs," 773-4.

36 "Goud" is likely to be a corruption of *gauda*, meaning village headman. See Chitnis, *Keḷadi Polity*, xvii.

37 Studies of Ikkeri's temple architecture also suggest that these Nayakas sought to connect themselves with the Hoysalas, as well as the Chalukyas of Kalyana. See: Amita Kanekar, "Two Temples of the

who worship the deity and build him a temple (first of straw and then of stone), and obtain prosperity in return.

The stories contain several natural miracles: Chaudappa's special status is signified by a snake that protects him; the site of the kingdom's second capital Ikkeri ("Ekaree") is indicated by a hare fighting a dog; and a cow shows the way to the *liṅgam*.[38] With regard to the acquisition of wealth, the discovery of a treasure provides Chaudappa with the means to increase his power and make the kingdom flourish. In the process, arable land is developed from the jungles around the *liṅgam* and buildings are constructed. Ikkeri's founders receive various symbols signifying their royal status, such as titles, arms (including the sword found with the *liṅgam*), jewellery, and a ring of a powerful sultan. Further, the continuation of the family's position as a hereditary dynasty is emphasised in passages mentioning Chaudappa's reception in Vijayanagara together with his brother Bhadrappa, his son Sadashiva's marriage to two virgins, and this son's ongoing close relations with the imperial rulers.

Only the motif of migration appears to be lacking here. Ikkeri's dynasty is presented as being of local descent and its founders need not travel further than the imperial capital (also located in the central Kannada area) and back to set up their kingdom. Finally, some stories contain an element that seems largely absent from the myths of other dynasties: the personal loyalty of the founder's subjects or followers and the great value this represents—or at least, that could be what the sacrifice of Chaudappa's servants Yadava and Murari symbolises. Through their extreme devotion, Ikkeri's Nayakas obtain the capital with which they can build up their polity.[39]

Ikkeri Nayakas," *South Asian Studies* 26, 2 (2010), 150-8, 159 (n. 11); idem, "Stylistic Origins and Change in the Temples of the Ikkeri Nayakas," 349, 352-3, 359-60. "Halabaidoo" may also refer to Hallibailu, directly south of Keladi.

[38] The common Indian story of a cow pouring milk often served to mark a spot where the divine and human worlds met. See Sohoni, "The Hunt for a Location," 217-18.

[39] One scholar points to a rarely cited version of Vijayanagara's foundation containing the same theme. Here, the goat-herd Meshapala offers to sacrifice himself so that Harihara and Bukka acquire a treasure. The source of this story is not given. See Naraharayya, "Keladi Dynasty" [pt. 1], 373. Similar stories are found in texts about the foundations of the town of Chandragiri and the Velugoti lineage, members of which served Vijayanagara's Aravidu house. In the former case, to appease local demons, the washermen Chandra and Giriya volunteer to die on the condition the town is named after them. See BL/AAS, MG, no. 9, pt. 2b: "Historical account of Chandragerry," ff. 11-12 (probably translated from a Tamil text, perhaps collected at Chandragiri in 1802; see Cotton, Charpentier, and Johnston, *Catalogue of Manuscripts in European Languages*, vol. I, pt. II, 78-9). For a similar text, see Subrahmanyam, *Explorations in Connected History: From the Tagus to the Ganges*, 86-9. For the Velugoti lineage, see Narayana Rao, Shulman, and Subrahmanyam, *Symbols of Substance*, 245-8, where sacrifice is associated not only with loyalty but also with ideals of land defence and prowess.

Nayakas of Tanjavur

We next move to the Tanjavur kingdom in the Tamil region's Kaveri River delta, once the heartland of the Chola realm (Cholamandalam) and conquered by Vijayanagara soon after its emergence. In the early modern period, Tanjavur was initially ruled by a Nayaka house, installed by Vijayanagara's Tuluvas. Again, little is known with any certainty about the foundation of this dynasty. Inscriptional sources suggest that its first ruler, Shevappa (or Cevvappa) Nayaka, belonged to a Telugu family of high military officers serving the Vijayanagara court and originally stationed in the north of the Tamil zone. Shevappa appears to have been appointed governor of the Tanjavur area by Emperor Achyuta Raya in or around the 1530s. He is believed to have ruled until the 1570s, when his son Achyutappa Nayaka succeeded him.[40]

Of the literary texts dealing with the beginnings of this dynasty, most relevant for our purpose seem to be the Telugu *Tañjāvūri āndhra rājula caritra*, the Sanskrit *Raghunāthābhyudayamu*, and the Telugu *Raghunāthanāyakābhyudayamu*. The first of these, composed by an unknown author probably at Tanjavur in the first half of the eighteenth century, is a chronicle relating the dynastic foundations of both Tanjavur's and Madurai's Nayakas. The second text is a kind of biography of Raghunatha Nayaka, the third of Tanjavur's Nayakas, written by his court poetess Ramabhadramba. The third work is largely devoted to describing a day in the life of Raghunatha and was authored by his son Vijayaraghava Nayaka.[41] Various other texts containing references to the dynasty's foundation are available in the English manuscripts of the Mackenzie collections, have been published, or are discussed in secondary literature.[42] Below we consider a composite, abridged version of the dynasty's origin myths, synthesised from all these sources.

[40] Vriddhagirisan, *The Nayaks of Tanjore*, 9-34; Heras, *The Aravidu Dynasty of Vijayanagara*, vol. I, 173-5, 286-7; Narayana Rao, Shulman, and Subrahmanyam, *Symbols of Substance*, 40.

[41] Vriddhagirisan, *The Nayaks of Tanjore*, 3-5; Narayana Rao, Shulman, and Subrahmanyam, *Symbols of Substance*, 44, 59, 335-6; idem, *Textures of Time*, 129-30; Krishnaswami Aiyangar, *Sources of Vijayanagar History*, 254, 284, 319; Heras, *The Aravidu Dynasty of Vijayanagara*, vol. I, 173.

[42] Vriddhagirisan, *The Nayaks of Tanjore*, 9-34; N.K. Venkatesam, "Govinda Deekshita: The Minister of the Tanjore Nayak Kings," *The Quarterly Journal of the Andhra Historical Research Society* II, 3-4 (1928), 221-3; P.R. Srinivasan and Marie-Louise Reiniche (eds), *Tiruvannamalai: A Śaiva Sacred Complex of South India*, vol. 1.1, *Inscriptions* (Pondicherry, 1990), 115; Heras, *The Aravidu Dynasty of Vijayanagara*, vol. I, 173; F.R. Hemingway, *Tanjore Gazetteer*, vol. I (Madras, 1906), 38; BL/AAS, MG, no. 1, pt. 8: "The Cheritee or actions of the Vadaka-Rajahs of Tanjore, Trichinopully & Madura," ff. 71-2; no. 1, pt. 24: "The Kyfeyat of Aachoota Bhoopal Naiq," f. 185 (translated from a Tamil text received in 1807 from someone employed at the Tanjavur palace); Mackenzie Miscellaneous collection (hereafter MM), no. 110, pt. 7 (at back of folder): "The Charythy of the Vadoka Raja of Tonjore, Trinchunnapully & Madura," ff. 2-3.

As some texts say, Govinda Dikshita, a young, knowledgeable Kannada Brahmin, moved to Vijayanagara city and was invited to Emperor Achyuta Raya's court. After a while, the Brahmin met Shevappa, an orphan of poor descent belonging to a Shudra caste, and took him into his service as a cowherd. When Govinda Dikshita once saw the boy sleeping while a cobra waved its hood over him, he knew a royal future awaited him. The Brahmin introduced Shevappa to the emperor—sometimes identified as Krishna Raya rather than Achyuta Raya—who appointed him as his personal betel-bearer.

Soon, according to one tradition, Shevappa distinguished himself intellectually and in battles, and also came to be cherished by the queen. He married Murtimamba, the younger sister of Achyuta Raya's consort Tirumalamba, and received the governorship of the Chola country as dowry. In this position, Shevappa built a fort and a water tank in his capital Tanjavur and restored and endowed temples. Towards the end of his peaceful reign, he installed his son Achyutappa Nayaka as *yuvarāja* (heir apparent) and made him responsible for the kingdom's administration. The Brahmin Govinda Dikshita continued to serve Tanjavur's Nayakas as general and minister.

On the whole, the origin myths of Tanjavur's Nayakas seem of a limited scale compared with those of other Vijayanagara successor states. Together, however, the different versions contain most motifs found in the texts discussed earlier, although the various stories do not agree on some points and none of them covers all stages of Shevappa's career. The texts are particularly unclear about Shevappa's ancestry and do not trace it back further than a few generations. Some sources state he was the son of a certain Timmappa Nayaka—door-keeper and warrior under Vijayanagara's Krishna Raya—and belonged to the Mannaru clan (*gotra*), whose similarly named tutelary deity was a form of Vishnu, residing at Mannargudi near Tanjavur.[43] Most stories mention his *nāyaka* descent and thus suggest that his immediate ancestors were warriors connected to the imperial court. At the same time, several texts emphasise a modest background, referring to Shevappa's poverty, his belonging to the low Shudra *varṇa* (caste category), and, in some cases, his orphaned status.

Shevappa displays his martial skills in the empire's battles. But before that, a close link is already established with Vijayanagara's Tuluva rulers when Shevappa is appointed to the honourable position of Achyuta Raya's personal betel-bearer. Later, the bond grows even more intimate when Shevappa marries the emperor's sister-in-law and consequently receives the government of what is called the Chola

[43] Vriddhagirisan, *The Nayaks of Tanjore*, 25-7; Srinivasan and Reiniche, *Tiruvannamalai*, vol. 1.1, 115; Heras, *The Aravidu Dynasty of Vijayanagara*, vol. I, 173.

country. It is probably far-fetched to interpret this appointment as an indication that Tanjavur's Nayakas claimed ties with the Chola dynasty. The same may apply to their association with Mannaru, whose temple at Mannargudi was first built by the Cholas. However, the family's relations with this deity demonstrate its religious connections, as does the role of the Brahmin Govinda Dikshita and Shevappa's sponsoring of temples.

While no natural wonder is needed to indicate the exceptional status of Tanjavur's location—having already served as the royal capital for many centuries—one tradition mentions the miracle of a snake protecting the future dynastic founder, foretelling his greatness. Migration is referred to both when Govinda Dikshita (originating in the Kannada region) travels to the imperial capital and when Shevappa moves from there to his new territory. Some texts further appear to emphasise the continuation of Shevappa's office as a hereditary function when they say he declares his son Achyutappa crown prince and gives him governmental responsibilities while he is still alive.

In contrast with other origin stories, the foundation myths of Tanjavur's Nayakas do not mention land development or the acquisition of wealth and royal symbols. These elements were maybe unnecessary because the Tanjavur region was already a political unit under the Cholas and Vijayanagara before Shevappa's installation—unlike Vijayanagara itself, Ikkeri, and Ariyalur. Therefore, Shevappa founded a dynasty rather than a kingdom. This ready availability of a state could account for the absence of references to land clearance and the acquisition of wealth. The fertile, heavily populated Kaveri River delta was already cultivated and yielded vast revenues. For these reasons, the mention of royal symbols was perhaps also less urgent than for other houses. Closely linked to the imperial family through both political and marital ties, and ruling a rich, well-institutionalised kingdom from the start, the Tanjavur Nayakas may have been secure in their regal position and felt little need to include symbols of royalty in their myths.

Bhonsles of Tanjavur

However, Tanjavur's Nayaka house was short-lived when compared with most other successor dynasties. As related in detail in the Epilogue, the family was terminated under its fifth ruler in 1673, when its namesakes from Madurai conquered the Tanjavur capital. Madurai then appointed a governor at Tanjavur, but an escaped son of Tanjavur's last Nayaka ruler tried to regain his ancestral throne. Assisted by the former Tanjavur courtier Venkanna, this prince, named Chengamaladasa, turned to the sultan of Bijapur for help, who sent his Maratha General Ekoji (alias Vyamkoji or Venkaji) Bhonsle. The Marathas originated in the Marathi-speaking region in western India and many of them served as warriors under various rulers.

Ekoji was a son of Shahaji—also a Bijapur general—by his second wife, and a half-brother of the well-known Maratha King Shivaji Bhonsle. In the 1640s, the family had been appointed governors of the Bangalore region.

Dispatched by his Bijapur overlord to Tanjavur, Ekoji Bhonsle expelled the Madurai forces. According to some sources, he installed Chengamaladasa on the Tanjavur throne, with his aide Venkanna as chief minister. Disagreements quickly arose between the new king and his minister, however, which would have led Venkanna to present the kingdom to Ekoji himself, no doubt in return for a new high position at court. The Maratha general is said to have accepted this offer, causing Chengamaladasa to flee Tanjavur. But soon after, Venkanna—considered an opportunistic traitor by Ekoji—also fled. Whether the Chengamaladasa interlude actually took place or not, by early 1676 Ekoji had assumed power in Tanjavur. He severed his ties with Bijapur, although his half-brother Shivaji, supposedly backed by the sultanate, now claimed to be his overlord, albeit with limited success.[44] Thus the Bhonsle dynasty of Tanjavur was established.[45]

Two literary works are particularly relevant for the foundation of this Bhonsle house. One is the abovementioned Telugu *Tañjāvūri āndhra rājula caritra*, thought to be composed under Tanjavur's Bhonsles. Besides the earlier Nayakas, it deals with the Bhonsle dynasty itself. The other text, in modern times given the title *Bhoṃsale vaṃśa caritra* (or, more commonly, *Bhonsle vamsa charitra*), is an exceedingly lengthy inscription in Marathi on the enclosing walls of the Brihadishvara Temple at Tanjavur (see illustration 2).[46] This family chronicle—completed (at least in its stone form) in December 1803—was composed by the royal Secretary (*chiṭnis*) Bapu Rao (or Babu Raya) and commissioned by Tanjavur's then Bhonsle ruler, Sarabhoji II.[47]

[44] Several sources suggest Ekoji took control of Tanjavur's capital in January-February 1676. A local text states that he conquered the town on 12 January and was installed as king on 5 March of that year. See: Jadunath Sarkar, *House of Shivaji* (3rd edition, Calcutta, 1955), 75; NA, VOC, no. 1321, f. 883: letter from Nagapattinam to Batavia, Aug. 1676; Tulajendra Rajah P. Bhosale, *Rajah Serfoji – II (With a Short History of Thanjavur Mahrattas)* (Tanjavur, 1999), 11; Martin, *India in the 17th Century*, vol. 1, pt. II, 511.

[45] Vriddhagirisan, *The Nayaks of Tanjore*, 149-54, 162-7; Subramanian, *The Maratha Rajas of Tanjore*, 1-12; Srinivasan, *Maratha Rule in the Carnatic*, 51, 123-34; Narayana Rao, Shulman, and Subrahmanyam, *Symbols of Substance*, 305-12; idem, *Textures of Time*, 130-5; Subrahmanyam, *Penumbral Visions*, 144-7; Tryambakayajvan, *The Perfect Wife (Strīdharmapaddhati)*, ed. I. Julia Leslie (New Delhi, 1995), 13-14.

[46] For images of the inscription, see also: George Michell and Indira Viswanathan Peterson, *The Great Temple at Thanjavur: One Thousand Years, 1010-2010* (Mumbai, 2010), 36-7; Usha Ramakrishna Ranade, "Comparative Study of Tanjore Marathi (1750-1850 A.D.) and Modern Marathi" (unpublished dissertation, Savitribai Phule Pune University, 1988).

[47] The text's genre has been characterised as a *bakhair* (narrative, memoir). For publications and discussions of the text, see: V. Srinivasachari and S. Gopalan (eds), *Bhonsle Vamsa Charitra: Being*

Illustration 2: Detail of the *Bhoṃsale vaṃśa caritra* inscription, Brihadishvara Temple (south and west enclosing walls), Tanjavur, 1803 (photo by the author).

Additionally, the English translations in the Mackenzie collections include an unpublished 211-page manuscript ending with a dedication to Sarabhoji II and a note saying this work was composed in March 1803 by "Cheetniss Bauboorau," a servant of Sarabhoji II.[48] With regard to both its overall structure and numerous

the Marathi Historical Inscription in the Big Temple, Tanjore, on the History of the Mahratta Rajas of Tanjore (3rd edition, Tanjavur, 1990); Sohoni, *The Great Inscription at Tanjore*; Vidya Gadgil, "The Bṛhadīśvara Temple Inscription of the Bhosales of Tanjore: A Critical Study," in R.K. Sharma and Devendra Handa (eds), *Revealing India's Past (Recent Trends in Art and Archaeology): Prof. Ajay Mitra Shastri Commemoration Volume*, vol. II (New Delhi, 2005); Ranade, "Comparative Study of Tanjore Marathi (1750-1850 A.D.) and Modern Marathi"; Sumit Guha, "The Frontiers of Memory: What the Marathas Remembered of Vijayanagara," *Modern Asian Studies* 43, 1 (2009), 277; idem, "Transitions and Translations," 30.

[48] BL/AAS, MT, class III, no. 87: "The historycal account of the Tonjore," ff. 31-136. The text is written in quaint English and some sections are hardly legible. The English translation probably dates from December 1804. Notably, this manuscript is filed under class III, indicating the original was in Tamil (the translation itself is silent on this), while the *Bhoṃsale vaṃśa caritra* inscription is in Marathi. Therefore, the original manuscript may be the Tamil version mentioned in Mahalingam, *Mackenzie Manuscripts*, vol. I, 142. That manuscript might in turn be a Tamil copy of a Marathi text. See also Sohoni, *The Great Inscription at Tanjore*. I have not been able to check how these texts relate to a chronicle on Tanjavur's Bhonsles written by one Babu Rao Chitnis in 1803 and published in K.M. Venkataramiah, *Tañcai Marāṭṭiya Maṉṉar Varalāṟu (History of the Maratha Rulers of Thanjavur,*

details, this text, titled "The historycal account of the Tonjore," greatly resembles the *Bhoṃsale vaṃśa caritra* inscription. Considering the contents, dates, and author's names of both works, it is likely that the original manuscript from which Mackenzie's translation was made, dating from March 1803, also served as the basis for the inscription, finished in December of that year. "The historycal account of the Tonjore" therefore is probably an English version of the *Bhoṃsale vaṃśa caritra*.

This text begins with a history of the ancestors of Tanjavur's Bhonsles going back to mythical times. Next, it describes in detail the lives of Ekoji Bhonsle's father and half-brother, Shahaji and Shivaji. The chronicle's last section deals with Ekoji himself and his descendants on the Tanjavur throne up to Sarabhoji II. What follows are several summarised excerpts (with the original English spelling of names) concerning Ekoji's ancestry and his foundation of the Bhonsle dynasty at Tanjavur.[49]

Living in the Maratta lands, many members of the Bhoosala race were famous kings, known for their valour, prowess, and virtues. In the Caleeyokum age (Kali Yuga or present era), King Sambhoo Rajah had a dream in which the deity Stree Sampooceva told him he would enjoy children and fortune. Soon, a son named Yacojee Rajah was born. The deity Stree Somuscondah Moorty appeared in a dream of the latter's son Surpah Rajah and gave him a secret mantra. Through this, he obtained the favour of the Badasha (Muslim ruler) of the southern country and was granted some land. Afterwards, Surpah Rajah assisted his Muslim overlord in a battle with 50,000 horses. To his son Yahajee Rajah appeared the deity Sambaceva who announced that his race would become Maharajahs or superior kings.

Several successors followed, some of whom fought against Muslim rulers. A descendant in the fourteenth generation, Mullojee Rajah, served in the army of the Nezam Badasha of Devagery Droog. He went to the fakir Sahasareef Banaly Colonder to express his worries about the lack of male offspring. The fakir predicted the birth of two sons who would become warriors, and presented him with two swords, two cloths, and an object ("punjau") of Hussan and Wossun, gods of the Mussulmans.

In the Shaka year 1531, Mullojee Rajah had two sons, one of whom was called Shahajee Rajah and married two women. He was appointed to rule his own kingdom with the consent of the Nezam Badasha. Shahajee was a great warrior and defeated the armies of Jahangeer Badash of Dilly and the Allyadulsha of Veejaeepoor. But a conflict at the Nezam Badasha's court made Shahajee return to his country Sattar and join the Allyadulsha. In the Shaka year 1551, Shahajee's second wife, Ceejawboy, gave birth to her second son named Seevajee Rajah. In the

Mackenzie manuscript D 3180) (Tanjavur, 1987). All three works may well be versions of the same text. See also: Subrahmanyam, *Penumbral Visions*, 242; Sascha Ebeling, *Colonizing the Realm of Words: The Transformation of Tamil Literature in Nineteenth-Century South India* (Albany, 2010), 117 (n. 17).

[49] For another brief summary of the *Bhoṃsale vaṃśa caritra*'s first part, see Guha, "The Frontiers of Memory," 277-8.

Shaka year 1552, Shahajee's first wife, Tookaboysaib, gave birth to her first son called Yakoojee Rajah, the fourth in the race bearing this name.

Now a war against the Allyadulsha and the Dilly Badasha followed in which Shahajee was joined by the ninety-five other Maratta officers, who descended from the Sun and the Moon. Later, when the Allyadulsha and Auvaringazabe of Dilly were displeased with each other, Shahajee assisted the former and defeated the Rajahs of Tonjore, Matoora, Chinjee, Veeteeyanagur, and other places. The Allyadulsha was extremely pleased and granted Bangalore to Shahajee, who moved there with his family. As Yakoojee Rajah was born to Shahajee's first wife and was her eldest son, he became the Youvarajee (heir apparent), inherited all titles, and was installed as Bangalore's governor. His half-brother Seevajee Rajah was appointed at Sattar and Poonah.

When Yakoojee was ruling the kingdom of Bangalore, the Naikers of Tonjore and Trichenapoly were displeased with each other. The latter wished to possess the country of Tonjore, and the former, unable to defend himself, asked the Allyadulsha of Veejaeepoor for help. Thereupon, the Allyadulsha dispatched two viziers to Yakoojee and ordered him to go to Tonjore and fight the Trichenapoly people. Having driven them out and reappointed the Tonjore people, Yakoojee encamped with his army in Treeroomoollyvoil. In a dream the deity Bawgavan told him to go back to Tonjore and, as the Tonjore people would ask him the next day, enjoy the kingdom for many generations. Accordingly, since the Naikers of Tonjore were in dispute with each other and their prime minister, the kingdom was offered to Yakoojee. He marched to the Tonjore fort and arrived at the gate at an auspicious time. There, some relatives and warriors of the Naikers attempted to prevent Yakoojee from entering, but he forced them to flee. The two viziers of the Allyadulsha, who had accompanied Yakoojee all this while, resolved that he was indeed the best person to reign over Tonjore.

Thus, in the Shaka year 1597, Yakoojee ascended the throne and sent presents to the Allyadulsha of Veejaeepoor. The latter was very pleased, replied that Yakoojee should enjoy the kingdom from generation to generation, and gave him valuable clothes. In the Shaka year 1604, Yakoojee departed his life and was succeeded by his eldest son Shahayee, the third king with this name.[50]

The *Tañjāvūri āndhra rājula caritra* has various details to add about the activities of Ekoji ("Yakoojee") Bhonsle after he ousted the forces of Madurai ("Trichenapoly," Tiruchirappalli) from Tanjavur ("Tonjore") and installed the young Nayaka Prince Chengamaladasa on the throne. He was given part of the buried treasure of the Tanjavur Nayakas in compensation for his expedition, and withdrew his troops to the nearby town of Kumbakonam. But soon, as related above, he was visited by Chengamaladasa's former adviser Venkanna, who had been dismissed from

[50] BL/AAS, MT, class III, no. 87: "The historycal account of the Tonjore," ff. 31-95; Srinivasachari and Gopalan, *Bhonsle Vamsa Charitra*, i-ix.

his ministerial post. Venkanna tried to persuade Ekoji to expel Chengamaladasa and take over Tanjavur's reign. As the text has it, Ekoji was initially reluctant to remove the prince he himself had enthroned and also claimed to be incapable of governing this southern land. Moreover, he needed permission from his overlord, the sultan of Bijapur, to ascend the throne. Then, however, news came that the sultan had been killed in battle, and so Venkanna could finally convince Ekoji to take the Tanjavur kingdom.[51]

Other texts broadly agree with the two works examined above. They further mention, for instance, that Ekoji, in addition to a share of the treasure, received splendid robes, ornaments, and lands from Chengamaladasa. Besides, once he started ruling, Ekoji subdued the chiefs in Tanjavur's vicinity and reconquered some territory taken by the neighbouring kingdom of Ramnad.[52]

Clearly, the origin stories of Tanjavur's Bhonsles differ a great deal from those of the other dynasties. Like his predecessors, Tanjavur's Nayakas, Ekoji Bhonsle did not found a new kingdom, but he did not even really found a new royal house either. He belonged to a family that considered itself to have been a dynasty since mythical times, as the various elements of the stories demonstrate. Ekoji's ancestry is traced back first to several legendary kings and then to more direct forefathers holding high military offices, all of whom are great warriors. Also, it is repeatedly foretold that more great kings and warriors will follow. Further, the Bhonsle family is said to belong to a group of ninety-six Maratha families descending from the Sun or the Moon.

By and large, Ekoji is simply the latest member of a long-existing line of ancestors and relatives holding political and (at times) royal power. Yet, he occupies a special position. Contrary to what is accepted as historically accurate, the *Bhoṃsale vaṃśa caritra* declares that Ekoji, rather than his half-brother Shivaji, is born of his father's first wife, as her eldest son, and therefore inherits all titles and the government of Bangalore. Therefore, he already holds a high rank when he arrives

[51] Krishnaswami Aiyangar, *Sources of Vijayanagar History*, 325-7; Narayana Rao, Shulman, and Subrahmanyam, *Textures of Time*, 132-4.

[52] See: Taylor, *Oriental Historical Manuscripts*, vol. II, 200-3 (it is unclear which text—in Telugu, despite the volume's title—has been translated here, but it seems to resemble the *Tañjāvūri āndhra rājula caritra*); idem, *Examination and Analysis of the Mackenzie Manuscripts Deposited in the Madras College Library* (Calcutta, 1838), 126-8; Śrīdhara Venkatēśa (Ayyaval), *Śāhendra Vilāsa (A Poem on the Life of King Śāhaji of Tanjore) (1684-1710)*, ed. V. Raghavan (Tanjavur, 1952), 5-6; Mahalingam, *Mackenzie Manuscripts*, vol. II, 345-7. For a partially different description of the events after Madurai was expelled from Tanjavur by Ekoji, suggesting the latter was not sufficiently indemnified by the Tanjavur court and therefore took over the kingdom, see BL/AAS, MT, class III, no. 32: "The History of the Tonjore Rajas," ff. 88-90v.

in Tanjavur. That Ekoji also possesses martial skills is obvious from his military position under Bijapur ("Veejaeepoor") and his defeat of Madurai's troops, the last remaining supporters of Tanjavur's Nayaka house, chiefs around Tanjavur, and Ramnad's forces.

The Bhonsle family maintains close ties with various dynasties over the course of time. In the first place, Ekoji, his father Shahaji, and his grandfather Maloji serve the Nizam Shah ("Nezam Badasha") of Ahmadnagar and the Adil Shah ("Allyadulsha") of Bijapur at various points.[53] Moreover, the *Bhoṃsale vaṃśa caritra* states that Ekoji is officially recognised as Tanjavur's ruler by the sultan of Bijapur, while the *Tañjāvūri āndhra rājula caritra* relates he is willing to ascend the throne only after his Bijapur overlord has deceased. In either case, assuming the reign over Tanjavur without claiming the sultan's consent was apparently problematic. Second, various stories appear to forge a link with the Nayaka predecessors, too. Ekoji receives robes, land, and other presents from Chengamaladasa and thus becomes part of the Nayaka realm to some extent.[54] However, no texts seem to seek any direct connection with Vijayanagara, apart from an inscription issued under Ekoji that mentions some of Tanjavur's earlier Chola, Vijayanagara, and Nayaka rulers.[55]

Religious appreciations of the Bhonsle dynasty's position are manifold. Throughout the family's history, Hindu deities appear in dreams with auspicious messages. Eventually, Ekoji himself has a dream in which the deity Vaidyanathasvami at Tirumalavadi ("Treeroomoollyvoil")—a form of Shiva—tells him to take and enjoy the Tanjavur kingdom.[56] There is also support from Islamic quarters when Ekoji's grandfather Maloji visits a Muslim saint and obtains swords, clothes, and an object called "punjau" that is associated with the Shiite martyrs Hasan and Husain ("Hussan and Wossun"), possibly denoting the *pañjā* or symbol of the hand representing the five members of the Prophet's family: Muhammad, Fatima, Ali, Hasan, and Husain.[57]

[53] Other corrupted names in the cited text include the following: Mughal Emperor Aurangzeb ("Auvaringazabe of Dilly"), Senji ("Chinjee"), Devagiri fort ("Devagery Droog"), Mughal Emperor Jahangir ("Jahangeer Badash of Dilly"), Madurai ("Matoora"), Pune ("Poonah"), Satara ("Sattar"), and perhaps Vijanayagara ("Veeteeyanagur"). See also the rest of the paragraph.

[54] For efforts in the multilingual dance drama *Mohinī vilāsa kuravañji* (c. 1700) to link the Bhonsles to this territory, see Seshan, "From Folk Culture to Court Culture," 333-4.

[55] C.R. Srinivasan, "Some Interesting Aspects of the Maratha Rule as Gleaned from the Tamil Copper-Plates of the Thanjavur Marathas," *Journal of the Epigraphical Society of India [Bharatiya Purabhilekha Patrika]* XI (1984), 42.

[56] See also Subrahmanyam, *Penumbral Visions*, 147.

[57] This saint or *pīr*, Shah Sharif Banali Qalandar, resided at Ahmadnagar. See William Hickey, *The Tanjore Mahratta Principality in Southern India: The Land of the Chola, the Eden of the South* (Madras,

Migration is a recurring motif in the Bhonsle foundation myths. Shahaji lives in the town of Satara in the Marathi-speaking region before he moves to Bangalore in the Kannada area, and his son Ekoji travels from there to Tanjavur in the Tamil south. The *Bhoṃsale vaṃśa caritra* puts much emphasis on the continuous and hereditary character of the Bhonsle dynasty. The births of Ekoji and his sons are all mentioned on separate occasions. Names like Shahaji, Ekoji, and Sarabhoji are borne by individuals of different generations and the text often specifies which consecutive number people with such names have, as in "Yakoojee Rajah number 5."[58] Finally, a few texts refer to royal symbols. Ekoji receives clothes and other insignia from his Nayaka predecessor and the Bijapur sultan, but these are not specified. It seems that since Ekoji's assumption of power in Tanjavur was basically the result of conquest, there was no truly rightful overlord from whom he would have received insignia that were worth describing in detail or could be specified at all.

As with Tanjavur's Nayakas, the motifs of natural miracles, land development, and the acquisition of wealth appear to be missing in the origin stories of Tanjavur's Bhonsles. With respect to wealth, Ekoji receives part of the former Nayaka treasure, but this is possibly meant to compensate for the expenses of his campaign rather than to serve as a financial basis for the new dynasty. The absence of these three elements could be explained by the same factors suggested for Tanjavur's Nayakas: Ekoji ascended the throne of a kingdom that had long existed, was already brought under cultivation, and produced great wealth.

Nayakas of Madurai

South-west of Tanjavur, at the tip of the Indian peninsula, lay the kingdom of Madurai. This Tamil-speaking region was traditionally the realm of the ancient Pandya dynasty. When Vijayanagara conquered the area in the late fourteenth century from the short-lived Madurai sultanate, the Pandyas initially remained on Madurai's throne as the empire's vassals. But in the early sixteenth century, Vijayanagara's Tuluvas replaced the Pandyas with a Nayaka governor from a Telugu-speaking background.

As with the other imperial heirs, the actual circumstances under which this Nayaka house came to power are obscure. Most historians agree that the dynasty's first ruler was Vishvanatha Nayaka, son of the imperial courtier and military officer Nagama Nayaka. He belonged to one of the Balija castes (part of the Shudra

1873), 70. I thank Subah Dayal for suggesting the possible meaning of "punjau." For both the saint and "punjau," see also Sohoni, *The Great Inscription at Tanjore*.

58 For some examples, see BL/AAS, MT, class III, no. 87: "The historycal account of the Tonjore," ff. 32-2v, 44v, 81v, 83, 95-6, 98.

varṇa or caste category), which originated in the Telugu region and whose members undertook both military and mercantile activities. Vishvanatha was possibly installed at Madurai around 1530 and reigned until c. 1563.[59]

There are several texts concerning the origins of Madurai's Nayakas. One elaborate version is found in the aforementioned Telugu work *Tañjāvūri āndhra rājula caritra*, thought to originate in eighteenth-century Tanjavur. In addition, a Tamil chronicle covers the house until its fall in the 1730s, and even up to the late eighteenth century when the dynasty's descendants attempted to regain the Madurai throne. This work has been published in Tamil with a full English translation, titled "History of the Carnataca Governors who ruled over the Pandya Mandalam."[60] Both that text and the section of the *Tañjāvūri āndhra rājula caritra* about this dynasty's foundation have been extensively summarised and analysed in secondary literature, and it seems the former work is a Tamil variant of the latter.[61] Further, the so-called Mrtyunjaya manuscripts—collected in the early nineteenth century by Madurai's chief Brahmin "Mirtanjeya-Pattar"—include a work resembling the two other texts to a considerable extent. This was published in its original Tamil with an English translation as "A description of the Carnataca Lords."[62] What follows is an abridged composite of these three works.

59 Sathyanatha Aiyar, *History of the Nayaks of Madura*, 48-67; Narayana Rao, Shulman, and Subrahmanyam, *Symbols of Substance*, 38-40; Heras, *The Aravidu Dynasty of Vijayanagara*, vol. I, 131-2; Rangachari, "The History of the Naik Kingdom of Madura," *Indian Antiquary* XLIII, 191-2, 218, 232, 258-60. But see also Nilakanta Sastri, *A History of South India*, 288, where Vishvanatha's founding of a dynastic governorship is doubted, as he may have been replaced by another officer rather than his son Kumara Krishnappa. The latter would have been installed later and only then started the hereditary line of Madurai's Nayakas.

60 Taylor, *Oriental Historical Manuscripts*, vol. II, 3-49. For another English translation of this Tamil text, see three more or less identical manuscript copies in: BL/AAS, MT, class III, no. 25: "History of the former Gentoo Rajahs who ruled over the Pandyan Mandalom," ff. 18-27; MG, no. 4, pt. 6a: "History of the former Rajahs of the Tellugoo nation who ruled over Paundium Mundalom," ff. 87-106; British Library: Manuscript and Map Collections, London (hereafter BL/MMC), Additional Manuscripts (hereafter AM), no. 18021, "History of Kurtakull" (translated in 1803, see f. 25). See also Cotton, Charpentier, and Johnston, *Catalogue of Manuscripts in European Languages*, vol. I, pt. II, 50-1.

61 Narayana Rao, Shulman, and Subrahmanyam, *Symbols of Substance*, 38-40, 44-56; Dirks, *The Hollow Crown*, 97-106; J.H. Nelson, *The Madura Country: A Manual* (Madras, 1868), vol. III, 87-97; Venkata Ramanayya, *Studies in the History of the Third Dynasty*, 453-5; Heras, *The Aravidu Dynasty of Vijayanagara*, vol. I, 133-7; Rangachari, "The History of the Naik Kingdom of Madura," *Indian Antiquary* XLIII, 191-2, 232, 253-7. Translated excerpts of the *Tañjāvūri āndhra rājula caritra* have been published in: Krishnaswami Aiyangar, *Sources of Vijayanagar History*, 319-27; Narayana Rao, Shulman, and Subrahmanyam, *Textures of Time*, 131-2, 134. See also: Mahalingam, *Mackenzie Manuscripts*, vol. II, 344-8; Chekuri, "'Fathers' and 'Sons'," 139-40.

62 Taylor, *Oriental Historical Manuscripts*, vol. II, 105-12. It is unclear where this text ends in Taylor's volume. Possibly, other sections of the work are published on 113-20, 147-67, 169-78, 182-217,

As the texts say, Nagama Nayaka was an important officer and revenue collector of the ruler of Vijayanagara. Since he had long been childless, he went on a pilgrimage to Benares, where he performed acts of charity and bathed in the Ganga River daily. After forty days, the deity Vishvanatha appeared to Nagama in a dream, announcing he would have a vision of the god the following day, whereupon he might return home and would have a son. The next morning, while Nagama was bathing in the Ganga, something underwater struck him, and he moved to another part of the river. There something struck him again. He now searched the riverbed and found an emerald *liṅgam* (Shiva's phallic symbol). Having thus viewed the god, Nagama went back to Vijayanagara and in due time a son was born, named Vishvanatha after the Benares deity. He grew up to be admired for his wisdom, prowess, and beauty.

When Vishvanatha was sixteen years old, a buffalo was sacrificed at Vijayanagara's annual Navaratri festival, devoted to the goddess Durga, as happened every year. Tradition required it to be beheaded with one single blow, but this year the buffalo was particularly strong, with horns extending all the way to its tail. Therefore, none of the king's men dared to perform this duty, lest the animal's head be not immediately severed and thus Vijayanagara's future be in peril. Now Vishvanatha, in a dream informed by the goddess of the king's concern, offered to carry out the sacrifice, provided he could choose a sword from the king's armoury. Though the king considered Vishvanatha too young, he let him select one of his weapons. As the goddess had predicted, Vishvanatha found a special sword lying on top of the others. He took this and with one blow cut off the buffalo's head. The king rewarded him with jewels and clothes, took him into his service, and promised him a kingdom. Later, Vishvanatha was sent north to subdue rebels, and having defeated them he received from the king all their banners and trophies, as well as some of the king's own emblems.

One day, as the texts continue, the Chola king of Tanjavur invaded the Madurai kingdom and dethroned its Pandya king. The latter sought help from his Vijayanagara overlord, Krishna Raya, who dispatched Vishvanatha's father Nagama Nayaka to drive off the invader and restore Madurai to its rightful ruler. Nagama marched southward and defeated the Chola king, but then installed himself on the Madurai throne and brought the kingdom under control. Receiving complaints from Madurai's expelled Pandya king again, Krishna Raya ordered Nagama to return to the imperial capital and give up the Madurai kingdom. The latter refused, arguing that he had spent a fortune on his campaign, whereas the Pandya king not

224-6, 229-35, 238-48, 252-64. But those texts may also be separate manuscripts in the Mrtyunjaya collection.

only had done nothing to keep his kingdom, but also was a low-caste bastard rather than a real Pandya and would not send revenues once reinstalled.

Infuriated, Krishna Raya invited his courtiers and officers to bring him the head of Nagama Nayaka. To his surprise, Nagama's son Vishvanatha Nayaka offered to do so, declaring that loyalty to his king was more important than loyalty to his father. Having travelled south and arrived near Madurai, Vishvanatha sent a note to his father saying that if he would reinstate the Pandya now, he could still be saved. But Nagama stuck to his position, stating he had conquered Madurai only for his son's sake and asking Vishvanatha to join him. The latter was equally resolute and so a battle was fought between father and son, won by Vishvanatha. Taken to Vijayanagara to be decapitated, Nagama was however pardoned by Krishna Raya, impressed as the emperor was by Vishvanatha's loyalty.

Since Vishvanatha Nayaka was to be rewarded with a kingdom of his own for his exceptional behaviour, Krishna Raya installed him at Madurai as Lord of the Southern or Pandya throne. According to some works, the grateful but incompetent and heirless Pandya king gave up his claims and adopted Vishvanatha as his son, giving him the Pandya crown, dagger, sceptre, seal, and fish umbrella. Krishna Raya presented the new king with an image of Durga, the goddess protecting Vijayanagara. Further, Vishvanatha received the wealth acquired by his father Nagama, who revealed that the Madurai goddess Minakshi had foretold his son's royal future in a dream. Vishvanatha then rebuilt Madurai's fort and temples, constructed irrigation facilities, founded new villages, subjugated robbing bands, and made the country's population increase.

He appointed seventy-two subordinate chiefs to each govern a part of his realm, collect revenues, and recruit troops. Five chiefs in the south, however, who were distant relatives of the former Pandya ruler, rebelled against the new king and a bloody war ensued. Eventually, Vishvanatha proposed to fight man to man with the chiefs. They delegated the strongest among them, but the king killed him, upon which the other rebels surrendered and flowers fell from heaven. After a long reign, Vishvanatha was succeeded by his son Kumara Krishnappa Nayaka.

Most other origin stories of Madurai's Nayakas basically agree with the texts synthesised above, although there are some variations. The Telugu *Balijavaṃśapurāṇam*, for example, states that once Vishvanatha had defeated his father Nagama, the Pandya king already adopted Vishvanatha as his successor. Another work declares the Pandya king was initially reinstalled by Vishvanatha, who only ascended the Madurai throne himself after the king and his son had passed away and the Pandya line became extinct. There is also a text saying that Nagama, after expelling the Chola ruler, killed the Pandya king and usurped the throne, which the Vijayanagara emperor then passed on to Vishvanatha. Yet another work extensively refers to the clearing of jungles under Vishvanatha's reign. Further, some traditions have it that the Nayakas did not only receive their sceptre from the local goddess Minakshi but were also born from her.[63]

Finally, a lengthy description of the Nayakas of Madurai compiled by the Dutch East India Company in 1677 includes a different version of the dynasty's foundation. In this work's opening lines, its author Adolph Bassingh writes that he was informed about the Nayakas' origins by "some old Brahmins from their chronicles." Thus apparently presenting a local tradition—perhaps the earliest surviving account—Bassingh's text relates that under Vijayanagara's first Tuluva rulers, Madurai was farmed out to a wealthy merchant, one Peda Chetti, who frequently lent money to the court. This office passed to his son, who was given greater authority over the area and received the title of Nayaka. He was in turn succeeded by his son, named Nagama Nayaka, who fell out of favour with the imperial court and was not succeeded by a relative after he died. Instead, the emperor appointed as Madurai's ruler his loyal servant and betel-bearer Vishvanatha Nayaka ("Wiesewenaden Naik") of the Balija ("Wellen Chitti") lineage, which had a higher status than the line of Nagama and his predecessors. Vishvanatha acquired the title of Nayaka when the king married him to a "daughter of princely blood." From him descended the successive Nayakas of Madurai.[64]

In these various texts, one encounters almost all the motifs identified in the origin stories of other dynasties. Beginning with the founder's ancestry, Vishvanatha's pedigree never seems to be traced back further than just one generation, apart from the claimed descent from the local goddess Minakshi. While one chronicle

[63] Nilakanta Sastri and Venkataramanayya, *Further Sources of Vijayanagara History*, vol. I, 239-41, vol. III, 177-8; BL/AAS, MT, class III, no. 25: "History of the former Gentoo Rajahs who ruled over the Pandyan Mandalom," f. 24; MG, no. 1, pt. 3: "An account of the Pandia Rajahs who reigned at Madurapuri," ff. 16-17; MM, no. 109, pt. 37: "The humble representation of ... Bangaroo Teeroomaly Nack," ff. 2-4 (compiled around 1800 by Bangaru Tirumalai, descendant of the expelled Nayakas of Madurai, see f. 1); no. 109, pt. 43: untitled document, ff. 1-4 (similar to MT, class III, no. 25); Mahalingam, *Mackenzie Manuscripts*, vol. I, 190-1; Shulman, *The King and the Clown*, 304; Venkata Ramanayya, *Studies in the History of the Third Dynasty*, 456-61; Rangachari, "The History of the Naik Kingdom of Madura," *Indian Antiquary* XLIII, 257-8, 261-2, XLIV (1915), 37-8. See also BL/AAS, MG, pt. 4, no. 4: "Mootiah's chronological & historical account of the modern kings of Madura," ff. 44-8 (based on a Tamil original). According to this text, it was Vishvanatha who was sent by Krishna Raya to Madurai to subdue some chiefs rebelling against the Pandya king (making the latter unable to pay tribute to the empire). Having disciplined the rebels, Vishvanatha usurped the Madurai government, imprisoned his father Nagama who had come to congratulate him, and massacred the entire Pandya family. After returning to Krishna Raya with treasures and repenting for his sins, Vishvanatha was crowned king of Madurai by the emperor. For a brief discussion of this text, see Dirks, *The Hollow Crown*, 76-7 (n. 42).

[64] Vink, *Mission to Madurai*, 284-8, 344-6.

suggests Vishvanatha belongs to a higher-ranking caste than Madurai's previous governors, virtually all texts agree he comes from a *nāyaka* or warrior background. His father Nagama is in charge of the imperial treasury but also serves as a general and defeats the Chola king. Vishvanatha himself possesses outstanding military skills: he beheads a formidable buffalo with one blow when he is sixteen years old, he overpowers his own rebellious father, and he kills a strong insurgent chief in a man-to-man fight.

The stories connect him firmly to the imperial Tuluva house. Possibly serving Krishna Raya as betel-bearer, Vishvanatha shows exceptional loyalty to the emperor, receives gifts from him, and is installed by him as king himself. An early tradition even suggests that he, like the founder of Tanjavur's Nayaka dynasty, married into the imperial family. Additionally, almost all texts establish some kind of continuation between Vishvanatha and his Pandya predecessors. Either adopted by the last Pandya king and receiving that dynasty's regalia—including the sceptre (*ceṅkōl*), a curved sword or scimitar, and the fish standard—or ascending the throne after the Pandya line has ended, Vishvanatha is portrayed as the rightful successor of Madurai's previous dynasty.[65]

There are also several instances of religious recognition. Vishvanatha's birth is foretold by his divine namesake residing in Benares (a form of Shiva), who manifests himself to his father Nagama in a dream and as a *liṅgam*. Vishvanatha's regal destiny is revealed to Nagama by Madurai's own goddess Minakshi (the local consort of Shiva), said by some to be the family's ancestress. And Durga, the protective goddess of Vijayanagara, moves with Vishvanatha to his new residence.

As with most other dynasties, Madurai's origin stories refer to southward migration. The Telugu-speaking Nagama and Vishvanatha move from the Deccan to the Tamil zone and the latter becomes "king of the south." With respect to wealth, when Vishvanatha ascends the throne, his father provides him with the capital acquired in his career so as to make the kingdom prosper. Unlike riverine, fertile, and densely inhabited Tanjavur, the Madurai territory requires further development, and texts mention the clearance of jungle areas, the population of new

[65] For other efforts by Madurai's Nayakas to forge links with the Pandyas, see: Branfoot, "Dynastic Genealogies," 336, 370-5; idem, "Imperial Memory," 330-3; idem, "Heroic Rulers and Devoted Servants," 173-4; Elaine M. Fisher, *Hindu Pluralism: Religion and the Public Sphere in Early Modern South India* (Oakland, 2017), 165; Gita V. Pai, "From Warrior Queen to Shiva's Consort to Political Pawn: The Genesis and Development of a Local Goddess in Madurai," in Diana Dimitrova and Tatiana Oranskaia (eds), *Divinizing in South Asian Traditions* (London/New York, 2018), 64-8; Sathyanatha Aiyar, *History of the Nayaks of Madura*, 87. For Vishvanatha being granted Pandya emblems and titles, see also: Mears, "Symbols of Coins of the Vijayanagara Empire," 79; idem, "Propaganda and Power: The Coinage of Vijayanagara," in Anila Verghese and Anna Libera Dallapiccola (eds), *South India under Vijayanagara: Art and Archaeology* (New Delhi, 2011), 287-8.

villages, and the construction of irrigation works. The realm is also clearly settled by way of a territorial division into seventy-two subordinate chiefdoms, whose chiefs are referred to as Palaiyakkarars (or in its anglicised form as "Poligars"). Some of the abovementioned elements also pertain to symbols of royalty, such as the acquisition of the Pandya regalia and the imperial Durga image. Besides, in an early stage Vishvanatha receives jewels, clothes, and emblems from the emperor, and banners and trophies of rebels he has subdued for his overlord.

The motifs of dynastic continuation and natural miracles are less conspicuous in the stories. The *Tañjāvūri āndhra rājula caritra* relates that Nagama Nayaka deliberately rebels against the emperor to give his son Vishvanatha the opportunity to show his loyalty and prowess and win himself a throne.[66] In that sense, Nagama can be said to aim at founding a hereditary dynasty. But unlike texts of other royal houses, Madurai's origin stories do not mention the founders' successors until these commence their reign. Natural wonders are also absent in the myths, apart from the moving *liṅgam* on the Ganga's riverbed predicting Vishvanatha's birth. This reminds us of the origin stories of Tanjavur's Nayakas and can be explained in the same way. While the dynastic founder's greatness is announced, his kingdom's special position need not be demonstrated by a miracle. The town of Madurai and its surroundings had long been the epicentre of the Pandya realm (Pandyamandalam). Vishvanatha takes over a throne instead of establishing one, thus founding a dynasty rather than a kingdom.

Setupatis of Ramnad

The last kingdom whose foundation stories are examined is Ramnad, situated in the far, somewhat marginal and desolate south-east of the Tamil zone. Once again, the origins of the kingdom's royal family are unclear. The first historical member of the line, Sadaika Tevar or Udaiyan, was installed around 1605 as a vassal of the Nayakas of Madurai, who then held sway over this region. Sadaika Tevar was a member of the Maravar caste (again belonging to the Shudra *varṇa* or caste category), which dominated the Ramnad area. Known for their martial skills, Maravars were involved in activities ranging from banditry to kingship.

Ramnad's royal house bore the title of Setupati, "Lord of the Bridge," referring to the Setu (bridge), the string of islets and sandbanks between the kingdom's south-eastern tip and Ceylon. The Setu was associated with events in the *Rāmāyaṇa* epic and had long been an important pilgrimage destination, in particular the Ramanathasvami Temple on Rameshvaram island. As their dynastic name indicates, the Setupatis acted as guardians of this sacred spot, and soon after his

66 Narayana Rao, Shulman, and Subrahmanyam, *Symbols of Substance*, 50.

instalment, Sadaika Tevar allegedly received a sceptre (*ceṅkōl*) from temple priests at Rameshvaram.[67]

Both texts produced by the Ramnad court itself and works deriving from the Madurai overlords deal with the Setupati's origins, but the focus lies here on the former category. Of these manuscripts, one Telugu work has been entirely published in an English translation (not in its original language) as "A chronicle of the acts of the Sethupathis." This text is thought to have been composed in the early nineteenth century.[68] The Mackenzie manuscripts include English translations of several other texts, the originals of which all seem to be in Tamil. Among these, one manuscript—probably dating from the late eighteenth century—stands out for its detail and length of thirty-one pages,[69] but a few other works, though much shorter, are also valuable.[70] Below follows a summary of the first section of the longest text (with the original spelling of names and some terms), titled "General history of the kings of Rama Naad or the Satoo-Putty Samastanum."

As the Ramayan mentions, in former ages Raavan-Eswar abducted Seeta Davee, the consort of Sree Ram, to the island of Lanka. Then Sree Ram gathered an army of monkeys ("vaanarah") and marched to the ocean's shore. There, digging up mountains from the sea, the monkey soldiers erected a bridge, called Satoo. Sree Ram presented the lands near the Satoo to one of the Maravaars residing in the forests. This Maravaar turned out to be a relation of Goohoodoor, an intimate friend of Sree Ram and chief commander of the Gunga River. Delighted, Sree Ram denominated the new king Ragoonaad Satooputty and proclaimed that all who came to bath

[67] Seshadri, "The Sētupatis of Ramnad," 5-20; Carol Appadurai Breckenridge, "From Protector to Litigant—Changing Relations between Hindu Temples and the Rājā of Ramnad," *The Indian Economic and Social History Review* 14, 1 (1977), 76, 81-2, 88-9; S. Thiruvenkatachari, *The Setupatis of Ramnad* (Karaikudi, 1959), 17-20; Sathyanatha Aiyar, *History of the Nayaks of Madura*, 89-93; Howes, *The Courts of Pre-Colonial South India*, 71-2, 83. For the Maravar caste, see for example: Edgar Thurston, *Castes and Tribes of Southern India* (Madras, 1909), vol. V, 22-48; Kadhirvel, *A History of the Maravas*, 6-17; Shulman, "On South Indian Bandits and Kings," 287-90; idem, *The King and the Clown*, 349-51, 364-5

[68] Taylor, *Oriental Historical Manuscripts*, vol. II, Appendix, 49-52. Despite its inclusion in Taylor's publication of Tamil texts, this work was originally written in Telugu. See also Seshadri, "The Sētupatis of Ramnad," 1.

[69] BL/AAS, MG, no. 4, pt. 8: "A general history of the kings of Rama Naad or the Satoo-Putty Samastanum," ff. 171-201. As stated on f. 201, the original text was compiled by "Soma-Soondara-Pillah," then "transmitted by Kylasputty from Madura," and in 1805 translated by Kavali Venkata (Borayya?), one of Mackenzie's assistants. Judging from its contents, the text was composed around the late eighteenth century. See also Cotton, Charpentier, and Johnston, *Catalogue of Manuscripts in European Languages*, vol. I, pt. II, 51-2

[70] For instance: BL/AAS, MG, no. 4, pt. 7: "Memoir of the Satoo-Putty or Ramnad Polligar," ff. 161-3 (likely translated from a Tamil text, see Cotton, Charpentier, and Johnston, *Catalogue of Manuscripts in European Languages*, vol. I, pt. II, 51); MM, no. 109, pt. 44: "Historical memoir of the Satoo-Samstaan," ff. 1-4.

in the waters of the Satoo must pay their respects to this king, lest their vows be of no effect. North of the Satoo, Sree Ram built a great city and installed Ragoonaad Satooputty as its ruler.

Now, with his army, Sree Ram crossed the ocean on the back of Hanoomunt to Lanka, extirpated all demons ("raachasas") and their King Raavan-Eswur, and liberated his consort Seeta Davee. Returning from Lanka and shooting his divine bow, he broke the Satoo at three places to prevent the demons from crossing. In compensation for killing Raavan-Eswur, who was a Brama, Sree Ram erected a lingum and a temple for the god Ram-Eswur at one of the Satoo's islands. Before he returned home, Sree Ram instructed Ragoonaad Satooputty to worship the god, govern the kingdom with care, and follow the Pandia king's orders. Ragoonaad Satooputty ruled his jungle kingdom, performing all charities as directed by Sree Ram. He visited the Pandia king and related all the gracious benefits conferred on him by Sree Ram. The Pandia king approved of this and, exempting Ragoonaad Satooputty from tribute, ordered him to cut down the jungle, establish new villages, populate them, and promote their prosperity. Ragoonaad Satooputty followed these instructions and built the town of Ramanaadpoor.

In the time of the third king of this race, Veera Goondoo Satooputty, the Pandia king was attacked by the Chola king. The Satooputty fought against the latter's army and threw it into great confusion. The grateful Pandia king granted him Tondi and two other ports, with the title of "Warden of the Tondi harbour." Later, the Carnatic king attacked and was about to kill the Pandia king. But the Satooputty saved him and defeated the enemy, for which he received some land and the title of "Establisher of the Pandia throne." Later again, the Andhra king invaded the Chola kingdom and its ruler fled to the Pandia king. Together with the latter, the Satooputty drove the Andhra king off and received from the Chola ruler the title of "Establisher of the Chola country." More fights and services followed, leading to titles like "Conqueror of all countries in sight, who never lets go conquered countries."

When Emperor Kistna Rayel was attacked by Muslim rulers ("Paadshahs"), the Pandia king sent Ranaputty Satooputty to assist him. During battle, the Chola king was imprisoned by the enemy, but the Satooputty liberated him and brought him back to Kistna Rayel's camp. As a reward, he received land from the Chola king and the Hanooma and Garooda standards from the emperor. After some time, the Pandia king grew apprehensive of the Satooputties' power and valour. He summoned Jayatoonga Ragoonaad Satooputty to Madura and put him and his pregnant wife in prison, where they died. The Pandia then tried to get possession of the country, but the strong Maravaars, entrenched in the jungle, warded him off. Finally, some agreement on the collection of revenues was reached between the Pandia king and the Maravaar chiefs.

One day, Jayatoonga-Tavadoo, of the race of the imprisoned and deceased Jayatoonga Ragoonaad Satooputty, had a dream in which the god Ramanaad-Swamy told him: "Your ancestors ruled this land and took care of my worship, food, and ceremonies, which have fallen into decline now. You shall have a son, who will obtain power and authority and will rule over the Satoo realm." A son named Vodeyar Tavur was born, who at the age of twelve married a Maravaar virgin and always worshipped Ramanaad-Swamy.

One night, his deity told him in a dream that his ancestors had buried money, which he should take to gather troops and acquire power over his country. Vodeyar dug up the money and sent a message to the Pandia king, saying that after his ancestors were removed from their position, all land revenues were taken by the king's officers, while the land had become desolate. The king replied that, since the officers had been appointed, he had not received revenues and therefore Vodeyar might now rule the country and deliver the money. Vodeyar then dismissed the king's officers, collected all revenues, cut down the jungles, repaired the roads to the Satoo, subdued robbers harassing pilgrims, and renewed the endowments to the god Ramanaad-Swamy. At that time, devotees of the god came from the north and urged the Pandia king to restore the Satoo realm and recognise Vodeyar as its lord. So did the Pandia king, exempting Vodeyar from tribute and presenting him clothes and gifts. The devotees from the north gave him a red umbrella to be preserved forever in their name. He then ruled over the country and was succeeded by his son Cootun.[71]

Other texts on the Setupatis' origin offer different versions of the story. "A chronicle of the acts of the Sethupathis" states that for many generations Ramnad had been governed by seven appointed guardians. Finally, their chief—"Sadaica Devaiyer" (Sadaika Tevar) or "Udiyan" ("Vodeyar" in the manuscript quoted above)—went to the Nayaka of Madurai and was appointed as the kingdom's ruler with the consent of the other guardians.[72] Another work claims that the Setupatis had once ruled for centuries over the Madurai and Tanjavur kingdoms and employed members of the Pandya dynasty as their ministers and generals, before they were treacherously subjugated by Vijayanagara and its Nayaka governors. The dynasty was reinstated only when 12,000 devotees from the north threatened to destroy the entire "Nayaka race" if the Nayaka of Madurai would not release the imprisoned former Setupati, Sadaika.[73] Also relevant in this regard are inscriptions issued by the Setupatis that contain long strings of dynastic titles. Several of these include such designations as "chief" or "ornament" of the *sūryavaṃśa* (sun lineage), suggesting that Ramnad's house considered itself part of the Solar line of kings.[74]

[71] BL/AAS, MG, no. 4, pt. 8: "A general history of the kings of Rama Naad or the Satoo-Putty Samastanum," ff. 171-9. For explanations of some of the titles mentioned, see Seshadri, "The Sētupatis of Ramnad," 228-32.

[72] Taylor, *Oriental Historical Manuscripts*, vol. II, Appendix, 49.

[73] BL/AAS, MG, no. 1, pt. 7C: "History of the Satoo-Putty of the Maravun Vumshum," ff. 61-5 (probably translated from a Tamil text, see Cotton, Charpentier, and Johnston, *Catalogue of Manuscripts in European Languages*, vol. I, pt. II, 7-8). See also: William Taylor (ed.), "Marava-Jathi-Vernanam," *Madras Journal of Literature and Science* IV (1836), 351; Wilson, *The Mackenzie Collection*, vol. I, 195.

[74] Jas. Burgess (ed.) and S.M. Naṭēśa Śāstrī (trans.), *Tamil and Sanskrit Inscriptions with Some Notes on Village Antiquities Collected Chiefly in the South of the Madras Presidency* (Madras, 1886), 71, 74, 77, 80, 83, 85, 92, 102.

Additionally, there are stories about the dynasty's foundation that are of unknown provenance but include noteworthy elements.[75] One tradition has it that the first Setupati, appointed by Rama, was Guha, who originated from the north and, as Rama's boatman, had rowed him across the Ganga River. Perhaps he can be identified with the abovementioned commander of the Ganga, "Goohoodoor." It is also said that the Maravar chief assisting Rama belonged to the Sembinattu sub-caste, from which the later, historical Setupatis sprang as well. Other stories claim that the dynasty was established by the Cholas or Ceylonese kings, or that the entire Maravar caste came from Ceylon. Yet another tradition holds that at the age of twelve Sadaika Tevar was found sleeping under a tamarind tree, while a cobra spread its hood over him.[76]

Finally, the "History of the Carnataca Governors who ruled over the Pandya Mandalam," a text deriving from Madurai's Nayaka court, contains a section on the foundation of the Setupati dynasty. It relates that in the early seventeenth century, during the reign of Muttu Krishnappa Nayaka, the Ramnad area was in a disorderly state. It paid no revenues and, being covered with forests, teemed with bandits who robbed pilgrims on their way to the Setu and Rameshvaram island. At that time, the chief *guru* (preceptor) of the Nayaka visited these sacred places and was safely escorted back and forth by the village chief of Pogalur, named Udaiyan (Sadaika Tevar). Udaiyan received land, clothes, and ornaments from the grateful Nayaka and returned to Ramnad. There he assembled troops, restored order, and collected revenues for the Nayaka. The latter then instructed Udaiyan to clear the forests, cultivate the newly available lands, and thus increase revenues. When these orders

[75] For surveys of such traditions, see: K. Seshradri, "The Origin and Restoration of the Setupatis," in Somalay (ed.), *The Saga of Rameswaram Temple: Kumbabishekam Souvenir* (Rameshvaram, 1975) (?); T. Raja Ram Rao, *Ramnad Manual* (Madras, 1889), 196-214; Nelson, *The Madura Country*, vol. III, 109-14; Heras, *The Aravidu Dynasty of Vijayanagara*, vol. I, 354-7; T.R. Rangaswami Ayyangar, "The Setupatis of Ramnad," *The Calcutta Review* (New Series) 32 (1920).

[76] Mahalingam, *Mackenzie Manuscripts*, vol. I, 59; N. Vanamamalai Pillai, *Temples of the Setu and Rameswaram* (Delhi, 1982; first published 1929), 108-9, 114-16; Raja Ram Rao, *Ramnad Manual*, 154, 213; Seshradri, "The Origin and Restoration of the Setupatis," 186f-g; Price, *Kingship and Political Practice in Colonial India*, 26, 37; Thiruvenkatachari, *The Setupatis of Ramnad*, 17; James Boyle, "Chronicles of Southern India: Part II.–The Marava Country," *Calcutta Review* 59, 117 (1874), 29-31, 37-8; J.L.W., "The Chronicles of the Marava Country in Southern India," *Calcutta Review* 66, 133 (1878), 447-9; Thurston, *Castes and Tribes of Southern India*, vol. V, 24-5; Rangachari, "The History of the Naik Kingdom of Madura," *Indian Antiquary* XLV (1916), 105; J.E. Tracy, "On the Coins of the Sethupatis [Sethupati Coins]," *The Madras Journal of Literature and Science* 32 (1889-94); Wilson, *The Mackenzie Collection*, vol. I, 195. See also: Anna Libera Dallapiccola, "Ramayana in Southern Indian Art," 184, 191, plate 6 (between 278-9); BL/AAS, MG, no. 1, pt. 7A: "Account of the Hindoo Rajium. The Raja-Cheritram or history of the ancient Rajahs of the Dutchana-Dickum or southern country of Pandia Mundalum, Colla-Mundalum & Tonda-Mundalum," ff. 52-3.

had been executed, the pleased Nayaka invested Udaiyan with the title of Setupati, presented him with elephants, horses, banners, and other gifts, and had him sprinkled with Ganga water as he installed him as governor. Udaiyan then built a mud fort at Ramanathapuram and ruled like a king.[77]

Although less value might be attached to the undocumented traditions and the Madurai text than to works deriving from Ramnad itself, if all sources are considered together, one observes all elements found in the origin stories of the other dynasties. Starting with the ancestry of the founder (Sadaika Tevar or Udaiyan), this is traced much further back than for most other heirs of Vijayanagara. Already in the mythical era of the *Rāmāyaṇa* epic, the first Setupati—either an anonymous member of the Maravar caste or boatman Guha—is installed by Vishnu's incarnation Rama ("Sree Ram") himself. His descendants are great warriors, possessing military skills surpassing those of neighbouring kings and earning them many rewards. Inscriptions further claim that the Setupatis belong to the Solar race. The dynasty falls into a temporary decline only because of treason.

The founder (or rather re-founder) Sadaika is also noted for his prowess as he subdues robbers, restores order, and protects the *guru* of Madurai's Nayaka. Ramnad's origin stories forge links with several earlier dynasties. Foremost are the so-called Pandyas of Madurai, a term initially referring to the actual Pandya house and later denoting the Madurai Nayakas. Both dynasties acknowledge the Setupatis as the rulers of Ramnad. Their power is also said to be recognised by the Cholas of Tanjavur and Krishna Raya of Vijayanagara's Tuluva house.

The Setupatis enjoy various religious credentials. To begin with, the foundation of their dynasty is interwoven with the *Rāmāyaṇa* episode of Rama's invasion of Lanka, by way of the Setu ("Satoo") bridge built by the Monkey-King Hanuman ("Hanoomunt"), to rescue his abducted wife Sita ("Seeta Davee") from the hands of Ravana ("Raavan-Eswar"), king of the demons. Further, the god Ramanathasvami ("Ram-Eswur" or "Ramanaad-Swamy," a form of Shiva), revered by Rama after his return from Lanka, appears in dreams of both Sadaika and his father and asks them to resume worshipping him. In fact, the guardianship of Ramanathasvami's sanctuaries is declared the Setupatis' *raison d'être*. A connection is also sought with the sacred Ganga River through the first Setupati, said to be either the oarsman Guha—a *Rāmāyaṇa* figure who rows Rama across the river—or a Maravar chief related to "Goohoodoor," chief commander of the Ganga.

[77] Taylor, *Oriental Historical Manuscripts*, vol. II, 27-9. A largely similar account is found in BL/AAS, MT, class III, no. 25: "History of the former Gentoo Rajahs who ruled over the Pandyan Mandalom," ff. 28v-9v. See also Rangachari, "The History of the Naik Kingdom of Madura," *Indian Antiquary* XLV, 105-6. For a discussion of this passage, see Dirks, *The Hollow Crown*, 105-6.

As for natural wonders, although its source is obscure, one tradition has it that Sadaika Tevar is sheltered by a snake, indicating his exceptional future, similar to the founders of Ikkeri's and Tanjavur's Nayaka houses. No miracle has to demonstrate Ramnad's special location, claimed as it is to have been the dynasty's kingdom since the events of the *Rāmāyaṇa*. Like most dynastic founders, Sadaika acquires a treasure that helps him increase his power. The motif of migration is less obvious as most texts say the Setupati house and its Maravar caste have local origins. Yet, a connection with the far north is established through the first Setupati who comes from the Ganga region himself or has a relative living there. Besides, the stories mention journeys of Sadaika and earlier Setupatis to the Nayaka and Pandya courts at Madurai, but as with Ikkeri, these are temporary and brief sojourns. In the end, the dynasty is founded at the place the founder comes from.

Land development figures prominently in Ramnad's origin stories. From the very start, the Setupatis are said to dwell in forests and to be instructed by their overlords to cultivate these lands. Thus, safety, population, and revenues are to be increased. Besides, Ramnad's territory is clearly marked, both by the construction of towns, forts, and roads, and by the lands and ports received from the Pandyas and the Cholas, whose locations are specifically mentioned.

Symbols of royalty frequently appear: the dynasty acquires titles from the Pandya and Chola kings, the standards of Hanuman and Garuda from Vijayanagara, and animals, clothes, banners, and other gifts from the Nayakas of Madurai. Finally, the hereditary continuation of the dynasty is emphasised, but this concerns Sadaika's predecessors rather than his successors—although he is also said to marry a Maravar virgin at the age of twelve. Most stories relate how Sadaika descends from the old, temporarily removed Setupati line. His birth and the re-establishment of the Ramnad realm are foretold in a dream of his father, himself "born in the race" of the previous Setupatis.

Conclusions

The previous sections have considered the origin myths of Vijayanagara and its heirs one by one and explained how certain motifs manifest themselves in all or most of these stories. The multitude of rulers, families, deities, animals, and other actors in the texts can all be linked to the elements that together form the myths, and so the stories of the various dynasties can be related to one another. This concluding section first considers how each of the motifs varies among the foundation stories and then compares the origin myths of the different royal houses as a whole.

With regard to the founders' ancestry, all dynasties refer to forefathers who had some form of politico-military power. Whether the family is traced back to a mythical age or just a few generations, every founder is said to descend from warriors, chiefs, kings, or at least a village headman. Fully-fledged royal ancestors, however, are claimed only by Vijayanagara's Saluvas and Aravidus (the Chalukyas of Kalyana), Tanjavur's Bhonsles, and Ramnad's Setupatis. The latter two families in fact maintain they are not new dynasties but continuations of ancient royal houses. In contrast, the Nayakas of Ikkeri, Tanjavur, and Madurai, all direct heirs of Vijayanagara, do not mention royal forefathers.

A comparable division is found for celestial descent, which is explicitly claimed by the imperial dynasties (the Lunar line), Ramnad's Setupatis (the Solar line), and Tanjavur's Bhonsles (mentioning both lines). Less unequivocally, only a few sources declare Madurai's and Ikkeri's Nayakas to have sprung from Minakshi and a form of Shiva, respectively. Caste does not appear to play a substantial role in the foundation myths, except in those of Ramnad, where the Maravar identity is brought up regularly. In sum, in all origin stories the founders share a martial background, but divine or royal ancestry is generally not referred to by Vijayanagara's direct, Nayaka heirs. In particular, the Telugu Nayakas in the Tamil region, appointed as non-local governors by the imperial rulers, usually trace their lineages to modest origins.

As for the physical skills of the founders themselves, all of them are portrayed as exceptional warriors. They conquer lands, perform martial feats, subdue enemies and rebels, and restore order, all in the service of their overlords, to whom they display great loyalty. These events usually mark the points in the stories where the founders in return acquire land, titles, honours, gifts, and the like. While some dynasties seem to stress the motif of the founders' prowess more than others, by and large the origin myths do not differ much in this respect.

All dynasties forge ties with other royal houses. Such links can be divided into two types, the first of which concerns bonds with the overlords whom the dynasties' founders initially serve and by whom they are sometimes actually installed or recognised. Thus, in their origin stories, Vijayanagara's houses refer to the sultan of Delhi (and the later imperial families also to the Sangamas), the Nayaka dynasties to Vijayanagara's Tuluvas, Tanjavur's Bhonsles to the sultan of Bijapur, and Ramnad's Setupatis to Madurai's Nayakas. A difference between the Nayakas of Ikkeri and those of Tanjavur and Madurai is that the former also mention Vijayanagara's Aravidus while the latter two do not, suggesting they did not wish to associate themselves with the last imperial family.[78]

[78] See also Wagoner, *Tidings of the King*, for instance 30-3.

The second kind of dynastic ties are those that are established with earlier royal houses that did not in fact install the dynasties' founders but were based in (more or less) the same area. Vijayanagara's dynasties look back to Kampili, the Chalukyas, the Hoysalas, or the Kakatiyas. While Ikkeri's Nayakas perhaps construct a link with the Hoysalas, Tanjavur's Bhonsles clearly refer to Tanjavur's Nayakas, and both Madurai's Nayakas and Ramnad's Setupatis to the Pandyas. The origin stories of Tanjavur's Nayakas seemingly do not mention an earlier local dynasty, but it has been suggested they saw themselves as heirs of the Cholas.[79] Overall, it appears that all dynasties seek to derive legitimacy from both their formal overlords—who can be seated in different regions—and more local predecessors who have become extinct.[80]

The element of religious recognition is found with every dynasty. All origin stories link the royal houses to deities, temples, or spiritual men. Nearly every founder (or sometimes their father) experiences dreams in which gods or goddesses foretell the dynasty's foundation, reveal a hidden treasure, or give orders to assemble troops or build temples. The deities who appear in these dreams or are otherwise connected to dynasties, for instance through temple worship or ancestry, often represent forms of Shiva. Shiva's *liṅgam* (phallic symbol) also figures regularly in the texts. In fact, in all but one case, the royal houses are associated with this pan-Indian god. His counterpart Vishnu is present in the stories of only the Nayakas of Tanjavur and—together with Shiva—the Saluvas of Vijayanagara and the Setupatis of Ramnad.[81] In all foundation stories, these great gods manifest themselves as local deities, connected to particular temples or sites.[82] This seems to be another way for royal houses to establish links with the area they rule over, in addition to ties with previous local dynasties.

79 Narayana Rao, Shulman, and Subrahmanyam, *Symbols of Substance*, 42. See also Vriddhagirisan, *The Nayaks of Tanjore*, 126.

80 See also Eaton and Wagoner, *Power, Memory, Architecture*, particularly sections II-III.

81 For the dynasties' religious affiliations, see also for example: Verghese, "Deities, Cults and Kings at Vijayanagara," 422; Ajay K. Rao, "A New Perspective on the Royal Rāma Cult at Vijayanagara," in Yigal Bronner, Whitney Cox, and Lawrence J. McCrea (eds), *South Asian Texts in History: Critical Engagements with Sheldon Pollock* (Ann Arbor, 2011); Chitnis, *Keḷadi Polity*, 53; Vriddhagirisan, *The Nayaks of Tanjore*, 124; Seshadri, "The Sētupatis of Ramnad," 82, 201, 203.

82 In the various origin stories, Shiva manifests himself as: Virupaksha and a *liṅgam* at Vijayanagara (Sangamas); Rameshvar and a *liṅgam* at Keladi (Ikkeri's Nayakas); Vaidyanathasvami at Tirumalavadi (Tanjavur's Bhonsles); Vishvanatha and a *liṅgam* at Benares and Minakshi at Madurai (Madurai's Nayakas); and Ramanathasvami and a *liṅgam* at Rameshvaram (Ramnad's Setupatis). Vishnu appears as: Narasimha (Vijayanagara's Saluvas); Mannaru at Mannargudi (Tanjavur's Nayakas); and Rama (Ramnad's Setupatis).

Finally, Islam, although an influential political and cultural factor in south India from the fourteenth century onward (see Chapter 5), is virtually absent in the texts as a legitimising force in a religious sense. The sole exception concerns one of the origin myths of Tanjavur's Bhonsles, which has the founder's grandfather seeking support and recognition from a Muslim shrine. Among Vijayanagara and its heirs, this seems an isolated case. The inclusion of this event in the Bhonsles' foundation story may well be related to the family's past as military commanders under the Deccan sultanates.

Natural miracles appear in the origin stories of most dynasties: Vijayanagara's Sangamas, Ikkeri's Nayakas, Tanjavur's Nayakas, Ramnad's Setupatis, and to some extent Madurai's Nayakas (as well as Ariyalur's rulers). The foundations of most of these houses coincide with the foundations of new kingdoms. The miracles signify the sites where capitals are to be built or the special status of the future founders. Vijayanagara's later dynasties and the houses of Tanjavur and Madurai are all founded in kingdoms that already exist and no miracle is needed to indicate the significance of these places.

It has been argued that natural miracles are of two kinds: those suspending the predatory order and those reversing it. The first sort is thought to denote spots with spiritual power, while the second type would refer to sites with worldly power.[83] To some extent, this model is applicable to the foundation myths analysed here. The three cases of snakes spreading their hoods over sleeping men—suspending the order—signify the exceptional talents of Chaudappa Nayaka of Ikkeri, Shevappa Nayaka of Tanjavur, and Sadaika Tevar of Ramnad. They are destined to found kingdoms or at least dynasties, which requires not only worldly (politico-military) skills but also spiritual qualities, such as pleasing deities, understanding omens, and endowing temples. The instances of hares (or lizards) turning against hunting dogs—reversing the order—indicate suitable places to establish capitals. Here, worldly factors seem more important than spiritual ones. Although the site of the Vijayanagara capital had strong religious connotations, its strategic position, both militarily and commercially, must have been decisive in its selection. Likewise, Keladi was replaced with Ikkeri as capital soon after the Nayaka dynasty's foundation, which was probably also determined by worldly rather than spiritual issues.

Some scholars have suggested that the myth of the hare and hounds symbolises the challenge and overthrow of the existing political order by a growing regional power, associated with a specific heroic location. The miracle would thus refer to the assertion of independence and the establishment of a new political landscape. Such an explanation certainly fits the foundation of Vijayanagara. Besides, in

83 Wagoner, *Tidings of the King*, 44-5.

this view the myth could recur among smaller principalities emerging under the empire's control, signifying a degree of autonomy granted by the imperial court. This model applies well to the Nayakas' move from Keladi to Ikkeri, representing the set-up of a new, royal centre that nevertheless was still loyal to the empire.[84]

It has been proposed that the tale of prey attacking a predator was part of the wide range of politico-cultural influences the Islamic world had on south India from the fourteenth century onward.[85] Local use of this story may seem older, however, as it figures, among many other instances, in the origin myths of Kampili and the Hoysalas. The latter's first capital was even called "City of the Hare," after a hare chasing a tiger.[86] But it is of course also possible that these references were introduced after the period they describe. In any case, the repetition of this tale could concern another effort by the rulers of Vijayanagara and Ikkeri to link themselves with the Hoysalas.

All but one foundation myth include the acquisition of wealth in some form. Several stories refer to the unearthing of a hidden treasure (Ikkeri, Ramnad), while other texts mention a heavenly shower of gold (Vijayanagara) or fortunes donated by the founder's father (Madurai). Nayaka Tanjavur is an exception, which could be related to the kingdom's fertile and densely populated territory, providing sufficient riches on its own. The role of wealth in the origin story of Tanjavur's Bhonsles, enjoying the same fruitful lands, is ambiguous. They obtain part of the former Nayaka treasure, but this may be an indemnification for their military expenses rather than capital to establish their rule. All other dynasties are specifically said to use the acquired money to strengthen their power, gather supporters, and make the kingdom prosper.

Migration occurs in almost all foundation stories. Ikkeri's Nayakas are the sole dynasty presented to be entirely of local origin. But Ramnad's Setupatis—even though some of their myths connect the primordial Setupati installed by Rama with the Ganga River—are also largely portrayed as having a local background. The texts of the Ikkeri and Ramnad houses just refer to a kind of "roundtrip," from

84 Suchitra Balasubrahmanyan, *The Myth of the Hare and Hounds: Making Sense of a Recurring City-Foundation Story* (New Delhi, 2014), 5-6, 10-14, 18-23, 31-4; Sohoni, "The Hunt for a Location," 219-20. For yet another interpretation, see Jackson, *Vijayanagara Voices*, 12, 48.

85 Sohoni, "The Hunt for a Location," passim, especially 219-20.

86 Venkata Ramanayya, *Kampili and Vijayanagara*, 6-7; Balasubrahmanyan, *The Myth of the Hare and Hounds*, 4-9, 14-31; Wagoner, *Tidings of the King*, 44-5, 176 (n. 38); Heras, *Beginnings of Vijayanagara History*, 9. This theme is also found in the foundation myth of the Bahmani sultanate. For another example of a future chief being protected by a snake, see Eaton and Wagoner, *Power, Memory, Architecture*, 166-7.

the family's native area to the overlord's court and back, instead of a permanent change of residence.[87] The myths of all other successor dynasties clearly speak of migration in some form. That is not surprising in the case of the Nayakas and the Bhonsles in the Tamil zone, of course, since they originated from other linguistic areas.

The origins of Vijayanagara's founders remain unclear, but they could have come from another region as well. At any rate, the standard myth relates that the Sangama brothers travel from Kampili to faraway Delhi and back before they set up their realm, while the sage Vidyaranya goes on a pilgrimage to equally distant Benares. The Saluva and Aravidu houses refer to Kalyana as their family's origin. Thus, migration, or at least a roundtrip, is an important element in Vijayanagara's foundation stories too. What nearly all dynastic movements—including that of Ariyalur—have in common is a southward direction. The foundation myths thereby reflect the general trend in late medieval and early modern south India of people (*nāyaka*s, *vaḍuga*s, Marathas) moving south in search of political and economic opportunities.

As with the acquisition of wealth, Tanjavur—both under the Nayakas and Bhonsles—is the only kingdom where land development is absent in foundation stories. This probably stems from the fact that its territory had already been brought under cultivation. Texts of all other dynasties refer to jungles that must be removed to populate the country, bring safety, and increase revenues. The lands thus obtained are usually marked with capitals, forts, villages, temples, and irrigation works. Territorial additions, such as land grants from overlords and conquests from enemies or rebels, are often specified in detail in the stories. All in all, the texts generally emphasise the acquisition of land, its geographic location, and its strategic and economic value.

Symbols of royalty are included in the origin myths of only some dynasties. Among them, the houses of Ikkeri and Ramnad (and Ariyalur) are most specific, referring in detail to titles, emblems, honours, and gifts received from their overlords. The other successor dynasties are usually less precise. Madurai's Nayakas list the Pandya regalia separately but describe the symbols granted by Vijayanagara in general terms. Tanjavur's Bhonsles mention clothes sent by the sultan of Bijapur, and robes and ornaments received from Chengamaladasa of the Tanjavur Nayakas, but do not give details. Tanjavur's Nayakas themselves, as well as Vijayanagara's dynasties, do not state anything in this regard.

[87] For the notion of a "roundtrip" between birthplace and royal city, see Ota, "Bēḍa Nāyakas and Their Historical Narratives," 174-6.

The general trend appears to be that dynasties of a local origin that are incorporated into their overlord's realm receive many royal symbols or at least attach much value to detailing them in their texts. For dynasties whose founders originate from the imperial court and are appointed as non-local governors (the Nayakas in the Tamil region), this seems unnecessary, or even inappropriate, because of their more direct bond with Vijayanagara. Tanjavur's Bhonsles obtain their kingdom through conquest, then sever their ties with Bijapur, and therefore have no overlord to receive symbols from. Vijayanagara's actual origins being obscure, little can be said about its founders in this respect. The Sangamas resemble both the Nayakas of Tanjavur and Madurai—in that they are appointed by Delhi and thus initially have close, hierarchical links with their overlord—and the Bhonsles, in that relations with Delhi have ended by the time the empire is founded and there is no overlord anymore to recognise them. Either way, the acquisition of symbols of royalty would seem less likely.

Finally, most origin stories emphasise the continuous, hereditary character of dynasties once they are established. Some royal houses are founded by several close relatives rather than one individual. Five sons of Sangama are involved in establishing Vijayanagara and its first ruler, Harihara, is succeeded by his brother Bukka (as happens in Ariyalur). The foundation of Madurai's Nayaka dynasty is the result of a complex interaction between father and son, Nagama and Vishvanatha. The same applies to Ikkeri, where Chaudappa's political activities—mostly undertaken with his brother Bhadrappa—are expanded by his son Sadashiva, fully securing the family's regal status.

Another effort to underline dynastic heredity concerns the stress Tanjavur's Bhonsles and Ramnad's Setupatis put on the great antiquity of their dynasties, to which they are rightful heirs. Further, Tanjavur's Nayakas mention that the founder Shevappa installs his son Achyutappa as crown prince and administrator while he is still in power. All these references to the continuation of family rule seem to express the desire of later rulers to emphasise their descent from the glorious founders and justify their position on the throne.

Having considered how the various elements manifest themselves in the dynasties' foundation stories, several patterns can be noticed. Some motifs are largely similar for each royal house: descent from warriors, the founder's own martial skills, links with overlords and preceding regional houses, ties with local deities connected to pan-Indian gods, and dynastic continuity. Thus, for these motifs, the myths of the heirs resemble those of the imperial houses, and these elements were apparently indispensable in the foundation stories of all dynasties.

Other elements occur in the texts in varying ways. All imperial families trace their forefathers to mythical times and the Moon, whereas their direct Nayaka heirs in Tanjavur and Madurai do not go further back than a few generations and mostly hint at a modest background. The indirect successors—and to a lesser extent Ikkeri's Nayakas—claim high antiquity or divine ancestry again. This pattern largely corresponds with the different stages of state formation: first the imperial houses, next the direct successors appointed by the imperial court in outlying provinces (the Nayakas in the Tamil zone), and finally locally installed heirs (Ikkeri's Nayakas) and indirect successors (the Bhonsles and the Setupatis) that seceded from or replaced the direct heirs.

Some motifs point to other divisions between the dynasties. Different sorts of natural miracles are necessary for new dynasties, for allegedly re-established houses, and for whole new states. Further, migration is largely missing in the myths of houses of local origin, which instead pay more attention to symbols of royalty than other dynasties. All these elements seem related to the question of whether dynastic founders originated from the Vijayanagara court or came from another background. Both the acquisition of wealth and the clearance of jungles are more or less absent from the foundation stories of Tanjavur's two dynasties, probably because of this country's exceptional geography and demography.

In short, some of the myths' motifs reflect general prerequisites for the foundation of a royal house, while other elements represent variations among the dynasties and their kingdoms. Because of this diversity, the foundation stories of the successor states differ from those of Vijayanagara and from each other. Therefore, these origin myths, including their "mythical" aspects, provide a fairly accurate picture of the actual background of each dynastic founder and the specific nature of his realm.[88]

Thus, the composers of the foundation stories of Vijayanagara's heirs seem to have followed traditions deriving from the empire—and perhaps from earlier polities—but chose from these traditions those elements, interpretations, and details that suited them best. The predatory hares of Vijayanagara's Sangamas and the Hoysalas may have been an inspiration for Ikkeri's Nayakas (and, in the shape of a lizard, for Ariyalur's chiefs) but were apparently of no use to the Nayakas of Tanjavur and Madurai. Likewise, the shower of gold falling on the sage Vidyaranya reappeared as the treasures found by Ikkeri's Chaudappa and Ramnad's Sadaika and the money offered to Madurai's Vishvanatha by his father, but was seemingly not deemed essential for Tanjavur's Shevappa and Ekoji.

[88] See also Ota, "Bēḍa Nāyakas and Their Historical Narratives," 187.

As explained in the Introduction, it has been argued that the main Nayaka dynasties in the Tamil region—Madurai, Tanjavur, and Senji—depended on five factors for the formation of their states: portable wealth, mobility, a territorial base, personal loyalty to a higher authority, and deities. At the same time, Brahmins, as ministers or priests, and exalted pedigrees are said to have been no longer necessary to create a kingdom, unlike before.[89]

Most of these factors can be linked to motifs in the origin stories of the Vijayanagara successor states. But looking at the heirs' individual foundation myths, one does not see those first five factors at work for every dynasty. Mobility did not play a substantial role in the origins of the Ikkeri and Ramnad houses. Portable wealth, as in moveable treasures, appears to be largely missing from the foundation stories of Tanjavur's Nayaka and Bhonsle dynasties, for whom land-based revenues rather than movable treasures seem to have been important. However, a territorial base, personal ties with higher authorities, and deities were evidently considered vital elements in the foundations of all royal houses, including the imperial families.[90]

Turning to the factors the Nayaka founders in the Tamil area are thought to have dispensed with—Brahmins and proper ancestry—these elements are certainly lacking in the origin stories of Ikkeri's Nayakas. However, at least some of the myths of Tanjavur's Nayakas do actually refer to the crucial role of the Brahmin Govinda Dikshita. Further, while Brahmins are largely absent from the foundation myths of Tanjavur's Bhonsles and Ramnad's Setupatis, those dynasties do claim to be of exalted descent.[91] Thus, based on the foundation myths discussed here, it can be concluded that the abovementioned basic elements of Nayaka statehood in the Tamil region are not entirely applicable to all Vijayanagara's heirs. Rather, all dynasties dealt with their own set of conditions, which affected the founding of their kingdoms and transpired in the varying origin stories.

The next chapter traces the fortunes of the dynasties after they were established, discussing all rulers who succeeded the dynastic founders.

89 Narayana Rao, Shulman, and Subrahmanyam, *Symbols of Substance*, 53-6. See also Narayana Rao and Subrahmanyam, "Ideologies of State Building," 225-8.

90 See also Wagoner, "Harihara, Bukka, and the Sultan," 314.

91 See also Narayana Rao and Subrahmanyam, "Ideologies of State Building," 228.

CHAPTER 2

Dynastic Successions[1]

In February 1689 the Dutch East India Company received a remarkable letter from a certain Sadashiva Nayaka, who introduced himself as the king of Ikkeri. He began his message with a list of his royal ancestors leading up to himself and his elder brother Shivappa, who had been king of Ikkeri in the past. Sadashiva next declared that since his brother had passed away, he was now the rightful heir to the kingdom. Besides, he claimed that he was beloved by all local chiefs and other distinguished people in Ikkeri, and that even the bravest warriors feared him when he went hunting in his lands. Furthermore, he stated repeatedly that it was inappropriate, in fact downright intolerable, for women to rule over his kingdom and over men in general. In sum, Sadashiva was an ideal king: a real man, of pure royal descent, first in the line of succession, held in high esteem, and commanding kingdom-wide support—and therefore wholly entitled to sit on the Ikkeri throne.[2]

Sadly for Sadashiva, as he had to admit in the same letter, already for nearly two decades the throne had been occupied by Chennammaji, who seems to have had few credentials to qualify as a monarch. First of all—to Sadashiva's horror—Chennammaji was a woman. She was the widow of a king who had been installed as a child, later went mad, and finally was murdered. Additionally, both Chennammaji and her deceased husband were said not to possess full royal blood but to have been born of an enslaved girl and another non-regal woman.

Yet, Chennammaji ruled as queen over Ikkeri, whereas Sadashiva was a powerless throne pretender on the run. Around early 1672, he and his elder brother Shivappa, the then king, had been imprisoned by rivals at the court, but some years later managed to flee to Mysore or one of the Deccan sultanates. Supposedly, Shivappa had escaped from being assassinated by leaving a look-alike in his room, who was then killed. After Shivappa himself died of chicken pox in the mid-1680s,

1 An early, much shorter version of this chapter appeared in Lennart Bes, "Toddlers, Widows, and Bastards Enthroned: Dynastic Successions in Early-Modern South India as Observed by the Dutch," *Leidschrift: Historisch Tijdschrift* 27, 1 (2012). The section on the eighteenth-century successions in Ramnad has partly been taken from: idem, "The Setupatis, the Dutch, and Other Bandits," 552-61; idem, "Friendship as Long as the Sun and Moon Shine," sections of chs 4-5, 7.

2 NA, VOC, no. 1463, ff. 437v-8, 440v-1: letter from "Sadaasjiwe Neijke king of Carnatica" at Vengurla to the Dutch commissioner-general (received at Nagapattinam), Feb. 1689.

Sadashiva took over his brother's quest to reclaim the Ikkeri throne. Since then, he had been wandering around south India with some dozen followers, looking for allies. His letter to the Dutch was actually a request for military assistance to expel Queen Chennammaji and help him become king, in exchange for which Sadashiva promised to grant unprecedented trade privileges to the VOC once he ruled Ikkeri. The mention of all his regal qualities was evidently meant to convince the Company of his rights.[3] But apparently, the men who should be king were not always the men—or women—who would be king.

This discrepancy between ideas of rightful succession, on the one hand, and the reality of succession struggles between rivals and the enthronement of illegitimate or puppet rulers on the other, is one of this chapter's topics. After discussing the founders of Vijayanagara and its heirs in the previous chapter, here we analyse the fortunes of their descendants on the throne—totalling almost thirty imperial rulers and, until the 1760s, over sixty monarchs in the successor states under study. Central questions concern how individual successions proceeded, which broad patterns can be discerned for each dynasty, and how the kingdoms differed from one another.

This chapter starts with a general overview of ideas on succession in India, held by ancient Indian thinkers and modern scholars. Subsequently, it considers the sources for successions, comprising local texts and images as well as European records. The chapter next treats the dynasties individually, dealing with local notions on legitimate heirship, the actual practices accompanying each transition, and overall tendencies. This part begins with the successions in Vijayanagara, about whose later houses relatively much is already known. Then, the successor dynasties are examined in more detail, since European sources contain much previously unknown information about these kingdoms. All successions under the last

[3] It is uncertain who this Sadashiva and his brother Shivappa were. Sadashiva and some of the ancestors mentioned in his letter do not seem to be listed in any published genealogical trees of Ikkeri's Nayakas, while his brother Shivappa possibly appears in only two of these pedigrees. See: C. Hayavadana Rao, *History of Mysore (1399-1799 A.D.)*, vol. III (Bangalore, 1948), 1287; Sundara, *The Keḷadi Nāyakas*, ix. But these brothers were likely great-great-grandsons of King Venkatappa Nayaka I (r. c. 1585-1629); see the section on Ikkeri successions in this chapter. This Shivappa should not be confused with his well-known namesake ruling Ikkeri in c. 1644-60. The former Shivappa also seems to be the fugitive Ikkeri king sheltered from c. 1683 by the Mysore court under Chikkadevaraja Wodeyar. For Dutch records on these brothers, see: NA, VOC, no. 1388, f. 1976; no. 1396, f. 655v; no. 1463, ff. 438-41v; no. 1474, ff. 210v-13, 329-32: letters from Cochin to Batavia and Gentlemen XVII, from "Sadaasjiwe Neijke king of Carnatica" at Vengurla to the Dutch commissioner-general, from the *commandeur* at Quilon to Commissioner Van Rheede, report on Vengurla and "Canara," July 1683, Jan. 1684, Feb.-Mar., June 1689; Coolhaas *et al.*, *Generale Missiven*, vol. IV (The Hague, 1971), 670. See also the last footnote of this chapter.

two imperial houses and in the successor states are also included in tables, listing for every monarch their dates of reign, kinship with earlier rulers (focussing on immediate predecessors), and other basic facts.[4] The sections narrating the actual successions may make for repetitive, tedious reading, but this fittingly illustrates the frequent competition for thrones and the succession patterns that resurfaced time and again. The chapter concludes with three comparisons, all revealing clear differences: between the various types of sources, between rules and reality, and between the dynasties. But below, it first considers traditional and modern views on royal succession in India in general.

The *Mahābhārata*, one of India's classical epics (fifth century BCE to fourth century CE?, ascribed to the sage Vyasa), would not have approved of Queen Chennammaji's reign. It strongly advises against the rule of women, gamblers, and children, under whom countries are bound to "sink like stone boats in a river" (V 38:40). Besides, it urges kings to securely install their son or another appropriate successor as their heir before their own death (XII 63:19). This advice, in order to avoid succession struggles, certainly made sense in the early modern period, for the epic also allows any suitable chief, even of the Shudra *varṇa* (lowest caste category), to take the throne in times of political disorder, like contested kingship or external threats (XII 79:34-9)—conditions that often prevailed when a ruler died in Vijayanagara or its heirs.

The *Arthaśāstra*, the ancient discourse on statecraft (traditionally ascribed to the Brahmin Minister Kautilya under the Maurya dynasty in the fourth century BCE, but thought to partly date from around 300 CE), recommends that a king passing away unexpectedly be succeeded by a son with a suitable personality, preferably the eldest. Should such a son be lacking, a faultless prince, a princess, or a pregnant queen can be chosen, although eventually a male member of the royal family must become the ruler again. Further, a weak but rightful king is preferred over a usurper (V 6:1-48; VIII 2:20-4). The *Nītivākyāmṛta*, a tenth-century political thesis by the south Indian Jain monk Somadevasuri, confirms the necessity of the king being succeeded by his most capable son, because both descent and personal abilities are considered essential for the throne (5:32, 36).[5]

[4] I use dynastic tables rather than genealogical trees because the exact kinship relations between consecutive rulers are often uncertain.

[5] Scharfe, *The State in Indian Tradition*, 55 (n. 234), 57, 62, 63 (n. 287), 122 (n. 752); Daud Ali, *Courtly Culture and Political Life in Early Medieval India* (Cambridge, 2004), 53, 71 (n. 11), 277; Vyasa, *The Mahābhārata*, vol. 3, book 5, *The Book of the Effort*, ed. J.A.B. van Buitenen, 279, vol. 7, book 12 (pt. 1), *The Book of Peace*, ed. James L. Fitzgerald (Chicago/London, 1978, 2004), 322, 367-8; Kautilya, *The Kauṭilīya Arthaśāstra*, pt. II, ed. R.P. Kangle (Bombay, 1963), 359-63, 453-4; De Casparis, "Inscriptions and South Asian Dynastic Traditions," 116-20. See also Mr. Colebrooke, "A Disquisition on Regal Succession, by Jaganatha Tercapanchanana: From the Digest of Hindu Law, Translated from the Original Sanscrit,"

Finally, the *Śukranīti*, a *śāstra* (treatise) perhaps written—or reworked—in the nineteenth century in west India by a certain Shukracharya, and dealing with a range of subjects including the state, is relatively explicit on who is eligible for succession. Also emphasising both ancestry and individual skills, it states that the king should preferably select as *yuvarāja* (heir apparent, literally "young king") a male descendant of a legally married wife able to fulfil his duties without idleness. In addition, this text provides a series of candidates for the position of crown prince. The list begins with the eldest son of the king, but if a son is unavailable or incapable, a paternal uncle younger than the king may be chosen, or else a younger brother of the king, a son's son, an elder brother's son, an adopted son, a daughter's son, or finally a sister's son (I 342-4; II 14-15).[6]

One may doubt whether any of these works—all in Sanskrit but from very different backgrounds and ages—played a normative role in Vijayanagara and its heirs with respect to successions, or indeed other subjects discussed in the present study.[7] However, together these texts provide some insight into political notions held in India over the course of time. At any rate, it seems that Indian works treating principles of succession in detail are rare. Those that do address this topic often leave room for broad interpretation and occasionally contradict one another. Most passages above agree that a legitimate son of the king with the right capacities is the preferred successor, thus valuing a combination of birth and personality and disfavouring minors, unlawful offspring, or women on the throne. Hardly any text refers to privileges of the eldest son over his younger brothers, so primogeniture is unlikely to have been an important concept.

But opinions start to diverge strongly when the question arises of who must be selected if a competent son is unavailable. Whereas one of the texts sanctions the rule of even a low-born but suitable Shudra if need be—favouring practical needs

in *The Asiatic Annual Register, or, a View of the History of Hindustan, and of the Politics, Commerce and Literature of Asia, for the Year 1800* (London, 1801), section "Miscellaneous Tracts."

[6] Shukracharya, *The Śukranītiḥ (Original Sanskrit Text with Translation into English)*, ed. Krishna Lal, trans. Benoy Kumar Sarkar (Delhi, 2005), 93, 115 (see also 116-25); Vandana Nagar, *Kingship in the Śukra-Nīti* (Delhi, 1992), 10, 63-4, 70-1; Lallanji Gopal, "The *Śukranīti*—A Nineteenth-Century Text," *Bulletin of the School of Oriental and African Studies* 25, 1/3 (1962), 535; Scharfe, *The State in Indian Tradition*, 25; Mahalingam, *South Indian Polity*, 92, 413; Chitnis, *Keḷadi Polity*, 44. The *Śukranīti* may have been composed much earlier than the nineteenth century. See: Nagar, *Kingship in the Śukra-Nīti*, 7-9; Saran Suebsantiwongse, "Dating and Locating the *Sāmrājyalakṣmīpīṭhikā*: A Hybrid Manual on Kingship and Tantric Practices," *Thai Prajñā: International Journal of Indology and Culture* I (2017), 250; Gopal, "The *Śukranīti*."

[7] See for instance: Donald R. Davis, Jr, *The Spirit of Hindu Law* (Cambridge, 2010), 14-15; Narayana Rao, "Coconut and Honey," 155-6; Sheldon Pollock, "Playing by the Rules: Śāstra and Sanskrit Literature," in Anna Libera Dallapiccola, Christine Walter-Mendy, and Stephanie Zingel-Avé Lallement (eds), *Shastric Traditions in Indian Arts* (Stuttgart, 1989), vol. 1.

over conventional ideas—another work advocates the rule of a weak but legitimate king rather than an illegitimate one, regardless of who is more capable. Likewise, one text states that female members of the royal family can serve as temporary alternatives to male successors, while another work allows the enthronement of all sorts of relatives but clearly excludes women. Altogether, there appear to have been certain general notions about rightful succession, as Ikkeri's unfortunate pretender to the throne Sadashiva Nayaka himself explained, but these became ambiguous and contradictory if the most obvious heir, a suitable son, was absent or when several such sons were on hand.[8]

Scholars have conducted only limited systematic research into dynastic successions in Vijayanagara and its heirs. Based on local sources, they often conclude that many such transitions were unchallenged and proceeded peacefully. Further, some historians have constructed sets of regulations that would have governed successions under the individual houses. But since contemporary normative texts with specific instructions in this regard are scarce or non-existent, these rules have chiefly been deduced from observed practices. The regulations thus pieced together, albeit slightly different for each kingdom, can be summarised as follows: the king's sons had preference over his brothers, elder relatives over younger ones, adults over minors, the direct family line over collateral branches, men over women, and biological relatives over adopted ones.[9] Despite these supposed preferences, however, and even when capable sons of the king were actually available, many a succession in Vijayanagara and its heirs was contested, as especially reported in European sources.

As a result—and much against the *Mahābhārata*'s advice—the approximately ninety monarchs under study include a substantial number of widows, minors, bastards, and other unlikely figures, instead of mature, legitimate sons of previous rulers. Such disqualified candidates for the throne frequently succeeded their predecessors after fierce clashes between rival claimants. For Vijayanagara it has been argued that, although succession struggles and the accompanying violence could cause instability or even dynastic collapse, they were also essential to generate processes of political transition. Such periods often witnessed changes in the court's internal and external relations, extending and renewing networks, providing career opportunities to ambitious, competent courtiers and chiefs, and

[8] See also: Chekuri, "Between Family and Empire," 47-8, 209; Robbins Burling, *The Passage of Power: Studies in Political Succession* (New York/London, 1974), 61, 63, 84; Ali, *Courtly Culture and Political Life*, 54; N. Subrahmaniam, "The Question of Succession to the Throne in the History of Tamilnad," *Proceedings of the Indian History Congress* 37 (1976).

[9] See for instance: Burling, *The Passage of Power*, 58-61; Scharfe, *The State in Indian Tradition*, 26-7, 55-6; Mahalingam, *South Indian Polity*, 32; and the literature on the individual dynasties treated below.

generally accelerating a restructuring of the balance of power.[10] As this chapter also concludes for Vijayanagara's heirs, struggles for the throne were therefore of an ambiguous nature: hazardous to the continuation of royal houses but instrumental in political developments.

Ambivalence also characterises the observations of the seventeenth- and early eighteenth-century Venetian gunner and traveller Niccolao Manucci (or Niccolò Manuzzi) about successions in India. Referring to "Hindu" kingdoms, Manucci states that rulers of such polities commonly imprisoned those destined to succeed them in order to avoid treachery and untimely regime changes. Only when a king died, would his successor be released and enthroned by prominent courtiers. Yet, as Manucci notes, these measures could not prevent dynastic instability from posing a continuous threat.[11] Although in Vijayanagara and its successors just a few heirs apparent were actually locked up, Manucci's remarks underscore the ambiguity of successions when it came to the rules devised for these occasions and the way matters unfolded in practice.

With regard to minors on the throne, it is unclear until what age minority lasted at early modern south Indian courts. Some sources suggest it differed for the various dynasties and that adulthood was attained in stages. One such phase appears to have started at the age of twelve. In 1741, when he was about twelve years old, King Sivakumara Muttu Vijaya Raghunatha Setupati of Ramnad (r. 1735-48) wrote to the Dutch that he had recently acquired new powers and honours through a special temple ceremony. According to the VOC, this event indicated a transition from a merely nominal royal position to a more substantial form of kingship. The same age figures in some of Ramnad's foundation myths, stating that the first historical Setupati, Sadaika Tevar (r. c. 1605-22), was found asleep guarded by a snake—announcing his exceptional status—and got married, both when he was twelve years old. Another local text says that the career of Ariyanatha Mudaliyar, a courtier helping Madurai's Vishvanatha Nayaka establish his kingdom, began at this age too.[12]

In all these instances, the age of twelve apparently marked a phase in the trajectory to maturity that initiated one's professional and marital life. Perhaps, this was related to the reception of the *upavīta* or consecrated cord by males belonging (or claiming to belong) to high castes. Usually taking place at the age of eight to

10 Chekuri, "Between Family and Empire," 10-11, 47, 52, 209. See also: Flores, "'I Will Do as My Father Did'," 1-2; Burling, *The Passage of Power*, 71.

11 Niccolao Manucci, *Storia do Mogor or Mogul India 1653–1708*, ed. William Irvine, vol. III (London, 1907), 52.

12 For Sivakumara Muttu Vijaya Raghunatha Setupati's temple ceremony and the text on Ariyanatha Mudaliyar, see respectively this chapter's section on Ramnad and the introduction to Chapter 3.

twelve, this ritual symbolised a second, spiritual birth after one's physical birth and denoted the beginning of one's formal education.

An event insinuating that complete adulthood came only later, concerns the temporary regency over Madurai's minor King Vijayaranga Chokkanatha Nayaka (r. 1707-32) by his grandmother Mangammal. This term ended when Vijayaranga Chokkanatha turned about seventeen, suggesting he had now become an adult and could reign on his own.[13] This ties in with a passage in Kautilya's *Arthaśāstra* (III 3:1) saying that men reach maturity at the age of sixteen, at least for legal transactions like marriage. But according to classical Indian notions on the *āśramas* or stages of life, the transition from student (*brahmacarya*) to householder (*gṛhastha*)—the start of one's own family and career—could happen later still. Ancient philosophical and medical texts variously place this shift at one's sixteenth, twenty-fifth, or thirtieth year or even at an older age.[14] All in all, it seems that no clear, single moment marked the change from minority to adulthood and that maturity arrived step by step, with the approximate ages of twelve and sixteen often considered significant.

However, since many references to south Indian kings being minors are found in European rather than Indian sources, early modern European ideas about adulthood must also be taken into account. By and large, these appear to have resembled Indian notions in that maturity was reached in stages, with the corresponding ages differing for various European courts. As in India, it seems that important transitions commonly occurred when princes were about twelve to fourteen years old and again at the approximate age of sixteen to twenty.[15] One can thus surmise that according to both Indian and European ideas, full adulthood was usually not attained before one turned sixteen. Therefore, in the following sections this age is regarded as the demarcation between minority and maturity.

South Indian sources for individual successions can be divided into two kinds: those that directly concern these events; and those that refer to such transitions indirectly as they contain the earliest mention of a certain ruler, suggesting that the previous one had been succeeded. The latter type of source has often been used to determine which monarch reigned when. Many studies of dynastic histories have been based chiefly on the inscriptions issued by each ruler, using their earliest and latest dates to ascertain the minimum period of each reign. In fact, these epigraphic texts—mostly proclamations of an administrative, commemorative, or religious

[13] For Vijayaranga Chokkanatha Nayaka's reign and Mangammal's regency, see this chapter's section on Madurai.

[14] Kautilya, *The Kauṭilīya Arthaśāstra*, pt. II, 232; Patrick Olivelle, *The* Āśrama *System: The History and Hermeneutics of a Religious Institution* (New York/Oxford, 1993), 132-3, 138-9, 165, 167. I thank Patrick Olivelle and Nikhil Bellarykar for discussing this with me.

[15] Duindam, *Dynasties*, 57-8, 60, 68-70. I am grateful to Jeroen Duindam and Judith Pollmann for sharing their ideas about this issue.

nature—are often the only sources to establish the approximate succession dates of the early rulers of Vijayanagara and its heirs. Since many inscriptions include royal pedigrees, they inform us about the relationships between consecutive monarchs, too, or at least how these were presented by those commissioning the inscriptions.[16]

Dynastic family relations are also frequently mentioned in local literary works such as chronicles and biographies. These texts sometimes refer directly to specific successions as well. But since all these sources were usually written under the auspices of particular rulers or even pretenders to the throne, they are likely to contain subjective views on the sequence and legitimacy of previous monarchs. Thus, the texts may establish fictitious family relationships, exaggerate reigning periods, or entirely leave out what were considered usurpers or rulers belonging to competing branches of the dynasty. Moreover, these sources are not always precise with respect to dates. Similar complications are encountered with the few visual sources on successions, available for several of Vijayanagara's heirs. These materials consist of painted or sculptured dynastic galleries, depicting only monarchs regarded as rightful predecessors by the kings commissioning such works. Some rulers were not included in these portrait groups and seem to have been considered unlawful occupants of the throne.

Besides the views of court poets, artists, and those who patronised them, there are many descriptions of successions in Vijayanagara and its heirs by Dutchmen and other Europeans. Such reporting often started as soon as vacant thrones were anticipated and continued while struggles between contenders were actually going on. On other occasions, accounts were compiled shortly after the events, when a new ruler had just been installed. Consequently, those documents usually relate in detail how such transitions unfolded over time, at least as understood by these external observers.

Dutchmen were never present at the courts in question (let alone actively involved) when successions occurred, so they drew up their accounts largely on the basis of local contacts, hearsay, or letters received from the courts themselves—thus recording information that was mostly provided by south Indian parties and represented their perspectives, but which could not easily be verified. If stories proved false later on, however, they were corrected in subsequent reports. In any case, for a number of successions European accounts are the only sources. In many other instances, these documents depict successions radically differently from what local chronicles and inscriptions suggest—as becomes clear in the sections on the individual courts below.

16 See also Chekuri, "Between Family and Empire," 65-79.

Vijayanagara

The first rulers of Vijayanagara's initial dynasty, the Sangama brothers Harihara and Bukka, were succeeded by about a dozen descendants, altogether reigning approximately one and a half centuries. Three other dynasties followed, numbering at least two, five, and seven emperors, and lasting around twenty, sixty-five, and eighty to ninety years, respectively.[17] Altogether, these thirty or so men ruled more than three centuries, from around the 1340s to the 1660s—although the fourth and final house, the Aravidus, continued to exist long after its expulsion from the last imperial capital, Vellore, only commanding some local power in its various places of exile.

Relatively little has been written on succession norms at the Vijayanagara court, by both contemporaries and modern scholars, and it seems such rules were neither elaborate nor strict. Some inscriptions and literary texts suggest that under all imperial houses, rulers generally nominated a *yuvarāja* (heir apparent), who sometimes also served as a co-ruler. This was frequently the emperor's eldest son, as for instance the Portuguese traveller Duarte Barbosa wrote in the 1510s, but it could also be another son, a brother, or any other male family member. *Yuvarājas* and other relatives of the ruler were often dispatched to outlying provinces and ruled those territories fairly autonomously, using imperial titles themselves. The resultant overlap of contemporaneous claims to authority found in inscriptions has been interpreted by some historians as a sign of joint-rule.[18] Others have argued that these competing claims reflected opposition between various pretenders to

[17] For a comparative survey of Vijayanagara's rulers and their regnal periods as proposed by five different scholars (including Sewell, Nilakanta Sastri, and Rāma Sharma), see Bridges White, "Beyond Empire," 48-52. For various (partly outdated or fictional) genealogical trees of one or more of Vijayanagara's dynasties, see: Nilakanta Sastri, *A History of South India*, 310-12; H.M. Nagaraju, *Devaraya II and His Times (History of Vijayanagara)* (Mysore, 1991), between 192-3; Eaton, *A Social History of the Deccan*, 89; Krishnaswami Aiyangar, *Sources of Vijayanagar History*, xi-iv; T.V. Mahalingam, *Administration and Social Life under Vijayanagar* (Madras, 1940), pt. II, 415-18; Rama Sarma, *Saluva Dynasty of Vijayanagar*, between 69-70; P. Sumabala (ed.), "Perundevi Samudram, Devaraja Samudram and Accharavakkam Grants of Srirangaraya III (or VI) of Aravidu Dynasty," *Journal of Indian History and Culture* 13 (2006), 147; V. Vijayaraghavacharya (ed.), *Inscriptions of Venkatapatiraya's Time* (Madras, 1937), 12; Butterworth and Venugopaul Chetty, *A Collection of the Inscriptions on Copper-Plates and Stones in the Nellore District*, pt. I, 53; V. Vijayaraghavacharya (ed.), *Epigraphical Glossary on Inscriptions* (Madras, 1938), 17-18, 25-6, 92-7; B. Suryanarain Row, *A History of Vijayanagar: The Never to Be Forgotten Empire* (Madras, 1905), Appendix, ii; Hayavadana Rao, *History of Mysore*, vol. III, 1286; Sewell, *A Forgotten Empire*, 214; idem, *The Historical Inscriptions of Southern India*, 387-8, 400-2; idem, *Lists of Inscriptions*, 3, 12-14, 16, 18, 30, 243-4, 248, 252-3; H. Krishna Sastri, "The Second Vijayanagara Dynasty: Its Viceroys and Ministers," *Annual Report 1908-9: Archæological Survey of India* (Calcutta, n.d.), 168, 201.

[18] Mahalingam, *Administration and Social Life under Vijayanagar*, pt. I, 11-16; Patil, *Court Life under the Vijayanagar Rulers*, 55-8; Nilakanta Sastri, *A History of South India*, 265-7; Nilakanta Sastri and Venkataramanayya, *Further Sources of Vijayanagara History*, vol. I, 78; Duarte Barbosa, *A Description*

the throne. These different interpretations do not necessarily exclude each other, as co-rulers could easily turn into rivals. The apparent lack of distinct succession principles must have made such struggles all the more ferocious.[19]

Sangamas and Saluvas

It has been estimated that the average rule of a king in pre-colonial India lasted slightly over twenty years.[20] As the high frequency of very brief reigns described below indicates, this period was much shorter under Vijayanagara's first dynasty, the Sangamas (c. 1340s-1485). If we just count the Sangama rulers whose reigns are acknowledged by all historians, we find that the average rule lasted just under thirteen years. If we include all fifteen possible emperors listed below, this length decreases to less than a decade. The many short reigns also hint at regular dynastic instability at the Sangama court. In fact, most Sangamas seem to have been murdered or dethroned in other ways.

Little is known about this dynasty, however, and information about successions in this period is found chiefly in inscriptions, to a lesser extent in literary texts—produced at both Vijayanagara and adjacent sultanate courts—and in a few accounts of foreign visitors. Besides, the sources, and by extension historians, do not entirely agree on the composition of the Sangama house. But by and large, the dozen or so successions appear to have proceeded as follows.

Already the first transition, from Harihara (r. c. 1340s-55) to Bukka (r. c. 1355-77)—initially perhaps co-rulers—is said to have been contested by the sons of one of their brothers, albeit in vain. Bukka was followed by his son Harihara II (r. 1377-1404), upon whose death at least three sons competed for the throne. It seems that two of them, Virupaksha (r. c. 1404-5) and Bukka II (r. 1405-6?), briefly ruled, before the third brother, Deva Raya (r. 1406-22), ousted them and remained in power for a substantial period. However, early in his reign he may have been temporarily deposed by a fourth brother, Sadashiva (r. 1408?). Most scholars presume that upon Deva Raya's passing, his son Ramachandra (r. 1422?) took over but died after a few months, to be replaced by another son, Vijaya alias Bukka III, whose rule lasted one or two years (r. c. 1422-3?).

of the Coasts of East Africa and Malabar in the Beginning of the Sixteenth Century, ed. H.E.J. Stanley (London, 1866), 88.

[19] Chekuri, "Between Family and Empire," 47-8, 51, 65-7, 78-9; idem, "'Fathers' and 'Sons'," 148-9; Patil, *Court Life under the Vijayanagar Rulers*, 57-8, 132, 145-6; Stein, *Vijayanagara*, 27-8, 91-3; Saletore, *Social and Political Life in the Vijayanagara Empire*, vol. I, 303-6; Nilakanta Sastri, *A History of South India*, 305-6.

[20] Thomas R. Trautmann, "Length of Generation and Reign in Ancient India," *Journal of the American Oriental Society* 89, 3 (1969); Scharfe, *The State in Indian Tradition*, 26.

The few sources on this earliest period contain no specific references to violence accompanying this series of quick successions, but a plot in the 1440s to murder Vijaya's son Deva Raya II (r. c. 1423-46) resulted in a bloodbath. Accounts by the Timurid ambassador Kamaluddin Abd al-Razzaq Samarqandi and the Portuguese horse trader Fernão Nunes both report that in an effort to seize the throne, a brother or a nephew of the emperor hosted a banquet for the entire court. During the deliberately noisy festivities, he invited the courtiers one by one into a separate room and had them all silently killed, while Deva Raya II himself barely survived an assassination attempt in his palace.

The latter's eventual death in 1446 was perhaps followed by the brief reign of his younger brother, Vijaya II alias Deva Raya III (r. 1446-7?), whose demise is thought to have led to a succession struggle between his own son Virupaksha II and a son of Deva Raya II, Mallikarjuna. The former may initially have sat on the throne for a short time but was soon expelled by his rival. When Mallikarjuna passed away after a long reign (c. 1447-65), he was possibly briefly succeeded by his son, Ramashekara or Ramachandra (r. 1465?). However, the earlier claimant Virupaksha II now invaded the capital, murdered all his opponents, and became emperor (r. c. 1465-85). In what seems to have been an effort to legitimise his usurpation, Virupaksha II omitted his cousin Mallikarjuna from the pedigrees in his inscriptions, suggesting he was the successor of Deva Raya II. But a chronicle that in its English manuscript form is titled "Hurry-Hurra Royer Vumshum" (*Harihara rāya vaṃśam*?) leaves out Virupaksha II instead, perhaps considering him an unlawful ruler. Further, some inscriptions by Mallikarjuna and his son Ramashekara seem to date from Virupaksha II's reign, suggesting they had not died and in fact maintained their claim to the throne.

In any case, Emperor Virupaksha II was assassinated by his own son, who could reportedly no longer bear his father's whimsical and cruel rule. Repenting for his sin, this son refused to ascend the throne and passed it to his younger brother Praudha (r. c. 1485?). Fearing his elder brother's brutality, Praudha in turn had him killed as well. Soon after, however, he was dethroned by the empire's most powerful general, Saluva Narasimha, which meant the end of the Sangama dynasty.[21]

[21] Rāma Sharma, *The History of the Vijayanagar Empire*, vol. I, 44-8, 50, 54-5, 60-1, 66-7, 70, 73, 81-2; Nilakanta Sastri and Venkataramanayya, *Further Sources of Vijayanagara History*, vol. I, 85-6, 93-4, 112, 122-5, 139-40; Krishnaswami Aiyangar, *Sources of Vijayanagar History*, 68-9; Nilakanta Sastri, *A History of South India*, 268-9, 271-3; Venkata Ramanayya, *Vijayanagara*, 126-7; Kumari Jhansi Lakshmi, "The Chronology of the Sangama Dynasty," *Proceedings of the Indian History Congress* 21 (1958); BL/AAS, MG, no. 3, pt. 4c: "Hurry-Hurra Royer Vumshum," f. 134; W.M. Thackston (ed.), *A Century of Princes: Sources on Timurid History and Art* (Cambridge (MA), 1989), 311-12; R.H. Major (ed.), *India in the Fifteenth Century: Being a Collection of Narratives of Voyages to India, in the Century Preceding the Portuguese Discovery of the Cape of Good Hope* (London, 1857), pt. I, 33-5; Joan-Pau Rubiés, "Late Medieval Ambassadors and

Although perhaps somewhat overwhelming, this summary makes clear that under the Sangama house all rulers were succeeded by sons or brothers, with only one exception, when a cousin took over. Sources do not mention any minors, queens, or illegitimate sons on the throne. Thus, this pattern appears to adhere neatly to the advice of Indian treatises on statecraft. Nevertheless it was virtually always fraternal competition that led to violence and caused dynastic instability. This friction probably also resulted in the Sangamas' demise, as it seemingly provided Generalissimo Saluva Narasimha with the opportunity to oust Praudha and assume imperial authority himself.[22]

Saluva Narasimha, founder of Vijayanagara's Saluva dynasty (c. 1485-1503), appears in inscriptions from the 1450s onward. The generalissimo initially served as the governor of the empire's Chandragiri province and was related to the Sangama house through his uncle's marriage to a sister of Deva Raya II. Earlier members of the Saluva family also held military functions under the Sangamas and intermarried with them. It is thought that already in 1459, under the weak reign of Mallikarjuna, Narasimha practically took over the emperor's powers, but allowed him and his few successors to maintain their formal position.[23] However, after Narasimha officially ascended the Vijayanagara throne, both his own reign and his dynasty turned out to be short-lived, as demonstrated by the few successions under the Saluva house, described below.

Probably of an advanced age by now, Narasimha passed away after a rather brief reign (c. 1485-91). It is not entirely clear what happened next, but his sons—possibly all minors—seem to have been the object of competition between various courtiers. Before his death, Narasimha had entrusted the care of these princes to his General Narasa Nayaka, who placed one of them on the throne. But this ruler, perhaps called Timmabhupa, died very soon and it is generally assumed he was murdered by an opponent of Narasa. A second son may have followed, suffering a similar fate.

the Practice of Cross-Cultural Encounters, 1250–1450," in Palmira Brummett (ed.), *The "Book" of Travels: Genre, Ethnology, and Pilgrimage, 1250-1700* (Leiden, 2009), 86-7; Stein, *Vijayanagara*, 92; Patil, *Court Life under the Vijayanagar Rulers*, 132-4; Chekuri, "Between Family and Empire," 52-4; Nagaraju, *Devaraya II and His Times*, 20-1 and between 192-3; Rama Sarma, *Saluva Dynasty of Vijayanagar*, 72-6, 175-82; Sewell, *The Historical Inscriptions of Southern India*, 193; Dodamani, *Gaṅgādevī's Madhurāvijayaṁ*, 29-30; Madhav N. Katti, "Some Important Epigraphs of the Sangama Dynasty," in Dikshit, *Early Vijayanagara*, 150. For discussions of the writings of Fernão Nunes, see: Rubiés, *Travel and Ethnology in the Renaissance*, ch. 8 (first part); Subrahmanyam, *Penumbral Visions*, 188-92.

22 Stein, *Vijayanagara*, 30.

23 For references, see the next footnote.

Eventually, another of Narasimha's sons, Immadi Narasimha, was installed as emperor and reigned for a longer period (c. 1491-1503), albeit under the regency of Narasa, whose own titles displayed growing imperial ambitions. All real power being in Narasa's hands, relations between the ruler and his regent gradually deteriorated and at one point Immadi Narasimha was even removed from the capital to the town of Penukonda to be kept under tight control. Again, sources and scholars disagree on the subsequent course of events, but sometime between 1501 and 1505 Immadi Narasimha was killed, signalling the end of the Saluvas.[24]

The Saluva house lasted too briefly to allow general conclusions, but it seems to have been characterised by instability. The dynastic founder was probably succeeded only by minor sons and these two or three successions apparently witnessed much brutality and the strong involvement of rivalling courtiers.

Tuluvas

The violence and factionalism at the Sangama and Saluva courts continued under the third imperial family, the Tuluvas (c. 1503-70), especially during later decades. The beginnings of this dynasty are somewhat obscure, despite the emergence of regular European records on south India in this period. Historians differ on the question of whether the aforementioned General Narasa Nayaka, founder of the Tuluva house, was involved in the assassination of the last Saluva ruler. Further, there is no consensus about whether he officially assumed imperial status, despite the fact that some texts claim he did ascend the throne. Finally, it is not clear if Narasa was related to the Saluva dynasty, although one literary work states his father's father was Saluva Narasimha's elder brother.[25] In any case, after Narasa's death in 1503, the Tuluvas counted at least five rulers (see table 2 towards the end of this section), who succeeded one another in the following way.

The dynasty began with the consecutive reigns of three sons of Narasa Nayaka, the eldest of whom, Vira Narasimha (r. c. 1503-9), was initially and unsuccessfully

[24] Rama Sarma, *Saluva Dynasty of Vijayanagar*, 39-40, between 69-70, 193-206, 223-6; G. Anjaiah, "Saluva Usurpation and Its Historical Importance in the History of Vijayanagar Empire," *Itihas: Journal of the Andhra Pradesh State Archives & Research Institute* XXVII, 1-2 (2001); Rāma Sharma, *The History of the Vijayanagar Empire*, vol. I, 69-70, 82, 87-8, 92-5, 97-8; Nilakanta Sastri and Venkataramanayya, *Further Sources of Vijayanagara History*, vol. I, 141, 150-6, 164-6, 177; Nilakanta Sastri, *A History of South India*, 274-6; Patil, *Court Life under the Vijayanagar Rulers*, 134-7; Sewell, *The Historical Inscriptions of Southern India*, 230.

[25] For references, see the next footnote.

opposed by a son of the last Saluva ruler.[26] At the end of his rule, as the Portuguese merchant Fernão Nunes reported, Vira Narasimha wished to be succeeded by his minor son rather than his half-brother Krishna(deva) Raya. On his death-bed, he ordered his Minister Saluva Timmarasu to have Krishna Raya blinded and thus render him unfit for the throne. The minister pretended he had carried out the demand by showing the eyes of a goat to Vira Narasimha, who then passed away contented.

No other sources confirm this story and various literary works in fact declare that Vira Narasimha installed Krishna Raya as his successor, according to the Telugu *Rāyavācakamu* and the Kannada *Śrī kṛṣṇadēvarāyaṇa dinacārī* by handing over the imperial diadem or ring. Some sources even suggest they were joint rulers for a while. There are also texts, however, that leave out Vira Narasimha's reign and place Krishna Raya's accession directly after the rule of his father (there also called Vira Narasimha), suggesting an attempt to stress Krishna Raya's monarchical claims rather than those of his predecessor.[27]

Whether there was friction between the half-brothers or not, Krishna Raya was next to sit on the throne (r. c. 1509-29).[28] But according to several texts, including one in Persian, he was not of full royal blood.[29] For example, a Mackenzie manuscript

[26] Rama Sarma, *Saluva Dynasty of Vijayanagar*, 223-6; Rāma Sharma, *The History of the Vijayanagar Empire*, vol. I, 97-107; Krishnaswami Aiyangar, *Sources of Vijayanagar History*, 106; Nilakanta Sastri and Venkataramanayya, *Further Sources of Vijayanagara History*, vol. I, 176-9; BL/AAS, MG, no. 10, pt. 11: "Kaalaganum," ff. 213-15 (translated from a Kannada text found in 1801 at "Gutpurtee" near Chitradurga "among some rubbish thrown out of a house after the ruins of the village by one of those plundering parties of Marattas that at one period overrun the country"; see f. 218 and Cotton, Charpentier, and Johnston, *Catalogue of Manuscripts in European Languages*, vol. I, pt. II, 95); Nilakanta Sastri, *A History of South India*, 276; Kamath, *Krishnadevaraya of Vijayanagara*, 21, 23.

[27] Sewell, *A Forgotten Empire*, 314-15; Wagoner, *Tidings of the King*, 87; BL/AAS, MG, no. 11, pt. 18a: "Historical account of Panoo Conda," f. 167 (compiled in 1801 by Mackenzie's assistant Borayya Kavali Venkata at Penukonda "from information collected there," see f. 163); no. 40, last pt.: "History of the kings of Beejayanagurr," f. 373; Krishnaswami Aiyangar, *Sources of Vijayanagar History*, 111, 129; Mahalingam, *Mackenzie Manuscripts*, vol. II, 45; Rāma Sharma, *The History of the Vijayanagar Empire*, vol. I, 109-110; Nilakanta Sastri and Venkataramanayya, *Further Sources of Vijayanagara History*, vol. I, 186-8; Narayana Rao, Shulman, and Subrahmanyam, "A New Imperial Idiom," 77; Nilakanta Sastri, *A History of South India*, 277; Patil, *Court Life under the Vijayanagar Rulers*, 132-3. See also: H.K. Narasimhaswami (ed.), *South-Indian Inscriptions*, vol. XVI, *Telugu Inscriptions of the Vijayanagara Dynasty* (New Delhi, 1972), iv; Kamath, *Krishnadevaraya of Vijayanagara*, 26-7, 29.

[28] Krishna Raya's reign is generally thought to have commenced on 8 August 1509, but it has also been argued it started on 24 January 1510. See D.V. Devaraj, "Date of Krishnadevaraya's Coronation," *The Quarterly Journal of the Mythic Society* XCIX, 1 (2008).

[29] Wilson, *The Mackenzie Collection*, vol. I, *288, 295-6;* Srinivas Sistla, "Allegory in Telugu Poetry during the Time of Krishnadevaraya," in Anila Verghese (ed.), *Krishnadevaraya and His Times* (Mumbai, 2013), 104, 107; Krishna(deva) Raya, *Sri Krishna Deva Raya: Āmuktamālyada*, 83-5, 112; Sri Sri Sri Raja Saheb, "The Origin of Vizayanagar in Kalinga," 282, 284; BL/AAS, MT, class I (Persian), no. 18: "The Keefeyet of Panoocundah," f. 43; MG, no. 10, pt. 4a: "Account of Bisnagur," ff. 64-5; no. 11, pt. 2:

titled "Kyfieth of Roya Vellore" (*Kaifīyat* of the Rayas of Vellore?), translated from a Tamil original, contains an extensive explanation of his supposed illegitimate descent. Starting with Krishna Raya's father—here again named Vira Narasimha instead of Narasa Nayaka—the story can be summarised thus (retaining the original spelling of names):

King Narasimmah had two sons: Mookoondaraja and Achooda-raja.[30] Astrologers predicted that these princes would die young, making the king worry about who should succeed him. After extensive consultations, the astrologers advised Narasimmah to unite with a queen during the fourth day of her monthly cycle, thus enabling him to beget a long-living and wise son, who was to enjoy many victories and great fame. The king now requested one of his wives, who happened to meet the stipulated condition, to prepare for an amorous encounter. But she took such a long time washing and beautifying herself for the occasion, that Narasimmah feared the auspicious moment might pass before she got ready. At that instant, a maidservant named Deebalanaikee entered the king's room to light the candles, and he begged her to bring him any woman who was in the fourth day of her monthly cycle. Upon her reply that nobody in the palace but she satisfied this demand, he hugged her and lay beside her at the right moment, nine months after which she gave birth to a son possessing the thirty-two royal attributes.

When the Pattastree [lawful queen] heard about this, she ordered Appajee [Minister Saluva Timmarasu] to kill the child, but he hid the boy in his house, slaying another child instead. The Pattastree found out about this too and Appajee then secretly sent the boy to Tirooppadee [Tirupati], where he was educated in many subjects. When he turned seven years old, the other two sons of Narasimmah died, as foretold by the astrologers, and some days later the king passed away as well. Realising with grief there was no rightful successor to the throne, the various Pattastrees regretted the murdering of Deebalanaikee's son, who could have been crowned now. Then Appajee revealed the boy was alive, and after the Pattastrees promised not to kill him, he was summoned from Tirooppadee and placed on the throne as a full sovereign, with the title of Kishtna-Royer.[31]

Giving a slightly different version of the tale, the Telugu poem *Kṛṣṇa rāya caritra* states that it was the mother of Vira Narasimha—here Krishna Raya's predecessor and elder half-brother—who ordered Krishna Raya's killing as she was jealous of

"Preliminary note to the historical account of the kings of Beejanagur," f. 8; no. 11, pt. 3b: "History of the kings of Beejanagur & Anagoondy," f. 18 (see also Mackenzie, "History of the Kings of Veejanagur"). See also Ilanit Loewy Shacham, "Expanding Domains and the Personal, Imperial Style of Kṛṣṇadevarāya," *The Indian Economic and Social History Review* 56, 3 (2019), 334.

30 It is unclear to me which princes these names refer to. "Achooda-raja" may be associated with Krishna Raya's half-brother and successor Achyuta Raya, but it seems illogical that a text would suggest he died before Krishna Raya came to power, and no other sources seemingly do so.

31 BL/AAS, MT, class II (Tamil: Tonda Mandalam), no. 12: "Kyfieth of Roya Vellore," ff. 11-21.

his great qualities, which surpassed those of her son.[32] Other traditions have it that Krishna Raya was not entitled to succeed Vira Narasimha because his other half-brother Achyuta(deva) Raya was older than he. Further, at the end of his reign, Krishna Raya would have accused his Minister Saluva Timmarasu of unlawfully installing him as emperor instead of Vira Narasimha's son, thereby committing treason.[33] These stories, while mostly acknowledging Krishna Raya's greatness, apparently aim at portraying him as an illegitimate or under-aged ruler, although most other sources declare he was a son of one of his father's official queens and had reached maturity when he ascended the throne.

Perhaps these attempts date from the reign of the next emperor, Achyuta Raya (r. 1529-42), who was possibly not Krishna Raya's preferred heir and therefore may have wished to downplay his predecessor. Indeed, there are even texts that entirely ignore Krishna Raya's reign and move straight from his father Narasa Nayaka to his successor Achyuta Raya.[34] Local inscriptions and Fernão Nunes' writings suggest that in 1524 Krishna Raya designated his minor son Tirumalai as *yuvarāja* (heir apparent). During the subsequent coronation festivities, however, the young prince fell sick and died, supposedly being poisoned by order of Minister Saluva Timmarasu, whose influence had decreased after Tirumalai's rise.[35] Now left with the choice between another, even younger son and a half-brother, Krishna Raya shortly before his death appointed the latter, Achyuta Raya, as his successor.[36]

But Vijayanagara's Generalissimo Rama Raya, who was married to one of Krishna Raya's daughters (earning him the name Aliya or son-in-law), favoured Krishna Raya's remaining infant son. While Rama Raya tried to enthrone this boy, the nominated Achyuta Raya hurried to the imperial capital from Chandragiri, where Krishna Raya had detained him earlier. On the way, Achyuta Raya performed coronation ceremonies at two different places—Tirupati and Kalahasti, its temples devoted to Vishnu and Shiva respectively—in an effort to bolster his claims. In the

[32] Wilson, *The Mackenzie Collection*, vol. I, 295-6. For yet another version, see Velcheru Narayana Rao and David Shulman (eds), *A Poem at the Right Moment: Remembered Verses from Premodern South India* (Delhi, 1999), 130-1. For still more stories on competition between Vira Narasimha and Krishna Raya, see Reddy, *Raya*, 8-10.

[33] K.G. Gopala Krishna Rao, "Krishnaraya as a Great King in Politics and Warfare," in Anila Verghese (ed.), *Krishnadevaraya and His Times* (Mumbai, 2013), 30-1.

[34] Krishnaswami Aiyangar, *Sources of Vijayanagar History*, 172, 176. See also Kamath, *Krishnadevaraya of Vijayanagara*, 74.

[35] Some scholars claim the Portuguese were involved in Tirumalai's death, hoping to cause Saluva Timmarasu's downfall. See Gopala Krishna Rao, "Krishnaraya as a Great King in Politics and Warfare," 47-8.

[36] Given the lack of sources on Krishna Raya's death, he may have retired and renounced the court rather than passed away before he was succeeded. See Loewy Shacham, "Expanding Domains and the Personal, Imperial Style of Kṛṣṇadevarāya," 334-5.

end, the two parties resolved that Achyuta Raya would be the formal emperor, yet share much of his power with Rama Raya. But although the infant son of Krishna Raya died soon after, Achyuta Raya's position remained insecure. Rama Raya may even have removed him briefly from the throne, initially to sit on it himself, and after courtiers had objected against this, to temporarily install a son of Achyuta Raya's brother Ranga, named Sadashiva.[37]

When Achyuta Raya passed away, he was succeeded by his minor son and alleged *Yuvarāja* Venkatadri (r. 1542), reigning under the regency of his maternal uncle Salakaraju China Tirumala. This arrangement was however opposed by Venkatadri's mother (Salakaraju China Tirumala's sister), many courtiers, and Generalissimo Rama Raya, who all took turns seeking the assistance of the sultan of Bijapur to defeat their rivals. A brief period of rapid and violent developments ensued, with the Bijapur army invading and having to retreat thrice. Although Rama Raya proclaimed Achyuta Raya's minor nephew Sadashiva emperor, the capital's inhabitants are said to have chosen as their ruler Salakaraju China Tirumala, who then had his sister's son Venkatadri—the designated ruler—and several of his relatives assassinated. Salakaraju China Tirumala's possible (but in any case very brief) reign is acknowledged in a few literary texts, but Rama Raya eventually killed him and performed the coronation of Sadashiva (r. c. 1542-70), whose regent he became.

While all power now lay with Rama Raya, Sadashiva was to be the last ruler of the Tuluva house and acted as emperor in name only, placed as he was under strict surveillance, especially when he grew older and more assertive. Once a year, Rama Raya and his brothers Tirumala and Venkatadri (not to be confused with abovementioned people with similar names) publicly prostrated themselves before Sadashiva and formally recognised him as their overlord. Yet, Rama Raya assumed a kind of imperial status himself in the course of Sadashiva's reign, and several literary texts and inscriptions state he did actually take the throne. Emperor Sadashiva died in or around 1570, perhaps by murder and probably still in confinement. Five

37 Rāma Sharma, *The History of the Vijayanagar Empire*, vol. I, 113-14, 145-6, 149, 171, 174-5; Chekuri, "Between Family and Empire," 55-9; Rubiés, *Travel and Ethnology in the Renaissance*, 271-3; Stein, *Vijayanagara*, 113; Nilakanta Sastri, *A History of South India*, 283-7; Sewell, *A Forgotten Empire*, 359-61, 366-7; Nilakanta Sastri and Venkataramanayya, *Further Sources of Vijayanagara History*, vol. I, 232, 234-8; Patil, *Court Life under the Vijayanagar Rulers*, 137-40; Venkata Ramanayya, *Studies in the History of the Third Dynasty*, 3-15, 56-75; T.V. Mahalingam, "Tirumalaideva Maharaya," *Journal of Indian History* XVII, 1 (1938); idem, *Readings in South Indian History*, 124-6. For Achyuta Raya's double coronation, see also: Lidia Sudyka, "A War Expedition or a Pilgrimage? Acyutarāya's Southern Campaign as Depicted in the *Acyutarāyābhyudaya*," in idem and Anna Nitecka (eds), *Cracow Indological Studies*, vol. XV, *History and Society as Depicted in Indian Literature and Art*, pt. II, *ŚRĀVYA: Poetry & Prose* (Cracow, 2013), 87-8; Jackson, *Vijayanagara Voices*, 181-93.

Table 2: Tuluvas of Vijayanagara, regnal years, relations to predecessors, and further remarks.

	name	accession date	ending date	relation to predecessors	remarks († = natural death at end of reign)
0	Narasa Nayaka	1490s?	1503?	— (founder)	†, general under Saluvas, formal reign unsure
1	Vira Narasimha	c. 1503	c. 1509	1st son of 0	†, contested by son of last Saluva
2	Krishna(deva) Raya	c. 1509	1529	half-brother of 1 & 2nd son of 0	†, contested minor son of 1?
3	Achyuta(deva) Raya	1529	1542	half-brother of 2 & 1, & 3rd son of 0	†, contested son of 2, contested himself by Rama Raya
4	Venkatadri	1542	1542	son of 3	minor, under regency of 5, killed by 5
5	Salakaraju China Tirumala	1542	1542	maternal uncle of 4 & brother-in-law of 3	formal reign unsure, contested and killed by Rama Raya
6	Sadashiva Raya	1542	c. 1570	nephew of 5 & brother's son of 3	†? minor at accession? under regency of Rama Raya, imprisoned by Aravidus during reign

For sources, see the references in the preceding section.

years earlier, Vijayanagara city had been sacked and Generalissimo Rama Raya killed by a coalition of several Deccan sultanates, after which the court, led by Rama Raya's brother Tirumala, had fled the capital. Tirumala was also Sadashiva's successor, becoming the first monarch of Vijayanagara's fourth and last dynasty, the Aravidus.[38]

[38] Nilakanta Sastri and Venkataramanayya, *Further Sources of Vijayanagara History*, vol. I, 238-9, 243, 291-4, 298-300, vol. III, 16, 185-7; BL/AAS, MG, no. 3, pt. 1: "Sketch of the general history of the peninsula," f. 48; no. 3, pt. 4d: "Veera Narasinga Royer Vumsham," f. 141; no. 10, pt. 11: "Kaalaganum," ff. 214-15; no. 11, pt. 3a: "History of the Anagoondy Rajahs," f. 10 (see also Mackenzie, "History of the Anagoondy Rajahs"); no. 11, pt. 3b: "History of the kings of Beejanagur & Anagoondy," f. 18 (see also Mackenzie, "History of the Kings of Veejanagur"); no. 11, pt. 18a: "Historical account of Panoo Conda," f. 170; Sewell, *The Historical Inscriptions of Southern India*, 257; Rubiés, *Travel and Ethnology in the Renaissance*, 274-6; Rāma Sharma, *The History of the Vijayanagar Empire*, vol. I, 181-3, 185-6, 219-26; Eaton, *A Social History of the Deccan*, 91-2, 95, 100-1; V. Srinivasan, "Disputed Succession after Achyutharaya," *The Quarterly Journal of the Mythic Society* LXIII, 1-4 (1972); Stein, *Vijayanagara*, 113-14, 119-20; Eaton and Wagoner, *Power, Memory, Architecture*, 114; Venkata Ramanayya, *Studies in the History of the Third Dynasty*, 76-90; Heras, *The Aravidu Dynasty of Vijayanagara*, vol. I, 1-17, 244-6, 511-12; Nilakanta Sastri, *A History of South India*, 288-9, 295; Krishnaswami Aiyangar, *Sources of Vijayanagar History*, 158, 170, 172; Patil, *Court Life under the Vijayanagar Rulers*, 140-2. For a different version of some of the events,

According to most historians, during the approximately sixty-five years of Tuluva rule (c. 1503-70) there were five emperors, whose reigns thus lasted an average of about thirteen years. Should one also count the possible rules of Narasa Nayaka and Salakaraju China Tirumala, this period would shrink to just over nine years. In both cases, the average reign under the Tuluvas was roughly as long as that under the initial Sangama house. Like the Sangamas, the Tuluva rulers were nearly always succeeded by their sons or brothers, and once by a cousin. In addition, Salakaraju China Tirumala—if we consider him a Tuluva monarch—was a maternal uncle of his predecessor and was followed by his nephew.

However, all successions under the Tuluvas appear to have been contested in one way or another. Krishna Raya was probably not Vira Narasimha's successor of choice and Krishna Raya himself detained Achyuta Raya since he wished his son to succeed him. Venkatadri and Sadashiva were minors when they ascended the throne, dominated by their regents, while Salakaraju China Tirumala was regarded by many as a usurper. Besides, it seems the latter three rulers were all assassinated. Although generally seen as presiding over Vijayanagara's most glorious phase, the Tuluva dynasty, like the Sangama house, can thus be regarded as rather unstable.

Aravidus

The empire's fourth dynasty, the Aravidus (or Aravitis, c. 1570-1660s) numbered seven "official" monarchs, but between the 1540s and 1565 Generalissimo Rama Raya was its first de facto ruler (see table 3 later in this section). Although regarded as a separate house, the Aravidu family was in fact very closely related to and partially overlapped with the preceding Tuluva dynasty, by both marital and blood ties. Rama Raya and his brother Tirumala were each married to a daughter of Krishna Raya. Consequently, all their sons, grandsons, and great-grandsons who became rulers under the Aravidus were direct descendants of this Tuluva emperor, albeit through the female line.

Literary works composed under or otherwise concerning the Aravidus make much of their connections with the preceding house. Several texts state that Rama Raya bestowed the sovereignty of the empire on the last Tuluva, Sadashiva, or was appointed *yuvarāja* (heir apparent) under him. According to another work, Rama Raya's brother Tirumala served as Sadashiva's *yuvarāja*. Still other texts claim that Rama Raya already acquired this status from Krishna Raya, the latter having no male offspring. As remarked in the previous chapter, one work even declares that

partially exchanging the roles of Salakaraju China Tirumala and Achyuta Raya's brother Ranga, see Rāma Sharma, *The History of the Vijayanagar Empire*, vol. I, 180-1.

Rama Raya was Krishna Raya's son.[39] These may all have been efforts to legitimise the Aravidus' takeover of imperial sovereignty from the Tuluvas.

Turning to the successions under the Aravidus, in the five years between the ransacking of Vijayanagara city (1565) and the formal beginning of Aravidu rule, the dynasty's first official monarch, Tirumala (r. c. 1570-2), tried to resettle at the former imperial capital. But the remaining citizens there preferred that Rama Raya's son Peda (who was also Krishna Raya's grandson) rather than Tirumala be the regent of the last Tuluva emperor, Sadashiva. While Tirumala then established his court—in name still under Sadashiva—around 1567 at Penukonda, his nephew Peda enlisted the support of the Deccan sultanates to claim the regency. This proved to be fruitless, and in 1570 Tirumala had himself proclaimed emperor, to retire only two years later.

His *yuvarāja* and successor was his eldest surviving son, Sriranga (r. c. 1572-85), who, dying childless, was succeeded by his youngest brother, Venkata (r. c. 1585-1614). During his reign, the imperial capital was first moved from Penukonda to Chandragiri (c. 1592), close to the peninsula's eastern shore and the important Tirupati sanctity, and subsequently to nearby Vellore (c. 1604), although the court would continue to shift regularly between these towns. At the end of his long rule, Venkata nominated his middle brother's son, Sriranga II (r. 1614), as his successor. In a ceremony described by the Jesuit Manuel Barradas, the emperor passed to his nephew the imperial regalia, including the so-called ring of state, other jewellery, and a precious robe.[40]

Despite this official transfer, the succession was heavily contested. The same Jesuit account has it that because Venkata had no sons, his Queen Obamamba (or

[39] Nilakanta Sastri and Venkataramanayya, *Further Sources of Vijayanagara History*, vol. III, 168, 182-3, 186, 199-200, 250; BL/AAS, MG, no. 3, pt. 4d: "Veera Narasinga Royer Vumsham," f. 141; no. 11, pt. 3a: "History of the Anagoondy Rajahs," f. 10 (see also Mackenzie, "History of the Anagoondy Rajahs"); no. 11, pt. 3b: "History of the kings of Beejanagur & Anagoondy," f. 18 (see also Mackenzie, "History of the Kings of Veejanagur"); no. 11, pt. 18a: "Historical account of Panoo Conda," f. 169; Mahalingam, *Mackenzie Manuscripts*, vol. II, 312.

[40] Heras, *The Aravidu Dynasty of Vijayanagara*, vol. I, 221-3, 229-37, 248-50, 260, 264-6, 277, 300-4, 310-12, 320, 506-8; idem, "Venkatapatiraya I and the Portuguese," *The Quarterly Journal of the Mythic Society* XIV, 4 (1924), 313-14; Cesare Frederici, "The Voyage of Master Cesar Frederick into the East India, and beyonde the Indies, Anno 1563," in Richard Hakluyt (ed.), *The Principal Navigations Voyages Traffiques & Discoveries of the English Nation ...*, ed. John Masefield (London, 1927), vol. III, 213, 216; Nilakanta Sastri and Venkataramanayya, *Further Sources of Vijayanagara History*, vol. I, 294-9, 301-2, 308-11, 325, vol. III, 254, 266; Rāma Sharma, *The History of the Vijayanagar Empire*, vol. I, 224-5, vol. II (Bombay, 1980), 1-2, 14, 38-9, 91-2; Eaton and Wagoner, *Power, Memory, Architecture*, 115-16; Sewell, *A Forgotten Empire*, 223-4; Krishnaswami Aiyangar, *Sources of Vijayanagar History*, 217, 244; Rubiés, *Travel and Ethnology in the Renaissance*, 304-5; Stein, *Vijayanagara*, 120; Nilakanta Sastri, *A History of South India*, 295-9; Patil, *Court Life under the Vijayanagar Rulers*, 141-3.

Bayamma) passed off the son of a Brahmin woman in the imperial household as her own. But the emperor reportedly saw through this and perhaps for that very reason wanted his nephew to succeed him. Once on the throne, Sriranga II seems to have disregarded a number of courtiers and fell out with them. Also, the new ruler was allegedly considered to maintain too close links with Tanjavur's Raghunatha Nayaka, whose kinship with Vijayanagara's former Tulava dynasty—his father being Achyuta Raya's brother-in-law—made him suspect to most members of the Aravidu house.

Subsequently, one court faction, headed by the queen's brother Gobburi Jagga Raya, imprisoned Sriranga II with his close relatives and enthroned the queen's putative son, Chikka Raya (r. c. 1614-16). Another faction, led by the chief Velugoti Yacama Nayaka, favoured the now jailed monarch and made several unsuccessful attempts to free him. Eventually, Jagga Raya had Sriranga II and his family killed, save for a minor son named Ramadeva, who was supposedly smuggled out of prison by a washerman.[41]

When Velugoti Yacama proclaimed this boy emperor, the resultant rivalry between the two young pretenders and their supporters reached beyond the Vijayanagara court, involving the formally still subordinate Nayaka rulers of Tanjavur, Senji, and Madurai. Although the latter two supported Jagga Raya and his protégé Chikka Raya, in a battle at Toppur village around 1616 Tanjavur-backed Velugoti Yacama defeated Jagga Raya and most of his allies. The victor acquired the imperial treasure and regalia, and made Ramadeva access the throne at the approximate age of fourteen.

After the death of his rival Chikka Raya in 1619, the emperor came to an agreement with Etiraja, brother of the murdered Jagga Raya, and even married the former's daughter, thus finally concluding this succession struggle. Although the young Ramadeva consolidated his position in the following years, his reign (c. 1616-30) continued to be contested by a grandson and a great-grandson of the dynasty's founder Rama Raya. The former, Peda Venkata, assumed imperial titles and was acknowledged as the rightful emperor by several chiefs, including even the Nayaka of Madurai.[42]

[41] The escape of royal heirs with the help of washermen seems a recurring theme in south Indian dynastic histories. For a Dutch account hinting at such an escape by a young Tuluva prince, see Vink, *Mission to Madurai*, 290, 346.

[42] Sewell, *A Forgotten Empire*, 222-30; idem, *The Historical Inscriptions of Southern India*, 271; Narayana Rao, Shulman, and Subrahmanyam, *Symbols of Substance*, 252-6; Subrahmanyam, *Improvising Empire*, 259; Heras, *The Aravidu Dynasty of Vijayanagara*, vol. I, 494-505; Rāma Sharma, *The History of the Vijayanagar Empire*, vol. II, 69-70, 91-2, 126-30, 136-9, 144-6, 155-7; Stein, *Vijayanagara*, 122-3; Nilakanta Sastri and Venkataramanayya, *Further Sources of Vijayanagara History*, vol. I, 326-34; Foster, *The English Factories in India 1624–1629: A Calendar of Documents in the India Office, etc.* (Oxford, 1909), 346-7; Chekuri, "Between Family and Empire," 60-4; Nilakanta Sastri, *A History of South India*,

According to Dutch reports, Ramadeva died on 24 May 1630, having fallen very ill. As the seventeenth-century Dutch Pastor Abraham Rogerius wrote in his treatise on south Indian Hinduism, some believed the emperor's early passing was caused by his taking of the ruby crown and other treasures belonging to the deity of the Tirupati Temple. Whatever the reason for his death, historians disagree on its consequences. Some say that by the time Ramadeva's end was nearing, so many chiefs had switched allegiance to his second cousin Peda Venkata or Venkata II (r. 1630-42), a grandson of Rama Raya, that the emperor had no choice but to pass the throne to him. Others say that since Ramadeva had no sons or brothers, he voluntarily nominated Venkata II as his successor—a view also found in VOC documents (referring to the new ruler as "Anij Goundij Pederagie," or Anegondi Peda Raja). Although nowhere explicitly stated, Venkata II alias Peda Venkata was probably identical to Ramadeva's rival pretender mentioned in the previous paragraph, as they bore the same name and were both grandsons of Rama Raya.

However, as various accounts say, the new emperor was challenged by Ramadeva's paternal uncle Timma Raja, an imperial general, who took control of the government for a while. Some sources claim that Venkata II stayed near Vijayanagara city during this period, but the Dutch wrote in 1632 that Timma Raja held Venkata II in captivity. In any case, since several courtiers and also the Nayakas of Madurai, Tanjavur, and Senji considered Timma Raja a usurper, they backed Venkata II, who eventually defeated his opponent and commenced his actual rule in 1635.[43]

The next and final succession under the Aravidus occurred in 1642, when Venkata II passed away. The VOC reported that on 10 October, he died of a high fever combined with what may have been loose bowels (*loop*), and left only a "pet child or bastard" (*speelkindt off bastaert*) behind, who "according to the customs and laws of this land" could not succeed him. Meanwhile, what remained of the empire was rapidly disintegrating, as the Bijapur and Golkonda sultanates were repeatedly invading it, while many subordinate chiefs—including Vijayanagara's larger successor states—grew increasingly disloyal. Some of them supported Sriranga III, son of Venkata II's younger brother, who had opposed his uncle since

300-2; R. Sathianathaier, *Tamiḻaham in the 17th Century* (Madras, 1956), 28-30; Patil, *Court Life under the Vijayanagar Rulers*, 142-5.

43 NA, VOC, no. 1100, ff. 95v, 99: letters from Pulicat, May, Aug. 1630; BL/AAS, Mackenzie Private collection, no. 47, pt. 1: final report (*memorie van overgave*) of Coromandel Governor Maerten IJsbrantsz, July 1632 (copy from c. 1740), f. 8; Mac Leod, *De Oost-Indische Compagnie*, vol. I, 491; Abraham Rogerius, *De open-deure tot het verborgen heydendom*, ed. W. Caland (The Hague, 1915), 123-4; Rāma Sharma, *The History of the Vijayanagar Empire*, vol. II, 163, 167-70, 200-2; Nilakanta Sastri and Venkataramanayya, *Further Sources of Vijayanagara History*, vol. I, 338-40; Nilakanta Sastri, *A History of South India*, 302-3. See also *Beknopte historie*, 22-4.

Table 3: Aravidus of Vijayanagara, regnal years, relations to predecessors, and further remarks.

	name	accession date	ending date	relation to predecessors	remarks († = natural death at end of reign)
0	Rama Raya	c. 1540s	1565	son-in-law of Krishna Raya of Tuluvas	formal reign unsure, killed in battle with Deccan sultanates
1	Tirumala	1565, formally in 1570	1572	brother of 0	†, contested by nephew
2	Sriranga	1572	1585	son of 1	†, childless
3	Venkata	1585	1614	youngest brother of 2 & son of 1	†, childless
4	Sriranga II	1614	1614	son of middle brother of 3 & 2	contested by 5, imprisoned, killed by uncle-in-law
5	Chikka Raya	c. 1614	c. 1616	"cousin" of 4 & putative son of queen of 3	minor? dethroned for 6
6	Ramadeva	c. 1616	1630	distant "nephew" of 5 & son of 4	†, minor at accession, contested by descendants of 0
7	Timma Raja	c. 1630	c. 1635	paternal uncle of 6	formal reign unsure, imprisoned 8, dethroned for 8
8	(Peda) Venkata II	1635, formally in 1630	1642	second cousin of 6 & grandson of 0	†, no legitimate sons, contested by 7 & 9
9	Sriranga III	1642 & 1650s	c. 1646 & c. 1660s	brother's son of 8	initially dethroned by Bijapur

For sources, see the references in the preceding section and the Epilogue.

the late 1630s and in fact was instrumental in Bijapur's invasions. Upon Venkata II's death, however, Sriranga III deserted the Bijapur troops, presented himself as the imperial heir, and was proclaimed emperor (r. c. 1642-6, 1650s-60s) on 29 October, with, as the Dutch wrote, the usual ceremonies.[44]

[44] NA, VOC, no. 1151, f. 725v: letter from Pulicat to Batavia, Jan. 1643; Colenbrander *et al.*, *Dagh-register gehouden int Casteel Batavia ... anno 1643–1644* (The Hague, 1902), 244; Mac Leod, *De*

He was the last ruler who could claim this title with any justification. After Bijapur drove Sriranga III away from the capital Vellore around 1646, the empire gradually collapsed over the next two decades, although the Aravidu house itself continued to exist for a much longer period. For these later fortunes of the final imperial family, see the Epilogue.

The Aravidus are generally considered to have included seven truly imperial rulers, reigning from approximately 1570 to the 1640s, so their average reign would have lasted slightly over eleven years. But if Timma Raja is counted too—who after all belonged to the Aravidu family and briefly sat on the throne—this time span dwindles to just under a decade. Should we also regard as Aravidu emperors the dynasty's de facto founder Rama Raya (say, from Sadashiva's reign onward) and Venkata's putative son Chikka Raya, the length would grow again, but by no more than a few years. Thus, on average, reigns under the Aravidus were about as long as those under the Tuluvas and the Sangamas.

During the first half of its existence, the Aravidu dynasty appears to have been rather stable, as the initial rulers were succeeded by sons or brothers, without violent rivalries, regicides, or infants on the throne. With the death of the childless Venkata in 1614, all this changed. The subsequent emperors included two minors (if Chikka Raya is counted) and only one ruler who was succeeded by his son. In the other successions, nephews, (distant) cousins, and an uncle followed their predecessors. All these later reigns were contested by relatives, leading to several bloody usurpations and two assassinated monarchs.

This period also witnessed a shift between the family's two branches, replacing the descendants of Tirumala with those of his brother Rama Raya. The latter had never forfeited their claim to the throne and finally won it back during the empire's last two decades. Furthermore, it appears that these developments were increasingly influenced by parties beyond the dynasty: courtiers, formally subordinate chiefs—including Vijayanagara's successor states—and the Deccan sultanates.

***

Oost-Indische Compagnie, vol. II, 173, 176-7; S. Krishnasvami Aiyangar, "Srirangarayalu: The Last Emperor of Vijayanagar," *Journal of Indian History* XVIII, 1 (1939), 21-4; Rāma Sharma, *The History of the Vijayanagar Empire*, vol. II, 234-8, 268-9; Nilakanta Sastri and Venkataramanayya, *Further Sources of Vijayanagara History*, vol. I, 346-8; Nilakanta Sastri, *A History of South India*, 302-3; Saulière, "The Revolt of the Southern Nayaks" [pt. 1], 93 (n. 12).

If one compares successions under the consecutive imperial dynasties, similarities seem more numerous than differences. Depending on which rulers are counted as formal emperors, for each house the average reign lasted between slightly less than a decade and about twelve years, around half the length of the estimated average rule in pre-colonial India. Under each dynasty, this short time span was largely the result of the many contested successions, which often led to brief reigns ending with dethronements or assassinations. Some historians have concluded that violent transitions even outnumbered harmonious ones.[45]

Notably, few of these rivalries resulted from cases where the imperial court ignored the advice of the *Mahābhārata* and other texts to exclude women, children, and illegitimate offspring from the throne. In fact, none of Vijayanagara's dynasties included female reigns, while just two rulers, Krishna Raya and Chikka Raya, have been portrayed as bastards. Since the former bastard case is contradicted by numerous sources, there probably was only one instance of an unlawful son becoming emperor. Infant monarchs were not common either, with just four out of around thirty accessions reportedly involving minors. Indeed, nearly all successions under the Sangamas, Saluvas, and Tuluvas—and half of the successions under the Aravidus—proceeded from father to son or from brother to brother.

Therefore, it seems that it was precisely those transitions that regularly instigated conflicts. As principles of heirship were ambiguous, all the ruler's sons might claim the throne, causing opposition between brothers or, when a son succeeded, between uncles and nephews. Thus, rivalry could arise between different branches of a dynasty, often continuing into later generations, as happened under the last Sangama emperors and throughout the Aravidu house.

For as long as a dynasty lasted, however, pretenders to the throne had to be related by blood to former rulers. If someone took the throne who did not meet that condition, this was regarded as the beginning of another dynasty, even if that ruler had marital ties with the previous house. Thus, the Aravidu rulers Rama Raya and his brother Tirumala, although sons-in-law of the Tuluva emperor Krishna Raya, were considered founders of a new house—or that is at least the view of modern historians. However, we have seen that texts produced under Vijayanagara's successive dynasties made great efforts to establish family ties with previous houses and thereby emphasised dynastic continuation.

Finally, under the later dynasties, when more varied sources become available, one notes a growing number of references to the interventions of courtiers, regional chiefs, and neighbouring states in successions. In addition to the three generalissimos who founded new imperial houses, courtiers often exerted decisive influence from at least the first Tuluvas onward. Usurpation attempts in particular

45 Patil, *Court Life under the Vijayanagar Rulers*, 123, 145; Stein, *Vijayanagara*, 92.

seem to have been successful only if backed by a court majority. Subordinate chiefs, including rulers of the successor states, appear to have played a similar role each time they recognised one of several pretenders and thus improved his chances of becoming emperor.[46] In contrast, interventions of the Deccan sultanates (especially Bijapur and Golkonda), although frequent and weakening the empire as a whole, were seemingly insignificant for the outcome of succession struggles. Sultanate armies invading Vijayanagara to support pretenders to the throne were usually repulsed or, in one case, deserted by the pretender himself.

Successor States

As shown above, sources on successions in Vijayanagara become increasingly varied and detailed around the turn of the sixteenth century. For the successor states, only in the seventeenth century do sources begin to shed more light on successions. From roughly 1650 on, inscriptions and literary texts of local origin are supplemented with regular accounts by the Dutch. In addition to reconstructing the successions themselves, the sections below examine how various sources complement and contradict each other. Again, Ikkeri in the Kannada region is discussed first, followed by Tanjavur (under both royal houses), Madurai, and Ramnad in the Tamil area.

Nayakas of Ikkeri

As told in the origin stories of Ikkeri's Nayakas, the dynasty and its kingdom were founded by Chaudappa and his son Sadashiva Nayaka. They were succeeded by fifteen descendants, although this number is subjective, depending on the criteria used to count monarchs. To begin with, in one case, historians do not agree on whether certain names and titles refer to one single king or denote two or even three different rulers. Further, a few kings are mentioned in just one or two sources, while others reigned only over outlying parts of the kingdom, competing with the central court. Here, monarchs are defined as people who occupied the capital's throne as the main ruler for any length of time. During this dynasty's lifespan, from the early 1500s to 1763, seventeen persons seem to have met these admittedly arbitrary conditions (see table 4 towards the end of this section).[47]

[46] See also Stein, *Vijayanagara*, 91-5, 109.

[47] For a comparative survey of Ikkeri's rulers and their regnal periods as proposed by five different scholars (including Swaminathan, Chitnis, and Naraharayya), see Bridges White, "Beyond Empire" 80-4. See also the genealogical table in G. Kuppuram, "The Genealogy and Chronology of Keḷadi Rulers: A Review," *The Quarterly Journal of the Mythic Society* LXIX, 1-2 (1978), 71. For various

Scholars have tried to establish Ikkeri's succession principles. These alleged rules are constructed on the basis of actual practices, however, instead of normative texts concerning successions. In fact, Ikkeri's main literary work dealing with statecraft, the early eighteenth-century Sanskrit *Śivatattva ratnākara* by King Basavappa Nayaka, describes royal duties and qualities at length but seems to provide no guidelines for selecting a successor to the throne. It merely mentions the capacities required of princes, confirming the importance that earlier Sanskrit texts attach to a combination of descent and personality (V 15:35-6).[48]

Scholars who have reconstructed regulations for successions in Ikkeri argue that primogeniture was the preferred procedure and that in the absence of an able son a brother could be selected. But they also note that these rules were regularly bent. Perhaps as a consequence, some historians observe a beneficial flexibility that allegedly characterised Ikkeri's successions. Joint-rule, voluntary abdications, early nomination of *yuvarājas* (heirs apparent), queens' regencies, adoptions, and regular shifts between different family branches are all said to have been conscious, peaceful, and usually effective strategies to accommodate various pretenders and minimise the risk of destabilising struggles for the throne.[49] However, the survey of successions that follows demonstrates that more often than not successions were accompanied by violent clashes between rival claimants.

Much about Ikkeri's Nayaka house during its first century or so remains unclear. This includes a number of successions and even some of the first kings themselves. All inscriptions and literary texts agree that the dynastic founder Chaudappa Nayaka (r. c. 1500-30?) was succeeded by a son, generally known as Sadashiva

(partly outdated) genealogical trees, see: Swaminathan, *The Nāyakas of Ikkēri*, between 280-1; Chitnis, *Keḷadi Polity*, 57 and between 224-5; Hayavadana Rao, *History of Mysore*, vol. III, 1287; Lennart Bes, "The Ambiguities of Female Rule in Nayaka South India, Seventeenth to Eighteenth Centuries," in Elena Woodacre (ed.), *A Companion to Global Queenship* (Kalamazoo/Bradford, 2018), 212; Gopal, "A Note on the Genealogy of the Early Chiefs of Keḷadi," 31, 58; N. Lakshminarayan Rao, "The Nayakas of Keladi," in S. Krishnaswami Aiyangar *et al.* (eds), *Vijayanagara Sexcentenary Commemoration Volume* (Dharwar, 1936), 269; Sundara, *The Keḷadi Nāyakas*, viii-ix; K. Gunda Jois (ed.), "Keladi Inscriptions on Gold Sandals and Pinnacles," *The Quarterly Journal of the Mythic Society* LXXXII, 1-2 (1991), 66; Krishnaswami Aiyangar, *Sources of Vijayanagar History*, xv; Lewis Rice, *Mysore and Coorg*, 157; L.D. Barnett, "The Keladi Rajas of Ikkeri and Bednur," *Journal of the Royal Asiatic Society* (New Series) 42, 1 (1910), 150; Sewell, *The Historical Inscriptions of Southern India*, 359-60; idem, *Lists of Inscriptions*, 177-8.

[48] Krishnamurthy, *Sivatattva Ratnākara of Keladi Basavaraja*, 23-71; Chitnis, *Keḷadi Polity*, 62-6; idem, "Sivatattvaratnakara with Special Reference to Polity."

[49] G. Kuppuram, "Principles of Succession under Keladi Rule," *Bulletin of the Institute of Traditional Cultures* 71 (1979); Chitnis, *Keḷadi Polity*, 39-41, 43-51; Swaminathan, *The Nāyakas of Ikkēri*, 163-4; Krishnamurthy, *Sivatattva Ratnākara of Keladi Basavaraja*, 124-5; S.N. Naraharayya, "Keladi Dynasty" [pt. 2], *The Quarterly Journal of the Mythic Society* XXII, 1 (1931), 73.

Nayaka (r. c. 1530-65?).[50] But at this point the sources become ambiguous and modern analyses begin to diverge. According to the dynasty's main chronicles, by his two wives Sadashiva had two sons, Dodda Sankanna Nayaka (r. c. 1565-70?) and Chikka Sankanna Nayaka (r. c. 1570-80), succeeding their father one after another. Next, the throne was consecutively occupied by two of Dodda Sankanna's sons, Ramaraja Nayaka (r. c. 1570-85) and Venkatappa Nayaka (r. c. 1585-1629), the former probably initially co-ruling with his uncle Chikka Sankanna.[51] Most modern studies adopt this version of the dynasty's early genealogy.[52]

But all important chronicles, although they refer to events in the sixteenth century, date from the eighteenth century. Questioning the reliability of these late texts, it has been suggested on the basis of contemporary inscriptions that Sadashiva and Dodda Sankanna were one single person. Originally called (Dodda) Sankanna, this son of the founder Chaudappa would have assumed the name (Immadi) Sadashiva to show his loyalty to Vijayanagara's similarly named emperor Sadashiva Raya, and by extension to the empire's de facto ruler Rama Raya. Consequently, Chikka Sankanna as well as Ramaraja and Venkatappa would all have been sons of Dodda Sankanna alias Sadashiva.[53] Whatever were the exact family relations, during this period most rulers were apparently succeeded by sons or brothers, with elder ones probably preceding younger ones.

[50] BL/AAS, MG, no. 6, pt. 11: "Historical account of Beedoonoor or Caladee Samstanum" (*Keḷadi arasara vaṃśāvaḷi*), ff. 62, 65v; Krishnaswami Aiyangar, *Sources of Vijayanagar History*, 194-5; Nilakanta Sastri and Venkataramanayya, *Further Sources of Vijayanagara History*, vol. III, 97, 189-90; Krishnamurthy, *Sivatattva Ratnākara of Keladi Basavaraja*, 104, 106; Gopal, "A Note on the Genealogy of the Early Chiefs of Keḷadi," 18-26; Kuppuram, "The Genealogy and Chronology of Keḷadi Rulers," 59-60.

[51] BL/AAS, MG, no. 6, pt. 11: "Historical account of Beedoonoor or Caladee Samstanum," ff. 65v, 67v-8, 70, 71; Krishnaswami Aiyangar, *Sources of Vijayanagar History*, 194-6, 337-9; Nilakanta Sastri and Venkataramanayya, *Further Sources of Vijayanagara History*, vol. III, 193-4; Krishnamurthy, *Sivatattva Ratnākara of Keladi Basavaraja*, 104, 106-8; Kuppuram, "The Genealogy and Chronology of Keḷadi Rulers," 60-3.

[52] See: Swaminathan, *The Nāyakas of Ikkēri*, 19-21, 30-2, 34-40; Chitnis, *Keḷadi Polity*, 12-14, 39, 43-6, 50; Lakshminarayan Rao, "The Nayakas of Keladi," 256-62; Naraharayya, "Keladi Dynasty" [pt. 1], 378-9; idem, "Keladi Dynasty" [pt. 2], 72-3. The last work claims Sadashiva was first succeeded by his brother Bhadrappa, who then installed Sadashiva's son Dodda Sankanna when he reached maturity.

[53] Gopal, "A Note on the Genealogy of the Early Chiefs of Keḷadi," passim, especially 35, 37. For a local account also suggesting there was only one ruler called Sankanna, see Mahalingam, *Mackenzie Manuscripts*, vol. II, 420-1. See also Lakshminarayan Rao, "The Nayakas of Keladi," 259, where Dodda Sankanna is identified with Immadi Sadashiva, the latter however thought to be different from Sadashiva himself. For these and other interpretations, see also B.S. Subhadra, "Art and Architecture of the Keḷadi Nāyakas" (unpublished dissertation, Karnatak University, 1991), 34-7. The names Ramaraja and Venkatappa were possibly also expressions of loyalty to the roughly contemporary Vijayanagara rulers Rama Raya (fl. 1542-65) and Venkata I (r. 1585-1614) of the Aravidu dynasty. See also Naraharayya, "Keladi Dynasty" [pt. 2], 74.

That does not mean these successions were uncontested. While the treatise *Śivatattva ratnākara* declares that Chikka Sankanna installed Venkatappa as his successor and Ramaraja as *yuvarāja*, the chronicle *Keḷadinṛpa vijayam* asserts that Chikka Sankanna was murdered by his successor Ramaraja.[54] There are no further texts either supporting or negating the latter story, but with the reigns of Venkatappa and his successor, his son's son Virabhadra Nayaka (c. 1629-44), European sources become available, which underscore that competition for the throne was often fierce. The Italian traveller Pietro Della Valle, visiting the Ikkeri court in 1623, reported that although Venkatappa was preparing Virabhadra to be his successor, this transition would likely be challenged, since another of Venkatappa's grandsons, Sadasivayya (born of one of his daughters), wanted to be king too. Besides, as the Italian traveller wrote, two sons of Venkatappa's brother and predecessor Ramaraja had been imprisoned out of fear that they would claim the throne as well.[55]

As Della Valle expected, Virabhadra's succession in 1629 was disputed. The Portuguese recorded that the eldest of Ramaraja's jailed sons, Vira (or Virappa) Vodeyar, escaped and had himself installed as king, probably while Virabhadra was away from the capital on a military campaign. In 1631, the Portuguese viceroy at Goa even concluded a treaty with Vira Vodeyar, regarding him as the legitimate king. He died a few months later, however, making Virabhadra the sole monarch. But in 1635, according to the Portuguese, another pretender took advantage of the king's absence from the capital and spent six months on the throne before Virabhadra ousted him.[56] This usurper was in all likelihood Sadasivayya, the other grandson of Venkatappa whom Della Valle thought to be harbouring royal ambitions.

That is at least suggested by the chronicle *Keḷadi arasara vaṃśāvaḷi*, which relates that, when Virabhadra was out of the capital, first his "uncle Veeravadeyaloo" (Vira Vodeyar) and next his brother-in-law "Sadaseeva" (Sadasivayya) were crowned king, although both of them passed away soon after. The *Śivatattva ratnākara* and the *Keḷadinṛpa vijayam* largely confirm these events, the latter adding that Sadasivayya mutilated Vira Vodeyar's brother

[54] Krishnaswami Aiyangar, *Sources of Vijayanagar History*, 339; Krishnamurthy, *Sivatattva Ratnākara of Keladi Basavaraja*, 108; Narasimhachar, "The Keladi Rajas of Ikkeri and Bednur," 190; Gopal, "A Note on the Genealogy of the Early Chiefs of Keḷadi," 30; Swaminathan, *The Nāyakas of Ikkēri*, 38, 87; Chitnis, *Keḷadi Polity*, 50.

[55] Pietro Della Valle, *The Travels of Pietro Della Valle in India: From the Old English Translation of 1644 by G. Havers*, ed. Edward Grey (London, 1892), vol. II, 262, 284. See also Chitnis, *Keḷadi Polity*, 47-8.

[56] Shastry, *Goa-Kanara Portuguese Relations*, 156, 158, 167; Pinto, *History of Christians in Coastal Karnataka*, 66-77; Subrahmanyam, *The Political Economy of Commerce*, 234-5; Teotonio R. de Souza, *Medieval Goa: A Socio-Economic History* (New Delhi, 1979), 36.

Basavalinga to prevent him from turning into a rival.[57] Perhaps as a consequence, in or around 1639, Virabhadra shifted the capital from Ikkeri to nearby Bednur (also Bidrur), considered a location with better strategic and mercantile advantages.[58]

While many texts thus mention the competition Virabhadra faced from certain family members, literary works unanimously praise the assistance he received from his relative Shivappa Nayaka, a powerful general. The latter is usually referred to as a (grand-)uncle of the king, but since he was a grandson of the former ruler Chikka Sankanna, he may actually have been a second cousin of Virabhadra. The *Keḷadi arasara vaṃśāvaḷi* describes a short period during which Shivappa was disloyal to Virabhadra. Having subsequently fled the capital, Shivappa was nevertheless caught but then forgiven because of his great stature, and even appointed governor of an important fort.[59] Apart from this episode, the text agrees with the other main works that Shivappa was a highly trusted servant and played an essential role in the kingdom's administration and defence. At the end of his reign, Virabhadra allegedly voluntarily withdrew from worldly affairs or died a natural death, and, as he had no sons, Shivappa would have been acknowledged as the new ruler (r. c. 1644-60).[60]

But a chronicle of the Wodeyar dynasty ruling neighbouring Mysore, the Kannada *Chikkadēvarāya vaṃśāvaḷi*, declares that Shivappa took the Ikkeri throne by killing Virabhadra.[61] Most historians consider this improbable because other Indian sources do not mention a violent take-over and in fact all glorify Shivappa's achievements. And since Ikkeri's chronicle *Keḷadinṛpa vijayam* does not conceal

[57] BL/AAS, MG, no. 6, pt. 11: "Historical account of Beedoonoor or Caladee Samstanum," ff. 74v-5; Narasimhachar, "The Keladi Rajas of Ikkeri and Bednur," 190-1; Krishnaswami Aiyangar, *Sources of Vijayanagar History*, 344, 346; Krishnamurthy, *Sivatattva Ratnākara of Keladi Basavaraja*, 110; Kuppuram, "The Genealogy and Chronology of Keḷadi Rulers," 63. Sadasivayya was not only a grandson of Venkatappa I like Virabhadra himself, but also the latter's brother-in-law. See also: Swaminathan, *The Nāyakas of Ikkēri*, 52, 67-72; Chitnis, *Keḷadi Polity*, 17-18, 44, 48.

[58] Swaminathan, *The Nāyakas of Ikkēri*, 82-3; BL/AAS, MG, no. 6, pt. 11: "Historical account of Beedoonoor or Caladee Samstanum," ff. 74v, 77; Bridges White, "Beyond Empire," 110, 208.

[59] BL/AAS, MG, no. 6, pt. 11: "Historical account of Beedoonoor or Caladee Samstanum," ff. 76-6v.

[60] Krishnaswami Aiyangar, *Sources of Vijayanagar History*, 346; Krishnamurthy, *Sivatattva Ratnākara of Keladi Basavaraja*, 110-11; BL/AAS, MG, no. 6, pt. 11: "Historical account of Beedoonoor or Caladee Samstanum," ff. 74v, 77-7v; Swaminathan, *The Nāyakas of Ikkēri*, 86;. Chitnis, *Keḷadi Polity*, 50; Kuppuram, "The Genealogy and Chronology of Keḷadi Rulers," 63-4. See also the remarks about Virabhadra in the mid-1630s in Peter Mundy, *The Travels of Peter Mundy in Europe and Asia, 1608-1667*, vol. III, pt. I, ed. Richard Carnac Temple (London, 1919), 82.

[61] Krishnaswami Aiyangar, *Sources of Vijayanagar History*, 309. See also Hayavadana Rao, *History of Mysore*, vol. I (Bangalore, 1943), 3.

Ramaraja's murder of Chikka Sankanna in the late sixteenth century, it would be unlikely to ignore Shivappa's assassination of Virabhadra.[62]

However, Portuguese, Jesuit, and Dutch reports all indicate that the Mysore text is probably correct. Either of these European documents say that in mid-1644 Shivappa besieged a fortress where Virabhadra was staying and reportedly had him poisoned. As the Jesuit Simon Martins put it some years later: "Xinapa Naique, who, having been captain general in Canara [Ikkeri] and desiring to get the sceptre, deprived of his life the lawful king, and by force of arms crowned himself king." In 1672 the Dutch phrased it largely similarly: "Sivapanijcq" had "usurped the sovereignty" from "his natural lord" and "repudiated the rightful heirs" (*de reghte erven verstooten*).[63]

These views—that other members of the Nayaka house had stronger claims to the throne than Shivappa—are shared by modern historians. They regard Shivappa's reign as the start of the domination of the family's collateral line. Despite the praise of some scholars for a supposedly regular and cordial alternation between the dynasty's two branches, in fact no member of the initial line ever ruled again, with one very brief exception. This more or less definite shift could explain why none of the literary works refers to Shivappa's killing of Virabhadra: these texts were all composed or commissioned by the former's descendants, who owed their place on the throne to Shivappa's usurpation and probably preferred to portray that transition as legitimate and peaceful. For the same reason, it did make sense to include Ramaraja's murder of Chikka Sankanna in the *Keḷadinṛpa vijayam*, as the latter was Shivappa's grandfather, whose reign was allegedly brutally ended by a member of the family's competing branch.

In late 1660, at the approximate age of sixty, Shivappa passed away after a long sickbed, perhaps again caused by poison, as a rumour recorded by Jesuits had it. He was succeeded by his younger brother Venkatappa Nayaka II (r. 1660-1), who according to some literary texts had already partaken in his predecessor's reign. Such co-rulership is also referred to in Dutch reports stating that Venkatappa II reigned together with Shivappa's son Bhadrappa Nayaka, who served as the second king. One VOC document even speaks of a diplomatic mission to "greet these two kings in their new reign."[64] However, within a year after his accession, in September 1661, Venkatappa II died and was succeeded by his nephew and co-ruler Bhadrappa (r. 1661-4).

62 Chitnis, *Keḷadi Polity*, 47; Swaminathan, *The Nāyakas of Ikkēri*, 87; Kuppuram, "Principles of Succession under Keladi Rule," 77.

63 NA, VOC, no. 1224, f. 76; no. 1288, f. 635v: report on "Canara," July 1657, letter from Cochin to Batavia, July 1672; D. Ferroli, *The Jesuits in Mysore* (Kozhikode, 1955), 30-1; Shastry, *Goa-Kanara Portuguese Relations*, 176-7, 179 (n. 68).

64 NA, VOC, no. 1236, ff. 35, 191-3: letters from Vengurla to Batavia, Oct. 1660, Jan. 1661; BL/AAS, MG, no. 6, pt. 11: "Historical account of Beedoonoor or Caladee Samstanum," ff. 77-7v, 78v-9; Krishnaswami Aiyangar, *Sources of Vijayanagar History*, 346-7; Krishnamurthy, *Sivatattva Ratnākara of Keladi*

This is another case in which eighteenth-century court chronicles present the transition as a tranquil affair, with Venkatappa II himself crowning Bhadrappa as the new king,[65] while Dutch and Jesuit sources have an entirely different story to tell. A letter sent from the VOC settlement at Vengurla to the Company's headquarters at Batavia in May 1662, only eight months after the event, deserves a lengthy quotation for its detailed coverage of the developments. As this account explains, the succession to the throne occurred:

> ... because that Ventapanijck [Venkatappa Nayaka II] loved the single-headed reign too much, which not only made him forget to pay appropriate respect to the said prince [Bhadrappa Nayaka] and general [named Shivalinga],[66] but moreover he secretly decided to take Sivalingia's life and Badrapanijck's sight. But they, observing matters were not right, wangled for so long that they found out about the secret, and seeing the approaching danger that threatened them, they resolved to make a virtue of necessity [*de noot een deucht te maken*] and let Ventapanijck fall into the trap that was set for them [*vallen in den strick die haer geschooren was*]...
>
> On 8 September last, the aforesaid prince and general, both provided with a good sabre, without any retinue but 2 or 3 trusted guards, moved in the morning at dawn to the palace of Ventapanijck, whom they caught in his bedroom as he was waking up, accompanied by the chief councillor and a chamberlain. Grasping the betrayal, the king called for his hand-gun, but jumping to him, Sivalingia dealt Ventapanijck a blow on the head so heavy that he fell on the ground and vomited his soul right away [*zijn ziel aenstonts uijt braeckte*]. The councillor and chamberlain, who tried to protect the king, were also hacked down. Seeing their intention accomplished as desired, they hastily commanded that the gates of the palace be closed and reinforced with trusted guards, until order had been restored. In the late afternoon a mandate was proclaimed around the entire town of Bidroer [Bednur] that Badrapanijck had been inaugurated [*gehult*] in his lord father's [Shivappa] place as king over the Cannarase realm [Ikkeri]. And although a great tumult ensued because of this murder, this was halted without further bloodshed.
>
> But we can suspect that this deed will drag along some difficulties, of which the first signs appear already. Because some time ago we heard that in early February the said Badrapanijck went to Tirthallij [Tirthahalli] (which that nation considers a holy place) and

Basavaraja, 113; Ferroli, *The Jesuits in Mysore*, 56; Shastry, *Goa-Kanara Portuguese Relations*, 184, 191, 202-3, 207; Swaminathan, *The Nāyakas of Ikkēri*, 101-2; Chitnis, *Keḷadi Polity*, 19.

[65] BL/AAS, MG, no. 6, pt. 11: "Historical account of Beedoonoor or Caladee Samstanum," ff. 77v, 79; Krishnaswami Aiyangar, *Sources of Vijayanagar History*, 347-8; Krishnamurthy, *Sivatattva Ratnākara of Keladi Basavaraja*, 111, 113; Swaminathan, *The Nāyakas of Ikkēri*, 104-5.

[66] According to the *Keḷadinṛpa vijayam*, Shivalinga Nayaka (also Sivalingaiya) was a son-in-law of Shivappa Nayaka I. The general died in 1662 in a battle with Mysore. See Swaminathan, *The Nāyakas of Ikkēri*, 104-6.

there gave 500 cows as charity [*aelmoes*], besides much handed-out cash money, to ask for forgiveness of his sins, to which end that Neijck [Nayaka] would also have executed some person there, as a sacrifice of life. This became known in the town of Bidroer, whereupon it was decided to stop His Majesty from entering his palace, with the intention to forcibly crown the brother's son of a former king named Vira Bhadranijck [Virabhadra Nayaka] (since this Badrapanijck did not reign well) and declare him king of the lands.

The houweldaer [*havāldār*, commander] in Bidroer, being informed of this intention, immediately had the king's palace secured and the doors closed, and wrote some letters to advise His Highness Badrapanijck, who after their reception hastily went to Bidroer. But he found the town gates closed and the people out and about [*d'gemeente op de been*], who prevented him from entering. He treated them very friendly, pledging that he would renounce whatever displeased them and that they would receive complete satisfaction from him. With these and other amicable words he got into his palace, where without delay he had called the aforementioned brother's son, named Alij Venttaija [unidentified prince], who was asked about all that had passed. But he answered that he had no guilt nor gave cause for this revolt, but that they wanted to put him on the throne with force, which he had not accepted, and he asked for permission to leave.

The following day, the king noticed that the revolting people, some 8,000 men strong, still continued their rebellion in order to crown the other, whom he summoned for the second time. But he ["Alij Venttaija"] appeared only after a long search (as he had hidden out of fear of being harmed), when he, by order of the aforementioned Badrapanijck, was robbed of his sight, which was cut out with red-hot piercers, but shortly afterwards he hanged himself out of misery. The common mob [*gemeene graeuw*] did not calm down because of this but started running around, so that several groups, 7 to 8 thousand heads strong, trooped up and stopped all distinguished persons who travelled from and to Bidroer, which made the roads very unsafe. Also, all letters reaching their hands were held up, but although these disturbances have been smoothed and silenced, we trust that the mentioned kingdom will not remain calm for long, since a great hatred has arisen between the General Sivalingia (who already draws the power quite to himself) and Badrapanijck, for which one of the two will likely have to pay with his life ...[67]

Other VOC letters add that the court merchant Mallappa Malu was closely involved in the conspiracy against Venkatappa II and served as an indispensable aide to the subsequent reign of Bhadrappa. It was even rumoured that Mallappa Malu had poisoned Bhadrappa's father Shivappa one year before.[68] In any case, the usurpation by Bhadrappa and his supporters clearly did not go uncontested. Apparently, the capital's

67 NA, VOC, no. 1240, ff. 584-7: letter from Vengurla to Batavia, May 1662 (translation mine).

68 NA, VOC, no. 1240, ff. 532-3, 602-3: letters from Vengurla to Batavia, May, Dec. 1662; Coolhaas *et al.*, *Generale Missiven*, vol. III, 434-5; Ferroli, *The Jesuits in Mysore*, 56.

angered inhabitants attempted to install another king, whose identity is uncertain but who seemingly was a nephew of the former ruler Virabhadra and therefore belonged to the dynasty's other branch, which originally governed the kingdom.

The Dutch documents concerning this succession are typical for the sort of descriptions these records provide about such occasions. The reports relate developments in great detail but do not explain how the VOC acquired this knowledge and how reliable its sources were. However, these accounts most probably contain information received from south Indian parties and therefore largely present local interpretations of the affairs. Anyhow, although the precise course of events cannot be verified, several elements can be distinguished in this source material, many of which seem typical for most successions in Ikkeri. These include rivalry and violence between members of the royal family and different dynastic lines, influence of court factions, some form of engagement by the common people, an apparent need to do penance for one's sins,[69] and, soon after the instalment of a new king, rising tensions once again.

As the Dutch had anticipated, Bhadrappa's reign did not last long: he died within three years, around mid-1664. The *Śivatattva ratnākara* and *Keḷadi arasara vaṃśāvaḷi* state that the childless Bhadrappa, having co-ruled with his half-brother Somashekara Nayaka, nominated him as his successor and before his death even handed over the kingdom to him (r. 1664-71).[70] But according to Dutch, Portuguese, and English sources, courtiers—reportedly involving some Brahmins—poisoned Bhadrappa and replaced him with Somashekara ("Esomsackernijck"), who was eight or nine years old. Bhadrappa's death initially caused disorder and threatened the position of the powerful court merchants Mallappa Malu and his brother Narayana Malu. Still, the latter supposedly managed to create stability and took the minor Somashekara under his protection.[71] However, the death of this young ruler only seven years later, in December 1671,[72] led to perhaps the most instable period in the dynasty's history.

The various sources offer quite different and often somewhat confused descriptions of this episode, although many accounts agree that Somashekara went mad

[69] See also Lewis Rice, *Mysore and Coorg*, 159, saying Basavappa I (r. 1697-1713) raised money to feed pilgrims as a penance for the murder of Somashekara I (r. 1664-71).

[70] Krishnamurthy, *Sivatattva Ratnākara of Keladi Basavaraja*, 112-13; Krishnaswami Aiyangar, *Sources of Vijayanagar History*, 348; BL/AAS, MG, no. 6, pt. 11: "Historical account of Beedoonoor or Caladee Samstanum," ff. 77v, 79, 80.

[71] NA, VOC, no. 1246, ff. 1619-20: report on Vengurla, July 1664; Foster, *The English Factories in India 1661–64* (Oxford, 1923), 343; Shastry, *Goa-Kanara Portuguese Relations*, 209-10; Swaminathan, *The Nāyakas of Ikkēri*, 108-9; Chitnis, *Keḷadi Polity*, 20, 39, 46, 48; Pinto, *History of Christians in Coastal Karnataka*, 82.

[72] Shastry, *Goa-Kanara Portuguese Relations*, 216; De Souza, *Medieval Goa*, 38.

during his reign. Local chronicles attribute this to the consumption of elephant medicine, opium, or another intoxicant that, so the young king was assured, improved his physical condition. The VOC reported instead that Somashekara spent much time tending animals while others actually ruled the kingdom.[73] In any case, as most sources have it, the king was killed by some courtiers, in the wake of which several years of violence ensued, involving a whole range of pretenders to the throne and their supporters.

The Dutch wrote in July 1672 that before Somashekara's death one court faction asked the neighbouring, dominating Bijapur sultanate to overthrow Ikkeri's alleged puppet government, whereupon the sultan sent an ambassador with 1,600 troops. When Somashekara resisted the subsequent takeover by the envoy and his local supporters, he was assassinated, which led to great tumult. Many courtiers were killed, while the Bijapur ambassador was forced to hastily return home, with only 400 men left. Amidst the confusion a new king had to be crowned, for which—still according to the Dutch—the options were either the nearest heir of Somashekara, from the dynasty's collateral branch of Shivappa Nayaka, or someone from the original, "rightful" line, which had ended with Virabhadra Nayaka around 1644. The choice fell on a member of the latter branch, a fourteen-year old boy named Shivappa (r. c. 1672).[74]

This Shivappa Nayaka II was in all probability the elder brother of Sadashiva Nayaka who in 1689 approached the VOC for military assistance, as related at the outset of this chapter. The *Keḷadinṛpa vijayam* says Shivappa II was a grandson of Sadasivayya, who in the mid-1630s had competed with King Virabhadra Nayaka for the throne and himself was a grandson of King Venkatappa Nayaka I (r. c. 1585-1629). Thus, Shivappa II would indeed have been a member of the initial ruling line of the Nayaka dynasty.[75] Dutch accounts dating from 1672 and 1673 describe how upon Shivappa II's instalment many more people were murdered, including all close relatives of the previous ruler Somashekara. Around the same time, Ikkeri was attacked by the still disgruntled sultan of Bijapur and the rulers of the adjacent Mysore and Kannur (or Cannanore) kingdoms. On top of all this, some Ikkeri courtiers, among whom court merchant Narayana Malu and General Timmanna, started backing another pretender to the throne.

The aspirant in question was a son of a certain Kasiyya Bhadrayya ("Cassibadria" as the Dutch called him), who also belonged to the dynasty's original branch.

[73] BL/AAS, MG, no. 6, pt. 11: "Historical account of Beedoonoor or Caladee Samstanum," f. 80; Buchanan, *A Journey from Madras*, vol. III, 127-8; Swaminathan, *The Nāyakas of Ikkēri*, 115; Mahalingam, *Mackenzie Manuscripts*, vol. II, 418; NA, VOC, no. 1288, f. 635: letter from Cochin to Batavia, July 1672.

[74] NA, VOC, no. 1288, ff. 635-5v: letter from Cochin to Batavia, July 1672. See also Fawcett, *The English Factories in India* (New Series), vol. I, 308-9.

[75] Chitnis, *Keḷadi Polity*, 48-9. See also Shama Shastry, "Malnad Chiefs," 49.

Assisted by Bijapur, this coalition dethroned the young Shivappa II soon after his accession, locked him up together with his brother Sadashiva and their blinded father, and cut off Shivappa II's right little finger, thus forever rendering him unfit to become king. While preparations were next made to crown Kasiyya Bhadrayya's son, Kasiyya Bhadrayya himself fell out with General Timmanna, disagreeing about the spending of Ikkeri's treasure. The general subsequently put the father and son in jail and removed from the latter not only a finger but an ear too. Despite this measure, it transpired that Kasiyya Bhadrayya and his son still commanded support among some of the kingdom's local chiefs. Timmanna then had both beheaded and nearly all other members of their dynastic line killed as well. Probably in an effort to prevent yet other assaults by aspiring royals on his power, by early 1673 the general had installed a new monarch on Ikkeri's now long-vacant throne: the widow of the former ruler Somashekara.[76]

That widow was Queen Chennammaji (r. c. 1673-97), whose rule horrified the escaped pretender Sadashiva Nayaka, as he wrote to the VOC. But in spite of his view on female rule, she would become one of Ikkeri's longest ruling monarchs. In a report written shortly after her death, the Dutch explain that the queen had achieved her power by what they called a "very political trick" (*seer politijcque streek*). When Chennammaji's husband Somashekara was killed in 1671, she was supposed to commit *satī* and die on his funeral pyre. She pretended to be pregnant, however, and was thus able to postpone her death by giving people hope she would give birth to a son and heir to the throne. Meanwhile, she forged such strong ties with parties at court that once her pregnancy proved false, no one could remove her from her ruling position and force her to perform *satī*.[77]

Initially, her most important ally was doubtlessly General Timmanna, who seems to have emerged from the tumultuous early 1670s as the kingdom's most powerful courtier and allegedly had Chennammaji crowned. He apparently harboured royal ambitions too, having himself addressed as the Nayaka of Ikkeri, and the queen and the general gradually turned into rivals, even engaging in military clashes. But Chennammaji remained seated on the throne and grew increasingly powerful, especially after Timmanna's death around mid-1676.[78] When she passed away herself, in early 1697, she had presided over a quarter-century of relative

[76] NA, VOC, no. 1288, ff. 636-8v; no. 1291, ff. 586v-7v; no. 1295, ff. 264v-6; no. 1299, f. 484; no. 1474, ff. 329-9v: letters from Cochin to Batavia and Gentlemen XVII, July 1672, Apr., Nov. 1673, Nov. 1674, report on Vengurla and "Canara," Mar. 1689.

[77] NA, VOC, no. 1593, ff. 876-6v: diary of Commissioner Zwaardekroon's tour in Malabar, Sept. 1697.

[78] NA, VOC, no. 1291, f. 587; no. 1308, ff. 642v-3; no. 1315, f. 740; no. 1321, f. 953; no. 1329, f. 1331-1v: letters from Cochin to Gentlemen XVII and Batavia, Nov. 1673, Apr. 1675, June 1676, Feb.-Mar. 1677; Coolhaas *et al.*, *Generale Missiven*, vol. IV, 119-20; Fawcett, *The English Factories in India* (New Series), vol. I, 337. See also: Shastry, *Goa-Kanara Portuguese Relations*, 216-18; John Fryer, *A New Account of East-India and*

dynastic stability, following a decade that witnessed three regicides, two pretenders mutilated, and the enthronement of two minors.

It would lead too far to discuss here all details other sources offer on the upheavals between Somashekara's death and Chennammaji's ascendancy. For example, various texts, including VOC documents,[79] mention yet more royal aspirants—including an in-law of the queen named Basavalinga—and yet more killing or, in the case of this Basavalinga, mutilation and exile. But what seems most notable is that the chronicles produced under Chennammaji's descendants paint a much rosier picture of the commencement of her reign than Dutch records do. According to the *Keḷadi arasara vaṃśāvaḷi* and the *Keḷadinṛpa vijayam*, Chennammaji took over the rule of her husband Somashekara as soon as he became mad. The queen is next said to have defeated or briefly tolerated Shivappa II, Kasiyya Bhadrayya's son, and other short-lasting pretenders. And she would herself have actively enlisted General Timmanna's assistance in her actions, after she had temporarily fled Bednur.

Further, these texts do mention the invasion of Bijapur, but state that Chennammaji warded off or bribed the sultanate's officers and made them return home. The *Śivatattva ratnākara* simply ignores the succession struggles of the early 1670s, declaring that Somashekara first co-ruled with his wife Chennammaji and then, shortly before his death, entrusted the kingdom to her.[80] In his letter to the VOC, Shivappa II's brother Sadashiva presented yet another version of the events. Besides what we read in this chapter's introduction, Sadashiva claimed that his brother, in his youthful naivety, had appointed General Timmanna, and that "son-of-a-slave" Somashekara had lived through all the turmoil to eventually dethrone Shivappa II himself and subsequently, on Timmanna's advice, pass the throne to Chennammaji.[81]

Whatever the reliability of these various documents with their competing claims, they obviously represent attempts to stress the legitimacy of each dynastic line, pointing to the defects of the opponents and glorifying their own power, status, and descent. Besides such usage of texts to bolster claims to kingship, this episode also points to another element that could play a role in successions: the influence of neighbouring kingdoms, in this case the Bijapur sultanate, to which Ikkeri had become tributary.

Persia in Eight Letters Being Nine Years Travels, Begun 1672, and Finished 1681 (London, 1698), 162. See also Bes, "The Ambiguities of Female Rule in Nayaka South India."

79 NA, VOC, no. 1593, f. 876v: diary of Commissioner Zwaardekroon's tour in Malabar, Sept. 1697.

80 BL/AAS, MG, no. 6, pt. 11: "Historical account of Beedoonoor or Caladee Samstanum," ff. 80-80v; Narasimhachar, "The Keladi Rajas of Ikkeri and Bednur," 192; Swaminathan, *The Nāyakas of Ikkēri*, 115-18; Chitnis, *Keḷadi Polity*, 20, 48-9; Krishnaswami Aiyangar, *Sources of Vijayanagar History*, 349; Krishnamurthy, *Sivatattva Ratnākara of Keladi Basavaraja*, 114; Kuppuram, "The Genealogy and Chronology of Keḷadi Rulers," 65, 69 (n. 52); Shama Shastry, "Malnad Chiefs," 49.

81 NA, VOC, no. 1463, ff. 438-8v: letter from "Sadaasjiwe Neijke king of Carnatica" at Vengurla to the Dutch commissioner-general, Feb. 1689.

Looking at the Nayakas' seven successions between the late sixteenth and late seventeenth centuries, from Venkatappa I to Chennammaji, one observes that the throne no longer always passed to a son or brother of the king, as happened in the dynasty's first century. Instead, in more than half of these cases, successors were the previous ruler's grandson, second cousin or grand-uncle, even more distant cousin, or widow. Furthermore, of the three kings who were their predecessor's son or brother, one was a minor. The five successions following Chennammaji's death continued this eclectic pattern.

Chennammaji and her deceased husband Somashekara being childless, the queen adopted a boy named Basavappa and acted as his regent until he would be old enough to rule alone.[82] The *Keḷadinṛpa vijayam* declares that Basavappa was a distant relative of the royal house, being the sister's son of the wife of King Bhadrappa Nayaka (r. 1661-4), who in turn was a half-brother of Somashekara.[83] Notably, a Dutch letter of 1673 mentions a three-year old boy kept by Chennammaji to be crowned in the future, who supposedly was one of the few remaining members of the dynasty's first branch.[84] This may well have been Basavappa, although there is no further evidence he descended from Ikkeri's originally ruling line. The *Keḷadi arasara vaṃśāvaḷi* has the following to say (in its English manuscript translation) about Basavappa's adoption:

> When some time had passed, Chinnamaujee resolved to adopt a successor in the government of the state & accordingly after consideration adopted the son of Badrapa-Naik, called Bawapah-Naik [Basavappa Nayaka], a near cousin of Somasakar-Naik, her husband, & acknowledged him as the legal head of the kingdom with the consent of all the citizens, relations of the family, & the principal officers ... She then embraced him as her own son and named him Caladeevroopaula-Baswapa-Naik, the true Rajah of the Caladee [Ikkeri] kingdom; she prayed that he might reign over the kingdom as happily as his ancestors.[85]

Remarkably, several of these claims presenting Basavappa's succession as rightful—stressing royal descent, formal recognition, and public, familial, and courtly consent—seem to be lacking in the work written by Basavappa himself, the *Śivatattva ratnākara*. Possibly seeking legitimation through a direct relationship with a male ruler, Basavappa instead declares he was both adopted and crowned

[82] Chitnis, *Keḷadi Polity*, 21, 45-7; Swaminathan, *The Nāyakas of Ikkēri*, 124-6; Fryer, *A New Account of East-India and Persia*, 162.

[83] Narasimhachar, "The Keladi Rajas of Ikkeri and Bednur," 189; Chitnis, *Keḷadi Polity*, 40, 57.

[84] NA, VOC, no. 1291, ff. 586v-7v: letter from Cochin to Gentlemen XVII, Nov. 1673.

[85] BL/AAS, MG, no. 6, pt. 11: "Historical account of Beedoonoor or Caladee Samstanum," ff. 80v-1 (original spelling retained).

by Somashekara, who had subsequently instructed his wife Chennammaji to take care of the boy and the kingdom until the former could reign over the latter.[86]

VOC records have several matters to add. The Dutch called Basavappa ("Bassap Neijk") a "supposed" (*suppositijf*) and unlawful king, who descended from a non-royal or "private house" (*particulier huijs*), since he was a nephew of a certain Mannappa Chetti. The latter was probably a brother of Mariyappa "Setti," mentioned as Basavappa's biological father in the *Keḷadinṛpa vijayam*. Judging from their second name, these brothers were merchants. According to the Dutch, Mannappa was a rich, important courtier of Queen Chennammaji, who managed to have his nephew Basavappa installed as king and himself became Ikkeri's most powerful man. However, soon after Chennammaji's death, in July 1698, Mannappa Chetti died as well, reputedly poisoned by rivals who hated him for his greed.

It seems that not long after Chennammaji ascended the throne, the young Basavappa was crowned king. Perhaps born around 1670, Basavappa is already referred to as "the Nayaka" in VOC documents of the late 1670s. During a VOC embassy to Bednur in 1684, he appeared as the official king beside Chennammaji and several times negotiations were conducted, and gifts presented, in his name. The English traveller John Fryer, calling at one of Ikkeri's ports in the mid-1670s, also reported that Basavappa, although a minor, was considered the king.[87] The adoption of this young and distant cousin as Ikkeri's new ruler could have been orchestrated by his uncle Mannappa Chetti to enhance his own power, but for Chennammaji it may have served as a way to legitimise her position, functioning as the king's regent and securing the dynasty's continuity.

After Chennammaji died, Basavappa Nayaka became Ikkeri's sole monarch (r. 1697-1713). Still, in 1703 the Dutch wrote that his father Mariyappa Chetti ("Mariap Chittij") was thought to actually control the kingdom.[88] Basavappa passed away in January 1713 after, as the *Keḷadinṛpa vijayam* has it, crowning his eldest son as Somashekara Nayaka II (r. 1713-39) shortly before his death.[89] The *Keḷadi arasara vaṃśāvaḷi* and VOC records are both somewhat confused in their portrayal of this succession. The chronicle seems to have mixed up the names of Basavappa and

[86] Krishnaswami Aiyangar, *Sources of Vijayanagar History*, 349-50; Krishnamurthy, *Sivatattva Ratnākara of Keladi Basavaraja*, 114-15.

[87] NA, VOC, no. 1406, ff. 913, 920v, 923v, 931v; no.1593, ff. 7-7v, 864, 872v, 876v, 901, 928; no. 1606, f. 98v; no. 1607, f. 90v: diary of mission to Ikkeri, Apr.-May 1684, diary of Commissioner Zwaardekroon's tour in Malabar, Aug.-Oct. 1697, letters from Cochin to Batavia, Dec. 1697, Dec. 1698, instructions of Zwaardekroon to Cochin, May 1698; s'Jacob, *De Nederlanders in Kerala*, 192; Fryer, *A New Account of East-India and Persia*, 57-8, 162.

[88] Shastry, *Goa-Kanara Portuguese Relations*, 222; NA, VOC, no. 1593, ff. 7, 864, 872v, 876, 901; no. 1694, f. 74: letter from Cochin to Batavia, Dec. 1697, diary of Commissioner Zwaardekroon's tour in Malabar, Aug.-Sept. 1697, report on the renewed trade in Ikkeri, Mar. 1703.

[89] Swaminathan, *The Nāyakas of Ikkēri*, 129-31; Chitnis, *Keḷadi Polity*, 22.

Somashekara II's younger brother Virabhadra. If that is really the case, the text confirms that Basavappa was succeeded by his son Somashekara II.[90] Dutch accounts speak of the death of the "state governor of Ikkeri" (*rijcx bestierder van Canara*), named Mariyappa Chetti, on 9 January. His successor is referred to as his son, the "long ignored" (*langh agter de banck verschovene*) Somashekara ("Cham Chanker"), who had now become the "lawful king and regent" (*wettige koningh en regent*).[91] It seems the VOC still associated the deceased Basavappa with his biological father and uncle, Mariyappa and Mannappa Chetti, thought to have forced him on the throne, thus making him a mere governor rather than a rightful king in the eyes of the Dutch. But now that Basavappa's son had been crowned, the family line was apparently considered to have become legitimate.

By all accounts, the following succession, in July 1739, was uneventful. The local chronicles agree with the VOC records that the childless Somashekara II fell ill, passed away at the age of about fifty-five, and was succeeded by Basavappa Nayaka II (r. c. 1739-54), the son of his brother Virabhadra and aged about twenty years old. Dutch reports further mention that Somashekara II had long suffered from a tumour in his lower back, and that already in late 1737 the recently matured Basavappa II was expected to become his successor, rather than another candidate, Somashekara II's sister's son—perhaps another indication of the preference for succession through male lines.[92]

Basavappa II remained childless too and therefore adopted a young boy, Chenna Basavappa Nayaka. None of the sources seem to indicate how or even if he was biologically related to the royal family, except for one short local text stating he was a grandson of Somashekara II's chief minister ("duwan").[93] However, both the main chronicles and VOC documents say that when Chenna Basavappa succeeded his adoptive father around late 1754 (r. c. 1754-7), he was still a minor and Basavappa II's widow Virammaji would serve as his regent, ruling in his name.[94]

[90] BL/AAS, MG, no. 6, pt. 11: "Historical account of Beedoonoor or Caladee Samstanum," ff. 82-2v.

[91] NA, VOC, no. 1838, ff. 178v-9: letter from Cochin to Batavia, Apr. 1713; Coolhaas *et al.*, *Generale Missiven*, vol. VII (The Hague, 1979), 30.

[92] BL/AAS, MG, no. 6, pt. 11: "Historical account of Beedoonoor or Caladee Samstanum," ff. 82v-3; Swaminathan, *The Nāyakas of Ikkēri*, 129, 143-4; Chitnis, *Keḷadi Polity*, 22; NA, VOC, no. 2201, f. 1898; no. 2432, f. 79; no. 2433, ff. 443v-4, 505v; no. 2435, ff. 2233v-4; no. 2446, f. 1098; no. 2461, f. 21v: Cochin diary, Apr. 1730, letters from Cochin to Batavia and Gentlemen XVII, from Basrur to Cochin, Mar.-Apr. 1738, Oct. 1739, report of meeting with Ikkeri's envoy, Dec. 1737, letter from Basrur interpreters, Jan. 1738 (both in "indigenous" diary (*inheems dagregister*), Oct. 1737-Nov. 1738), instructions for mission to Ikkeri, Mar. 1738.

[93] BL/AAS, MG, no. 25, pt. 27: "Memoir of Barkoor," f. 209 (compiled by "the Curneeck Ramiah" in 1800, from a copy provided by the British official Thomas Munro; see f. 207).

[94] BL/AAS, MG, no. 6, pt. 11: "Historical account of Beedoonoor or Caladee Samstanum," ff. 83-3v; Narasimhachar, "The Keladi Rajas of Ikkeri and Bednur," 189; Swaminathan, *The Nāyakas of Ikkēri*, 149-51; Chitnis, *Keḷadi Polity*, 23, 40; NA, VOC, no. 2857, f. 36: letter from Cochin to Batavia, Mar. 1755.

The next and final succession in Ikkeri occurred soon after, when Chenna Basavappa died on 17 July 1757. The *Keḷadi arasara vaṃśāvaḷi* and the *Keḷadinṛpa vijayam* simply declare that he passed away, but according to the Kannada *Haidar nāma*, a work composed in Mysore in the 1780s, this succession was once more accompanied by violence. Supposedly, the widowed Queen Virammaji had fallen in love with an enslaved man, and the ensuing scandal made Chenna Basavappa protest against her loose manners. Rumour had it that the young king was then strangled in bath or buried alive with broken limbs by an athlete who used to soap him. British sources and a local text mention the murder of Chenna Basavappa too and hold the queen responsible.

In any case, the main chronicles go on to say that Virammaji next consulted with the principal courtiers and adopted another boy. This new king—a son of the queen's maternal uncle or her father's brother-in-law—was installed as Somashekara Nayaka III, again under Virammaji's regency (r. 1757-63). One text adds that from now on she reigned in her own name. Dutch records confirm that because of Somashekara III's minority, the queen continued to be the main ruler, assisted by courtiers.[95] Notwithstanding, less than six years later, in January 1763, both the Ikkeri kingdom and the Nayaka dynasty came to an end when Mysore's new ruler Haidar Ali Khan conquered Bednur. The subsequent demise of the royal family is treated in the Epilogue.

Reflecting on Ikkeri's sixteen successions, one notices several patterns and developments. During the approximately 260 years of its existence, seventeen persons ruled the kingdom, meaning that the average period between successions lasted about one and a half decades. This time span is significantly influenced by the four brief reigns in the 1660s-70s and 1750s, which all ended with the king being killed or put in prison. But rulers sitting on the throne for more than a few years were also often removed. In fact, just about half of the monarchs died a natural death at the end of their reign, while the others were all dethroned, with almost nobody surviving the occasion.

95 BL/AAS, MG, no. 6, pt. 11: "Historical account of Beedoonoor or Caladee Samstanum," f. 83v; no. 25, pt. 27: "Memoir of Barkoor," f. 209; Swaminathan, *The Nāyakas of Ikkēri*, 151-2; Chitnis, *Keḷadi Polity*, 23, 40-1, 47, 49, 238; Nair, "Eighteenth-Century Passages to a *History of Mysore*," 81-3; Mahalingam, *Mackenzie Manuscripts*, vol. II, 431; Buchanan, *A Journey from Madras*, vol. III, 128; Lewis Rice, *Mysore and Coorg*, 160; NA, VOC, no. 2928, f. 93; no. 2929, f. 248: secret letter from Cochin to Batavia, Apr. 1758, Cochin proceedings (*resoluties*), June 1758; Godefridus Weijerman, *Memoir of Commandeur Godefridus Weijerman Delivered to His Successor Cornelis Breekpot ...*, ed. P. Groot (Madras, 1910), 53; Adriaan Moens, *Memoir Written in the Year 1781 A.D., by Adriaan Moens ...*, ed. P. Groot (Madras, 1908), 55; Hayavadana Rao, *History of Mysore*, vol. II (Bangalore, 1945), 453-4. See also: Mahalingam, *Mackenzie Manuscripts*, vol. II, 405; Bes, "The Ambiguities of Female Rule in Nayaka South India."

Table 4: Nayakas of Ikkeri, regnal dates, relations to predecessors, and further remarks.

	name	accession date	ending date	relation to predecessors	remarks († = natural death at end of reign)
1	Chaudappa Nayaka	c. 1500	c. 1530?	— (founder)	†, son of village headman
2 a	(Immadi) Sadashiva Nayaka	c. 1530?	c. 1565?	(1st?) son of 1	†, a & b same person, or father and son
b	Dodda Sankanna Nayaka	c. 1565?	c. 1570		
3	Chikka Sankanna Nayaka	c. 1570	1580	1st son of 2, or brother of 2b	killed by 4?
4	Ramaraja Nayaka	c. 1570	c. 1585	brother or nephew of 3 & son of 2(b)	†, co-rule with 3?
5	Venkatappa Nayaka	c. 1585	1629, Nov. 10	brother of 4 & son of 2(b)	†
6	Virabhadra Nayaka	1629	c. 1644	son's son of 5	two brief usurpations by relatives, childless, poisoned by 7?
7	Shivappa Nayaka	c. 1644	late 1660	grand-uncle or 2nd cousin of 6 & son's son of 3	†? 1st of collateral branch
8	(Chikka) Venkatappa Nayaka II	late 1660	1661, Sept. 8	brother of 7 & son's son of 3	co-rule with 7? killed by 9
9	Bhadrappa Nayaka	1661, Sept. 8	mid-1664	nephew of 8 & 1st son of 7	co-rule with 8, childless, poisoned
10	Somashekara Nayaka	mid-1664	1671, Dec.	half-brother of 9 & son of 7	minor at accession, no sons, killed
11	Shivappa Nayaka II	c. early 1672	c. early 1672	great-great-grandson of 5?	minor at accession, dethroned, finger cut
12	Chennammaji	c. early 1673	early 1697	widow of 10	†, female, temporary co-rule with 13
13	Basavappa Nayaka	early 1697	1713, Jan. 9	adopted by 12 & nephew of 9 (9 was brother-in-law of 12)	†, co-rule (partially as minor) with 12

	name	accession date	ending date	relation to predecessors	remarks († = natural death at end of reign)
14	Somashekara Nayaka II	1713, c. Jan. 9	1739, July	1st son of 13	†, no sons
15	(Kiriya) Basavappa Nayaka II	1739, c. July	c. late 1754	half-brother's son of 14	†, no sons
16	Chenna Basavappa Nayaka	c. late 1754	1757, July 17	adopted by 15	minor at accession, killed by 17?
17	Virammaji	1757, c. July 17	1763, Jan.	widow of 15	female, co-rule with adopted cousin Somashekara III, dethroned by Mysore

For sources, see the references in the preceding section, Chapter 1, and the Epilogue.

Only around five rulers were sons of their immediate predecessors and two of these were adopted minors. Some eight kings were (half-)brothers or grandsons of previous rulers, the former group often also being sons of non-immediate predecessors. The other monarchs comprised two widows and one distant cousin. Altogether, five minors ascended the throne, including Basavappa and Somashekara III who commenced their reigns under the regencies of their adoptive mothers Chennammaji and Virammaji respectively. By and large, the recommendations on succession in the *Mahābhārata*, *Arthaśāstra*, and other such texts appear to have been paid little heed.

This is particularly true for the second half of the dynasty's existence. The first 130 years or so seem to have been relatively stable, with just five or six successions—all by sons or brothers of predecessors and with only one assassination—resulting in an average reign of close to a quarter of a century. But when European sources become available, around the 1620s, we observe a rise in regicides, much shorter reigns (averaging about a decade), and unlikely throne occupants. For this latter period, it turns out that Ikkeri's literary texts often portray successions differently from European reports. The local chronicles were apparently written with the descent of the then ruler in mind, ignoring murders, usurpations, or even kings themselves. These texts depict transitions as peaceful and focus on dynastic continuity, frequently referring to periods of joint-rule by consecutive monarchs. They also emphasise the exalted ancestry and qualities of the kings' wives and mothers, stressing the family's royal purity.[96] As said earlier, more or less contemporaneous

[96] For references to rulers' wives and mothers, see BL/AAS, MG, no. 6, pt. 11: "Historical account of Beedoonoor or Caladee Samstanum," ff. 61, 62, 65v, 71, 74, 77v, 80, 81v-2, 83.

inscriptions in the name of different kings are often thought to point to co-rulership as well.[97]

VOC records never speak of joint-rule, with the exception of Venkatappa II and his nephew Bhadrappa, and Chennammaji and her adopted son Basavappa. Instead, these and other external sources emphasise dynastic instability, competition, and violence. Although European materials may have exaggerated or misunderstood succession struggles, it is unlikely these transitions were the harmonious events that local sources purport them to be. Thus, the abovementioned inscriptions could signify competing claims rather than cordial co-rulership.[98] We should therefore ask what picture would emerge of the dynasty's earlier successions if sources other than local ones were available for that period.

In any case, when sources grow more varied, several patterns become apparent. Most striking are the fierce rivalry within the dynasty, the influence of courtiers, some form of participation by the common people, and the interference of neighbouring kingdoms. The latter two factors are occasionally mentioned in sources, but on the whole their effect seems to have been limited. Bijapur was engaged in the assassination of Somashekara I in 1671, Shivappa II's subsequent brief reign, and the rise of Queen Chennammaji. The kingdom of Mysore appears to have been involved, too, as it probably sheltered Shivappa II after his escape from Bednur and later his brother Sadashiva.[99] These were isolated events, however, without far-reaching consequences. As for Ikkeri's common people, in 1662 they allegedly opposed Bhadrappa and tried to have another member of the royal family crowned, all in vain. And according to one chronicle, public consent was sought for Chennammaji's adoption of Basavappa. But these cases also seem to have been exceptions rather than the rule.

Much more constant and influential were conflicts between pretenders to the throne and the role of court factions. These factors were interrelated, heightening their impact. Courtiers could exploit competition within the dynasty, and royal aspirants could take advantage of rivalry among court factions. From the moment the VOC started reporting on successions, in the 1660s, one notices the close and persistent involvement of courtiers. Chapter 3 discusses these people in detail, but the events described above make clear they frequently played a decisive part in the outcome of succession struggles.

97 Swaminathan, *The Nāyakas of Ikkēri*, 36, 164; Chitnis, *Keḷadi Polity*, 14, 45-7; Kuppuram, "Principles of Succession under Keladi Rule," 75-7.

98 See also Chekuri, "Between Family and Empire," 78-9.

99 See the third and last notes of this chapter.

One significant element in these clashes was the coexistence of two opposed dynastic branches, which had its roots in the dynasty's early phase. When King Chikka Sankanna died in 1580, possibly by murder, his descendants saw the throne being transferred to Chikka Sankanna's brother or nephew and his close relatives. Chikka Sankanna's grandson Shivappa must have literally felt passed over and around 1644 he acquired the throne for his line, probably by force, and thus initiated what is generally called the collateral branch. With one very brief exception, members of the other line never ruled again, but they remained threatening rivals for a substantial period. This was probably an important cause for the dynastic crises in the 1660s and 1670s, no matter how hard court chroniclers attempted to write it out of their accounts. Only the extinction of nearly all members of one of the branches around 1673 brought this destabilising competition to a brutal end.

Nayakas of Tanjavur

With regard to both the way successions proceeded and the availability of sources, Tanjavur's Nayakas stand in contrast with their Ikkeri namesakes. Between the installation of this dynasty by Vijayanagara in the 1530s and its dethronement by Madurai in 1673, probably just five men ruled, perhaps later followed by a brief reign of the house's last scion (see table 5 at the end of this section).[100] Few sources discuss the four successions in question. Local literary works and inscriptions can be corroborated with only a small number of European accounts, most importantly Jesuit and Danish reports.

Neither contemporary texts nor modern historiography seem to have treated the principles of succession in Nayaka Tanjavur in much detail. Based on the successions themselves, modern scholarship simply has concluded that the transfer of royal power was hereditary. *Yuvarājas* (heirs apparent) are thought to have been nominated quite a long time before they ascended the throne, until then functioning as co-rulers. Voluntary abdication to make space for successors is said to have been common practice.[101]

[100] For genealogical trees of Tanjavur's Nayakas, see: S. Srikantha Sastri, "Development of Sanskrit Literature under Vijayanagara," in S. Krishnaswami Aiyangar *et al.* (eds), *Vijayanagara Sexcentenary Commemoration Volume* (Dharwar, 1936), 324; Krishnaswami Aiyangar, *Sources of Vijayanagar History*, 254; Vijayaraghavacharya, *Epigraphical Glossary on Inscriptions*, 101; N. Venkata Rao, *The Southern School in Telugu Literature* (Madras, 1978), 22; Pradeep Chakravarthy and Vikram Sathyanathan, *Thanjavur: A Cultural History* (New Delhi, 2010), 188; Sewell, *The Historical Inscriptions of Southern India*, 394.

[101] Vriddhagirisan, *The Nayaks of Tanjore*, 169.

Little is known with certainty about the individual successions, even with respect to dates. But in most cases, the king appears to have died a natural death after a long reign and been succeeded by an adult son without much disorder at court. That is at least the picture presented by inscriptions and the main literary works produced in the kingdom. The latter include the earlier mentioned *Raghunāthanāyakābhyudayamu*, *Raghunāthābhyudayamu*, and *Tañjāvūri āndhra rājula caritra*—as well as the Sanskrit poem *Sāhitya ratnākara*, dealing with the dynasty's third ruler Raghunatha Nayaka and written by Yagnanarayana Dikshita, son of the well-known Minister Govinda Dikshita. According to these texts, only four men sat on the throne. The dynastic founder Shevappa Nayaka (r. c. 1530s-70s) was succeeded by his son Achyutappa Nayaka, who was followed by his son Raghunatha Nayaka, whose place was taken by his son Vijayaraghava Nayaka.

As claimed by the literary works and suggested by simultaneous inscriptions of different rulers, each king appointed his son as *yuvarāja* early in his reign, whereupon a period of joint rule began in which the father gradually passed royal duties to his son. The *Sāhitya ratnākara* states that Achyutappa (r. c. 1570s-97?) even formally abdicated, had his son Raghunatha crowned (r. c. 1597?-1626), and retired to a religious life. The Icelander Jón Ólafsson, staying in Tanjavur in the early 1620s as servant of the Danes at the port of Tranquebar, also relates that the then king (Raghunatha) had nominated a son as his heir apparent. As Ólafsson writes, portraits of the ruler and his intended successor even hung in the Danish church at Tranquebar.[102]

There are also sources, south Indian and European, that present a different picture of some successions. Several Jesuit letters confirm that Achyutappa resigned to make way for Raghunatha, in or shortly before 1597, but they also declare that Raghunatha was not the eldest son. Reportedly, his anonymous elder brother had been imprisoned during his father's reign and was killed soon after his brother's accession. With regard to the next succession, Jesuit, Dutch, and Danish accounts as well as some south Indian texts say Raghunatha also had several sons, including Ramabhadra and the younger Vijayaraghava. Additionally, Danish documents of the 1620s and early 1630s indicate that Ramabhadra, rather than the often mentioned Vijayaraghava, was the *yuvarāja* and became king when his father passed away on 25 November 1626 (see illustration 3).

Ramabhadra's reign is also specifically mentioned in several less well-known local texts and a Dutch work of the 1750s. Moreover, although not giving personal

[102] Krishnaswami Aiyangar, *Sources of Vijayanagar History*, 255, 269-70, 273, 285-6, 323-4; Vriddhagirisan, *The Nayaks of Tanjore*, 34-5, 57-66, 125-30; Heras, *The Aravidu Dynasty of Vijayanagara*, vol. I, 287, 399-402; Jón Ólafsson, *The Life of the Icelander Jón Ólafsson: Traveller to India*, vol. II, ed. Bertha S. Phillpotts, Richard Temple, and Lavinia Mary Anstrey (London, 1932), 114.

Illustration 3: Address of a letter of April 1631 by Christian IV of Denmark to "The mighty high-born prince, lord Rambadro Naico [Ramabhadra Nayaka], king of Taniura [Tanjavur], our specially good friend," *Rigsarkivet*, Copenhagen, *Den Ledreborgske Dokumentsamling (1466-1701)*, no. 89 (11 April 1631) (photo by P.S. Ramanujam, courtesy *Rigsarkivet*).

names, contemporary VOC records report that on 24 January 1631, the Nayaka of Tanjavur died after a reign of three years. If correct, this could refer to neither Raghunatha nor Vijayaraghava and must have denoted Ramabhadra. The Dutch account further claims that this ruler had earlier blinded his elder brother—who subsequently poisoned himself—and was now succeeded by a younger brother of fifteen or sixteen years old. This should have been Vijayaraghava, who supposedly was a minor when he ascended the throne. However, Jesuit materials declare it actually was Vijayaraghava who around 1630 blinded two brothers—in all likelihood including Ramabhadra—and subsequently put them in jail.[103] In sum,

[103] Saulière, "The Revolt of the Southern Nayaks" [pt. 2], 178; P.S. Ramanujam, *Unheard Voices: A Tranquebarian Stroll* (Odense, 2021), ch. 1 (fig. 1.6); *Rigsarkivet*, Copenhagen (hereafter RA), *Den Ledreborgske Dokumentsamling (1466-1701)* (The Ledreborg document collection), no. 89: letter from Christian IV to Ramabhadra Nayaka, 11 Apr. 1631; Johann Heinrich Schlegel, *Samlung zur Dänischen Geschichte, Münzkenntniß, Oekonomie und Sprache*, vol. I, pt. 4 (Copenhagen, 1773), 162-3; "The Indo-Danish Connect," *The Hindu* (3 May 2015) (discussing research by P.S. Ramanujam); NA, VOC, no. 1103, ff. 131-1v: letter from Pulicat to Batavia, Feb. 1631; Mac Leod, *De Oost-Indische Compagnie*, vol. I, 492;

while sources do not fully agree, it seems certain that Ramabhadra succeeded his father Raghunatha first and reigned over Tanjavur (1626-31) before his brother Vijayaraghava took over (1631-73), and that either one or both of these transitions was accompanied by violence.

After a long reign, Vijayaraghava, the dynasty's last real king, died in 1673 on the battlefield together with his eldest son Mannarudeva (or Mannarudasa) when Tanjavur was besieged by the Nayakas of Madurai. Mannarudeva had been released from jail by his father just before this battle. It was said he was imprisoned after inappropriate advances towards a daughter of Minister Govinda Dikshita.[104] But given this dynasty's tradition of appointing *yuvarājas* early and letting them co-rule, and Vijayaraghava's advanced age at this time, one would think there was a more pressing reason to lock up what must have been the heir apparent. Perhaps this was another example of a Tanjavur Nayaka preventing a possible rival from taking his place, in this case his own son.

Anyhow, Madurai's invasion virtually terminated Tanjavur's Nayaka house as only an infant prince—named Chengamaladasa and probably a younger son of Vijayaraghava—managed to escape from the siege. The dynasty's last surviving member, this boy perhaps briefly sat on Tanjavur's throne two years later and he certainly played an important role in the kingdom's transfer to the Bhonsle house. But for a discussion of the Nayakas' fall and the exploits of Chengamaladasa and his descendants, see the Epilogue.

An analysis of the successions in Nayaka Tanjavur reveals substantial differences between how they are depicted in the main court chronicles and in other sources, including European materials—at least from the late sixteenth century onward. The former texts portray Raghunatha and Vijayaraghava as rightful successors and ignore Raghunatha's anonymous brother and Ramabhadra. One historian has

Srinivasan, "Some Interesting Aspects of the Maratha Rule," 45; S. Raju (ed.), *Tañcai Marāṭṭiyar Ceppēṭukaḷ-50* (Tanjavur, 1983), 112 and subsequent pages; Heras, *The Aravidu Dynasty of Vijayanagara*, vol. I, 399-402; Vriddhagirisan, *The Nayaks of Tanjore*, 127-8; Sathianathaier, *Tamiḻaham in the 17th Century*, 59-60; BL/AAS, MG, no. 1, pt. 6: "A brief account of the ancient Rajahs in the Solah Dhesam," f. 38; no. 1, pt. 8: "The Cheritee or actions of the Vadaka-Rajahs of Tanjore, Trichinopully & Madura," f. 72; MM, no. 110, pt. 7: "The Charythy of the Vadoka Raja of Tonjore, Trinchunnapully & Madura," ff. 3-4; no. 118, pt. 74: "Names of the Rayers who have reigned Techanautterady," f. 3; Hickey, *The Tanjore Mahratta Principality*, 36-7; *Beknopte historie*, 96. Not mentioning its sources, the latter Dutch work gives the following succession dates: Achyutappa, 1553; Raghunatha, 1588; Ramabhadra, 1626; Vijayaraghava, 1629. See also: Valentijn, *Oud en Nieuw Oost-Indiën*, vol. 5, 1st book, 4, which mentions "Ramapattiza" but places him before Achyutappa. Several less well-known local texts also have it that Achyutappa was not Shevappa's son but his younger brother.

104 Vriddhagirisan, *The Nayaks of Tanjore*, 153 (including n. 16); Narayana Rao, Shulman, and Subrahmanyam, *Symbols of Substance*, 306 (n. 3).

Table 5: Nayakas of Tanjavur, regnal dates, relations to predecessors, and further remarks.

	name	accession date	ending date	relation to predecessors	remarks († = natural death at end of or after reign)
1	Shevappa Nayaka	c. 1530s	c. 1570s	— (founder)	†, former courtier at Vijayanagara, married into Tuluva house
2	Achyutappa Nayaka	c. 1570s	c. 1597?	son of 1	†, co-rule with 1? abdicated
3	Raghunatha Nayaka	c. 1597?	1626, Nov. 25	(2nd?) son of 2	†, co-rule with 2? killed brother?
4	Ramabhadra Nayaka	1626, c. Nov. 25	1631, Jan. 24	(2nd?) son of 3	blinded elder brother? jailed and blinded by 5?
5	Vijayaraghava Nayaka	1631, c. Jan. 24	1673, Sept. 29	brother of 4, (3rd?) son of 3	minor at accession? jailed or blinded 4, another elder brother, and 1st son? killed by Madurai
6	Chengamaladasa	c. 1675?	c. 1675?	later son of 5	installed and dethroned as a minor by Ekoji Bhonsle? reign unsure

For sources, see the references in the preceding section, Chapter 1, and the Epilogue.

fiercely criticised Jesuit observations as being unreliable,[105] but as in Ikkeri, court chronicles were written from the author's or commissioner's point of view. In the case of Tanjavur's Nayakas, such works were compiled by Vijayaraghava himself and by the court poets Ramabhadramba and Yagnanarayana Dikshita, whose patron was Raghunatha. It is unlikely these texts would mention opposition from the rulers' brothers, let alone the blinding or killing of these brothers.

Therefore, as Jesuit, Danish, and Dutch documents indicate, competition probably did arise between pretenders on several occasions. Even so, those rivalries appear to have been limited to what most Indian treatises on statecraft consider rightful heirs to the throne: the king's sons. Furthermore, these fraternal struggles were settled relatively fast—if brutally—seemingly without widespread violence at court or the involvement of neighbouring kingdoms. For want of detailed sources, little, if anything, can be said about the role of courtiers in those events. But compared to their Ikkeri counterparts, Tanjavur's Nayakas formed a stable dynasty, as almost all rulers occupied a secure position until their death and were succeeded by a son. Further—if we discount the infant Chengamaladasa—they ruled for an average of around twenty-eight years. That was about twice the length

105 Vriddhagirisan, *The Nayaks of Tanjore*, 59-61.

of the average reign in Ikkeri, and also in Tanjavur under its next dynasty, the Bhonsles.

Bhonsles of Tanjavur

The Maratha Bhonsle house of Tanjavur reigned from 1676, when the Bijapur General Ekoji assumed power, to 1855, when the last ruler, Shivaji II, passed away. The dynasty was then pensioned off by the British colonial government on the pretext that there was no direct male successor. But in 1773 already, King Tuljaji II was removed for three years by the Nawab (ruler) of Arcot. The latter was backed by the British, who in the last decades of the eighteenth century grew increasingly powerful in Tanjavur and in the 1790s even took over its administration.[106]

Therefore, this study only considers the successions until Tuljaji II's accession in 1763, after which the Bhonsles soon lost much of their autonomy. From the 1670s to the 1760s, eight men and one woman ruled the kingdom (see table 6 towards the end of this section).[107] For almost all their successions, both Indian and European sources are available, including court chronicles, Dutch accounts, and a few nineteenth-century series of dynastic portrait murals, one of which includes captions mentioning the relationships between consecutive monarchs (see illustration 4).

There seem to be very few works, contemporary or modern, that refer to rules of succession under Tanjavur's Bhonsles. One rare case is an anonymous Tamil chronicle collected and translated in the early 1810s, titled "The history of the Tonjore Rajas." According to a passage in this text, the "rule of the law" dictated that a successor be the son of a real queen rather than of a so-called sword-wife (*khāṇḍārāṇī*). The latter held not the king's hand but a royal sword during her wedding, and in a sense was married to this sword rather than the monarch. Sword-wives, and their offspring, had a lower status than queens and their progeny. Referring to the rule of Ekoji II (1735-6), the chronicle explains that even though the conduct of this son of a queen was considered inappropriate,

[106] Subramanian, *The Maratha Rajas of Tanjore*, 61-76; Srinivasan, *Maratha Rule in the Carnatic*, 301-41; Subrahmanyam, *Penumbral Visions*, 151-2, 156-75, 183-5.

[107] For (partly outdated) genealogical trees of Tanjavur's Bhonsles, see: Bhosale, *Rajah Serfoji – II*, 152-3; Srinivasan, *Maratha Rule in the Carnatic*, 30; Tryambakayajvan, *The Perfect Wife*, 13, 15; Pratap Sinh Serfoji Raje Bhosle, *Contributions of Thanjavur Maratha Kings* (2nd edition, Chennai, 2017), 21, 302-3; *Beknopte historie*, between 76-7; Chakravarthy and Sathyanathan, *Thanjavur: A Cultural History*, 189; Sewell, *The Historical Inscriptions of Southern India*, 395; idem, *List of Inscriptions*, 193; T. Venkasami Row, *A Manual of the District of Tanjore, in the Madras Presidency* (Madras, 1883), 764.

Illustration 4: Murals depicting Sarabhoji Bhonsle I (left) and Sujana Bai Bhonsle (right) of Tanjavur, Subrahmanya shrine, Brihadishvara Temple, Tanjavur, mid-19th century (left image: photo by Pulavar N. Thyagarajan, source: George Michell and Indira Viswanathan Peterson, *The Great Temple at Thanjavur: One Thousand Years, 1010-2010* (Mumbai: Marg Publications, 2010), 30, courtesy The Marg Foundation; right image: courtesy Clare Arni).

his reign was preferred over that of his elder half-brothers who were born of sword-wives.[108]

Further, some modern studies discuss principles of succession under this house, but, as with other dynasties, this is based on observed practices rather than contemporary normative texts. In brief, it is thought that rulers were preferably succeeded by their eldest son (previously functioning as *yuvarāja* or heir apparent), or else another son, a younger brother, a prince adopted from a collateral dynastic branch, or the chief queen.[109] Literature dealing with successions among other

[108] BL/AAS, MT, class III, no. 32: "The History of the Tonjore Rajas," ff. 91v-2. See also: BL/AAS, MG, no. 4, pt. 9: "History of Tanjore," f. 220 (probably translated from a Marathi text); Subramanian, *The Maratha Rajas of Tanjore*, 23. For sword-wives in Tanjavur, see: Vidayanand Swami Shrivastavya, "Are Maratha-Rajput Marriages Morganatic?," in Usha Sharma (ed.), *Marriage in Indian Society: From Tradition to Modernity* (New Delhi, 2005), vol. I, 172-3; Gadgil, "The Bṛhadīśvara Temple Inscription of the Bhosales of Tanjore," 300. One tradition has it that one of the wives of Vijayanagara's Krishna Raya, a daughter of Orissa's Gajapati ruler called Lakshmi, was also married to the emperor's sword. See Sistla, "Allegory in Telugu Poetry during the Time of Krishnadevaraya," 104.

[109] K. Manamalar, "Administration and Social Life under the Mahrathas of Thanjavur" (unpublished dissertation, Bharathidasan University, 1995), 12-14; Gadgil, "The Bṛhadīśvara Temple Inscription of the Bhosales of Tanjore," 299.

Maratha houses, in western India, broadly agrees with these regulations as well as with ideas advocated in general Indian discourses on politics, requiring the king to be succeeded by sons rather than brothers, by elder rather than younger relatives, by men rather than women, and so on.[110]

During the initial phase of Tanjavur's Bhonsle house, these notions were well adhered to. The dynasty's founder Ekoji (r. 1676-84) was succeeded by three sons one after another. Dutch records report that on 25 December 1684, after a period of illness, Ekoji summoned his eldest son Shahaji (r. 1684-1711) before him, transferred "all his jewels, riches, etc." to him, and died three hours later. Some time before, still according to the VOC, the sick king had already passed the actual rule of the kingdom to his son. This may account for the statement that Ekoji had abdicated in favour of Shahaji, found in several literary texts, such as the *Śāhendra vilāsa* (I 98), a Sanskrit poem by Sridhara Venkatesa (alias Ayyaval) glorifying Shahaji's life.

Another local work, the *Tañcai marāṭṭiya maṉṉar varalāṟu*, says that while the new king resided in Tanjavur town, his brothers Sarabhoji (or Serfoji) and Tukkoji (or Tuljaji) became governors in the kingdom's northern and southern regions respectively, seated at Tiruvidaimaruthur (north-east of Kumbakonam) and Mahadevipatnam (perhaps fifteen miles south of Adirampatnam). According to some literature Shahaji was about twelve to fourteen years old when he ascended the throne, but VOC documents declare that his age was thought to be nineteen. In any case, as both local and Dutch sources mention, from the beginning the young king was assisted by powerful courtiers and his influential mother Dipamba Bai.[111]

The latter seems to have played an important role in the next succession too, which occurred, as VOC letters state, after Shahaji died on 28 September 1711 at the approximate age of forty-five, having long suffered from dropsy, tuberculosis, and other ailments. Since Shahaji had no children, the elder of his two full brothers, Sarabhoji, was placed on the throne, showered with 10,000 *pardao* coins, and thus installed as the new ruler (r. 1711-29), upon which all the kingdom's chiefs and

110 Burling, *The Passage of Power*, 58-61.

111 NA, VOC, no. 1398, f. 406v; no. 1411, ff. 96v, 103-4v, 303-3v: letters from Nagapattinam and Pulicat to Batavia, Oct. 1684, Feb. 1685, "register of news," Jan. 1685; BL/AAS, MT, class III, no. 87: "The historycal account of the Tonjore" (*Bhoṃsale vaṃśa caritra*), ff. 81v (?), 95; class III, no. 32: "The History of the Tonjore Rajas," ff. 90v-1; Śrīdhara Venkatēśa, *Śāhendra Vilāsa*, 1, 4-5, 7; Michael Christian Linderman, "Charity's Venue: Representing Indian Kingship in the Monumental Pilgrim Rest Houses of the Maratha Rajas of Tanjavur, 1761-1832" (unpublished dissertation, University of Pennsylvania, 2009), 158; Subramanian, *The Maratha Rajas of Tanjore*, 18-19, 28; Srinivasan, *Maratha Rule in the Carnatic*, 171-2, 228; Velcheru Narayana Rao and David Shulman (eds), *Classical Telugu Poetry: An Anthology* (New Delhi, 2002), 354; Bhosale, *Rajah Serfoji – II*, 24-5.

officers came to swear allegiance to him.[112] The court chronicle *Bhoṃsale vaṃśa caritra* and other works portray this succession as a peaceful event, proceeding with the consent of the third brother, Tukkoji, who was allegedly only two years younger. Literary texts and an inscription from 1718 state that the latter even functioned as co-ruler.[113]

Upon Sarabhoji's accession, the Tanjavur court informed the Dutch that Tukkoji had indeed been given control over some southern coastal districts, as well as 1,000 horsemen and 2,000 foot soldiers, to enable him to maintain his state.[114] As it turned out, however, he was discontented with his brother's succession and rumours said he had tried to prevent it.[115] After the throne passed to Sarabhoji, Tukkoji at first apparently accepted the situation and maintained more or less cordial relations with his brother, which the Dutch ascribed to the skills of their mother Dipamba Bai. By now of advanced age, she was said to command great respect at court while making continuous efforts to keep her sons on friendly terms. Her prominence also transpires from local literary works, mentioning her as a patron of art and learning, and her entitlement to the revenues of certain districts.[116] Yet, in the subsequent years the brothers fell out with each other, arguing about land rents and revenues, and in 1723 Tukkoji demanded half of the kingdom. Sarabhoji's refusal had Tukkoji retreat to a fort near Adirampatnam in Tanjavur's far south (possibly the abovementioned Mahadevipatnam) and gather around him other opponents to the king.

112 NA, VOC, no. 1329, f. 1172v; no. 1803, ff. 98, 302v-3, 467-7v: report of mission to Tanjavur, Jan. 1677, letters from Nagapattinam to Batavia, July, Sept., Nov. 1711.

113 BL/AAS, MT, class III, no. 87: "The historycal account of the Tonjore," ff. 83, 94v, 95v; class III, no. 32: "The History of the Tonjore Rajas," ff. 90v-1; Subramanian, *The Maratha Rajas of Tanjore*, 26; Srinivasan, *Maratha Rule in the Carnatic*, 230; Bhosale, *Rajah Serfoji – II*, 28; Sewell, *List of Inscriptions*, 2; idem, *The Historical Inscriptions of Southern India*, 294. A few south Indian texts say Shahaji nominated as his successor one Anna Sahib, a son of Tukkoji. But their mother (Dipamba Bai) intervened and had Sarabhoji placed on the throne. See BL/AAS, MG, no. 1, pt. 8: "The Cheritee or actions of the Vadaka-Rajahs of Tanjore, Trichinopully & Madura," f. 73; MM, no. 110, pt. 7: "The Charythy of the Vadoka Raja of Tonjore, Trinchunnapully & Madura," f. 7.

114 The districts presented to Tukkoji were Kivalur, Katchanam, and what is perhaps Kadambadi ("Kadaramban"), all in the vicinity of (but excluding) Nagapattinam. See NA, VOC, no. 1803, ff. 467, 469: letter from Nagapattinam to Batavia, Nov. 1711.

115 Already in 1710, the Dutch reported there were conflicts between Shahaji, Sarabhoji, and Tukkoji, causing some political instability. See NA, VOC, no. 1796, f. 119: letter from Nagapattinam to Batavia, Aug. 1710.

116 She also managed to reconcile Ekoji with his half-brother Shivaji in the late 1670s. For Dipamba Bai, see: P.K. Gode, "Raghunātha, a Protégé of Queen Dīpābāi of Tanjore, and His Works – Between A. D. 1675-1712," in idem, *Studies in Indian Literary History*, vol. II (Bombay, 1954), 393-7; idem, "The Identification of Raghunātha, the Protégé of Queen Dīpābāi of Tanjore and His Contact with Saint Rāmadāsa – Between A. D. 1648 and 1682," in idem, 414; Tryambakayajvan, *The Perfect Wife*, 14, 20-2.

When two years later Sarabhoji, having no legitimate children, adopted a boy—apparently to become his heir—Tukkoji protested, claiming that according to an earlier agreement his own sons would succeed to the throne. Ignored again, he now retired from court altogether, although he still had the decency to ask Sarabhoji for permission to leave. This was granted with all due honours and Tukkoji then straightaway departed with his troops. But when the king came to know that his brother was about to enter the Bijapur sultanate, looking to team up with other Maratha bands, Sarabhoji went after him in an attempt to solve their differences. Although Tukkoji tried to evade an encounter, his brother eventually tracked him down near the town of Tiruvarur and managed to make him return to the court voluntarily. This seems to have soothed the dispute only temporarily, because soon the Dutch reported that the succession struggle had not terminated.[117]

A few years later, on 17 November 1729, Sarabhoji passed away, aged around sixty. Hereupon Tukkoji finally ascended the throne (r. 1729-35), with, as VOC records say, the usual ceremonies and his subjects' consent. But these documents also state that the court was not in full agreement on Tukkoji's right to succeed, several courtiers preferring the abovementioned boy adopted by Sarabhoji. Even though the succession dispute between Sarabhoji and Tukkoji had been settled some years earlier, the child was considered the rightful successor by both the deceased king and a large court faction. Still, Tukkoji became the new ruler, supported in exchange for 3.5 million *rupees* by Arcot's Nawab Sa'adatullah Khan, who was campaigning in the region to enforce peace between Tanjavur, Madurai, and Ramnad, and collect tribute.[118] In contrast to the Dutch accounts, local chronicles present this succession again as largely harmonious, as they do with the next transition in 1735.[119]

On 23 July of that year, at the age of about sixty-four, Tukkoji died and was succeeded by his eldest son born of an official queen, Baba Sahib alias Ekoji II (r. 1735-6). Like his father, Ekoji II had already been given control over some lands prior to his accession to the throne, perhaps denoting his status as *yuvarāja*, but again this had led to disagreements about revenues between the king and his son.

[117] NA, VOC, no. 1803, ff. 467-9; no. 1819, f. 42v; no. 1849, ff. 319v-20; no. 1997, ff. 22-3, 18 (2nd numeration); no. 2031, ff. 436-8, 1359; no. 2043, f. 144v; no. 8844, f. 45: letters from Nagapattinam to Batavia, Nov. 1711, May 1712, Aug. 1714, May, Sept. 1723, May, Aug. 1725, May, Oct. 1726; *Beknopte historie*, 97. See also Subrahmanyam, *Penumbral Visions*, 149-50.

[118] NA, VOC, no. 1329, f. 1172v; no. 2147, f. 4833v; no. 2166, ff. 69-71: report of mission to Tanjavur, Jan. 1677, Nagapattinam proceedings and letter from there to Batavia, Mar. 1730; *Beknopte historie*, 97; Subrahmanyam, *Penumbral Visions*, 150-1. See also Love, *Vestiges of Old Madras*, vol. II, 251.

[119] BL/AAS, MT, class III, no. 87: "The historycal account of the Tonjore," ff. 95v-6, 97v-8; class III, no. 32: "The History of the Tonjore Rajas," ff. 91-2; Subramanian, *The Maratha Rajas of Tanjore*, 40, 42-3; Srinivasan, *Maratha Rule in the Carnatic*, 236, 242-3; Bhosale, *Rajah Serfoji – II*, 29-32.

Before Ekoji II could now ascend the throne himself, however, he had to undergo a test—so Lutheran missionaries reported—where he was blindfolded and had to select one of three objects: rice, coal, and a dagger.[120] Although he picked the last, considered a bad omen as it represented war and calamities, Ekoji II commenced his reign on 14 August. As VOC documents specifically mention, the Nawab of Arcot did not object to Ekoji II's succession, indicating that this kingdom's role in Tukkoji's enthronement was not a one-time affair.[121]

The rule of Ekoji II marked the beginning of a short, atypical period of dynastic instability. Several brief reigns followed each other in quick succession, seeing one widow and two low-born princes ascending the throne, one of the latter with considerable aggression. On 1 August 1736, less than a year after his coronation, Ekoji II passed away without issue, leaving behind, as Dutch records say, a half-brother born of a concubine and two pregnant wives. The eldest of these queens, Sujana Bai, was installed as regent (r. 1736-8), but this was soon contested by courtiers supporting Ekoji II's half-brother, perhaps named Siddhoji Dada. This dispute made some Arcot troops, camping nearby, march to the capital to collect tribute and force the court factions to agree that, until a new heir was born, Queen Sujana Bai would reign, albeit with the half-brother's assistance.[122] Local texts also speak of one Siddhoji—possibly Ekoji II's half-brother referred to by the Dutch—mentioning him as a very important courtier, but they ignore both any rivalry with Sujana Bai and Arcot's role in solving it.[123]

With respect to the next two successions, not only VOC documents but also court chronicles point to accompanying conflicts, considering the first transition a usurpation. Yet, the sources give divergent and sometimes slightly confused accounts and

120 This seems to have been an ancient ritual for newly selected kings. See Gonda, *Ancient Indian Kingship*, 92.

121 NA, VOC, no. 1329, f. 1172v; no. 2350, ff. 118, 438-41, 578-9; no. 2351, ff. 3994-5; no. 8866, f. 129: report of mission to Tanjavur, Jan. 1677, letter from Nagapattinam to Batavia, Aug. 1735, Nagapattinam proceedings, Jan., Apr., Oct. 1735; Axel Utz, "Cultural Exchange, Imperialist Violence, and Pious Missions: Local Perspectives from Tanjavur and Lenape Country, 1720-1760" (unpublished dissertation, Pennsylvania State University, 2011), 35; *Beknopte historie*, 97-8; Subrahmanyam, *Penumbral Visions*, 153.

122 NA, VOC, no. 2387, ff. 94-5; no. 2443, f. 2690; no. 2538, f. 1619: letter from Nagapattinam to Batavia, Sept. 1736, final report of Coromandel *Commandeur* Elias Guillot, Sept. 1738, instructions for mission to the Tanjavur king (in Nagapattinam proceedings), May 1741. See also: *Beknopte historie*, 98; Utz, "Cultural Exchange, Imperialist Violence, and Pious Missions," 35; Subrahmanyam, *Penumbral Visions*, 153.

123 BL/AAS, MT, class III, no. 87: "The historycal account of the Tonjore," ff. 98v-9; class III, no. 32: "The History of the Tonjore Rajas," ff. 92-2v; Subramanian, *The Maratha Rajas of Tanjore*, 43; Srinivasan, *Maratha Rule in the Carnatic*, 243; Bhosale, *Rajah Serfoji – II*, 32-3.

historians disagree on the most likely course of events. For both successions, we first examine the VOC records and then discuss how other sources differ from them.

The reign of Queen Sujana Bai was, again, short-lived and ended violently. As the Dutch reported, in June 1738 a pretender to the throne approached Tanjavur with troops. He declared he was Shahaji, the aforementioned adopted son of Sarabhoji (r. 1711-29), and that his right to succeed his father had been denied by Sarabhoji's brother Tukkoji (r. 1729-35). The latter had claimed that this boy was actually the son of a Brahmin, presented by one of Sarabhoji's queens as her own child, while in fact she had given birth to a daughter. At his accession, Tukkoji's son Ekoji II (r. 1735-6) had ordered that the boy be killed, but it was said his executioner had spared him and entrusted him to the care of a local chief outside Tanjavur. Now the pretender had come back to take what was rightfully his. When he was nearing the capital, Sujana Bai's forces refused to fight, thinking his army was stronger. Moreover, all the queen's courtiers, except for her aide Siddhoji Dada, went over to her opponent. Thus, in July he took Tanjavur without resistance, ascended the throne as Shahaji II (r. 1738-9), and had Siddhoji and some supporters murdered. Sujana Bai, in order to escape a dishonourable death, poisoned herself.[124]

Court chronicles such as the *Bhoṃsale vaṃśa caritra* and "The history of the Tonjore Rajas" have much to add. One or both of these works have it that the boy adopted by Sarabhoji was the son of a Shudra woman—not a Brahmin—and had been killed by Sarabhoji himself when his identity was discovered. The pretender who dethroned Queen Sujana Bai was just a young betel-keeping servant born of an enslaved or washer woman and exploited by a courtier named Koyaji Kattigai, who was displeased with Sujana Bai's reign. According to the chronicles, this courtier pretended that the betel-keeping servant was Sarabhoji's adopted son and convinced various parties, including the British and the Dutch ("Volandan"), to support him financially in order to raise troops. Koyaji Kattigai also allied himself with the commander of Tanjavur town, Sayyid, and thus managed to enthrone his protégé as Shahaji II. Some local texts seem to emphasise this king's illegitimate status by saying that, since he supposedly had spent years hiding in the woods, people mockingly called him "Kattu Raja," or jungle king, which was a mark of contempt.[125]

[124] NA, VOC, no. 2427, ff. 425, 435v, 441v; no. 2442, ff. 608-10, 633; no. 2443, ff. 1963, 2035, 2690-1; no. 2538, f. 1619: Nagapattinam proceedings extract, July 1738, letter from Porto Novo to Nagapattinam, July 1738, letter from the Tanjavur court to Nagapattinam (in Nagapattinam proceedings extract), July 1738, letters from Nagapattinam to Batavia, June, Sept. 1738, instructions for mission to the Tanjavur king, May 1741, final report of Guillot, Sept. 1738; *Beknopte historie*, 98.

[125] BL/AAS, MT, class III, no. 87: "The historycal account of the Tonjore," ff. 97-7v, 99-100v; class III, no. 32: "The History of the Tonjore Rajas," ff. 92v-4v; MG, no. 4, pt. 9: "History of Tanjore," f. 219; Orme Collection, India series (hereafter OI), no. I, pt. 27: "Morratoe kings of Tanjore" [3rd pt.], f. 244.

There is considerable confusion about Shahaji II's reign. Some sources claim he actually ruled for two brief periods, securing his second accession to the throne with French help. Other works state that Queen Sujana Bai was first succeeded by one Saiyaji, a legitimate son of Tukkoji, before Shahaji II became king. It has also been suggested that Saiyaji and Shahaji II were the same person.[126] However, no Saiyaji is mentioned in either the chronicles or Dutch documents, nor does he figure in two portrait galleries of the Bhonsle house: one in the Subrahmanya shrine on the grounds of Tanjavur's Brihadishvara Temple, and the other in the audience hall of the royal palace. As for Shahaji II, while he does figure in the *Bhoṃsale vaṃśa caritra*, compiled around 1800—albeit as some kind of usurper—he too is ignored in both sets of dynastic murals, executed in the nineteenth century. This is particularly obvious in the temple series, where Sujana Bai's portrait is directly followed by that of Pratapasimha (r. 1739-63), suggesting he succeeded her.[127] Apparently, the later Bhonsles did not consider Shahaji II and the possible Saiyaji as members of their dynasty, or at least did not recognise their reigns as rightful.[128]

In any case, Shahaji II occupied the throne for an even shorter period than Sujana Bai. According to the VOC, he used opium and spent all his time pursuing "sensualities" (*wellustigheeden*). Moreover, he soon got into disputes with the town-commander Sayyid, as well as with the French and Arcot. A general of that kingdom, Chanda Sahib, had arrived to collect tribute from the new king, who seemed unwilling to pay. At the same time, the French wanted permission to settle at the port of Karaikal, promised to them in return for financial assistance. But Shahaji II argued he had already conquered Tanjavur without their backing, so there was no need for compensation. Consequently, as the Dutch wrote in around

See also: Subrahmanyam, *Penumbral Visions*, 154; Subramanian, *The Maratha Rajas of Tanjore*, 40, 43-6; Srinivasan, *Maratha Rule in the Carnatic*, 235-6, 243-8; Bhosale, *Rajah Serfoji – II*, 33-4; Hemingway, *Tanjore Gazetteer*, vol. I, 44-5.

126 Srinivasan, *Maratha Rule in the Carnatic*, 242-8; Subramanian, *The Maratha Rajas of Tanjore*, 43-6; Hemingway, *Tanjore Gazetteer*, vol. I, 44-6. See also Srinivasachari, *Ananda Ranga Pillai*, 93-5 (n. 18), 393 (n. 1).

127 Michell and Peterson, *The Great Temple at Thanjavur*, 30-1, 35, 153-9; *Annual Report on South-Indian Epigraphy for the Year Ending 31st March 1925* (Madras, 1926), 61-2 (nos 863-74). In the palace murals, Queen Sujana Bai appears to be missing as well, as is the case in at least one inscription from 1758, for which see Raju, *Tañcai Marāṭṭiyar Ceppēṭukaḷ-50*, xliv (no. 22). For more reproductions of some of the portraits, see: Indira Viswanathan Peterson, "Portraiture at the Tanjore Maratha Court: Toward Modernity in the Early 19th Century," in Rosie Llewellyn-Jones (ed.), *Portraits in Princely India 1700-1947* (Mumbai, 2008), 55-6; Daud Ali, "Tanjavur: Capital of the Delta," in George Michell (ed.), *Eternal Kaveri: Historical Sites along South India's Greatest River* (Mumbai, 1999), 104-5; Chakravarthy and Sathyanathan, *Thanjavur: A Cultural History*, 10, 34.

128 See also Srinivasan, *Maratha Rule in the Carnatic*, 247-8

August 1738, Arcot's Chanda Sahib and the French planned to attack Tanjavur together, no doubt finding Sayyid a useful ally at the court.[129]

Thus, the king was overthrown within a year. VOC documents say that in July 1739, on the instigation of the invading General Chanda Sahib, Shahaji II was imprisoned by town-commander Sayyid, considered as he was to be not of royal blood but born of an enslaved woman. His actual parents, interrogated about this, had admitted that Shahaji II was their child. Sayyid now wanted to enthrone Tukkoji's son Pratapasimha, who, although of royal descent, was reluctant to become king. With some amazement the Dutch reported that Pratapasimha visited Shahaji II in prison, telling him he could not ascend the throne unless his predecessor formally renounced it to him. Shahaji II's reply came clearly: "If you do not accept the reign we shall both lose our heads, but if we stay alive we can see what will be next, therefore go and sit on the throne," advice which Pratapasimha duly followed (r. 1739-63).

It was also said that another Arcot general, Safdar Ali Khan, had made an offer to Shahaji II to reinstall him in exchange for a financial reward. However, around early September Tanjavur and Arcot concluded a peace treaty, stipulating that the former kingdom would pay the latter six million *rupee*s in cash, elephants, horses, and jewellery, as well as the revenues of several districts. Besides, it was agreed that Pratapasimha would remain on the throne while town-commander Sayyid actually governed the kingdom, and that Shahaji II would be given some lands to live off. An agreement was also reached with the French, allowing them to stay at Karaikal, much to the VOC's dismay.[130]

Local chronicles mostly agree with the Dutch accounts and add some dynastic details. All texts state that Pratapasimha was born of a sword-wife of Tukkoji, not of a formal queen. But according to the *Bhoṃsale vaṃśa caritra*, this sword-wife, named Annapurna Bai, belonged to a Maratha caste rather than a south Indian one.[131] That background, and Pratapasimha's alleged physical resemblance to his father,

129 NA, VOC, no. 2427, ff. 425-5v, 435-6, 471-2, 478-9v, 530v-1; no. 2443, ff. 2034-67: Nagapattinam proceedings extract, July-Aug. 1738, letters from Porto Novo and Teganapatnam to Nagapattinam, from Nagapattinam to Colombo and Batavia, July-Sept. 1738; *Beknopte historie*, 98; V.G. Hatalkar, *Relations between the French and the Marathas (1668-1815)* (Bombay, 1958), 62.

130 NA, VOC, no. 2470, ff. 70-2, 75-7, 303, 323, 355-7; no. 2471, ff. 51-2; no. 2538, f. 1620: letters from Nagapattinam to Batavia, July, Sept. 1739, Nagapattinam proceedings, Mar.-May 1739, instructions for mission to the Tanjavur king, May 1741; *Beknopte historie*, 98-9; text of first VOC letter also in Tamil Nadu Archives, Chennai (hereafter: TNA), Dutch records (hereafter: DR), no. 282, ff. 54v-61v: letter from Nagapattinam to Cochin, July 1739; Aniruddha Ray, "French Establishment at Karikkal: Early Efforts," *Proceedings of the Indian History Congress* 62 (2001), 268-75; K. Rajayyan, *A History of British Diplomacy in Tanjore* (Mysore, 1969), 23-5; quote of Shahaji II also in Subramanian, *The Maratha Rajas of Tanjore*, 44.

131 See also Shrivastavya, "Are Maratha-Rajput Marriages Morganatic?," 173.

rendered him an acceptable monarch. "The history of the Tonjore Rajas" has it that his lower descent was even the very reason that town-commander Sayyid chose him as the new king. His imperfect royal status supposedly made him vulnerable to other pretenders and therefore dependent on, and obedient to, Sayyid. The fact that the town-commander had proven himself a traitor could explain Pratapasimha's hesitation to accept the throne. However, he still ascended it around July 1739 and, perhaps not surprisingly, after some time had Sayyid executed.[132]

Some local texts say that before Pratapasimha was installed, his predecessor Shahaji II was killed by Sayyid.[133] This is improbable because during the subsequent decades many attempts were made to dislodge Pratapasimha, including several by what appears to have been Shahaji II himself. Indeed, this made the king remark in 1757 that he had dealt with no fewer than twenty-five opponents so far.[134] One such endeavour took place in 1749,[135] when the British received a request from Shahaji II that greatly resembles the plea made by Ikkeri's pretender Sadashiva Nayaka to the Dutch, mentioned at this chapter's beginning. As the British reported:

> In April 1749, Sahagie Maha Rajah [Shahaji II] applyd to the [British] president & co. at Fort St. David, setting forth that he had been deprived of his right as lawful king of Tanjour [Tanjavur] about seven years [ago] by an illegitimate brother [Pratapasimha], representing the latter as a tyrant & much dislik'd by the subjects of that kingdom, that ever since he [Shahaji II] had been dethron'd, he had been oblig'd to keep himself very private, fearing his brothers resentment, but that very lately having rec. [received] letters & agents from several of the great officers & others at Tanjour, who gave him assurances of their assistance in being reinstated in his kingdom, provided he could engage any nation to join him, that no great force was required, as they (his friends) would immediately join him upon his appearing in arms in that kingdom, where he assur'd us he was greatly beloved

132 BL/AAS, MT, class III, no. 87: "The historycal account of the Tonjore," ff. 96-6v, 100-1, 102v-3; class III, no. 32: "The History of the Tonjore Rajas," ff. 91v, 93, 94v-6v; MG, no. 4, pt. 9: "History of Tanjore," ff. 219-20; Subramanian, *The Maratha Rajas of Tanjore*, 42, 44-9; Srinivasan, *Maratha Rule in the Carnatic*, 242-3, 245-6, 248-51; Subrahmanyam, *Penumbral Visions*, 151, 153-4; Bhosale, *Rajah Serfoji – II*, 30, 34; Hemingway, *Tanjore Gazetteer*, vol. I, 44-6.

133 BL/AAS, MT, class III, no. 32: "The History of the Tonjore Rajas," f. 94v; MG, no. 4, pt. 9: "History of Tanjore," f. 219.

134 Subramanian, *The Maratha Rajas of Tanjore*, 47-54; Srinivasan, *Maratha Rule in the Carnatic*, 248, 250, 253, 261-4, 279-80; Subrahmanyam, *Penumbral Visions*, 154-8. The latter two works respectively say that Pratapasimha was temporarily pensioned off by Arcot around 1740 and replaced by Shahaji II in 1740-2. See: Srinivasan, *Maratha Rule in the Carnatic*, 252-3; Subrahmanyam, *Penumbral Visions*, 154. Dutch records seem to make no mention of this. See: NA, VOC, nos 2489, 2505-6, 2556, 2573-4, 2608, 2631; Coolhaas *et al.*, *Generale Missiven*, vols X (The Hague, 1997), XI.

135 For an effort by Shahaji II in 1746, involving Arcot and the French, see Ananda Ranga Pillai, *The Private Diary*, vol. I, 356-8, 389.

> & did not in the least doubt his being reinstated in the possession of that kingdom, without effussion of blood ...[136]

This is another case of a pretender declaring himself the rightful monarch while an unlawful relative was occupying the throne against the will of the common people and most courtiers, who would welcome him, should he have the opportunity to dislodge the alleged usurper. Unlike the Dutch with Sadashiva Nayaka, the British sympathised with Shahaji II and decided to assist him with troops, no doubt encouraged by his offer to hand over the fort of Devikottai and the revenues of the surrounding land in return. But Pratapasimha's position turned out not to be as unstable as Shahaji II made his allies believe. The British report continues:

> ... upon marching into the Tanjour country, the English were in hourly expectation of being join'd (according to Sahagee Maha Rajah's frequent assurances that it would be so) by the grandees of that kingdom, but not a man came over to him & we were soon informed that he had not a friend among them, that he certainly was the right & lawful heir to the kingdom of Tanjour & was in the possession thereof, but was so very weak a prince & gave himself up to the guidance of favorites of low condition, thereby causing great confusion in that kingdom, that the great men dethroned him & set up his brother [Pratapasimha] who has the character of a very brave man & [is held] in great esteem with his subjects.[137]

Thus it seems Shahaji II was actually considered Tanjavur's rightful king because of his descent, but had proven to be an unsuitable ruler, whereas his "brother" Pratapasimha did meet the requirements regarded as more essential than ancestry: appropriate skills and the people's respect. Despite the recommendation of many Indian treatises that kings combine proper descent and correct personality, in this case the latter aspect was apparently favoured. At any rate, Shahaji II never regained the throne. After the failed expedition of 1749, Pratapasimha agreed to provide Shahaji II with an annual income on the condition that the British henceforth be responsible for him and guarantee he caused no more disturbances.[138]

136 BL/AAS, OOV, no. 247, pt. 1: "Application to Fort St. David by Sahajee ... for assistance to recover his rights at Tanjore," ff. 1-2. For published descriptions by the collector of the manuscripts mentioned here and in the following footnotes, see Orme, *A History of the Military Transactions*, vol. 1, 111-22.

137 BL/AAS, OOV, no. 247, pt. 1: "Application to Fort St. David by Sahajee ... for assistance to recover his rights at Tanjore," f. 3; OI, no. II, pt. 33: "Account of the pretender to Tanjore & the expedition to Devi Cotah in 1749...," f. 452. For extensive descriptions of the British campaign in support of Shahaji, see: BL/AAS, OI, no. I, pt. 17: "Devi Cotah, Lord Clive," ff. 219-25; Hemingway, *Tanjore Gazetteer*, vol. I, 255-6.

138 BL/AAS, OI, no. I, pt. 17: "Devi Cotah, Lord Clive," f. 225; no. II, pt. 33: "Account of the pretender to Tanjore & the expedition to Devi Cotah in 1749...," f. 452; OOV, no. 247, pt. 1: "Application to Fort St. David by Sahajee ... for assistance to recover his rights at Tanjore," f. 4; Subramanian, *The Maratha Rajas of*

The last succession discussed here occurred when Pratapasimha passed away on 15 or 16 December 1763, upon which his only son, Tuljaji II (r. 1763-73, 1776-87), took his place at the approximate age of twenty-five. Local chronicles and VOC records offer different versions of the event, with regard to both internal and external factors. The *Bhoṃsale vaṃśa caritra* and "The history of the Tonjore Rajas" relate that Pratapasimha, when he felt his death was near, appointed his son as successor and advised him, together with his minister or *dabīr*, on the future government of the kingdom. When Tuljaji II ascended the throne, Nawab Muhammad Ali Khan of Arcot sent him letters, clothing, and a large bird "as tall as one and a half man with the legs of a camel', perhaps an ostrich.[139]

But the Dutch wrote that as soon as news about Pratapasimha's death reached Arcot, the Nawab hurried to Tanjavur and intervened in disputes arising at court after the king's demise. Tuljaji II was apparently Arcot's preferred successor, but he reportedly behaved like a bully and led a lecherous (*wulps*) life, being dominated by courtiers, in particular *Dabīr* Naro Pandidar.[140] Despite the differences between these sources, this clearly was another succession in which both Tanjavur's court factions and Arcot played a large or even decisive role, foreshadowing the end of the dynasty's formal autonomy, which was soon to come. That last phase is discussed in the Epilogue.

From the eight successions under Tanjavur's Bhonsles until Tuljaji II, one gets the impression of a relatively secure dynasty, which suffered a brief, uncharacteristic period of instability in the late 1730s. Leaving out Tuljaji II's long but interrupted reign, between 1676 and 1763 eight monarchs sat on the throne, resulting in an average rule of just over a decade. This is much shorter than under Tanjavur's Nayakas and rather resembles the situation under Ikkeri's later Nayakas. But whereas Ikkeri—and Madurai and Ramnad, as shown below—saw more than one series of quickly succeeding rulers, this happened only once in Tanjavur. If one therefore considers the reigns of Sujana Bai and Shahaji II unrepresentative and counts only the other six kings, the average rule lasted almost one and a half decades.

Tanjore, 50-2; Srinivasan, *Maratha Rule in the Carnatic*, 262-4; Rajayyan, *A History of British Diplomacy in Tanjore*, 27-30; Hemingway, *Tanjore Gazetteer*, vol. I, 45-6; *Beknopte historie*, 99. For a reference to Shahaji II from 1758, see Orme, *A History of the Military Transactions*, vol. 2 (London, 1778), 318.

139 BL/AAS, MT, class III, no. 87: "The historycal account of the Tonjore," ff. 100, 120; class III, no. 32: "The History of the Tonjore Rajas," ff. 96v-8; MG, no. 4, pt. 9: "History of Tanjore," f. 221; Subramanian, *The Maratha Rajas of Tanjore*, 57-8, 66; Srinivasan, *Maratha Rule in the Carnatic*, 293-4, 313; Subrahmanyam, *Penumbral Visions*, 151, 183; Bhosale, *Rajah Serfoji – II*, 37-8. See also Utz, "Cultural Exchange, Imperialist Violence, and Pious Missions," 36.

140 NA, VOC, no. 3077, ff. 433-3v; no. 3108, ff. 23-4, 29-30, 92: letter from Nagapattinam to Batavia, Dec. 1763, Nagapattinam proceedings (with instructions and report concerning mission to Tanjavur), Feb. 1764.

Table 6: Bhonsles of Tanjavur (until 1780s), regnal dates, relations to predecessors, and further remarks.

	name	accession date	ending date	relation to predecessors	remarks († = natural death at end of reign)
1	Ekoji / Venkaji / Vyamkoji	1676, Mar. 5?	1684, Dec. 25	— (founder)	†, former general of Bijapur
2	Shahaji	1684, Dec. 25	1711, Sept. 28	1st son of 1	†, minor at accession? childless
3	Sarabhoji / Serfoji	1711, c. Sept. 28	1729, Nov. 17	brother of 2 & 2nd son of 1	†, contested by 4
4	Tukkoji / Tuljaji	1729, c. Nov. 17	1735, July 23	brother of 3 & 2, & 3rd son of 1	†, contested by 7
5	Ekoji II / Baba Sahib	1735, Aug. 14	1736, Aug. 1	son of 4	†, childless
6	Sujana Bai	1736, c. Aug. 1	1738, July	widow of 5	female, dethroned by 7
7	(Savai) Shahaji II / Kattu Raja	1738, July	1739, July	alleged adopted son of 3	"usurper," dethroned for 8
8	Pratapasimha	1739, July	1763, Dec. 15/16	low-born son of 4 & half-brother of 5	†, contested by 7 until late 1750s
9	Tuljaji II	1763, c. Dec. 15/16 & 1776, Apr.	1773, Sept. & 1787, Jan. 31	son of 8	†, interlude of rule by Arcot in 1773-6

For sources, see the references in the preceding section, Chapter 1, and the Epilogue.

During the tumultuous late 1730s, rulers not only lasted briefly, they also fell short of the usual requirements to ascend the throne, being female or lacking full royal blood. The remainder of the kings were all legitimate adult sons or brothers of their predecessors. Yet, as elsewhere, royal brothers could become opponents and such conflicts tended to spill over into subsequent generations. The rivalry between Sarabhoji and Tukkoji in the 1710s-20s led to competition between their (real or alleged) sons Ekoji II, Shahaji II, and Pratapasimha in the 1730s-50s.

In Tanjavur, this pattern was further complicated by the co-existence of official queens and different categories of sword-wives, the latter occupying varying positions between queen and concubine, which gave their sons an ambiguous standing. The *Bhoṃsale vaṃśa caritra* explicitly mentions the names and castes of all queens and sword-wives, probably to indicate the status of their offspring. The fact that

Pratapasimha's mother was a sword-wife belonging to a Maratha caste is stated to have made him an acceptable king.[141] Another sword-wife of Tukkoji was member of a "Nayaka caste," perhaps reflecting an effort of the Bhonsles to forge marital ties with local families remaining from Tanjavur's Nayaka period.[142]

As Dutch accounts in particular make clear, two other factors were instrumental in the outcome of succession struggles: courtiers and external powers. The former group played an essential role in each succession, with powerful figures ranging from women, like Queen-Mother Dipamba Bai, to Muslims, such as town-commander Sayyid. Outside powers are first referred to during Tukkoji's enthronement, which was backed by Arcot. The Nawabs and some of their generals grew increasingly influential in the selection of successors and often exploited their rivalry to extract tribute.[143] From the late 1730s on, the French and the British also became involved when they supported the pretender Shahaji II. These foreign interventions, eventually contributing to the dynasty's downfall, must have been facilitated by the ongoing fraternal feuds.

Excessive violence was rare, however. Most successions were accompanied by friction, but this was usually resolved relatively peacefully. The opposition between Sarabhoji and Tukkoji, for example, led to bitterness and estrangement, but many efforts were made to accommodate Tukkoji's grievances, thus avoiding large-scale hostilities. After Shahaji II's reign—itself resulting from what probably was the sole episode of real bloodshed—this usurper also adopted a conciliatory or at least practical approach when he advised his successor Pratapasimha to accept the throne, thus sparing both their lives, winning his own freedom, and, of course, gaining new opportunities to dislodge his rival.

Nayakas of Madurai

After Vishvanatha founded the Nayaka house of Madurai around 1530, he was succeeded by approximately fifteen monarchs until the dynasty's fall in about 1739. Then followed one or two more rulers reigning for brief periods until the early 1750s (see table 7 at the end of this section).[144] As with other royal houses, con-

[141] It appears that under other Maratha dynasties, too, mothers absolutely had to belong to the appropriate caste for their sons to be able to claim the throne. See Burling, *The Passage of Power*, 60.

[142] BL/AAS, MT, class III, no. 87: "The historycal account of the Tonjore," ff. 94v, 95v-6v; MG, no. 4, pt. 9: "History of Tanjore," f. 220.

[143] See also Subrahmanyam, *Penumbral Visions*, 154.

[144] For (partly outdated) genealogical trees of the Madurai Nayakas, see: Sathyanatha Aiyar, *History of the Nayaks of Madura*, ix; Bes, "The Ambiguities of Female Rule in Nayaka South India," 214; Venkata Rao, *The Southern School in Telugu Literature*, 37-8; Sewell, *The Historical Inscriptions of Southern India*, 364; idem, *List of Inscriptions*, 200.

temporary works providing guidelines for succession seem virtually non-existent, apart perhaps from one chronicle—in its English translation called "Account of the Rajas who held the government of Madura"—that contains a short remark saying a childless king could be followed by his brother's son. Therefore, once again, in modern historiography, principles supposedly governing successions in Madurai have been reconstructed on the basis of actual events rather than normative texts. These reconstructions, however, are limited in both number and extent.

In brief, all the king's sons are said to have been co-heirs, with a certain preference for the eldest son of the chief queen, if he possessed the right qualities. If adult sons were not available, the king might be succeeded by a brother, an uncle, or someone belonging to a collateral branch of the family—or by a queen, as happened twice during the dynasty's last phase. If the king's son was still a minor, a temporary regent could be appointed, for example the chief minister or the queen-mother.

Further, some sources state that, especially during the first half of the dynasty's existence, younger brothers of the king often functioned as co-rulers—sometimes referred to as *ciṉṉa turai* ("small lord") or "second in command"—and held important offices. It appears that from around the 1660s onward this position became hereditary from father to son, thus passing through a collateral line of the Nayaka house.[145] It is not clear what this function exactly entailed, for example what claim its holders could lay to the throne. At any rate, these secondary rulers generally seem to have played a marginal role, except for a few cases discussed below.

Sources on the first few successions are relatively scarce. These comprise the usual inscriptions and literary texts, but also a few sets of dynastic portrait sculptures in and around Madurai town, as well as the local chronicle recorded by the Dutch, mentioned in the previous chapter. For the years until the early 1600s, there is some disagreement between scholars about who exactly sat on this Nayaka throne. From the seventeenth century onward, Jesuit and VOC accounts have much to add to the other source materials, and for this period the consecution of rulers can be more clearly established.

By all available accounts, the dynasty's founder Vishvanatha Nayaka (r. c. 1530-63) was succeeded by his son Kumara Krishnappa Nayaka (r. c. 1563-72), who was followed by his son Virappa Nayaka (r. c. 1572-95). The latter may have temporarily

145 BL/AAS, MT, class III, no. 82: "Account of the Rajas who held the government of Madura," f. 110 (compiled in 1806 by Bangaru Tirumalai of Madurai's expelled Nayaka line, see ff. 133-4); Aseem Banu, "Polity under the Nayaks of Madurai," 22-3; C. Chandra, "The Cultural History of the Nayaks of Madurai" (unpublished dissertation, Madurai Kamaraj University, 2006), 59-60; Sathyanatha Aiyar, *History of the Nayaks of Madura*, 77-8, 260-1; Rangachari, "The History of the Naik Kingdom of Madura," *Indian Antiquary* XLIV, 118, XLV, 81, XLVI, 215. See also: Taylor, *Oriental Historical Manuscripts*, vol. II, 235; Nelson, *The Madura Country*, vol. III, 252-4.

ruled jointly with a brother named Vishvanatha Nayaka II, a statue of whom is included in the dynastic portrait gallery at the Putu Mandapa festival hall near the Minakshi Sundareshvara Temple in Madurai town (see illustration 5). Both successions seem to have proceeded peacefully. According to the Dutch chronicle on the Nayakas, Virappa married a Tanjavur princess, acquiring as dowry the lands of Tiruchirappalli, the dynasty's future capital.[146]

With Virappa's death around 1595, the consecution of rulers becomes less clear. This king left three sons: Vishvappa Nayaka, Kumara Krishnappa Nayaka II, and Kasturi Rangappa Nayaka. They may all have ascended the throne, but only the second son is accepted by all historians as a formal ruler. According to the better-known historiography, there is no evidence for Vishvappa's reign, while Kasturi Rangappa was only a very short-lasting usurper.[147]

But many literary texts state that after their father's passing, Vishvappa (r. c. 1595) first sat on the throne, albeit briefly, with his (probably younger) brother Kumara Krishnappa II as a secondary ruler. Upon Vishvappa's death, Kumara Krishnappa II became king (r. c. 1595-1601), with the third brother Kasturi Rangappa occupying the second place. When Kumara Krishnappa II passed away a few years later, probably leaving no sons behind, he was also succeeded by his co-ruler, Kasturi Rangappa (r. 1601). This last brother died very soon, whereupon Vishvappa's son Muttu Krishnappa Nayaka was crowned (r. 1601-6).

The texts differ on the question of whether the two latter successions were harmonious events. Some works have it that upon Kumara Krishnappa II's passing, Kasturi Rangappa ascended the throne only because his nephew Muttu Krishnappa was still a minor. He would thus have functioned as a regent and died an untimely but natural death. Other sources say that Kumara Krishnappa II's demise led to a succession struggle between the young Muttu Krishnappa and his uncle Kasturi Rangappa. The latter won, but was considered a usurper by some courtiers and assassinated within a few days, to be replaced by his nephew.

[146] Heras, *The Aravidu Dynasty of Vijayanagara*, vol. I, 165-6, 281-3; Sathyanatha Aiyar, *History of the Nayaks of Madura*, 65-8, 75-80; Rangachari, "The History of the Naik Kingdom of Madura," *Indian Antiquary* XLV, 82, 90-1; Nelson, *The Madura Country*, vol. III, 101, 105; Henry Heras, "The Statues of the Nayaks of Madura in the Pudu Mantapam," *The Quarterly Journal of the Mythic Society* XV, 3 (1925), 210-13; T.G. Aravamuthan, *Portrait Sculpture in South India* (London, 1931), 50; Vink, *Mission to Madurai*, 288, 292, 346-7; *Beknopte historie*, 87; Taylor, *Oriental Historical Manuscripts*, vol. I, 38, 205, vol. II, 23, 111, 117, 119; Mahalingam, *Mackenzie Manuscripts*, vol. I, 192-4. One text says that Vishvanatha and Kumara Krishnappa both died prematurely—the former because of his sins, the latter through suicide out of grief over his father's death—and that Kumara Krishnappa and Virappa were minors, ruling under the regency of Vishvanatha's father Nagama Nayaka (apparently still alive) and the powerful courtier Ariyanatha Mudaliyar. See BL/AAS, MG, no. 4, pt. 4: "Mootiah's chronological & historical account of the modern kings of Madura," ff. 50-3.

[147] See Sathyanatha Aiyar, *History of the Nayaks of Madura*, 83-9.

Illustration 5: Statues of some of the Nayakas of Madurai, including Tirumalai Nayaka on the right, Putu Mandapa, Madurai, c. 1630s (courtesy Crispin Branfoot).

The Dutch chronicle only refers to the reigns of the second and third of the three brothers, stating that the latter, Kasturi Rangappa, died young after ruling just some days, reportedly being poisoned. Additionally, all three brothers are probably portrayed in the dynastic sculpture gallery in Madurai (see illustration 5), which was commissioned by King Tirumalai Nayaka (r. c. 1623-59). Considering all sources, it seems that all three brothers did sit on the throne, however briefly, and were regarded as rightful monarchs, even Kasturi Rangappa. Had he been a usurper, opposing his nephew Muttu Krishnappa, it is unlikely that Tirumalai—who was Muttu Krishnappa's second son—would have included him in the portrait gallery of his predecessors. However, given the rumour concerning Kasturi Rangappa's violent death recorded in the Dutch chronicle, his short rule may have been accompanied by friction.[148]

[148] BL/AAS, MT, class III, no. 25: "History of the former Gentoo Rajahs who ruled over the Pandyan Mandalom," ff. 28-8v; Taylor, *Oriental Historical Manuscripts*, vol. I, 38, 205-6, vol. II, 25, 119; Mahalingam, *Mackenzie Manuscripts*, vol. I, 195; Heras, *The Aravidu Dynasty of Vijayanagara*, vol. I, 343-5, 350-1; Rangachari, "The History of the Naik Kingdom of Madura," *Indian Antiquary* XLV, 100-3; Vink, *Mission to Madurai*, 293-4, 348; *Beknopte historie*, 87; Heras, "The Statues of the Nayaks of Madura," 213-15; Aravamuthan, *Portrait Sculpture in South India*, 49-50; Crispin Branfoot, "Royal Portrait Sculpture in the South Indian Temple," *South Asian Studies* 16, 1 (2000), 22-3; idem, "Dynastic Genealogies," 330-5, fig. 30; Michell, *Architecture and Art of Southern India*, 184; Nelson, *The Madura Country*, vol. III, 106-9.

Muttu Krishnappa reigned only a few years and, as the Jesuit Robert de Nobili reported, passed away in the night of 6 to 7 December 1606. He was succeeded by the eldest of his three sons, Muttu Virappa (r. c. 1606-23), with, as some texts say, the second son Tirumalai functioning as the secondary ruler. During this reign, the capital was shifted north from Madurai town to Tiruchirappalli, possibly because of a war against nearby Tanjavur. At Muttu Virappa's death, or perhaps a few years earlier already, his younger brother Tirumalai became king at the approximate age of forty (r. c. 1623-59), while the third brother, Kumara Muttu, now supposedly assumed the secondary position.

Tirumalai moved the capital back to Madurai, probably again for strategic purposes, although tradition has it that Madurai's deities asked him to do so after curing him of a disease. Even though the court was again transferred to Tiruchirappalli in the 1660s,[149] Madurai town henceforth remained the place where kings were usually installed and received the royal sceptre in the presence of the local goddess Minakshi.[150] As the Dutch reported, Tirumalai died in early February 1659. Some sources say this happened suddenly and according to one tradition he was murdered by a Hindu priest resenting the king's sympathy with Christianity or his

In addition, various texts with short dynastic lists include Vishvappa, Kasturi Rangappa, or both, as fully-fledged rulers. See: BL/AAS, MM, no. 109, pt. 37: "The humble representation of ... Bangaroo Teeroomaly Nack," f. 4; MT, class III, no. 90: "The genelogical account of the Madura Vadoka Rajahs," ff. 162-3 (collected in 1809); OI, no. I, pt. 22: "Kings of Tritchanopoly from 1509," ff. 239-40 (related by a Brahmin at Tiruchirappalli); Mahalingam, *Mackenzie Manuscripts*, vol. I, 13; W. Francis, *Madura Gazetteer* (Madras, 1906), 42. A Dutch overview from 1762 (probably based on the Dutch chronicle) mentions Kumara Krishnappa II and Kasturi Rangappa while omitting Vishvappa. See Schreuder, *Memoir of Jan Schreuder*, 34.

149 Jesuit sources suggest Tiruchirappalli became the capital because Madurai town had suffered badly from an invasion by Mysore. See *Lettres édifiantes et curieuses*, vol. XIII, 131.

150 Heras, *The Aravidu Dynasty of Vijayanagara*, vol. I, 351, 359; Sathyanatha Aiyar, *History of the Nayaks of Madura*, 89, 97-8, 103, 109-15, 160-1; Rangachari, "The History of the Naik Kingdom of Madura," *Indian Antiquary* XLV, 103-4, 132, 149-50; Nelson, *The Madura Country*, vol. III, 109, 115, 119, 121-4; Mahalingam, *Mackenzie Manuscripts*, vol. I, 195; A. Saulière, "The Date of Accession of Muttu Vīrappa Nāyaka I of Madurai Settled by Letters of His Contemporary Fr. Robert de Nobili," *Journal of Indian History* XXXII, I (1954), 83-4; K. Rajaram, *History of Thirumalai Nayak* (Madurai, 1982), 8-11; Taylor, *Oriental Historical Manuscripts*, vol. I, 38, 206, vol. II, 25, 29-31, 119, 147; BL/AAS, MT, class III, no. 25: "History of the former Gentoo Rajahs who ruled over the Pandyan Mandalom," f. 30; Vink, *Mission to Madurai*, 294, 296, 348. For textual references to the Nayakas' sceptre and installation at Madurai town, see also: BL/AAS, MG, no. 4, pt. 4: "Mootiah's chronological & historical account of the modern kings of Madura," ff. 48, 51, 57, 70-1, 73; MM, no. 109, pt. 37: "The humble representation of ... Bangaroo Teeroomaly Nack," ff. 3-4; MT, class III, no. 25: "History of the former Gentoo Rajahs who ruled over the Pandyan Mandalom," f. 24v; Taylor, *Oriental Historical Manuscripts*, vol. II, 109, 153, 255; Vink, *Mission to Madurai*, 302-3, 351-2; NA, VOC, no. 1756, f. 1219v; no. 8923, f. 317; no. 11306, ff. 120-2: report of mission to Ramnad, Oct. 1708, letter from Colombo to Batavia, Feb. 1708, description of the Nayakas of Madurai by Holst, 1762.

intimacy with the priest's wife. None of the local chronicles nor Dutch accounts refer to an assassination, however, although the latter records confirm Tirumalai passed away suddenly. Perhaps, this was related to an abscess on his head, mentioned by the Jesuit Antony de Proença in 1656, which was rumoured to be the result of a curse inflicted by some pretender to the throne.[151]

The succession of Tirumalai's son Muttu Virappa Nayaka II (r. 1659-60) led to a brief struggle. According to VOC documents, shortly before his death Tirumalai had installed Muttu Virappa II, between twenty-five and thirty years old, as his successor. But as the latter was allegedly born of a concubine, a son of Tirumalai's brother called Muttu Allappa Nayaka (spelled "Moutalle Appa Naijcq" by the Dutch) contested this appointment, claiming he was first in the line of succession. Muttu Allappa had long been staying with King Vijayaraghava Nayaka of Tanjavur, to whom he was related, and with the expelled Vijayanagara Emperor Sriranga III. Supported by troops of Tanjavur, Mysore, and unspecified "Moors" (probably Bijapur or Golkonda), he marched to Madurai to take the throne from Muttu Virappa II, who was aided by the Setupati of Ramnad among other rulers. By late February, however, the rivals had solved their differences, and Muttu Virappa II remained king.

This alliance was further cemented by the engagement of two sons of Muttu Virappa II with two daughters of Muttu Allappa's foremost supporter at the Madurai court, a friend or relative called Kati Alakadri Nayaka ("Catiallagatris Naijcquen") in the VOC records. This Dutch account is largely similar to what appears in other sources. Although most of these do not mention Muttu Virappa II's supposed illegitimate descent, many confirm that his instalment was opposed by a close relative, here referred to as Kumara Muttu, who was probably identical to the abovementioned nephew of Tirumalai, Muttu Allappa. In this version of the events, peace was achieved when Kumara Muttu was given control over some lands in the kingdom's south and his son Kumara Rangappa anointed as second ruler beside Muttu Virappa II.[152]

151 NA, VOC, no. 1231, ff. 131, 406, 627: letters from Colombo to Batavia, from Tuticorin to Colombo, Mar., May-June 1659; Vink, *Mission to Madurai*, 297, 349; *Beknopte historie*, 87; Vink, "Encounters on the Opposite Coast," 236; Saulière, "The Revolt of the Southern Nayaks" [pt. 2], 174; Sathyanatha Aiyar, *History of the Nayaks of Madura*, 147-49; Rangachari, "The History of the Naik Kingdom of Madura," *Indian Antiquary* XLVI, 27-8, 36; Rajaram, *History of Thirumalai Nayak*, 18-22; Nelson, *The Madura Country*, vol. III, 139-42; Taylor, *Oriental Historical Manuscripts*, vol. I, 39, vol. II, 33-5, 119, 175, 183; BL/AAS, MT, class III, no. 25: "History of the former Gentoo Rajahs who ruled over the Pandyan Mandalom," f. 32; MG, no. 4, pt. 4: "Mootiah's chronological & historical account of the modern kings of Madura," ff. 62-3.

152 NA, VOC, no. 1231, ff. 131-1v, 406-9, 413: letters from Colombo to Batavia, from Tuticorin and Kayalpatnam to Colombo, Mar., May 1659; Van Dam, *Beschryvinge van de Oostindische Compagnie*,

Once firmly on the throne, however, Muttu Virappa II reigned only about a year. In July 1660 the Dutch wrote that the recently installed Nayaka had passed away and been succeeded by his eldest son Chokkanatha Nayaka (r. 1660-77, 1680-2), aged about fourteen, with the consent of the most important courtiers. But according to the Dutch chronicle and the literary work titled "A description of the Carnataca Lords," he was not of pure royal descent. While the latter source has it that Chokkanatha was adopted by his father, the Dutch chronicle says his mother was a concubine rather than a queen, as she belonged to the agricultural Vellala caste. Another text, called "History of the Carnataca Governors who ruled over the Pandya Mandalam," adds that the position of second in power was now kept by Kumara Tirumalai, son of the abovementioned Kumara Rangappa (who previously held that function), thereby starting some sort of dynasty that provided a line of secondary rulers and lasted into the eighteenth century.[153]

It may have been descendants of this collateral branch—from the 1730s onward claiming the Madurai throne and even briefly occupying it—who commissioned texts declaring that Chokkanatha and his father Muttu Virappa II were illegitimate sons of their predecessors, in order to strengthen their own rights to kingship. It has also been suggested that Chokkanatha's temporary successor, his brother Muttu Linga Nayaka, downplayed Chokkanatha's ancestry to legitimise his own rule. The Madurai chronicle recorded by the Dutch was compiled during Muttu Linga's reign and could have been influenced by the latter's preferred version of the dynasty's genealogy.[154]

In any case, other sources, in particular Jesuit letters, also state that Chokkanatha was a minor at his accession, whereas the kingdom's de facto rulers comprised a court faction including the *pradhāni* (prime or financial minister), *daḷavāy* (chief general), and *rāyasam* (royal secretary). This situation soon created tensions as the young Chokkanatha objected to the tight control under which he was put. A subsequent plot to replace the king with his younger brother is said to have been revealed to him by a court lady, upon which he gathered his own supporters and in

vol. 2.2, 281; Vink, "Encounters on the Opposite Coast," 236; Sathyanatha Aiyar, *History of the Nayaks of Madura*, 150-1; Rangachari, "The History of the Naik Kingdom of Madura," *Indian Antiquary* XLVI, 37-8; Nelson, *The Madura Country*, vol. III, 178; Taylor, *Oriental Historical Manuscripts*, vol. II, 33, 175-7, 183-4.

[153] See also Rangachari, "The History of the Naik Kingdom of Madura," *Indian Antiquary* XLVI, 215. According to some local texts, Kumara Tirumalai was a younger brother of Chokkanatha. See: BL/AAS, MT, class III, no. 82: "Account of the Rajas who held the government of Madura," f. 109v; Taylor, *Oriental Historical Manuscripts*, vol. II, 190.

[154] For this latter suggestion, see: Vink, "Encounters on the Opposite Coast," 346 (n. 27); idem, *Mission to Madurai*, 63.

mid-1662 had the *rāyasam* murdered and the *pradhāni* blinded, while the *daḷavāy* fled to Tanjavur.[155]

This appears to have secured Chokkanatha's place on the throne for quite some time, yet in early 1677 he was forced to abdicate and make place for his younger brother Muttu Linga Nayaka (alias Muttu Alakadri Nayaka, r. 1677-80). The Dutch chronicle relates that the royal sceptre and crown were transported from the Minakshi Sundareshvara Temple in Madurai town to the capital Tiruchirappalli for Muttu Linga's coronation ceremony. This unusual procedure was perhaps organised to prevent Chokkanatha from retaking the throne while his brother would have been absent from the capital.[156]

Sources do not agree on the cause of Chokkanatha's dethronement, but all European accounts state he did not function well. His allegedly indolent and capricious conduct estranged courtiers, subordinate chiefs, common subjects, and neighbouring rulers. The Dutch wrote that some close relatives, with their troops, had even shifted allegiance to Tanjavur's King Ekoji Bhonsle. This made Chokkanatha attempt in vain to stab himself to death, after which the throne was transferred to Muttu Linga, supposedly with Chokkanatha's consent. But many local texts entirely ignore Muttu Linga's reign, while one work says that Chokkanatha himself, in his wisdom, crowned his younger brother because he wished to spend all his time studying religious works.

Whatever the exact circumstances, in September 1677 the Dutch noted that Chokkanatha had started opposing this transition and his subsequent house arrest, and, still controlling the royal treasure, was fighting a street war in the capital against his younger brother. Yet, Muttu Linga managed to remain on the throne for a few years, although his reign reportedly was no better than that of Chokkanatha, and the fraternal friction appears to have continued all the while. In mid-1680, however, Muttu Linga was removed in his turn and expelled to Tanjavur by his own General Rustam Khan, who had usurped all power at court and now reinstalled Chokkanatha, with himself as the de facto ruler. But Rustam Khan's own fall came soon too, when around February 1682 he was killed, either by his own allegedly

155 NA, VOC, no. 1233, f. 43v: letter from Pulicat to Batavia, July 1660; Coolhaas *et al.*, *Generale Missiven*, vol. III, 337; Vink, *Mission to Madurai*, 63, 141, 213, 297, 349; A. Saulier (ed.), "Madurai and Tanjore, 1659-1666," *Journal of Indian History* XLIV, III (1966), 779-81; Taylor, *Oriental Historical Manuscripts*, vol. I, 39, vol. II, 33-5, 119; Sathyanatha Aiyar, *History of the Nayaks of Madura*, 153-6; Rangachari, "The History of the Naik Kingdom of Madura," *Indian Antiquary* XLVI, 40-2; Nelson, *The Madura Country*, vol. III, 182-5; Vink, "Encounters on the Opposite Coast," 236-7; *Beknopte historie*, 87; BL/AAS, MT, class III, no. 25: "History of the former Gentoo Rajahs who ruled over the Pandyan Mandalom," f. 32.

156 One Dutch document however says Muttu Linga did actually travel to Madurai to receive (or at least collect) the royal sceptre. See NA, VOC, no. 1333, f. 24: letter from Galle to Batavia, May 1678.

underpaid men (as the Dutch wrote), a coalition of courtiers and subordinate chiefs (according to local texts), or Chokkanatha himself (as a Jesuit report has it)—three versions that do not necessarily exclude one another.[157]

Having finally gotten rid of his rivals, Chokkanatha had little time to enjoy this new phase. A VOC letter from January 1683 declares that Chokkanatha had passed away a few months earlier, after which his twelve-year old son Muttu Virappa Nayaka III (alias Ranga Krishna, r. 1682-91) was proclaimed king. Further, the "History of the Carnataca Governors who ruled over the Pandya Mandalam" states that during this reign, the son of the secondary ruler Kumara Tirumalai, Bangaru Tirumalai, succeeded his father in that position.

Muttu Virappa III himself was initially placed under the regency of *Daḷavāy* Tubaki Anandappa Nayaka, a brother of the king's mother Mangammal. Like her contemporary Chennammaji, queen of Ikkeri, this widow of Chokkanatha escaped death on her husband's funeral pyre (*satī*) by claiming that nobody but she could raise the young king. Tubaki Anandappa's regency lasted until 1686, when Muttu Virappa III discovered the *daḷavāy* was part of a conspiracy to dethrone him and reinstall his father's brother Muttu Linga. Having fled the kingdom, three years later Tubaki Anandappa became involved in a similar plot, this time resulting in his being caught by Muttu Virappa III and subsequently executed, along with Muttu Linga himself.[158]

On 9 March 1691, as the Dutch wrote, Muttu Virappa III passed away and was cremated on the 13th "without any marks of honour," perhaps because he had

157 NA, VOC, no. 1316, f. 304; no. 1324, ff. 17-17v, 40v; no. 1333, f. 28v; no. 1373, f. 433v: letters from Tuticorin to Colombo, Jan. 1677, from Colombo and Pulicat to Batavia, Mar., June 1677, June 1678, Feb. 1682; Vink, "Encounters on the Opposite Coast," 291-2, 346 (n. 27), 372-3; idem, *Mission to Madurai*, 63-4, 301-3, 351-2, 366-7, 373-4; Taylor, *Oriental Historical Manuscripts*, vol. I, 206, vol. II, 35, 119, 203; Mahalingam, *Mackenzie Manuscripts*, vol. I, 13; BL/AAS, MT, class III, no. 90: "The genelogical account of the Madura Vadoka Rajahs," ff. 162-3; class III, no. 25: "History of the former Gentoo Rajahs who ruled over the Pandyan Mandalom," ff. 32-2v; MM, no. 109, pt. 37: "The humble representation of ... Bangaroo Teeroomaly Nack," f. 4; Martin, *India in the 17th Century*, vol. 1, pt. II, 566; Sathyanatha Aiyar, *History of the Nayaks of Madura*, 180-2; Rangachari, "The History of the Naik Kingdom of Madura," *Indian Antiquary* XLVI, 96-7; Nelson, *The Madura Country*, vol. III, 201-2.

158 NA, VOC, no. 1373, f. 91; no. 11306, ff. 39-40: letter from Colombo to Gentlemen XVII, Jan. 1683, description of the Nayakas of Madurai by Holst, 1762; Vink, "Encounters on the Opposite Coast," 374-7; idem, *Mission to Madurai*, 63, 157 (n. 111), 181 (n. 170), 399 (n. 69), 470 (n. 226); Taylor, *Oriental Historical Manuscripts*, vol. I, 39, vol. II, 35, 119; BL/AAS, MG, no. 4, pt. 4: "Mootiah's chronological & historical account of the modern kings of Madura," ff. 66-8; MT, class III, no. 25: "History of the former Gentoo Rajahs who ruled over the Pandyan Mandalom," f. 32v; Sathyanatha Aiyar, *History of the Nayaks of Madura*, 190-3; Rangachari, "The History of the Naik Kingdom of Madura," *Indian Antiquary* XLVI, 104; Nelson, *The Madura Country*, vol. III, 204, 207. Another literary work mentions one Kumara Muttula as Muttu Virappa III's secondary ruler. See Taylor, *Oriental Historical Manuscripts*, vol. II, 205.

been poisoned by Brahmins, as some rumours had it, although a letter by the Jesuit Peter Martin of 1700 and other accounts claim he died of smallpox. His mother Mangammal reportedly objected to the installation of a new king and with the help of some courtiers took control of the government. Mangammal was now to rule the kingdom (1691-1707) until the recently born son of the deceased Muttu Virappa III, Vijayaranga Chokkanatha Nayaka, would reach maturity. According to other sources, including the abovementioned Jesuit letter, this child actually ascended the throne when he was three months old, while his grandmother Mangammal served as his guardian, holding the prince "in her lap" (as some local texts put it), while the then *daḷavāy* was said to be entrusted with the kingdom's administration.

However, a mural in the Unjal Mandapa hall at Madurai's Minakshi Sundareshvara Temple shows the local goddess Minakshi presenting the dynasty's sceptre to Mangammal through what must have been a Brahmin priest, suggesting she attained or at least claimed fully-fledged regal status herself (see illustration 6, left). Additionally, an adjacent painting (see illustration 6, right) and some statues in other buildings, all portraying Mangammal together with her grandson Vijayaranga Chokkanatha, depict the queen twice as large as the young king, which is thought to indicate her superior powers rather than their age difference.[159]

All this suggests she became an influential figure at court. Indeed, it was said that Mangammal—whose beauty was described as "angelic" (in a local text) and "of wondrousness" (*van wonderschoonht.*, in a Dutch report of 1668)—already held considerable power during the rule of her husband Chokkanatha. Nevertheless, during her own reign, Mangammal seems to have shared much of her might with Brahmin courtiers and representatives around the kingdom, or that is at least the complaint found in VOC documents and Jesuit letters dating from the last phase of her rule.[160]

[159] For online images of these murals, see: southindianpaintings.art/monuments/madurai-minakshi-sundareshvara-temple.

[160] NA, VOC, no. 1492, ff. 250-50v; no. 8921, ff. 163-4; no. 11306, f. 40: letter from Tuticorin to Batavia, May 1691, final report of Tuticorin's chief (*opperhoofd*) Nicolaas Welter, Oct. 1705, description of the Nayakas of Madurai by Holst, 1762; Vink, *Mission to Madurai*, 64, 166 (n. 128), 204, 258, 474 (n. 237); Taylor, *Oriental Historical Manuscripts*, vol. I, 39, vol. II, 35, 119, 216-17; BL/AAS, MG, no. 4, pt. 4: "Mootiah's chronological & historical account of the modern kings of Madura," ff. 66, 69-70; MT, class III, no. 25: "History of the former Gentoo Rajahs who ruled over the Pandyan Mandalom," ff. 32v-3; Crispin Branfoot, "Mangammal of Madurai and South Indian Portraiture," *East and West* 51, 3-4 (2001), 371-6, figs 1-3, 5, 8; idem, "Royal Portrait Sculpture in the South Indian Temple," 19-21 (figs 6-7); R. Nagaswamy, *Studies in Ancient Tamil Law and Society* (n.p., 1978), 124-6; Chandra, "The Cultural History of the Nayaks of Madurai," Appendix, plate II B; Calambur Sivaramamurti, *Vijayanagara Paintings* (New Delhi, 1985), 46-7, 84 (plate XXIV); J. Lockman (ed.), *Travels of the Jesuits into Various Parts of the World*, vol. I (London, 1743), 460-1; Sathyanatha Aiyar, *History of the Nayaks of Madura*, 203-4, 377-8; Rangachari, "The History of the Naik Kingdom of Madura," *Indian Antiquary* XLVI, 124, 156; Nelson, *The Madura Country*, vol. III, 214-16. See also Bes, "The Ambiguities of Female Rule in Nayaka South India."

Illustration 6: Details of murals depicting Queen Mangammal of Madurai receiving the royal sceptre from the local goddess Minakshi through a priest (left), and attending a divine wedding with her grandson Vijayaranga Chokkanatha Nayaka (right), Unjal Mandapa (central ceiling), Minakshi Sundareshvara Temple, Madurai, c. 1700? (courtesy *Institut Français de Pondichéry* / British Library EAP 692).

In February 1707, the Dutch wrote that the young Nayaka prince, Muttu Virappa III's son Vijayaranga Chokkanatha, now about seventeen years old, had reached the age to assume the government and many courtiers wished him to do so. Yet, it was thought he was unwilling to ascend the throne before the release of a *daḷavāy* who had been imprisoned by his grandmother, much to the pleasure of "deceitful" Brahmins. But in late July, news came that Mangammal had indeed been dethroned and replaced with Vijayaranga Chokkanatha (r. 1707-32). Some months later, the Dutch heard that the queen was presumably poisoned by order of the new king and the now released *daḷavāy*. This remained a rumour, however, since some years later it was reported she had fled from Madurai to Tanjavur, hoping to find shelter with the VOC at Nagapattinam. But Company documents from that town do not seem to mention her appearance there.[161]

[161] NA, VOC, no. 1756, f. 1193; no. 8595, f. 129; no. 8922, ff. 71, 249; no. 8923, ff. 314-15: letters from Tuticorin to Colombo, Jan. 1708, from Colombo to Batavia and Gentlemen XVII, Feb., Aug., Nov. 1707, Feb. 1708; Coolhaas *et al.*, *Generale Missiven*, vol. VI, 555, 821; J.S. Chandler, *History of the Jesuit Mission in Madura, South India, in the Seveneenth and Eighteenth Centuries* (Madras, 1909), 55. For Mangammal's possible escape to Nagapattinam, see also the section on Madurai in Chapter 4.

While some other accounts agree that Mangammal was reluctant to abdicate in favour of her grandson and therefore was deposed and killed by him, most local texts declare that the queen voluntarily vacated the throne before she passed away. But one south Indian work, "Mootiah's chronological & historical account of the modern kings of Madura," describes the friction between the two in detail. It relates that towards the end of her reign, Mangammal was charmed by the amorous songs of a musician. Informed about this by *Daḷavāy* Kasturi Ranga Ayyan, Vijayaranga Chokkanatha became furious and had the singer tortured. The queen then imprisoned the prince and the *daḷavāy*, but when they escaped after three years, Vijayaranga Chokkanatha seized the royal sceptre and paraded through the streets on an elephant. Having thus shown he was now the king, he jailed Mangammal, who died soon after.

According to another tradition, the queen had an affair with a courtier, weakening her position among her subjects and necessitating her removal. Additionally, a Telugu text called *Madura mangāpumścalī līlavilāsamu*—perhaps composed by the poet Vikatakavi Gopalakavi, who had fallen out with Mangammal—portrays her reign as cruel and immoral. It is possible that these three sources derive from the same origin and that the musician, the courtier, and the poet were the same person. In any case, these stories may well have stemmed from efforts by Vijayaranga Chokkanatha to discredit his predecessor and legitimise his take-over.[162]

The final succession in Madurai dealt with in this chapter took place on 25 February 1732, when Vijayaranga Chokkanatha passed away. As VOC documents explain, his son and heir apparent had already died in 1721, and so he was succeeded by his first queen, Minakshi (r. c. 1732-9).[163] She was spared of committing *satī* because she was—or pretended to be—seven months pregnant. Although her unborn child was destined to become king if it was a male, Minakshi herself was allegedly formally recognised as queen by the courtiers and the common people.

162 Taylor, *Oriental Historical Manuscripts*, vol. I, 39, vol. II, 37, 119, 229; BL/AAS, MG, no. 4, pt. 4: "Mootiah's chronological & historical account of the modern kings of Madura," f. 71; MT, class III, no. 25: "History of the former Gentoo Rajahs who ruled over the Pandyan Mandalom," f. 33v; Timmavajjhala Kodandaramaiah, *The Telugu Poets of Madura and Tanjore* (Hyderabad, n.d. [c. 1975]), 30, Appendix V (no. 4); Venkata Rao, *The Southern School in Telugu Literature*, 143-4; Sathyanatha Aiyar, *History of the Nayaks of Madura*, 220-3; Rangachari, "The History of the Naik Kingdom of Madura," *Indian Antiquary* XLVI, 184-6; Nelson, *The Madura Country*, vol. III, 237, 239-40; Francis, *Madura Gazetteer*, 55. According to the supplement by G.F. Holst to the Dutch chronicle of the Nayakas of Madurai, dating from 1762, Mangammal had peacefully passed the government to Vijayaranga Chokkanatha just before her death. See NA, VOC, no. 11306, f. 47, and also *Beknopte historie*, 89.

163 Minakshi may have belonged to the Tubaki family (like Queen Mangammal and her brother Anandappa, see also Chapter 3), as one local text says she was a daughter of "Toopaukela Ramalingama." See BL/AAS, MG, no. 4, pt. 4: "Mootiah's chronological & historical account of the modern kings of Madura," ff. 71-2.

Yet, as various sources mention, her rule was contested by her distant cousin Bangaru Tirumalai, most probably the aforementioned secondary ruler under Muttu Virappa III in the 1680s. Even though Minakshi is thought to have adopted Bangaru Tirumalai's son Vijayakumara Nayaka as her future successor, Bangaru Tirumalai himself—aided by Madurai's *daḷavāy* and seemingly Arcot and Mysore too—attempted to dislodge the queen, claiming the throne since he belonged to the family's collateral line. According to some local texts, Bangaru Tirumalai came to exercise all control, enjoyed the support of most courtiers, and resided in a new palace, whereas the treasure, the regalia, and the old palace were in the possession of Minakshi and her influential brothers. Other literary works have it that the queen not only adopted Bangaru Tirumalai's son Vijayakumara but also installed him as king, whose regent she would be, while Bangaru Tirumalai assumed actual governmental authority.

However, some generals of Arcot became closely involved in this succession struggle, which around 1739 led to Minakshi's death and the demise of the Nayaka dynasty, save for the brief reigns of, perhaps, Bangaru Tirumalai around 1740 and of his son Vijayakumara in the early 1750s.[164] These events are discussed in the Epilogue.

Considering the successions under Madurai's Nayakas until the reign of Minakshi, one gains a picture of a dynasty that frequently suffered instability, yet lasted much longer than the two other Nayaka dynasties in the Tamil region, those of Senji (until 1649) and Tanjavur (until 1673). Not counting the later rulers Bangaru Tirumalai and Vijayakumara, but including all three sons of Virappa, sixteen monarchs occupied the throne between c. 1530 and 1739. Their average rule thus lasted nearly thirteen years, or slightly under fifteen years if we discount the two sons of Virappa whose reigns are doubted by some historians.

In both cases, this period differs little from the average length under most other dynasties. In Madurai, this relatively brief span was partly the result of a few short-lived reigns, occurring throughout the dynasty's existence. Their very brevity indicates that most of these reigns were opposed and ended violently. From

164 NA, VOC, no. 2318, f. 2646-7; no. 8958, ff. 672-3, 701; no. 11306, ff. 47-8, 53-4: letters from Tuticorin to Colombo, from Nagapattinam to Batavia, Mar., Oct. 1732, Sept. 1734, description of the Nayakas of Madurai by Holst, 1762; Coolhaas *et al.*, *Generale Missiven*, vol. VII, 567, vol. IX (The Hague, 1988), 393; *Beknopte historie*, 89; Taylor, *Oriental Historical Manuscripts*, vol. I, 40, vol. II, 37-43, 232-5; BL/AAS, MG, no. 4, pt. 4: "Mootiah's chronological & historical account of the modern kings of Madura," ff. 72-4; MT, class III, no. 25: "History of the former Gentoo Rajahs who ruled over the Pandyan Mandalom," ff. 33v-6v; class III, no. 82: "Account of the Rajas who held the government of Madura," ff. 109v-14; Sathyanatha Aiyar, *History of the Nayaks of Madura*, 230-4; Rangachari, "The History of the Naik Kingdom of Madura," *Indian Antiquary* XLVI, 189, 213-19, 237-41; Nelson, *The Madura Country*, vol. III, 251-60. See also Bes, "The Ambiguities of Female Rule in Nayaka South India."

Table 7: Nayakas of Madurai, regnal dates, relations to predecessors, and further remarks.

	name	accession date	ending date	relation to predecessors	remarks († = natural death at end of reign)
1	Vishvanatha Nayaka	c. 1530?	c. 1563	— (founder)	†, son of Nagama, Vijayanagara general
2	(Periya) Kumara Krishnappa Nayaka	c. 1563	c. 1572	son of 1	†
3	(Periya) Virappa (Krishnappa) Nayaka	c. 1572	1595	son of 2	†, co-rule with 2 and brother Vishvanatha II?
4	Vishvappa / Bisvama / Vishvanatha Nayaka	1595	c. 1595	1st son of 3	†, co-rule with 3?
5	(Kumara) Krishnappa Nayaka II / Lingama / Lingappa / Lingaya	c. 1595	c. 1601	brother of 4 & 2nd son of 3	†, co-rule with 4? no sons?
6	Kasturi Rangappa Nayaka	c. 1601	c. 1601	brother of 5 & 3rd son of 3	co-rule with 5? contested by 7, killed?
7	Muttu Krishnappa Nayaka	c. 1601	1606, Dec. 6/7	nephew of 6 & son of 4	†
8	Muttu Virappa Nayaka	1606, c. Dec. 6/7	c. 1623	1st son of 7	†
9	Tirumalai Nayaka	c. 1623	1659, early Feb.	brother of 8 & 2nd son of 7	†? co-rule with 8?
10	Muttu Virappa Nayaka II / Muttu Alakadri	1659, early Feb.	c. early 1660	(low-born?) son of 9	†, contested by nephew of 9
11	Chokkanatha Nayaka	c. early 1660 & mid-1680	1677, c. Feb. & mid/late 1682	(low-born?) 1st son of 10	†, minor at accession, temporarily dethroned for 12
12	Muttu Linga Nayaka / Muttu Alakadri	1677, c. Feb.	mid-1680	brother of 11 & 2nd son of 10	contested by and dethroned for 11

	name	accession date	ending date	relation to predecessors	remarks († = natural death at end of reign)
13	(Ranga Krishna) Muttu Virappa Nayaka III	mid/late 1682	1691, Mar. 9	son of 11	minor at accession, contested by 12, poisoned?
14	Mangammal	1691, c. Mar. 9	1707, c. July	mother of 13 & widow of 11	female, maybe regent of 15, poisoned by 15?
15	Vijayaranga Chokkanatha Nayaka	1707, c. July	1732, Feb. 25	grandson of 14 & son of 13	†, minor at possible accession in 1691, no sons
16	Minakshi	1732, c. Feb. 25	c. early 1739	widow of 15	female, contested by 17, dethroned by Arcot
17	Bangaru Tirumalai	c. mid-1739?	c. 1739?	great-grandson of brother of 9	enthroned by Arcot, reign unsure
18	Vijayakumara Nayaka	c. 1750 & c. 1753	c. 1751 & c. 1754	son of 17, adopted by 16	enthroned and dethroned by Arcot defectors, enthroned by Ramnad and Shivagangai, dethroned by Arcot defectors

For sources, see the references in the preceding section, Chapter 1, and the Epilogue.

around the mid-seventeenth century, when sources become more diverse, almost every succession appears to have been contested. This suggests that also during the dynasty's earlier phase competition for the throne was common. It can therefore be concluded that about half of the rulers were assassinated or dethroned. Still, until the dynasty's last few decades, virtually all kings were sons or brothers of predecessors. Only from around 1660 do we see two widows, about three minors, and perhaps two low-born sons ascending the throne.

Thus, the number of "unqualified" monarchs was limited, and often it was the traditionally recommended successions by sons or brothers that caused conflicts. An early instance of this is perhaps found with Virappa's three sons, two of whom ruled for only about a year and the third for just six years. Fraternal and filial clashes certainly became prominent later on. One example concerns the career of Muttu Linga, who in the late 1670s temporarily replaced his elder brother Chokkanatha, and in the 1680s attempted twice to usurp the throne from his nephew Muttu Virappa III.

An even longer lasting rivalry commenced when in 1659 Muttu Virappa II's accession was contested by his cousin Kumara Muttu (or Muttu Allappa). He eventually gave up his demands but had his son Kumara Rangappa installed as second in power. From him sprang the collateral, hereditary line of secondary kings, the last of whom, Bangaru Tirumalai, claimed the throne upon Vijayaranga Chokkanatha's death in 1732. As described in the Epilogue, the competition between him and Minakshi contributed in large measure to the dynasty's demise. The latter's gender likely weakened her position and emboldened her opponent, as was probably the case for Mangammal when her grandson Vijayaranga Chokkanatha reached maturity and her reign, under the guise of regency, was no longer accepted. As elsewhere, these rivalries were often instigated or exploited by parties around the royal house: court factions, subordinate chieftaincies, and neighbouring kingdoms.

Setupatis of Ramnad

Originally installed by Muttu Krishnappa Nayaka of Madurai around 1605, the first clearly historical Setupatis were local chiefs of the Ramnad area. During the seventeenth and early eighteenth centuries, they became ever more assertive and gradually achieved a de facto independent position, in particular after the fall of the Madurai Nayakas around 1739. The Setupatis' fully-fledged royal status lasted until the turn of the nineteenth century, when the British designated the family as *zamīndār*s (revenue-paying landholders) over the Ramnad "Estate." But in 1772 already, the kingdom was conquered by the combined forces of Arcot and the British and was subsequently ruled by the Nawab for nearly a decade.[165] Therefore, this survey only concerns successions until 1763, the year of accession of Muttu Ramalinga Setupati, who was deposed during the Anglo-Arcot invasion. Up to and including his reign, sixteen men ruled Ramnad (see table 8 towards the end of this section).[166]

Sources for the successions during this period include inscriptions, literary works (produced at both the Ramnad and Madurai courts), Jesuit letters, and, from the mid-seventeenth century on, Dutch records. In addition, there are sculptural dynastic galleries in several temples. These include the Ramanathasvami Temple on Rameshvaram island, where most statues were executed in the seventeenth and

[165] Seshadri, "The Sētupatis of Ramnad," 127-45; Thiruvenkatachari, *The Setupatis of Ramnad*, 53-71; Kadhirvel, *A History of the Maravas*, 159-68, 181-5, 190-3, 202-3; K. Rajayyan, *History of Madurai (1736-1801)* (Madurai, 1974), 258-62, 276-8, 329-33, 402-7.

[166] For (partly outdated) genealogical trees of Ramnad's Setupatis, see: Seshadri, "The Sētupatis of Ramnad," between 182-3; Bes, "Friendship as Long as the Sun and Moon Shine," ix; Sewell, *The Historical Inscriptions of Southern India*, 391; idem, *List of Inscriptions*, 228.

Illustration 7: Statues of the Setupatis of Ramnad, Kalyana Mandapa, Ramanathasvami Temple, Rameshvaram, 18th-19th centuries (courtesy R.K.K. Rajarajan).

eighteenth centuries, but some sculptures portray Setupatis up to the twentieth century (see illustration 7).[167]

In contrast to the royal houses considered before, several historians have discussed the principles of succession under the Setupatis in some detail. They state that traditionally the king was to be succeeded by the eldest son born of a wife belonging to the king's Maravar sub-caste, the Sembinattu. In the absence of such a son, the throne would allegedly fall to a daughter of similar ancestry. Next in line were the king's brothers or else other close paternal relatives. The king could also adopt a successor, and finally, if no heir was available at all, Maravar chiefs had to select a new monarch.[168] It is not entirely clear whether these specific regulations were recorded in contemporary texts, but in any case the rules were often bent, as the following events demonstrate.

All sources agree that the first Setupati of the modern, historical line, Sadaika Tevar (r. c. 1605-22), whose regal name was Udaiyan Setupati, died about 1622 and was succeeded by his eldest son Kuttan Tevar (r. c. 1622-36). But from that point until the 1720s, relations between consecutive Setupatis are largely unclear since sources

[167] Bes and Branfoot, "'From All Quarters of the Indian World'"; Branfoot, "Heroic Rulers and Devoted Servants," 179-85, 189-91, 196 (n. 48); G. Sethuraman, *Ramesvaram Temple (History, Art and Architecture)* (Madurai, 1998), 190-2, 212, 216; Michell, *Architecture and Art of Southern India*, 118, 184; Jas. Burgess, "The Ritual of Râmêśvaram," *The Indian Antiquary: A Journal of Oriental Research* XII (1883), 316, 326; Vanamamalai Pillai, *Temples of the Setu and Rameswaram*, 75; Burgess and Naṭēśa Śāstrī, *Tamil and Sanskrit Inscriptions*, 57; and personal observation (Sept. 1997).

[168] Kadhirvel, *A History of the Maravas*, 34 (n. 4); Seshadri, "The Sētupatis of Ramnad," 183-4; Price, *Kingship and Political Practice in Colonial India*, 35-7.

often contradict one another. Kuttan, perhaps dying childless around 1636, was followed by Sadaika Tevar II, also known under his regal name Dalavay Setupati (r. c. 1636-40, 1640-5). Dalavay was his predecessor's younger brother or his son, possibly by adoption. Some local texts say that when Dalavay nominated his sister's son Raghunatha as his future successor, this was contested by his illegitimate half-brother Peddanna Nayaka Tevar, alias Tambi, born of an enslaved woman according to one chronicle. To realise his claims to the throne, Tambi enlisted the support of King Tirumalai Nayaka of Madurai, resulting in hostilities between Dalavay and the Madurai General Ramappaiya.

This conflict is extensively described in the Tamil poem *Rāmappaiyaṉ ammāṉai* (probably dating from the second half of the eighteenth century), which relates that Dalavay fled across the Pamban Channel to Rameshvaram island. As a poetic reference to the episode in the *Rāmāyaṇa* epic of Rama using a monkey-built bridge to cross these same waters to Lanka, the *Rāmappaiyaṉ ammāṉai* says that Madurai's General Ramappaiya now had a causeway constructed across the channel. Soon, Dalavay was defeated, imprisoned in Madurai, and replaced with his rival Tambi (r. c. 1640).

The new, low-born Setupati proved an incapable ruler, however, who was opposed by his courtiers and subjects alike. This was one reason why Madurai's Tirumalai Nayaka soon reinstalled Dalavay, although—as the *Rāmappaiyaṉ ammāṉai* relates—the god Vishnu's personal breaking of the prisoner's chains also prompted the Nayaka to do so. Other literary texts, mostly deriving from Madurai, state that Tirumalai Nayaka's removal of the Setupati was caused by the latter's refusal to pay tribute and his discourteous behaviour towards his overlord's representatives. But when Ramnad subsequently fell into disorder, and pilgrims to Rameshvaram island complained about the lack of safety and demanded the Setupati's return, the Nayaka reappointed Dalavay.[169]

[169] BL/AAS, MG, no. 4, pt. 8: "A general history of the kings of Rama Naad or the Satoo-Putty Samastanum," ff. 179-81; MT, class III, no. 25: "History of the former Gentoo Rajahs who ruled over the Pandyan Mandalom," ff. 29v-31; T.V. Mahalingam, "Historical Material in the Ramappayyan Ammanai," *Proceedings of the Indian History Congress* 10 (1947); K.C. Kamaliah, "Anatomy of *Rāmappaiyaṉ Ammāṉai*," *Journal of Tamil Studies* 7 (1975); Howes, *The Courts of Pre-Colonial South India*, 86; Mahalingam, *Readings in South Indian History*, 186-91; Taylor, *Oriental Historical Manuscripts*, vol. II, 29-31, 175, 180-1, Appendix, 49-51; Mahalingam, *Mackenzie Manuscripts*, vol. I, 60, 180; Price, *Kingship and Political Practice in Colonial India*, 19-25; Seshadri, "The Sētupatis of Ramnad," 20, 23-31; Thiruvenkatachari, *The Setupatis of Ramnad*, 20-2; Raja Ram Rao, *Ramnad Manual*, 213-16; Sathyanatha Aiyar, *History of the Nayaks of Madura*, 93, 122-5; Rangachari, "The History of the Naik Kingdom of Madura," *Indian Antiquary* XLV, 106, 169-71, 178-85; Nelson, *The Madura Country*, vol. III, 128-30. One inscription has it that Raghunatha Setupati was the son of Dalavay Setupati. See Sewell, *The Historical Inscriptions of Southern India*, 284.

The VOC archives contain another local account of these developments. The Madurai General Tirumalai Kulantha Pillai presented this version in written form to the Company's official Hendrik Adriaan van Rheede at Tuticorin in 1665, when the Dutch attempted to mediate in a conflict between Madurai and Ramnad about the latter's arrears in tribute. This report, recorded twenty-five years after the events, was clearly meant as Madurai's justification for its grievances. Yet, the account, titled "Origin of the war and rise of the Teuver [Tevar, the Setupati]," appears to combine parts of all abovementioned texts, including some of the more "epic" elements:

> Oerienchedupadij [Udaiyan Setupati or Sadaika Tevar], being the grand uncle of the Raganoeda Teuver [Raghunatha Tevar, the Setupati who reigned when the report was written], ... was by one of the Neijke [Nayakas] of Madure appointed head and supervisor of some lands, whose son named Talavaij Chedupadij Teuver [Dalavay Setupati] in the course of time took control of a few places, of which the rulers were tributaries of the Neijck, and after a while crept across ... some boundaries that even belonged to the Neijck.
>
> Because of this, the Neijck resolved to drive him away and give his office [*bediening*] to someone else, choosing for that end Chedapadij Theuver [Tambi]—being the brother's son of the abovementioned Thalawaija Chedupadij Theuver—sending him to wage war against his uncle with a large army under a general named Ramapaijen, who, closing the channel of Outiaer [Pamban] with a dam, crossed it to Ramanocoijl [Rameshvaram] where Thalawaij Chedupadij Tever (and ... 3 nephews named Tauwcatta Teuver, Araijanatwer, and this Ranganoeda Tevar, being three brothers) had fled with their families, all of whom were taken prisoner to Madure ... while Chedepadie Tever [Tambi] remained, ruling as governor of the conquered lands under firm promises of tribute.
>
> Seeing himself established in this government, he revolted against the Naijck and refused to pay the tribute, for which reasons the Naijck set free the imprisoned Talavaij Chedupadij Thever, under the condition that he, being in the government, would pay one lack or 100,000 ditto [currency unclear] and regular tribute to the Neijck of Madure, keeping as hostages for this promise this Setupati [Raghunatha, ruling in 1665] with his brothers and family ...[170]

Thus, in the view of the Madurai court, the cause for Dalavay's temporary removal from the Ramnad throne was his encroachment upon lands of the Nayaka and his subordinates. Nothing is said about Tambi objecting to Dalavay's supposed nomination of his sister's son Raghunatha, and Tambi is here Dalavay's brother's son instead of his illegitimate half-brother—perhaps giving him a better claim to the throne than Raghunatha. Further, Tambi was soon re-exchanged with Dalavay

[170] NA, VOC, no. 1251, ff. 743-4: report of mission to Travancore, Madurai, and Ramnad, Mar.-Oct. 1665 (translation mine). See also Vink, "Encounters on the Opposite Coast," 227 (n. 13).

again, simply because the former proved as disobedient as the latter, unwilling to deliver the agreed tribute. Moreover, the mention of a bridge to Rameshvaram in the poem *Rāmappaiyaṉ ammāṉai* may not have merely been a lyrical effort to liken Madurai's General Ramappaiya to the *Rāmāyaṇa*'s Rama, but a reference to an actual crossing of the Pamban Channel by way of a constructed dam.

All in all, it seems that while in Madurai the developments were seen as a partially successful suppression of two consecutive disloyal Ramnad chieftains, texts from Ramnad itself mostly attempted to portray Dalavay as an obedient ruler, whose low-born rival dethroned him, but who was soon reinstalled when the Nayaka realised he was the rightful monarch. This version of the events was probably propagated by the later Setupatis, who descended from Dalavay's nominee Raghunatha. In this respect, it is perhaps telling that in at least one of the sculptural portrait galleries of Ramnad's house—located at the Kalyana Mandapa hall of Rameshvaram's Ramanathasvami Temple and including name labels (see illustration 7)—Tambi is one of only two Setupatis who appear to have been left out.[171] Even though these labels may have been added as late as the twentieth century, they seem to reflect a tradition that did not acknowledge Tambi as a Setupati.

In any case, the next succession in Ramnad is also dealt with in Madurai's account recorded by the Dutch:

> Some time later, Thalavaij Chedupadij Teuver was treacherously killed by his brother's son … Chedupadij Teuver [Tambi], whereupon the Naijck set free all the deceased's imprisoned friends as revenge for the treason, moreover sending an army that, by the violence of arms, forced the rebel to hand over everything. The Neijck then took his lands …, distributing the remainder among the Teuver [Raghunatha Setupati] and his two brothers, with the order to pay tribute as obedient subjects …[172]

This description of Dalavay's demise after a few more years on the throne and the kingdom's subsequent partition agrees fairly well with most other sources. According to some accounts, Dalavay died a natural death rather than a violent one at Tambi's hands, but almost all texts say or at least suggest that his passing led to a succession struggle. For Tirumalai Nayaka of Madurai interfered again and divided Ramnad into three, the central part to be governed by Dalavay's nominee Raghunatha (Tirumalai) Setupati (r. c. 1645-73) and the other parts by Tambi and Raghunatha's two brothers respectively. This does not seem to have made all these rulers more willing to pay tribute, since the pages of the Dutch-recorded Madurai report are full of complaints in this regard. Indeed, VOC sources indicate that the chiefs of Ramnad's

171 Personal observation (Sept. 1997).

172 NA, VOC, no. 1251, f. 744 (translation mine).

seceded portions were courted by the Nayaka of Tanjavur and the Portuguese as part of their animosity against Madurai. But after some time, these chiefs passed away or perhaps were dethroned and the Ramnad kingdom was reunited under Raghunatha's allegedly loyal reign, probably around 1658 as Dutch records suggest.[173]

By almost all local accounts, Raghunatha Setupati died peacefully and was succeeded by Surya Tevar (r. 1673), although sources differ on the date of this transition and the question of whether the latter was the former's son or nephew. The Dutch wrote in April 1673 that the Setupati was recently deceased and had been succeeded by his brother's son. Another VOC letter mentions that this new ruler had imprisoned one of his brothers, perhaps indicating a succession struggle. In any case, Surya's reign was short-lived. As reported by the Dutch, during the then growing tension between the Madurai and Tanjavur Nayakas—leading to the fall of the latter in September 1673—the Setupati supported Tanjavur. He was subsequently caught by Madurai troops and drawn and quartered at Tiruchirappalli around October.[174]

His successor was Athana Tevar (r. 1673), whose relationship with Surya is not quite agreed upon by local sources. These accounts variously designate Athana as his predecessor's brother, adopted cousin, uncle, or distant relative, or even as a wholly unrelated, elected ruler. VOC reports declare that upon Surya's death, Maravar chiefs chose his ten-year old brother (Athana) as Setupati, for want of a more suitable relative, since Surya had killed three other brothers some months earlier. The young Athana spent even less time on the throne than Surya. As Dutch records state, within weeks the minor ruler was also captured and killed by Madurai.

A VOC document of January 1674 mentions as the kingdom's next ruler a certain Raghunatha, probably the earliest Dutch reference to the Setupati better known under his nickname Kilavan ("old man") Tevar (r. 1673-1710). Remarkably, in a letter written to the VOC soon after, Kilavan explained in some detail how his predecessors

[173] BL/AAS, MG, no. 4, pt. 8: "A general history of the kings of Rama Naad or the Satoo-Putty Samastanum," ff. 181, 191; MT, class III, no. 25: "History of the former Gentoo Rajahs who ruled over the Pandyan Mandalom," f. 31; NA, HRB, no. 542 (unpaginated, 1st document, c. halfway, section "Teuverslant"): description of Ceylon, Madurai, south Coromandel, Malabar, and Kanara by Rijcklof van Goens, Sept. 1675; Taylor, *Oriental Historical Manuscripts*, vol. II, 31-3, Appendix, 51; Mahalingam, *Mackenzie Manuscripts*, vol. I, 180; Seshadri, "The Sētupatis of Ramnad," 31-3, 37; Thiruvenkatachari, *The Setupatis of Ramnad*, 23-4; Raja Ram Rao, *Ramnad Manual*, 216-18; Sathyanatha Aiyar, *History of the Nayaks of Madura*, 125; Nelson, *The Madura Country*, vol. III, 130-1.

[174] It may well be the execution of Surya Tevar that the Venetian traveller Niccolao Manucci mentions in his account of a clash between Madurai's Nayaka and the Setupati. This is also logical considering Manucci's reference to Madurai's General Chinna Tambi Mudaliyar (prominent in the late 1660s–early 1670s), whom the modern-day editor of Manucci's work probably erroneously has identified as Tambi, Ramnad's pretender to the throne around 1640. See Manucci, *Storia do Mogor*, vol. III, 100-2. For what is likely another description of Surya Tevar's death, see Jeyaraj and Young, *Hindu-Christian Epistolary Self-Disclosures*, 263-4

Surya and Athana had met their end, but was silent about how he had become king or was related to the previous Setupatis. This unusual omission of the ruler's credentials can well be linked to two factors appearing from other accounts: Kilavan's alleged illegitimate descent and the bloodshed that accompanied his accession to the throne.

Again, sources do not agree on the kinship between Kilavan and his predecessors. Some suggest he was a relative of Surya and Athana, although, as the Jesuit John de Britto wrote, he had a low status because his mother did not belong to the appropriate Maravar sub-caste. In contrast, the Telugu text called "A chronicle of the acts of the Sethupathis" declares that Kilavan was elected by Maravar chiefs since neither Surya nor Athana nor any of their siblings had left children. According to a Tamil work translated as "A general history of the Kings of Rama Naad or the Satoo-Putty Samastanum," he was a cousin of Surya, had gone into hiding for some time, and was recognised as the rightful new Setupati once he reappeared at court.

Despite their differences, all these accounts have in common that upon Athana's death, Kilavan's coming to power was not a foregone conclusion and had to be negotiated and acknowledged. Dutch records seem entirely silent on Kilavan's ancestry, but they extensively relate the violence with which he eliminated all possible opposition. In the first years of his reign he killed his General Chandra Servaikkarar and several other courtiers, while members of the royal family—including relatives of the deceased Raghunatha Setupati—were quietened through marital alliances or by force.

Further, as reported by De Britto again, Kilavan married a woman of the Sembinattu sub-caste, thereby strengthening his legitimacy. He is also thought to have moved the kingdom's capital from Pogalur to Ramanathapuram, which he fortified with stone walls.[175] Despite several endeavours to dislodge him in the 1670s and 1680s—variously involving subordinate chiefs, Madurai, Tanjavur, and Pudukkottai—Kilavan achieved practical autonomy from Madurai and became one of Ramnad's most powerful rulers, and in any case he was the longest reigning Setupati until the twentieth century.[176]

175 For Pogalur, see one of the footnotes in the section on Sivakumara Muttu Vijaya Raghunatha Setupati (r. 1735-48) below.

176 NA, VOC, no. 1291, ff. 515v, 594v; no. 1292, ff. 180-80v; no. 1295, ff. 82, 127-7v, 144-4v, 707v; no. 1298, ff. 292v-3, 325v; no. 1302, ff. 613-13v, 618; no. 1316, ff. 331v-2: letters from superintendent Rijcklof van Goens to Surya Tevar (in proceedings of the Dutch fleet and Colombo), from Cochin to Gentlemen XVII, from Pulicat, Nagapattinam, and Colombo to Batavia, from Nagapattinam to Van Goens, Apr.-May, Aug., Oct.-Nov. 1673, Jan. 1674, Dec. 1676 (letter of Oct. 1673 partly translated in Narayana Rao, Shulman, and Subrahmanyam, *Symbols of Substance*, 310), correspondence between Kilavan Tevar and Van Goens, June 1674; Vink, "Encounters on the Opposite Coast," 289-90, 292-3, 377; idem, *Mission to Madurai*, 73-4; BL/AAS, MG, no. 4, pt. 8: "A general history of the kings of Rama Naad or the Satoo-Putty Samastanum," ff. 183-7; Taylor, *Oriental Historical Manuscripts*, vol. II, Appendix, 51; Seshadri, "The

Kilavan's demise on 12 October 1710, at the approximate age of seventy, gave rise to a series of succession disputes that lasted into the 1730s and eventually caused another partition of the kingdom, this time for good. According to "A chronicle of the acts of the Sethupathis" and other sources, Kilavan's son Bhavani Shankara Tevar could not succeed him since his mother's caste was not appropriate. Yet, as "A general history of the Kings of Rama Naad or the Satoo-Putty Samastanum" adds, several relatives, courtiers, and chiefs wanted him to ascend the throne and he supposedly sat on it for a few days while Kilavan was deathly ill.

This proved unacceptable to other parties, and the Dutch wrote that on the day Kilavan died, he had his daughter married to the man who now succeeded him: Tiru Udaya Tevar, also known under his regal name Muttu Vijaya Raghunatha Setupati (r. 1710-25). Besides son-in-law, the new Setupati was probably also a nephew of his predecessor. Further, as he claimed in a letter to the VOC, he was a grandson of Raghunatha Setupati (r. c. 1645-73). Passed over, Bhavani Shankara left Ramnad and in the subsequent years tried to dislodge Muttu Vijaya Raghunatha with the aid of Tanjavur and others on several occasions. But his attempts remained unsuccessful until Muttu Vijaya Raghunatha passed away—on 8 April 1725, at 4 o'clock in the afternoon, as Dutch records specify—at the northern town of Arantangi, where he was defending Ramnad against yet another attack by his rival Bhavani Shankara.

Sources differ on what happened afterwards. According to several texts, Muttu Vijaya Raghunatha left no legitimate children and was succeeded by Tanda Tevar alias Sundareshvara (r. 1725), either his sister's son, son-in-law, or distant cousin. "A general history of the Kings of Rama Naad or the Satoo-Putty Samastanum" says that Muttu Vijaya Raghunatha had formally nominated Tanda as his successor. When the Setupati lay dying, however, his favourite concubine, whose niece was married to Bhavani Shankara, secretly mixed a drug through his medicine, making him forget this nomination. Thus, Bhavani Shankara became the new ruler, but he was dislodged within a month by Tanda—himself dethroned by Bhavani Shankara again after a few more months. While the latter was thus victorious in the end, this work suggests that Tanda was the rightful successor.

Dutch records give another account of the events. While upon Muttu Vijaya Raghunatha's death Tanda probably ascended the throne in the capital Ramanathapuram, Bhavani Shankara straightaway attacked Arantangi, where the deceased king's retinue and troops were still gathered. Assisted by Tanjavur,

Sētupatis of Ramnad," 43-4, 50-4, 74; Kadhirvel, *A History of the Maravas*, 33-5; Thiruvenkatachari, *The Setupatis of Ramnad*, 27-30, 37; Raja Ram Rao, *Ramnad Manual*, 221-3; Shulman and Subrahmanyam, "Prince of Poets and Ports," 506-7; Sathyanatha Aiyar, *History of the Nayaks of Madura*, 184, 214; Rangachari, "The History of the Naik Kingdom of Madura," *Indian Antiquary* XLVI, 45; Nelson, *The Madura Country*, vol. III, 205-6, 217.

Bhavani Shankara conquered the town in a matter of days and most of Ramnad's officials there recognised him as the new Setupati (r. 1725-9) by raising both their hands and worshipping him. But other courtiers refused to acknowledge him and some members of the royal family even feared his rule and fled the kingdom or entrenched themselves at the capital. Although backed by Madurai, Tanda was defeated by Bhavani Shankara in August.

Next—as Bhavani Shankara wrote in detail to the VOC in October—while marching with Tanjavur's troops to Ramanathapuram, he caught some hostile chiefs in possession of Ramnad's regalia, including the royal elephant, golden palanquin, throne (*periyapērikai*), umbrella (*kuṭai*), and drum (*mēlsalli*).[177] Having confiscated these which the Dutch called "stately things," Bhavani Shankara took the capital from another opponent in September. In early October, as he again informed the VOC, he performed the "water-bathing" ceremony, probably a reference to the Navaratri festival. Some accounts say that in the meantime he had married the niece or daughter of what was probably Kilavan Setupati's chief concubine. No doubt, the regalia, the festival, and the wedding were all meant to consolidate his royal aspirations. Nevertheless, Bhavani Shankara seems to have been considered a usurper by most, and besides Tambi (ruling in the 1640s) he is the only Setupati appearing to be lacking in at least one of the dynasty's sculpture galleries, the aforementioned statues with name labels at the Kalyana Mandapa in Rameshvaram's Ramanathasvami Temple (see illustration 7).[178]

Among the courtiers who escaped from Ramnad upon Bhavani Shankara's accession to the throne was Kattaya Tevar, chief at Arantangi, maternal uncle of the murdered Tanda Tevar, and married to a daughter of the late Muttu Vijaya Raghunatha Setupati. Perhaps surprisingly, Kattaya fled to Tanjavur, whose ruler Sarabhoji Bhonsle had just assisted this fugitive's opponent Bhavani Shankara. Kattaya was nonetheless welcomed at Tanjavur and later joined by another refugee from Ramnad, Sasivarna Tevar. The latter was related to the royal family through his marriage with another of Muttu Vijaya Raghunatha's daughters, albeit a low-born one, as some sources have it. One text suggests that Sasivarna's father was a milk-brother of the Setupati Kilavan, as both had been breastfed by the former's mother. Like his ancestors, Sasivarna was the chief of the town of Nalkottai in north-west Ramnad, but he had now been dislodged by Bhavani Shankara. Kattaya and Sasivarna thus proved useful allies to one another.

177 I thank A. Govindankutty Menon for making sense of the Dutch renderings of these Tamil words. The original VOC corruptions are "perieperigij," "koede," and "meelsjalli."

178 Personal observation (Sept. 1997).

At the Tanjavur court, both men, particularly Sasivarna, stood out for their valour.[179] Literary works relate that a dangerous tiger was killed, combat duels were won, and an assassination attempt on King Sarabhoji was thwarted by either one of them. Impressed, the king decided to help them attack their rival Bhavani Shankara, who had not fulfilled his promise to Sarabhoji that, once on the throne, he would return some land taken from Tanjavur by Kilavan Tevar. Sarabhoji now attached the same condition to his support of Kattaya and Sasivarna, and in 1729 they invaded Ramnad with Tanjavur's troops. Dutch records however explain that after the kingdom's north was conquered, Sarabhoji literally tried to divide and rule. Similarly to Madurai's strategy a century before, he made Bhavani Shankara a proposal that Ramnad be partitioned and distributed among the three contenders, obviously excluding the lands claimed by Tanjavur. Bhavani Sankara refused and was soon defeated and deported to Tanjavur, whereupon Kattaya was installed as Setupati on 17 September (r. 1729-35).

According to virtually all sources, including accounts of the Tanjavur court and the British of several decades later, Ramnad was now divided into five parts, two of which were given to Sasivarna in gratitude for his assistance, while the remainder went to Kattaya. But Dutch reports state that matters did not actually proceed in such an amicable way. They claim that, once Bhavani Shankara was dethroned, Tanjavur's Sarabhoji handed Ramnad over as a land grant to Kattaya and Sasivarna—except the Setupati seat Ramanathapuram, which was assigned to the former—with the instruction to divide it equally between them.

Like the Tanjavur king may have expected, his ambiguous order caused friction between Kattaya and Sasivarna, and the latter was discontented with the arrangement, seemingly aspiring to the Ramnad throne himself. He settled near a town called "Pativenalur" by the Dutch,[180] important for its weekly market, and started opposing Kattaya until Sarabhoji would specify the areas granted to each of them, which never happened. Both men tried to enlist the support of what the VOC termed "Marrua robber-leaders," local chieftains and commanders of roaming bands belonging to the Maravar caste. The two rivals were apparently so dependent on these chiefs and warriors for the consolidation of their power, that Kattaya invited some of the most important among them to his capital to pardon them for certain crimes and thus win them over.

[179] For an origin myth about Sasivarna Tevar's rise to power, mentioning his heroic deeds in Tanjavur, see Price, *Kingship and Political Practice in Colonial India*, 108. See also J.L.W., "Chronicles of the Marava Country," *Calcutta Review* 75, 149 (1882), 126.

[180] "Pativenalur" is perhaps modern-day Partibanur, roughly halfway between Ramnad and Madurai. For more information on this place, see Bes, "The Setupatis, the Dutch, and Other Bandits," 551 (including n. 20).

But in the course of time, many chiefs, courtiers, and common subjects sided with Sasivarna, who took possession of the "Pativenalur" market town and grew increasingly powerful. While Kattaya still relied on Tanjavur, Sasivarna allied himself with Madurai. Luckily for the former, disagreements arose among the Maravar chiefs and some went back to Kattaya. Besides, he begot a son "from the direct Marrua [Maravar] line," which according to the Dutch was of great importance in securing his position. Thus, two kingdoms gradually emerged from the tumult after Bhavani Shankara's defeat: Shivagangai, centred on the eponymous town and its environs, including "Pativenalur," ruled by Sasivarna Tevar, who assumed the title Udaya Raja; and a much shrunken Ramnad, with the old capital Ramanathapuram and the sacred Rameshvaram island, ruled by Kattaya Tevar, the Setupati, who took as his regal name Kumara Muttu Vijaya Raghunatha.[181] Nevertheless, Sasivarna, who died in 1739, and his dynasty maintained their claim to the Setupati throne for decades and waged many a war against Ramnad.[182]

[181] NA, VOC, no. 1771, f. 1499; no. 1788, f. 1493; no. 1805, ff. 1039v-40; no. 1865, ff. 869v-70; no. 2026, ff. 834v-5; no. 2044, ff. 94v-5; no. 2046, ff. 762-2v; no. 2158, ff. 945-57v: report of mission to Ramnad, letters from Kilakkarai to Tuticorin, from Muttu Vijaya Raghunatha to Nagapattinam, from Tuticorin and Bhavani Shankara to Colombo, from Colombo to Batavia, report on mission of envoys from Ramnad to Colombo, May 1709, Oct. 1710, Feb. 1711, July 1715, Apr., Oct. 1725, Apr. 1726, Sept. 1729-May 1730; BL/AAS, MG, no. 4, pt. 8: "A general history of the kings of Rama Naad or the Satoo-Putty Samastanum," ff. 187-93; no. 49, pt. 2: "Abstract history of the Marawar," ff. 27-9 (compiled by the British official S. Lushington in 1800, see f. 5); MT, class III, no. 77: "Regarding the Zemindars of Ramnad," ff. 73-3v (translated from Tamil in 1817 by one Mr Wheatby, see f. 72); OOV, no. 10, pt. 19: letter from General Joseph Smith at Madras to Brigadier-General Richard Smith concerning Tanjavur's expedition against Ramnad, Mar. 1771, ff. 225-6; no. 33, pt. 11 (1): extract diary and proceedings, Fort St. George, 1771, "concerning the state of affairs and quarrel between the Nawab and the king of Tanjore," ff. 162-5 (containing a somewhat confused letter of King Tuljaji II of Tanjavur, c. 1771); no. 33, pt. 11 (2): extract consultations, Fort St. George, 1771, "concerning the origin and state of the Maravars ...," ff. 169-75; Taylor, *Oriental Historical Manuscripts*, vol. II, Appendix, 51; Mahalingam, *Mackenzie Manuscripts*, vol. I, 180, 226, 243-4; Bes, "The Setupatis, the Dutch, and Other Bandits," 552-6; Price, *Kingship and Political Practice in Colonial India*, 27-8; K.V.S. Maruthumohan, "Sasivarna Thevar and Formation of Sivagangai Seemai," *The Quarterly Journal of the Mythic Society* XCVII, 3 (2006), 14-18; Subrahmanyam, *Penumbral Visions*, 160-1; Seshadri, "The Sētupatis of Ramnad," 72, 77-82, 84, 87-92, 94; Kadhirvel, *A History of the Maravas*, 50-61; Thiruvenkatachari, *The Setupatis of Ramnad*, 45-50; Raja Ram Rao, *Ramnad Manual*, 230-1, 233-6; Sathyanatha Aiyar, *History of the Nayaks of Madura*, 224-9; Rangachari, "The History of the Naik Kingdom of Madura," *Indian Antiquary* XLVI, 209-13; Nelson, *The Madura Country*, vol. III, 247-50.

[182] NA, VOC, no. 2337, ff. 1543v-7v; no. 2403, ff. 1938-8v; no. 2456, f. 217; no. 2459, f. 1599v; no. 2523, ff. 1425-5v; no. 2599, ff. 2310v-1; no. 2666, ff. 2321-3: letter from the king of Shivagangai to Tuticorin, June 1746, correspondence between Tuticorin, Colombo, and Batavia, Aug.-Sept. 1735, May 1737, Mar., May 1739, July 1741, Apr. 1743; DNA, DCGCC, no. 2691, f. 11: final report of Tuticorin's chief Noël Anthony Lebeck, June 1745. Around 1800, the British official S. Lushington remarked that disagreements on the use of water from the Vaigai River had also caused frequent violent clashes between Ramnad and Shivagangai. See BL/AAS, MG, no. 49, pt. 2: "Abstract history of the Marawar," f. 29.

It is perhaps not surprising that sources from Ramnad itself portray this partition as a peaceful affair. With the accession of Kattaya, the kingdom lost a considerable part of its territory and power, and in literary works commissioned by him or his successors it may have been tempting to present Shivagangai's secession as a mutual agreement instead of the unwanted outcome of a succession struggle. In any case, Kattaya's kingship remained precarious during the subsequent years. In 1732, he was attacked twice by Tanjavur for not paying the 50,000 *pardao*s promised in return for military assistance against Bhavani Shankara. Indeed, Tanjavur now supported Bhavani Shankara again, who made another effort to gain the Setupati throne.

But Kattaya stayed in power until he died on 12 August 1735, as VOC records say, from a cold, a fever, and a lump on one of his thighs. Two days later, his five- or six-year old son Sivakumara Muttu Vijaya Raghunatha was installed as Setupati (r. 1735-48) and recognised by all courtiers and present Maravar chiefs. During his minority his regent would be the *Daḷavāy* (general) Vairavanatha (or Vairavar) Servaikkarar, although the Dutch would occasionally also report that the regency was in the hands of the boy's mother, probably named Chalabara Nachiar.

Upon Kattaya's passing, Sasivarna, still ruling Shivagangai, sent envoys to Ramnad with the message that he would approve of this succession under the condition that the most important jewels and the golden palanquin of the deceased ruler—together with two elephants, 10,000 *pardao*s, and a fortress—be handed over to him. Although this demand would obviously never be complied with, it demonstrated Sasivarna's continuing claim to Setupati kingship. For, as the Ramnad court wrote to the VOC, at his accession the young Sivakumara Muttu Vijaya Raghunatha received this golden palanquin himself, as well as the red umbrella ("quipezo"),[183] both signifying Setupati status. His kingship was further consolidated when he celebrated Vijayadasami ("wesiji desemi," as the Dutch spelled it), the tenth and final day of the Navaratri festival.

In late 1741, when Sivakumara Muttu Vijaya Raghunatha was about twelve years old, he performed another ceremony at the Ramanathasvami Temple in Rameshvaram. As he informed the VOC, on this occasion the temple deity bestowed on him great power, a sceptre, various titles, and a palanquin with "curved bamboo." Indian Company employees explained to their superiors that hitherto the young Setupati had been considered a reigning king only in name, whereas now, "following

[183] I thank Herman Tieken for identifying this term. See also: Herman Tieken (ed.), *Between Colombo and the Cape: Letters in Tamil, Dutch and Sinhala, Sent to Nicolaas Ondaatje from Ceylon, Exile at the Cape of Good Hope (1728-1737)* (New Delhi, 2015), 148-9; Lodewijk Wagenaar, *Galle, VOC-vestiging in Ceylon: Beschrijving van een koloniale samenleving aan de vooravond van de Singalese opstand tegen het Nederlandse gezag, 1760* (Amsterdam, 1994), 222. One Setupati title also calls them "holders of the red umbrella." See: Seshadri, "The Sētupatis of Ramnad," 233; Burgess and Naṭēśa Śāstrī, *Tamil and Sanskrit Inscriptions*, 102.

the old custom," he was inaugurated as a real monarch and then publicly recognised by the people.[184] Earlier Setupatis had usually also been installed at Rameshvaram, and apparently Sivakumara Muttu Vijaya Raghunatha had to reach a certain stage of maturity before he could undergo this procedure and receive all regalia and titles.[185]

On 24 December 1748, Sivakumara Muttu Vijaya Raghunatha passed away childless at the approximate age of eighteen. Dutch records do not give the cause of his demise and just mention it happened very unexpectedly, making one wonder whether he died a natural death. The new Setupati, Rakka Tevar (r. 1748-9), one of his predecessor's cousins, was appointed two days later, on the orders of Ramnad's powerful *Daḷavāy* Vellaiyan Servaikkarar and the mother of the deceased ruler, as some local sources say. Nevertheless, VOC documents state that Rakka's accession was soon opposed by a court faction favouring another pretender to the throne, the twelve-year old Sella Tevar, probably a more distant cousin of the previous ruler.

Although Sella was initially forced to flee to Tanjavur, by early December 1749 Rakka had been "kicked out of the throne" by the *daḷavāy*, as the Dutch put it. Thereupon the young Sella was installed as Setupati under his regal name Vijaya Raghunatha (r. 1749-63), with consent of the community. Both "A chronicle of the acts of the Sethupathis" and "A general history of the Kings of Rama Naad or the Satoo-Putty Samastanum" have it that Rakka was dislodged precisely because he did not enjoy this popular consent. Those texts may however have exaggerated this concern with the common people in an effort to conceal another account saying Rakka was simply dethroned because he had turned against the dominating *daḷavāy*.[186]

184 NA, VOC, no. 2185, ff. 1167-7v; no. 2224, ff. 1611v-19; no. 2290, f. 254; no. 2291, ff. 497-8; no. 2337, ff. 1543-4, 1546v-7v, 1579-80v; no. 2523, f. 1426; no. 2559, f. 1472; no. 8958, ff. 752, 754: report of mission to Ramnad, Feb. 1731, letters from the Ramnad court to Tuticorin and Colombo, Aug. 1735, Jan. 1742, letters from Kilakkarai to Tuticorin, from Tuticorin to Colombo, May-Nov. 1732, Jan., Mar. 1733, Aug.-Sept. 1735, Nov. 1741; BL/AAS, MG, no. 4, pt. 8: "A general history of the kings of Rama Naad or the Satoo-Putty Samastanum," f. 193; MT, class III, no. 77: "Regarding the Zemindars of Ramnad," f. 73v; Mahalingam, *Mackenzie Manuscripts*, vol. I, 164 (note *); Bes, "Friendship as Long as the Sun and Moon Shine," 46, 54-5; Seshadri, "The Sētupatis of Ramnad," 97-8, 100; Thiruvenkatachari, *The Setupatis of Ramnad*, 50; Raja Ram Rao, *Ramnad Manual*, 236.

185 According to some traditions, the Setupatis were also installed or received the royal sceptre in Pogalur, about ten miles west of Ramanathapuram, thought to have been Ramnad's initial capital and the place where the first Setupatis originated. See, for example: "Account of the Province of Rámnád, Southern Peninsula of India," *Journal of the Royal Asiatic Society* 3, 5 (1836), 174; Boyle, "Chronicles of Southern India," 45; J.L.W., "The Chronicles of the Marava Country," 449. Dutch sources however never seem to refer to Pogalur.

186 NA, VOC, no. 2733, ff. 18-18v, 33v; no. 2735, ff. 1052v-3v; no. 2757, f. 1474: letters from Tuticorin to Colombo, from Colombo to Batavia, Feb., May 1749, Jan. 1750; BL/AAS, MG, no. 4, pt. 8: "A general history of the kings of Rama Naad or the Satoo-Putty Samastanum," ff. 193-4; *Beknopte historie*, 94; Taylor, *Oriental Historical Manuscripts*, vol. II, Appendix, 52; Bes, "Friendship as Long as the Sun and Moon Shine," 83-4; idem, "The Setupatis, the Dutch, and Other Bandits," 560; Seshadri, "The Sētupatis

The years 1763-4 saw the last succession discussed here. As extensively described in VOC documents, Sella died on 30 January 1763, which led to a succession struggle between three court factions, each with its own figurehead. One party consisted of the former *Pradhāni* (prime or financial minister) Damodaram Pillai and the son of the now deceased *Daḷavāy* Vellaiyan Servaikkarar, the second group of the current *pradhāni* and his supporters, and the third faction of yet other courtiers. At some point, Damodaram managed to place the two-month old Muttu Ramalinga Tevar on the throne (r. 1763-72, 1781-95), who was the sister's son of the previous Setupati. After this infant had been acknowledged by the leading Maravars, Damodaram himself was reinstalled in his former office of *pradhāni*, while Muttu Ramalinga's father, Mappillai Tevar, was to act as his son's regent. To end all competition at court, the other pretenders to the throne and several of their followers were beheaded.

But, still according to the Dutch, animosity immediately arose between Damodaram and Mappillai too. While leading Ramnad's troops in a war against Tanjavur, the former scented a plot hatched by the latter to have him killed on the battlefield. Damodaram then made peace with Tanjavur, enlisted the support of Madurai—now annexed by Arcot—and several Maravar chiefs, and marched towards Ramanathapuram to oust his opponent. In fear, Mappillai had some more competitors decapitated and jailed Damodaram's family. The Nawab of Arcot attempted to mediate between the two rivals, but after Mappillai proved unwilling to cooperate, Damodaram returned to him the signet ring and sword received in his capacity as *pradhāni*, thus entirely withdrawing himself from the court's service. When he subsequently laid siege to the royal fort, Mappillai asked the Dutch for military assistance, but in December 1763 he suddenly died of chicken pox or poison. With no serious competition left, Damodaram now took control of the kingdom. The minor Muttu Ramalinga (Mappillai's son) remained Setupati, however, since Damodaram did not belong to the Maravar caste and therefore could not become king, while his own favourite for the throne was unacceptable to Arcot and the increasingly influential British.[187]

Most local texts and secondary literature present slightly different versions of the events. For example, some works state that Muttu Ramalinga's regent was his mother Muttu Tiruvayi Nachiar, sister of the former ruler, whereas other accounts

of Ramnad," 100-2, 104; Kadhirvel, *A History of the Maravas*, 84; Thiruvenkatachari, *The Setupatis of Ramnad*, 51; Raja Ram Rao, *Ramnad Manual*, 237; Nelson, *The Madura Country*, vol. III, 293-4.

187 DNA, DCGCC, no. 2705, ff. 12-14v: final report of Tuticorin's chief Godfried Sweepe, Feb. 1765; NA, VOC, no. 3082, ff. 1157-62, 1453-6: letters from Tuticorin to Colombo, from Colombo to Batavia, Feb.-Mar., Sept.-Oct. 1763, Jan. 1764; Bes, "The Setupatis, the Dutch, and Other Bandits," 561. The accounts in the various Dutch documents differ slightly from each other. Muttu Ramalinga may have been two years old, instead of two months, when he ascended the throne, while Mappillai Tevar perhaps died in Dec. 1764 rather than 1763.

Table 8: Setupatis of Ramnad (until 1790s), regnal dates, relations to predecessors, and further remarks.

	name (regal / personal)	accession date	ending date	relation to predecessors	remarks († = natural death at end of reign)
1	Udaiyan Setupati / Sadaika Tevar	c. 1605	c. 1622	descendant of mythical line	†, installed by Madurai Nayakas
2	Kuttan Setupati	c. 1622	c. 1636	1st son of 1	†, childless?
3	Dalavay Setupati / Sadaika Tevar II	c. 1636 & c. 1640	c. 1640 & c. 1645	brother of 2 & 2nd son of 1, or adopted son of 2	his nomination of 5 contested by 4, dethroned and re-installed by Madurai, murdered by 4?
4	Peddanna Nayaka Tevar alias Tambi	c. 1640	c. 1640	low-born half-brother of 3 & son of 1 or 2, or brother's son of 3	installed and dethroned by Madurai
5	Raghunatha (Tirumalai) Setupati	c. 1645	1673, c. Apr.	sister's son or son-in-law of 3	†, parts of Ramnad first ruled by 4 and brothers of 5
6	Surya Tevar	1673, c. Apr.	1673, c. Oct.	(half-)brother's son or 1st son of 5	childless, killed by Madurai
7	Athana Tevar	1673, c. Oct.	late 1673	brother of 6 & son of 5, uncle or cousin of 6, distant relative, or unrelated	minor, killed by Madurai
8	Raghunatha Setupati / Kilavan Tevar	late 1673	1710, Oct. 12	low-born son or cousin of 6, or uncle's grandson of 7, or unrelated	†, elected? contested by several
9	Muttu Vijaya Raghunatha Setupati / Tiru Udaya Tevar	1710, Oct. 12	1725, Apr. 8 (4 pm)	sister's son & son-in-law of 8, & adopted by 8? grandson of 5?	†, contested by 11, childless?
10	Sundareshvara Setupati / Tanda Tevar	1725, Apr.	1725, Aug.	sister's son or son-in-law of 9, or great-grandson of 8's father	killed by 11 and Tanjavur

	name (regal / personal)	accession date	ending date	relation to predecessors	remarks († = natural death at end of reign)
11	Bhavani Shankara Tevar	1725, Apr./ Aug.	1729, Sept.	low-born son of 8, "in-law" of 9 through concubine?	dethroned by 12 and Tanjavur
12	Kumara Muttu Vijaya Raghunatha Setupati / Kattaya Tevar	1729, Sept. 17	1735, Aug. 12	maternal uncle of 10 & son-in-law of 9	†, contested, leading to secession of Shivagangai at accession
13	Sivakumara Muttu Vijaya Raghunatha Setupati	1735, Aug. 14	1748, Dec. 24	son of 12	†? minor at accession, childless
14	Rakka Tevar	1748, Dec. 26	1749, c. Dec.	cousin of 13 or 12	dethroned for 15
15	Vijaya Raghunatha Setupati / Sella Tevar	1749, c. Dec.	1763, Jan. 30	aunt's grandson of 13	†? minor at accession, no sons
16	Muttu Ramalinga Setupati	1763, c. Feb. & 1781, Apr.	1772, June & 1795, Mar.	sister's son of 15	minor at accession, contested, dethroned twice by Arcot and British, interlude of Arcot rule in 1772-80

For sources, see the references in the preceding section, Chapter 1, and the Epilogue.

say this position fell to the young king's uncle, who wished to become Setupati himself and imprisoned the boy. Despite such differences, nearly all sources, including even most local chronicles, refer to the rivalry and brutalities accompanying this succession. The violence was apparently so excessive that only one or two texts, among which "A chronicle of the acts of the Sethupathis," chose to fully ignore it.[188] The further fortunes of Muttu Ramalinga—in 1772 temporarily deposed by a coalition of Arcot and the British—and his successors are briefly considered in the Epilogue.

188 BL/AAS, MG, no. 4, pt. 8: "A general history of the kings of Rama Naad or the Satoo-Putty Samastanum," ff. 194-6; MT, class III, no. 77: "Regarding the Zemindars of Ramnad," f. 74; Taylor, *Oriental Historical Manuscripts*, vol. II, Appendix, 52; Mahalingam, *Mackenzie Manuscripts*, vol. I, 180; Seshadri, "The Sētupatis of Ramnad," 116-17, 120-3; Kadhirvel, *A History of the Maravas*, 142-6, 160; Thiruvenkatachari, *The Setupatis of Ramnad*, 52; Raja Ram Rao, *Ramnad Manual*, 239-40; Nelson, *The Madura Country*, vol. III, 294.

Looking at successions in Ramnad until the 1760s, one gets the impression of a dynasty characterised by almost continuous instability that nevertheless held its own against many internal and external threats for over one and a half centuries. Leaving out Muttu Ramalinga's interrupted rule but including the brief take-over by Tambi, fifteen Setupatis sat on the throne between approximately 1605 and 1763. The average reign thus covered slightly over a decade, placing these men among the shortest ruling kings discussed here.

This low average is not merely the result of the five reigns that lasted no longer than a year. It appears that virtually every succession was opposed and only about six rulers died a natural death. The few uncontested transitions nearly always resulted in a minor (and once even a suckling) becoming king, under the regency of the most powerful courtier. But besides these four infants, there were only a few other dynasts who did not fully qualify for the throne. These were the two or three men regarded as low-born sons of previous Setupatis. As for women rulers, despite the alleged succession rule that in the absence of a king's son, a king's daughter was the first heir, no queen ever reigned over Ramnad during the period under study, while there was just one possible case of female regency.

Thus, the dynasty's volatile nature did not wholly stem from ignoring the recommendations in political discourses not to crown women or illegitimate children. Rather, other succession patterns were prominent in Ramnad, apart from the usual role of courtiers. First, successions from father to son or from brother to brother were relatively rare, especially in the eighteenth century. Instead, quite a number of rulers were followed by cousins or nephews (four of these probably being sister's sons), various in-laws, or more distant relatives. The pool of candidates for the throne was apparently larger in Ramnad than in the other kingdoms, and therefore the potential for clashes was probably higher.

Second, various sources state that subjects from beyond court circles, like local Maravar chiefs, had some say in the installation of new kings, or were even entitled to choose them. Dutch records in particular refer to this. They mention kings who needed "permission of the community" (*toestemming der gemeente*), were "publicly introduced to the people" in the capital (*den volke aldaar publicq voorgestelt*), or were "recognised and accepted as their legitimate monarch" (*voor haaren wettigen vorst erkent en aangenomen*) by Maravar leaders from around the kingdom. The documents also speak of a ceremony where courtiers and warrior chiefs publicly acknowledged the new ruler by raising both hands and worshipping him. VOC documents on the other kingdoms never refer to anything comparable. Admittedly, these occasions could have been orchestrated, but it was apparently important to engage the wider public when a Setupati ascended the throne.[189] The prominent role of Maravar commanders in Shivagangai's secession from Ramnad is likely an indication of this involvement as well.

Third, the great influence of neighbouring kingdoms stands out. Initially, the Nayakas of Madurai played a decisive part in many successions, first installing the Setupati dynasty, then appointing and dethroning several rulers, next temporarily dividing the kingdom into three, and finally assassinating two kings. When Ramnad had largely broken away from Madurai at the turn of the eighteenth century, the Tanjavur Bhonsles came to interfere in succession struggles, shifting their support between whichever contender promised them land and tribute in return, and managing to partition the kingdom permanently. In the course of the eighteenth century, as Tanjavur's power diminished, Arcot took over this role and even removed the Setupati house for some time.

Altogether, an exceptionally wide range of parties was involved in Ramnad's successions: the extended royal family, local leaders, neighbouring kingdoms, and of course courtiers. This seems to have accounted for the instability of the Setupati dynasty and the often violent transitions between its consecutive rulers.

Conclusions

After discussing around ninety successions under nine dynasties in five states, this chapter concludes with a general analysis of these events by making three comparisons: between sources, between rules and reality, and between dynasties.

Starting with the various kinds of sources, we have seen that events as they are described in European documents differ from how they are portrayed in south Indian accounts, like literary and epigraphic texts. It has also become clear that significant variations exist within these two sets of sources, particularly among those deriving from courts. Chronicles, inscriptions, and visual materials all reflect the views of the rulers patronising those sources. Therefore, these materials may label earlier kings as unlawful usurpers and even leave them out, or, on the contrary, depict usurpers as peacefully installed rulers. Monarchs portrayed as legitimate heirs in one text can be presented as low-born violators in another. That becomes manifest, for instance, when two collateral dynastic lines competed with one another, as happened with almost all royal houses under consideration. Often, however, sources created by individuals or family branches who lost succession

189 NA, VOC, no. 2026, f. 834v; no. 2158, f. 950v; no. 2337, f. 1543v; no. 2757, f. 1474. But see also Scharfe, *The State in Indian Tradition*, 65-6.

struggles appear not to have survived. As a consequence, many remaining dynastic chronicles, usually created under the last few rulers, give versions of past successions favouring those later kings and the lines of their direct ancestors.

But at the same time, these works thereby show how rulers attempted to legitimise their own and their forefathers' positions and how they downplayed opponents. The main elements employed here are legitimate descent and nomination by predecessors, ascribed rather than achieved characteristics. These qualities were apparently considered most important to justify one's place on the throne—despite the emphasis in political treatises on a combination of ancestry and ability. Whereas references to achieved attributes like valour, wisdom, and physical strength are common in dynastic foundation stories, those motifs rarely figure in textual passages claiming right of succession. It seems that once a dynasty was established, personal capacities were no longer considered as significant as ancestry. Of course, in reality these aspects were often essential, as European accounts attest.

The previous sections demonstrate how Dutch and other European accounts contribute to our knowledge of successions. Those "foreign" sources obviously had their own limitations: their authors may have misunderstood certain court machinations, been misinformed by local rumours, or intentionally exaggerated political upheavals to explain lulls in trade or cover up corruption. Still, these documents make sufficiently clear that more often than not, transitions described as peaceful in south Indian texts were in fact violent conflicts. According to European records, the outcomes of succession struggles were not principally determined by descent and nomination, but equally by ambitions, strategies, networks, and plain fate. Thus, external sources do not merely show that south Indian texts were constructions endorsed by their patrons, but also which events local works chose to ignore, and by consequence, what purposes these texts served.

With regard to the discrepancy between formal succession principles and the actual unfolding of succession struggles, two matters stand out. First, under all dynasties of Vijayanagara and its heirs, notions on succession rights appear to have been rather unspecific and flexible, and also were not clearly documented, at least not in surviving texts. Based on both pre-modern Indian works on statecraft and modern reconstructions by historians, it seems there was a general preference for adult sons or brothers, born of official queens, as successors. If these were unavailable, other legitimate male family members were acceptable, often without much further prioritising.[190] Ramnad may have been somewhat exceptional, but it is unclear whether its alleged succession rules were actually recorded somewhere.

[190] See also Burling, *The Passage of Power*, 58.

By and large, however, the courts appear not to have been deeply concerned with principles of succession. Extensive discourses on politics by some of the kings themselves—such as the *Āmuktamālyada* by Vijayanagara's Krishna Raya and the *Śivatattva ratnākara* by Ikkeri's Basavappa Nayaka I—largely ignore the subject. It is of course possible that this vagueness was deliberate, allowing the most capable member of the royal family to ascend the throne, thereby aiming at dynastic continuation.

Second, insofar as preferences did exist, they were frequently disregarded. Under the last two Vijayanagara houses (for which substantial information is available) and all but one of the successor dynasties, only about one-fifth to one-third of the successions involved fathers and mature legitimate sons. Transitions between mature legitimate brothers occurred even less often. In many other instances, successions went against all supposed principles. Together, the imperial Tuluva and Aravidu houses and the succeeding dynasties included around fifteen minors, five women, and six low-born relatives on the throne, accounting for about one-third of all rulers. The remainder mostly comprised paternal and maternal cousins, nephews, uncles, and grandsons—successions not discouraged, but not recommended either, in political treatises.

The relative paucity of successions by sons or brothers under these houses is surprising when compared with the alleged high frequency of such transitions among other dynasties throughout India's past. Modern-day surveys of relationships between consecutive rulers from antiquity until the early modern period show an overwhelming majority of filial and fraternal successors. In the same vein, much secondary literature on individual dynasties preceding Vijayanagara claims that successions were largely peaceful.[191]

Therefore, either Vijayanagara and its heirs were exceptional in this regard, or the south Indian sources on which those surveys are based portray successions in subjective ways, aiming at legitimising the rulers who commissioned these sources through supposedly direct descent from predecessors. The latter option seems more likely, considering the differences between local and external sources discussed

191 For surveys of large numbers of dynasties, see: C.H. Philips (ed.), *Handbook of Oriental History* (London, 1963), 82-94; S.B. Bhattacherje, *Encyclopaedia of Indian Events and Dates* (New Delhi, 1995), C7-51; David Henige, *Princely States of India: A Guide to Chronology and Rulers* (Bangkok, 2004), passim, especially 3-4. For individual pre-Vijayanagara dynasties, see, for instance: K.R. Basava Raja, "The Central Government under the Chālukyas of Kalyāṇa," in M.S. Nagaraja Rao (ed.), *The Chālukyas of Kalyāṇa (Seminar Papers)* (Bangalore, 1983), 91-3; K.A. Nilakanta Sastri, "The Chāḷukyas of Kalyāṇi," in G. Yazdani (ed.), *The Early History of the Deccan* (London, 1960), pts I-VI, 382; A.S. Altekar, "The Yādavas of Seuṇadeśa," in idem, pts VII-XI, 557; N. Venkataramanayya and M. Somasekhara Sarma, "The Kākatīyas of Warangal," in idem, 670-1; Y. Subbarayalu, *South India under the Cholas* (New Delhi, 2012), 212.

above. In that case, successions under dynasties before Vijayanagara did not generally proceed differently from those investigated in the present study—and thus also regularly witnessed rulers not favoured by political treatises, likely installed after violent competition—in spite of what the only available, local sources may claim.

If one succession principle can be deduced from the events described in the previous sections, it simply is the condition that a new ruler be part of the royal family.[192] All dynasts, including those two dozen minors, widows, and bastards, were somehow related to previous kings. But even this guideline was interpreted in different ways, as appears from instances where in-laws ascended the throne. While in Vijayanagara succession through the female line was reason to speak of a new dynasty—demonstrated by the transition from the Tuluvas to the Aravidus—in Ramnad this was not considered a change of dynasty, as several cases there illustrate.

Anyhow, each and every succession could be contested, including those following the rules set by discourses on statecraft. Thus, mature legitimate sons of former rulers were dethroned, brothers succeeded even when sons fitting all requirements were available, and long-reigning family branches were deposed by collateral lines. On the whole, principles of succession appear to have been neither elaborate nor effective under any of the imperial and successor dynasties.[193]

The last comparison discussed here is that between the royal houses. In general, some dynasties were more secure than others, for example with regard to the length of reigns, the frequency and intensity of successions struggles, and kinship relations between consecutive rulers. Under the rather stable Tanjavur Nayakas, the average king ruled for nearly thirty years, competition was of a limited scale, and successors—and even their rivals—were all sons of previous rulers. The dynasty that came next in Tanjavur, the Bhonsle house, was more volatile but still relatively stable. Apart from a short, atypical interlude of some violent successions and brief reigns by a widow and a putative son, the Bhonsles ruled for about fifteen years on an average, accessions to the throne were contested only in some cases and without much impact beyond the royal family, and all kings were sons or brothers of their predecessors. Besides, almost all Bhonsle rulers died a natural death.

At the other end of the spectrum were the Setupatis of Ramnad, whose average reign lasted about a decade, whose consecutive rulers were often distant relatives, and under whom nearly every succession was opposed—often leading to widespread confusion and twice even to the kingdom's division. Further, about half of

[192] See also Burling, *The Passage of Power*, 58.

[193] For a somewhat different view, see Narayana Rao and Subrahmanyam, "Ideologies of State Building," 231.

the Setupatis were killed or otherwise dislodged, and with four infants and two low-born sons this house numbered comparatively many "unqualified" kings.

Between these extremes, one can place the houses of Vijayanagara, Ikkeri, and Madurai, each for different reasons. In the two latter kingdoms, monarchs occupied the throne for relatively long periods, close to fifteen years on an average. But of the approximately seventeen rulers under both Nayaka dynasties, just around ten died a natural death while seven faced opposition when ascending the throne. Under both houses, about half of the successors were their predecessors' sons or brothers, while in each kingdom "unqualified" monarchs included two females and three or four minors. An additional complication, especially in Ikkeri, was long-lasting competition between dynastic branches.

Vijayanagara's dynasties all witnessed substantially shorter average reigns, hovering around a decade, and accessions to the throne were often contested, frequently leading to dethronements and assassinations. Successions from father to son or from brother to brother were about as common as in Ikkeri and Madurai, however, while under the four imperial houses together there were only about five cases of minors or illegitimate relatives on the throne and queens never reigned at all. The number of "unqualified" emperors was therefore very low.

In sum: it appears that with regard to succession practices and dynastic stability, Vijayanagara, Ikkeri, and Madurai were positioned more or less in the middle, whereas Tanjavur and Ramnad occupied opposite ends of the scale. There may be several reasons why these two kingdoms stood out. In Ramnad, an unusually large number of parties were involved in court politics: a very extended royal family, various kinds of courtiers, local Maravar chieftains, and several neighbouring kingdoms. Therefore, the potential for competition between pretenders and for the exploitation of this rivalry by others was high. With large pools of both candidates for the throne and external parties, conflicts could easily arise and then quickly expand. Both groups appear to have been smaller in the other kingdoms—especially Tanjavur—generally seeing fewer royal contenders, interfering neighbours, or independent-minded local chiefs. These chiefs were however an important factor in the vast Vijayanagara empire, where many a pretender could build up a local power base far away from the capital, either to seize the throne or assume regional autonomy.

Ramnad's and Tanjavur's exceptional positions might be related to their geography and demography. Located in a zone of dry wasteland and forests, Ramnad was thinly inhabited and roving groups of warriors and herders were common. Such mobile, autonomous bands were instrumental in the kingdom's final partition. Its political structure seems to have been relatively open and flexible, making access to the court comparatively easy. Tanjavur, by contrast, was based in the fertile Kaveri delta, dominated by farmland and sedentary communities, resulting in a high population density. Thus, its society was highly stratified, preventing social mobility, and had long been controlled by an elite of kings and priests solidly institutionalised and religiously sanctioned. This could have curtailed the influence of outsiders on dormant tensions at court and kept succession struggles limited in terms of both participants and impact.[194]

We now return to the discussion on the ambiguity of succession struggles, mentioned in this chapter's introduction. Did such clashes actually threaten dynasties or did they serve as necessary periods of transition, testing the court's balance of power and reshuffling the political landscape? As this chapter demonstrates, succession struggles did both. They provided opportunities for capable people—on and around the throne—to increase their influence, do away with incapable rivals, reset internal and external relations, and thereby secure the continuity of the dynasty, the court, and the state. The lack of specific and forceful succession principles may therefore have had some positive consequences, allowing for flexibility and progress.

However, opposition between pretenders could also lead to political fragmentation and even dynastic demise. Further, although brothers were generally considered to be among the most preferred successors, hostilities were often the result of fraternal friction. Indeed, rivalry between brothers—regularly spilling over into subsequent generations and causing long-lasting, potentially dangerous collateral lines—seems to have been the most common and significant form of competition under all royal houses. These conflicts would usually come to involve courtiers, local chiefs, and neighbouring kingdoms, sometimes with fatal consequences for the dynasties.

It appears that the various royal families adopted different strategies to deal with opposing relatives and collateral branches. Madurai's Nayakas chose an incorporative approach by recognising a hereditary line of secondary rulers, which however eventually contributed to the dynasty's fall. Ikkeri's Nayakas, by contrast, seem to have left this issue unaddressed for a long time, until one branch almost entirely annihilated the other. While most houses resorted to bloody confrontations only intermittently, Tanjavur's Nayakas appear to have dealt with the problem most effectively—if most violently—by killing, imprisoning, or blinding rivalling brothers on a seemingly regular basis. All in all, both succession principles and succession struggles remained ambivalent phenomena,[195] for which Vijayanagara and its heirs apparently never managed to develop satisfactory solutions.

194 For discussions on geographic, demographic, and societal zones in Ramnad and Tanjavur, see for instance: Price, *Kingship and Political Practice in Colonial India*, 9-10; Bes, "The Setupatis, the Dutch, and Other Bandits," 545-6, 563-6; Shulman, "On South Indian Bandits and Kings," 288-90, 301-6; Subrahmanyam, *Penumbral Visions*, 226. See also Chapter 1.

195 See also Burling, *The Passage of Power*, 67. For a Eurasia-wide perspective, see Duindam, "The Court as a Meeting Point," 34-5.

***

One more question has remained unanswered in this chapter: what became of Sadashiva Nayaka, the wandering prince who possessed so many qualifications to sit on Ikkeri's throne and yet was outsmarted by Queen Chennammaji? His request for military assistance was politely turned down by the Dutch, as it was by the Portuguese and the Maratha King Sambhaji, although a representative of the latter provided him with a guard of twenty men. Pointing to his succession rights, Sadashiva even contacted the Ikkeri court itself, including Chennammaji. She was courteous enough to send him a handsome sum of money, 2,000 *pagodas*, to enable him to support himself. All the Dutch did was lend him 25 *pagodas*, present him with a small gift of spices, and allow him to camp on the grounds of their factory in Vengurla for a few days.

Thus, Sadashiva had no choice but to continue moving around south India, looking for allies and devising strategies to become king.[196] He would never be one, however, lacking a healthy dose of luck and, especially, the right connections. The people forming the bulk of such connections, courtiers of all ranks and kinds, are investigated in the next chapter.

196 NA, VOC, no. 1463, ff. 439v-40; no. 1474, ff. 210v-13, 329v-32; no. 1593, ff. 7-7v: letters from "Sadaasjiwe Neijke king of Carnatica" at Vengurla to the Dutch commissioner-general, from the *commandeur* at Quilon to Commissioner Van Rheede, from Cochin to Batavia, report on Vengurla and "Canara," Feb.-Mar., June 1689, Dec. 1697. See also Shastry, *Goa-Kanara Portuguese Relations*, 216. A VOC document from 1703 mentions a son of Shivappa II's brother (Sadashiva?), Kasiyya Bhadrayya, whom the Dutch considered the rightful heir to Ikkeri's throne. Backed by Mughal troops, he invaded Ikkeri and nearly besieged Bednur. In spite of this and efforts to win Ikkeri's subjects over, the pretender was defeated by King Basavappa, as the Mughal troops were withdrawn to fight the Maratha King Shivaji. See NA, VOC, no. 1694, ff. 75-6: report on trade in Ikkeri, Mar. 1703. For a Dutch reference from 1697 to what probably was the same person, then supported by Mysore, see NA, VOC, no. 1593, f. 7v: letter from Cochin to Batavia, Dec. 1697.

CHAPTER 3

The Power of Courtiers[1]

One day, at the age of twelve, Ariyanatha Mudaliyar was sleeping outside when a passing Brahmin spotted a cobra using its hood to protect the boy from the rays of the sun. Feeling that this auspicious sign foretold a glorious future, the Brahmin paid his respect to Ariyanatha, saluting and feeding him. Later, on the Brahmin's advice, Ariyanatha travelled north, where he entered into service with a Vijayanagara courtier. At the imperial court, Ariyanatha soon stood out for his wisdom and prowess. He accurately analysed the emperor's horoscope and explained how the head of a buffalo must be cut off with one blow. Ariyanatha was then employed as a courtier himself and displayed his magnificence by bestowing numerous gifts. Next, he crushed disorders in Madurai and reinstalled its Pandya king. Leading several other victorious battles for Vijayanagara, guided by the goddess Durga, he was adopted as the emperor's son. But rather than ascending the imperial throne, Ariyanatha divided the realm into three parts and appointed rulers in Madurai, Tanjavur, and Mysore, while he himself remained the chief commander of all those kingdoms. Subsequently, he fought more wars, fortified towns, installed local chiefs, cultivated lands, and endowed temples and Brahmins.[2]

Reading this summarised Tamil account of Ariyanatha Mudaliyar's career, one might be excused for thinking that this man was well on his way to found yet another house ruling one of Vijayanagara's successor states. Many elements here remind us of the dynastic origin myths discussed in Chapter 1. Like the heroes in those texts, Ariyanatha is associated with martial feats, ties to the imperial house, recognition of a religious kind, natural miracles, migration, and the cultivation of land.

Other stories glorify Ariyanatha even more, saying he cut off the buffalo's head himself, surpassed all Vijayanagara officials in mathematical skills, received special honours from the emperor, won a wrestling contest, built Madurai's future capital Tiruchirappalli, and served the Madurai, Tanjavur, and Mysore kingdoms not only as generalissimo but as chief minister, too. It is also said that Madurai's

[1] This chapter's section on Ramnad is partly based on: Bes, "The Setupatis, the Dutch, and Other Bandits," 550-2, 556-64; idem, "Friendship as Long as the Sun and Moon Shine," sections of chs 3-5, 7.

[2] Taylor, *Oriental Historical Manuscripts*, vol. II, 113-16. This text belongs to the so-called Mrtyunjaya manuscripts, collected by Madurai's chief Brahmin in the early nineteenth century.

first Nayaka, Vishvanatha, presented Ariyanatha with two rings symbolising this double military-civilian dignity, as well as other jewels, valuable clothes including a quadrangular turban, and the privilege of adorning his forehead with a "civet beauty spot." Notwithstanding all this, however, he never was to assume royal status because, according to one text, his background as a farmer (belonging to the Vellala caste) precluded that.[3]

Rather, as historians believe, Ariyanatha Mudaliyar was a very powerful courtier under Madurai's first few Nayakas from the mid- to the late sixteenth century. While there is little evidence for activities at the Vijayanagara court, his influence and stature in Madurai were exceptional indeed. He is thought to have held two of the kingdom's most important positions—*pradhāni* (prime or finance minister) and *daḷavāy* (chief general)—for several decades and to have played a major role in organising Madurai's territorial division among the Palaiyakkarars (subordinate chieftains). Further, he commissioned several temple buildings and was co-granter of religious endowments alongside the king.[4]

As such, Ariyanatha Mudaliar provides an example of a courtier who grew so powerful that his position appeared to nearly match that of a king, or that is what the texts praising him seem to suggest. His exalted status, albeit non-regal, evidently justified the composition of such laudatory works. But Ariyanatha was not the only official in the Vijayanagara successor states whose standing was glorified in literary texts. Two other examples concern heirs of the empire not systematically discussed in this study: Mysore and Senji. Under the Nayakas of the latter kingdom, a whole dynasty of ministers legitimised its prominence through a tale that again brings royal foundation myths to mind. One version of this story has been translated in a manuscript titled "Historical account of Gingee." It relates Senji's history from the fifteenth century, when it is described as a village of herdsmen under Tanjavur rule, up to its fortunes as a kingdom until the late eighteenth century. A summary of the text's initial sections, with the original spelling of names, runs as follows:

[3] BL/AAS, OI, no. I, pt. 22: "Kings of Tritchanopoly from 1509," f. 239; MG, no. 4, pt. 4: "Mootiah's chronological & historical account of the modern kings of Madura," f. 48; Rangachari, "The History of the Naik Kingdom of Madura," *Indian Antiquary* XLIV, 62-5, XLV, 83-7; Nelson, *The Madura Country*, vol. III, 90-1, 104; Taylor, *Oriental Historical Manuscripts*, vol. II, 117-20.

[4] Sathyanatha Aiyar, *History of the Nayaks of Madura*, 51-3, 58-62, 73-4, 79-80, 84-6, 236, 340, 342; Susan Bayly, *Saints, Goddesses and Kings: Muslims and Christians in South Indian Society, 1700-1900* (Cambridge, 1989), 211-12; Heras, *The Aravidu Dynasty of Vijayanagara*, vol. I, 139, 345-6; Francis, *Madura Gazetteer*, 42-3; Sewell, *List of Inscriptions*, 2. It is said that an equestrian statue in the thousand-pillared hall of the Minakshi Sundareshvara Temple at Madurai town portrays Ariyanatha Mudaliyar, but this claim has been contested. See Nagaswamy, *Studies in Ancient Tamil Law and Society*, 113.

One day, a herdsman from Chenjee [Senji] named Aununda Coana [Anandakona] brought his sheep to an overgrown hill. There, some of his animals went missing. Unable to find them, the herdsman returned home with the rest of his flock. Four years later, when Aununda Coana let his sheep graze at the same place, he chanced upon his lost animals, who had remained on the hill. Trying to drive them down, he found a den in which a holy man was living. The later explained to Aununda Coana it was his task to develop this land, and revealed to him the location of a nearby treasure of money and precious stones, to be used to build a fort, temples, and agraharoms [*agrahārams*, lands donated for Brahmin settlements]. The herdsman should go to Tanjore [Tanjavur] to inform Veejaya Renga Naik [Vijayaranga Nayaka, unidentified ruler] of these matters, whereupon, so the holy men predicted, Veejaya Renga Naik's and Aununda Coana's descendants would rule as respectively king and minister of the new Chenjee kingdom for eleven generations.

Although feeling insecure and reluctant, the herdsman travelled to Tanjore and spoke to Veejaya Renga Naik, who was greatly pleased and presented him and his own son, Vyapa Naik [Vaiyappa Nayaka], with cloths and jewels. In the Mussulman year 852 [c. 1442 CE], accompanied by military forces, Aununda Coana and Vyapa Naik arrived in Chenjee. Having recovered the treasure, they employed people to remove the jungle, cut stones, and erect three enclosing fortifications, as well as palaces, offices, and houses. Further, Aununda Coana commanded his own troops and installed his son Kistnapilla [Krishna Pillai] as pradhaunee [*pradhāni*]. Thus his house was established.[5]

The text goes on to list the successors of King Vaiyappa Nayaka (possibly the historical founder of Senji's Nayaka house)[6] and of *Pradhāni* Krishna Pillai, all the sons of their predecessors. As foretold by the holy man, both the royal and ministerial houses continue for ten more generations, spanning 225 years, after which the Mughals are stated to have conquered Senji in 1667.[7]

[5] BL/AAS, MG, no. 9, pt. 13e: "Historical account of Gingee," ff. 138-41. This work, whose original language is unknown (possibly Marathi), labels itself as *kaifiyat-bakhair* ("kyfyat bakhyr"), which might be literally translated as "compiled local narrative." For a comparable manuscript account, see BL/AAS, MM, no. 118, 1st pt.: "Kypheat of Gingee." See also MG, no. 9, pt. 13a: "Kyfyat of Gingee," ff. 121-2. For discussions of these and related texts, see: S.M. Edwardes (ed.), "A Manuscript History of the Rulers of Jinji," *The Indian Antiquary: A Journal of Oriental Research* LV (1926); C.S. Srinivasachari, *A History of Gingee and Its Rulers* (Annamalainagar, 1943), 80-92; Subrahmanyam, *Penumbral Visions*, 207-17; Alf C. Hiltebeitel, *The Cult of Draupadī*, vol. 1, *Mythologies: From Gingee to Kurukṣetra* (Chicago, 1988), 17-19, 57-9; Cotton, Charpentier, and Johnston, *Catalogue of Manuscripts in European Languages*, vol. I, pt. II, 85-7; Narayana Rao, Shulman, and Subrahmanyam, *Textures of Time*, 151 (n. 14).

[6] For Vaiyappa Nayaka, see: A. Krishnaswami, *The Tamil Country under Vijayanagar* (Annamalainagar, 1964), 246-50; Nobuhiro Ota, "A Study of Two *Nāyaka* Families in the Vijayanagara Kingdom in the Sixteenth Century," *Memoirs of the Research Department of the Toyo Bunko* 66 (2008), 111-18; Karashima, *Towards a New Formation*, 17, 22, 40 (n. 18); Srinivasachari, *A History of Gingee*, 78-82.

[7] BL/AAS, MG, no. 9, pt. 13e: "Historical account of Gingee," ff. 141-4.

This work appears somewhat confused in its erroneous dates and it is difficult to identify some people with historical persons. Also, the story of Anandakona's rise to power is not supported by other sources. Indeed, his very existence, and that of his successors, is uncertain. Besides, the text's original version may have been corrupted with a particular agenda in mind, considering it was obtained in 1803 from someone claiming descent from the line of Anandakona. Yet, this account is another instance of courtiers attaining an exalted standing that is linked to motifs also found in royal foundation myths. In addition to a natural miracle, religious acknowledgement, ties to a royal family, and land development—figuring in texts on Madurai's Minister Ariyanatha Mudaliyar, too—one now encounters the acquisition of wealth and even hereditary continuity.

One more example of a courtiers' dynasty with its own foundation story is the Kalale family, which provided Mysore's Wodeyar rulers with *daḷavāy*s during major parts of the seventeenth and eighteenth centuries. Indeed, according to some texts the Kalales had a formal agreement with the Wodeyar dynasty stipulating that only they were entitled to serve as *daḷavāy*. Between the 1730s and 1750s, they came to dominate the Mysore court, imprisoning and installing kings as they pleased. Unsurprisingly, boosting their status, literary works on the family's origins include the motifs of descent from chieftains, military achievements, southward migration,[8] and dynastic links through marital ties with the Wodeyars themselves.

The Kalales' perception of their own position seems well illustrated in a drawing on the frontispiece of a Kannada manuscript chronicle of the house, the *Kaḷale doregaḷa vaṃśāvaḷi*, recorded around 1800. As the drawing's captions explain, it depicts the Wodeyar ruler Krishnaraja II (r. 1734-66) and two members of the Kalale house, *Daḷavāy* Devarajayya and his brother, Chief Minister Nanjarajayya (active in the 1720s-50s). While the king's official status is recognised by the fact that only he is shown sitting on a kind of throne and being attended by a servant, the Kalale brothers are drawn much larger, hold swords (unlike the king), and clearly dominate the scene (see illustration 8).[9]

[8] The family's founding brothers are said to have moved from Dvaraka in Gujarat (north-west India) to the Kannada region. Interestingly, the same is stated about Mysore's Wodeyars themselves in their origin myths. See, for example, Caleb Simmons, "The Goddess and the King: Cāmuṇḍēśvari and the Fashioning of the Woḍeyar Court of Mysore" (unpublished dissertation, University of Florida, 2014), 109-12.

[9] For literary works on the Kalale family, see: M.H. Krishna, "The Dalavāi Family of Mysore," in N.K. Sidhanta *et al.* (ed.), *Bhārata-Kaumudī: Studies in Indology in Honour of Dr. Radha Kumud Mookerji*, pt. I (Allahabad, 1945); "The Dynasty of Kaḷale," *Annual Report of the Mysore Archæological Department for the Year 1942* (Mysore, 1943), 78-99, plate XIII. For the Kalales, see also: A. Satyanarayana, *History of the Wodeyars of Mysore (1610-1748)* (Mysore, 1996), 111, 116-22, 131, 225-7; K.C. Prashanth, "The Dalavai Project in Trichinopoly: The Evaluation of a Mysore Historian," *The Quarterly Journal of the Mythic*

Illustration 8: Drawing of Krishnaraja Wodeyar II of Mysore with courtiers Devarajayya and Nanjarajayya of the Kalale family, frontispiece of the *Kaḷale doregaḷa vaṃśāvaḷi*, c. 1800 (source: "The Dynasty of Kaḷale," *Annual Report of the Mysore Archæological Department for the Year 1942* (Mysore: University of Mysore, 1943), plate XIII, no. 2).

In fact, the long-lasting hereditary offices of Mysore's Kalale and (perhaps) Senji's Pillai lineages and the exalted standing of Madurai's Ariyanatha Mudaliyar, as well as the glorification of these officials in literary works, were not that common among Vijayanagara's heirs.[10] Yet, together these examples indicate various general aspects of the position of courtiers in these kingdoms: some of these men—and occasionally women—became exceedingly prominent, regardless of their official function; courtiers might hold different positions at the same time; kinship could be an important factor in their careers; and rivalry easily emerged between individuals or factions at the court. As shown in Chapter 2, courtiers played an important part in succession struggles. But both Indian and foreign sources make

Society XCVI, 1-2 (2005); Simmons, "The Goddess and the King," ch. 4; Hayavadana Rao, *History of Mysore*, vols I-II; Vikram Sampath, *Splendours of Royal Mysore: The Untold Story of the Wodeyars* (New Delhi, 2008), 129-37; Mark Wilks, *Historical Sketches of the South of India in an Attempt to Trace the History of Mysore from the Origin of the Hindu Government of that State, to the Extinction of the Mohammedan Dynasty in 1799*, ed. Murray Hammick (n.p., 1810), vol. I, 251-5.

10 But see also the *Rāmappaiyaṉ ammāṉai*, dealing with Madurai's *Daḷavāy* Ramappaiya, referred to in the section on Ramnad in Chapter 2.

clear that in between these transitions they were equally influential in dynastic and other political developments.

Therefore, the present chapter focuses on the role of courtiers in court politics. Central questions are how courtiers acquired their positions, how their formal functions were related to their actual activities and influence, how their power was manifested, and how they interacted with one another and with their rulers. Neither for Vijayanagara nor for its heirs have courtiers as a group been the subject of systematic research. Historians have looked at several individual courtiers, however, and demonstrated for instance that they could become very influential, combined different kinds of activities, and came from diverse backgrounds.[11] The findings of this chapter confirm these conclusions but also expand on them.

The composition and terminology of offices at south Indian courts varied over time and space, but functionaries generally comprised ministers and other councillors, treasurers and chancellors, secretaries, military commanders, poets and other artists, provincial governors and revenue-farmers, people with religious or mercantile duties, and ambassadors—as well as personal assistants of the ruler, including chamberlains, bodyguards, and bearers of regal paraphernalia such as fans, betel-leaves, spittoons, parasols, and fly-whisks. Further, some functions existed among the king's close relatives, like crown prince (*yuvarāja*), queen-mother, and chief queen. Moreover, members of the royal family could occupy regular court positions, for instance councillor, governor, and general. Additionally, outside the court proper, there were all sorts of subordinate chiefs and other leading figures with regional power who occasionally stayed at court.[12]

Therefore, in this study the term "courtiers"—used in the absence of a better word—denotes a very heterogeneous group of people, that could include members of dynasties (blood relatives and in-laws), court functionaries of various kinds and ranks (civil and military), personal servants, local chiefs and representatives, court

[11] For the successor states, see for example: Sanjay Subrahmanyam and C.A. Bayly, "Portfolio Capitalists and the Political Economy of Early Modern India," *The Indian Economic and Social History Review* 25, 4 (1988), 406-8, 411-12; Shulman and Subrahmanyam, "Prince of Poets and Ports"; Subrahmanyam, *The Political Economy of Commerce*, ch. 6, especially 298-300; C.S. Srinivasachariar, "Muslim Adventurers in the Kingdoms of Tanjore and Madura," in S.M. Katre and P.K. Gode (eds), *A Volume of Indian and Iranian Studies: Presented to Sir E. Denison Ross* ... (Bombay, 1939); Venkatesam, "Govinda Deekshita"; Vink, "Encounters on the Opposite Coast"; S. Somasundra Desikar, "Viceroys of the Nayaks of Madura," *Journal of Indian History* XVII, 2 (1938). For a critique of the first three works, see Kanakalatha Mukund, *The Trading World of the Tamil Merchant: Evolution of Merchant Capitalism in the Coromandel* (London, 1999), 60-1, 164-5. See also Radhika Seshan, *Trade and Politics on the Coromandel Coast: Seventeenth and Early Eighteenth Centuries* (Delhi, 2012), 65-7.

[12] See for instance: Ali, *Courtly Culture and Political Life*, 44-5, 52, 56-7; Scharfe, *The State in Indian Tradition*, 148-52; Mahalingam, *South Indian Polity*, 18, 60-5, 104-27, 132-3, 141-52.

merchants, and heads of professional and religious groups. Basically, "courtier" refers here to anyone present at court other than the monarch.[13]

As this chapter shows, the distinction between "official" courtiers and "unofficial" ones (influential persons from beyond strictly courtly confines) does not appear to have been sharp. For example, regional chieftains and heads of mercantile communities could have influential positions at court, even if they did not occupy clearly defined court ranks. Neither was the division between the abovementioned offices absolute, since different functions could well be held by one person at the same time. Adding to the fluid nature of the body of courtiers, the power that came with particular positions varied greatly, both among different individuals and over time. Unlike Ariyanatha Mudaliyar and the Kalale and Pillai families, most courtiers never earned something of an exalted reputation or managed to establish a kind of dynastic continuity over several generations. But several grew so powerful that they overshadowed their kings or queens, practically ruling the kingdom, reducing the monarch to a formal figure, and shaping court politics according to their will.

This chapter is largely organised in the same manner as the previous one. It first considers the sources, which comprise Indian texts—including political treatises on the power of courtiers in general—and European reports. Subsequently, it zooms in on the individual states, discussing the organisation of court offices, the fortunes and influences of various individuals, and long-term patterns. The chapter's conclusion compares the courts, attempts to explain differences and similarities, and analyses the overall role of courtiers in court politics.

Unlike the preceding chapter, which covers all rulers, the present one cannot be exhaustive. It is impossible to treat every courtier of some standing in Vijayanagara and its heirs during their entire existence. Not only would this amount to hundreds of people, but the sources, particularly European materials, contain far too many references to all be analysed here. Besides, it appears that numerous courtiers do not figure in the surviving sources and we rarely have something approaching a complete picture of a court's prosopographical composition. Therefore, the focus lies on particular careers and moments that, first, emerge clearly from the source materials on hand and, second, seem illustrative of general developments or provide noteworthy exceptions.

Because of the paucity of texts specially devoted to courtiers—like those described at the beginning of this chapter—references in local sources are somewhat scarce and rather scattered. Chronicles, inscriptions, and other south Indian works tend to mention courtiers only intermittently and seldom list large numbers

13 For a discussion of the term "courtier" and the need to define it, see: Duindam, "The Court as a Meeting Point," 80; Duindam, *Dynasties*, 235-6.

of them in a single occasion. Aimed at the glorification of dynasties, these texts focus on monarchs and their close relatives. In the rare cases where courtiers are included, it is mostly because they stood out for heroic deeds, or, in a few instances, usurped the throne. Courtiers who largely stuck to performing their duties or dominated the court without formally deposing the ruler, were frequently left out of south Indian sources or appear only in the margins of dynastic narratives.[14]

While local texts are comparatively silent on individual courtiers, several Indian treatises discuss the role of this group in general. An often recurring notion in this literature is that of the kingdom's seven limbs or constituents (*aṅga*, *prakṛti*). Mentioned already in such ancient Indian texts as the *Mahābhārata* (XII 59:51, 69:62-3), the *Manusmṛti* or *Mānavadharmaśāstra* (IX 294-7; VII 157), and the *Arthaśāstra* (VI 1:1-18), this idea holds that a polity consisted of seven essential elements, arranged according to their importance: king, minister, territory, fort, treasury, army, and ally. Listed as second, the minister (*amātya*, *mantri*) was apparently seen as one of the kingdom's mightiest limbs.

This concept appears in several later texts too, including works produced at the courts of Vijayanagara and its heirs. It is briefly referred to in the Telugu *Āmuktamālyada* (IV 211) of Emperor Krishna Raya (r. c. 1509-29), elaborated upon in the Kannada text *Śrī kṛṣṇadēvarāyaṇa dinacārī* (I)—probably dating from his reign as well—and mentioned in passing in the Telugu *Rāyavācakamu*, thought to be composed at Madurai's Nayaka court. In his Sanskrit poem *Śivatattva ratnākara*, Ikkeri's ruler Basavappa Nayaka I (r. 1697-1713) presents an alternative version of the model, now comprising seven limbs of the king himself: queen, heir apparent, wealth, sword, minister, horse, and elephant (V 15:29-30). Although here placed as fifth, ministers were evidently regarded as a principal factor in Ikkeri, too. That Basavappa Nayaka seemed well aware of the ambivalence of the courtiers' central position, however, transpires from his warning that the worst kingdoms are those governed not by kings but by ministers alone (V 7:4-12).[15]

14 See also Talbot, *Precolonial India in Practice*, 150.

15 Krishnamurthy, *Sivatattva Ratnākara of Keladi Basavaraja*, 23, 35-6, 59; Chitnis, "Sivatattvaratnakara with Special Reference to Polity," 220; Krishna(deva) Raya, *Sri Krishna Deva Raya: Āmuktamālyada*, 315; A. Rangasvami Sarasvati, "Political Maxims of the Emperor-Poet, Krishnadeva Raya," *Journal of Indian History* IV, III (1926), 65; Wagoner, *Tidings of the King*, 89; Vyasa, *The Mahābhārata*, vol. 7, book 12 (pt. 1), *The Book of Peace*, 307, 344; Wendy Doniger and Brian K. Smith (eds), *The Laws of Manu* (New Delhi, 1991), 144, 229; Kautilya, *The Kauṭilīya Arthaśāstra*, pt. II, 364-7; Shukracharya, *The Śukranītiḥ*, 20; Nagar, *Kingship in the Śukra-Nīti*, 37-8; Ali, *Courtly Culture and Political Life*, 73; B.A. Saletore, *Ancient Indian Political Thought and Institutions* (Bombay, 1963), 293-8, 344; Dallapiccola and Kotraiah, *King, Court and Capital*, 151, 165; Chitnis, *Keḷadi Polity*, 62. See also V. Balambal, "The Saptanga Theory and the State in the Sangam Age" [summary], *Proceedings of the Indian History Congress* 52 (1991).

Several political discourses consider the delicate relationship between kings and courtiers. They regard the king as the sovereign and foundation of the realm, but also recommend that he share his powers and duties with his ministers, thereby benefitting from their expertise, reducing his own burden, and demonstrating his superior status. As a consequence, however, while the king is thus formally recognised as the sole embodiment of royal sovereignty and courtiers presumably act only in his name, the latter are likely to exercise much effective power, resulting in a high potential for friction between the monarch and his ministers.[16] An observation in a Dutch report from 1677 about the delegation of authority among courtiers in Madurai underscores the risks involved:

> The Naiken [Nayakas], or kings of Madura, executed over the ... lands and people a ... sovereign government [*souveraine regeering*]. But as these heathen kings seldom took a fixed decision about a matter, and did not or little interfere with the government, the courtiers [*hovelingen*], and principally the Braminees [Brahmins], who by their nature possess sharp ingenuity and are no less sly and cunning, had the heart of the king and the government entirely in their hands ...[17]

The danger of courtiers growing too mighty is also acknowledged in Indian treatises. Indeed, the *Arthaśāstra* states that the most serious threat to the king are his close officials, rather than his common subjects or foreign powers (VIII 2:2-4; IX 3:9-19). Other texts give advice on how to keep ministers under control. According to the *Śukranīti*, functionaries should be checked by peers and rotated regularly to curb their power (II 109-17). The section on *rāja-nīti* ("king's policy") in Krishna Raya's *Āmuktamālyada* proposes that trustworthy Brahmins be appointed to important positions, for instance as commanders of forts, because they are knowledgeable, legitimise kings rather than strive to replace them, and are not rooted in particular lands (IV 207, 217, 261). Other passages in this work recommend that officials be watched by spies and promoted only gradually to avoid arrogance and allow time to test their loyalty (IV 208, 238, 260, 265). Both this text (IV 254) and Somadevasuri's *Nītivākyāmṛta* (XVIII 66) urge kings to exploit envy and rivalry among courtiers, for then they do their best to stand out and their activities will not remain hidden.[18] As the *Āmuktamālyada* phrases this last suggestion:

[16] Ali, *Courtly Culture and Political Life*, 57-60; Saletore, *Ancient Indian Political Thought and Institutions*, 344-5; Shukracharya, *The Śukranītiḥ*, 108-14, 134-83; Burling, *The Passage of Power*, 81; Venkata Ramanayya, *Studies in the History of the Third Dynasty*, 95-6.

[17] NA, VOC, no. 11306, ff. 122-3: description of the Nayakas of Madurai by Holst, 1762 (citing Adolph Bassingh's description of 1677); Vink, *Mission to Madurai*, 309, 353 (translation by Vink and myself).

[18] Scharfe, *The State in Indian Tradition*, 59, 67-8, 152, 158; Mahalingam, *South Indian Polity*, 128-30; idem, *Administration and Social Life under Vijayanagar*, pt. I, 30-1; Kautilya, *The Kauṭilīya Arthaśāstra*,

> The king should encourage competition among subordinates and soldiers.
> That is how their qualities, good and bad, will come out.
> They will be so obsessed with winning the king's attention and honour,
> that they will have no time for treacherous plots.[19]

Another quote from the abovementioned VOC report shows that this divisive strategy was in fact tested by Madurai's Nayakas. As for its effectiveness, the Dutch author arrived at a different conclusion from the one reached by Krishna Raya:

> The councillors [*raads personen*] whom these kings used were neither chosen nor appointed ... But they [the kings] took those whom they deemed fit, today these, tomorrow others again—so that the courtiers were generally possessed by very great jealousy, sprouting from the imagined envy or hate or friendship the one enjoyed over the other. They never were just friend or enemy among each other, but both at the same time.
>
> The king speculated on this and thus relied on his courtiers all the more, thinking that because they were very jealous of each other, therefore they—each out of fear of being spied on by the others—would dare to undertake nothing to the damage or detriment of the lands and him [the king]. In this he was gravely mistaken, so that the political government of the lands was owned more by the courtiers than by the kings ...[20]

Apparently, at least according to the Dutch, following recommendations from political treatises did little to curb the courtiers' powers in Madurai. Besides, the Dutch report's first quote suggests that the very Brahmins advocated by Krishna Raya controlled not only the government but the king as well. As the later sections of this chapter demonstrate, events regularly followed a similar course in Vijayanagara's other heirs.

pt. II, 451-2, 479-80; Nagar, *Kingship in the Śukra-Nīti*, 78-9, 132; Shukracharya, *The Śukranītiḥ*, 146-8; Narayana Rao, Shulman, and Subrahmanyam, "A New Imperial Idiom," 83, 88, 90-2, 97, 100-2; Krishna(deva) Raya, *Sri Krishna Deva Raya: Āmuktamālyada*, 313-16, 326, 328-9; Rangasvami Sarasvati, "Political Maxims of the Emperor-Poet," 65-6, 72-3; Nilakanta Sastri and Venkataramanayya, *Further Sources of Vijayanagara History*, vol. III, 153-4, 162; Narayana Rao and Subrahmanyam, "Ideologies of State Building," 221-2. See also idem, "History and Politics in the Vernacular," 46, 49-50, 56, and its slightly modified version, "Notes on Political Thought in Medieval and Early Modern India," 195, 198-9, 201, 205.

19 Narayana Rao, Shulman, and Subrahmanyam, "A New Imperial Idiom," 100 (IV 254). See also: Krishna(deva) Raya, *Sri Krishna Deva Raya: Āmuktamālyada*, 328; Rangasvami Sarasvati, "Political Maxims of the Emperor-Poet," 71; Nilakanta Sastri and Venkataramanayya, *Further Sources of Vijayanagara History*, vol. III, 161.

20 NA, VOC, no. 11306, ff. 123-4: description of the Nayakas of Madurai by Holst, 1762 (citing Adolph Bassingh's description of 1677); Vink, *Mission to Madurai*, 309, 353 (translation by Vink and myself).

We know this mostly from Dutch and other European sources, because unlike many south Indian texts, this material contains a wealth of information on individual courtiers. Their contacts with Europeans were both frequent and diverse: in day-to-day business, during diplomatic missions, and in times of conflict, courtiers of ranks high and low served as intermediaries between European powers and south Indian parties ranging from royals to craftsmen. References in the Dutch records are legion and allow us to trace the careers of several courtiers simultaneously, thus providing insight into the often changing relations between them.

One illuminating class of VOC documents are lists of gifts presented by the Company to courtiers during its embassies to the courts. The distribution of those gifts among different individuals reflected the standing and influence of each of them, at least as perceived by the Dutch.[21] Naturally, monarchs always received the most precious and numerous presents, but otherwise their worth and quantity depended on the courtiers' actual power rather than their official functions. The VOC's views in this regard generally seem to have been quite accurate. The many complaints by court functionaries about the Company's gifts usually pertained to their value, number, and kind, but rarely concerned their distribution among courtiers. The presents were often inspected beforehand by the court and only in a few cases do embassy reports mention requests to adjust this distribution.

Notwithstanding, it must be kept in mind that the Dutch (and other Europeans) got in touch chiefly with certain kinds of courtiers. These comprised provincial governors and other local representatives in coastal regions where the VOC maintained settlements, and functionaries at the central court dealing with affairs related to the Company's activities, such as commercial, diplomatic, and military matters. In fact, courtiers regularly combined such central and local offices. People in the capital with other portfolios and officials in inland areas stood a much smaller chance of figuring in the VOC archives.

One example is a certain Vira Tevar ("Werra Teuver"), who according to a Dutch source served as a general (*velt-oversten*) of Tanjavur's ruler Ekoji Bhonsle I for a considerable period. Despite his prominent position, it seems that Vira Tevar is not mentioned in regular VOC documents. The reason we know of him is because in November 1678, after he had died in battle, eight of his widows performed *satī* (death on a husband's funeral pyre). This event was deemed so shocking by some VOC servants who witnessed it, that when a personal account by one of them reached the Dutch Republic in 1680, it appeared there in print in an eight-page

21 For a similar Portuguese approach, see Melo, "Seeking Prestige and Survival," 678.

pamphlet.[22] If it were not for this newsletter, Tanjavur's General Vira Tevar would likely have remained absent from surviving sources, like so many other courtiers.

In addition to being limited, VOC sources are not always clear or consistent in their terminology for courtiers. Functions are sometimes mistaken for personal names and vice versa, south Indian court and governmental terms may be corrupted beyond recognition, and some Dutch translations or interpretations of these words provide little clue to their originals. Thus, one comes across vague or fabricated designations like "state governor" (*rijxbestierder*), "state confidant" (*rijxvertrouwder*), "ordain-it-all" (*albeschik*), and the often-used generic "greats of the court" (*hofsgrooten*). Yet, although these and other European sources can be confused and incomplete, they still give a picture of the dynamic relations between courtiers and of their dominant role at court.

Vijayanagara

In the empire, the group of people who may be termed courtiers (as defined above) was probably even more varied than in the successor states. Besides all sorts of functionaries in the capital, Vijayanagara's extensive territory included numerous regional officials and subordinate chiefs, who possessed greatly varying levels of power and autonomy. For example, several of the most distinguished provincial governors—*mahāmaṇḍalēśvaras*, often called viceroys in secondary literature—were members of the imperial family, by blood or through marriage. Some of them, in particular the emperors' sons and brothers, were among the first in the line of royal succession and might ascend the throne themselves. As mentioned in the previous chapter, one prominent provincial governor, Saluva Narasimha, was related to the imperial dynasty only through a somewhat distant marital link but became such a powerful general that he simply took the throne and founded Vijayanagara's second house. The third and fourth imperial dynasties were also established by courtiers, the Generals Narasa Nayaka and Rama Raya respectively, after they took over the central court.

Some other provincial governors founded local dynasties, which turned into the royal houses reigning over the empire's successor states. Yet, on certain

[22] *Vrije Universiteit* (VU) Library, Amsterdam, Special Collections, no. XW.07161.-: "Waarachtig verhael van 't schrikkelijck en vrywilligh verbranden van acht vrouwen, van seker velt-oversten, van den vorst Egosia Ragie, genaemt Werra Teuver, …" [True story of the terrible and voluntary burning of eight women, of a certain field-lord, of the King Ekoji Raja, named Vira Tevar, …], c. 1680, ff. 1-8. Vira Tevar is perhaps very briefly mentioned in the VOC archives as Ekoji's commander "Weta Teuver," killed in a war against Ramnad in late 1678. See NA, VOC, no. 1333, f. 294: letter from Nagapattinam to Colombo, Dec. 1678.

occasions these rulers were still expected to fulfil duties at Vijayanagara's court. The Nayakas of Senji, Tanjavur, and Madurai continued to symbolically occupy the imperial offices of bearers of the betel box, fan, and spittoon, traditionally held by their founding fathers as the emperor's personal servants. One of Ikkeri's early Nayakas, Sadashiva, also had a formal rank at the imperial court according to some local literature, serving as the main *daḷavāy* (general) of Vijayanagara's Rama Raya during the latter's final battle in 1565.[23]

Thus, on the one hand, imperial courtiers could become so powerful that they replaced the reigning dynasty, subsequently were recognised as sovereign rulers themselves, and even seemed to be considered more or less direct successors to the previous house, thereby continuing the empire's existence. Apparently, dynastic usurpation from within the court was not perceived as a fundamental rupture leading to a new state. On the other hand, the empire's courtiers included many men stationed so far away from the capital that they could build up their own power base and grow into largely autonomous rulers—of which the Nayaka houses studied here are obvious examples.[24]

Both observations, while typical for Vijayanagara, do not, or hardly, apply to its heirs. There, no courtier ever managed to formally take over the throne to establish a new dynasty, despite the exalted position of people like Madurai's Ariyanatha Mudaliyar and the Kalale and Pillai families in Mysore and Senji. Because of the relatively small size of these kingdoms, courtiers attaining regional autonomy and threatening the central court were also very rare. Clearly, in those respects Vijayanagara and its successors differed considerably and cannot be well compared. Therefore, this section focuses on prominent offices and persons at Vijayanagara's central court, allowing for a valuable comparison, and pays little attention to provincial governors and other regional representatives.[25] It does however consider those few exceptional men who crossed the divide between minister and monarch.

23 BL/AAS, MG, no. 3, pt. 5: "Ram-Rajah Cheritra," f. 180. This account of Rama Raya's last period in power exists in several versions and languages, for which see the section on Vijayanagara in Chapter 4.

24 See for instance also: Stein, *Vijayanagara*, 92; Mahalingam, *Administration and Social Life under Vijayanagar*, pt. I, 26-8.

25 For general overviews of provincial government in Vijayanagara, see for example: Venkata Ramanayya, *Studies in the History of the Third Dynasty*, 143-59; Mahalingam, *Administration and Social Life under Vijayanagar*, pt. I, 175-205; Y. Subbarayalu, "Administrative Divisions of the Vijayanagara State," in P. Shanmugam and Srinivasan Srinivasan (eds), *Recent Advances in Vijayanagara Studies* (Chennai, 2006). For extensive lists of provincial governors, see also: H. Krishna Sastri, "The First Vijayanagara Dynasty: Its Viceroys and Ministers," *Annual Report 1907-8: Archæological Survey of India* (Calcutta, 1911); idem, "The Second Vijayanagara Dynasty"; idem, "The Third Vijayanagara Dynasty: Its Viceroys and Ministers," *Annual Report 1911-12: Archæological Survey of India*, ed. John Marshall (Calcutta, 1915).

Unfortunately, we do not have a complete picture of Vijayanagara's courtiers at any given time. Inscriptions, literary works, and visitor's accounts only mention certain functions and individuals, rather than providing detailed and comprehensive surveys. Besides, it seems that various terms were used for largely similar offices or the same term could refer to different functions. Furthermore, the composition of court ranks is likely to have changed during the empire's three centuries of existence. Nevertheless, these sources give at least an idea of the most significant and powerful positions at court.

There was some sort of ministerial council, possibly numbering between eight and twenty persons, which comprised officials with administrative or military duties and members of the royal family. One literary text claims that Rama Raya, founder of the Aravidu dynasty, had eight chief ministers and seven heads of "the great departments," the latter dealing with fortifications, other defensive works, justice, armed forces, intelligence, towns, and religious buildings. The *Sāmrājyalakṣmīpīṭhikā* section of the anonymous Sanskrit work *Ākāśabhairavakalpa*—thought to be connected to Vijayanagara's Tuluva court—lists no less than seventy-two court functions and mentions that the king should meet every day with four or eight ministers as well as other officials, such as the treasurer (63:4-17, 70:23-50, 76:3-10, 77:4-8).

The term *daṇḍanāyaka* was probably used as a general denomination for the highest court ranks, one of which was the (*mahā*)*pradhāni* or *pradhāna*, the chief minister heading the empire's overall administration. An important scribal function was known as *rāyasam*, usually translated as (royal) secretary. Its place in the hierarchy appears not to have been entirely fixed, and some people in this role may have acted as prominent ministers. Besides, treasurers of several ranks were designated as *bhāṇḍāgārika* or *samprati*.

As for military positions, while various kinds of courtiers could be assigned temporary military tasks—for example to lead one particular campaign—permanent commanders-in-chief were usually called *daḷavāy*. In the religious sphere we find the *rājaguru* (king's preceptor) and the *purōhita* (royal or family priest). Further, some sources mention the *vāśal*(*kāriyam*), the door-keeper or head of the palace guard, regulating access to the king. Finally, the fourteenth-century Sanskrit poem *Madhurāvijaya* by Gangadevi speaks of a *vidūṣaka* or court jester under the early Sangamas, and many later stories refer to the Brahmin jester Tenali Rama, who served Emperor Krishna Raya. But there seems no proof that either this function or Tenali Rama actually existed.[26] Obviously, there were numerous other functions

[26] Neither Indian nor European sources appear to refer to real court jesters in Vijayanagara's successor states. For Vijayanagara court jesters, see for example: Shulman, *The King and the Clown*, 180-200; Narayana Rao and Shulman, *A Poem at the Right Moment*, 180-5; Narayana Rao, "Multiple

at Vijayanagara's court, for instance dealing with judicial, fiscal, commercial, and diplomatic affairs, but the abovementioned offices appear to have been the most influential and constant ones.[27]

For most of Vijayanagara's existence, little is known of the individuals occupying these central positions, let alone how actual power was divided among them. Epigraphic records give the names of many chief ministers, generals, and other dignitaries at the capital. But in most cases, these sources are silent on their backgrounds and how their careers developed. Since personal names and official designations seem to have been used interchangeably, it is often unclear whether certain courtiers were relatives. Thus, some terms suggest that the people using them belonged to the same family, but they could also merely denote a similar rank. These complications concern the empire's first two dynasties in particular.

Sangamas and Saluvas

Under Vijayanagara's initial Sangama house (c. 1340s-1485), there were few courtiers for whom the sources provide much context. One of them is Vidyaranya, a minister under Emperor Bukka (r. c. 1355-77). Some scholars claim he was also the Brahmin sage of that name mentioned in Vijayanagara's foundation stories. If true, he combined political and religious duties. We know a bit more about General Kumara Kampana, a son of Bukka, who around the 1360s subjugated the Indian peninsula's far south for Vijayanagara. He is one of the few courtiers whose achievements are glorified in a literary work, in this case the *Madhurāvijaya* (or *Kamparāyacharitram*), composed by his wife Gangadevi. She relates how Kumara

Literary Cultures in Telugu," 66-8; Narayana Rao and Shulman, *Classical Telugu Poetry*, 292; D. Sridhara Babu, "Kingship: State and Religion in South India According to South Indian Historical Biographies of Kings (Madhurāvijaya, Acyutarāyābhyudaya and Vemabhūpālacarita)" (unpublished dissertation, Georg-August-Universität Göttingen, 1975), 125; Artatrana Sarangi, *A Treasure of Tāntric Ideas: A Study of the Sāmrājyalakṣmīpīṭhikā* (Calcutta, 1993), 288-9.

27 Mahalingam, *Administration and Social Life under Vijayanagar*, pt. I, 28-39; Saletore, *Social and Political Life in the Vijayanagara Empire*, vol. I, 253-6, 261-73; Venkata Ramanayya, *Studies in the History of the Third Dynasty*, 95-119; Sridhara Babu, "Kingship: State and Religion in South India," 123-8; Sarangi, *A Treasure of Tāntric Ideas*, 282, 284-5, 301-6; Gode, "Ākāśabhairava-Kalpa," 122-3, 126-7, 136; Ganesh Thite, "Sāmrājyalakṣmīpīṭhikā of Ākāśabhairavakalpa: A Tāntric Encyclopaedia of Magicoreligion," *Sambodhi* 7, 1-4 (1978-9), 43, 47; BL/AAS, MG, no. 3, pt. 5: "Ram-Rajah Cheritra," f. 173; Sewell, *A Forgotten Empire*, 384-9; Patil, *Court Life under the Vijayanagar Rulers*, 60-6; Rao, "A New Perspective on the Royal Rāma Cult at Vijayanagara," 31-3. For discussions of connections between the *Ākāśabhairavakalpa* or *Sāmrājyalakṣmīpīṭhikā* and Vijayanagara—as well as Tanjavur's Bhonsles and Ikkeri's Basavappa Nayaka I and his *Śivatattva ratnākara*—see also: Suebsantiwongse, "Dating and Locating the *Sāmrājyalakṣmīpīṭhikā*"; Dinnell, "*Sāmrājyalakṣmīpīṭhikā*," 16-20; Sarangi, *A Treasure of Tāntric Ideas*, ch. 1.

Kampana grew up excelling in both learning and martial skills, and later became provincial governor at the newly conquered town of Kanchipuram. Next, he liberated Madurai from its short-lived dynasty of sultans with a sword presented by the Madurai goddess. In addition, inscriptions designate him with exalted titles like "lord of the great province" (*mahāmaṇḍaḷēśvara*) and "lord of the eastern, southern, western, and northern four oceans" (*pūrva dekṣiṇa pachchima uttara nālu semudrādhipati*).

Another early notable military commander was Saluva Mangappa (or Mangu or Mangi) Dandanatha, who accompanied Kumara Kampana on his southern campaign, during which he acquired the family title "Saluva" (hawk). His descendants also served the Sangamas, and even married into the imperial family, until his great-grandson General Saluva Narasimha replaced the dynasty with his own Saluva house.

Under the reign of Deva Raya II (r. c. 1423-46), Lakkanna Danda Nayaka appears to have been a particularly influential figure. Functioning as chief minister (*pradhāni*), general, and provincial governor (*mahāmaṇḍalēśvara*), he played an instrumental role in the emperor's switch from the Vaishnava to the Shaiva strand of Hinduism, thereby promoting his own interests. Demonstrating his might, in a religious Kannada work Lakkanna Danda styled himself as Deva Raya II's "increaser of wealth" and "intimate friend" (*unnata kēḷaya*), while inscriptions call him "lord of the southern ocean" (*dakṣiṇa samudrādhipati*) and someone "who knows the art of strengthening the seven organs of state" (*saptānga rājya vardhana kaḷādhara*). Moreover, he was entitled to issue his own coins.[28]

During the brief rule of the Saluva dynasty (c. 1485-1503), again only some courtiers stand out. One was Thimma Raja, whose precise court rank seems unknown but who was powerful enough to command his own troops. After the death of Saluva Narasimha, Thimma wanted the emperor's eldest son to ascend the throne. But he faced competition from General Narasa Nayaka, who favoured another prince, had Thimma killed, and thus solved the succession struggle. Narasa Nayaka was the son of one of two other generals who were prominent at the Saluva court: Ishvara Nayaka and Aravidi Bukka, whose offspring founded the third and fourth imperial houses respectively.[29]

[28] For references, see the next footnote.

[29] Rāma Sharma, *The History of the Vijayanagar Empire*, vol. I, 29-31, 38, 42, 58-9, 64, 88; Saletore, *Social and Political Life in the Vijayanagara Empire*, vol. I, 256-60; Krishna Sastri, "The First Vijayanagara Dynasty"; idem, "The Second Vijayanagara Dynasty," 165-9; Vasundhara Filliozat, "Relatives and Officers of Ballala III and IV Who Accepted Service under the Kings of Vijayanagara," *Itihas: Journal of the Andhra Pradesh Archives* I, 2 (1973); Dodamani, *Gaṅgādevī's Madhurāvijayaṁ*, passim, especially 14-21, 30-7; Krishnaswami Aiyangar, *Sources of Vijayanagar History*, 23-4; Audrey Truschke, *The*

Other than this handful of ministers and commanders, there were few or no courtiers under the Sangamas and Saluvas of whom more is known than their name and designation. Occasionally, ministers and generals are stated to be uncles, nephews, or other relatives of the emperor, and for some officials their kinship to other, non-royal functionaries is mentioned. Despite this fragmented information, one can surmise that during the first half of Vijayanagara's existence, it was regularly military men—and sometimes ministers with other portfolios or people combining different tasks—who became particularly powerful courtiers, capable of eliminating rivals at court and influencing the emperor himself. They were often members of prominent court families, frequently of a Brahmin background or belonging to the rulers' caste, considering their blood or marital relations with them.

Tuluvas

By and large, these conclusions are applicable to Vijayanagara's next one-and-a-half centuries, too, for which period more sources are available. A very prominent minister under the first two emperors of the Tuluva house (c. 1503-70)—Vira Narasimha (r. c. 1503-9) and Krishna Raya (r. c. 1509-29)—was the Brahmin Saluva Timmarasu. Despite his first name, he was not related to the Saluva dynasty and one text claims he came from a poor background. During Krishna Raya's many military campaigns, Timmarasu further held the office of general and served as a provincial governor as well. Also called Appaji (father), he may be the courtier with the most exalted status in the empire's history. Many inscriptions and literary works refer to the sound advice and noble deeds of this *mahāpradhāna* (great minister) and the great respect Krishna Raya had for him. As part of a ceremony to honour him, Timmarasu's name appeared with that of the emperor on a specially issued coin. The Portuguese horse trader Domingo Paes, visiting the capital in this period, wrote that Timmarasu commanded the entire court and that all officials behaved with him as they did with Krishna Raya himself.

As the Telugu work *Rāyavācakamu* has it, Timmarasu was the courtier to whom Krishna Raya famously complained about being controlled by his ministers,

Language of History: Sanskrit Narratives of Indo-Muslim Rule (New York, 2021), 76-89; Ajay K. Rao, "From Fear to Hostility: Responses to the Conquests of Madurai," *South Asian Studies* 32, 1 (2016), 72-6; *Epigraphia Carnatica*, vol. X, *Inscriptions in the Kolar District*, ed. B. Lewis Rice (Mangalore, 1905), 70 (1st numeration), 61 (2nd numeration) (both no. 203); Narayana Rao, Shulman, and Subrahmanyam, *Symbols of Substance*, 28-9; Mahalingam, *Administration and Social Life under Vijayanagar*, pt. I, 30-1; S. Srikanta Sastri, "Deva Raya II," *The Indian Antiquary: A Journal of Oriental Research* LVII (1928), 77-81; Dębicka-Borek, "The Bravery of Sāḷuva Narasiṃha," 65; Chekuri, "Between Family and Empire," 82; idem, "'Fathers' and 'Sons'," 137-8; Devadevan, *A Prehistory of Hinduism*, 70; Venkata Ramanayya, *Studies in the History of the Third Dynasty*, 93-4.

making him wonder what his royal sovereignty really meant. The emperor would have sighed that were he to attempt to exercise his authority, the court would just ignore him. Some historians regard Krishna Raya's grievances as an indication of the courtiers' great powers in Vijayanagara during this period. But since it has been shown that the *Rāyavācakamu* was composed under the Nayakas of Madurai, this episode may say more about the might of court officials in Madurai than in the empire. In any case, after a tenure of about two decades, Timmarasu fell from grace, accused of being involved in the death of Krishna Raya's minor son and designated successor. Together with his own son and brother, the latter himself an important functionary, Timmarasu was blinded and imprisoned—for life, as some sources say, although several inscriptions suggest he was later set free and lived on until the 1530s.

Another key official during Krishna Raya's reign was the Brahmin *Rāyasam* (secretary) Kondamarasu, again an administrator serving as a general too. Not only does he prominently figure in the *Rāyavācakamu* as an advisor to the emperor, he is also mentioned in the account of the Portuguese merchant Fernão Nunes, staying in Vijayanagara around the early 1530s. According to Nunes, when Krishna Raya marched out of the capital to wage war against the Bijapur sultanate, he was followed by dozens of dignitaries, each accompanied by their own troops. In this procession, Kondamarasu allegedly headed 120,000 foot soldiers, 6,000 horsemen, and sixty elephants, more than any other official.[30]

Nunes further wrote that Kondamarasu's son Ayyapparasu was chosen to succeed Saluva Timmarasu as chief minister and that Ayyapparasu had killed one of the sons and successors of Emperor Saluva Narasimha, founder of the previous dynasty.[31] This courtiers' duo of father and son thus seems to have gone to great lengths to increase their power at the Vijayanagara court and to have done so successfully, securing their position especially after the downfall of Minister Saluva

[30] For other officials mentioned by Nunes, including the rebellious provincial governor of the Tamil region, Saluva Narasingha Nayaka alias Chellappa, see Stein, *Vijayanagara*, 48-51, 57, 98-9.

[31] Rāma Sharma, *The History of the Vijayanagar Empire*, vol. I, 98, 122, 145-7; Wagoner, *Tidings of the King*, 47-9, 89, 101-4, 112-13, 142, 152, 160, 235, 245; V. Vijayaraghavacharya (ed.), *Inscriptions of Krishnaraya's Time from 1509 A.D. to 1531 A.D.* (Madras, 1935), 94, 96, 276; Narayana Rao, Shulman, and Subrahmanyam, *Textures of Time*, 122-5; Krishna Sastri, "The Second Vijayanagara Dynasty," 172-4, 183, 191-2; Sewell, *A Forgotten Empire*, 250, 310-15, 322, 326-7, 359-61; K. Veeresha, "Saluva-Timmarasu the Crafty Prime-Minister of Krsnadeva Raya," *Itihas: Journal of the Andhra Pradesh State Archives & Research Institute* XXI, 1-2 (1995); Chekuri, "'Fathers' and 'Sons'," 152-7; Venkata Ramanayya, *Studies in the History of the Third Dynasty*, 96; Saletore, *Social and Political Life in the Vijayanagara Empire*, vol. I, 260-1. For a discussion of the account of Domingo Paes, see Rubiés, *Travel and Ethnology in the Renaissance*, ch. 7.

Timmarasu. Upon Krishna Raya's death, however, they fell out of favour as other courtiers rose to prominence.[32]

These included the Salakaraju brothers and their rival Rama Raya, who all had close marital ties with the imperial Tuluva family. A sister of the Salakaraju brothers was the wife of Emperor Achyuta Raya (half-brother and successor of Krishna Raya), while Rama Raya had married one of Krishna Raya's daughters. The elder Salakaraju brother, Peda Tirumala, first appears to have become prominent during Achyuta Raya's reign. Having earlier served as a provincial governor and military commander, he was installed as *pradhāna* in 1534 and further promoted in the subsequent years. His younger brother China Tirumala seems to have functioned as general or perhaps treasurer.

Together, they came to dominate the court in the 1530s, backing the claims to the throne of their brother-in-law Achyuta Raya and his infant son and *yuvarāja* (heir apparent) Venkatadri. When Peda Tirumala and Achyuta Raya died soon after each other (around 1540 and in 1542 respectively), Salakaraju China Tirumala no longer supported his sister's son, the new, minor ruler Venkatadri. As explained in Chapter 2, he usurped all power, became Venkatadri's regent but then killed him, and next was probably proclaimed emperor himself. His own death came soon, however, when he finally lost the power struggle against Rama Raya that had been going on all the while.[33]

The later part of Rama Raya's career has also been related in the previous chapter. While he ended up as Vijayanagara's de facto—and perhaps de jure—emperor between the 1540s and 1565 and founded the Aravidu house, he started out as a rather ordinary warrior, originally not even employed in Vijayanagara. In the early 1510s, Rama Raya served the Golkonda sultanate as a military commander and landholder, despite his ancestors' past as high generals in the imperial armies, who included his father, the aforementioned Aravidi Bukka. Offering his military skills to Vijayanagara in 1515, Rama Raya stood out for his exceptional prowess in Krishna Raya's campaigns, making the emperor give him his daughter's hand.

[32] For the strong influence at Krishna Raya's court of a religious leader, the Brahmin monastic head Vyasatirtha, see Valerie Stoker, *Polemics and Patronage in the City of Victory: Vyāsatīrtha, Hindu Sectarianism, and the Sixteenth-Century Vijayanagara Court* (Oakland, 2016).

[33] See in particular Venkata Ramanayya, *Studies in the History of the Third Dynasty*, 12, 18, 31-2, 56-7, 61-2, 74-89. The following literature sometimes speaks of only one Salakaraju brother or seems to confuse the elder and younger: Rāma Sharma, *The History of the Vijayanagar Empire*, vol. I, 171, 175, 180-3; Heras, *The Aravidu Dynasty of Vijayanagara*, vol. I, 4-12; Krishna Sastri, "The Second Vijayanagara Dynasty," 190; Saletore, *Social and Political Life in the Vijayanagara Empire*, vol. I, 261; Patil, *Court Life under the Vijayanagar Rulers*, 139-41; Nilakanta Sastri, *A History of South India*, 288-9.

From then on, Rama Raya increased his power, appointing relatives at strategic posts, endowing temples, and exploiting conflicts between and within the Deccan sultanates. Despite these activities and his position as minister, he initially faced strong competition from Emperor Achyuta Raya and many courtiers, particularly the Salakaraju brothers. But in 1542 Rama Raya defeated all his remaining opponents, placed his protégé Sadashiva on the throne, and became this minor ruler's regent. Besides, he installed his two brothers in the court's highest offices: Tirumala as chief minister and Venkatadri as commander-in-chief. As the empire's central figure Rama Raya was now in full control, gradually replacing Sadashiva as Vijayanagara's emperor during the next two decades.[34]

Aravidus

When Tirumala became emperor, soon after the court fled Vijayanagara city in 1565, the rule of the Aravidu house (c. 1570-1660s) formally commenced. Despite the increasingly many European sources on south India for this period, we still know little more of most courtiers than their names. By and large, however, one observes the same patterns for this phase as for the earlier dynasties. The family of Gobburi Jagga Raya—mentioned in Chapter 2 for its role in the succession struggle following Emperor Venkata's death in 1614—serves as an example.

Jagga Raya was a son of Gobburi Oba Raya, a very prominent courtier and high military commander. In 1608, the Italian Jesuit Antonio Rubino described Oba Raya as the most significant among the dozens of the emperor's "captains," calling him "the right arm of the king [*braccio diritto del re*] in important matters." His exalted position also transpires from other Jesuit reports, stating that he enjoyed the rare privilege of sitting on the same carpet as the emperor. Besides, Oba Raya held close marital ties with the Aravidus: his daughter Obamamba (alias Bayamma) was an influential queen of Emperor Venkata, while his wife is thought to have been a daughter of Rama Raya.

Jagga Raya's own court office is not entirely clear but he is said to have controlled large quantities of troops as well as revenues, and may have held the rank of *daḷavāy* (general), as a text praising his opponent Velugoti Yacama Nayaka suggests. Further, he, his siblings, and their associates dominated the commercially significant region around the port of Pulicat, where the VOC set up a factory in

[34] Eaton, *A Social History of the Deccan*, 78-80, 87-8, 90-2; Stein, *Vijayanagara*, 113-20; Heras, *The Aravidu Dynasty of Vijayanagara*, vol. I, 27-40; P. Sree Rama Sarma, "Rāma Rāya's Policy," *Proceedings of the Indian History Congress* 36 (1975); Rāma Sharma, *The History of the Vijayanagar Empire*, vol. I, 185-6; Nilakanta Sastri, *A History of South India*, 285-9; Krishna Sastri, "The Third Vijayanagara Dynasty," 178-80; Saletore, *Social and Political Life in the Vijayanagara Empire*, vol. I, 261.

1610. While Jagga Raya governed the surrounding area, his sister Obamamba had received Pulicat itself as dowry. Here, this powerful queen had appointed her own "Governess" (*gouvernante*) Kondama, as the Dutch and the English called her, whom they considered a major figure at the court too. Furthermore, this governess' son was the port's *shāhbandar* ("harbour master"), supervising all mercantile activities and the collection of customs duties. When the Dutch got Emperor Venkata's permission to settle in Pulicat, their Portuguese rivals offered the influential Jagga Raya 5,000 *pagodas* (later supposedly raised to 200,000) to use his connections to have the VOC expelled again. The Dutch could only prevent this by sending several embassies and expensive gifts to the emperor.

Some years later, after Jagga Raya was killed in the empire's succession struggle of the mid-1610s, the daughter of his brother Etiraja was wedded to the new emperor, Ramadeva—marking the third generation of marital alliances between the Gobburi and Aravidu families. As the Dutch and English wrote, Etiraja now became governor of the Pulicat area and seems have been an important courtier in the following years, accompanying the emperor on military campaigns and peace negotiations.[35] Thus, while Jagga Raya had personally failed to hold full sway over the Vijayanagara court, the Gobburi family as a whole kept its powerful position, maintaining close links with the imperial house, holding a range of court positions, and controlling a region of great economic importance.

***

35 NA, VOC, no. 1055, ff. 103-5, 149, 169-71, 174-5, 189-90; no. 1056, ff. 151-3v: letters from Pulicat and Vellore to Banten and Masulipatam, May, July, Sept.-Nov. 1610, Aug. 1613, Pulicat proceedings (*resoluties*), Aug. 1610; Joan-Pau Rubiés, "The Jesuit Discovery of Hinduism: Antonio Rubino's Account of the History and Religion of Vijayanagara (1608)," *Archiv für Religionsgeschichte* 3, 1 (2001), 248; Frederick Charles Danvers and William Foster (eds), *Letters Received by the East India Company from its Servants in the East ...*, vol. I (London, 1896), 134; Foster, *The English Factories in India 1622–1623: A Calendar of Documents in the India Office and British Museum* (Oxford, 1908), 106, 139-40; Narayana Rao, Shulman, and Subrahmanyam, *Symbols of Substance*, 103, 252-5; Sewell, *A Forgotten Empire*, 224; Heras, *The Aravidu Dynasty of Vijayanagara*, vol. I, 24-5, 307, 465-7, 496-501; Nilakanta Sastri and Venkataramanayya, *Further Sources of Vijayanagara History*, vol. I, 326-7; Rāma Sharma, *The History of the Vijayanagar Empire*, vol. II, 69, 91, 127; L.C.D. van Dijk, *Zes jaren uit het leven van Wemmer van Berchem, gevolgd door iets over onze vroegste betrekkingen met Japan, twee geschiedkundige bijdragen* (Amsterdam, 1858), 24, 27-8, 30; Mac Leod, *De Oost-Indische Compagnie*, vol. I, 134, 212, 452, 456, 464-7, 487, 491; Raychaudhuri, *Jan Company in Coromandel*, 22, 36; Terpstra, *De vestiging van de Nederlanders aan de kust van Koromandel*, 130, 132; Subrahmanyam, *Improvising Empire*, 196-202; Van Dam, *Beschryvinge van de Oostindische Compagnie*, vol. 2.2, 102; Om Prakash (ed.), *The Dutch Factories in India: A Collection of Dutch East India Company Documents Pertaining to India, Vol. II (1624-1627)* (New Delhi, 2007), 103, 114, 149, 158.

From this brief overview of courtiers under the empire's four dynasties, some general and continuous tendencies can be deduced. Powerful courtiers often occupied various ranks over time or simultaneously, regularly held family ties with the royal houses and nearly always with other courtiers, at least in some instances operated from a regional power base providing them with financial and personal support, and frequently got involved in rivalry, among themselves and with the emperors.[36] Among these people were men, and sometimes women, of various backgrounds. A fair number of officials—seemingly mostly in administrative functions like *pradhāni* (chief minister) and *rāyasam* (secretary)—were Brahmins. But others, many of them military commanders, evidently were not Brahmins since they or their relatives were able to marry into the imperial families, who belonged to Shudra or (as they claimed) Kshatriya castes. All in all, it appears that one's court function and caste ranking were hardly the main factors that determined how much power one wielded. At least as important seem to have been one's connections (familial or otherwise), ambitions, strategic skills, material means, and good fortune.

Successor States

The following sections analyse the positions of courtiers in Ikkeri, Tanjavur, Madurai, and Ramnad. Although we must focus on certain periods and people, the close relations of these courts with the Dutch and other Europeans allow us to go into much more detail than is possible for Vijayanagara. For each dynasty, we examine the system of court positions in general—largely on the basis of secondary literature—followed by discussions of the careers of some individual courtiers and the balance of power at court at a few specific moments.

Nayakas of Ikkeri

In his early eighteenth-century *Śivatattva ratnākara*, Ikkeri's ruler Basavappa Nayaka devotes considerable attention to courtiers. Besides explaining on which matters a king must consult with his ministers (*mantrin, saciva*) (V 7:16-37), he lists about twenty different court offices and the qualities these require (V 15:46-105). Among the main officials are the *purōhita* (family priest), *jyotiṣika* (astrologer), *senāpati* (chief commander), *daṇḍadhara* (administrator of justice), and *kośādhyakṣa* (treasurer). He also refers to various lower positions, ranging from bodyguards and gatekeepers to physicians and cooks. It seems the *Śivatattva*

36 See also Chekuri, "'Fathers' and 'Sons'," especially 155-6.

ratnākara portrays an idealised court, however, based on ancient political discourses, since other types of functionaries figure in inscriptions and chronicles produced under Ikkeri's Nayakas.

Most of those positions also existed in one or another form at the Vijayanagara court, such as the *pradhāni* (chief minister), *daḷavāy* (or *daḷavāyi*, general), *rājaguru* (king's preceptor), and *rāyasam* (secretary). Other officials appear to be typical of Ikkeri, including the *bokkasa* officer or (amongst other terms) *sēnabōva* (both treasurer or finance minister), *karaṇika* (accountant, scribe), *sabbunīsa* (high military commander), and *subēdār* (governor)—the latter two positions of Persian origin.[37]

For Ikkeri's early period there is little information about the people in these functions besides their names. Even less is known about the influence of particular courtiers in relation to others and the king himself.[38] But from the mid-seventeenth century on, the increasing volume of European sources provides enough details to partially reconstruct the fortunes of some prominent functionaries over longer periods and the distribution of power among courtiers at certain moments. Obviously, those occasions and people concern cases in which Europeans were closely involved. Therefore, the following paragraphs are chiefly based on observations during diplomatic missions and other dealings with officials likely to come into contact with Europeans.

Given these limitations, the earliest courtiers in Ikkeri one can study in some depth are members of the Malu family. Active at least during the quarter-century between the early 1650s and the mid-1670s, they served under five kings and one queen. While they were primarily merchants, belonging to the community of Sarasvat Brahmins, they rose to great heights in Ikkeri's political constellation. First appearing in Portuguese documents, initially Vitthala Malu grew influential at court, selected by King Shivappa Nayaka to head an embassy to the Portuguese at Goa in 1652 and again the following year. In 1654, these sources mention his son Mallappa Malu as Ikkeri's representative to conduct peace negotiations with the Portuguese, while English records state he was authorised to actually conclude treaties.

In the period around the first Dutch-Ikkeri agreement in 1657, Mallappa begins to figure extensively in VOC records. He was the main or sole merchant with whom the Dutch were allowed to do business and their letters refer to him as "the king's trader." In the subsequent years, he and his brother Narayana Malu strengthened

[37] Krishnamurthy, *Sivatattva Ratnākara of Keladi Basavaraja*, 36-9, 60-4, 404-5; Chitnis, *Keḷadi Polity*, 67-73, 77-82, 164-7; Swaminathan, *The Nāyakas of Ikkēri*, 166-8.

[38] But see BL/AAS, MG, no. 6, pt. 11: "Historical account of Beedoonoor or Caladee Samstanum," f. 72v, for a passage in the *Keḷadi arasara vaṃśāvaḷi* about a minister attempting to overthrow King Venkatappa Nayaka I (r. c. 1585-1629).

their position in Ikkeri. VOC documents from 1660-1 describe Mallappa as the kingdom's most prominent merchant, who controlled the rice trade, was "mighty rich," enjoyed a good reputation with the king, had easy access to the court, and was privileged to travel by palanquin.

That the Malu brothers harboured not just commercial but also political ambitions, becomes clear from Mallappa's role in Ikkeri's succession struggles, related in Chapter 2. After King Venkatappa Nayaka II was killed and succeeded by his cousin Bhadrappa Nayaka in 1661, rumour had it that Mallappa had instigated both this violent transition and the alleged poisoning of the previous ruler Shivappa Nayaka in 1660. In any case, as the VOC reported, Mallappa's position at court was formally raised (*in qualiteijt verhoocht*) once the throne was occupied by Bhadrappa, who seemed entirely dependent on him. Thus, the merchant's power increased to such an extent that in 1662 the Dutch considered the Malu brothers to "have the kingdom's helm in their hands."

But King Bhadrappa's passing around mid-1664 and the following power struggles made them temporarily fall from grace. Apparently, as soon as their protégé on the throne had gone, other courtiers could contest their position. VOC documents state that while Mallappa had conveniently left Ikkeri to head another embassy to Goa—supposedly deliberately planned by him as he foresaw the king's death and the resultant troubles—his brother Narayana found himself stuck at court with his rivals and barely survived the ensuing clash, suffering severe head wounds and being stripped of all his designations. Mallappa, extending his stay with the Portuguese as long as possible, eventually returned home, but, having fallen ill on the way back, died in July 1664.

This was far from the end of the Malu family's influence. Only a few months later, the Dutch and Portuguese both reported that Narayana Malu had replaced his brother as the chief broker between Ikkeri and European powers. Some sources claim that he himself re-established order at the capital and now became the protector of the new king, Somashekara Nayaka. However Narayana regained power, his subsequent career included more ups and downs. In April-May 1668, during a VOC embassy to Ikkeri's capital Bednur, he served as the main contact between the court and the Dutch and received more gifts from them than any other courtier (see table 9). Additionally, he and one Vitthala Malu—possibly his father or the son of his deceased brother Mallappa—were called the "court merchants" with whom the VOC was to conduct its trade. The Company's estimation of Narayana's high standing was proved accurate when in 1670 the Dutch received news that:

> ... His Highness Somsecraneijcq [Somashekara Nayaka] has honoured Narnamaloe [Narayana Malu] ..., above the quality of state merchant [*rijcx coopman*], with the seat [*zitplaats*]—in His Highness' presence—of councillor [*raats hr.*], which puts the mentioned

> Narnamoele in greater esteem [*aensien*] by the realm of Canara [Ikkeri] than any of his ancestors have had before.[39]

While the king and the merchant-courtier thus maintained a close relationship, both fared badly during the succession struggles in the next year. In Somashekara's case, competition between courtiers, the involvement of the Bijapur sultanate, and his madness and absence from court led to his assassination. With respect to Narayana—said to be instrumental in the king's downfall by luring him from the countryside to the capital and delivering him to Bijapur's troops—the Dutch initially wrote that the new ruler, probably Shivappa Nayaka II, confirmed the merchant's privileges and bestowed even more honours on him.

The position of this king and his supporters quickly grew weak, however, making Narayana leave the court, store his possessions at the VOC factory in Basrur, and back another contender to the throne, the son of Kasiyya Bhadrayya, a member of the royal family. With him, Narayana returned to Bednur around mid-1672, but here he fell victim to the ongoing power struggles during the following years. When Kasiyya Bhadrayya clashed with a coalition of General Timmanna, Widow-Queen Chennammaji, and "state secretary" Krishnayya (*'s rijx schrijver* "Crusnia"), Narayana shifted allegiance to this faction.

Nevertheless, there was no trust within this coalition. Allegedly, Narayana and Krishnayya dared to appear at court only with a group of warriors to protect them. True enough, when General Timmanna finally convinced the two men to dismiss their bodyguards and they next paid a visit to the queen all by themselves, they were locked up and severely tortured. Accused of secretly supporting Kasiyya Bhadrayya, Narayana and Krishnayya were sentenced to donate large sums of money to finance the war against Kasiyya Bhadrayya. Having consented to do so, they were released and by November 1673 had been reinstalled as court merchant and state secretary respectively. Soon after, still according to VOC reports, Narayana was even dispatched as head of a military expedition against the Nayaka of Sonda, given back his money, and offered the post of governor of the Kalluru province. Perhaps impressed by Narayana's diverse and resilient career, the Dutch now called him "that politic man" (*dien politeijcken man*).

But Narayana's third rise to power would be his last. The campaign he led against the Sonda kingdom failed and he declined the office of provincial governor because, as the Dutch guessed, he preferred to oversee trade rather than lands. Narayana may indeed have grown tired of Ikkeri's court politics, which in the mid-1670s centred on the competition between Queen Chennammaji and General Timmanna. VOC documents from late 1675 declare that Narayana, who generally favoured Chennammaji,

[39] NA, VOC, no. 1274, f. 171: Basrur diary extract, June 1670 (translation mine).

felt so miserable because of this rivalry that he stopped eating and eventually poisoned himself. Counter-poison saved him just in time, but his misfortune did not end there. Together with Chennammaji, Narayana was now summoned by Timmanna to accompany him on an expedition against Mysore, so as to prevent the merchant and the queen from creating trouble during the general's absence. Less than two months later, in early 1676, the Dutch reported that Narayana had been put in prison, with all his possessions taken from him and "his entire family effectively ruined and scattered," while another court merchant was appointed in his stead.

By mid-1676 Narayana had died, as had Timmanna, who was killed in a battle that year.[40] The Malu family's great influence had now really ended. The VOC wrote that following Narayana's passing his nephew or cousin Venkatesh Malu ("Winkittezy Maloe") would possibly be installed by the queen as court merchant. Dutch records also refer to several other people bearing the name Malu until at least the 1730s, including men called Vitthala, Narayana, and Venkatesh, serving the Ikkeri court as brokers, governors, commanders, or (court) merchants. But there is no indication that these people were related to the erstwhile mighty Malu family, and after Narayana nobody named Malu seems to have attained a prominent and lasting position at court anyway.[41]

The precise reasons for Narayana's final downfall and the cause of his death are unknown. In fact, many details of his life are uncertain since they are only

40 NA, VOC, no. 1231, ff. 515-16v; no. 1233, f. 595v; no. 1236, ff. 205-7; no. 1240, ff. 532-3, 602-3; no. 1245, ff. 355, 499; no. 1246, ff. 1399, 1432, 1445, 1619-20; no. 1268, ff. 1111-17; no. 1288, ff. 635-8; no. 1291, ff. 586v-7; no. 1295, ff. 264v-9; no. 1299, ff. 345v-7v, 406v-7v; no. 1304, f. 393; no. 1308, ff. 642v-3, 743, 746v, 777; no. 1315, f. 740; no. 1321, ff. 957, 961: letters of Shivappa Nayaka and Mallappa Malu to superintendent Rijcklof van Goens, from Barkur ("Backanoor"), Vengurla, Cochin, and Basrur to Batavia, Kannur (Cannanore), and Gentlemen XVII, from VOC merchant Lefer off the Kanara Coast to Batavia, from a VOC spy at Goa to Vengurla, Apr. 1659, Feb. 1661, May, Dec. 1662, Apr., Aug., Nov. 1664, July 1672, Apr., Nov. 1673, Feb., Dec. 1674, Apr., Oct.-Dec. 1675, Jan. 1676, Feb. 1677, report by *Commandeur* Adriaen Roothaes, June 1660, reports on Vengurla and Ikkeri, July 1664, May 1676, agreements with Ikkeri, May 1668, report of mission to Ikkeri, Apr.-May 1668; Coolhaas *et al.*, *Generale Missiven*, vol. IV, 120; Shastry, *Goa-Kanara Portuguese Relations*, 184, 192-5, 209-15, 218, 304-5; Foster, *The English Factories in India 1661–64*, 120, 343-4, 346, 349 (referring to Mallappa Malu as "Malik Mulla" and "Mollup Molla"), idem, *1668–1669*, 109, 111-12, 124-5, 268, 270-1; Fawcett, *The English Factories in India* (New Series), vol. I, 298, 308-9, 320, 328, 337; Sanjay Subrahmanyam, "The Portuguese, the Port of Basrur, and the Rice Trade, 1600-50," in idem (ed.), *Merchants, Markets and the State in Early Modern India* (Delhi, 1990), 38, 44; R.J. Barendse, *The Arabian Seas: The Indian Ocean World of the Seventeenth Century* (New Delhi, 2002), 213; Rao, *Craft Production and Trade in South Kanara*, 61-2, 159-63; Pinto, *History of Christians in Coastal Karnataka*, 80-1, 86, 96-8, 109; Chitnis, *Keḷadi Polity*, 48, 79-80, 184-5; Swaminathan, *The Nāyakas of Ikkēri*, 107-9, 113.

41 NA, VOC, no. 1406, ff. 920, 925; no. 2231, f. 2982; no. 2414, ff. 520-2, 541: report of mission to Ikkeri, May 1684, letters from broker Narayana Malu and merchant Venkatesh Malu to VOC official Hendrix and Cochin, Mar. 1732, Jan. 1737, report on meeting with Ikkeri envoys, Nov. 1736; Coolhaas *et al.*, *Generale Missiven*, vol. IV, 120; s'Jacob, *De Nederlanders in Kerala*, 273.

mentioned in VOC reports or in his own letters to the Dutch, both of which sources may not be entirely reliable. However, it is clear that the Malu brothers and their father held multiple, and sometimes simultaneous, functions at the Ikkeri court, acting as trader, ambassador, councillor, general, and—had Narayana accepted the offer—provincial governor. Their prominence as courtiers initially derived from their commercial enterprise, including their monopoly on the kingdom's rice export. Their mercantile connections with European powers appear to have paved the way for their diplomatic undertakings, in turn leading to other ranks and more power at the court—and to greater vulnerability for that matter. Narayana seemed well aware that his political adventures could backfire on his original economic activities. After his second comeback, he refused a position as governor, apparently preferring trade over rule, and the machinations at court frustrated him to the point of a suicide attempt. At any rate, his demise involved both his political and commercial careers, which had evidently grown intertwined.

The great but oscillating power of the Malu family left ample room for other courtiers. As noted in Chapter 2, while Mallappa Malu was allegedly involved in the murder of Venkatappa Nayaka II in 1661, General Shivalinga actually killed this king and initially took charge of the court. Further, Portuguese sources from late 1664 speak of hostilities between King Somashekara Nayaka's brother-in-law and the powerful Secretary Govayya and his brother, governor at the important port of Mangalore.[42]

General Timmanna dominated the court in the early 1670s, eliminating pretenders to the throne, installing Chennammaji as puppet queen, and locking up officials. Indeed, the English voyager John Fryer reported that Timmanna had raised himself from a "toddy-man" (palm-wine trader) to the kingdom's "protector" and travelled with great pomp and circumstance, and the Dutch claimed he had himself saluted as the Nayaka of Ikkeri.[43] Thus, during much of the period of the Malu brothers' activities, power was shared by and fluctuated among different courtiers. Some insight into how influence was divided over various court factions about a decade later, when Chennammaji still sat on the throne, is provided by two VOC reports of 1683 and 1684.

The first of these documents relates that Ikkeri's then General Krishnappayya ("Crustnapaija") fell out with a group of courtiers, including Queen Chennammaji's father Sidappa Chetti ("Sidapchittij") and other associates of hers. They had grown

[42] Shastry, *Goa-Kanara Portuguese Relations*, 209-12.

[43] It has been argued that in 1672-3 Queen Chennammaji sought and received assistance of the Maratha King Shivaji in tempering General Timmanna's power, but Dutch sources make no mention of this. See Suryanath U. Kamath, "Keladi Nayakas and Marathas," *The Quarterly Journal of the Mythic Society* LXI, 1-4 (1970), 66-7.

envious of Krishnappayya, who was leading a successful military campaign against Golkonda and Mysore. This jealousy developing into downright distrust, the queen allegedly felt compelled to issue a secret written order to have the general killed, but this document fell into the very hands of Krishnappayya. First contemplating not returning from his expedition and avoiding the capital, he eventually ensured himself of the support of his friends and troops, and then visited the queen. Chennammaji received him most courteously and presented a robe of honour (*eercleet*) to him. Krishnappayya politely rejected it, showed the paper ordering his assassination, and asked if that document was not a suitable enough robe of honour. This caused great distress and countless apologies were made to the general. He appears to have accepted these, as he remained Ikkeri's general for some time to come, but Chennammaji and many courtiers now feared his power all the more and worried he might start backing another pretender to the throne.[44] Adding to the tension, around the same time a former court merchant, considered a favourite of Krishnappayya, was stabbed to death just outside the Bednur palace.[45]

This state of affairs seems to have been largely unchanged when less than a year later the VOC envoy Jacob Wilcken embarked on a diplomatic mission to Ikkeri. In April 1684 he arrived at the capital with the aim of obtaining better trading privileges than the Dutch had enjoyed so far. The Company wanted to pay lower tolls and get permission to buy rice from any trader rather than only the court's agents. The embassy proved problematic from the start. General Krishnappayya was supposed to serve as the court's contact for Wilcken, but he had little time to discuss matters, repeatedly saying he did not feel well or was busy entertaining an ambassador from the Golkonda sultanate. At one of his few meetings with Wilcken, the general made clear that he was personally well-disposed towards the VOC but had to reckon with other courtiers.

After a week without any progress, let alone an audience with Queen Chennammaji, Wilcken sought support from another influential courtier. This was, quite exceptionally, a woman, referred to by the Dutch as "Governess" (*gouvernante*) Maribasvama ("Maribassuama"). The VOC ambassador had hitherto refrained from contacting her, fearing this might offend Krishnappayya, but he changed his mind when he found out that the general and the governess were close friends. Wilcken's talks with Maribasvama were equally fruitless, however, revolving around the question of whether lowered tolls would reduce the court's

[44] This was possibly Shivappa Nayaka II, who seems to have escaped from his imprisonment in Ikkeri in this period. See the introduction and Ikkeri section of Chapter 2.

[45] NA, VOC, no. 1388, ff. 1975v-6: letter from Cochin to Batavia, July 1683; Fryer, *A New Account of East-India and Persia*, 58, 162. See also NA, VOC, no. 1379, ff. 2355-5v: letter from Cochin to Batavia, May 1682.

income or stimulate trade and thus increase profits. In the end, the governess repeated Krishnappayya's remark that much depended on other courtiers and she recommended Wilcken to stay in touch with the general and no one else.

Finally, two weeks after his arrival in Bednur, the Dutch envoy secured his first audience with the queen. She was accompanied by Krishnappayya, Maribasvama, and an official named Bhadrayya ("Badriaia"), described by Wilcken as "supreme governor" (*opperste gouverneur*). After consultations with the queen, all three courtiers said they largely supported the Company's wishes but that things could be finalised only when the court merchant Siddabasayya ("Zidbasia") returned. This man was currently staying in Ikkeri's former capital Keladi to perform annual royal ceremonies and would be back within a few days. When some time later news came that Siddabasayya had proceeded from Keladi to inspect border fortresses, Wilcken became impatient and, slightly insulted, informed Krishnapayya he would not stay in Bednur much longer. This led to further deliberations with the general, who now seemed somewhat insecure about his own position at court, saying he was willing to force the acceptance of the VOC's demands if only he could be sure this would not prove a bad decision later on.

But soon after, during another audience with Chennammaji—now accompanied by her minor, adopted son, the future King Basavappa Nayaka—Krishnappayya made a different impression. Declaring to speak on behalf of the young king, the general assumed a harsh tone against Wilcken and the meeting turned into an argument in which the Dutch envoy and the courtiers repeated their viewpoints without making any progress. In the subsequent weeks, yet more futile discussions with various functionaries followed and audiences with the queen were endlessly postponed, while the court merchant Siddabasayya never appeared to settle matters during Wilcken's sojourn. Eventually, the envoy returned home without any of the VOC's requests having been granted.[46]

Disappointing though this mission was to Wilcken, his report gives an idea of the relations between various court officials, at least those involved in Ikkeri's contacts with the VOC and thus having a say in commercial, diplomatic, and military affairs. Much less is known about the background and careers of these people than about the Malu brothers. Yet, to some extent one can deduce the functions and power they held and reconstruct the court factions they belonged to.

First, there was a coalition of General Krishnappayya, "Governess" Maribasvama, and possibly "Chief Governor" Bhadrayya, which essentially favoured the VOC. Krishnappayya was referred to as "field lord" (*veltoverste*), indicating a high military commander. According to the chronicle *Keḷadinṛpa vijayam*, Krishnappayya had occupied the position of *sabbunīsa* since the reign of Somashekara Nayaka.

[46] NA, VOC, no. 1406, ff. 909v-33: report of mission to Ikkeri, Apr.-May 1684.

This military rank came just below the *daḷavāy*, but in Ikkeri it had a more or less equal standing.[47] It is unclear which functions Maribasvama and Bhadrayya held, but the former is mentioned in Dutch records as an important figure for trade matters between at least 1681 and 1684, while the latter was obviously considered a very highly placed person, perhaps the chief minister or *pradhāni*.[48] In spite of their prominence, however, these courtiers could not force decisions without getting other functionaries on their side, or so reported ambassador Wilcken.

Those other officials apparently belonged to a second, opposing faction, less clearly defined in Wilcken's account. It may well be that these were the people who had tried to eliminate Krishnappayya the year before. Judging from Wilcken's quote below, this group included the court merchant Siddabasayya, some relatives of the king, the governor of the port of Mangalore, and—as Wilcken suggested elsewhere in his report—several Brahmin traders. Of these, Siddabasayya seems to have been particularly powerful, although his exact function is, again, unclear. In the period of Wilcken's mission, he likely was the court's chief rice merchant and probably also held other posts, considering his performance of a royal ceremony in the old capital Keladi and examination of defence works.

A third party can perhaps be said to have consisted of Queen Chennammaji and her minor son, as there is no indication the queen associated herself with either of the main factions in this period. How influential Chennammaji actually was, is hard to determine, but from Wilcken's account it appears she occasionally took part in negotiations with the VOC envoy and had to give her consent to certain decisions.

In any case, during Wilcken's stay in Bednur, none of these alliances seems to have been dominant and all had to reckon with one another. As the Dutch envoy concluded:

> ... the field lord [General Krishnappayya]—as we could not have noticed differently—has done his best, with sincere intentions, to advance the Company's free trade. And although that lord, in our presence, has displayed himself in the opposite way before the queen and others, that happened in order to show that he sought not to lessen the

[47] Swaminathan, *The Nāyakas of Ikkēri*, 112, 116-19; Chitnis, *Keḷadi Polity*, 165-6. See also BL/AAS, MG, no. 6, pt. 11: "Historical account of Beedoonoor or Caladee Samstanum," ff. 80v-1v, where *Sabbunīsa* Krishnappayya seems to be referred to as "Sabneveesoo Croostapiah."

[48] I have found no clear references to Maribasvama and Bhadrayya in Indian sources or secondary literature. Wilcken's report does not give Maribasvama's name, but it appears in other VOC documents. See NA, VOC, no. 1370, f. 2083v; no. 1373, ff. 361v, 370v; no. 1379, f. 2411v: letters from Cochin to Gentlemen XVII, Vengurla, and Basrur, Jan. 1681, Dec. 1682, memorandum for Basrur and Vengurla, Mar. 1682. This Bhadrayya should not be confused with Kasiyya Bhadrayya who attempted to install his son on the throne in the early 1670s.

> king's revenues—which, as some troublemakers [*dwarsdrijvers*] suggest, would be the consequence of the free trade. And we know for sure that, in our absence, His Excellency [Krishnappayya] has made enough effort with the queen—for the benefit of the Company's business—to bring to reason the troublemakers or opponents [*tegenstrevers*], of whom the king's father and brother [Mariyappa and Mannappa Chetti], as well as the court's rice trader Zidbasuwaia [Siddabasayya] and the Mangeloorse governor, are the principal ones ...[49]

Thus can be explained Krishnappayya's behaviour of privately professing support for the VOC and publicly showing toughness. He surely was a powerful official, considering for instance that he conducted some of Ikkeri's correspondence with the Dutch and that they believed gifts to him could make the whole court comply with their wishes.[50] Moreover, he commanded a great number of troops. But in his efforts to realise his goals, he had to beware of becoming even more suspect in the eyes of his rivals, as he admitted to Wilcken. Indeed, during the latter's visit, the general's influence had probably diminished already. The soured Dutch-Ikkeri relations in the subsequent years appear to confirm this. Since its requests were not granted, the VOC even temporarily closed its factory at Basrur and trade came to a near standstill.[51] Apparently, Krishnappayya remained unable to win over other courtiers.

It is of course also possible that the court simply feigned internal disagreement to Wilcken in an attempt to reject the Company's demands without embittering it too much, presenting Krishnappayya as a friend of the Dutch, whose advice could be trusted. But whether the general faced competition at court or not, after 1684 he disappears from the VOC archives, while the overall political patterns sketched above continue to figure in those records for many more decades. For instance, these documents suggest that from the mid-1680s the court merchant Siddabasayya consolidated his position and dominated the court. Until his death around 1696, Dutch references to most probably the same man call him the "state governor" (*rijcxbestierder*, possibly *pradhāni*), and say he clashed with Queen Chennammaji at least once.[52]

49 NA, VOC, no. 1406, f. 932 (translation mine).

50 NA, VOC, no. 1379, ff. 2353v, 2411v-12: letter from Cochin to Batavia, May 1682, memorandum for Basrur and Vengurla, Mar. 1682.

51 Coolhaas *et al.*, *Generale Missiven*, vol. IV, 824, vol. V (The Hague, 1975), 61.

52 NA, VOC, no. 1463, ff. 439-9v; no. 1474, ff. 15, 116-17, 191, 315, 329v, 336v: letters from Sadashiva Nayaka to Nagapattinam, from Basrur to Cochin, from Cochin to Gentlemen XVII, from "Sidij Bassuaija" to Cochin, Jan., May-June, Dec. 1689, Jan. 1690, report on Vengurla and Ikkeri, Mar. 1689; Coolhaas *et al.*, *Generale Missiven*, vol. V, 802. Siddabasayya may be the same person as one of Chennammaji's important officers, perhaps a treasurer, known as (Bokkasada) Siddabasavayya. See: Swaminathan, *The Nāyakas of Ikkēri*, 124; Chitnis, *Keḷadi Polity*, 71.

Eighteenth-century Ikkeri saw many courtiers whose careers were as diverse, illustrious, or volatile as those of Narayana Malu, Krishnappayya, or Siddabasayya. While these officials are too numerous to even list here, one example that should be briefly mentioned is Nirvanayya. From the 1710s to the 1730s he held various offices, including that of "state governor" (*rijxbestierder*), and maintained his own ships for overseas horse trading. Figuring in both local and European sources, he further stands out because in 1722 his daughter Nilammaji was married in a grandiose wedding ceremony to King Somashekara Nayaka II, as was another daughter on a separate occasion.

In 1730, however, the VOC reported that disagreements had arisen between Nirvanayya ("Nerwanea") and his royal son-in-law. The marriages between Somashekara II and Nirvanayya's daughters had produced no children and opinions differed on who should be considered the heir apparent. Whereas Somashekara II preferred his nephew, Nirvanayya favoured his own son, Sangana Basappa, thus bluntly disregarding the king's wish. After this confrontation, Nirvanayya's prominence diminshed. During VOC embassies to Ikkeri in 1735 and 1738, Dutch envoys were discouraged from presenting gifts to him or even visiting him. Indeed, Somashekara II's hatred of Nirvanayya reached such heights that nobody at court dared to mention his name, while his possessions had been confiscated in the hope he would "lay his head down."[53] Clearly, marital ties to a dynasty would not always prevent courtiers from falling out of favour, but could actually contribute to it.

This survey concludes by considering how the Dutch distributed gifts among courtiers each time they sent an embassy to Ikkeri, thus providing a series of snapshots of the court's balance of power, as the VOC saw it. This information is available for only three missions, as lists of presents during other missions have not survived. Further, because Dutch-Ikkeri relations were deeply troubled during the embassy

53 NA, VOC, no. 1852, ff. 60-2; no. 1977, ff. 110-10v; no. 2130, f. 53; no. 2187, ff. 9-11v, 148-8v; no. 2187, f. 222; no. 2200, ff. 1134, 1257; no. 2201, ff. 1897-9; no. 2228, ff. 949-50, 952, 955-5v; no. 2229, ff. 2031-1v, 2035; no. 2231, ff. 2891-2v, 2964; no. 2232, ff. 3593-8; no. 2354, ff. 1535, 1578, 1604, 1606-7: letters from Cochin to Batavia and Gentlemen XVII, from Basrur to Cochin, from Nirvanayya and merchant "Sunderdas Wistnadas" to the VOC, May 1714, May 1722, Apr. 1729, Sept., Nov. 1730, May, c. Sept.-Oct., Dec. 1731, Apr. 1732, Cochin diary, Apr. 1730, report on Malabar, May 1732, reports of missions to Ikkeri, Oct.-Dec. 1731, Jan.-Mar. 1735; TNA, DR, no. 257, ff. 9, 17-23: report of mission to Ikkeri, Apr.-May 1738 (also available in NA, VOC, no. 2435, ff. 2236-69); Pinto, *History of Christians in Coastal Karnataka*, 91; *Annual Report of the Mysore Archæological Department for the Year 1915-16* (Bangalore, 1916), 68; *Epigraphia Carnatica*, vol. VIII, *Inscriptions in the Shimoga District (Part II)*, ed. B. Lewis Rice (Bangalore, 1904), 294, 324, 361-2; R.S. Siva Ganesha Murthy, "Sanskrit Literature under Keḷadi Rule," in G.S. Dikshit (ed.), *Studies in Keladi History (Seminar Papers)* (Bangalore, 1981), 102; Swaminathan, *The Nāyakas of Ikkēri*, 141-2, 149, 224, Appendix B (between 280-1); Chitnis, *Keḷadi Polity*, 40, 69-71, 116; Shastry, *Goa-Kanara Portuguese Relations*, 232, 237-8, 291; Guha, "Transitions and Translations," 29.

in 1684 (described above), no gifts were brought on that mission, save for some minor ones for Queen Chennammaji.

Table 9 ranks people according to the value of the presents they each received, indicating who were considered most influential by the VOC—or, in 1738, by the court itself. The embassy in that year was one of the rare occasions on which Dutch envoys were urged to distribute their gifts differently than initially planned. They intended to donate the most valuable presents to "former state governor" Nirvanayya and General Raghunatha Odduru ("Regenade Odderoe"). But a court's representative sent to discuss this, explained that Chief Minister Devappa ("state governor Dewapa") and Secretary Paramasarayya ("Parmasaraija") now dominated the court. Not honouring these men with gifts would damage the VOC's interests. Like Nirvanayya, General Raghunatha Odduru had recently fallen from grace. In 1734 he had single-handedly concluded an unfavourable peace treaty with the Dutch and he was suspected of silently allowing the Portuguese to build a fortress at Mangalore, of which port he was the governor. Therefore—although he still enjoyed the privilege of sitting one step below the king during audiences, together with Devappa—Raghunatha Odduru should receive fewer presents than other, more prominent officials.[54]

Despite its limited coverage, table 9 underscores the dynamics transpiring from the preceding paragraphs. While the monarch naturally always received the most presents, the order of other offices differed with each embassy, suggesting these functions did not always ensure the same levels of power. In 1668, court merchant Narayana Malu received the second most valuable gifts, followed by various councillors and, at the bottom of the list, a secretary. In contrast, in 1735 a secretary occupied second place, with a treasurer coming next. Only three years later, the then secretary had moved to third place, since Chief Minister Devappa was now most honoured after the king.[55] The general, often the most powerful official in Ikkeri's history, received the least during this mission.

[54] TNA, DR, no. 257, ff. 9, 17-23: report of mission to Ikkeri, Apr.-May 1738. For General Raghunatha Odduru, see: NA, VOC, no. 2226, ff. 54, 57; no. 2340, ff. 410v-18; no. 2354, ff. 1535, 1547, 1573-7, 1591-3; no. 2414, ff. 529, 531; no. 2432, f. 75v; no. 2433, ff. 231-32v, 245v, 436v, 504v, 512v-13, 538, 540v; no. 2435, f. 2232v; no. 2462, ff. 157, 371-1v, 433-3v: letters from Cochin to Gentlemen XVII and Batavia, Oct. 1732, Mar. 1738, final report (*memorie van overgave*) of Malabar *Commandeur* Adriaan Maten, Jan. 1735, report of mission to Ikkeri, Jan.-Mar. 1735, report on meeting with envoys from Ikkeri, Nov. 1736, "indigenous" diary (*inheems dagregister*, with correspondence and reports), Oct.-Dec. 1737, Jan. 1738, Nov. 1738, instructions for mission to Ikkeri, Mar. 1738; Heeres and Stapel, *Corpus diplomaticum Neerlando-Indicum*, vol. 5 (The Hague, 1938), 199-203; Chitnis, *Keḷadi Polity*, 160-1, 167-8, 172-3, 183, 190; Swaminathan, *The Nāyakas of Ikkēri*, 132, 137. For violent Dutch-Ikkeri conflicts in this period, see NA, VOC, no. 2320, ff. 1507-698; no. 2414, ff. 137-477: reports concerning expeditions against Ikkeri, etc., c. 1734, Apr. 1736.

[55] It is not clear whether Devappayya ("Deopaja"), treasurer in 1735, was the same person as Devappa ("Dewapa"), chief minister in 1738.

Table 9: Distribution of gifts among prominent courtiers during Dutch missions to Ikkeri, in order of value, 1668-1738.

1668	1735	1738
king Somashekara	*king* Somashekara II	*king* Somashekara II
court merchant Narayana Malu	*secretary* Chanappayya	*chief minister* Devappa
chief councillor "Jantopaneijck"	*treasurer* Devappayya	*secretary* Paramasarayya
second councillor "Marij Boeij"		*general & governor* Raghunatha Odduru
two *councillors* & a *secretary*		

Sources: NA, VOC, no. 1268, ff. 1113v-4v; no. 2354, ff. 1537-45, 1550-2; TNA, DR, no. 257, ff. 17-24.

Obviously, the balance of power suggested by table 9 is largely based on Dutch observations and gives an incomplete picture, like all events discussed in this section. There were of course other officials in prominent positions, whom the VOC did not meet or write about. Further, the Dutch stayed in Ikkeri only during the second half of the kingdom's existence and even then they were absent from the court for long periods. Nevertheless, for all their limitations these sources reveal certain tendencies.

First, the courtiers thought to have been most influential over the years comprise a diverse group. Little is known about the background of most: we are aware only that the Malu family was of Brahmin descent,[56] and that Nirvanayya was probably a Lingayat, like Ikkeri's Nayakas, considering his daughters' marriages to the king. However, a survey of the positions held by the most prominent courtiers over time gives an idea of the variety among these ranks. At the very least, this list contains merchants Mallappa and Narayana Malu, General Timmanna, merchant Siddabasayya, "state governor" Nirvanayya, Secretary Chanappayya, and Chief Minister Devappa. One can add members of the royal family who, in the name of their relative on the throne, controlled the kingdom, like Basavappa Nayaka's father and uncle, Mariyappa and Mannappa Chetti. Some treasurers and various governors—including provincial ones and a woman—also exercised substantial power. Clearly, the formal positions of these courtiers bore little relation to their actual might. Offices could be very prominent when occupied by one person and much less significant when held by another. Between the 1660s and 1680s, the most influential

[56] Many more Ikkeri courtiers (not treated here) were Brahmins. See Swaminathan, *The Nāyakas of Ikkēri*, 183.

courtiers were court merchants and generals. In the 1730s, people in these positions were less important, the court now being dominated by a secretary and a treasurer.

Further, courtiers moved between or combined functions to increase their power. Court merchants Narayana Malu and Siddabasayya acquired governmental and military ranks, and General Raghunatha Odduru served as the governor of Mangalore. With extra offices came more authority, status, servants, connections, resources, information, and therefore influence. Exploiting family relations or forging ties with prominent persons were additional means to advance one's position. The Malu family is just one example of the former kind of bonds. VOC documents abound with important people who were brothers, cousins, or other blood-relatives of one another. When General Timmanna died in 1676, his competitor Queen Chennammaji imprisoned some of his family members. Their considerable possessions, confiscated at this time, suggest they had risen to power in Timmanna's wake. In the 1720s, when "state governor" Nirvanayya was at his most powerful, his brother and his son received gifts from the Dutch on various occasions, indicating their high status. And in 1737, the brother of the influential Secretary Devappa was installed as general, governor of Mangalore, or both, albeit for a brief period.[57] As for links between non-blood-related courtiers, the report of the VOC mission in 1684 mentions several coalitions between courtiers who seemingly were not biological relatives. Nirvanayya was particularly effective in establishing such ties when he had his daughters marry the king.

Yet, as Nirvanayya's case demonstrates, no career step guaranteed security. Court factions obviously emerged—and fell apart—depending on the advantages they yielded. All officials ran the risk of losing their power, and many did so, sometimes even more than once. Narayana Malu repeatedly supported unsuccessful pretenders to throne, Krishnappayya annoyed jealous opponents, Nirvanayya grew overconfident, Raghunatha Odduru behaved too independently—all contributing to their downfall. Very few people kept their position for long. Career lengths cannot be determined with much precision, but no courtier considered above seems to have maintained great influence for longer than two decades. For most, their period in power was much shorter.

Nayakas of Tanjavur

It is impossible to arrive at such specific conclusions for courtiers serving under Tanjavur's Nayaka house, because for most of its existence one depends on south Indian sources. Intensive contacts between this court and the VOC lasted no longer

[57] NA, VOC, no. 1315, f. 740; no. 1977, ff. 110-10v; no. 2130, ff. 323v-4; no. 2433, ff. 436-6v: letters from Cochin to Gentlemen XVII and Batavia, Feb. 1677, May 1722, Cochin proceedings, Jan. 1729, "indigenous" diary, Dec. 1737.

than fifteen years: from 1658, when the Dutch captured the port of Nagapattinam, to 1673, when the Tanjavur Nayakas were dethroned by Madurai. But even VOC records of that period are not particularly rich when it comes to Tanjavur officials. There are, for instance, no Dutch embassy reports to throw light on the court's composition and its internal power relations. Therefore, this section only discusses a courtier dominating Tanjavur's early phase—based on local texts—and what little VOC documents say on functionaries during the Nayakas' last few decades.

First, we briefly inventory which important positions are thought to have existed in this kingdom, as listed in secondary literature based on south Indian sources. Like in Ikkeri, courtiers or ministers were referred to as *mantri* and *saciva*. Most prominent would have been three officials also encountered in Vijayanagara and Ikkeri. In descending order, these were the *pradhāni* (chief minister), the *daḷavāy* or *senāpati* (general), and, quite a bit lower in rank, the *rāyasam* (secretary), the first of which posts was allegedly always held by a Brahmin. Then followed some financial officers, including the *aṭṭavaṇai* (chief accountant of the revenue department) and the *tōshikāna adhikāri* (head of the treasury).[58] Judging from this literature, it is unclear which other types of high functionaries existed.

During almost half of this dynasty's relatively short span of about 140 years, one courtier stood out above everyone else: Govinda Dikshita. Indeed, his exalted position seems on par with that of his contemporary Ariyanatha Mudaliar, Madurai's powerful minister introduced at this chapter's beginning. Govinda is also mentioned in Chapter 1, as he figures in the origin stories of Tanjavur's Nayakas. One tradition traces the earliest career phase of this Brahmin, who came from the Kannada-speaking region, to Vijayanagara. Visiting the imperial court, he impressed the ruler Achyuta Raya (r. 1529-42) with his knowledge of religious texts and astrology, and was then employed as a courtier.

At Vijayanagara Govinda met the young Shevappa Nayaka, future founder of Tanjavur's Nayaka house. Recognising Shevappa's potential, Govinda introduced him to the emperor, who took him into his service. After military feats and marrying the emperor's sister-in-law, Shevappa became governor of Tanjavur, taking Govinda with him as his minister. Legend has it that Shevappa even offered his own position to Govinda, but he declined this since Brahmins were not to harbour royal ambitions. Instead, he served as the main official not only of Shevappa (r. c. 1530s-70s) but of several of his descendants, too.[59] Thus, some texts suggest that

[58] Vriddhagirisan, *The Nayaks of Tanjore*, 169-71.

[59] In addition to the sources and literature mentioned in Chapter 1, see Mahalingam, *Mackenzie Manuscripts*, vol. II, 344, for a text saying Govinda Dikshita even served under the dynasty's last real ruler, Vijayaraghava Nayaka (r. 1631-73).

Govinda was a courtier under this dynasty right from its beginning and lived and worked for an exceptionally long time.

Historians presume Govinda was in fact chiefly active during the reigns of Achyutappa Nayaka (c. 1570s-97?) and Raghunatha Nayaka (c. 1597?-1626). He is mentioned in inscriptions from the years between 1588 and 1634, and works like the *Raghunāthābhyudayamu* also link him to these rulers. Thus, he was still active for an exceedingly long period, compared with officials in Ikkeri. Little is known of Govinda's actual life, but a number of texts together suggest he held several court offices over time. The Sanskrit *Sāhitya ratnākara*, written by Govinda's son Yagnanarayana Dikshita, calls him *guru* (preceptor) and it is likely he was the Nayakas' *purōhita* (royal or family priest), in which capacity he may have crowned Raghunatha. The same work declares that he functioned as regent of Tanjavur when Raghunatha left the capital for a military campaign. In an inscription of 1631 he is specifically referred to as *pradhāni*, while the Telugu *Tañjāvūri āndhra rājula caritra* seems to mention Govinda as both minster and general. So perhaps at one point he occupied the combined ranks of *pradhāni* and *daḷavāy*, like Madurai's Ariyanatha Mudaliar supposedly did.

In addition, Govinda built religious edifices, made gifts, and composed philosophical works. His prominence is further demonstrated by texts stating that he was allowed to sit on the same seat as Raghunatha while watching a play, and that this king held an umbrella—symbol of royalty—over Govinda's head when the latter performed a sacrifice. In short, both before and after his death, he enjoyed an illustrious reputation and over the years achieved some kind of saintly status (see illustration 9).[60]

Based on this scant information, certain aspects of Govinda Dikshita's life as a courtier remind us of the Vijayanagara and Ikkeri courts. First, he clearly became a very powerful figure, outshining other officials and being glorified in literature and inscriptions. According to the *Sāhitya ratnākara*, Govinda not only arranged the coronation of Raghunatha, but also initiated the abdication of his predecessor Achyutappa, suggesting he played an influential role in this succession, like so many courtiers did in Vijayanagara and its heirs. Second, he apparently held several offices, simultaneously or consecutively, involving administrative, religious, and perhaps military duties. Third, Govinda's family ties played an

[60] Krishnaswami Aiyangar, *Sources of Vijayanagar History*, 267-74, 323; Venkatesam, "Govinda Deekshita"; Vriddhagirisan, *The Nayaks of Tanjore*, 54, 74, 105, 113-25, 170, 185-7 (nos 34, 36, 40, 46-7, 50, 54-5); Heras, *The Aravidu Dynasty of Vijayanagara*, vol. I, 288, 399-401, 522; Narayana Rao, Shulman, and Subrahmanyam, *Symbols of Substance*, 40, 248; M. Krishnamachariar, *History of Classical Sanskrit Literature ...* (Madras, 1937), 231-4; P.V. Jagadisa Ayyar, *South Indian Shrines* (Madras, 1920), 76; Padma Seshadri and Padma Malini Sundararaghavan, *It Happened along the Kaveri: A Journey through Space and Time* (New Delhi, 2012), 267.

Illustration 9: Statue of the Tanjavur courtier Govinda Dikshita, Amman Shrine Mandapa, Thenupurisvarar Temple, Pattisvaram (photo by Ssriram mt, source: en.wikipedia.org/wiki/Govinda_Dikshita).

important role, since several of his sons rose to prominence, too. One text claims that Venkateshvara Dikshita served as a minister under Vijayaraghava Nayaka (r. 1631-73), while Yagnanarayana Dikshita was a celebrated court poet during Raghunatha's reign.[61] Notwithstanding all this, we read nothing about rivalry with other courtiers, temporary or permanent downfalls, or other troubles. Govinda's

[61] Vriddhagirisan, *The Nayaks of Tanjore*, 4-5, 59, 116, 118, 122-4; Krishnaswami Aiyangar, *Sources of Vijayanagar History*, 252, 269, 273.

career was a smooth one, local sources lead us to believe. But obviously, not all of Tanjavur's officials, or perhaps none at all, shared that experience. That, at least, is what the few Dutch records on functionaries under these Nayakas indicate.

The first Tanjavur courtiers the VOC archives refer to, albeit very briefly, include some *daḷavāys*. In 1652 it was noted that "dalleweij" Narayanappa Nayaka ("Narnapaneijcq") had been dismissed, for reasons unknown. Six years later, a message was received from an official described as the "dalleweij and great governor of the lowlands [*beneden landen*, coastal areas]" and probably called Kumarappa Nayaka ("Commerapaneijck"). In 1663, Tanjavur's chief general (*veltoverste*) was reported to be Tubaki Lingama Nayaka, the former *daḷavāy* of Madurai, who had fled that kingdom in the previous year but would return to his former position in the following year. As for local sources, an inscription of 1644 speaks of *Daḷavāy* Venkatadri Nayaka, while the *Tañjāvūri āndhra rājula caritra* mentions Rangappa Nayaka in this function during Tanjavur's conquest by Madurai in 1673.[62] These scattered references suggest there were at least four and probably five *daḷavāys* during the Nayakas' last three decades, implying they generally did not occupy this rank for long. Besides, one of them was apparently both general and coastal provincial governor, thus combining military and administrative functions.

More is known about another courtier of sorts, the magnate Chinanna Chetti, often called Malaya ("Maleije") in Dutch and English documents. Like some Nayaka houses, he belonged to one of the Balija castes, originating in the Telugu zone and engaged in both mercantile and military activities. Much of Chinanna's career has been described elsewhere,[63] but here his familial connections and many different positions are important. Similar to Ikkeri's Malu brothers, Chinanna was part of a family of merchants who branched off into a whole range of other enterprises.

His brother Achyutappa Chetti, also referred to as Malaya in European sources, was the first to grow prominent. While in the early seventeenth century he still worked as an intermediary between the Senji Nayakas and the VOC, in the 1620s and 1630s Achyutappa had become not only a powerful merchant, sending ships overseas, but also a dealer in arms and horses, a diplomat active at the courts

[62] NA, VOC, no. 1195, f. 504; no. 1227, f. 5v; no. 1231, ff. 151, 154, 167; no. 1240, ff. 378-9; no. 1243, f. 186; no. 1246, f. 498: letters from Pulicat to Batavia, from merchant-envoy Chinanna Chetti and King Vijayaraghava Nayaka to Admiral Van Goens, from Jaffna to Pulicat, Aug. 1652, Jan., Sept.-Oct. 1658, Feb. 1662, Jan. 1663, Feb. 1664; Vriddhagirisan, *The Nayaks of Tanjore*, 153 (n. 15), 188 (no. 58). For Tubaki Lingama Nayaka, father of Madurai's Queen Mangammal (r. 1691-1707) and brother of Senji's *Daḷavāy* Tubaki Krishnappa Nayaka, see also the section on Madurai below.

[63] See: Subrahmanyam, *The Political Economy of Commerce*, 300-14; Mukund, *The Trading World of the Tamil Merchant*, 62-6; Joseph J. Brennig, "Chief Merchants and the European Enclaves of Seventeenth-Century Coromandel," *Modern Asian Studies* 11, 3 (1977), 323-8; Seshan, *Trade and Politics on the Coromandel Coast*, 62-7.

of Vijayanagara (at Chandragiri) and Madurai, a revenue-farmer administering extensive coastal areas, and a broker for the English.

Chinanna, initially an agent for his brother, was heavily involved in politics as well. Since the 1620s he had been an influential figure at the Senji court. After Achyutappa's passing in 1634, Chinanna took over his brother's role as the VOC's main broker on the Coromandel Coast. Around the same time, he captured a fort in which Vijayanagara's Timma Raja had entrenched himself, thus ending the latter's succession struggle with Emperor Venkata II. In 1637 this ruler requested Chinanna to mediate in conflicts between Tanjavur, Madurai, and Senji. In 1642 Vijayanagara's Emperor Sriranga III presented some fortresses and villages to him and in 1646 he escorted that ruler on a mission to the Dutch settlement at Pulicat. As the English wrote in the mid-1640s, Chinanna was held in such high esteem by Sriranga III that he was made the emperor's treasurer and "ruleth both king and contry." Apparently quick to forge ties with newly arrived powers, in the late 1640s he farmed revenue in some coastal territories recently conquered by the Bijapur sultanate. Meanwhile, Chinanna's large-scale seaborne trade continued to flourish, although he faced heavy and at times violent competition from some relatives and Senji's powerful *Daḷavāy* Tubaki Krishnappa Nayaka.[64]

Originally chiefly active in other kingdoms, Chinanna became some kind of courtier in Tanjavur only very late in his life. Nevertheless, he seemed well on his way to acquire a special position there. In September 1658, following their conquest of Nagapattinam from the Portuguese, the Dutch sent him to Tanjavur's King Vijayaraghava Nayaka to discuss a treaty that would formally recognise the VOC's possession of the port. According to Chinanna's own account of this mission, the actual negotiations about Nagapattinam progressed with some difficulty. But Chinanna himself was allegedly treated with great respect by the Nayaka. During the first audience, he received several marks of honour and talked with the king about the "olden times" and the days of Chinanna's father. Vijayaraghava then announced he would place some lands under Chinanna's administration, while a few days later, at a more intimate audience, he once more stated he held Chinanna in high esteem. Confirming the merchant's own remarks about his standing with

[64] Subrahmanyam, *The Political Economy of Commerce*, 300-14; Mukund, *The Trading World of the Tamil Merchant*, 65-6; Brennig, "Chief Merchants and the European Enclaves of Seventeenth-Century Coromandel," passim, especially 323-8; Raychaudhuri, *Jan Company in Coromandel*, 42-4, 52-6; Mac Leod, *De Oost-Indische Compagnie*, vol. II, 13-15, 170-1, 183-93; NA, VOC, no. 1231, f. 146v: instructions by Admiral Van Goens to Nagapattinam, Sept. 1658; Colenbrander *et al.*, *Dagh-register gehouden int Casteel Batavia ... anno 1643–1644*, 244. For English references to the Chetti brothers, see: Foster, *The English Factories in India 1622–1623*, 122, 141, 238, idem, *1624–1629*, 9, 16, 131, 358, idem, *1642–1645*, 154, 279-80, 285, 290.

Vijayaraghava, the VOC wrote that Chinanna had free access to the king because of his long-existing prestige at court.

That Vijayaraghava's compliments were not mere words became clear when by January 1659 the supervision of all the kingdom's ports had been leased to Chinanna. But his rise to prominence was not confined to commerce, administration, and diplomacy. In October 1658 he informed the Dutch that the Nayaka had agreed to marry Chinanna's daughter and let his own daughter marry Chinanna's son.[65] Later VOC records suggest these weddings really took place, and at any rate this agreement further indicated that Chinanna's power at court was quickly increasing and expanding. Having served several dynasties, he now established familial connections with one of them. He could not enjoy this status for long, however. In April 1659 he passed away and, in true courtly style, was cremated together with thirty-three of his wives.[66] Had he lived longer, he probably would have become a fully-fledged Tanjavur courtier, at least in the sense of the term adopted here.

The last official under Tanjavur's Nayakas considered here is a somewhat obscure one. Referred to by the Dutch as "old court woman" (*oude hooffse wijff*) and named Vengamma ("Wengama"), this ambassadress was repeatedly dispatched by Vijayaraghava Nayaka to the VOC to discuss outstanding debts, overdue gifts, and withheld tolls. Vengamma's exact position at court is not clear, but she was active at least between 1658—taking part in Tanjavur's negotiations with Chinanna about the VOC's control of Nagapattinam—and 1666, when she last appears in Dutch records.

Having first visited the VOC at Pulicat in 1661, in early 1664 Vengamma travelled there again and also called at Nagapattinam to collect money for the Nayaka, to return to Pulicat once more in the middle of that year. The Tanjavur court had given her a limited mandate, however. Her embassies seemed chiefly meant as a charm offensive, launched, the VOC presumed, because Vijayaraghava was in great need of money and elephants. The Dutch further suspected that the ambassadress pursued personal interests as well, trying to increase her status in the eyes of both the Nayaka and the VOC. When she visited Pulicat again a few months later with another overly friendly letter from the court, the Dutch even started wondering if this correspondence was fabricated by her.

Since all this made the Company exercise restraint, Vengamma's missions achieved little, apparently making her insecure. In mid-1665, she was delegated

65 This seems to confirm that Tanjavur's Nayakas and Chinanna Chetti's family both belonged to Balija castes.

66 NA, VOC, no. 1231, ff. 146v, 149, 150v, 186, 632, 642v, 711, 712-12v; no. 8925, ff. 147-8: instructions by Admiral Van Goens to Nagapattinam, Sept. 1658, correspondence between Chinanna Chetti, Van Goens, Pulicat, and Batavia, Sept.-Oct. 1658, Jan. 1659, report of Kandy envoys received at Nagapattinam, Feb. 1710.

once more, now to Nagapattinam, but lingered in the nearby town of Kivalur, hesitant to risk an embassy proving as fruitless as the previous ones. In the end, she just returned home, mission wholly unaccomplished. In the following months, the court and the Company exchanged several letters—the former requesting that Vengamma be received by the Dutch governor in Pulicat, the latter replying that although she might visit the subordinate Nagapattinam settlement, this would be useless without her being granted proper powers of attorney. Eventually, in late 1666, when Vengamma had yet again embarked on a mission to the Dutch and pleaded with them that she did not dare appear before her king without bringing money back, they gave in and provided her with some capital due to Tanjavur for the lease of a few villages. She left Nagapattinam for good on that same day.[67]

Vengamma seems to have been a courtier with little power. Whether she was acting on the Nayaka's orders or also on her own behalf, she lacked the authority to operate effectively and reach her goals. Tanjavur may have chosen a woman as representative in the hope of creating leniency among the Dutch, but since she had no real mandate to bargain, they could not consider her a serious negotiator, giving them an easy excuse to ignore the Nayaka's demands. As a consequence, Vengamma got stuck between the king and the VOC, unable to fulfil the expectations of either party and thereby employ her diplomatic activities to attain more standing at court. Thus, she did not join the ranks of the other discussed Tanjavur officials, who grew increasingly influential and often shifted between different functions.

Although there is little information about courtiers in Nayaka Tanjavur, these examples suggest that careers here largely resembled those in Ikkeri and Vijayanagara. People like Govinda Dikshita and Chinanna Chetti combined various functions, relied on family relations, played an important part in dynastic developments, and held great power, although it is unclear if they dominated the entire court, including the king himself. Further, judging from the brief survey of Tanjavur's last few *daḷavāy*s, most careers seem not to have lasted long. For one aspect, Nayaka Tanjavur appears to have differed from Ikkeri: courtiers shifting allegiance between courts. Tubaki Lingama Nayaka was *daḷavāy* in Madurai, Tanjavur, and Madurai again, and merchant Chinanna Chetti served at least three other states—Senji, Vijayanagara, and Bijapur—as diplomat, military officer, and revenue-farmer before he rose to prominence in Tanjavur.

[67] NA, VOC, no. 1234, f. 133; no. 1236, f. 922; no. 1246, ff. 498, 565, 1514; no. 1248, ff. 1968-71, 2338-9; no. 1252, ff. 871-2, 1112; no. 1253, f. 1769; no. 1254, ff. 512-14; no. 1256, f. 728: letters from Pulicat and Nagapattinam to Gentlemen XVII and Batavia, from Nagapattinam to Pulicat, Sept. 1661, Feb.-Mar., June-July, Oct. 1664, May-June, Oct.-Nov. 1665, Sept. 1666; Heeres and Stapel, *Corpus diplomaticum Neerlando-Indicum*, vol. 2, 190.

Bhonsles of Tanjavur

Research of courtiers at Tanjavur's Bhonsle court, for which many sources have survived, reveals some elements not encountered so far. That is not surprising, considering the origins of this house in Maratha western India and its past under various Deccan sultanates. According to secondary literature, the council of ministers at this court chiefly consisted of heads of various departments, generally well-educated men from upper classes. The Sanskrit text *Strīdharmapaddhati*—probably composed by Tanjavur's courtier Tryambaka Makhi in the first half of the eighteenth century—adds that the king should meet with his ministers and his general every afternoon, at half past one and half past four, respectively.

Unlike in other kingdoms, the term *mantri* (or *maṇtrī*) did not primarily refer to any high official but rather denoted the chief minister. The word *khārbārī* seems to have been sometimes used for this function too. The second most important post was that of *daḷavāy* (also *senāpati*, general), which was occasionally occupied by the *mantri* himself, in that case holding both the main administrative and military powers. Next came the *dīwān* or *pradhāni*, who was responsible for the collection of revenue—the second designation thus having a somewhat different connotation than at the other courts. It appears that two distinct names were also employed for the rank of chief accountant: *samprati* and *dabīr*, but the latter word could refer to a secretary as well. The use of different terms for what seem to have been largely similar offices was no doubt often the result of the convergence in Bhonsle Tanjavur of Indic traditions and Persian influences in political organisation and terminology.

Other prominent functionaries included the *rāyasam* (secretary), *purōhita* (royal priest), and *qiladār* or *killedār* (commander of the fort, here Tanjavur town). Introduced around the mid-eighteenth century, according to a British report, was the office of *sar-i-khail*, a term for which various meanings are given, such as chancellor, troop commander, and chamberlain. Besides, there were various *sūbadārs*, governors of the kingdom's five or six *sūbas* or provinces. Finally, the term *peśvā* (more commonly *peshwa*), which in other Maratha states usually indicated the chief minister, appears not to have been a regular rank in Bhonsle Tanjavur but used as a more personal name or title.[68]

[68] Subramanian, *The Maratha Rajas of Tanjore*, 77-81; Srinivasan, *Maratha Rule in the Carnatic*, 347-54; Tryambakayajvan, *The Perfect Wife*, 3, 10-12, 46; Subrahmanyam, *Penumbral Visions*, 156, 159, 162, 177; Hickey, *The Tanjore Mahratta Principality*, 42-5; Manamalar, "Administration and Social Life under the Mahrathas of Thanjavur," 17-22; BL/AAS, MM, no. 77, pt. 23: "Tanjour report," f. 7 (compiled in 1798-9 by a British commission consisting of the officials Torin, Harris, and Stratton; see Cotton, Charpentier, and Johnston, *Catalogue of Manuscripts in European Languages*, vol. I, pt. II, 605); NA, VOC, no. 3108, f. 89: report of mission to Tanjavur, Feb. 1764.

European records, and to a lesser extent south Indian sources, contain many references to courtiers serving the Bhonsles of Tanjavur, and only a fraction of them can be considered here. An early glimpse of the Bhonsle court is offered in the account of a VOC mission to Tanjavur in December 1676, less than a year after the kingdom's conquest by the dynasty's founder Ekoji. This document mentions the following officials as most influential: "governor Saijbo"; Treasurer (*tresaurier*) Koneri; "councillors" Gopala Pandit and Rangasaya; and Ekoji's brother "Pardane Ragia," possibly the *pradhāni*.

These names and ranks, corrupted by the Dutch, are hard to link to other sources. For example, a later Bhonsle chronicle—called "The history of the Tonjore Rajas" in its English manuscript version—suggests that Ekoji appointed four chief functionaries: Sayyid ("Syed") as *qiladār*, maybe identical to the VOC's "governor Saijbo"; "Bashvah" as *pradhāni*; "Cojee" Pandit possibly as *mantri*, stated to be in charge of "country domination"; and "Conra [or Coura] Mahadave" as what is called *vakil*, a judicial office. Additionally, Dutch records from the subsequent decade refer to Koneri Pandidar ("Conerij Pandidaer") as the kingdom's chancellor (*rijx cancelier*) and its most important "state minister." He was probably the same person as the Treasurer Koneri in the VOC report of 1676 and the *vakil* "Conra Mahadave" in the Bhonsle chronicle.[69]

While these local and VOC sources differ with respect to certain offices and individuals, it appears there were several Pandits, or Brahmins, among Tanjavur's most prominent officials in this period. Indeed, in 1678 the Dutch complained that the "Pandigens" exercised so much influence that little could be achieved without them. But the highest courtiers included at least one Muslim, too, if "Syed" and "Saijbo" indeed refer to Sayyid. The Dutch account also explains that the Brahmin Venkanna, former *rāyasam* of Tanjavur's Nayakas, was still active during this time, serving as a broker between the VOC ambassadors and the court. As seen in Chapter 1 and the Epilogue, Venkanna had tried to maintain his position by helping the last Nayaka scion Chengamaladasa regain his family's throne after Madurai's invasion and, when this failed, by presenting the kingdom to Ekoji. But the latter regarded him as a traitor, causing Venkanna to flee Tanjavur soon after, which meant the end of his career.[70]

[69] The *Mujumdār* (auditing official) Konher Mahadev mentioned in the Marathi text *Sabhāsad bakhar* on the Maratha King Shivaji, authored by Krishnaji Anant Sabhasad, may be the same person. See: Surendranath Sen (ed.), *Śiva Chhatrapati. Being a Translation of Sabhāsad Bakhar with Extracts from Chiṭṇīs and Śivadigvijaya, with Notes* (Calcutta, 1920), 125.

[70] BL/AAS, MT, class III, no. 32: "The history of the Tonjore Rajas," ff. 90-90v; NA, VOC, no. 1329, ff. 1169v-76v; no. 1333, ff. 284v, 290; no. 1355, f. 163; no. 1398, f. 171; no. 1405, f. 1592; no. 1411, f. 96: reports of missions to Tanjavur, Dec. 1676-Jan. 1677, Mar. 1684, letters from Nagapattinam to Colombo, from Pulicat to Batavia, Oct.-Nov. 1678, Dec. 1680, Apr. 1684, news register, Jan. 1685. For possibly another

The Dutch embassy report of 1676 is silent on two Brahmin courtiers named Baboji Pandidar and Ragoji Pandidar ("Wawosi Pandidaer" and "Regosie Pandidaer").[71] Yet, they are worth being discussed in detail. Both start to figure prominently in the VOC archives in the late 1670s, so they began their careers in Tanjavur more or less simultaneously with Ekoji. Described as an eminent chief (*aensienel. hoofd*), Baboji held a function the Dutch labelled "regent" or governor of the southern "lowlands" (*beneden landen*). Generally based at Tiruvarur, a dozen miles inland from Nagapattinam, Baboji controlled Tanjavur's southern coastal region up to the port of Naguru (or Nagore) and the Vettar River. Beyond lay the northern "lowlands," stretching at least as far as the Kollidam (or Coleroon) River and administered by "regent" Ragoji.

Judging from their activities, Baboji and Ragoji served as revenue-farmers. That these were powerful positions transpires from the fact Baboji established his own mint at Tiruvarur in 1685. In his own words, in a letter to the VOC of 1688, he was "not an ordinary local revenue collector [*gemenen* "manigaar," *māṇigār*] or ambassador ... but ... in supreme command [*oppergesag*] of a region of 24 miles ... alongside a prominent fortress."[72] According to the Dutch, both "regents" commanded more or less equal authority and power, but whereas Baboji seemed a protégé of "chancellor" Koneri Pandidar, Ragoji was said to be held in high esteem by the king himself.

When Ekoji died in late 1684, however, it was reportedly Baboji and one Narasimharaya who received orders from the new, young ruler Shahaji to keep the government in "state and shape" (*staat en postuijer*). Thus, Baboji assumed political duties covering the entire kingdom, at least temporarily. At the same time, both Baboji and Ragoji continued their control of the littoral areas, while a Muslim (*moor*) remained the *qiladār* (*slotvoogt*, "fort-commander") of Tanjavur town. He was probably the Sayyid referred to above, now called "Saijed" and "Zayet" by the VOC.

Soon after, in 1685, Baboji expanded his range of activities again when he led a military expedition against Ramnad. This was apparently not a one-time affair because the Dutch referred to him as a general in the late 1680s, too. But in this period it was also rumoured that Ragoji enjoyed so much prestige with Shahaji that

reference to Koneri Pandidar ("Conery Pantulo"), see Fawcett, *The English Factories in India* (New Series, 1670-7), vol. II (The Eastern Coast and Bengal) (Oxford, 1952), 188.

71 Baboji's name is also spelled Balogi, Vagogi, Bavaji, and the like in primary sources and secondary literature.

72 NA, VOC, no. 1454, ff. 1017-17v: letter from Baboji Pandidar to Nagapattinam, Aug. 1688. It is unclear which fortress and what type of miles are referred to. If Dutch or Rhineland miles are meant, the mentioned distance seems to amount to about 80 modern miles, which is unlikely considering Tanjavur's size.

the king had given his own "state" palanquin to him, along with many other marks of honour. Evidently, Baboji and Ragoji both grew increasingly prominent—the VOC now called them "the two greatest Pandits"—but did so in different ways, each with their own patronage network.

Although Dutch records do not mention an open clash between them, the two men seem to have been rivals rather than allies. They courted different European trading companies, causing a struggle that was often expressed through protocolar insults. Baboji supported the Dutch, demanding that no other European power be allowed to trade in Tanjavur, as agreed in the treaties. Ragoji, assisted by his son, favoured the French, who wished to establish a trading station in the coastal region he supervised. Although Baboji had some backing from "chancellor" Koneri, Ragoji humiliated him and the Dutch on several occasions. Around mid-1688 Ragoji had knocked down the VOC's flags at the Company's building in the important inland market town Darasuram, on the outskirts of Kumbakonam. And when in early 1689 Baboji's representative in the capital wanted to visit the king to discuss the demands of his master and the Dutch, Ragoji and a courtier named Tryambaka waylaid him in front of the royal residence and turned him away.

Because of these conflicts, the distribution of presents to Tanjavur's courtiers during a VOC embassy in November-December 1688 was probably determined as much by the wish to strengthen ties with the Company's allies as by the actual balance of power at court. "Regent" Baboji, "chancellor" Koneri, and "governor" Sayyid all received gifts, but "regent" Ragoji, also attending audiences during this embassy, was given nothing at all, despite his influential position (see table 10) .

Another courtier the VOC did not honour with presents on this occasion was Tryambaka ("Triemboe Ragoe"), referred to above. That is surprising because, although apparently an ally of Ragoji, he was far less hostile towards the Dutch. This powerful Brahmin may have been quite receptive to presents and willing to consider the VOC's wishes. Yet, his name is absent from the Dutch embassy report and perhaps he was away from Tanjavur's capital around this time. In any case, Ragoji disappeared from the VOC records soon after, for reasons unknown, while "chancellor" Koneri's influence also seemed to be waning and the French received no permission to set up a factory. Tryambaka now became a very prominent official and while his exact position is not clear, the Dutch described him as the "second in power" (*secunde*) and an eminent councillor of the king who "executed everything." Local texts relate that Tryambaka, bearing the additional name Makhi or Makhin, was also a court poet, patronised scholars, and performed religious sacrifices.

These works reveal the prominence at court of Tryambaka's family as a whole, too, for instance in the *Śāhendra vilāsa*, dealing with King Shahaji (VI 40-5). The courtier Narasimharaya—together with Baboji in charge of the central government when Shahaji commenced his reign—was an elder brother of Tryambaka. Their father Gangadhara and younger brother Bhagavantaraya were ministers too, and Narasimharaya's son, Anandaraya, became a celebrated general, as discussed below. Finally, the latter's sons (two of them also named Tryambaka and Narasimharaya) were important courtiers in the late 1730s, said to be held in high esteem by the king and receiving gifts from the Dutch and the French. All or most of these men combined political and literary qualities.[73]

During the 1690s and early 1700s, Tryambaka and Baboji remained influential. In 1693 Baboji served as an ambassador to the Dutch with full powers of attorney to sign a contract. In mid-1700, according to VOC sources, he was a general in an unsuccessful war against Madurai, while some of his responsibilities as "regent" had been taken over by his brother-in-law Ranga Pandidar. In 1702 he commanded another campaign against Ramnad. In addition, around the years 1701-3 both Dutch and Jesuit documents mention him as the kingdom's first minister. Thus, Baboji continued to combine mercantile, diplomatic, governmental, and military functions until he passed away in 1703, by which time his son Gangadri Pandidar had acquired a high military rank.

Tryambaka's activities were almost equally diverse. In November 1700 he was dispatched to negotiate a peace treaty with Madurai. He promised to settle an agreement within ten days on the condition that he be given control over some lands around Mannargudi and Kumbakonam. Since those areas were administered by Baboji and Ranga Pandidar, Tryambaka's demand may point to rivalry with Baboji. By 1709 Tryambaka had become chief minister himself and in 1711, when King Shahaji felt his end was near, he was even invested by the monarch with what the Dutch called the "principal government" (*principaal bewind*), apparently to oversee the imminent royal succession. Indeed, after Sarabhoji ascended the Tanjavur throne, Tryambaka's position seemed stronger than ever. In 1712 local scholars told German Pietist missionaries that "Istriburaier" (a corruption similar to the Dutch "Triemboe Ragoe") controlled "the heart of the king" and the kingdom was reigned "according to his will and pleasure."[74]

[73] For genealogical trees of this family, see: Tryambakayajvan, *The Perfect Wife*, 18; Krishnamachariar, *History of Classical Sanskrit Literature*, 246.

[74] NA, VOC, no. 1329, f. 1167v; no. 1333, ff. 294v-5; no. 1349, f. 1402; no. 1355, ff. 163-4v; no. 1411, ff. 96v, 103-3v, 135v-7, 142, 343v, 346v; no. 1448, ff. 294-7, 304, 319v, 324, 326-35; no. 1454, ff. 1009v, 1014v-17; no. 1456, ff. 2081-1v; no. 1463, ff. 169, 171v, 205-13v, 427v-8; no. 1526, ff. 250-50v; no. 1633, ff. 122v-3, 126-8v, 143-7; no. 1638, f. 189; no. 1645, ff. 150-1v; no. 1649, f. 58; no. 1657, ff. 74, 142v, no. 1664, f. 177; no. 1678, ff. 338, 353 (latter folio 2nd numeration); no. 1778, f. 104; no. 1803, f. 303; no. 2369, f. 117 (and possibly subsequent folios); no. 2387, ff. 322-3: instructions for mission to Tanjavur, Dec. 1676, correspondence between Nagapattinam, Pulicat, Sadras, Colombo, Batavia, and Gentlemen XVII, letters from commander Floris Blom to Baboji Pandidar, from Baboji to Nagapattinam, from VOC envoys Rangappa and "Wieragua" to

After Tryambaka no prominent courtiers seem to really stand out in the VOC archives until the decades around the mid-eighteenth century, when the partially overlapping careers of several courtiers can be traced. One of them was a Muslim called Imam (or Iman) Khan Kurush Sahib ("Iman Chan Koroosje Sahib") in Dutch documents, who appears not to figure in local sources. In 1730 he was installed by King Tukkoji as a supervisor, probably *sūbadār*, over the lands around Mannargudi. Only a year later, the VOC began to describe him as "state minister" and especially as Tanjavur's *albeschik*. Literally meaning "all-ordainer," the latter term seems to have denoted someone holding great effective power or at least interfering in all sorts of matters, but it has also been translated as factotum, suggesting a more executive role.[75] Exactly what the Dutch referred to is unclear, nor whether this was an actual function or an umbrella term for whoever exercised most control.[76] But certainly any person given this label must have been influential.

In the 1730s Imam Khan Kurush conducted nearly all of the court's correspondence with the VOC, which annually presented costly gifts to him. As another instance of a courtier expanding his range of activities, in 1731 he both led a siege of the Danish settlement at Tranquebar and travelled south to conclude treaties with Ramnad and Shivagangai about their tribute-paying to Tanjavur. Although in 1733 the Dutch wrote that Tukkoji had reshuffled both the structure and the staff of his government, Imam Khan Kurush's position appears to have gone unchallenged since the VOC still called him "ordain-it-all" in subsequent years.

In the same period, as the Dutch reported, the position of chief minister was occupied by the Brahmin Anandaraya ("Anandaraijer") Makhi, perhaps better

commander Blom, from "Wengerawaddij" to his master captain Ramanatha Nayaka at Nagapattinam, from "Candae Rague" to his master Baboji, from a VOC spy in Tirumullaivasal to Nagapattinam, Dec. 1678, Dec. 1680, July 1685, Aug., Oct., Dec. 1688, Jan.-Feb., July 1689, Dec. 1693, Aug.-Nov. 1700, June, Oct. 1701, May, Sept. 1702, Apr., Oct. 1703, May 1709, Sept. 1711, Oct. 1736, reports on Tanjavur, May 1679, Aug. 1688, news register, Jan., Apr.-May 1685, instructions to VOC envoy "Wiereragua," Aug. 1688, report of mission to Tanjavur, Nov.-Dec. 1688, Nagapattinam proceedings, June 1736; *Arsip Nasional Republik Indonesia*, Jakarta (hereafter ANRI), *Buitenland* collection ("foreign countries," access no. K.48, hereafter BC), no. 150e (unpaginated, entry of 29 June): Nagapattinam diary extract, June 1688; Jeyaraj and Young, *Hindu-Christian Epistolary Self-Disclosures*, 266; Śrīdhara Venkatēśa, *Śāhendra Vilāsa*, 11, 25-6; Tryambakayajvan, *The Perfect Wife*, 3, 10-13, 17-19, 24-5; Krishnamachariar, *History of Classical Sanskrit Literature*, 246-7; Ananda Ranga Pillai, *The Private Diary of Ananda Ranga Pillai, Dubash to Joseph François Dupleix, Knight of the Order of St. Michael, and Governor of Pondichery* ..., ed. J. Frederick Price and K. Rangachari, vol. I (Madras, 1904), 50; Lockman, *Travels of the Jesuits*, vol. II, 286-7; Subramanian, *The Maratha Rajas of Tanjore*, 18, 30-1, 77-8, 87; Srinivasan, *Maratha Rule in the Carnatic*, 225, 228, 373; Bhosale, *Rajah Serfoji – II*, 24, 27.

75 For the latter translation, see Subrahmanyam, *Penumbral Visions*, 105-6, 120, 138, 153.

76 Perhaps the term derived from the function of *harakāra*, literally "do-all," which referred to messengers and information-gatherers. See Subrahmanyam, *Penumbral Visions*, 239.

known as the often victorious *Daḷavāy* Ananda Rao Peshwa, and a son and a nephew of the courtiers Narasimharaya and Tryambaka Makhi, respectively. Other sources add that he had already held the office of *daḷavāy* since the reign of Shahaji. Also a patron of literature, Anandaraya thus combined various functions over time, involving both governmental and military duties, and may have succeeded his uncle Tryambaka as chief minister or *mantri*. In 1734, however, he died in a war against Arcot.

"Ordain-it-all" Imam Khan Kurush remained one of the court's most influential men for the rest of the 1730s, enjoying much respect from the king—at least according to the VOC, which during an embassy in 1735 presented most of the gifts for courtiers to him and his son Husain Khan (see table 10). Imam Khan Kurush is further mentioned in a grant issued by Ekoji II to the Dutch following their mission. In all likelihood, he was also the prominent courtier called "General Khan Sahib" in the report of a Danish embassy to Ekoji II in 1735, suggesting his duties included military activities at this time. When the Danes reached the capital, not only the king but this courtier, too, sent representatives to welcome them. His son Husain Khan ("Usenhan") played an important role during this mission as well.[77] As VOC records suggest, Imam Khan Kurush maintained his position during the troubled years of 1736-9, when Queen Sujana Bai and "usurper" Shahaji II briefly sat on the throne. Under the former he still was referred to as "ordain-it-all," while under the latter he additionally served as the chief governor of the coastal region around the northern town of Mayuram.

The post of "ordain-it-all" was however now also ascribed to Siddhoji Dada, Sujana Bai's chief minister and favourite, and Imam Khan Kurush's influence may have diminished during her rule. Soon after Pratapasimha commenced his reign, he appears to have lost most or even all power. In May 1740, the Dutch reported that the new king had installed one Annappa Rao Shetke as his "ordain-it-all." For unknown reasons, around the same time Imam Khan Kurush disappears abruptly from the VOC documents, the last mention of his name dating from July of that year.[78]

[77] For these Danish references, see Kay Larsen, "En dansk Gesandtskabrejse i Indien (1735)," *Historisk Tidsskrift* 8, 3 (1910-12), 59-67.

[78] NA, VOC, no. 2166, f. 554; no. 2198, ff. 12, 14, 43, 64, 194-202 (2nd numeration); no. 2243, f. 558; no. 2244, ff. 48, 61, 1272-7, 766 (latter folio 2nd numeration); no. 2289, ff. 105-6; no. 2304, ff. 232-3v (?); no. 2317, ff. 192-3; no. 2318, ff. 2281-3; no. 2334, f. 182v; no. 2350, ff. 118, 438-41; no. 2351, ff. 3994, 3997-8; no. 2352B, f. 528; no. 2386, ff. 65-72, 164-8, 905-6, 943-4; no. 2387, f. 209; no. 2399, ff. 301-1v; no. 2412, ff. 56-7, 371-4, 436, 62, 273-4, 1983 (latter folios 2nd numeration); no. 2427, ff. 431v-3, 441-2, 465-9, 517-18v; no. 2442, ff. 45, 609, 799, 2028, 2035, 2038; no. 2443, ff. 311-14 (2nd numeration); no. 2455, ff. 447, 459v-61, 462v-4, 475v-6, 519v-20; no. 2471, ff. 1225, 1232; no. 2505, ff. 82, 1655-6; no. 8866, ff. 123-4: letters from Nagapattinam to Batavia, Sept. 1730, Sept. 1731, Sept. 1732, Oct. 1734, Aug., Oct. 1735, Nov. 1736, June, Oct.

Another courtier faring badly after Pratapasimha's accession was the last person in what seems to have been a hereditary succession of Muslim functionaries. Both the previous and present chapter already discussed members of this dynasty of sorts, which probably provided the Tanjavur Bhonsles with *qiladārs* for almost three-quarters of a century and figures extensively in both local and European sources. All designated as Sayyid, these men were apparently of high ancestry, possibly claiming descent from Prophet Muhammad. In 1735, the Dutch described one of them as:

> ... the fort-supervisor [*slot voogd*] or killedaar, and recruiter of the soldiers, on horseback as well as on foot, a man of great prestige [*aansien*] from the Said's or priestly house ...[79]

One of the Bhonsle chronicles—in its English manuscript translation titled "Account of the Tanjore Samastanums"—has less kind things to say about these *qiladārs*. Covering the decades between the 1680s and 1740s, and mixing up the consecutive reigns of Shahaji, Sarabhoji, and Tukkoji, some excerpts from this text run as follows:

> ... When the Toocojee Rajah [Tukkoji] mounted on the throne, he then appointed Sydahaneef [Sayyid Hanif] as a Killadar or commander of the fort. While he was ruling the kingdom, the said Syeed sent for a fakeer ... While it was so the Rajah [king] had born no childrins, then by the power of the ... muntra [magical spell] of that fakeer, he had borne 2 sons named Shankar & Shareef. Thus he ... ruled the kingdom & departed his life. Also the said Syda Haneef was died, but he had born a son named Syda Boorahun [Sayyid Burhan], who had continued the same service. He succeeded [made succeed] the Shahajee Rajah [Shahaji] to the throne & himself ... acted [in] the Deevanyeerey [office of *dīwān*] or prime ministership.
>
> When the Shahajee Rajah grow big ..., he began to manage the affairs of the countries. Then the abovementioned Syad give poison and killed the Rajah & seated his young brother Sharafoujee Rajah [Sarabhoji] on the throne. When [Sarabhoji] grow big, then the Syad struck of the head of him & succeeded [made succeed] one of their realation named

1737, June, Sept. 1738, July 1740, Nagapattinam proceedings, Apr.-May 1731, Mar. 1733, Jan., Oct.-Nov. 1735, Mar., Sept., Dec. 1736, May 1737, Feb., July-Aug. 1738, correspondence with Imam Khan Kurush Sahib, Apr.-June 1731, Apr. 1732, July, Oct.-Nov. 1735, July-Aug. 1738, Jan.-Feb., June 1739, lists of gifts presented in Coromandel, 1730-9, report on visit of Tanjavur envoys to Jaffna, Apr.-Aug. 1734, report of mission to Tanjavur, Nov. 1735, grant of Ekoji II to VOC, Nov. 1735, Nagapattinam diary, May 1740; S. Raju (ed.), *Tañcai Marāṭṭiyar Kalveṭṭukkaḷ / Inscriptions of the Marathas of Thanjavur* (Tanjavur, 1987), xlviii (no. 99); idem, *Tañcai Marāṭṭiyar Ceppēṭukaḷ-50*, xlvii-viii (nos 35, 37); Subramanian, *The Maratha Rajas of Tanjore*, 31-2, 37-8, 77-8; Srinivasan, *Maratha Rule in the Carnatic*, 231-3, 240-1, 349; Bhosale, *Rajah Serfoji – II*, 28; Subrahmanyam, *Penumbral Visions*, 153-4, 160.

[79] NA, VOC, no. 2386, f. 167: report of mission to Tanjavur, Nov. 1735 (translation mine).

Baw Baw Saib [Baba Sahib, Ekoji II] to the throne ... Afterward he succeeded one of their realation named Annah Saib [unidentified ruler, perhaps Tukkoji's son Anna Sahib, who in fact never became king] to the throne.

In the course of that time the Syad was died, but he had borned a son named Syad Mahamud [Sayyid Muhammad], who followed the custom of his fathers & had killed the said Annah Saib. Then being nobody to succeed the throne, then the wife of the Rajahs—her named Soojan Banye [Sujana Bai]—was ruling the kingdom. Sometimes after she was departed her life, then Syada Mahamada considered in his mind: if he [made] succeed any of a realation of the Rajahs to the throne, he would happen any trouble by it. Having this considered, he catch and brought a lad from the wood and told he is the son of the Rajahs: "formerly Baw Baw Saibs [Ekoji II's] son would mix poison to him, therefore he running now, [but] he was caught by me." So that he succeeded him to the throne.

While he was ruling the kingdom for some time, this Cottirajah [Kattu Raja, Shahaji II] considered in his mind: "... this Syad had distroyed many Rajahs, likewise he will do to me." Having this considered, he given the Deevangerry or prime ministership to the Annapa Shatunga [Annappa Rao Shetke?] & only continued the service of the Killadary to the Syad. The Syada then having resented much, suddenly went with some peons in to the Mahall [palace] of the Rajahs & murdered the Rajah. Whereupon he ... considered: as there was nobody to succeed the throne but the Pratapa Singa [Pratapasimha], son of Rackey or concubine of the Toccojee Rajah, ... whom he intended to succeed to the throne. Then the lad [Pratapasimha] being afraid in thinking: "... he [Sayyid] will kill me like the others." He [Sayyid] then incouraged him [Pratapasimha] very much & seated him on the throne. Pratapa Singa considered in his mind: if he keeps the Annapa Shatunga & Syada, they will kill him. [Therefore] he confined the Syad and killed him. Also he sent a number of the army and murdered the Annapa Shatunga ...[80]

Here we read an occasionally confused account of three generations of the Sayyid family: first Hanif, next his son Burhan, and last Burhan's son Muhammad. Their influence on the Bhonsle dynasty is presented as all-pervasive, with Hanif employing a "fakir" to guarantee royal offspring, and Burhan and Muhammad killing and enthroning kings at will. But as shown before, according to other sources these Sayyids initially were not as omnipresent—let alone as murderous—as the quoted text leads us to believe. This work apparently projects the might and aggression of the last Sayyid, from the mid-1730s onward, to his much less influential and bloodthirsty predecessors. However, as Dutch records also imply, the post of *qiladār* was probably indeed passed between several men called Sayyid from the start of Bhonsle rule in the mid-1670s until King Pratapasimha had the last of them executed in the early 1740s.

[80] BL/AAS, MT, class III, no. 88: "Account of the Tanjore Samastanums," ff. 140-1v.

Both local and VOC sources suggest that the first Sayyid, maybe the above-mentioned Hanif, was appointed right upon Ekoji's conquest of Tanjavur. Later Dutch documents, mostly from the 1680s, regularly refer to a "fort-supervisor" or "governor" called "Saijed," "Zayet," and the like, possibly Hanif or Burhan. And VOC records of the late 1730s in particular report about the then active *qiladār*. Perhaps indicative of his growing influence, in 1738 the Dutch asked him to forestall another French effort to settle in Tanjavur. Since the VOC addressed him as Sayyid Qasim Sahib ("Saijd Casim Sahib") and he signed his reply with Mirza Sayyid al-Yusuf ("Miera Sei-Iedoe Ischieph"), it is not clear if this person can be identified with Burhan or Muhammad in the cited text.

In any case, in September of that year, just after Shahaji II had taken the throne, the VOC thought that *Qiladār* Sayyid commanded most power (*vermogen*) at court and, as discussed in Chapter 2, may have been instrumental in this king's instalment. Around the same time, a French embassy to the court presented him with the most expensive gifts among all courtiers. In July 1739 the Dutch remarked that Shahaji II's dethronement within a year was a "betrayal by the fort-commander," further demonstrating the *qiladār*'s great role in court politics. Indeed, two months later, the VOC reported that an agreement had been reached stipulating that, although Pratapasimha had now been crowned king, Sayyid would hold the "government of everything." A Marathi text of about forty-five years later portrays the relationship between these two men thus:

> For a very considerable time, Pretap-cen-veh [Pratapasimha] enjoyed nothing but the name of Rajee [king], & experienced every degree of mortification & insult from Sied [Sayyid], who now possessed a most unbounded power. He had the horse [riders] & foot [soldiers] under his command—the former amounting to 4,000 men—the keys of the fort, & was besides Cerkeel [*sar-i-khail*] or Duan [*dīwān*?]. When the Rajee rode out, Sied attended him in the greatest state, & on their return, while the Rajee was obliged to go to his palace with only two or three attendants, Sied would go to his own house attended by all the guards.[81]

But this division of formal kingship and actual power was not to last and, as the earlier-cited "Account of the Tanjore Samastanums" suggests, the *qiladār* overplayed his hand, making Pratapasimha distrust him. Soon after, the Dutch wrote that the aforementioned Annappa Rao Shetke had become "the principal person at court, after whose will all matters were governed." In fact, after 1739 *Qiladār* Sayyid figures no more in the VOC records and perhaps Pratapasimha had already disposed of this king-maker by then. The Marathi text quoted above declares:

[81] BL/AAS, MG, no. 4, pt. 9: "History of Tanjore," f. 220; Cotton, Charpentier, and Johnston, *Catalogue of Manuscripts in European Languages*, vol. I, pt. II, 52.

> ... being apprehensive from the fate of his predecessors for his life, he [Pratapasimha] consulted with his confident Annapah Centa-ghee [Annappa Rao Shetke], ... having determined to take off Sied [Sayyid], it was accomplished in the following manner. The Rajee [king] feigned to have received a letter from Poonah [Maratha capital Pune] of importance, and retired to read it with Sied in a private garden of the palace, where a tent had been previously prepared. After being a little seated, the Rajee got up & went to the door, upon which men who had been placed for the purpose between the walls, rushed out & dispatched Sied, which occasioned some commotion amongst the troops at first & the gates of the fort were kept shut for three days, at the end of which time they returned to their duty. Annapah Centa-ghee was for his services created Cerkeel [*sar-i-khail*].[82]

Thus, the peak of Sayyid's career, although high, was also short and signalled the end of his line's position.[83] In September 1740 the Dutch reported that the post of *qiladār* was held by Mallarji Gadi Rao ("Khatte Rauw"), the king's brother-in-law, who seemingly kept it until at least the 1760s. Signifying his status, this man's partaking in several battles earned him inclusion in the *Pratāpasimhendra vijaya prabandha* (55), a Marathi poem by Ramakrishna Kavi Pandit glorifying one of Pratapasimha's military expeditions.[84]

As brief and turbulent as Sayyid's zenith, was the period in power of Annappa Rao Shetke (also Sedge or Setage) and his brothers Govinda Rao and Ayyannar Rao, the last Tanjavur courtiers considered here. Annappa, besides taking over Sayyid's position as the court's most influential man, also replaced Imam Khan Kurush Sahib as the king's "ordain-it-all." Annappa and his brothers appear to have risen to prominence very suddenly and from a low position. In May 1740 the Dutch described this event as follows:

> ... the currently reigning king Pretappa Singa Raasja [Pratapasimha Raja] raised to stately service the three brothers Rouw Sahib, Anna Chetke, and Aijnaar Rouw Chetke—who,

[82] BL/AAS, MG, no. 4, pt. 9: "History of Tanjore," ff. 220-1.

[83] Several other local texts refer in detail to the dominance and death of *Qiladār* Sayyid. See: BL/AAS, MT, class III, no. 32: "The History of the Tonjore Rajas," ff. 92v-5v; class III, no. 87: "The historycal account of the Tonjore" (*Bhoṃsale vaṃśa caritra*), ff. 99v-103; OI, no. I, pt. 24: "Morratoe kings of Tanjore" [II], f. 242.

[84] NA, VOC, no. 2427, ff. 431v-3, 437-8v, 470-70v; no. 2443, ff. 2038, 2040; no. 2470, f. 70; no. 2471, ff. 51-2; no. 2506, ff. 58-9, 86; no. 3108, f. 98: Nagapattinam proceedings, July 1738, Aug.-Sept. 1740, Feb. 1764, correspondence with *Qiladār* Sayyid, July-Aug. 1738, letters from Nagapattinam to Batavia, Sept. 1738, July, Sept. 1739; TNA, DR, no. 282, ff. 54v-61v: letter from Nagapattinam to Cochin, Dec. 1738; Ramakrishna Kavi Pandit, *Pratapasimhendra Vijaya Prabandha*, ed. A. Krishnaswamy Mahadick Rao Sahib (Tanjore, 1950), 30; Ananda Ranga Pillai, *The Private Diary*, vol. I, 50; Subramanian, *The Maratha Rajas of Tanjore*, 43-4, 48-9, 54, 60; Srinivasan, *Maratha Rule in the Carnatic*, 242-4, 250-1; Bhosale, *Rajah Serfoji – II*, 32-5; Subrahmanyam, *Penumbral Visions*, 153.

> like all their ancestors, since long years have served the consecutive Tansjourse kings like slaves by carrying their spittoon, slippers or papoesen, etc.—namely: the first-mentioned, Rouw Sahib, as chief regent over Combagonna [Kumbakonam] and its subordinate lands; the second, Anna Chitke, as his carbarrie [*khārbārī*, chief minister] or ordain-it-all at his court; and the third or last-mentioned, Aijnaar Rauw Chitke, also as chief regent over the Manaargoijl [Mannargudi] and Maijoeramse [Mayuram's] lands ...[85]

Apparently coming from a family of personal servants of the Bhonsles, the Shetke brothers entirely dominated Tanjavur in the subsequent years. The VOC called Annappa both chief minister and even "supreme ordain-it-all" (*oppersten albeschik*) and he was said to hold so much power that he "ruled over the king." A royal grant to the Dutch was co-issued by him, and when King Pratapasimha visited Tiruvarur and Nagapattinam in 1741, he received the most gifts from the VOC of all courtiers (see table 10 below and illustration 12 in Chapter 4). Further, he conducted part of the court's correspondence with the Dutch, the French, and the Danes—to the last designating himself as "revenue officer in charge"—and figures in the abovementioned *Pratāpasimhendra vijaya prabandha* (55) as a "resolute and courageous" army commander.

His brother Ayyannar Rao Shetke, who in addition to his regency led several military campaigns, grew powerful as well. He felt strong enough to let his men intimidate the Dutch and the French on several occasions, destroying their property, beating up their personnel, confiscating their merchandise, and laying siege to their settlements. But the third Shetke, Govinda Rao, seems to have become the most influential brother over the years, taking over the label of "supreme ordain-it-all" from Annappa, increasingly dominating the king, and regulating all access to him. Not surprisingly, tension arose between Pratapasimha and the Shetkes, and the "evil" Ayyannar, as the VOC called him, was even temporarily jailed.[86]

85 NA, VOC, no. 2505, ff. 1655-6: Nagapattinam diary, May 1740 (translation mine).

86 NA, VOC, no. 2505, ff. 1656-80; no. 2506, ff. 29-32, 58-61, 85-6; no. 2538, ff. 11-13, 1615, 1622; no. 2539, ff. 2486-8, 2490, 2629, 2671; no. 2556, ff. 669v, 679v; no. 2574, ff. 43-5, 88-94; no. 2575, ff. 2049-51; no. 2594, f. 497; no. 2608, ff. 83-90, 388-92: Nagapattinam diary, May-July 1740, Nagapattinam proceedings, July-Sept. 1740, May, Aug.-Sept. 1741, letters from Nagapattinam to Batavia and Gentlemen XVII, Feb. 1741, Oct. 1742, Mar., July, Oct. 1743, grant by Tanjavur, May 1741, lists of gifts presented during royal visits to Tiruvarur and Nagapattinam, May 1741, letter from Annappa Rao Shetke to Nagapattinam, Oct. 1742; *Lettres & conventions des gouverneurs de Pondichéry avec differents princes hindous 1666 à 1793* (Pondicherry, 1911-14), 133-5, 236-8, 240; Elisabeth Strandberg (ed.), *The Moḍī Documents from Tanjore in Danish Collections* (Wiesbaden, 1983), 90-3, 285-6; Ramakrishna Kavi Pandit, *Pratapasimhendra Vijaya Prabandha*, 31; Coolhaas *et al.*, *Generale Missiven*, vol. XI, 275; Srinivasan, *Maratha Rule in the Carnatic*, 352. For references to Annappa Rao Shetke in south Indian texts, see: BL/AAS, MT, class III, no. 32: "The History of the Tonjore Rajas," ff. 95v, 97; class III, no. 87: "The historycal account of the Tonjore," ff. 102v-3, 105v-6; Raju, *Tañcai Marāṭṭiyar Ceppēṭukaḷ-50*, xlviii (no. 42).

Finally, in 1746 an opportunity presented itself to rid Tanjavur of their influence once and for all. The Shetke brothers' fall was as steep and rapid as their rise and merits another quote from the VOC records:

> ... the so-called supreme ordain-it-all of that court, Gowinda Rauw Chetke, by whom the king was entirely governed, died in the month of April. Because of that, the way to His Highness' throne was opened again for several well-intentioned [people], to enable [them] to inform him how his subjects were exploited and also exhausted by the deceased and his two brothers Annaji Rauw and Aijna Rauw Chetke—without spending any of that [extorted income], but only to gather great riches for themselves. And because those brothers ... pretended there was no money in the treasury ... to pay overdue salary to the horsemen, His Highness had them and some of their heralds caught and robbed of their riches. And [having] afterwards also intercepted a letter sent by them to the king of the Marattijs [Marathas] at Satara to the detriment of His Highness, in mid-August His Highness had their heads placed before their feet.[87]

But this time, perhaps because of the violent career endings of Sayyid and the Shetkes, it proved not so easy to find people willing to fill the positions that now became vacant—a situation, however, the Dutch deemed most beneficial:

> ... the king has offered the government of affairs to one of his relatives named Manosie Rauw Jagataap, but he has requested to be excused from that, and so until now the king continues to manage everything himself, and it is to be wished this would carry on.[88]

Still, despite the managerial qualities that the king himself may have possessed, powerful courtiers of course kept coming and going under Pratapasimha and his successors,[89] as they had always done. This rotation is also illustrated in table 10, which shows the distribution of presents among Tanjavur officials during seven VOC embassies between 1677 and 1764. Admittedly, in some cases there were gaps of several decades between missions, making changes among the courtiers only logical. Besides, three of these embassies were dispatched to Tiruvarur or Naguru while the king visited these towns, during which trips several important functionaries remained in the capital and would not receive gifts anyhow.[90]

Yet, the table makes clear that in Bhonsle-ruled Tanjavur neither particular ranks nor certain individuals were automatically honoured with presents and

[87] NA, VOC, no. 2677, ff. 256-7: letter from Nagapattinam to Batavia, Oct. 1746 (translation mine).

[88] NA, VOC, no. 2677, f. 257: letter from Nagapattinam to Batavia, Oct. 1746 (translation mine).

[89] See for instance Orme, *A History of the Military Transactions*, vol. 1, 290.

[90] See for example NA, VOC, no. 2386, ff. 67, 70: Nagapattinam proceedings, Nov. 1735.

Table 10: Distribution of gifts among prominent courtiers during Dutch missions to Bhonsle Tanjavur, in order of value, 1677-1764.

1677	1688	1725	1730	1735	1741	1764
king Ekoji	*king* Shahaji	*king* Sarabhoji	*king* Tukkoji	*king* Ekoji II	*king* Pratapasimha	*king* Tuljaji II
governor *(qiladār?)* Sayyid (?)	*chancellor* Koneri Pandidar	*sūbadār* Nanaji Babaji	*minister* Siddhoji Dada	*"ordain-it-all"* Imam Khan Kurush Sahib	*"supreme* *ordain-it-all"* Annappa Rao Shetke	*qiladār* Katta Rao
treasurer Koneri (Pandidar?)	*regent* Baboji Pandidar	*"assembaij"* *(?)* (name unknown)	*sūbadār* Govinda Damodra Pandidar	*son of* *"ordain-it-all"* Husain Khan	*regent* Ayyangar	*dabīr* Naro Pandidar
councillor Gopala Pandit	*governor* *(qiladār?)* Sayyid		*secretary* *(rāyasam?)* Naroji Pandit	*qiladār* "from Said's house"	*regent* Ragoji	*head of* *cavalry* Manoji Appan
councillor Rangasaya			*sūbadār's envoy* Jagannath Narasimha		*dabīr* (name unknown)	*rāyasam* Amboji Pandidar
pradhāni (?) "Ragia"			*minister's* *servant* Venkappa Ayyar Karwari		*regent* Ayyannar Rao Shetke (?)	*sūbadār* "Arnegeri- appen"
"broker" Venkanna						

Notes: in 1677 the differences between nos 2 to 5 were very small, and nos 3 and 4 were virtually equal; in 1688 the differences between nos 2 to 4 were small; in 1730 nos 3 and 4 received equally much; the reception of gifts by no. 4 in 1735 is probable but not certain; in 1741 nos 5 and 6 received equally much; the missions of 1725, 1730, and 1741 were dispatched to Tiruvarur or Naguru when the king visited those towns; the *sūbadār*s mentioned here were always seated in Mannargudi.

Sources: NA, VOC, no. 1329, ff. 1169v-76v; no. 1463, ff. 205-13v; no. 2031, ff. 1119, 1299-300; no. 2166, ff. 392-9; no. 2386, ff. 66-71, 167; no. 2539, ff. 2487-9; no. 3108, ff. 97-101.

therefore considered influential by the Dutch. Rather, on each occasion different positions and different persons obtained the most valuable gifts after the king. For instance, what were probably several members of the Sayyid line, each holding the post of *qiladār*, received the second most expensive presents in 1677 but were listed as fourth in 1688 and 1735. In 1764 a *qiladār* belonging to the royal family came second again. Likewise, in 1725, 1730, and 1764, various *sūbadār*s ranked second, third, and sixth respectively, while the *dabīr* moved from the fifth to the third place during the last two embassies. And some positions, such as "son of the ordain-it-all" (in 1735) and head of the cavalry (in 1764), appear in the table only once, underlining that power resided in people rather than offices.[91]

The previous paragraphs describe patterns partly similar to those observed at other courts. Thus in Bhonsle-ruled Tanjavur some officials—holding various ranks—grew exceedingly powerful, to the point of overshadowing the king. But such periods of dominance generally were quite short, as demonstrated by the brief, tumultuous careers of the last *Qiladār* Sayyid and the Shetke brothers. Functionaries wielding substantial but not overarching influence, and for longer periods, seem to have been more common. The relatively stable and lengthy careers of men like "regent" Baboji Pandidar, Minister Tryambaka, "ordain-it-all" Imam Khan Kurush Sahib, and the earlier Sayyid *qiladār*s are exemplary. Further, many courtiers shifted between or combined different portfolios. Baboji, initially a revenue-farmer, later served as a military commander, ambassador, and chief minister as well. Tryambaka Makhi acted as chief minister, envoy, and some sort of provincial governor over the years. And Imam Khan Kurush, who also started out as a local administrator, soon assumed governmental, military, and diplomatic responsibilities.

Other aspects of Tanjavur's courtiers appear to be more specific to this kingdom. To start with, competition between functionaries seems to have been less intense and violent than at other courts. Apart from the political upheavals around 1740, we read little about court factions expelling, imprisoning, or killing opponents, when compared to Ikkeri for example. Competition did of course exist: Baboji Pandidar faced it first from the "northern regent" Ragoji Pandidar and later from Tryambaka. Yet, such rivalry apparently seldom led to large-scale, vicious clashes.[92]

[91] It is not clear whether Treasurer Koneri (1677) was the same person—with the same function—as Chancellor Koneri Pandidar (1688), nor if Secretary Naroji Pandit (1730) was the same person as *Dabīr* Naro Pandidar (1764).

[92] See also Narayana Rao, Shulman, and Subrahmanyam, *Symbols of Substance*, 96.

Another outstanding element is the strong and long-lasting presence of a relatively small number of families. Kinship relations were important at all courts, but under the Bhonsles power passed between family generations especially often. Perhaps most notable in this respect are the (probably) three men of the Sayyid line, who likely held the position of *qiladār* for almost seven decades, and the Makhi family—most prominently Tryambaka, Narasimharaya, and Anandaraya (Ananda Rao Peshwa)—which spanned at least four generations. But blood ties also played an essential role for the Shetke brothers, as well as for Baboji and Imam Khan Kurush and their respective sons, Gangadri and Husain.

Further, unlike in Vijayanagara, Ikkeri, and Nayaka-ruled Tanjavur, there seem no instances of marital ties between courtiers and the royal house. The distinct backgrounds of many functionaries may have precluded such liaisons. Judging from the discussed officials, a fair number of courtiers were Brahmins or Muslims, while the Bhonsle family belonged to a Shudra caste that perhaps claimed Kshatriya status. Finally, the influential and enduring presence of Muslims, probably related to the dynasty's past under various Deccan sultanates, is another element setting this court apart.

Nayakas of Madurai

Several terms for functions at the Madurai court are also found for other Nayaka courts, but in Madurai their exact nature appears to have been somewhat different. According to secondary literature, the most distinguished official was generally the *daḷavāy*, a post frequently occupied by Brahmins. Formally, this term denoted the commander-in-chief, but in Madurai it is thought to have often included the supervision of civilian affairs, too. As a consequence, two ranks that traditionally represented the division between these portfolios, *mantri* (minister or chief minister) and *senāpati* (general), seem to have been less significant or even not in use here. Another important position was that of *pradhāni*, in Madurai the finance minister rather than the chief minister, who was responsible for the collection and expenditure of revenues and exercised great influence on the kingdom's administration. As with Ariyanatha Mudaliyar, the Madurai courtier discussed at the outset of this chapter, the offices of *daḷavāy* and *pradhāni* could at times be combined in one person. Third in the supposed ranking order came the *rāyasam* (royal secretary), also closely involved in administrative matters.

Other high functions, not necessarily existing throughout the Nayaka period, included the *kaṇakkan* (chief accountant), *daḷakartan* (commander of the capital's fort, akin to Tanjavur's *qiladār*), *sthānāpati* (foreign secretary, ambassador), and *ācārya* (royal preceptor). Further, there were about seven provincial governors, the one residing at Tirunelveli—a vast distance south of the capitals Madurai and

Tiruchirappalli—often being very prominent. Finally, as explained in Chapter 2 and unique to Madurai, the royal family provided not only regular monarchs but also a continuous line of secondary rulers, whose influence was occasionally far-reaching.[93]

Again, there is only space to consider a limited number of courtiers here. To begin with, a chronicle compiled around 1800 discusses many of the *daḷavāys* under Madurai's Nayakas over time. As the text goes, after *Daḷavāy*-cum-*Pradhāni* Ariyanatha Mudaliyar's passing, two uterine brothers took over his ministerial offices, probably serving as the *pradhāni* and *daḷavāy* respectively. Supposedly, the latter was the celebrated Ramappaiya, mentioned in the previous chapter as the general who around 1640 invaded Ramnad to capture the Setupati and said to have served as Madurai's ambassador to Goa in 1639.[94] The chronicle next refers to Ramappaiya's son-in-law and successor Kondappaiya, active under King Tirumalai Nayaka (r. c. 1623-59) and praised as the conqueror of Ceylon.

We then read of a general called Tutu Tirumalai Nayaka, maybe identical to the *Daḷavāy*-cum-poet Venkata Krishnappa Nayaka. A former betel-bearer promoted by King Chokkanatha Nayaka (r. 1660-77, 1680-2),[95] he and his assistant Chinna Tambi Mudaliyar allegedly fought against the Nayaka Prince Chengamaladasa of Tanjavur. Remarkably, the significant role they probably played in the fall of Tanjavur's Nayaka house in 1673 is more or less ignored here. Instead, the text relates that on this occasion, Chokkanatha dispatched a hundred tall, plump prostitutes with the order to show their naked bodies to his own unsuccessful and unmotivated soldiers. Utterly disgraced, the Madurai troops now desperately fled towards the hostile Tanjavur army, hoping at least to die an honourable death on the battlefield, but entirely routing the enemy in the process.

After this episode, the first mentioned general is Kasturi Ranga Ayyan, initially serving Queen Mangammal (r. 1691-1707) but later backing her grandson and rival Vijayaranga Chokkanatha (r. 1707-32). The text suggests that Kasturi Ranga held a minister's post as well, possibly combining the functions of *daḷavāy* and *pradhāni*. However, he was later imprisoned by Vijayaranga Chokkanatha and replaced with General Govindappa Ayyan. The chronicle ends with the last real Nayaka

[93] Sathyanatha Aiyar, *History of the Nayaks of Madura*, 235-43; Rangachari, "The History of the Naik Kingdom of Madura," *Indian Antiquary* XLIV, 113-16; Nelson, *The Madura Country*, vol. III, 144-7; Aseem Banu, "Polity under the Nayaks of Madurai," 26-35, 39-42; Chandra, "The Cultural History of the Nayaks of Madurai," 52, 61-6, 72-3, 78-9; Vink, *Mission to Madurai*, 53, 58-62, 309-15, 353-6; Mahalingam, *South Indian Polity*, 117.

[94] Mahalingam, "Historical Material in the Ramappayyan Ammanai," 389, 391.

[95] The text has "budget bearer," thought to refer to "betel bearer." See BL/AAS, MG, no. 4, pt. 4: "Mootiah's chronological & historical account of the modern kings of Madura," f. 43 (footnote).

ruler, Queen Minakshi (r. c. 1732-9), under whom a few more, competing generals follow. These include Minakshi's aid Ravanaiya—another *daḷavāy* who was also a minister—and his opponent Muttu Svami Ayya (perhaps to be identified with Venkatacharya), supporter of the queen's rival Bangaru Tirumalai and son of yet another general, probably named Narasappa Ayyan.[96]

This text is rather confused, mixing up several people and events, and clearly omitting a number of *daḷavāys*. Still, it implies that many characteristics of courtiers found at other courts also existed in Madurai. The chronicle repeatedly mentions functionaries occupying different offices simultaneously, profiting from family connections, competing among each other, falling from grace, and influencing dynastic developments. All these observations are underscored by Dutch reports on this Nayaka court.

But before turning to those accounts, we briefly consider another succession of officials initiated by Madurai's first great courtier, Ariyanatha Mudaliyar. Not only did he commence the *daḷavāy* and *pradhāni* lines at the central court, he supposedly also established a hereditary governorship at the town of Tirunelveli in the far south when he was dispatched to subdue that region. This lineage allegedly came to be known as the Medai Dalavay Mudaliyars, the word *mēḍai* referring to the high platform on which the governors sat when receiving their subordinates, and the second term denoting the high military office held by the family founder. Perhaps because of this tradition, Tirunelveli emerged as a secondary political and courtly centre in Madurai, according to some local texts complete with a sumptuous display of might, riches, and status.[97]

Around the mid-seventeenth century, by the time the VOC settled down on Madurai's shores, these two nodes of power—the main court (alternating between Madurai town and Tiruchirappalli) and the southern governor's seat at Tirunelveli—still shaped the kingdom's politics. For, as Dutch records suggest, this period saw the domination of two families of courtiers, one stationed at the capital, the other based in the Tirunelveli region. The former, the Tubaki family, included several individuals already mentioned. Central among them was Tubaki Lingama (or Lingappa) Nayaka, who around 1663 briefly served as a *daḷavāy* under the Nayakas of Tanjavur, both after and before holding the same post in Madurai. He was a younger brother of Tubaki Krishnappa Nayaka, the *daḷavāy* of Senji, whose

[96] BL/AAS, MG, no. 4, pt. 4: "Mootiah's chronological & historical account of the modern kings of Madura," ff. 59, 61, 64-5, 71-4. For the identification of some of these generals see Sathyanatha Aiyar, *History of the Nayaks of Madura*, 165, 231, 232, 234, 236-7.

[97] Kadhirvel, *A History of the Maravas*, 67; Ludden, *Peasant History in South India*, 69-70, 99, 189; Narayana Rao, Shulman, and Subrahmanyam, *Symbols of Substance*, 39-40, 95; Taylor, *Oriental Historical Manuscripts*, vol. II, 213-15; Sathyanatha Aiyar, *History of the Nayaks of Madura*, 53.

power was feared more than that of the Senji Nayaka himself, at least according to a Dutch letter of 1644.[98]

When Krishnappa died in 1659, his brother Lingama offered his services and troops to the Nayakas of Madurai. There, already in 1660, he was instrumental in the succession following King Muttu Virappa Nayaka II's passing. He acquired the offices of *daḷavāy* and governor of the province bordering Tanjavur soon after and held great power at court during much of the 1660s while the young Chokkanatha Nayaka sat on the throne. In the beginning of that decade, Lingama was involved in a plot with the *pradhāni* and the *rāyasam* to replace Chokkanatha with his younger brother. Its timely discovery explains why Lingama fled to Tanjavur and became *daḷavāy* there. But his surprisingly quick return to Madurai to resume this rank under Chokkanatha—after a short stint in prison—shows the might and prestige he continued to enjoy in these years.

Indeed, in 1665 Chokkanatha married Lingama's daughter Mangammal, thought to wield great influence on her husband through her legendary beauty. Lingama's son Tubaki Anandappa (or Antappa) Nayaka, now brother-in-law of the king, became a prominent courtier too, later occupying the office of *daḷavāy* himself.[99] The Tubakis were a highly influential family, then, centred on the brothers Lingama and Krishnappa, who in the course of time were employed by all three Nayaka houses in the Tamil area in various, mostly military, offices, and even managed to establish marital ties with one of these dynasties.

In the same period, another Madurai official with a strong family network rose to great heights. This was Vadamalaiyappa Pillai, who according to the Dutch came from the Tanjavur region and belonged to the Vellala caste. At least from the late 1640s on, he served the Nayakas of Madurai, intermittently holding the positions of governor of the southern Tiruvallur province—seated at Tirunelveli—and of

[98] NA, VOC, no. 1147, ff. 535-5v: letter from Pulicat to Batavia, Jan. 1644. For Senji's *daḷavāys*, in Dutch records often referred to as "the great Aija," see: Srinivasachari, *A History of Gingee*, 114-19; Philippus Baldaeus, *Naauwkeurige beschryvinge van Malabar en Choromandel, der zelver aangrenzende ryken, en het machtige eyland Ceylon. Nevens een omstandige en grondigh doorzochte ontdekking en wederlegginge van de afgoderye der Oost-Indische heydenen …* (Amsterdam, 1672), 1st pt., 158; Subrahmanyam, *The Political Economy of Commerce*, 310-11; Narayana Rao, Shulman, and Subrahmanyam, *Symbols of Substance*, 96; Om Prakash (ed.), *The Dutch Factories in India 1617-1623: A Collection of Dutch East India Company Documents Pertaining to India* (New Delhi, 1984), 32 (n. 2); idem, *The Dutch Factories in India … Vol. II*, 159; Terpstra, *De vestiging van de Nederlanders aan de kust van Koromandel*, 89; Raychaudhuri, *Jan Company in Coromandel*, 19-20, 43-4, 53-4; Colenbrander *et al.*, *Dagh-register gehouden int Casteel Batavia* and Coolhaas *et al.*, *Generale Missiven*, both series first few volumes.

[99] Vink, *Mission to Madurai*, 58-9, 63, 150 (n. 100), 157 (n. 111), 163 (n. 124), 166 (n. 128), 176 (n. 157), 177; NA, VOC, no. 1233, f. 43v: letter from Pulicat to Batavia, July 1660; Saulier, "Madurai and Tanjore," 778-83; Sathyanatha Aiyar, *History of the Nayaks of Madura*, 155-6, 192; Rangachari, "The History of the Naik Kingdom of Madura," *Indian Antiquary* XLVI, 41-2.

pradhāni at the central court. It is unclear whether he was related to the Tirunelveli-based Medai Dalavay Mudaliyar line of governors supposedly founded by the celebrated Ariyanatha Mudaliyar. In any case, Vadamalaiyappa appears to have initially operated as a revenue collector in this area, which likely formed his power base. Inscriptions, temple paintings, and literary works glorify his beneficent rule and exalted deeds, including his divinely-guided recovery of the deity statues seized by the VOC from the coastal Subrahmanya Svami Temple at Tiruchendur in 1649, during a Dutch-Madurai conflict (see illustration 10).

By the 1660s, he exercised great control in the central capital as the kingdom's *pradhāni*, while his son or son-in-law Tirumalai Kulantha Pillai had taken his place as governor at Tirunelveli. A brother of Vadamalaiyappa and a nephew of Tirumalai Kulantha later occupied this office, too, and in 1665 the Dutch referred to Tirumalai Kulantha as "the second of the court" and head of the army. Vadamalaiyappa's own influence was still strong in this period, since in 1670 the VOC called him the "land regent" or provincial governor, who also functioned as "the ordain-it-all [*albeschick*] of all the Nayaka's lands." In addition to holding political power, most members of the Pillai family acted as patrons of letters or were poets themselves.[100]

An impression of how the powerful Tubaki and Pillai families coexisted is provided by the account of a Dutch mission to Tiruchirappalli in February-May 1668. The VOC's ambassador, Hendrik Adriaan van Rheede, wrote that upon his arrival at the capital he first contacted Vadamalaiyappa Pillai ("Barmialappa Pulle" in Dutch records), then *pradhāni* and considered the kingdom's second man. As he reportedly supervised all matters at the central court and personally governed the southern coast, where the Company had settled, nothing could be achieved without his help. In fact, during this embassy, the *pradhāni* literally controlled access to King Chokkanatha Nayaka as his troops guarded the royal residence.

While envoy Van Rheede therefore mostly negotiated with Vadamalaiyappa, on separate occasions he met with a few other courtiers. One of them was Tubaki Lingama's son, Anandappa Nayaka. Although only in his early twenties and seemingly not holding a specific court function yet, according to the Dutch he already wielded substantial influence through his sister Queen Mangammal. Lingama

100 Vink, *Mission to Madurai*, 48, 54, 59-60, 127 (n. 7), 132 (n. 34), 136 (n. 46), 162 (n. 119), 163-4 (ns 123-4), 179 (n. 166); NA, VOC, no. 1251, f. 741; no. 1277, f. 1603: report of mission to Travancore, Madurai, and Ramnad, Mar.-Oct. 1665, instructions for mission to land regent Vadamalaiyappa Pillai, Feb. 1670; *Travancore Archæological Series*, vol. V, pt. III, ed. A.S. Ramanatha Ayyar (Trivandrum, 1927), 200-1; Somasundra Desikar, "Viceroys of the Nayaks of Madura," 175-80; Mac Leod, *De Oost-Indische Compagnie*, vol. II, 382-3; Bauke van der Pol, *The Dutch East India Company in India: A Heritage Tour through Gujarat, Malabar, Coromandel and Bengal* (Bath, 2004), 160. For the Tiruchendur Temple murals portraying Vadamalaiyappa Pillai recovering the statues from the VOC through divine intervention, see: tiruchendur.org/dutch_gallery.htm.

Illustration 10: Painting depicting the Madurai courtier Vadamalaiyappa Pillai recovering deity statues seized by the Dutch, Subrahmanya Svami (Murugan) Temple, Tiruchendur, 20th century? (photo by Patrick Harrigan, courtesy Sri Subrahmanya Swami Devasthanam, source: tiruchendur.org/dutch/dream-9.htm).

himself, despite being Chokkanatha's father-in-law, had lately fallen out of the ruler's favour and lost his position of *daḷavāy*, accused—through instigations of *Pradhāni* Vadamalaiyappa—of treason, allegedly conspiring with Mysore, Tanjavur, Ramnad, and Bijapur. As a consequence, the standing of his son Anandappa had also suffered, even though he had been raised together with Chokkanatha.

During Van Rheede's stay in Tiruchirappalli, the tension at court increased when Tubaki Lingama announced that if his former functions and designations were not returned to him, he would look for employment at other courts. Because of his family ties with the king, Lingama was permitted to depart on the condition he left his capital and possessions behind. As it was thought unlikely he would comply, Tiruchirappalli was secured with soldiers to prevent him from escaping, while Lingama himself permanently kept some 1,500 personal guards with him. Matters quieted down a bit when Chokkanatha gave Lingama command over a number of the kingdom's troops again, according to the Dutch because Queen Mangammal had threatened to commit suicide if her father left Madurai. Yet, *Pradhāni* Vadamalaiyappa appears to have remained in charge—supposedly through massive bribery of the king—and he entirely dominated the sole audience the VOC envoy secured with Chokkanatha. Not surprisingly, a few days later it turned out Lingama had fled the kingdom after all.

This did not prove an unequivocal victory for Vadamalaiyappa. Left with no general to oversee the war against Mysore, a group of courtiers managed to have the *pradhāni* himself sent to the battlefield as commander. These officials, belonging to neither the Pillai nor the Tubaki faction, included the councillor Chinna Tambi Mudaliyar and chief chamberlain Kumara Rangappa Nayaka. The former was another military official disposed of by Vadamalaiyappa, who nevertheless would serve as both *daḷavāy* and *pradhāni* a few years later, while the latter was a close and perhaps illegitimate relative of the king and was much favoured by him.[101] That these men held some power of their own, is suggested by the fact that Van Rheede presented them with gifts, albeit of less value than what Vadamalaiyappa and Anandappa Nayaka received (see table 11 below). In any case, Vadamalaiyappa soon returned from the war front, claiming to have fallen ill, but no doubt eager to keep the court under control.[102]

Whereas during the following four decades two members of the Tubaki family rose to great heights, the Pillai family gradually lost its prominence. In the early 1670s, Vadamalaiyappa was imprisoned twice, reportedly with the aim to confiscate his riches. After his first time in jail, he had to endure the presence of two Brahmins sent from the central court to Tirunelveli to monitor him. After he died in 1675, in the 1680s his functions of *pradhāni* and governor of Tirunelveli were both held by the Brahmin Tiruvenkatanatha Ayya. Like Vadamalaiyappa, he originated from Tanjavur and had enjoyed a high court position there before he and his sons moved to Madurai to offer their administrative and fiscal skills. Local sources suggest that Tiruvenkatanatha had already been governor at Tirunelveli around the mid-seventeenth century and that his son Venkatesha later occupied this position, while other sons served as a *pradhāni* or provincial governor elsewhere. Like the Pillai family, these men patronised poets and composed texts themselves. Some literature even portrays them as behaving like fully-fledged royals, holding court and lavishly parading around town. Confirming this local view, in 1705 the Dutch wrote that the governors of Tirunelveli—whom they called "great land regents"—might be considered "viceroys" (*onder coningen*), for the Nayakas had permitted them to "maintain their own court" (*hoff te houden*).

While these Brahmins operated from their southern power base until the 1690s, Tubaki Anandappa Nayaka became a powerful *daḷavāy* based at the capital, and so the coexistence of two political centres in the kingdom continued. Perhaps as a consequence of this rivalry, Anandappa's career kept oscillating. After his stature

101 This Kumara Rangappa Nayaka was possibly the same person as the eponymous member of Madurai's secondary line of rulers, mentioned in Chapter 2.

102 Vink, *Mission to Madurai*, 144-8, 157-8, 160, 165-8 (ns 130-1), 172-7, 180, 190, 193-4, 196, 201-5, 214-17, 221-4, 227-8, 232-7, 246-7, 249-50, 252, 255-60.

had briefly diminished in 1668 when his father Lingama was accused of treason, in 1677 he temporarily shifted allegiance to Tanjavur, now under Ekoji Bhonsle. Back in Madurai—being the uncle of Chokkanatha's successor Muttu Virappa Nayaka III—from 1682 on Anandappa acted as the regent of this underaged ruler, in which capacity he dominated the court.[103] But in 1686, losing a battle against the Maratha King Shivaji, he fell out of favour once more. Finally, in 1689, upon the discovery that he was part of a plot to assassinate the king, he was executed together with dozens of other members of the Tubaki family.[104]

Anandappa's sister Mangammal fared better. After her son Muttu Virappa III died in 1691, she effectively reigned over Madurai as a widowed queen, installing her infant grandson Vijayaranga Chokkanatha as formal co-ruler. Only when the latter reached maturity and dethroned his grandmother in 1707, the might of the Tubaki family at last came to an end.[105]

Of course, there were numerous other courtiers to fill their place, most of whom must go unmentioned here. Some deserve brief reference, however, as they provide us with further illustrative examples of the fortunes of Madurai officials. One of them was Kavita Nayaka, who was married to a sister of King Chokkanatha Nayaka and around 1674 served as both a *daḷavāy* and the governor of the briefly occupied Tanjavur coast. His son Pradhani Nayaka (alias Bodi Alagiri), the ruler's nephew, initially succeeded Vadamalaiyappa Pillai as governor in Tirunelveli and was thought by the Dutch to dominate the court in the mid-1670s.

The Muslim general or *daḷakartan* (commander of the capital's fort) Rustam Khan, allegedly adopted and raised by Chokkanatha, usurped the kingdom in 1680. Once in power, he appointed his followers to important positions, locked Chokkanatha up in the palace, and reportedly appropriated all the king's privileges and possessions, including the royal women—until he was assassinated in 1682. During an embassy in 1689, the Dutch considered the *Pradhāni* Raghava Ayya the most powerful courtier, judging from their distribution of gifts (see table 11). But just as this mission was taking place, Raghava lost his position when the

[103] Notably, like Queen Mangammal, the wife of this young king, Muttammal, was the daughter of a Madurai *daḷavāy*, Venkata Krishnappa Nayaka, who in 1673 defeated the Nayakas of Tanjavur.

[104] Vink, *Mission to Madurai*, 59-62, 157 (n. 111), 168, 174, 204, 228, 233-4, 258, 262 (n. 2), 312 (n. 196), 377-8 (n. 4), 464, 476-7, 548, 556-7; NA, VOC, no. 1292, ff. 24, 214v; no. 1274, ff. 81, 303; no. 8921, f. 163: letters from Colombo to Gentlemen XVII and Batavia, Dec. 1670, Jan. 1671, Feb., May 1673, final report of Tuticorin's chief (*opperhoofd*) Nicolaas Welter, Oct. 1705; DNA, DCGCC, no. 2672, ff. 9v-10v: final report of Tuticorin's chief Laurens Pijl, Dec. 1672; S. Somasundra Desikar, "Tiruvēṅkaṭanātha of Mātai," *Journal of Indian History* XVI, 2 (1937), 133-6; idem, "Venkatesa, Viceroy of Rangakrishna Muttuvirappa III," *Journal of Indian History* XVI, 3 (1937), 304-9; Taylor, *Oriental Historical Manuscripts*, vol. II, 213-15.

[105] Madurai's Queen Minakshi (r. c. 1732-9) may however have belonged to the Tubaki family as well. See the Madurai section in Chapter 2.

abovementioned Tiruvenkatanatha Ayya was suddenly reinstalled as *pradhāni* again, necessitating the Dutch to quickly produce extra presents for the latter.[106]

Around the turn of the eighteenth century the court was dominated by two Brahmin *daḷavāy*s, father and son Narasappa Ayyan and Kasturi Ranga Ayyan, who figure prominently in both local and VOC sources. The former, a favourite of Queen Mangammal, grew so influential that Jesuit missionaries called him the "prince-regent." But his great influence, and—as the VOC claimed—his Tamil background, caused resentment and fear among Madurai's Telugu-speaking courtiers, many of whom allegedly sought asylum in Ariyalur. When Narasappa died in battle in 1702, his son Kasturi Ranga seems to have taken over his father's great might. His was an unstable career, however. He was first imprisoned by Mangammal and later, under her successor Vijayaranga Chokkanatha Nayaka, he fled to Tanjavur to serve Shahaji Bhonsle. But in both cases, Kasturi Ranga was soon reinstalled in Madurai as *daḷavāy*, the second time supposedly with the help of the Nawab of Arcot in return for 400,000 *rupees*—another instance of the strongly fluctuating powers of some courtiers and the ongoing involvement of neighbouring kingdoms.[107]

Until the fall of the Nayakas around 1739, more courtiers followed. Some appear in table 11, which lists the officials receiving the most valuable gifts from the Dutch at seven diplomatic meetings between Madurai's monarchs and the VOC during the period 1668-1731, mostly in the early eighteenth century. As in this chapter's other tables, there are great changes in the distribution of presents with each

[106] For Kavita Nayaka, Pradhani Nayaka, and Raghava Ayya, see: Vink, *Mission to Madurai*, 64, 269 (n. 22), 378 (n. 4), 384 (n. 9), 409-10, 499-500, 571-2; NA, VOC, no. 1304, ff. 281v, 323; no. 1316, f. 302: letters from Nagapattinam to Batavia, from Tuticorin to Colombo, Sept. 1674, Dec. 1676, report of Tuticorin's chief, Mar. 1674. For Rustam Khan, see: Srinivasachariar, "Muslim Adventurers in the Kingdoms of Tanjore and Madura," 389-92; Taylor, *Oriental Historical Manuscripts*, vol. II, 35; Sathyanatha Aiyar, *History of the Nayaks of Madura*, 180-2, 286; Vink, *Mission to Madurai*, 314 (n. 211), 396 (n. 61); idem, "Encounters on the Opposite Coast," 372-3; Rangachari, "The History of the Naik Kingdom of Madura," *Indian Antiquary* XLVI, 96-9.

[107] For Narasappa Ayyan and Kasturi Ranga Ayyan, see: NA, VOC, no. 1617, f. 67v; no. 1664, f. 177; no. 1706, ff. 1040v, 1047-50v; no. 1756, ff. 1195-6v, 1205-8v; no. 1778, ff. 103-4; no. 1803, ff. 102-3v; no. 1893, ff. 1050v-3v; no. 8595, ff. 129-30; no. 8924, ff. 201-2; no. 11306, ff. 43-5: letters from Nagapattinam and Colombo to Batavia, from Tuticorin to Colombo, June 1699, May 1702, Feb. 1707, May 1709, July 1711, July 1717, reports of meetings with Madurai rulers, July 1705, July 1708, report on the Nayaka's imminent visit to Tuticorin, Apr. 1709, description of the Nayakas of Madurai by Holst, 1762; BL/AAS, MG, no. 4, pt. 4: "Mootiah's chronological & historical account of the modern kings of Madura," f. 71; Coolhaas *et al.*, *Generale Missiven*, vol. VI, 593, 779; Vink, *Mission to Madurai*, 38, 64, 474-5 (n. 237); Venkata Rao, *The Southern School in Telugu Literature*, 144; Sathyanatha Aiyar, *History of the Nayaks of Madura*, 209-10, 213, 217-19, 223, 295, 305-11, 316-17, 366 (nos 216, 218); Burgess and Naṭēśa Śāstrī, *Tamil and Sanskrit Inscriptions*, 110-11; Nelson, *The Madura Country*, vol. III, 230-5, 240; Rangachari, "The History of the Naik Kingdom of Madura," *Indian Antiquary* XLVI, 162-3, 183, 187-8.

Table 11: Distribution of gifts among prominent courtiers during Dutch missions to Madurai, in order of value, 1668-1731.

1668	1689	1705	1708	1717	1720	1731
king Chokkanatha	*king* Muttu Virappa III	*queen* Mangammal	*king* Vijayaranga Chokkanatha	*king* Vijayaranga Chokkanatha	*king* Vijayaranga Chokkanatha	*king* Vijayaranga Chokkanatha
pradhāni Vadamalai- yappa Pillai	*pradhāni* Raghava Ayya	*daḷavāy* Kasturi Ranga Ayyan	*daḷavāy* Kasturi Ranga Ayyan	*daḷavāy (& pradhāni?)* Rajasam	*pradhāni* Sambu Ayyan	*daḷavāy* Govindappa Ayyan
king's brother Achyutappa Nayaka	*lowlands regent* Alagiri Nayaka	*"favourite"* Pattavirama Ayyan	*royal in-law* Achyutapati Nayaka	*deputy general* Sambu Ayyan	*royal in-law* Periya Mappil- lai Nayaka	*"favourite"* Ananda Raghu Ayyan
town governor Chokkalinga Nayaka	*(new) pradhāni* Tiruvenkata- natha Ayya	*royal in-law* Lakshminan Nayaka	*royal in-law* Lakshmipati Nayaka	*councillor* Venkatesa Ariyar	*state minister* Venkatesa Ariyar	*courtier* Polamara Chetti Ayyan
courtier Tubaki Anandappa	*regent's envoy* Mutti Mudaliyar	*councillor* Vadamalai- yappa Pillai	*lowl. regent* Ananda Pat- panatha Pillai	*lowl. regent* Alagappa Mudaliyar	*regent's in-law* Kumara Svami Mudaliyar	*lowl. regent* Chetti Raja Ayyan
councillor Chinna Tambi Mudaliyar	*captain* Venkatapati Nayaka		*rāyasam (?)* Govindappa Ayyan		*court merchant* Sundardasu Ayyan	*minister* Venketa Raghava Ariyar
chamberlain Rangappa Nayaka					*royal relative* Chagavada Ayyan	*deputy regent* Lingaraja Ayyan

Notes: in 1668 the order between nos 3 and 4 and between nos 5 and 6 is not certain; in 1689 gifts for no. 4 had to be improvised during the mission after his sudden installation and the demotion of nos 2 and 3; in 1705 nos 3 and 4 received equally much, while the difference with no. 5 was very small; in 1708 nos 3 and 4 as well as nos 5 and 6 received equally much; in 1717 no. 2 was not present, nos 4 and 5 received equally much, and the difference between them and no. 3 was very small; in 1720 nos 3 and 4 received equally much; all missions from 1705 to 1731 were dispatched to Melur, on the outskirts of Tuticorin, when the monarch visited that town.
Sources: Vink, *Mission to Madurai*, 199-203, 254-7, 382-4, 408-10, 450-1, 459, 461-3, 499-500, 537-8, 544, 546-7, 571-2; NA, VOC, no. 1706, ff. 1040v-50v, 1054v-5; no. 1756, ff. 1198v-208; no. 1893, ff. 1050v-5v; no. 1941, ff. 927v-9, 931, 939-45; no. 2185, ff. 1009v-11.

new encounter. Since the first embassies were decades apart, those differences should maybe not surprise us. Besides, the eighteenth-century missions all took place during royal tours to Madurai's Fishery Coast, so courtiers staying back at the capital were generally not honoured with gifts. Yet, the table underscores some of the patterns seen above.

Most notably, the men who over the decades were given the most valuable presents after the king or queen were two *pradhāni*s, two *daḷavāy*s, another *pradhāni*, and a *daḷavāy* again. The first of these *pradhāni*s, Vadamalaiyappa Pillai, was also governor of Tirunelveli, or "regent of the lowlands," as the Dutch called this function. But people holding only this regional post never made it to the highest level in the VOC's ranking order, although they were still regularly presented with gifts, often occupying the third or fifth position. Another category that frequently received presents, unlike in the other kingdoms, comprised relatives of the monarch, including a brother and several in-laws, positioned anywhere between the third and seventh place.

Most other functions—including some unclear Dutch classifications like "councillor," "minister," "favourite" (*gunsteling*), or simply "courtier"—occur just once in the table, indicating the transitory power of these offices. A special case concerns the royal tour in 1717, when *Daḷavāy* Rajasam—who may have been *pradhāni* too since the Dutch called him "Prodani Raijasam"—received the most gifts of all courtiers. The fact that he did not actually accompany the king on this trip, shows all the more the great influence he wielded according to the VOC.

All this suggests that one's formal office said little about one's effective power, at least in the eyes of the Dutch. Tellingly, while in this table the position of either *pradhāni* or *daḷavāy* always comes second, these offices never appear together in a single list. Thus, whenever the *pradhāni* was honoured with the most gifts after the monarch, the *daḷavāy* was given nothing at all, and so it was the other way round. It seems that someone holding one of these ranks was either very powerful or lacked much influence, perhaps pointing to a general fierce rivalry between these potentially most prominent functions.

Although the preceding pages have discussed only some of Madurai's courtiers, several characteristics can be deduced from the examples. Some of these are common for all courts, while others seem more typical for Madurai. Starting with the latter, this was the only kingdom among Vijayanagara's heirs that long harboured two strong political centres or—as some contemporaries called it—two courts: the capital, at Madurai town or more northerly Tiruchirappalli; and the governor's seat at Tirunelveli in the far south. Several southern governors, such as Vadamalaiyappa Pillai, Pradhani Nayaka, and Tiruvenkatanatha Ayya, also occupied important positions at the central court, usually as *pradhāni*. Control of the Tirunelveli region, and the wealth gained from revenue collection there, likely often served as a power base for the acquisition of influence at the capital.

This coexistence of two nodes of power, and the resultant great potential for competition, may have contributed to another phenomenon occurring often in Madurai: the movement of courtiers to or from other kingdoms. Tubaki Lingama Nayaka and his son Anandappa, Vadamalaiyappa Pillai, Tiruvenkatanatha Ayya, Raghava Ayya, and Kasturi Ranga Ayyan, all *daḷavāys* or *pradhānis*, each left this Nayaka court to seek employment or asylum at Tanjavur or Ariyalur—usually to soon return—or first arrived in Madurai from elsewhere in search of political and economic opportunities, found at both the capital and Tirunelveli.

Another point on which Madurai seems to stand out is the relatively limited diversity of the courtiers' backgrounds. Most officials were either members of various Brahmin communities or, judging from their many marital liaisons with the royal family, belonged to the Balija castes, like the Nayakas themselves. The considerable size of the second group may also explain the fair number of royal in-laws mentioned in table 11. In contrast, and unlike in Bhonsle-ruled Tanjavur, few or no Muslims are found among Madurai's prominent functionaries, with the notable exception of Rustam Khan.

Other aspects are more common for all courts. Madurai courtiers frequently held various offices consecutively or simultaneously, in the latter instance often combining a function in the capital with a regional governorship. Besides the aforementioned cases, table 11 shows that in 1717 Sambu Ayyan was a deputy general (*onder veltheer*), while three years later he held the more civilian post of *pradhāni*. Climbing in the opposite direction—from an administrative to a military rank—Govindappa Ayyan, *rāyasam* in 1708, was probably the same person who acted as *daḷavāy* in 1731. Further, in Madurai, too, careers were not only diverse but also oscillating. Tubaki Lingama, Vadamalaiyappa Pillai, Raghava Ayya, and Kasturi Ranga Ayyan rose to prominence and fell from grace at least twice, and Tubaki Anandappa did so no fewer than three times. Apparently, demotion, imprisonment, or even defection hardly ever signalled the end of one's possibilities at this court. Anandappa seems a rare example of a Madurai courtier whose career ended with his execution.

Another element shared with other successor states is the prominent role of kinship. In Madurai, a handful of Brahmin and (probably) Balija families dominated the kingdom from the moment the VOC began to report about it. These included the Tubaki and Pillai houses, Tiruvenkatanatha Ayya and Kavita Nayaka with their respective sons, and father and son Narasappa and Kasturi Ranga Ayyan. The Tubaki and Pillai lines were especially long-lasting, active during at least the years 1660-1707 and 1640s-1705 respectively.[108] Equally common was the strong opposi-

108 For this last year, when a relative of Vadamalaiyappa Pillai held an important post, see table 11.

tion between these families and among individual courtiers. The power struggle between the Tubaki and Pillai families during the 1660s and 1670s and the rivalry between the "Tamil" *Daḷavāy* Narasappa Ayyan and Telugu-speaking officials in the 1690s are just two examples of the regular competition at the Madurai court, in which nearly every courtier somehow seemed involved.

Setupatis of Ramnad

The composition of high functionaries in Ramnad appears to be largely modelled on its parental state Madurai. Secondary literature states that Ramnad's most prominent courtier was the *daḷavāy*, who combined the highest military and civilian duties, serving as both the chief minister and supreme general. It has been suggested this office was only introduced here in the early 1680s, when Madurai's King Chokkanatha Nayaka presented his *Daḷavāy* Kumara Pillai to Ramnad's Setupati Kilavan Tevar, showing his appreciation for the latter's assistance in assassinating Madurai's usurper Rustam Khan. But Dutch records refer to a *daḷavāy* in Ramnad at least from 1674 on, so the function may have been in use since the court's beginnings.

The *pradhāni* is thought to have been the next most important official, controlling financial matters, revenue collection, and the state's internal administration. The third court rank was the *rāyasam*, the king's secretary. Further, VOC documents speak of a "treasurer" (*schatbewaarder*), probably the *sarvādhikāri* mentioned in secondary literature, and several *sērvaikkārars* ("cheerwegaren"), a term that in Ramnad seems to have indicated military officers of various ranks.[109] Besides, there were provincial governors, including the functionary the Dutch called "regent of the lowlands," the revenue-farmer of the region along the kingdom's southern shore.[110]

[109] The word *sērvaikkārar* as used by the VOC chiefly denoted a high military post, but it had in fact several meanings depending on the context. Besides a military or political designation—commander or chief—it was a title of members of the Ahambadiya caste (closely related to the Maravars and Kallars), the name of a Maravar sub-caste, and a term for male offspring of Setupatis and junior wives of the Ahambadiya caste. Such progeny was disqualified from kingship but it is thought courtiers were often recruited from this group. It is unclear whether the officials called *sērvaikkārar* in this chapter came from this background. See: Dirks, *The Hollow Crown*, 72 (n. 35), 173-4, 268-9 (n. 7); Kadhirvel, *A History of the Maravas*, 9-10; Thurston, *Castes and Tribes of Southern India*, vol. V, 48, vol. VI, 362; Mahalingam, *Mackenzie Manuscripts*, vol. I, 238; Ludden, *Peasant History in South India*, 72; Raja Ram Rao, *Ramnad Manual*, 33.

[110] For the size and composition of the entire palace staff and other servants in late eighteenth-century Ramnad and (in more detail) its off-shoot Pudukkottai in the nineteenth and early twentieth centuries, see respectively: Howes, *The Courts of Pre-Colonial South India*, 146-7, 166, 169; Joanne Punzo Waghorne, *The Raja's Magic Clothes: Re-visioning Kingship and Divinity in England's India* (University Park, 1994), chs 5-7.

The focus lies here on the period from the last decades of the seventeenth century onward, because the VOC only permanently settled down in Ramnad in 1690, leading to closer and more continuous contacts with courtiers than before. Moreover, the 1680s seem to mark the kingdom's achievement of practical autonomy from Madurai, as it was in these years that King Kilavan Tevar no longer supported his Nayaka overlord but, on the contrary, joined Madurai's opponents and conquered part of the Nayaka's lands.[111] Thus, starting around 1690, one can both study an independently functioning court and consult sources that deal intensively and uninterruptedly with this kingdom's courtiers.[112]

Among the limited number of Ramnad officials who can be discussed here are various members of the family of Shaykh Abd al-Qadir, like the Dutch based at the town of Kilakkarai. This port had long been home to communities of Muslim merchants—some claiming Arab descent—who designated themselves as Maraikkayars, Labbais, or both.[113] Belonging to the former group, Abd al-Qadir and several relatives consecutively bore the title of *periya tambi* or "great brother," denoting their prominent position among Kilakkarai's inhabitants and at the Ramnad court. At least active from the 1670s, the initial *periya tambi* was Abd al-Qadir's uncle or elder brother, who served as the Setupati's chief merchant and in his capacity as revenue-farmer controlled Ramnad's Fishery Coast, including Kilakkarai. Like in Madurai and Tanjavur, the Dutch called this coastal representative "regent of the lowlands."

As with many other magnates, in the wake of the *periya tambis*' extensive commercial enterprise—including large-scale overseas trade—came political power. The standing of the first *periya tambi* at the Ramnad court transpires from the fact that during a VOC mission in 1683 he was one of the two courtiers conducting the negotiations in between the formal audiences with the king. But his great influence and mercantile activities led to clashes with the Dutch, who, after a military confrontation with Ramnad in 1685, forced the Setupati to sign a treaty that removed the *periya tambi* and his relatives from their administrative positions. Like with

111 Seshadri, "The Sētupatis of Ramnad," 55-8, 184-6; Shulman and Subrahmanyam, "Prince of Poets and Ports," 505-6; Vink, *Mission to Madurai*, 73-4, 470 (n. 226); Kadhirvel, *A History of the Maravas*, 37-49; NA, VOC, no. 2956, f. 1223: diary of mission to Ramnad, June 1759.

112 For courtiers in Ramnad up to the 1680s, see: Vink, "Encounters on the Opposite Coast," 288-9, 292-3, 372, 376-7; idem, *Mission to Madurai*, 73-4; Shulman and Subrahmanyam, "Prince of Poets and Ports," 506-7; Seshadri, "The Sētupatis of Ramnad," 29-30, 56-7.

113 While the term "Maraikkayar" generally denoted a higher status than "Labbai," this distinction appears not to have always been observed in Ramnad in this period. At any rate, someone like Labbai Nayinar Maraikkayar (see below) apparently bore both titles.

many other such agreements, however, this stipulation was more or less ignored by the Ramnad court.

Consequently, when the first *periya tambi* died in 1688, his various functions passed to a family member who was probably his brother's younger son, or perhaps his brother himself, called Citakkati Pillai (the former term a Tamilisation of "Shaykh Abd al-Qadir"). Although facing opposition from not just the Dutch but also other Muslims traders and court officials, Citakkati became the most powerful person in Ramnad after the king. Illustrative of his high position was the permission he, and maybe already his predecessor, received to bear the names "Vijaya Raghunatha," used by Ramnad's royal family. This sharing of names—thereby establishing fictional kinship—was an effort by the Setupati Kilavan Tevar to incorporate the powerful *periya tambi*s and Kilakkarai's Muslim community at large, binding them with moral obligations. One reason why the king wished to maintain such close relations was his desire to conduct overseas trade himself, for which Kilakkarai's merchants served as valuable middlemen.

Further conflicts with the VOC, however, resulted in another Dutch-Ramnad contract in 1690, once more stating that the *periya tambi* family be excluded from political functions. During the signing of this treaty, Kilavan swore on his gun that this time he would stick to the clause and even put the hands of the *periya tambi*'s son and the Dutch envoys together in his own hands "as a sign of friendship." Despite all that, this stipulation was again hardly adhered to as by the mid-1690s Citakkati resurfaced in VOC documents, dominating Kilakkarai and wielding great influence at court.

After Citakkati Pillai passed away in 1698, he was succeeded by a close relative, also named Abd al-Qadir. This third *periya tambi* grew even more influential than his predecessors. Said by the Dutch to possess the king's mind (*gemoet*) and be consulted by him on all important affairs, Abd al-Qadir served as a revenue-farmer, court merchant, ship and arms supplier, and diplomatic intermediary between the court and the VOC, besides his own commercial activities. As with very powerful courtiers in Tanjavur and Madurai, the Dutch referred to Abd al-Qadir as the Setupati's "ordain-it-all" (*albeschik*). One tradition has it that he or his predecessor also helped the king fund the construction of the capital's fort and palace hall, in return for which he was allowed to reside in a nearby palatial building.

In addition, Abd al-Qadir, his predecessor Citakkati Pillai, and possibly the other *periya tambi*s were patrons of Tamil Muslim literature. Such texts portray them variously as heroic warriors, religious devotees, and even kingly figures holding court with all due pomp and circumstance. Thus, this family provides another example of traders whose wealth and network made them attain political power and rise to great prominence as courtiers, in this case complete with royal trappings.

Nevertheless, when Abd al-Qadir died in 1708 and his place was filled by his young son, the end of the family's power was near. The son got involved in yet more discord with the VOC and on one occasion had his men attack not only Dutch property but also delegates of the Setupati. Therefore, in 1709 the VOC could finally convince the court to strip the *periya tambi* line of its political power. A Dutch-Ramnad treaty in that year stipulated that all relatives and descendants of Abd al-Qadir's family be perpetually excluded from governmental positions. Soon after, under the reign of Muttu Vijaya Raghunatha Setupati, the Dutch reported that the fourth *periya tambi* had still engaged himself in the succession struggle between this ruler and his opponent Bhavani Shankara, financially backing the latter's supporters Madurai and Pudukkottai. After severe punishment, Abd al-Qadir's son allegedly died in 1710 and in the following years his family largely disappeared from the VOC archives, a return to power seemingly impossible.

However, much to the VOC's dismay, a mission sent in 1739 by Ramnad to the Dutch at Colombo was headed by another member of Abd al-Qadir's house. Like his predecessors, this man, perhaps a son of the fourth *periya tambi*, served as the "regent of the lowlands" and was entitled to bear the royal names "Vijaya Raghunatha." Yet, he never acquired the great powers of his ancestors and after the Colombo embassy the VOC records are silent on him.[114]

Thus, in short, Ramnad's court on the one hand profited from the economic skills of the *periya tambis* and other Maraikkayars and Labbais, but on the other hand faced competition for political power from these Muslim communities. The Setupatis' efforts to incorporate their leaders—for instance through administrative appointments and name-sharing—were therefore moves to control them, which they were more than willing to accept because this only increased their influence and prestige. As with Abd al-Qadir's family, however, there was always the risk of growing too powerful, overplaying one's hand, and falling from grace.[115]

[114] As late as around the mid-nineteenth century, this family continued to use the Setupatis' dynastic names, like "Ravikula Muttu Vijaya Raghunatha." Other Muslim families at Kilakkarai bore the Setupati designation "Hiranya Garbhayaji" (for which title see Chapter 5). See Bayly, *Saints, Goddesses and Kings*, 83-4.

[115] Shulman and Subrahmanyam, "Prince of Poets and Ports"; Vink, *Mission to Madurai*, 77-80; idem, "Encounters on the Opposite Coast," 293-4; Bayly, *Saints, Goddesses and Kings*, 78-90; Raja Ram Rao, *Ramnad Manual*, 228; Thiruvenkatachari, *The Setupatis of Ramnad*, 45, 150 (n. 51); Bes, "The Setupatis, the Dutch, and Other Bandits," 548, 550-2; P. Sabapathy, "Muslims under the Setupatis of Ramnad: A Study in the Socio-Cultural History of Tamilnadu (17th and 18th Centuries)," *Proceedings of the Indian History Congress* 60 (1999), 386; J.L.W., "The Chronicles of the Marava Country," 456; NA, VOC, no. 1383, f. 554v; no. 1479, f. 403v; no. 1615C, f. 653; no. 2457, ff. 1026v-7, 1030; no. 2459, ff. 1613v, 1617v-20v, 1623-4; no. 8595, f. 133: reports of missions to Ramnad, May-June 1683, Sep. 1690, Feb. 1699, letters from Colombo to Batavia, from Sivakumara Muttu Vijaya Raghunatha Setupati to Colombo, Feb. 1707, Apr., Aug. 1739, diary of visit of Ramnad envoys to Colombo, May-June 1739; Heeres and Stapel,

Hence, around 1710 the *periya tambis* were replaced with other distinguished Muslims, initially one Adam Labbai, and in 1715 Labbai Nayinar Maraikkayar. The career of the latter, although seemingly a less prominent man than Citakkati Pillai and Abd al-Qadir, had much in common with the fortunes of the *periya tambis*. As stated in poetry sponsored by him, Labbai Nayinar ("Lebbe Neijna Marca" in Dutch documents) descended from both important mercantile families and leading religious figures.[116] Like the *periya tambis*, he was appointed tax-farmer of the Kilakkarai area—"regent of the lowlands"—and after a temporary loss of the function regained it in 1723. He was also permitted to use the Setupati's names "Vijaya Raghunatha." These attempts by the king to monitor another mighty, and possibly threatening, figure again proved hazardous since Labbai Nayinar did indeed turn out to be a threat.

In the report of a VOC embassy to Ramnad in January 1731, envoy Reijnier Helmondt wrote that the lowlands regent was the kingdom's most powerful man, enjoyed the protection of Tanjavur's King Tukkoji Bhonsle, and completely dominated the new Setupati, Kattaya Tevar. Even though the mission was partially dispatched to protest against Labbai Nayinar's frequent violations of the Dutch-Ramnad treaties, the regent himself was present at all audiences, turning Kattaya against the VOC or bluntly interrupting the king and taking over the negotiations. According to envoy Helmondt it was obvious that Labbai Nayinar, and indeed most other courtiers, kept the Setupati in the dark. Kattaya was illiterate and as a newcomer to the capital had little idea what agreements had been made with the VOC. In a letter of August 1731, Tuticorin's Dutch chief Daniel Overbeek drew a picture of the balance of power at the Ramnad court in no uncertain terms:

> The cannecappel [*kaṇakkuppiḷḷai*, local clerk] whom I have sent to the court of the Theuver [Kattaya Tevar] has not been able to achieve anything, other than that he has noticed that even the lowest betel-bearer there understands more than His Excellency the lord of the woods [*woudheer*, Kattaya] himself. Yes! So much so, that a pupil of that idiot [Kattaya], in his own face and in the presence of all courtiers, nullified the word that had been given by that king to the delegated cannecappel Philip and that had already been signed on a blank ola [*ōlai*, palm-leaf letter] to the effect that his subjects were all ordered to pay [their debts

Corpus diplomaticum Neerlando-Indicum, vol. 4 (The Hague, 1935), 328-30. The first two secondary works mentioned above partly disagree on the number of and relationship between the *periya tambis*. I largely follow Vink's more recent findings here.

116 Labbai Nayinar Maraikkayar was perhaps even a close relative of the *periya tambis*, his paternal grandfather possibly being a younger brother of Citakkati Pillai. See Torsten Tschacher, "Challenging Orders: *Ṭarīqas* and Muslim Society in Southeastern India and Laṅkā, ca. 1400–1950," in R. Michael Feener and Anne M. Blackburn (eds), *Buddhist and Islamic Orders in Southern Asia: Comparative Perspectives* (Honolulu, 2019), 88.

> to the VOC]. [This nullification happened] under the pretext that if those people were to fail [to pay], the Honourable Company [VOC] would always hold His Excellency responsible. Thus, that ola was destroyed ...[117]

While this sarcastic portrayal may reflect the VOC's frustration with Ramnad's opposition as much as the actual situation at court, Kattaya appears to have held little authority in this period. However, in the following years Labbai Nayinar's own position proved insecure as well. When the VOC had difficulties collecting debts owed by the Setupati, several courtiers, and others, the lowlands regent discretely endeavoured to mediate between the Dutch and some of the debtors, foremost the king himself. The VOC thought Labbai Nayinar's sudden cooperation highly dubious, wondering whether he was sincerely trying to solve the disputes or actually safeguarding his own interests, bearing in mind Kattaya's reign was still unstable. On one occasion, the regent hinted that if the Dutch wished to build a fort at Kilakkarai, the Setupati might not object, adding that he himself would always support the VOC, even if Kattaya was dethroned. The Dutch ignored this offer, suspecting it was the king rather than the regent who suggested the construction of a fort, because a Dutch stronghold on Ramnad territory might serve as a safe retreat should the Setupati be attacked.

Whether Labbai Nayinar acted on Kattaya's behalf or not, he was walking a tightrope. He could not exert his influence on the king too openly in favour of the VOC, as he faced competition from other courtiers, who might accuse him of disloyalty. At the same time, winning the confidence of the Dutch was not only important in case the Setupati lost his throne but also to partake in the next, VOC-controlled pearl fishery. In the end, however, it was Kattaya who dropped Labbai Nayinar. If the regent had really approached the Dutch in the king's name, he had achieved very little. If he had acted on his own behalf, his courting of the VOC while the Setupati's reign was under threat had probably not passed unnoticed. In either case, Labbai Nayinar no longer served a purpose and was blamed for having made problems between the court and the Dutch worse. Thus, around March 1734, after an earlier temporary suspension, this regent, too, was removed from office in perpetuity, as a consequence, it seems, of a combination of wrong assessments, exploitation by his overlord, and competition from other courtiers.[118]

[117] NA, VOC, no. 2186, ff. 1307-8: letter from Tuticorin to Colombo, Aug. 1731 (translation mine).

[118] NA, VOC, no. 1992, ff. 843-3v; no. 2068, ff. 1375-5v; no. 2185, ff. 1053v-62, 1167-85; no. 2186, ff. 1215-34, 1265v, 1274-80v, 1312-12v; no. 2224, ff. 1508-9, 1623-8; no. 2245, ff. 328-9; no. 2291, ff. 499-500, 508-9, 517; no. 2308, ff. 2056v-83v: correspondence between Kilakkarai, Tuticorin, and Colombo, Aug. 1723, Aug.-Oct., Dec. 1731, Jan.-Feb. 1732, May, July, Nov. 1733, Feb.-May 1734, judicial document, Mar. 1727, letters from Kattaya Tevar to Colombo, from Labbai Nayinar Maraikkayar to Tuticorin, Feb. 1731, Apr. 1734, report and diary of mission to Ramnad, Jan.-Feb. 1731, report of journey of Ceylon Governor

Nevertheless, a son of Labbai Nayinar probably functioned as the king's representative in Kilakkarai from around 1745. In his correspondence with the Dutch, this man signed as Kumara Muttu Vijaya Raghunatha Labbai Nayinar Maraikkayar, apparently referring to symbolic kinship ties with the Setupati Sivakumara Muttu Vijaya Raghunatha. His career seems to have been steady for a quite some time, since he led a mission to the Dutch in 1750, still using these royal names, and he is mentioned as a courtier in the diary of a VOC embassy to Ramnad in 1759.[119]

After Labbai Nayinar's fall in 1734, the regency of the lowlands was held by a sequence of people quickly replacing each other. Their different backgrounds make clear this office was not reserved for notables from Kilakkarai's Muslim community, but simply for the highest-bidding aspiring tax-farmer. Among others, the VOC records mention as regents the Brahmin Veda alias Chinna Ayyan (1735), the Muslim Chinna Maraikkayar, who was perhaps Labbai Nayinar's brother (1737, holding the post for the second time), the Brahmin Ramalinga Pillai (1739), the Muslim Shaykh Ibrahim Maraikkayar (1739, also acting as envoy to the VOC in this year), and the Hindu Svaminathan (twice, including the late 1750s). No one among this wide range of people, however, appears to have attained the influence and prestige at court enjoyed by the *periya tambi*s and Labbai Nayinar.[120] Between the mid-1730s and the early 1760s, courtiers in other functions rose to prominence and, moreover, they managed to keep their position for longer periods.

One of them was Muttu Vairavanatha (or Vairavar) Servaikkarar ("Moettoe Waijrewenaden Cheerwegaren" in VOC records), who held the office of *daḷavāy* and thus functioned as both prime minister and commander-in-chief. He was probably identical to the prominent but not particularly powerful *sērvaikkārar* or military officer Muttu Vaira Tevar mentioned in a Dutch report of 1709. The latter was Kilavan Tevar's brother-in-law and consequently must have belonged to the Maravar caste like Ramnad's rulers themselves. Besides holding a military rank, in this period he served as the revenue-farmer of lands near the Pamban Channel.

In any case, by the early 1730s Muttu Vairavanatha Servaikkarar had become Ramnad's *daḷavāy*, although, judging from the distribution of gifts during a VOC

Versluys to the Fishery Coast, Feb. 1732. See also: Bes, "The Setupatis, the Dutch, and Other Bandits," 556-8; idem, "Friendship as Long as the Sun and Moon Shine," 30, 34-44.

119 NA, VOC, no. 2473, f. 97; no. 2666, ff. 2209, 2211; no. 2757, ff. 1457, 1465v-6, 1480v; no. 2956, ff. 1228v-30: letters from Tuticorin to Colombo, from Kilakkarai to Tuticorin, Aug. 1739, Sept. 1750, correspondence between the VOC and Labbai Nayinar Maraikkayar, Dec. 1745, Jan. 1746, diary of visit of Ramnad envoys to Tuticorin, Apr. 1750, diary of mission to Ramnad, June-July 1759.

120 For these regents, see NA, VOC, no. 2015, ff. 577, 672, 686; no. 2337, ff. 1519-19v, 1521v, 1524-5, 1530v-1, 1540; no. 2403, ff. 1974, 1980-80v; no. 2459, f. 1617; no. 2925, f. 842v: diary of mission to Ramnad, Feb.-May 1724, correspondence between Tuticorin and Colombo, Mar.-Apr., June-July 1735, Aug., Oct. 1737, Feb. 1758, report on visit of Ramnad's envoys to Colombo, May 1739.

mission in 1731, at this time the regent Labbai Nayinar Maraikkayar was still considered more influential (see table 12). Vairavanatha's chance to become the kingdom's mightiest courtier arrived when the Setupati Kattaya died in 1735. The latter's son, the five- or six-year old Sivakumara Muttu Vijaya Raghunatha, was installed as king with the provision that during his minority Vairavanatha would be his guardian and rule Ramnad in his name.

Henceforth, the *daḷavāy* appears to have considered the kingdom his own. Like several Setupatis before him, he selected a prominent Muslim, Nongu Muttu, as his protégé and appointed him supervisor of the lucrative conch shell diving. According to the Dutch, Vairavanatha provided his protection in exchange for part of the profits made by Nongu Muttu on the shells, the trade of which was supposed to be the VOC's monopoly. *Pradhāni* Ramalingam Pillai was occasionally given some money, too, to enlist his support. This man seems to have held little power of his own, however, said to be unwilling to discuss even the smallest matter as long as Vairavanatha was away on the battlefield. In any case, when the Dutch in 1736 dispatched an embassy to the court to complain about Nongu Muttu's diving, Vairavanatha and Ramalingam simply told envoy Wouter Trek they wished to receive extra gifts, over and above the regular presents, before they could grant an audience with the minor Setupati, at which the *daḷavāy* would lead the negotiations anyhow.

To the VOC's indignation, the same demand was made in 1741 when it requested a reduction of the tolls levied at Kilakkarai. These had been raised on the occasion of the consecration of Sivakumara, now about twelve years old, as Setupati. Although this marked a new stage towards the king's adulthood, Vairavanatha remained Ramnad's most powerful person, according to both the VOC—calling him the court's "ordain-it-all" in these years—and other courtiers the Dutch met. For at a VOC mission in June 1743, the official Kadamba Tevar, inspecting the gifts brought along by the Dutch, suggested that Vairavanatha's share be increased even though he would already receive the most of all courtiers anyway.

Further exemplifying the *daḷavāy*'s wide-ranging powers and exalted status, he maintained his own ships for overseas trade and built or endowed several temples, as well as a pilgrim rest house on Rameshvaram island with, according to a VOC report of 1746, a statue depicting him. Even the fact that Vairavanatha grew blind over the years—the Dutch now described him as "that fickle, cross-eyed field-lord"—did not threaten his unshakeable position. His dominance only came to an end when he died in a battle with Shivagangai around April 1745.[121]

[121] For Muttu Vairavanatha Servaikkarar, see: NA, VOC, no. 1771, ff. 1494-5, 1499, 1501, 1516, 1528v, 1547, 1555, 1581v; no. 2015, f. 680; no. 2185, ff. 1186-7v; no. 2224, f. 1613; no. 2337, ff. 1543-3v; no. 2374, ff. 2041-73v; no. 2388, ff. 1392-3; no. 2400, ff. 411-11v; no. 2403, f. 1971v; no. 2523, f. 1400; no. 2559, ff. 1463, 1485;

Vairavanatha's apparent impregnability did not mean that he faced no rivalry at court. Probably the strongest opposition came from a somewhat unexpected corner: the young Setupati's mother, Kattaya Tevar's widow. While Dutch records refer to her just as the king's mother (*Theuvers moeder*), an English corruption in a translated Tamil text suggests her name was Chalabara Nachiar. During the VOC embassy to Ramnad in 1736, envoy Wouter Trek was approached by her several times. First, through an interpreter, she let Trek know that he could be assured of her respect, that from now on she regarded him as her eldest son, and that it was therefore his duty to strive for harmony between the Dutch and Ramnad. Later, Chalabara, who did not attend the audiences with the minor king, herself visited the VOC ambassador. She asked him not to be offended should he not be received with the proper respect, and urged him to consider her son's tender years.

It is likely the queen-mother was dismayed to see how *Daḷavāy* Vairavanatha dominated her son and she probably hoped the Dutch could counterbalance his power. Calling Trek her eldest son seems to have been yet another effort to create a bond through fictional kinship—this time between a Dutchman and the Setupati dynasty—in order to involve the VOC in her struggle against her opponents. Trek may not have been fully aware of it, but in a sense Sivakumara Setupati had become his younger brother, whom he was supposed to protect. In 1739, these family ties were apparently extended to the envoy's superiors when the Dutch governor of Ceylon, Gustaaf Willem van Imhoff, was invited as Sivakumara's "eldest brother" for the Setupati's wedding. However, Van Imhoff bluntly replied that the king should pay more respect to his Dutch brothers and comply with the VOC's demands.

Although Chalabara never became a serious threat to *Daḷavāy* Vairavanatha, she still maintained influence at court, as scattered references in VOC and local sources suggest. In 1739 she sent delegates and gifts to the Dutch governor at Colombo to apologise for Ramnad's repeated offences, and in 1746 a local VOC representative was received by the Setupati in the company of his mother. When in

no. 2599, ff. 2107-59, 2175-88, 2201v-2; no. 2621, ff. 2190-5, 2212; no. 2642, ff. 141v-2, 176v; no. 2666, f. 2357v: diaries of missions to Ramnad, May-July 1709, Feb.-May 1724, correspondence between VOC envoys at Ramnad and Colombo, June 1709, letters from Tuticorin to Colombo, from Colombo to Batavia and Nagapattinam, June 1732, Aug. 1735, Sept. 1736, June-July 1737, Feb. 1741, Nov. 1742, Jan.-Feb., Sept. 1743, Jan. 1744, Apr., June 1745, list of gifts distributed during mission to Ramnad, Feb. 1731, reports and diaries of missions to Ramnad, Nov. 1736, Apr.-July 1743, letter from Colombo to Ramnad court, Oct. 1742, correspondence between Colombo and Vairavanatha Servaikkarar, July-Aug. 1744, diary of visit to Rameshvaram ("Pamban") island, Aug. 1746; TNA, DR, no. 353, ff. 6, 91-5: letter from Tuticorin to Cochin, Jan. 1743, report of visit to Ramnad, Nov.-Dec. 1742; Raja Ram Rao, *Ramnad Manual*, 96, 236, 270; Seshadri, "The Sētupatis of Ramnad," 97. See also: Bes, "The Setupatis, the Dutch, and Other Bandits," 558-9, 564; idem, "Friendship as Long as the Sun and Moon Shine," 46-73. Temples were also sponsored by *Pradhāni* Ramalingam Pillai. See: Raja Ram Rao, *Ramnad Manual*, 81; Seshadri, "The Sētupatis of Ramnad," 97.

1742 a VOC interpreter was dispatched to Ramnad with a letter of protest because of another conflict, Chalabara openly sided with the Dutch. As the interpreter wrote, she ordered Vairavanatha to comply with the VOC's requests, but he did not take the slightest notice of her commands.

Nevertheless, around the same time several Dutch officials stated that Ramnad was ruled by courtiers but also by the queen-mother, and in 1744 she reportedly sanctioned the plundering of lands in Madurai by Ramnad's troops. Besides, during the Dutch mission in 1743, Chalabara received the most gifts after the king and the *daḷavāy*, more than the *pradhāni* (see table 12). Rather than her actual power, this perhaps reflected the VOC's wish to raise the prestige of this ally at court, but in any case no objections were made against this distribution. Further, both Dutch records and the Tamil *Māduraittala varalāṟu*, a history of Madurai town, claim that she was involved in selecting Rakka Tevar as Setupati in 1748. However, following this succession she does not appear in any source. After what seems to have been an insecure and isolated career, Chalabara must have either passed away or lost all power in the 1750s, when her son no longer sat on the throne.[122]

A few other illustrative careers must be briefly mentioned here. Muttu Vairavanatha Servaikkarar was succeeded as *daḷavāy* by Vellaiyan Servaikkarar ("Willejen Cheerwegaren"), who according to Dutch reports grew equally powerful. As Chapter 2 explains, he was instrumental in the dynastic successions in the late 1740s. He built temples and pilgrim rest houses and figures prominently in the abovementioned *Māduraittala varalāṟu* for his efforts to re-establish Madurai's Nayakas after their demise (see the Epilogue). One tradition has it that he, despite his non-royal status, forced subordinate chiefs to prostrate themselves before him, right where mud had been thrown on the ground. After his passing around 1760, his son also served as a general but most power now was held by a *pradhāni*, Damodaram Pillai, also discussed in the previous chapter.

122 NA, VOC, no. 2374, ff. 2052, 2059-60, 2073, 2075-6v; no. 2457, ff. 874-6v; no. 2459, ff. 1615-15v, 1618-18v, 1624, 1628; no. 2559, ff. 1463, 1491-2v, 1502v-3; no. 2599, ff. 2139, 2141v, 2149-9v, 2150v, 2160-2v; no. 2665, f. 2010v: diaries of missions to Ramnad with lists of gifts, Nov. 1736, June-July 1743, report on visit of Ramnad's envoys to Colombo, May-June 1739, Colombo proceedings (with correspondence with Sivakumara Muttu Vijaya Raghunatha Setupati), June 1739, correspondence between the VOC and the Setupati, July 1739, and between Tuticorin and Colombo, Oct. 1742, letter from Colombo to the Setupati and his mother, Oct. 1742, report of VOC's *arachi* (local captain) in Ramnad, Sept. 1746; TNA, DR, no. 334, f. 305; no. 353, ff. 89-94: (secret) reports of VOC's *arachi* in Ramnad, Dec. 1742, June 1744; DNA, DCGCC, no. 85, f. 116v: Colombo proceedings (with letter to the Setupati and his mother), Oct. 1742; BL/AAS, MG, no. 4, pt. 8: "A general history of the kings of Rama Naad or the Satoo-Putty Samastanum," f. 194; *Beknopte historie*, 94; Daniel Overbeek, *Memoir of Daniel Overbeek, Governor of Ceylon, 1742 – 1743, for His Successor Julius Stein van Gollenesse, 22 April 1743*, ed. K.D. Paranavitana (Colombo, 2009), 50, 97. See also: Bes, "The Setupatis, the Dutch, and Other Bandits," 540-1 (n. 1), 559-60, 568; idem, "Friendship as Long as the Sun and Moon Shine," 48, 50, 58-9, 66, 68, 70.

An important courtier in the 1730s and 1740s was an official the Dutch referred to as the "Moorish" Ravuttan Servaikkarar ("Rauten Cheerwegaren"), probably the captain of the Setupati's bodyguards. His name or title suggests that Muslims, too, could attain high military ranks in Ramnad. Another eminent man during this period was Kadamba Tevar, son of Muttu Vijaya Raghunatha Setupati. As governor of the town of Tiruppullani (between the capital and Kilakkarai), Kadamba did not occupy a particularly high post, but as "prince" (as the Dutch called him) he nevertheless proved influential when he solved several disputes between the court and the VOC.

Finally, Chalabara Nachiar was not the only prominent queen-mother in this kingdom. Already in 1685, the Dutch delegated a Brahmin envoy to present gifts not just to Kilavan Tevar and some of his courtiers but to his mother as well. And according to several local texts, the sister of the former Setupati Sella Tevar, Muttu Tiruvayi Nachiar, initially acted as regent when her minor son Muttu Ramalinga Tevar ascended the throne in 1763.[123]

This survey concludes with an analysis of the distribution of gifts during four VOC embassies to Ramnad between 1724 and 1743 (see table 12). These are the only missions from which lists of presents remain, while on the embassy in 1759 the VOC brought no gifts anyway—apart from a few minor "private presents" for the Setupati—to express its annoyance with Ramnad's violations of the treaties. Still, the available lists are worth analysing because they tie in with the developments discussed above.

In 1724, a *rāyasam*, and what the Dutch called a eunuch (*cappater*), a "distinguished councillor," and a "treasurer-cum-state cashier" (*schat bewaarder en rijxcassier*, perhaps *sarvādhikāri* or *pradhāni*), received the most gifts. The regent

[123] NA, VOC, no. 2185, f. 1172v; no. 2308, ff. 2060v-1, 2064v; no. 2374, ff. 2055v-6, 2060v-4v; no. 2492, f. 1471v; no. 2559, f. 1498; no. 2599, ff. 2108v, 2128-30v, 2136, 2148v-50v, 2152-3, 2192v-3v, 2196v; no. 2621, f. 2222; no. 2666, ff. 2215-15v, 2227-7v, 2235-7v; no. 2757, ff. 1470v, 1474-4v, 1477-8v; no. 2774, f. 1326; no. 2812, f. 230; no. 11306, f. 113: diaries and reports of missions to Ramnad, Jan. 1731, Nov. 1736, June-July 1743, correspondence between Tuticorin, Manapadu, and Colombo, Mar., May 1734, May 1742, Apr. 1743, May 1744, Jan., Apr.-June 1750, Aug. 1751, Jan. 1754, letters from Sivakumara Muttu Vijaya Raghunatha Setupati and Vellaiyan Servaikkarar to the VOC, Feb. 1740, Jan., Mar. 1746, description of the Nayakas of Madurai by Holst, 1762; TNA, DR, no. 334, ff. 305-6: secret report of VOC's *arachi* in Ramnad, June 1744; DNA, DCGCC, no. 29, f. 28v: Colombo proceedings, May 1685; BL/AAS, MG, no. 4, pt. 8: "A general history of the kings of Rama Naad or the Satoo-Putty Samastanum," ff. 194-7; Taylor, *Oriental Historical Manuscripts*, vol. II, Appendix, 52; Srinivasachari, *Ananda Ranga Pillai*, 115 (n. 17); Raja Ram Rao, *Ramnad Manual*, 82, 96, 110, 237-9, 239-40; Nelson, *The Madura Country*, vol. III, 292-4; Seshadri, "The Sētupatis of Ramnad," 101-2, 104-5, 115-17, 120-1, 126-8; Thiruvenkatachari, *The Setupatis of Ramnad*, 51-2; Kadhirvel, *A History of the Maravas*, 84, 86-7, 91-3, 99-100; Sathyanatha Aiyar, *History of the Nayaks of Madura*, 378-81; Burgess and Naṭēśa Śāstrī, *Tamil and Sanskrit Inscriptions*, 57. See also: Bes, "The Setupatis, the Dutch, and Other Bandits," 540-1 (n. 1), 559-60, 568; idem, "Friendship as Long as the Sun and Moon Shine," 58-9, 73, 83-5.

Table 12: Distribution of gifts among prominent courtiers during Dutch missions to Ramnad, in order of value, 1724-43.

1724	1731	1736	1743
king Muttu Vijaya Raghunatha	*king* Kattaya Tevar	*king* Sivakumara Muttu Vijaya Raghunatha	*king* Sivakumara Muttu Vijaya Raghunatha
rāyasam Adi Narayana	*lowlands regent* Labbai Nayinar Maraikkayar	*daḷavāy* Vairavanatha Servaikkarar	*daḷavāy* Vairavanatha Servaikkarar
eunuch Raja Gopala Ayyan	*pradhāni* Ramalingam Pillai	*pradhāni* Ramalingam Pillai	*queen-mother* Chalabara Nachiar
"distinguished councillor" Avirikutti (?) Ayyan	*daḷavāy* Vairavanatha Servaikkarar	*queen-mother* Chalabara Nachiar	*pradhāni* Ramalingam Pillai
sarvādhikāri / pradhāni (?) Subrahmanya Pillai	*rāyasam* Karuppa Pillai	*rāyasam* Karuppa Pillai	*rāyasam* Karuppa Pillai
lowlands regent Labbai Nayinar Maraikkayar		*royal guard's captain* Ravuttan Servaikkarar	
regent's brother Chinna Maraikkayar		*chancellor / eunuch* "Teijve Chidamanniaijer"	

Notes: the mission of 1724 was dispatched to Arantangi where the Setupati prepared for battle; for this year the differences between nos 2 to 5 are not entirely clear; in 1731 nos 4 and 5 received equally much; in 1736 nos 2 and 3 as well as nos 5 to 7 received equally much.
Sources: NA, VOC, no. 2015, ff. 573-4, 603-4, 643, 672, 677-9, 689-92; no. 2185, ff. 1170, 1186-7v; no. 2374, ff. 2060v, 2064v, 2075-6v; no. 2599, ff. 2160-2v.

of the lowlands, Labbai Nayinar Maraikkayar, and his brother were listed last. Less than a decade later, in 1731, the same regent was honoured with the most presents, followed by *Pradhāni* Ramalingam Pillai, whereas the *daḷavāy* and *rāyasam* now occupied the last places. After only five more years, this *daḷavāy*, Vairavanatha Servaikkarar, shared the highest position with the *pradhāni*, followed by Queen-Mother Chalabara Nachiar. The *rāyasam*, Karuppa Pillai, still came in last (together with two others), while the then regent of the lowlands was not even mentioned.

The distribution among the higher-ranking courtiers hardly changed in 1743, when only the positions of the *pradhāni* and the queen-mother were swapped.[124]

Thus, while at first no presents were allotted to the *daḷavāy* and the queen-mother, later people in these positions received valuable goods. Conversely, the *rāyasam* was initially honoured with many gifts, whereas his successor during the following embassies each time ranked low. The "regent of the lowlands" was even less sure of Dutch presents, consecutively receiving nearly the least of all, the most of all, and nothing at all. In addition, some people appear only once in the table, providing still more examples of officials whose functions were apparently hardly related to their actual influence.

These lists therefore show the rapidly changing balance of power in Ramnad during this quarter-century, as perceived by the Dutch. The court initially appears somewhat unstable here, as witnessed by Labbai Nayinar Maraikkayar's fast rise to prominence and equally quick fall. Subsequently, there seems to be a phase of consolidation, judging from the steadier careers of Vairavanatha Servaikkarar, Chalabara Nachiar, Ramalingam Pillai, and Karuppa Pillai, who each more or less maintained their place in Ramnad's political constellation.

The preceding overview of Ramnad's courtiers suggests that this kingdom, too, shared certain matters with the earlier discussed successor states, while other characteristics were less common. Elements found everywhere include the great power courtiers could acquire, the absence of a clear relationship between such influence and formal positions, combinations of different functions, the oscillating nature of some careers, the importance of family ties, and competition between individuals and factions.

Thus, between the 1680s and 1760s the court often was dominated by individual courtiers, including the *periya tambis*, Labbai Nayinar Maraikkayar, Vairavanatha Servaikkarar, perhaps Chalabara Nachiar, Vellaiyan Servaikkarar, and Damodaram Pillai. They all appeared to wield more influence than the Setupatis at some point, regardless of their official designations. Between them they occupied a wide range of functions, the first few men serving as "regents of the lowlands," followed by a *daḷavāy*, a queen-mother, another *daḷavāy*, and a *pradhāni*. Some engaged in different activities at the same time. The *periya tambis* and Labbai Nayinar Maraikkayar started as merchants and assumed administrative duties as revenue-farmers, sometimes also acting as councillors and ambassadors. In turn, Vairavanatha

[124] NA, VOC, no. 2015, ff. 573, 603-4, 643, 672, 677-9, 689-92; no. 2185, ff. 1170, 1186-7v; no. 2374, ff. 2060v, 2064v, 2075-6v; no. 2599, ff. 2160-2v; no. 2956, ff. 1234, 1237-7v: diaries and reports of missions to Ramnad, Feb.-May 1724, Jan. 1731, Nov. 1736, June 1759, lists of gifts distributed at VOC mission to Ramnad, May 1724, Feb. 1731, Nov. 1736, July 1743.

Servaikkarar held a military rank but also got involved in commercial enterprise. While the careers of the *daḷavāys* in particular were stable, the fortunes of the "regents of the lowlands" fluctuated wildly, eventually falling to such depths that they were forever excluded from official functions. Yet, a few decades later their sons were again accepted in administrative and diplomatic positions, illustrating the importance of family relations.

Other instances of the strong role of kinship include the prominence of Labbai Nayinar Maraikkayar's brother, Vellaiyan Servaikkarar's son, and royal family members Chalabara Nachiar and Kadamba Tevar. Possibly Kilavan Tevar's brother-in-law, *Daḷavāy* Vairavanatha Servaikkarar may have had family ties with the Setupati house, too. Further, rivalry between courtiers was ever present. The competition faced by "regents of the lowlands" from other officials and the opposition between the *daḷavāys* and Queen-Mother Chalabara Nachiar are cases in point. The nearly always tumultuous successions to the throne provide many other examples of rivalling court factions.

In certain respects, Ramnad's courtiers clearly differed from those in other kingdoms. First, the great variety of their backgrounds is striking. As at all courts, Brahmins and the ruling family's caste—here the Maravars—were well-represented. All or most *pradhānis* and *rāyasams* belonged to the former group, while *daḷavāys* chiefly were Maravars, at least in the eighteenth century. Additionally, however, several coastal Muslim merchants served as revenue-farmers and some grew very influential in this capacity. Besides, there were Muslims based at the capital, including Ravuttan Servaikkarar, captain of the royal guard, and Labbai Nayinar Maraikkayar junior, simply called "courtier" by the Dutch. Possibly related to this was the presence of eunuchs at court, which has been interpreted as a sign of Muslim influence,[125] although those mentioned in table 12 bear Hindu names. In any case, it appears Muslims played a more significant political role in Ramnad than in the other kingdoms, apart from Bhonsle-ruled Tanjavur.

Another aspect typical of Ramnad's courtiers was the regular occurrence of name-sharing and fictional kinship relations, employed between various parties. Several Muslim merchants-cum-revenue-farmers had permission to bear the Setupati dynasty's Hindu names, while a Dutch ambassador and his superior in Colombo were designated as sons by the queen-mother, making them elder brothers of the king. These were all efforts to bind powerful people in order to control them or win them over.[126]

[125] Shulman and Subrahmanyam, "Prince of Poets and Ports," 505.

[126] See Chapter 6 for an example concerning the Setupatis and the Nayakas of Madurai in the 1650s.

Finally, the position of queen-mothers in Ramnad stands out compared to other kingdoms. Both Dutch records and local texts refer to the influence some of them wielded, opposing other parties, manipulating successions, and dispatching embassies. With the exception of the five queens reigning over Ikkeri, Bhonsle Tanjavur, and Madurai, very few such references are found for Vijayanagara's other heirs. This difference may be related to the relatively great autonomy enjoyed by widows—and women in general—belonging to the caste of the Setupatis, the Maravars.[127]

Conclusions

Much of the information about the dozens of courtiers discussed in this chapter derives from VOC documents. These sources often portray them in a negative way: violently opposing rivals, dominating or even dethroning their kings, extorting gifts and cash from whomever they could, and generally creating political instability. A question that must be asked, therefore, is whether the Dutch may have misunderstood or exaggerated matters and how ill-informed and biased their accounts possibly are. To address that issue, this section first briefly considers the only embassy the VOC ever dispatched to the successor state of Mysore, ruled by the Wodeyar dynasty. The report of this mission, lasting from December 1680 to February 1681, serves as a valuable counterpoint because of its rather impartial description of Mysore's courtiers, with none of whom the Dutch had interacted before.

The VOC's ambassador Jan van Raasvelt was dispatched to Mysore's capital Srirangapatnam to secure an audience with King Chikkadevaraja Wodeyar (r. 1673-1704) and investigate commercial opportunities in this landlocked kingdom. Mysore had already invited the Dutch to do so in 1679, eager as it was to purchase war horses and elephants. Yet, the mission proved unsuccessful. Unfamiliar with the maritime world, the court was reluctant to follow Van Raasvelt's suggestion that Mysore representatives sail with the VOC to Ceylon to select elephants. Even the idea of boarding a ship made the king and courtiers uncomfortable and afraid of losing money.

The Dutch, in turn, were unwilling to venture into areas beyond their control, preferring to conduct trade from their factory at the port of Kannur (Cannanore). Also, they suspected Chikkadevaraja was chiefly interested in receiving VOC delegations to enhance his prestige among other rulers. Moreover, it was impossible to deliver the hundreds of horses he so adamantly asked for. Consequently, Dutch-Wodeyar contacts evaporated soon and from the mid-1680s Mysore largely disappeared from the Company records.

127 For Maravar women, see: Thurston, *Castes and Tribes of Southern India*, vol. V, 39-40; Taylor, "Marava-Jathi-Vernanam," 354.

Nonetheless, Van Raasvelt's report is an exceptional description of an early modern south Indian court. For, unlike other accounts of Dutch embassies to Vijayanagara's heirs, it gives a rather positive impression of the king and his courtiers. Chikkadevaraja is portrayed as friendly and attentive, albeit slightly eccentric, and his officials as competent and courteous. Most powerful among the latter appears to have been the king's father-in-law and *Daḷavāy* (general) Kumarayya. The Dutch referred to him with the exalted term "governor-general," not used by them for any other courtier in the successor states. His influence is manifest in his prominent role during audiences, his physical proximity to Chikkadevaraja on these occasions, and his overall control of access to the king. Kumarayya's paramount position perhaps foreshadowed the great dominance of his Kalale family over Mysore as *daḷavāy*s in the early eighteenth century, discussed in this chapter's introduction.[128] Other important courtiers the Dutch envoy encountered were the *Rāyasam* Nagappayya (*secretaris* "Negapaja"), the king's brother-in-law Balayya ("Ballia"), and Doddayya ("Dordia"), Kumarayya's son or nephew, who replaced him when he was sent into battle against Madurai.[129]

Although Van Raasvelt spent a full month at Srirangapatnam and met all these courtiers several times, he did not observe friction among these men or between them and the king. Only the merchant Chikkanna Chetti, the middleman between the court and the ambassador, caused some misunderstanding and was strongly reprimanded by Balayya for his delaying tactics and begging for gifts. Other than that, the complaints and general derogatory tone so often found in VOC documents about dealings with south Indian courts—commonly criticising ignorant kings and sly officials—are lacking in this mission's diary. In brief, the Dutch depicted the Wodeyar court of the early 1680s as orderly, stable, and reasonable.[130]

128 The VOC report does not mention the *daḷavāy*'s name, but "governor-general" doubtlessly refers to Kumarayya, Mysore's then *daḷavāy*. For more information on him, see: Satyanarayana, *History of the Wodeyars of Mysore*, 91-2, 225-7; Hayavadana Rao, *History of Mysore*, vol. I, 226-34, 263-77, 291-8; Sampath, *Splendours of Royal Mysore*, 105-6; Wilks, *Historical Sketches of the South of India*, vol. I, 114-15.

129 Unlike some secondary literature, the Dutch refer to Doddayya as Kumarayya's son. In any case, the former seems to have permanently replaced the latter as *daḷavāy* in 1682. See: Satyanarayana, *History of the Wodeyars of Mysore*, 89, 91, 226-7; Hayavadana Rao, *History of Mysore*, vol. I, 296-9, 311, 332-3; Sampath, *Splendours of Royal Mysore*, 106; Mahalingam, *Mackenzie Manuscripts*, vol. II, 448-9; Wilks, *Historical Sketches of the South of India*, vol. I, 115-17.

130 For the diary of the VOC mission to Mysore, see NA, VOC, no. 8985, ff. 104-20. For Dutch-Wodeyar relations, see also: NA, VOC, no. 1355, f. 437; no. 1370, ff. 2086v, 2099-9v, 2272-3: correspondence between Cochin and Mysore, Feb.-Mar. 1681, letters from Cochin to Gentlemen XVII, Jan., Mar. 1681, contracts regarding trade to Mysore, June 1681; Coolhaas *et al.*, *Generale Missiven*, vol. IV, 456-7, 577, 702, 824; Colenbrander *et al.*, *Dagh-register gehouden int Casteel Batavia ... anno 1681* (Batavia/The Hague, 1919), 563, 707; Mailaparambil, "The VOC and the Prospects of Trade between Cannanore and Mysore," 211-20; s'Jacob, *De Nederlanders in Kerala*, 218.

Regardless of the question of whether it really was all that, Van Raasvelt's account suggests VOC ambassadors were not always entirely prejudiced against the courts they visited. Even when a mission failed, as happened in Mysore, the Dutch apparently reported about their host in positive terms if they believed they were treated appropriately. It seems therefore that, although VOC officials no doubt misunderstood or overstated certain matters, their reports on south India's court politics cannot be discredited as merely subjective and ignorant opinions. To a certain extent, these writings also reflect functionaries' efforts to explain events to their best ability and provide reliable information for their fellow Company men. The VOC records thus give a valuable impression of at least some aspects of courtiers' powers, despite the one-sided view we are left with due to the scarcity of other sources.

Comparing the findings in this chapter, one observes many similarities but also differences between kingdoms. The main common elements can be summarised as follows. By way of career moves and personal connections, all kinds of courtiers could become exceedingly powerful, but, by the same token, they could also fall from grace because of competition.[131] At each court, people from different backgrounds, including Brahmins and people of the same castes as the rulers, often occupied various positions—most notably military, administrative, mercantile, and diplomatic functions—consecutively or simultaneously. In many cases one's official designation (if any) only partially covered one's actual activities. A number of women contributed to this diversity. Indeed, instances of female power were found in each kingdom. The courts of Vijayanagara, Ikkeri, Nayaka- and Bhonsle-ruled Tanjavur, and Ramnad all included women with substantial influence, acting as governess, ambassadress, or queen-mother, while Ikkeri, Bhonsle-ruled Tanjavur, and Madurai had female rulers.[132]

Clearly, power could be held not only by occupants of the standard offices mentioned in secondary literature—like *pradhāni* (chief or financial minister), *daḷavāy* (general), and *rāyasam* (secretary)—but also by persons in many other functions, such as court merchant, provincial governor, revenue-farmer, and *qiladār* (fort-commander). People of sword, pen, and coin could all become influential. Members of the royal families regularly occupied such posts, too, and thus acquired power in addition to the status they naturally enjoyed because of their descent.

131 For similar conclusions on other pre-modern Eurasian courts, see: Duindam, "The Court as a Meeting Point," 83-5; Flatt, *The Courts of the Deccan Sultanates*.

132 For female power in Bhonsle-ruled Tanjavur, see also the references in Chapter 2 to Queen-Mother Dipamba Bai. For an analysis of Ikkeri's and Madurai's ruling queens, see Bes, "The Ambiguities of Female Rule in Nayaka South India." See also Howes, *The Courts of Pre-Colonial South India*, 142.

On the whole, however, positions bore limited relation to ancestry. There seems to be some correlation between Brahmins and the *pradhāni* office and between members of the kings' castes and the *daḷavāy* rank, but few functions were strictly reserved for persons from particular backgrounds. Still, Brahmins (of various communities) probably made up the single largest group with important offices. Acclaimed by Vijayanagara's Krishna Raya and often despised by the Dutch, they occupied all sorts of posts, from *pradhāni*, *daḷavāy*, and *rāyasam* to provincial governor, ambassador, revenue-farmer, and merchant.

Frequently, combinations of positions enabled courtiers to increase their influence. Generals governed provinces and conducted trade, finance ministers led military campaigns, and merchants became diplomats and revenue-farmers. Bringing pen, sword, and coin together, courtiers expanded their power base through personal connections, military support, and financial means. Relationships were forged with anyone sharing political interests, but networks often included relatives in particular. There are numerous examples of officials whose power derived from blood or marital ties with eminent families, sometimes even the royal houses.

Yet, apart from a few exceptional cases—like Tanjavur's *qiladār*s, Ramnad's *periya tambi*s, and Mysore's *daḷavāy*s—prominent functions did not turn into long-lasting hereditary offices, and were rarely held by the same family for more than two generations. Family bonds generally helped one acquire influence in general rather than specific posts.[133] All in all, it seems power was attained through access to anyone else with power—the ruler, courtiers, parties beyond the court and the kingdom, and so on—rather than specifically the ruler, despite his or her sovereign status.[134]

In each kingdom some courtiers grew so powerful that they came to dominate the court, including the monarch. Dutch records contain many references to functionaries thought to practically rule the state. They eliminated competitors, removed kings or queens, and even appropriated symbols of royalty, such as dynastic titles, courtly pomp, and praises in literature hardly different from glorifications of rulers. But this competition also made careers insecure. Other courtiers, other courts, and the king himself were all potential rivals and many officials lost their power quickly—sometimes to rise to prominence again later.[135]

[133] But see also Burling, *The Passage of Power*, 62-3.

[134] Access to the ruler in particular is generally considered to have been important for gaining influence at pre-modern Eurasian courts. See for instance Duindam, "The Court as a Meeting Point," 103-4.

[135] See also: Shulman, "On South Indian Bandits and Kings," 304-6; Heesterman, *The Inner Conflict of Tradition*, 148.

In addition to these similarities between all courts, certain distinctions can be perceived. These are mostly related to the backgrounds and connections of courtiers. To begin with, whereas in Vijayanagara, Ikkeri, Nayaka-ruled Tanjavur, and Madurai no or very few Muslims ever became influential, they held considerable and lasting power in Ramnad and Bhonsle-ruled Tanjavur. There, they occupied varied posts, like *qiladār*, "ordain-it-all," "state minister," provincial governor, and revenue-farmer, and in some cases acquired so much influence that they were thought to overshadow the entire court, including the king. It is not surprising that Muslims grew prominent in these two states, considering the Bhonsles' past as generals in the Deccan sultanates, and the importance of Ramnad's Muslim traders.

In Ramnad, courtiers had relatively diverse backgrounds, coming from Muslim communities, Brahmin groups, and the royal family's caste. Less variety was seemingly found in Vijayanagara, Madurai, and perhaps Ikkeri and Nayaka-ruled Tanjavur, where most functionaries appear to have been Brahmins or—as regular marriages between the royal houses and courtiers' families show—members of the dynasties' castes. In Bhonsle-ruled Tanjavur probably few or no such marital ties were forged, and functionaries seem to have belonged chiefly to Brahmin and Muslim communities rather than to the caste of the royal house. There was apparently a lack of court families with whom the Bhonsles could intermarry and a certain distance may have existed between this dynasty and the court, although it is unclear which was the cause and which the effect.

Besides, this kingdom stands out for its relative absence of violence and of rapid changes among officials—setting aside the atypical turmoil around 1740. Like the Bhonsle rulers themselves, several courtiers here managed to stay in office for comparatively long periods and many belonged to a small pool of prominent families. Madurai witnessed the same dominance of a limited number of families, but there politics appear to have been more volatile, possibly related to the unusual coexistence of two political centres. For decades these were the power bases of fiercely competing families, leading to instability and even deserting officials. Desertion seems to have been especially common between Madurai and Tanjavur. A considerable number of courtiers from the former kingdom sought asylum in the latter, perhaps because several of them, or their direct ancestors, had arrived from Tanjavur in the first place. Many defectors soon returned to Madurai to assume high offices again and relations between the two courts must have been close and competitive at the same time.

Further, in none of the kingdoms relations between courtiers appear to have been strongly determined by religious, ethnic, linguistic, or caste factors. Apart from the opposition of Telugu-speaking officials to the Tamil *Daḷavāy* Narasappa Ayyan in Madurai around 1700, nothing suggests these aspects generally played a significant role in either alliances or hostilities at any of the courts. Brahmins, members of the rulers' castes, and Muslims might all collaborate in the same faction. Indeed, antagonism could rise within each of these social or religious groups, as demonstrated by the competition among, for example, Brahmins in Madurai and Bhonsle-ruled Tanjavur, Islamic merchants in Ramnad, and extended royal families at each court. Also, there seem to be few or no instances of such communities acting collectively against a common opponent.[136] As said, factional divisions and networks rather coincided with mutual political and economic interests and close family ties. After all, these were among the most significant elements in the acquisition of power by courtiers.

Finally, one may ask what all these findings say more generally about (south) Indian courtiers over time. For the early modern period, we have seen that while various south Indian sources occasionally refer to the might of courtiers, usually merely hinting at it, European records in particular show how powerful some of them actually grew and what mechanisms were behind this. For earlier historical phases, external documents are extremely scarce, but Indian sources from those periods at times also suggest courtiers could become highly influential as they—like their early modern successors—combined various offices, used family connections, married into royal families, and so on.[137]

Therefore, in this respect, the courts of Vijayanagara and its heirs probably did not differ much from those preceding them. The frequency of courtiers dominating

[136] Court factions based on ethnic, religious, or linguistic factors did however occur in several neighbouring kingdoms. For the Deccan sultanates, see: Roy S. Fischel, *Local States in an Imperial World: Identity, Society and Politics in the Early Modern Deccan* (Edinburgh, 2020), especially ch. 3; Kruijtzer, *Xenophobia in Seventeenth-Century India*, chs 2, 6. For Nayaka-ruled Kandy, see: Dewaraja, *The Kandyan Kingdom*, for instance 43, 92, 110-11, 114; Michael Roberts, *Sinhala Consciousness in the Kandyan Period 1590s to 1815* (Colombo, 2003), for example 48-52.

[137] For conclusions on courtiers in early medieval India largely similar to the present work's findings, see Ali, *Courtly Culture and Political Life*, 264-5. For glimpses of powerful courtiers under the Chalukyas of Kalyana, Hoysalas, Kakatiyas, Yadavas, Cholas, and Pandyas, see: Mahalingam, *South Indian Polity*, 48, 96, 105, 109-10, 113, 115-17, 122-3, 134; Nilakanta Sastri, "The Chāḷukyas of Kalyāṇi," 388-92, 395-8; Basava Raja, "The Central Government under the Chālukyas of Kalyāṇa," 98-100, 103-5; idem, "Qualifications of Ministers under Hoysaḷas," in B. Sheik Ali (ed.), *The Hoysaḷa Dynasty* (Mysore, 1972), 142-9; William Coelho, *The Hoysaḷa Vaṁśa* (Bombay, 1950), 97-106, 252, 266-7; Daud Ali, "Between Market and Court: The Careers of Two Courtier-Merchants in the Twelfth-Century Deccan," *Journal of the Economic and Social History of the Orient* 52, 4-5 (2009); Venkataramanayya and Somasekhara Sarma, "The Kākatīyas of Warangal," 596-7, 618-19, 641, 662-4; Talbot, *Precolonial India in Practice*, 159; A.V. Narasimha Murthy, *The Sevunas of Devagiri* (Mysore, 1971), 146-50; Altekar, "The Yādavas of Seuṇadeśa," 559-60; Veluthat, *The Political Structure of Early Medieval South India*, 109; Whitney Cox, *Politics, Kingship, and Poetry in Medieval South India: Moonset on Sunrise Mountain* (Cambridge, 2016), 167-70, 182-8; K.A. Nilakanta Sastri, *The Cōḷas* (Madras, 1935-7), vol. I, 279, vol. II, pt. I, 58-60, 89-92, 101-9, 222; idem, *The Pāṇḍyan Kingdom: From the Earliest Times to the Sixteenth Century* (London, 1929), 154; Karashima, *A Concise History of South India*, 143-4.

courts, the strategies they employed to this end, and the resultant fierce competition amongst them—it is likely that these aspects of court politics remained largely the same in the course of time (even though the arrival of European powers no doubt enhanced the opportunities of certain south Indian courtiers). If correct, this assumption has significant consequences for the historiography on courts predating the early modern period. The power of courtiers in Vijayanagara's predecessors would have been far greater than indicated by the available sources.

All facets of court politics considered in this chapter had strong repercussions on the position of the king in Vijayanagara and its successors. Of course, as Indian treatises on statecraft declare, the monarch embodied the kingdom's sovereignty and served as its foundation. The fact that at the courts under study no rulers were removed without being replaced more or less immediately demonstrates their essential role. After all, the king ranked first among the kingdom's seven limbs, coming before the minister. Further, the advice of political discourses that kings delegate their power and duties to courtiers was certainly followed, as illustrated by the efforts of Tanjavur's ruler Pratapasimha to find new functionaries after he eliminated the Shetke brothers. As the Dutch reported, while this search lasted he had to govern the kingdom himself, which he apparently deemed undesirable.

But as Indian treatises also warn, courtiers were prone to usurping the monarch's power rather than simply executing it in his name. That this was indeed a real danger is shown in this chapter by many such cases. These make clear that rulers were never assured of effective power, and in fact their influence fluctuated as much as that of courtiers. The complaint of Vijayanagara's Emperor Krishna Raya in the *Rāyavācakamu* about being dominated and ignored by his officials—whether it concerned his court or that of Madurai, where the text was composed—must have been shared by many of the kings of Vijayanagara's heirs.

Thus, despite his sovereignty, exalted descent, semi-divine status, and all other attributes of kingship, the monarch in Vijayanagara and its successor states was in many ways just one of the courtiers—or rather, just one of the contenders for power in the political arena that was the court.[138] Just as no court office granted actual political influence, so even the throne did not guarantee a powerful position, since this always depended on other parties. In all states, however, courtiers, although influential as a group, seldom operated in harmony and were usually divided. As

[138] For courts all over pre-modern Eurasia as arenas for power competition—played out in three partly overlapping hierarchies based on formal ranking, membership of decision-making bodies, and access to the monarch—see Duindam, "The Court as a Meeting Point," 100-14. Based on the available sources, it seems difficult to clearly identify and distinguish between these three domains at the south Indian courts under study.

shown by the VOC's comment on the Madurai court cited in this chapter's introduction, kings tried to benefit from the disagreements and jealousies among officials, playing them off against each other, thereby securing their own position.

Some rulers were much stronger than others. Several kings wielded concrete power and did not hesitate to rid themselves of threatening functionaries, whereas other monarchs lacked any authority, being barely tolerated by their ministers, their reigns often ending violently. In sum, the ruler's effective might was based on both his own capacities and the influence of others. One can therefore conclude that royal power in Vijayanagara and its heirs was largely shaped by the same factors that determined the powers of courtiers: personal ambitions and skills, connections within and outside the court, financial and other resources, and, of course, fate.

Obviously, kings differed from courtiers in certain other respects. Court politics were not all about plain ambitions and raw power. Just as the distribution of the VOC's gifts reflected the power balance between the court's officials, it also demonstrated the monarch's exceptional position. The Dutch always presented many more gifts to rulers than to courtiers, regardless of their effective power. The following chapter considers one of the aspects of court politics in which the king, or queen, occupied an exceptional place: court protocol.

CHAPTER 4

Court Protocol and Insults

Around early September 1674, when Madurai had eliminated Tanjavur's Nayaka dynasty and temporarily occupied the kingdom, this invader also threatened the Dutch settlement at Nagapattinam. Madurai's *Daḷavāy* (general) and regional Governor Kavita Nayaka appeared with 1,400 horsemen and 3,500 foot soldiers on the outskirts of the port. VOC records do not mention the *daḷavāy*'s motives for this siege, but his goal probably was to make the Company accept a new trade agreement more favourable to Madurai than the earlier treaty had been to Tanjavur's Nayakas.

With fewer troops at his disposal, the Dutch military commander, Lieutenant Davidt Butler, had received strict orders from his superiors not to move beyond the confines of Nagapattinam and just defend it from within its enclosure. But Butler, said to have fought "among the Muscovites," was not impressed by Madurai's army and ignored the instructions. Armed with a gun, a double-edged stick (*pedarm*), and a short spear, he stormed towards the approaching enemy. In no time, he mowed down nine of Madurai's "bravest assailants," while his thirty or so followers caused several dozen casualties, including the *daḷavāy*'s brother. Although these few Dutch soldiers were rapidly closed in by their opponents and some of them fell, they continued to offer fierce resistance. This, and advancing VOC reinforcements, so the Dutch wrote, caused panic among Madurai's forces, who quickly withdrew and made no further attempt to attack Nagapattinam.

In fact, *Daḷavāy* Kavita—brother-in-law of Madurai's king and considered the kingdom's most powerful person—visited the port soon after to settle the conflict with the VOC. But, although the Dutch thus won this confrontation, commander Butler had not survived it. Subsequently, however, an exceptional south Indian honour befell the dead VOC lieutenant. Despite their hasty retreat, the Madurai troops had taken the trouble to sever Butler's head and take it with them, while leaving some of their own killed and wounded men behind on the battlefield. As the Dutch were later notified by Kavita's envoy, Butler's head was shown to the *daḷavāy*, who wished to see the face of such a valiant warrior. Kavita next ordered the head to be embalmed and perfumed with incense, after which it was wrapped in silk and returned to the Dutch with great reverence, accompanied by drummers and horn-blowers.[1]

[1] NA, VOC, no. 1298, ff. 389v-90, 400-1: letter from Nagapattinam to Batavia, Sept. 1674.

This event demonstrates two matters. First, it shows the great value attached to protocol and honour in south India. The *daḷavāy*'s desire to see a dead but highly admired enemy, the hazardous effort to secure his head, and the extensive ritual to pay respect to it—these all signified the importance of marks of distinction. Second, this occasion indicates that foreigners could be part of south India's systems of protocol and honour. The fact Butler was a Dutchman was no reason for Kavita to deny him the deference and ceremonial due to great warriors of Indian origin. Also, the ritual transfer of Butler's head to the VOC suggests that the Dutch were supposed to understand the value of this ceremony. In south India, severing the head of one's enemy was a widespread custom, performed to manifest one's military and political power.[2] It therefore seems that Madurai's seizure of Butler's head was also meant as an act of triumph over this fearful adversary. Yet, at the same time, such a great soldier evidently deserved to be honoured, even if he was European.

Given their significance, the central question of this chapter is how court protocol and related aspects of honour reflected and shaped other elements of court politics. Protocol and honour can be regarded as symbolic expressions of establishing, confirming, altering, or ending relationships between rulers, courtiers, and others with political power.[3] Hence, protocol and honour often were manifestations of matters discussed in the other chapters: royal legitimation practices, power struggles at court, and inter-state relations. Indeed, protocol could display nuances not expressed in other ways, like subdued tensions, private preferences, and unuttered grievances. But it could also influence political developments and personal contacts, for better or for worse. For instance, diplomatic insults and humiliating ceremonies, intended primarily to indicate existing hierarchies

[2] Bayly, *Saints, Goddesses and Kings*, 53-4. The best-known case may be the beheading of Vijayanagara's ruler Rama Raya in 1565. See the section on Vijayanagara. Another example is found in a text saying that after Vijayanagara's courtier Gobburi Jagga Raya was defeated around 1616, his head was put in a palanquin and sent to his home. See Mahalingam, *Mackenzie Manuscripts*, vol. I, 280. In 1645, referring to a clash between Senji's Nayakas and General Tubaki Krishnappa Nayaka, the Dutch wrote that the heads of dozens of killed people were removed "as a sign of triumph." See Colenbrander *et al.*, *Dagh-register gehouden int Casteel Batavia ... anno 1644–1645* (The Hague, 1903), 334. The VOC reported in 1673 that the heads of Tanjavur's Vijayaraghava Nayaka and his son Mannarudeva were brought to Madurai's Chokkanatha Nayaka, maltreated, and shown to the imprisoned Setupati of Ramnad, probably Surya Tevar. See the section on Tanjavur's Nayakas in the Epilogue and Narayana Rao, Shulman, and Subrahmanyam, *Symbols of Substance*, 311. For other instances, see: Taylor, *Oriental Historical Manuscripts*, vol. II, 173; Nilakanta Sastri and Venkataramanayya, *Further Sources of Vijayanagara History*, vol. III, 86; Jeyaraj and Young, *Hindu-Christian Epistolary Self-Disclosures*, 265; Talbot, *Precolonial India in Practice*, 146; Narayana Rao, Shulman, and Subrahmanyam, *Symbols of Substance*, 77-8; Dodamani, *Gaṅgādevī's Madhurāvijayaṁ*, 20-1; BL/AAS, MG, no. 4, pt. 8: "A general history of the kings of Rama Naad or the Satoo-Putty Samastanum," f. 183.

[3] See also Duindam, "The Court as a Meeting Point," 87-9.

or discordance, could trigger or prolong conflicts or even lead to escalations. Considering this aspect of protocol, the present chapter aims at providing a view of courts that complements the findings in other chapters.

There are few or no studies of court protocol and insults in the successor states, but some historians have considered these matters for Vijayanagara. They point to the significant role diplomatic humiliation played in the empire's relations with the Deccan sultanates, but leave open the question of whether such breaching of protocol generated or reflected conflicts.[4] This chapter argues that, at the courts of Vijayanagara's heirs, insults were mostly expressions rather than causes of political tensions.

Below follows first an overview of sources for the study of protocol and honour in Vijayanagara and its successors. Based on south Indian texts, this section then discusses various elements of south Indian court ceremonial and the purposes these served. The chapter's central sections deal with the individual courts and examine local manifestations of protocol—which either adhered to or breached the required procedures—analysing what these signified and how they were related to political developments and interactions. This part contains only a selection of what the various sources have to offer, covering recurring and therefore typical situations as well as remarkable single occasions. The chapter's conclusion compares the courts and looks for general patterns.

South Indian sources like inscriptions and literary works seem to contain limited information on protocol in Vijayanagara's successor states. Local materials that do include references often pertain to Vijayanagara itself or earlier polities. But the VOC archives abound with descriptions of court ceremonial and the role of honour, especially in Vijayanagara's heirs. Apparently incorporated into south India's ritual world, the Dutch were frequently confronted with these aspects of court politics. In particular, reports of VOC embassies—but also letters exchanged with the courts, accounts of court missions to Dutch settlements, and many other VOC documents—extensively refer to welcoming rituals, procedures at royal audiences, gift-giving, seating arrangements, forms of address, diplomatic insults, and so on.

Obviously, these documents portray events as experienced and interpreted by "outsiders," but as Madurai's honouring of Davidt Butler's head suggests, the ceremonial practised at Indo-Dutch encounters was chiefly based on south Indian notions and customs. Except during meetings at large VOC establishments, such as Nagapattinam, Tuticorin, and Colombo, nothing of the described protocol indicates

4 See for instance: Subrahmanyam, *Courtly Encounters*, ch. 1, especially 102; Eaton and Wagoner, *Power, Memory, Architecture*, 135-6, 268-9, 299, 311-13.

it was partially adjusted to European conventions.[5] It is therefore likely that these Dutch accounts are illustrative of south Indian ceremonial in general, although one may wonder if the Dutch fully grasped all subtleties of the protocol and insults they encountered, such as the ambiguity of the treatment meted out to Butler. We return to this question at the end of the chapter.

Indian texts on specific dynasties, like chronicles and inscriptions, contain comparatively few explicit references to court protocol and honour, but several south Indian works relate to these matters in a more general way, directly or indirectly. One relevant political manual is the twelfth-century Sanskrit *Mānasollāsa*, composed by Someshvara III of the Chalukya dynasty of Kalyana, Vijayanagara's distant predecessor. It describes the way kings were to hold court, detailing the actions, positions, and roles of courtiers and visitors in the royal audience hall and how these reflected the bestowal of honours. The audience hall served both as symbol of the ruler's sovereignty and as the prime meeting place for participants in the kingdom's politics. One's status was manifested here in physical proximity to the king and permission to sit down. Located near the throne and allowed to sit—thus enjoying most prestige—were first princes, and next royal priests, the ruler's ministers and companions, and provincial and tributary lords or their representatives. Although the king's personal attendants, like whisk- and betel-bearers, his swordsmen or bodyguards, and palace women were situated closer, beside and behind him, they had to stand. Lower-ranked courtiers, placed further from the king than the abovementioned groups, were not permitted to sit either.

Honours and authority were also demonstrated in the audience hall through eloquent verbal interaction, bowing or prostration before the king, and exchanging presents. Such gifts could take the form of services, privileges, cash, or goods such as clothing, ornaments and jewellery, animals, land, and emblems. Services included symbolic duties—like attending to the king—performed by people not generally residing at court. All such protocol, described in the *Mānasollāsa* (III 1132-50, 1161, 1203-7, 1225-44, 1674-96) and other pre-Vijayanagara texts, served to express respect, loyalty, benevolence, recognition of hierarchies, and so on.[6]

Vijayanagara's best-known political discourse, the *rāja-nīti* ("king's policy") section in Krishna Raya's *Āmuktamālyada* (IV 204-85), contains little on protocol

[5] For similar conclusions with respect to Indo-Portuguese and Dutch-Mughal relations, see respectively: Melo, "Seeking Prestige and Survival"; Guido van Meersbergen, "The Diplomatic Repertoires of the East India Companies in Mughal South Asia, 1608-1717," *The Historical Journal* 62, 4 (2019); idem, "Kijken en bekeken worden: Een Nederlandse gezant in Delhi, 1677-1678," in Lodewijk Wagenaar (ed.), *Aan de overkant: Ontmoetingen in dienst van de VOC en WIC (1600-1800)* (Leiden, 2015), 205-11.

[6] Ali, *Courtly Culture and Political Life*, 111-32; Basava Raja, "The Central Government under the Chālukyas of Kalyāṇa," 95-6. See also Ronald Inden, "Hierarchies of Kings in Early Medieval India," *Contributions to Indian Sociology* 15, 1-2 (1981), 103-22.

and related aspects of honour.[7] But several other works from this period—such as the Kannada *Channabasava purāṇa* composed in 1585 by the Vijayanagara priest Virupaksha Pandita (VII 3-5, 8, 12-18)—describe seating positions in the audience hall. Largely agreeing with the *Mānasollāsa*, some of these make a further distinction between the king's left and right. While the former side was reserved for palace women according to a late-fifteenth-century text, the latter was often associated with the chief minister, subordinate rulers, officials, and famous scholars, possibly indicating a higher status.

Some works refer to royal gifts, which could be presented to everyone in the audience hall or to individuals, for instance a victorious general or an eloquent poet, and which comprised jewellery, garments, vehicles, lands, and *tāmbūla* (betel-leaves and areca-nuts). Other honours bestowed by kings included musical performances, elephant rides around town, permission to travel by palanquin, ministerial posts, retinues of personal attendants and military troops, and even marriages to princesses.[8]

Among texts of Vijayanagara's successor states, the early eighteenth-century Sanskrit *Śivatattva ratnākara* by Ikkeri's King Basavappa Nayaka I deals extensively with protocol. Having much in common with the *Mānasollāsa*, it discusses the distribution of people in the audience hall at length. The king on his throne formed the centre, in relation to which the status of others was indicated. Palace women were positioned closest to the king and in this text had permission to sit beside and behind him. Also near the throne, but standing, were the betel-bearer and swordsmen. Next came princes, royal priests, and ministers, followed by provincial governors and subordinate rulers, all sitting before the king or to his far left and right. At a further distance were lower officers, poets, musicians, magicians, and the like. An additional category consisted of rulers seeking refuge, who had to prostrate themselves before the king until being summoned to get up. All these groups were expected to be aware of their position in relation to the ruler and behave in a modest, dignified way (VII 1:6-71).

The *Śivatattva ratnākara* also treats the importance of gifts, deemed the best tools for kings to show benevolence and secure the loyalty of various people, including ministers, other servants, and potential allies. The text distinguishes several types of gifts, including lands and their produce, villages and ports, horses and

7 Narayana Rao, Shulman, and Subrahmanyam, "A New Imperial Idiom," 90-107; Krishna(deva) Raya, *Sri Krishna Deva Raya: Āmuktamālyada*, 313-36; Rangasvami Sarasvati, "Political Maxims of the Emperor-Poet," 64-77.

8 Dallapiccola and Kotraiah, *King, Court and Capital*, 39-41, 59-60, 145-6, 154; Virupaksha Pandita, "Channa-Basava Puráṇa of the Lingaits," ed. G. Würth, *Journal of the Bombay Branch of the Royal Asiatic Society* XXIV, VIII (1865), 128.

elephants, ornaments and jewellery, and royal privileges like the use of parasols and seats (V 12:76-98).[9]

The Sanskrit *Śukranīti*, possibly dating from the nineteenth century, underscores the ideas presented in earlier works. Although some details differ, once again the royal audience hall and the placement of various people around the king are extensively described. Further, it emphasises the value of kind speech, etiquette, and gifts, which all contribute to cordial relations—for instance between the king and his servants—while insults result in great hostility (I 217-50, 287-8, 353-63; V 7, 44-5, 47-8).[10]

Some other literary texts also refer to protocol and honour, although less explicitly. One example is the Tamil poem *Rāmappaiyaṉ ammāṉai*, which recounts the mid-seventeenth-century war between Madurai's General Ramappaiya and Ramnad's ruler Dalavay Setupati. This work points to specific moments at which honours were bestowed and gifts presented. These occasions can be classified as recognising someone's status and power, encouraging people to take certain action, commencing and ending missions, and beginning and concluding negotiations.[11]

Although the events in the *Rāmappaiyaṉ ammāṉai* mostly have military connotations, this categorisation can be applied more broadly to systems of honour and protocol at south Indian courts. Thus, together with the other discussed texts, this work suggests that many situations demanded ceremonial. Taking the form of gifts, rituals, rhetoric, or other manifestations, protocol was necessary whenever parties met or otherwise communicated in order to establish contacts, pay homage, confirm relationships, mark special moments, hold deliberations, ask favours, or express dissatisfaction.[12]

Given the similarities between the *Mānasollāsa, Śivatattva ratnākara, Śukranīti*, and other texts, the significance and nature of this protocol appear to have remained mostly unchanged during the existence of Vijayanagara and its heirs. Furthermore, the importance of protocol and honour meant that violations could have far-reaching consequences.

[9] Krishnamurthy, *Sivatattva Ratnākara of Keladi Basavaraja*, 49-50, 402-6. For suggestions that the *Sivatattva Ratnākara* was partly inspired by the *Mānasollāsa*, see, for instance, Krishnamurthy, *Sivatattva Ratnākara of Keladi Basavaraja*, 30, 32, 39, 47, 53, 66 (where *AC* refers to the *Abhilaṣitārtha cintāmaṇi*, as the *Mānasollāsa* is also known).

[10] Shukracharya, *The Śukranītiḥ*, 58-67, 76, 96-8, 566, 574-5.

[11] Price, *Kingship and Political Practice in Colonial India*, 19-25, especially 22.

[12] See also: Mahalingam, *South Indian Polity*, 57-62, 65, 75-7; Scharfe, *The State in Indian Tradition*, 86-7.

Vijayanagara

Sources on the Vijayanagara court refer to protocol and honour in several instances, all related to the above identified situations that require ceremonial. One early reference to the arrangement of people in the audience hall comes from the Timurid ambassador Kamaluddin Abd al-Razzaq Samarqandi. He briefly mentions that in 1442 Deva Raya II was seated amidst a crowd of courtiers, standing left and right of him in a circle, while the ambassador himself was honoured with a seat close to the emperor.

The Portuguese merchant Domingo Paes left a long description of Krishna Raya holding court around 1520, during the Navaratri festival. Beside the emperor sat what probably were close male relatives ("men who belong to his race"), including several fathers-in-law, who were local kings and chiefs themselves. Also near to the ruler, but standing, were personal attendants—holding his betel-leaves, sword, and other emblems—and Brahmin priests. Next came what Paes calls "captains" and "nobles," probably courtiers with military and administrative ranks. Others included soldiers and dancing women.[13] While this maybe was an uncommon audience, taking place during a festival, the distribution of people around the emperor largely agrees with notions found in political treatises. No doubt, in Krishna Raya's audience hall, too, closeness to the king and permission to sit served as symbols of prestige.

Both local and external sources mention other ceremonial occasions at the Vijayanagara court. During the reign of Achyuta Raya (1529-42), the Portuguese trader Fernão Nunes wrote that among the greatest honours the ruler could bestow on courtiers were presenting them with ornamented fans, jewellery, and scarves, and allowing them to kiss his feet. Several south Indian texts state how emperors and high ministers honoured servants, poets, and subordinate chiefs—including rulers of the empire's heirs—with gold, jewels, land, animals, clothes, umbrellas, palanquins, titles, and all sorts of privileges.

The Telugu poet Allasani Peddana is said to have been invited by Krishna Raya to sit together on the royal elephant. The emperor even personally carried a palanquin in which the poet was seated and, following an outstanding poetic improvisation, put a "hero's anklet" around his foot. According to the *Rāyavācakamu*, after an exceptionally rapid mobilisation of the imperial army, the courtier Appaji alias Saluva Timmarasu was awarded by Krishna Raya with the *saptānga* of honour, the

[13] Major, *India in the Fifteenth Century*, pt. I, 30-1; Sewell, *A Forgotten Empire*, 269-70; Rubiés, *Travel and Ethnology in the Renaissance*, 247. The *Rāyavācakamu* describes in detail who are present while Vira Narasimha (r. c. 1503-9) holds court, but omits to mention their spatial distribution and, therefore, who are most prominent. See Wagoner, *Tidings of the King*, 77-9, and this chapter's section on Madurai.

seven worthy gifts: cap, ornamental shirt, necklace, pearl earrings, golden-yellow shawl, fragrant musk, and *tāmbūla* (betel-leaves and areca-nuts).[14]

References to rulers presenting garments often denoted the *khil'at* ceremony, widely practised in the Islamic world and adopted by the Vijayanagara court. In this audience ritual, clothes, in particular long robes, served as the main presents to bind the donor (for instance a king or a chief) and the recipient in a reciprocal relationship. By accepting and wearing the dress, the latter attained honour while the former acquired recognition. In Vijayanagara such clothing came to take prominence over traditional audience gifts.[15]

Additionally, Vijayanagara's rulers gave presents to servants before military missions to encourage them and secure their loyalty, but also to demonstrate respect. One local work, included in the Mackenzie manuscript translations, describes in detail how Vijayanagara's Generalissimo Rama Raya honoured his commanders and troops with gifts just before the famed battle with the Deccan sultanates in 1565:

> ... he presented them with rich gifts & presents out of his jamdar-cana (wardrobe or treasury) of the most valuable cloths, silk & embroidered vests & jackets, atalash salas, & other costly stuffs with shawls of the various kinds called zaffaranee, lackee, goolabee & suffaid [different colours], printed chintzes of bunder & woollen cloths of various kinds as jancaroodee, sultanee, callapee, laharee & suffaid, wrought, embroidered & silk sashes & flowered hachadoms [silk cloths] & jewels, pearl toorayes [turban jewels] & chains, bracelets of precious stones & moohan-maala [necklaces], pattuks [gold necklaces with medals and jewellery] & various jewels of diamonds, emeralds, topazes, rubies, coral, onyx, pearl, goomakada & neelum [probably turquoises], with arms of all the various kinds of Hindoo construction ... [including shields, discuses, curved swords, sabres, clubs, bows

14 Sewell, *A Forgotten Empire*, 376; Krishnaswami Aiyangar, *Sources of Vijayanagar History*, 63, 66, 144, 152-3, 241-2; Nilakanta Sastri and Venkataramanayya, *Further Sources of Vijayanagara History*, vol. III, 103-4, 150-1; Narayana Rao and Shulman, *Classical Telugu Poetry*, 241-3; Narayana Rao, "Coconut and Honey," 160; Wagoner, *Tidings of the King*, 104-6 (see also 159); Mahalingam, *Mackenzie Manuscripts*, vol. I, 151, 166, 172-3; BL/AAS, MG, no. 11, pt. 12: "Kyfyat of Bellary," f. 86 (compiled at Bellary in 1801 by Mackenzie's assistant Borayya Kavali Venkata with information from "respectable native authority," see: f. 84; Cotton, Charpentier, and Johnston, *Catalogue of Manuscripts in European Languages*, vol. I, pt. II, 106-8). See also Allasani Peddana, *The Story of Manu*, xxv-vi, xxxvii.

15 Stewart Gordon, "A World of Investiture," in idem (ed.), *Robes and Honor: The Medieval World of Investiture* (New York, 2001); Phillip B. Wagoner, "'Sultan among Hindu Kings': Dress, Titles, and the Islamicization of Hindu Culture at Vijayanagara," *The Journal of Asian Studies* 55, 4 (1996), 866. For the adoption in south India of court culture from the Islamic world, see Chapter 5. For the *khil'at* ritual at both Muslim- and Hindu-ruled courts in late medieval and early modern India, see Stewart Gordon, "Robes of Honour: A 'Transactional' Kingly Ceremony," *The Indian Economic and Social History Review* 33, 3 (1996).

> and arrows, and iron chains]. Besides these, he distributed from his arsenal to the troops arms complete of the 32 known ayoodums [weapons]. He arranged them & recommended to the royal army courage, bravery, discretion, honor & fidelity, & settled annual & monthly allowances for their families.[16]

Although this account and several other mentioned texts date from long after the events they depict and may exaggerate or invent matters, they amply demonstrate the great value attached to honour, gifts, and ceremonial.

While such passages give an idea of the protocol to be observed, certain elements transpire especially clearly in cases where it was breached—deliberately or not—and where people were offended. Already for the first phase of Vijayanagara's Sangama dynasty, literary works refer to diplomatic insults, which often concerned the empire's intense and tumultuous relationship with the Bahmani sultanate. In his Persian *Tārīkh-i firishta* (early seventeenth century), the Bijapur chronicler Muhammad Qasim Firishta refers to earlier texts saying that during the reign of Bukka (c. 1355-77) political conflicts with the Bahmani rulers were expressed through ceremonial humiliations.[17] Around 1366 Bahmani envoys were reportedly dispatched to Vijayanagara with a draft on the empire's treasury, issued by the allegedly drunk Bahmani Sultan Muhammad I as a reward to musicians at his own court. In response to this offence, Bukka had the main Bahmani ambassador paraded on a donkey around the capital, after which he declared war.

About half a century later, another diplomatic insult intensified a conflict. Again according to Firishta, when Vijayanagara's Emperor Deva Raya I was forced to make peace with the Bahmanis following a war around 1406, he had to offer his daughter in marriage to Sultan Firuz. But after the latter had celebrated his wedding in the Vijayanagara capital, Deva Raya accompanied him only a few miles out of the city. This greatly offended Firuz and led to further discord, which was probably the reason that in 1423 Crown Prince Deva Raya II escorted the Bahmani Sultan Ahmad I all the way to Vijayanagara's border following peace negotiations at the imperial capital. However, when in the early sixteenth century Krishna Raya conquered Gulbarga, former capital of the now defunct Bahmani sultanate, he proclaimed a son of the last sultan the new Bahmani ruler and then had himself referred to as

[16] BL/AAS, MG, no. 3, pt. 5: "Ram-Rajah Cheritra," f. 172 (original spelling retained). See ff. 176-8, 190 for gifts by Rama Raya to his women, other relatives, and envoys. See also Nilakanta Sastri and Venkataramanayya, *Further Sources of Vijayanagara History*, vol. III, 214, 218, 236. For this text, see also below.

[17] For recent discussions of Firishta and his work, see: Subrahmanyam, *Courtly Encounters*, 45-56, 70-1, 78-80; Rubiés, *Travel and Ethnology in the Renaissance*, 279-85; Manan Ahmed Asif, *The Loss of Hindustan: The Invention of India* (Cambridge (MA)/London, 2020).

"establisher of Yavana [Muslim] rule." Thus, Krishna Raya both declared his control over the region and humiliated Vijayanagara's erstwhile opponents.[18]

The often deliberate breaches of protocol played an equally influential role in the relations Vijayanagara's Tuluva and Aravidu houses maintained with the Bahmanis' successors, in particular Bijapur and Ahmadnagar. As Fernão Nunes relates, after Krishna Raya won a battle against Bijapur in 1520, he disgraced an ambassador sent by that sultanate to claim back the lost territories. First, the emperor made the envoy wait for a month before granting him an audience. Next, Krishna Raya let him know he was willing to comply with Bijapur's requests, provided its sultan, Ismail Adil Shah, came to Vijayanagara to kiss the emperor's foot. While this was an honour to imperial courtiers, it would be an unacceptable submission for sovereign rulers. Informed of Krishna Raya's condition, Ismail diplomatically replied he would happily comply with it, were it not for the fact he could not legally enter another ruler's realm. In response, Krishna Raya suggested to meet at the common border to solve this problem and straightaway marched to Bijapur to confront the sultan. Showing the strong value attached to protocol—or, in this case, the great importance of avoiding a dishonourable ritual—Ismail chose to flee and leave his capital undefended rather than be forced to kiss the emperor's foot. As Nunes' account concludes, only when Krishna Raya withdrew his army did the sultan return home. But although Ismail had managed to evade a most embarrassing encounter, he was still deeply disgraced.[19]

Perhaps inspired by Krishna Raya, his military commander and son-in-law Rama Raya continued this policy of insult when he assumed power. He disgraced the Deccan sultans and their envoys time and again, thereby increasing or even creating tensions. Probably because of their far-reaching consequences, Rama Raya's diplomatic offences figure in many seventeenth- and eighteenth-century texts, in such diverse languages as Kannada, Telugu, Persian, Marathi, and Dakhani.

Matters were still very positive when in the late 1550s Rama Raya and Bijapur's Ali Adil Shah cemented their mutual interests with the help of ceremonial. According to both Firishta and the Bijapur courtier Rafi al-Din Ibrahim Shirazi in his Persian chronicle *Tazkirat al-mulūk* (early seventeenth century), during

[18] Muhammad Qasim Firishta, *Ferishta's History of the Dekkan from the First Mahummedan Conquests …*, ed. Jonathan Scott (Shrewsbury, 1794), vol. I, 23-4, 85-8, 101-2; Sewell, *A Forgotten Empire*, 32-9, 57-62, 69-70; Rāma Sharma, *The History of the Vijayanagar Empire*, vol. I, 28-30, 49-50, 56-7; Subrahmanyam, *Courtly Encounters*, 78; Nilakanta Sastri, *A History of South India*, 244, 247-9; Eaton, *India in the Persianate Age*, 163.

[19] Richard M. Eaton, "'Kiss My Foot,' Said the King: Firearms, Diplomacy, and the Battle for Raichur, 1520," *Modern Asian Studies* 43, 1 (2009), 306-8; Sewell, *A Forgotten Empire*, 349-58; Eaton and Wagoner, *Power, Memory, Architecture*, 268, 311-13; Rāma Sharma, *The History of the Vijayanagar Empire*, vol. I, 141-2.

a visit by the Bijapur sultan to Vijayanagara to condole with Rama Raya on the death of a son, he was received with great honours. Banquets were held, gifts were exchanged, and Ali was even admitted to the imperial harem and referred to by Rama Raya's wife as her own son. But, in a repetition of the early 1400s, when the sultan departed he was not accompanied back far enough by his host, resulting in strong and lasting bitterness—which certainly did not fade when later Rama Raya did not permit Ali's officers to sit down in his presence.

In the following years, Rama Raya kept on employing humiliating protocol, sometimes leading to escalations of mutual insults. After Rama Raya had conquered Ahmadnagar's capital in 1561, Firishta informs us, he let Sultan Husain Nizam Shah know that one of the conditions for peace was that Husain visit him and eat *pāṇ* (betel-leaf and areca-nut) from his hand. Since the latter had no choice but to obey, Rama Raya thus made the Ahmadnagar sultan kiss his hand as it were. Utterly disgraced, Husain immediately washed his hands in water after this encounter, an offence that Rama Raya returned by washing his hands as well.

Bijapur's chroniclers may have overstated these dishonourable practices of their lords' opponents, but even some sources from Vijayanagara itself mention its degrading conduct. The Telugu work *Narasabhūpālīyamu*, by the court poet Bhattu Murti, states that after Rama Raya's brother Venkatadri defeated Bijapur, he forced the sultan to prostrate before him and with his head touch his feet before peace would be restored.[20]

A last example of Rama Raya's politics of humiliation concerns the visit of a Bijapur envoy to Vijayanagara shortly before 1565. South Indian texts contain various accounts of this event. One version, recorded by Mackenzie's assistants in the capital region, runs thus:

> ... towards the conclusion of his reign, he [Rama Raya] was persuaded by some worthless wretches to provoke the resentment of all the Mussulman [Muslim] princes by some acts highly insulting to their religion. At last, a certain Mahaldar [*mahaldār*, envoy] coming to the Rajah on behalf of Aly Adil Shah Badsha of Beejapore [Sultan Ali Adil Shah of Bijapur] on some particular occasion, he happened to encounter near the public hall of audience a

[20] Subrahmanyam, *Courtly Encounters*, 77-87; Eaton and Wagoner, *Power, Memory, Architecture*, 135-6, 159 (n. 52), 268-9, 285 (n. 75), 299; Eaton, "'Kiss My Foot'," 308-9; idem, *A Social History of the Deccan*, 96-7; Rafi al-Din Ibrahim Shirazi, "A Portrayal of Vijayanagar by Rafiuddin Shirazi in Tadhkirattul Muluk," ed. Parveen Rukhsana, in P. Shanmugam and Srinivasan Srinivasan (eds), *Recent Advances in Vijayanagara Studies* (Chennai, 2006), 236-7; Rafi al-Din Ibrahim Shirazi, "History of Vijayanagara in *Tazkiratul Muluk* of Rafiuddin Shirazi," ed. Abdul Gani Imaratwale, in Shrinivas Ritti and Y. Subbarayalu (eds), *Vijayanagara and Kṛṣṇadēvarāya* (New Delhi/Bangalore, 2010), 106-7; Krishnaswami Aiyangar, *Sources of Vijayanagar History*, 224-5; Stein, *Vijayanagara*, 115-18; Rāma Sharma, *The History of the Vijayanagar Empire*, vol. I, 209-12; Nilakanta Sastri, *A History of South India*, 291-2.

> herd of swine, which were brought to be given to some Dommary [Domra caste] players (actors).[21] These creatures being held in abhorrence by Mussulmen, the Mahalldar, as he could not avoid them at the time, immediately shut his eyes to avoid the hateful sight & asked pardon of his God for his ... offence. Rama Rayaloo [Rama Raya], seeing what passed, rediculed him for his behaviour, [and] observed jestingly that the Mussulmen need not despise the food of the lower caste of Hindoos when they [Muslims] were wont to eat the fowls, which fed upon seeds taken out of the excrement of men & beasts.
>
> Not satisfied with these indiscreet words, he [Rama Raya] caused a number of hogs [pigs reared for meat] to be shut up in one certain place where they were plentifully fed with Joaree [*juār*, millet]. On the following day, he caused a number of fowls to be sent into the same place & introduced the Mussulman officer to behold them feeding on the seeds in the hog's dung, in evidence of what he had said, & rediculed him publicly & all of his religion. The Mahalldar lamented the affront & insult ... offered to his religion, & returning to his master [the Bijapur sultan], acquainted him of the affront put upon him by the Carnatic [Karnataka, Vijayanagara] people & urged him to punish Rama Rajah for the insult ...[22]

A largely similar story is found in the Kannada and Marathi versions of the better-known *Rāmarājana bakhairu*. All variations of the account continue by relating how after the humiliation of the Bijapur envoy the Deccan sultans united to attack Vijayanagara, leading to the killing of Rama Raya and the sacking of the capital in 1565.[23]

Other texts link this attack to the disgraceful treatment of a thirsty Muslim traveller—variously called "fakir" or "sayyid"—who arrived in Vijayanagara city from Delhi. Either because he used a covered city well, dived into a lake, or put his finger in a bowl with buttermilk, Rama Raya had his finger cut off or made him eat mutton secretly mixed with pork. Indeed, had not the sultans of Bijapur, Golkonda, and Ahmadnagar begged for his life, the Muslim traveller would have been beheaded.

21 Members of the low-status Domra caste were often musicians. See Henry Yule and A.C. Burnell, *Hobson-Jobson: The Anglo-Indian Dictionary* (London, 1886), 322.

22 BL/AAS, MG, no. 11, pt. 3b: "History of the kings of Beejanagur & Anagoondy," ff. 19-20 (original spelling retained) (see also Mackenzie, "History of the Kings of Veejanagur").

23 For a discussion of several of these versions (in Kannada, Marathi, and English), see: Guha, "The Frontiers of Memory," 283-5; idem, *History and Collective Memory in South Asia*, 148-50. See also: Subrahmanyam, *Courtly Encounters*, 81-2; Cotton, Charpentier, and Johnston, *Catalogue of Manuscripts in European Languages*, vol. I, pt. II, 36-9; Chekuri, "Between Family and Empire," 153-60. For English translations of (parts of) the Marathi and Kannada versions, see: BL/AAS, MG, no. 3, pt. 5: "Ram-Rajah Cheritra" (from Kannada and Marathi, see f. 195); Nilakanta Sastri and Venkataramanayya, *Further Sources of Vijayanagara History*, vol. III, 204-42 (from Kannada); Sumit Guha, "Literary Tropes and Historical Settings: A Study from Southern India," in Rajat Datta (ed.), *Rethinking a Millennium: Perspectives on Indian History from the Eighth to the Eighteenth Century: Essays for Harbans Mukhia* (Delhi, 2008), 110-18 (from Marathi and Kannada).

Yet another work has it that Rama Raya caused the war with the sultanates by "affronting their religion by killing a hog on the tomb of a Mussulman."[24]

All discussed texts likely date from long after Rama Raya's reign and contain historical inaccuracies, like portraying the Deccan sultans as servants in Vijayanagara or involving Delhi's Mughals in the battle of 1565. Still, together with Firishta's and Shirazi's writings, they suggest that, among other causes, honour and protocolar insults were seen as elemental factors in the growing tension between Rama Raya and the sultans, resulting in the destruction of Vijayanagara city and Rama Raya's decapitation—the latter probably by Ahmadnagar's greatly dishonoured Sultan Husain Nizam Shah himself.

Indeed, even after Rama Raya's death, protocol, humiliating or not, remained important with respect to his body. Reminding us of the Dutch Lieutenant Davidt Butler, Ikkeri's chronicle *Keḷadinṛpa vijayam* claims that Rama Raya's head was sent to the holy city of Benares on the Ganga River, while according to another tradition it was brought to Ahmadnagar and regularly displayed as a trophy, covered with oil and red pigment.[25]

Such disgrace did not befall Europeans visiting the Vijayanagara court, but those contacts, too, were governed by both the observance and breaching of protocol. During the sixteenth and early seventeenth centuries, several embassies were dispatched by the Portuguese and the Jesuits to the Tuluva and Aravidu emperors and vice versa. Reports by the former two parties about these Indo-European encounters refer to the same diplomatic ceremonial as was observed between south Indian parties. Thus, Portuguese envoys to Krishna Raya (r. c. 1509-29) and Venkata (r. 1585-1614) were welcomed with all due respect, being awaited at the capital by high officials, escorted by elephants, camels, horses, and kettle-drummers, and lodged in comfortable buildings.

It has been argued that since a king's body was considered sacred, very few people were permitted to touch or even come near him.[26] But at audiences with the Vijayanagara emperors, the Portuguese were permitted to approach them very closely and sit down. As Domingo Paes wrote, Krishna Raya even touched his Portuguese visitors, thereby greatly honouring them. Presents to the Portuguese

[24] BL/AAS, MG, no. 10, pt. 4b: "Bijanagar," ff. 69-70; no. 10, pt. 5: "Traditionary notices of the history of the country," ff. 78-9 (collected at Harihara in 1800); MT, class I, no. 18: "The Keefeyet of Panoocundah," ff. 52-3; MG, no. 3, pt. 1: "Sketch of the general history of the peninsula," f. 48; Guha, "The Frontiers of Memory," 281-2.

[25] Nilakanta Sastri and Venkataramanayya, *Further Sources of Vijayanagara History*, vol. III, 243; Eaton and Wagoner, *Power, Memory, Architecture*, 269, 285 (n. 77).

[26] Amin Jaffer, "Diplomatic Encounters: Europe and South Asia," in Anna Jackson and Amin Jaffer, *Encounters: The Meeting of Asia and Europe 1500–1800* (London, 2004), 78.

included jewellery, lands, royal-style garments, cloths, food, and other marks of distinction. Vira Narasimha (r. c. 1503-9) sent gifts not only to the Portuguese in Goa but also to the royal family in Portugal itself, proposing (in vain) that the Portuguese prince marry the emperor's only sister to strengthen the bond. In the mid-1540s, Rama Raya paid homage to the Portuguese by delegating a very high military commander as ambassador, together with an extensive retinue of courtiers and servants.

The Portuguese returned all these honours largely in a similar manner. They welcomed Vijayanagara's envoys with cannon fire, escorts, and music, placed them in chairs on canopied platforms, held pompous parties, and presented them and the emperors with gifts like horses, cloths, and exotic musical instruments. Luso-Vijayanagara diplomacy was not always cordial, however. Audiences to Portuguese ambassadors were sometimes considerably delayed or the emperor would simply ignore them. During a mission in 1510, the Franciscan Friar Luís do Salvador was entertained by prominent courtiers but is thought not to have been received by Emperor Krishna Raya himself.

Around the turn of the seventeenth century, during the reign of Venkata, the Jesuits maintained close relations with the court and encountered similar protocol. In 1598 Simão de Sa and Francesco Ricio visited the capital Chandragiri and were awaited by prominent courtiers, including a nephew of the emperor's brother-in-law Gobburi Oba Raya, together with elephants and horses. The emperor and Oba Raya himself received the Jesuits with great kindness, giving them silk cloths, land (to build a church on), and a golden palanquin—the last present no doubt a very high mark of distinction. In 1604 the Jesuit Alberto Laerzio was welcomed at the capital Vellore by Venkata in much the same way, being lodged in a house adjacent to the palace, treated with exquisite food, permitted to sit down right beside the imperial throne, and sent away with great honours.

The Flemish diamond trader Jaques de Coutre visited the court in the early 1610s. As he wrote, he presented the emperor—most likely still Venkata—with coral and enjoyed a long, informal conversation with him. Later, the Fleming met with what he called the ruler's cousin or nephew "Gopol Raya," probably Gobburi Oba Raya. De Coutre received from him a long tunic and high cap, both worked with gold, and was told that these royal garments were the highest honour that could be bestowed on someone. Continuing the reverence, on his departure he was placed in a palanquin, accompanied by horn-blowers.[27]

[27] Henry Heras, "Early Relations between Vijayanagara and Portugal," *The Quarterly Journal of the Mythic Society* XVI, 2 (1925), 66, 69, 72-4; idem, *The Aravidu Dynasty of Vijayanagara*, vol. I, 57-64, 68, 435-7, 459, 465-7, 473-7; idem, "Venkatapatiraya I and the Portuguese," 315; Sewell, *A Forgotten Empire*, 251-3; Maria Augusta Lima Cruz, "Notes on Portuguese Relations with Vijayanagara, 1500-1565,"

Finally, during the four decades the Dutch were active in Vijayanagara, they recorded comparable experiences with imperial protocol. In May 1610, envoys Arend Maertssen and Abraham Fontaine embarked on a mission to Venkata, seeking approval to establish a trading station at the port of Pulicat. They found the emperor in what probably was the village of Kaveripakkam ("Caueri Pacque"), some 25 miles east of Vellore. Although he welcomed them with a procession of horsemen and foot soldiers, he declined to meet them personally there and departed to Vellore that night. As courtiers informed Maertssen and Fontaine, it would be a disgrace for the emperor to grant an audience in this village. He wanted the VOC ambassadors to visit his capital and see what they described as "his magnificence and royal state, his superb castles and antique edifices."

Reaching Vellore on 27 May and securing an audience with Venkata on the 30th, the envoys obtained permission to settle at Pulicat, but only, as they wrote, because they had appeared in person before the emperor. Had they not paid this homage, the urgent Portuguese requests to the court to keep the Dutch away, supported by gifts and large donations of money, would have made Venkata decide against the VOC.

A Dutch mission to Vellore in August of the same year initially proceeded less smoothly. The ambassadors, Hans Marcellis and Abraham Fontaine, had to wait twelve days near the palace until Venkata received them, despite an effort to attract his attention by shouting at him when he appeared before his people. They presented the emperor, the queen, and some officials with two Ceylonese elephants, sandalwood, mace, porcelain cups, textiles, and cash. Probably because of a conflict between the emperor's brother-in-law and the captain of the royal guard, the envoys were only granted their farewell audience a month later. But then the mission took a more positive turn. Not only were the VOC's privileges at Pulicat confirmed, the ambassadors were also given two rings and a village,[28] and placed in palanquins to be paraded around town, escorted by elephants, musicians, and "nobles" (*edelluijden*). Although further visits and donations to Gobburi Oba

in Sanjay Subrahmanyam (ed.), *Sinners and Saints: The Successors of Vasco da Gama* (Delhi, 1998), 17-29; Rubiés, *Travel and Ethnology in the Renaissance*, 185-93, 322-7; Pinto, *History of Christians in Coastal Karnataka*, 25-6, 32-41, 46-7; Subrahmanyam, *Penumbral Visions*, 45-7; idem, *Courtly Encounters*, 13-14; Shastry, *Goa-Kanara Portuguese Relations*, 58-62; De Coutre, *Aziatische omzwervingen*, 166, 173, 196; S. Jeyaseela Stephen, *Expanding Portuguese Empire and the Tamil Economy (Sixteenth-Eighteenth Centuries)* (New Delhi, 2009), 201. For Venkata's diplomatic relations with the Mughals, Bijapur, and the English, see for example Rāma Sharma, *The History of the Vijayanagar Empire*, vol. II, 68-9, 72-4, 90-1.

28 This village, called "Averipaqque" and about "one hour" from Pulicat, may have been Avurivakkam, three miles west of the port. Three more villages near Pulicat were donated by the courtier Gobburi Jagga Raya to the Dutch ambassador Wemmer van Berchem in December 1612 or January 1613. See Van Dijk, *Zes jaren uit het leven van Wemmer van Berchem*, 27-8.

Raya and other courtiers were necessary to obtain the papers confirming the new agreements, this embassy eventually proved successful.[29]

During later Dutch embassies—to Venkata in December 1612, Ramadeva in October 1629, and Sriranga III around April 1645—the envoys were received with similar ceremonial, being presented with palanquins, lands, and what they called "tasserijffen" (*tashrīf*s), a term of Arabic origin for marks of honour.[30] Only for the mission of 1629 is a specific (albeit not extensive) report available, giving an idea of how it proceeded. At the first audience with Ramadeva, on 26 October, ambassador Carel Reijniersz presented the VOC's gifts, which included an Arakanese elephant, round mirrors, a Japanese suitcase, three paintings of which one depicted "Prince Hendrick" (probably Stadtholder Frederik Hendrik of the Dutch Republic), and what probably were two Chinese bed canopies (*Chineese verhemelten*), all gratefully received. The second meeting, two days later, focused on negotiations related to the ongoing Luso-Dutch competition at nearby Pulicat and St. Thome. The third and last audience, on the 31st, was largely ceremonial again, the emperor signing a new grant, presenting the envoy with honours, bidding him farewell, and placing his hand in that of the Brahmin accompanying the Dutch as a sign of his sincerity.[31]

Vijayanagara's rulers also visited the VOC in Pulicat a few times, such as in 1643 and 1646, when the touring Sriranga III was honoured with a cannonade. The former visit was announced only some days in advance, giving the Dutch little time to prepare suitable gifts. They eventually managed to gather presents worth 2,800 guilders, including two very mediocre Persian horses of which they felt rather ashamed. Still—although the VOC's gifts during missions to the court could amount to almost twice as much (5,100 guilders in 1645)—the emperor accepted everything with appreciation and issued a new grant. The Dutch had evidently followed the ceremonial to his satisfaction. The VOC sometimes also sent presents as part of its correspondence with the court, like horses, a gold necklace, mirrors, and binoculars, besides the usual spices and textiles. The English estimated that one of these

[29] NA, VOC, no. 1055, ff. 103-4, 149, 167-76, 189-90: letters from Pulicat and Vellore to Banten and Masulipatam, May, July, Sept.-Nov. 1610, Pulicat proceedings (*resolutie*), Aug. 1610; Terpstra, *De vestiging van de Nederlanders aan de kust van Koromandel*, 122-5, 129-32; Raychaudhuri, *Jan Company in Coromandel*, 20-2; Mac Leod, *De Oost-Indische Compagnie*, vol. I, 93-7; Jeyaseela Stephen, "Rise and Decline of Pulicat," 2, 14.

[30] For *tashrīf*, see the section on Tanjavur in Chapter 5.

[31] On earlier missions to Vijayanagara and also Senji, the Dutch received "hands of sandal" from the rulers, perhaps denoting hands of sandalwood, which may similarly have functioned as an assurance. See: NA, VOC, no. 1055, ff. 77, 102-3, 275; no. 1056, ff. 151-1v: letters from Tiruppapuliyar, Pulicat, and Masulipatam to Banten (?), May 1610, Oct. 1613, treaty concluded with Senji, Mar. 1610; Mac Leod, *De Oost-Indische Compagnie*, vol. I, 92-3; Van Dijk, *Zes jaren uit het leven van Wemmer van Berchem*, 25.

Dutch donations cost some 4,000 *pagodas*, around 20,000 guilders,[32] seemingly a fortune for mere flattering,[33] but yet considered a worthwhile investment.[34]

This overview of protocol and related matters of honour in Vijayanagara allows a few tentative conclusions. First, many elements remind us of the regulations and recommendations in works like the *Mānasollāsa* and *Śivatattva ratnākara*, for example the way status was expressed by proximity to the king and permission to sit down, the significance of mutual gifts, and the value attached to how people were received and dismissed. Second, the contacts between Vijayanagara and its sultanate neighbours show that insults reflected tensions but could also heighten or even create these and thus influence political developments. Third, the empire's relations with European powers suggest that foreigners were largely incorporated into south India's systems of protocol and honour. Ceremonies experienced by the Portuguese, the Jesuits, and the Dutch appear more or less similar to those practised among south Indian parties. Nothing seems to indicate that the Vijayanagara court adjusted its protocol when dealing with Europeans.

Successor States

To gain a picture of the role of protocol and honour at the courts of Vijayanagara's heirs, there are hardly such comprehensive local accounts as Firishta's *Tārīkh-i firishta* on Vijayanagara and the Deccan sultanates. Dynastic chronicles and other texts of the successor states generally contain brief and isolated references to these matters. Dutch records, however, provide much more detail on court protocol for

[32] For exchange rates in early modern south India, see, for example: Arasaratnam, *Merchants, Companies and Commerce*, 295, 306, 318-20; Vink, "Encounters on the Opposite Coast," 109-10; Subrahmanyam, "The Portuguese, the Port of Basrur, and the Rice Trade," 47; s'Jacob, *De Nederlanders in Kerala*, lxxxvii-ix; Bes, "The Setupatis, the Dutch, and Other Bandits," 551 (n. 20); NA, VOC, no. 1268, f. 997v; no. 1343, f. 85; no. 2130, ff. 23-3v; no. 2197, f. 578: letters from Pulicat, Nagapattinam, and Cochin to Batavia, Sept. 1668, July 1679, Mar. 1729, list of gifts presented in Coromandel, 1729-30.

[33] The purchasing power of 20,000 guilders in 1642 equalled that of 249,000 euros in 2018. See iisg.amsterdam/en/research/projects/hpw/calculate.php.

[34] NA, VOC, no. 1056, ff. 151-2; no. 1100, ff. 65v, 77-7v; no. 1151, ff. 776-6v; no. 1156, ff. 249v-50; no. 1161, ff. 988-8v: letters from Masulipatam and Pulicat to Banten and Batavia, Aug. 1613, Dec. 1629, June 1643, May 1645, report of mission to Vijayanagara, Oct. 1629, lease by Sriranga III concerning Pulicat, May 1646; Colenbrander *et al.*, *Dagh-register gehouden int Casteel Batavia ... anno 1636* (The Hague, 1899), 124-5, idem, *anno 1643–1644*, 244, idem, *anno 1644–1645*, 346; Van Dijk, *Zes jaren uit het leven van Wemmer van Berchem*, 24-8; Raychaudhuri, *Jan Company in Coromandel*, 22-3, 36-7, 52; Mac Leod, *De Oost-Indische Compagnie*, vol. I, 127, 489, vol. II, 174, 179-80, 186; Subrahmanyam, *The Political Economy of Commerce*, 312; Foster, *The English Factories in India 1642–1645*, 81.

these kingdoms than for Vijayanagara. The following pages contain a representative selection of what those documents offer, combined with what can be derived from south Indian sources. All sections begin with a discussion of audience rituals, gifts, welcoming and departure ceremonies, eloquence, and other marks of honour. The second part of each section deals with breaches of protocol and how such insults both reflected and influenced political relations.

Nayakas of Ikkeri

As discussed in this chapter's introduction, the *Śivatattva ratnākara* of Ikkeri's Basavappa Nayaka I (r. 1697-1713) specifies how people in the audience hall must behave and be positioned when the king holds court. Unfortunately, the Dutch did not dispatch any mission to Basavappa and no VOC documents relate how his audiences actually proceeded. But between the 1650s and 1730s the Dutch sent about a dozen embassies to other Ikkeri rulers, usually to renew treaties or complain about violations of agreements. Lengthy reports of five of these missions are still available. In addition, the travellers Pietro Della Valle and Peter Mundy left accounts of Portuguese and English embassies to the kingdom in the 1620s and 1630s.[35] None of the texts seems to cover all aspects of the ceremonial encountered during such trips, but by combining the reports a reasonable impression of Ikkeri's court protocol can be gained.

Starting with royal audiences, a series of such meetings is described in the diary of a VOC embassy to Somashekara Nayaka II in 1735, undertaken to restore relations with Ikkeri after a military confrontation.[36] An abridged version of the relevant passages runs as follows:

On 9 February, Corijn Stevens and Abraham Gosenson, like nearly all VOC envoys middle-ranking employees, arrived at the capital Bednur with five local assistants, two interpreters (for Kannada and Portuguese), fourteen soldiers, and several dozen men carrying their palanquins and gifts. One week later, the ambassadors were called for their first meeting with Somashekara Nayaka. In the late afternoon two horses sent by the king—soberly and badly decked out, according to Stevens—appeared before the lodging of the envoys, who then dispatched fifty-two porters with presents for the Nayaka to the court. A little later, escorted by

[35] NA, VOC, no. 1268, ff. 1113-17; no. 1406, ff. 909v-33; no. 2232, ff. 3593-8; no. 2354, ff. 1491-632: reports of missions to Ikkeri, Mar.-May 1668, Apr.-May 1684, Oct.-Dec. 1731, Jan.-Mar. 1735; TNA, DR, no. 257, ff. 1-84: report of mission to Ikkeri, Apr.-May 1738; Della Valle, *The Travels of Pietro Della Valle in India*, vol. II, 246-57, 263; Mundy, *The Travels of Peter Mundy*, vol. III, pt. I, 81-9.

[36] For this clash, see: NA, VOC, no. 2320, ff. 1507-698: report concerning a conflict between the Dutch and Ikkeri, c. 1734; Galletti, Van der Burg, and Groot, *The Dutch in Malabar*, 144-5.

Dutch soldiers and the king's two horses, chief ambassador Stevens followed in a palanquin, alone since Gosenson had fallen ill.

Around 6 o'clock in the evening, Stevens reached some kind of country estate (called "hosarmoni," perhaps a Dutch corruption of the Kannada words *hosa aramane*, new palace), about one hour from the main palace, where the Nayaka was temporarily holding court.[37] Between two rows of horsemen, the Dutch envoy was guided by the court merchant Gana Sinai to a tent and told to wait. When the VOC's gifts had been lined up in another tent, where the audience would take place, the court's Secretary Chanappayya informed Stevens that the presents were inadequate and urged him to add extra cash. Upon the ambassador's reply that he was not qualified to do so and that these were the most precious gifts the Dutch could gather, Chanappayya let the matter rest. By then, the king had arrived in the audience tent and told Gana Sinai to fetch the VOC envoy. Coming within the ruler's sight, Stevens had his soldiers present their arms and—being ordered to remove his cow-leather shoes, which were not to be shown to the Nayaka—he entered the tent.

Somashekara sat on a raised throne covered with golden cloth.[38] Behind him stood a crowd of servants (*menigte van dienaren*), while beside him sat "some state lords and highly ranked persons" (*eenige rijxgrooten en staaten*). Standing before the Nayaka together with Secretary Chanappayya, merchant Gana Sinai, and a few interpreters, Stevens saluted the king. The latter enquired about the health of the VOC's governor-general and councillors at the Company's headquarters in Batavia and asked whether the envoy had brought a letter from them. Stevens answered that they were all perfectly healthy but that he had no letter because the king had not responded to earlier letters. Somashekara expressed his happiness about the wellbeing of the VOC's directors but then fell silent. The envoy now said he had been delegated with valuable gifts as a sign of the Company's benevolent intent and wished to raise some points on his superiors' behalf, for which he sought the king's permission. The Nayaka replied this was a ceremonial audience and the VOC's interests would be considered later. Next, Stevens was asked to step slightly backwards and sit on a carpeted bench as the king was to inspect a military parade.

The ambassador saw several elephants with their drivers passing by the tent and honouring the Nayaka, followed by horsemen—creating a chaos, according to Stevens—and foot soldiers and other servants. Meanwhile, Somashekara had some of the VOC's gifts brought to him, including large glass and porcelain jugs and various textiles such as silk-like cloths (*armozijnen*), Persian velvet, and cloth worked with silver (*passement*). The remainder of the gifts, in which the king seemed less interested, consisted of other textiles, spices, sugar,

[37] Perhaps this was the Kumbathi Mahal, built by Shivappa Nayaka I near Bednur. See P.M. Veerendra, "Royal Farmhouse of Keladi Rulers is a Shambles," *The Hindu* (16 Dec. 2019). It may also refer to the palace built by Somashekara II himself at "Banglegadde." See Subhadra, "Art and Architecture of the Keḷadi Nāyakas," 333-4.

[38] For a full translation of the description, see the section on Ikkeri in Chapter 5.

rosewater, and nuts. After two hours had passed and the procession had ended, Somashekara wanted the Dutch soldiers to demonstrate their rifles and set off six volleys. When this was completed, about forty dancing girls (*baljaer meiden*) appeared to give a performance. Thereupon the Nayaka let Stevens know, through Secretary Chanappayya, that the envoy could now mention to the secretary the reasons for his mission.

Rising up and walking a few steps towards the king, Stevens brought up various issues, concerning money promised to the VOC in an agreement signed by Ikkeri's General Raghunatha Odduru, the confiscated cargo and papers of a stranded Company ship, and the court's overall adherence to the Dutch-Ikkeri treaties. Following a brief and private chat between Chanappayya and the Nayaka, the ambassador was informed that these issues would be discussed at another audience. After requesting—and being promised—that he would not be made to stay in Bednur longer than a few more days, Stevens and his retinue were presented with betel-leaves, dried areca-nuts, and flowers on behalf of the king. Finally, around 9 o'clock, the envoy returned to his lodging, escorted by four royal servants carrying torches.[39]

Despite Stevens' request that matters be dealt with rapidly, the ambassadors had to spend four more weeks in Bednur before they secured a second and final audience. Presents worth 265 guilders given to Secretary Chanappayya and Treasurer Devappayya in an effort to gain their support, hardly speeded things up. But Stevens still met the king twice before the farewell audience, when Somashekara passed by the envoys' residence and they were expected to stand outside to greet him. At the first of these encounters, Stevens had his soldiers present arms, while around fifty horsemen, some elephants (tusked and non-tusked) with bells and banners, and a camel carrying two drums rode by.

Then Someshekara appeared, seated on a non-tusked elephant in a canopied, open chair, covered with red cloth, with a servant sitting directly before and behind him. His elephant was surrounded by female dancers, musicians, and several courtiers on horseback. One of them was Secretary Chanappayya, who rode towards Stevens, alighted from his horse, and served as an interpreter when Stevens asked the Nayaka whether he was still in good health and if he would let him return home soon. Somashekara affirmed both questions and presented the ambassador with betel and flowers on a copper bowl. Stevens then wanted his men to set off three volleys, but this was discouraged by some courtiers. When the Nayaka reached his palace, however, he was saluted there with three gunshots.

Six days later, Somashekara passed the envoys' house again, accompanied by the same entourage but this time sitting on a black horse. Stevens now stood outside together with his recovered companion Abraham Gosenson. After an exchange of the usual courtesies, the Nayaka remarked he remembered Gosenson from an earlier embassy, whereupon he personally handed over a few flowers to the envoys and had his assistants give them betel. Somashekara then proceeded, but after about twenty steps a servant came back saying that the

39 NA, VOC, no. 2354, ff. 1519, 1526, 1536-50, 1630-2: report of mission to Ikkeri, Feb.-Mar. 1735.

king fancied the parasol (*sommereel*, from *sombareere*)[40] Stevens was carrying. The ambassador immediately offered it to the Nayaka, who let his attendant hold the Dutchman's parasol—a symbol of royalty in India—over his head.[41]

After several delays, the farewell audience took place on 17 March. In the afternoon, once more two royal horses arrived—in Stevens' opinion looking "indescribably bad"—and around 6 o'clock Stevens and Gosenson went by palanquin to the outlying country estate, where they had to sit in a separate tent again. Following a one-and-a-half hour long wait, they were guided by the merchant Gana Sinai to another tent for what was called a "secret conference." Somashekara now sat on a throne covered with velvet, behind which stood Treasurer Devappayya and only around five servants, while Secretary Chanappayya was standing "not far from" the king. Having greeted the Nayaka, Stevens enquired about his wellbeing, but Somashekara did not reply, instead letting his secretary ask whether the envoys had really come in friendship. At their reply that their gifts were proof of their sincere intentions, a debate ensued on the VOC's military actions in the previous year and the agreement it had allegedly forced upon Ikkeri's General Raghunatha Odduru. As this discussion, in which Somashekara also joined, led nowhere, the Nayaka at one point just declared that Stevens and Gosenson could return home the next day. They were presented with flowers, betel, areca, and cloths, and then escorted back to their lodging by four of the king's servants.[42]

Although none of these audiences was held at Bednur's main palace, reports of other embassies to Ikkeri make clear that the experiences of Stevens and Gosenson were typical for the protocol on such occasions. The functions of the various audiences, the kinds of gifts, and the welcome and departure ceremonies were largely the same at all embassies. As for audiences, Dutch and other accounts show that European missions to Ikkeri generally included two to four such meetings, which each served different goals. Initial audiences were mostly ceremonial: the court welcomed ambassadors, who then presented their gifts. As Ikkeri's courtiers assured VOC delegates in 1738, giving presents at the first meeting was an ancient and essential practice. The traveller Pietro Della Valle was told by the Portuguese that opening audiences were not meant to discuss business. At final meetings, rulers commonly gave presents to ambassadors and formally dismissed them, sometimes after talks about requests or grievances of either party. If other audiences took place—which was often the case—these were generally devoted to negotiations between the court and envoys, with fewer formalities.

40 For *sombareere* or *sombreer*, deriving from Portuguese, see: Coolhaas *et al.*, *Generale Missiven*, vol. VI, 21; Yule and Burnell, *Hobson-Jobson*, 851. I also thank Jorge Flores for discussing this term with me.

41 NA, VOC, no. 2354, ff. 1550-5, 1560-2: report of mission to Ikkeri, Feb. 1735.

42 NA, VOC, no. 2354, ff. 1593-604: report of mission to Ikkeri, Mar. 1735.

Dutch gifts to Ikkeri's rulers during embassies usually comprised both large quantities of bulk goods, like textiles and spices (often cloves, nutmeg, and mace), and smaller numbers of more valuable items, such as animals, weapons, jewellery, and exotic objects. Among the presents for Somashekara II in 1738 were a tusked elephant and a dog that could do tricks. Although satisfied, the Nayaka kept asking to be sent more curiosities, like greyhounds, other skilful (preferably curly-haired) dogs, a white elephant, silver plates (round and square), gilded mirrors, Chinese gold necklaces, enough pearls to cover a throne, and especially all sorts of glassware—like lamps, lanterns, and jugs—accompanied by a Dutch glassblower, who, once arrived in Ikkeri, should produce glass tableware, a glass house, and a glass elephant saddle (see illustration 11). Although the VOC could not possibly comply with these demands, exquisite and exceptional presents were evidently considered particularly appropriate for south Indian kings.[43] Thus, at two Dutch embassies to Ikkeri in the 1660s and 1680s, the costs of gifts amounted to around 2,500 guilders, nearly as much as was spent for Vijayanagara's Emperor Sriranga III in 1643.[44]

As for counter-gifts during embassies, besides the aforementioned betel-leaves, areca-nuts, and flowers, envoys of all European powers regularly received clothes to put on in the ruler's presence. VOC ambassadors in the 1660s and 1680s wrote that Ikkeri's monarchs hung around them a "covering robe" (*deckleet*) or "honour robes" (*eerkleden*)—in one case worth 16 *pagoda*s, about 80 guilders, according to the ever cost-conscious Dutch. As the English envoy Peter Mundy remarked about a similar occasion, this happened "after the countrie manner." These were no doubt references to the incorporative *khil'at* ritual.

Another common royal gift of sorts to envoys was a small sum of money, which the VOC sometimes referred to as *gastos* or *guastus*, a term probably deriving from Portuguese. This seems to have been a symbolic reimbursement of the ambassadors' expenditures. Thus, in 1660 or 1661 Dutch envoy Leendert Lenartsz received 50 *pagoda*s from King Venkatappa II, another honour said to follow the "land's manners" (*lants manieren*). When around the same time a representative of the Ikkeri court departed after a visit to the Dutch at Vengurla, they presented him "according to the land's usage" with a little gift they called "rice money." In 1681 in neighbouring Mysore, ambassador Jan van Raasvelt was given some cash by King Chikkadevaraja Wodeyar, too, now termed "betel money" and amounting to 20 *pardaos*.[45]

43 For similar Portuguese experiences, see Melo, "Seeking Prestige and Survival," 690-1.

44 The purchasing power of 2,500 guilders in 1660 equalled that of 24,500 euros in 2018. See iisg.amsterdam/en/research/projects/hpw/calculate.php.

45 NA, VOC, no. 1236, ff. 192, 204-5, 496; no. 1240, f. 532; no. 1268, ff. 1113-17; no. 1379, f. 2351v; no. 1406, ff. 909v-33; no. 2232, ff. 3593-8: letters from Barkur, Vengurla, and Cochin to Batavia, Jan.-Feb., Apr.

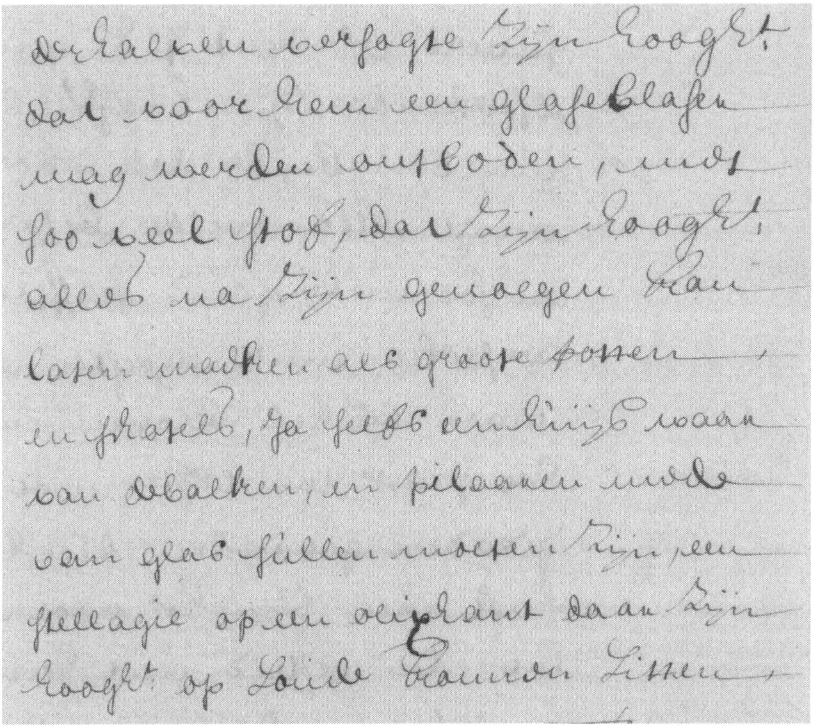
derhalven versogte Zijn Hoogh't:
dat voor hem een glaseblaser
mag werden ontboden, met
soo veel stof, dat Zijn Hoogh't:
alles na Zijn genoegen kan
laten maken als groote potten,
en schotels, ja selfs een huijs waar
van de balken, en pilaaren mede
van glas sullen moeten zijn, een
stellagie op een olijphant daar Zijn
Hoogh't: op soude kunnen sitten,

Illustration 11: Part of the report of the Dutch mission to Ikkeri in April 1738, describing Somashekara Nayaka II's desire to obtain glass objects: "therefore His Highness requested that a glassblower may be summoned for him, with so much material, that His Highness can have everything made to his pleasure, like big jars and dishes, yes, even a house of which the beams and pillars also will have to be glass, [and] a platform on an elephant on which His Highness would be able to sit," *Nationaal Archief*, The Hague, archives of the *Verenigde Oost-Indische Compagnie*, no. 2435, ff. 2240v-1 (courtesy *Nationaal Archief*, source: www.nationaalarchief.nl/onderzoeken/archief/1.04.02/invnr/2435/file).

The welcoming and seating arrangements at audiences described by envoys Stevens and Gosenson in 1735 are also rather similar to what other Europeans reported about Ikkeri. As Pietro Della Valle wrote, in 1623 the Portuguese ambassador João Fernandez Leitão was escorted to his first audience by local soldiers,

1661, Dec. 1662, May 1682, reports of missions to Ikkeri, Mar.-May 1668, Apr.-May 1684, Oct.-Dec. 1731; TNA, DR, no. 257, ff. 1-84: report of mission to Ikkeri, Apr.-May 1738; Colenbrander *et al.*, *Dagh-register gehouden int Casteel Batavia ... anno 1661* (Batavia/The Hague, 1889), 97; Della Valle, *The Travels of Pietro Della Valle in India*, vol. II, 253, 257; Mundy, *The Travels of Peter Mundy*, vol. III, pt. I, 83, 88. For a discussion of Della Valle's account, see Rubiés, *Travel and Ethnology in the Renaissance*, 359-63.

musicians, dancing women, and the Brahmin Vitula Sinai, himself a former envoy of Ikkeri. The most important men in Fernandez's retinue were granted the privilege of riding on horseback until the palace-fort's third gate, while King Venkatappa I was waiting beyond the fourth gate. For his second meeting, Fernandez was fetched by dancers and a palanquin.

In 1636 or 1637 the English envoy Mundy was also honoured with dancing men and women—as well as a play about "some antient history of those parts"—and in 1738 the escort of the VOC delegates Renicus Siersma and Joannes Mooijaart included another ambassador of Ikkeri, Sube Sinai. Upon entering the audience hall, envoys commonly greeted the rulers by taking off their hats, kneeling (perhaps only occasionally), and presenting gifts. Mundy and his companion Thomas Robinson, who carried the English letter to King Virabhadra on his head, also kissed the Nayaka's hand.

The European ambassadors generally found the king, or queen, sitting on a raised, carpeted, and canopied platform, resting on cushions or a chair, and surrounded by important courtiers, personal attendants, and, as Mundy wrote, dancing and singing women. Only the most prominent officials were seated, beside or behind the king. In 1623, just one courtier, probably Ikkeri's chief minister, was sitting, at some distance on Venkatappa I's right. In 1738, Chief Minister Devappa and General Raghunatha Odduru sat beside Somashekara II, but placed one step lower. All other local people had to stand, including soldiers, dancers, bearers of the king's fan, fly-whisk, betel, and spittoon, and even important men like ambassador Vitula Sinai.

European envoys were always invited to sit down, usually on a carpet or a carpeted bench. Whereas Siersma and Mooijaart were seated before the king, Fernandez was placed on his right-hand side, while Mundy sat "two yards away" from the Nayaka. Further, Fernandez was asked to sit under the king's canopy, but his entourage had to sit outside the canopied area. At initial audiences the king often continued his welcome with enquiries about personal matters, like the well-being of the ambassadors and their superiors in Asia and Europe, and questions about general political affairs.[46]

Much of the protocol encountered by Europeans during embassies was also adhered to in other instances. For example, Ikkeri's kings received presents from other south Indian rulers on all sorts of occasions. The *Keḷadi arasara vaṃśāvaḷi* and *Śivatattva ratnākara* relate that Vijayanagara's emperors honoured the Nayakas with palanquins, horses, weapons, jewels, betel, the privilege of being escorted

[46] NA, VOC, no. 2232, f. 3596: report of mission to Ikkeri, Nov. 1731; TNA, DR, no. 257, ff. 2-4, 9: report of mission to Ikkeri, Apr. 1738; Della Valle, *The Travels of Pietro Della Valle in India*, vol. II, 247-57, 263; Mundy, *The Travels of Peter Mundy*, vol. III, pt. I, 81-3, 88.

with a torch ("mashull") during daytime, an enemy's head, and royal insignia such as yak-tail fly-whisks ("chouries"), umbrellas, and the shell ("sankoo") and discus ("chakrum") emblems. The Nayakas received these gifts when summoned to the imperial capital, before and after assisting Vijayanagara in battle, and as a reward for providing protection.

Ikkeri's kings also donated gifts to other rulers in various situations, for instance to express gratitude or acknowledge their supremacy. Thus, the *kaifiyat* of the Harapanahalli principality states that after its chief Dassappa Nayaka declared allegiance to Ikkeri, the Nayaka gave him an elephant, banners, horses, and other valuables. And when around 1664 Mysore defeated Ikkeri and Somashekara I sued for peace, he sent elephants, horses, robes, and jewels to the Wodeyar court. Additionally, people staying at the court could receive gifts from the king after great achievements. According to the Sanskrit text *Vaiyākaraṇabhūṣaṇa* of the Benares-based scholar Kondabhatta, Venkatappa I awarded Kondabhatta's visiting father Rangojibhatta with the honour of using a palanquin after the latter defeated an opponent in a religious debate.[47]

Presents exchanged between Ikkeri and the Dutch on other occasions than embassies largely served the same purposes—and partly consisted of the same items—as gifts between Indian parties did. Upon concluding the first Dutch-Ikkeri treaty, in March 1657, Shivappa I presented the VOC with cardamom, pepper, pickle ("aetchiaer"), and rice. His successor Venkatappa II honoured the highest Dutch official in Asia, the governor-general at Batavia, with a diamond ring and robes of honour, while Someshekara II showed his deference for the governor-general by personally wrapping and sealing a present for him. Ikkeri's letters to the VOC were also often accompanied by cloths.[48]

[47] BL/AAS, MG, no. 6, pt. 11: "Historical account of Beedoonoor or Caladee Samstanum," ff. 64-5, 66-7; no. 11, pt. 15a: "Kyfyat of Harponelly," f. 126 (compiled in 1800 or 1801 by assistants of Mackenzie, see Cotton, Charpentier, and Johnston, *Catalogue of Manuscripts in European Languages*, vol. I, pt. II, 111-12); Krishnaswami Aiyangar, *Sources of Vijayanagar History*, 347; Hayavadana Rao, *History of Mysore*, vol. I, 221-2; P.K. Gode, "The Contact of Bhaṭṭoji Dīkṣita and Some Members of His Family with the Keḷadi Rulers of Ikkeri – Between c. A. D. 1592 and 1645," in idem, *Studies in Indian Literary History*, vol. III (Pune, 1956), 205. For some of the terms for royal gifts mentioned here, see: Yule and Burnell, *Hobson-Jobson*, 184-5, 214-15, 601; D.C. Sircar, *Indian Epigraphical Glossary* (Delhi, 1966), 64-5.

[48] For these and other examples, see: NA, VOC, no. 1224, f. 89; no. 1231, f. 515; no. 1233, ff. 595-5v; no. 1234, f. 127v; 1236, f. 431; no. 1240, ff. 531-2; no. 1274, f. 185v; no. 2432, f. 147: correspondence between VOC and Shivappa Nayaka, June 1656, Apr. 1659, reports of *Commandeur* Adriaen Roothaes, June 1660, May 1661, letters from Colombo to Gentlemen XVII or Batavia, from Vengurla to Batavia, from Cochin to Basrur and Batavia, Apr. 1661, Dec. 1662, Sept. 1670, May 1738; Colenbrander *et al.*, *Dagh-register gehouden int Casteel Batavia ... anno 1656–1657* (The Hague, 1904), 164; Heeres and Stapel, *Corpus diplomaticum Neerlando-Indicum*, vol. 2, 104-13.

Likewise, the VOC felt obliged to honour Ikkeri's monarchs and courtiers with gifts in various situations, including royal weddings and successions to the throne. When in April 1722 Somashekara II married the daughter of the courtier Nirvanayya, the Dutch sent presents to the king, his brother, Nirvanayya himself, and his brother, together costing 122 guilders. Around early 1662 the VOC presented the recently enthroned Bhadrappa with commodities worth over 500 guilders. Although this king wrote to the governor-general that he considered "true friendship the principal matter in gifting," presents were essential to keep relations friendly. This became clear when in 1674 court merchant Narayana Malu suggested to the Dutch they dispatch an envoy to Ikkeri with gifts for certain prominent courtiers to win them over. As Narayana argued, the previous embassy was six years ago and he could no longer exert his influence with only "idle words and empty hands."[49]

Visits by Ikkeri's kings and courtiers to Dutch settlements also required gifts and ceremonies. In 1703, when Basrur's VOC lodge re-opened after a closure of several years, Ikkeri sent an eminent courtier named Nagappayya to renew the Dutch-Ikkeri treaty. The VOC welcomed him and his retinue of about one hundred men with betel-leaves, areca-nuts, and dancing women both on his arrival and departure. But Nagappayya also insisted on receiving gifts for himself, the king, and the latter's father Mariyappa Chetti, who in fact ruled the kingdom. The Dutch were reluctant to do so, whereupon Nagappayya threatened not to sign the new agreement, forcing them to present spices, sandalwood, and sugar. When the courtier Nirvanayya called at Basrur on several occasions in the 1720s, the VOC honoured him with gun salutes, female dancers, and gifts, each time costing around 150 guilders. And in 1729 King Somashekara II—together with his queen, Crown Prince Basavappa, and several courtiers—visited the Dutch factory too, necessitating the VOC to spend over 200 guilders on presents and dance troupes. As the Dutch wrote, it was essential to honour the king and his entourage "after all old customs" to maintain their "respect for the Company."[50]

Finally, protocol also governed correspondence between Ikkeri and the VOC. Only some examples remain because the Dutch, to avoid repetition, usually left out

[49] For these and other examples, see: NA, VOC, no. 1240, f. 544; no. 1299, ff. 352v-3; no. 1582, f. 497; no. 1598, f. 131; no. 1977, ff. 110-11; no. 2834, ff. 76-6v: letters from Vengurla and Cochin to Batavia and Gentlemen XVII, May 1662, Dec. 1674, Oct., Dec. 1696, May 1722, Mar. 1754; DNA, DCGCC, no. 3396, f. 1: letter from Bhadrappa Nayaka to Batavia, 1662. For gifts and missions sent by the Portuguese to new Ikkeri kings, see Shastry, *Goa-Kanara Portuguese Relations*, 160, 222.

[50] NA, VOC, no. 1694, ff. 54-5, 57-8, 60-2, 77-8, 84; no. 1928, f. 68 (3rd numeration); no. 1942, ff. 266v-7; no. 1977, f. 90; no. 2130, ff. 53, 323v-4v, 499v-502: correspondence between Cochin and Ikkeri, report on renewed trade in Ikkeri, with memorandum of expenses, Mar.-Apr. 1703, letters from Cochin to Batavia, Mar. 1719, Apr. 1722, Apr. 1729; Cochin proceedings, Nov. 1719, Jan. 1729; s'Jacob, *De Nederlanders in Kerala*, 362-3.

ceremonial parts from the copies they made of these documents. But the surviving written courtesies suggest these largely consisted of standard phrases. At least four VOC letters to Somashekara II and Basavappa II, dating from between the 1730s and 1750s, begin as follows:

> To the great mighty monarch and lord Ghelada [Keladi] ... [personal name], king of the widely extending realm [*rijk*] of Cannara, holding court at Bidroer—whom are wished all sorts of pleasures, together with a fortunate reign over his subjects and an everlasting victory over his enemies, besides peace and quiet as well as contentment in this world for many long days—this letter of respect and affection is being written ...[51]

In addition, one of these letters ends thus:

> May God guard Your Highness for long years for the benefit of his realm and subjects, while [we], after kind salutation, remain Your Highness' obedient servants ...[52]

Further, the VOC likely used special paper for letters to Ikkeri's rulers—and other kings—to pay respect to them. The original documents sent to the Nayakas have been lost. Obviously, these are not found in the Company archives, which only contain copies on ordinary paper. But the very few original Dutch letters to south Indian rulers that still exist, received by the kings of Cochin in Malabar, are extensively embellished with gold-leaf floral patterns.[53] Rulers of powerful states like Ikkeri were probably honoured with similarly decorated paper.

Little has survived, too, of the written courtesies sent by the court to the Dutch, but these were equally polite. In 1647, King Shivappa concluded a letter by saying: "May God spare Your Honours in health for many years." In 1689, Ikkeri's pretender to the throne Sadashiva informed the VOC he was in good health and desired to know the state of health of the Dutch commissioner-general. In 1731, the courtier Nirvanayya used a comparable phrase.[54] Clearly, like during royal audiences, health

[51] NA, VOC, no. 2435, f. 2270; no. 2462, ff. 618-18v: letter from Cochin to Somashekara Nayaka II, June 1738, Jan. 1739; TNA, DR, no. 404, ff. 121, 155: letters from Cochin to Basavappa Nayaka II, June 1745, Dec. 1751 (translation mine).

[52] TNA, DR, no. 404, f. 161: letter from Cochin to Basavappa Nayaka II, Dec. 1751 (translation mine).

[53] For original letters to the kings of Cochin, see Regional Archives Ernakulam (Kochi), Dutch Records, no. D 64: letters from Batavia to Cochin's kings, c. 1706-89. For reproductions, see: Lennart Bes, "Gold-Leaf Flattery, Calcuttan Dust, and a Brand New Flagpole: Five Little-Known VOC Collections in Asia on India and Ceylon," *Itinerario: International Journal on the History of European Expansion and Global Interaction* 36, 1 (2012), 93; Van der Pol, *The Dutch East India Company in India*, 166.

[54] NA, VOC, no. 1170, f. 697; no. 1236, f. 204; no. 1463, f. 437v; no. 2187, f. 222: letters from Shivappa Nayaka and Sadashiva to Vengurla and the Dutch commissioner-general, May 1647, Feb. 1689, letters

often figured in expressions of deference, which enquired about one's wellbeing or wished someone good health. Although no examples remain of correspondence between Ikkeri's Nayakas and other Indian rulers, it seems this custom was a regular part of south Indian protocol.

The Ikkeri court used protocol not only to convey good intentions and build relationships, but also to express annoyance and humiliate other parties. All aspects considered above—seating arrangements, gifts, reception and departure rituals, the tone of conversations and correspondence, and so on—could and frequently would be employed to communicate negative sentiments, by breaching the protocol. Again, only a selection of cases can be discussed, aiming at being representative for court insults in Ikkeri.

The Dutch were regularly confronted with such offences, the most common of which probably was the recurring postponement of audiences during embassies. The reports of nearly all VOC missions to Ikkeri abound with complaints about endless delays of meetings with the monarch or courtiers, and the resultant obligation for envoys to spend weeks or even months in the capital. Illustrative is the embassy to Queen Chennammaji in 1684. The diary of ambassador Jacob Wilcken, some of whose experiences are related in Chapter 3, is dominated by days passed in lethargy and frustration as promised audiences were cancelled over and over again. Yet, it may be worthwhile to describe Wilcken's stay at Bednur in detail to give an idea of its progress—or rather the lack of it:

Wilcken arrived at the capital in the evening of 9 April. That night, however, Ikkeri's General Krishnappayya, the envoy's main contact person, was busy receiving an ambassador of the Golkonda sultanate. Therefore, the next morning Wilcken sent servants to inform Krishnappayya of his arrival and his wish not to be kept at Bednur too long since the ships waiting for him in the port of Basrur had to leave soon, because of imminent weather changes. The general replied he did not feel well but would invite Wilcken for a meeting that evening. As no invitation came, the following day the envoy sent servants to Krishnappayya again. They were refused entry, however, which Wilcken considered very unusual but attributed to the general's dealings with the Golkonda ambassador. The next afternoon, the Dutch envoy dispatched his interpreter to Krishnappayya, but he was not granted a meeting either.

Only the following morning, the interpreter was admitted to the general and told him Wilcken's stay had been fruitless so far, while things could no longer be postponed. Krishnappayya put his hand on his chest, declaring he would take care of everything and go

from Barkur to Batavia, from Nirvanayya to Cochin, Feb. 1661, Sept. 1731. Dutch letters to the rulers of the adjacent Sonda kingdom contain similar expressions. See NA, VOC, no. 1274, ff. 180-80v: Basrur diary extract, July 1670.

to court right away to arrange the matter. The following day, 14 April, Wilcken himself went to the general's house early in the morning and waited four hours until he could speak with him. Krishnappayya then explained that yesterday at court he had mentioned the envoy's visit and today would discuss it further. That evening Wilcken met the general again and could finally explain the objectives of his mission—a toll decrease and an open rice market—upon which Krishnappayya stated he would arrange an audience with Queen Chennammaji for tomorrow.

The following day, on Krishnappayya's advice, the VOC's interpreter waited almost the entire day near the fort-palace to see if a meeting with the queen would materialise, but the general was busy entertaining the Golkonda ambassador. On the 16th the interpreter was told that Wilcken should be patient for two more days, until the Golkonda ambassador departed. The Dutch envoy, figuring this was a pretext because the Golkonda ambassador was unlikely to leave soon, now turned to Governess Maribasvama for support. He sent his interpreter to her, together with a Brahmin to improve the chance of getting access. The governess was however "washing herself," as the mission report has it,[55] and postponed the meeting. Wilcken then went to Krishnappayya's house but found the door closed as the general was having dinner with the Golkonda ambassador and his wife.

The next morning, Krishnappayya suddenly informed Wilcken he should get to the fort and be ready to meet the queen. But after waiting for three hours, the envoy was asked to go to the house of Governess Maribasvama and discuss matters with her. When the governess appeared, after another one and a half hours, they had a long but fruitless talk about the VOC's requests, which ended with the ambassador asking to be granted at least a quick farewell audience with the queen. The following four days proceeded in the same manner. Wilcken and his interpreter had several encounters with Krishnappayya and Maribasvama, at which grievances about the VOC's behaviour were aired, the envoy was advised to have more patience, or the queen was said to have fallen ill.

Eventually, on 22 April, nearly two weeks after his arrival, and following another long wait at the fort, Wilcken secured his first audience with Chennammaji. After presenting his gifts—comprising merely some spices for the queen—the envoy discussed the VOC's demands with the attending courtiers, but was told matters could only be settled when the court merchant Siddabasayya returned to the capital. This would supposedly happen within a few days, but it soon turned out it would not. Wilcken let General Krishnappayya know he was not going to wait for Siddabasayya since the Company's ships could no longer postpone their departure, and if therefore the VOC's wishes were not honoured, the general should at least provide him with a letter stating the envoy had actually appeared at court. Krishnappayya promised Wilcken that another audience would be granted that same evening or early next morning, but for several days nothing happened apart from more deliberations with the general. Finally on 27 April, Wilcken was again received by the queen, now accompanied by her minor adopted

[55] This and other mentions of "washing" in Dutch records probably refer to religious ceremonies.

son, Basavappa I. Following an unproductive discussion and another request by Wilcken to be granted a farewell audience soon, the meeting was concluded.

Already the next morning, the envoy went to see Krishnappayya and pleaded for his support to arrange a rapid departure. The general suggested it might happen tomorrow, but as this would be a Saturday and therefore a "washing day in the fort," Wilcken knew the court would not convene. The envoy now asked why he was kept at the capital so long and if someone else was behind it. The general kept quiet and then denied this suggestion with a vague excuse, adding that Wilcken would surely be given a farewell audience. The next day, the envoy sent his interpreter to Krishnappayya, who stated it was a full moon today but that Wilcken would be able to travel to Basrur tomorrow morning without delay. That following morning, on 30 April, the envoy went to the general, ready to take his leave from the queen. Krishnappayya turned out to have left Bednur that night, however, to intercept the Golkonda ambassador, who had quietly gone home without informing the court.

This was the last drop in the bucket of Wilcken's frustrations. Straightaway, he and his party quickly and silently departed from the capital. But after a few hours of travelling, a court servant came hurriedly after them, requesting them in the queen's name to return to Bednur for an audience that evening or the next morning. When Wilcken declared he was unwilling to do so, a heated argument ensued, which ended with the court servant threatening to stop them by force and close a gate they were about to pass. The envoy could now only follow the servant back to the capital, although he refused to be escorted into town as if he and his men were "crooks or thieves" (*schelmen of dieven*).

Finding himself in Bednur once more, Wilcken noted nothing had changed. Governess Maribasvama informed him she considered his sudden departure rather dishonourable and two watchmen were appointed to prevent the envoy from escaping again. Meanwhile, Krishnappayya had also returned and let Wilcken know that matters would be promptly arranged and that some courtiers opposing the VOC would be of no harm anymore. After several more meetings with the general and the governess, Wilcken eventually secured a third audience with Chennammaji on 4 May, after a seven-hour wait at the fort. Krishnappayya now came with a new proposal regarding the VOC's wishes. When the envoy responded he was not authorised to accept it, the general said he would write to the Company's directors in Cochin and wait—together with the envoy—for their reply. This was unacceptable to Wilcken, whereupon it was decided that the envoy could leave two days later with letters of the court for Cochin.

While during the following days the weather deteriorated and Wilcken worried about the ships still waiting for him, he kept reminding Krishnappayya to prepare the letters for Cochin and arrange a farewell audience. His suggestion that he leave now and the letters be sent later, was strongly rejected. Soon after, Wilcken noticed that all roads out of the capital were guarded. On 7 May, he was informed that the queen could not yet authorise (*siapen*, chop?)[56] the letters as today was an inauspicious day, while on the 8th he was told the queen suffered from a

56 Literally: seal or print. See Yule and Burnell, *Hobson-Jobson*, 207-9.

swelling on her cheek and could not receive him. Nevertheless, Wilcken was asked to go to the fort, where he, after a few hours, was received by Krishnappayya and Governess Maribasvama, while the queen sat in a nearby room. The general explained that the letters were ready and would be authorised that night, so the envoy could collect them tomorrow morning and leave. Wilcken then requested permission to depart already and leave his interpreter behind to obtain the letters, which was granted to him. A robe of honour (*deckleet*) was now brought in from the queen's room for the envoy, but he refused to wear it. Strongly urged to accept the robe since it was given by the king, Wilcken grudgingly put it on. Following a hasty goodbye, he immediately left the capital, almost a month after he had arrived there.[57]

In this account, Wilcken's frustrations could have driven him to overstate matters, but it does not seem he misunderstood the local protocol. Clearly, he was humiliated by the court's disregard for the expected procedures. Not only had the envoy to wait constantly for audiences and thus prolong his sojourn in Bednur, but explicit promises were allegedly also broken. When Wilcken no longer accepted this and terminated his mission—as the Golkonda ambassador apparently did as well—he claims he was in effect taken hostage and even accused of acting dishonourably himself.

Obviously, this treatment was not an isolated event but part of a long-lasting confrontation between the court and the VOC. Tension had arisen after Ikkeri increased toll duties and the Dutch objected to them. In the years prior to Wilcken's mission, the VOC already dispatched several embassies to negotiate more favourable trade conditions, but these yielded little result, even though 2,632 guilders were spent on gifts for one of these trips. The Dutch lamented the court's lack of respect for their employees and letters. Indeed, relations deteriorated to a point that the VOC resolved that if Wilcken's mission was also a failure, the Basrur factory might be closed.

The breaches of protocol during this embassy appear to have both reflected the existing disagreements and further spoiled the relationship. Wilcken was maltreated by the court from the beginning, but his meagre gift of some spices to the queen only—itself meant to show the VOC's discontent—no doubt worsened matters. Thus, it seems, ensued an escalation: more postponements followed; Wilcken then departed without permission; the court next confined his movements; and at the end he initially refused to undergo the *khil'at* ritual. After the mission, this ceremonial stand-off reinforced the commercial dispute. In the mid-1680s, as the insulted Dutch minimised contact with Ikkeri, their trade at Basrur often came to a virtual standstill, a situation profitable to neither the Dutch nor the court.[58]

57 NA, VOC, no. 1406, ff. 909v-33: report of mission to Ikkeri, Apr.-May 1684.

58 NA, VOC, no. 1373, ff. 343-3v, 352v-3, 354v, 361; no. 1379, ff. 2327v-8, 2351v-7v; no. 1383, ff. 723-3v; no. 1388, ff. 1908, 1935v, 1945; no. 1396, ff. 655v, 729: letters from Cochin to Gentlemen XVII, Batavia,

While the delays during Wilcken's embassy can perhaps be attributed to internal disagreements at court, postponed audiences were also common during several other Dutch missions, when competition between courtiers seemed less pervasive. In 1658 and 1682, envoys were forced to stay at Bednur for several months until they secured a departure audience. In 1668 the ambassadors had to pretend to abort their mission, too, openly leaving the capital in their palanquins, before a farewell audience was arranged. Their patience was further tried when promised documents did not materialise and they had to hunt down King Somashekara I at the elephant stables to collect the papers and have them signed. In 1731 the envoy was told that if he intended to discuss grievances, he simply would not be granted an audience. He had to wait three weeks for a meeting with Somashekara II and was not allowed to mention the reason for his visit. When he still attempted to do so, the audience was terminated. Finally, when in 1738 ambassadors made clear they grew tired of waiting, the rowers they had hired to sail off were pressured by the court into withdrawing their service. Only when other rowers proved easily available, an audience was instantly organised.[59]

Court insults in Ikkeri could take multiple forms, as is demonstrated by the experiences of ambassadors Stevens and Gosenson in 1735, at least as they reported them. Having arrived at Basrur on 10 January, the next day they sent an interpreter to Bednur to announce their visit and ask for palanquins to get them there. But although it took just two or three days to reach the capital and a welcoming letter from the court arrived on the 19th, by 6 February still no palanquins had appeared. Thus, Stevens and Gosenson were forced to arrange palanquins themselves. When almost halfway, they ran into eighteen palanquin-bearers sent by the court but without palanquins. After replacing the hired porters with these men, the envoys arrived at Bednur's outskirts the following afternoon. There, they were stopped by courtiers who in the name of Secretary Chanappayya asked how they had dared to pass the so-called King's Gate, two hours from Bednur, without authorisation. Amazed, Stevens and Gosenson answered that the courtiers must certainly be aware of the written permission granted to them some weeks before. Undeterred, the courtiers replied that the ambassadors' lodging would be ready only by tomorrow and they had to spend the night in a church. But only after two more days, they

Vengurla, and Basrur, Nov. 1681, Feb.-Mar., May, Dec. 1682, Apr., Nov.-Dec. 1683, Jan.-Feb., July 1684; Coolhaas *et al.*, *Generale Missiven*, vol. IV, 577, 735, 824, vol. V, 61, 142, 239.

[59] For these and other examples, including Portuguese and English cases, see: Coolhaas *et al.*, *Generale Missiven*, vol. III, 222-3; NA, VOC, no. 1268, ff. 1113v-16; no. 1379, ff. 2328, 2351v; no. 2232, ff. 3593-8: reports of missions to Ikkeri, Apr. 1668, Oct.-Dec. 1731, letter from Cochin to Gentlemen XVII, Nov. 1681; TNA, DR, no. 257, ff. 46-9: diary of mission to Ikkeri, May 1738; Shastry, *Goa-Kanara Portuguese Relations*, 132, 135-6; Foster, *The English Factories in India 1651–1654: A Calendar of Documents in the India Office, Westminster* (Oxford, 1915), 75-6.

could enter their residence, which turned out to be devoid of any furniture and foods, forcing the envoys to gather their own provisions.

During the remainder of their sojourn at Bednur, various other insults followed—alternating with marks of honour—including long-delayed audiences, complaints about the VOC's "worthless" gifts, and refusals to speak with the Company's interpreters. Further, Secretary Chanappayya told the envoys' palanquin-bearers not to serve them anymore. Stevens and Gosenson attributed some humiliations to disputes and misunderstandings between Chanappayya and King Somashekara II. But it also became clear that the court was still annoyed by a recent military confrontation with the Dutch, when they had supported Ikkeri's opponent Kannur and allegedly forced Ikkeri's General Raghunatha Odduru into signing a degrading agreement. Thus, the envoys' experiences during this mission were another instance of protocol—or the breaching thereof—reflecting political issues.[60]

During the following decades, tensions between Ikkeri, Kannur, and the VOC continued to be expressed though violations of protocol, also by the Dutch themselves. In January 1738, at a meeting in Cochin with Ikkeri's envoy Dogu Sinai, the Dutch declined a gift sent by Raghunatha Odduru, calling the general a swindler (*bedrieger*). During a mission to Ikkeri later in 1738, envoys Siersma and Mooijaart refused betel and flowers from a courtier, much to his dismay.[61] Finally, referring to a border conflict between Ikkeri and the Ali Raja of Kannur, a Dutch letter of 1755 offers a rare glimpse of insults exchanged among south Indian rulers themselves, with their political repercussions. These seem to have differed little from humiliations meted out between Ikkeri and the VOC:

> … about this [the border conflict], he, Adij Ragia [Ali Raja], had sent his writers to the Bidroerse [Bednur's] court several times and had very seriously persisted in that. But eventually seeing the fruitlessness of this, and [seeing] that at the end of the passed summer time his letters about that matter, sent to the king of Canara [Ikkeri], were thrown on the ground with much scorn by the latter's state Governor [*rijksbestierder*] Dewapa [Devappa], and [seeing that] the deliverers of these were treated very disdainfully through words and deeds—all this has made him, Adij Ragia, resolve to … send vessels and troops with orders to, while lurching at one or another port of the mentioned Canara coast, demand satisfaction …, first amicably, but if that bears no fruit, then with force …[62]

[60] NA, VOC, no. 2187, f. 168; no. 2231, f. 2882v; no. 2354, ff. 1493-604: letter from Cochin to Batavia, May 1731, document concerning the Kanara Coast, Jan. 1732, diary of mission to Ikkeri, Jan.-Mar., 1735.

[61] NA, VOC, no. 2433, ff. 511-14: "indigenous" diary (*inheems dagregister*), Jan. 1738; TNA, DR, no. 257, f. 35: diary of mission to Ikkeri, Apr. 1738.

[62] NA, VOC, no. 2857, ff. 131v-2: secret letter from Cochin to Batavia, Oct. 1755 (translation mine).

In conclusion, the cases above suggest several patterns. To begin with, the protocol discussed here—chiefly on the basis of Dutch sources—largely agrees with ideas in Indian treatises on statecraft. All ceremonial served to acknowledge mutual relations, express gratitude, or persuade one another. Precisely because of these roles, protocol was frequently violated, by ignoring established norms (like postponing audiences) or even turning conventions into offensive acts (such as throwing letters down rather than accepting them respectfully). Further, protocol both reflected and influenced relations. The contacts between Ikkeri and the VOC are a clear example of a relationship in which diplomatic humiliations mirrored but also helped shape its volatile character. This is not surprising because the Dutch usually dispatched embassies to Ikkeri only when they wanted to complain, for instance about ignored treaties, unanswered letters, or military threats. The tensions that consequently characterised these missions must have significantly contributed to the frequent insulting of VOC envoys—the court assuming that its message was as clear to the Dutch as it would be to local parties.

Nayakas of Tanjavur

Compared with Ikkeri, there is little material to reconstruct and analyse protocol at Tanjavur's Nayaka court. South Indian texts appear to be scarce and it seems there are especially few sources, local or foreign, on the ceremonial practised when the king held court. A work like the Telugu *Raghunāthanāyakābhyudayamu*, describing a typical day in the life of Tanjavur's Raghunatha Nayaka, devotes little attention to meetings with courtiers and how they were positioned and honoured in the audience hall. Dutch records are also limited, chiefly dating from the brief period between the VOC's first settling in Tanjavur in 1644 and the fall of its Nayaka house in 1673. For the seventeenth century's early decades, however, there are references to protocol in accounts of other European powers.

Two reports of what may be the best documented European mission to these Nayakas have quite a bit to offer. As recorded by both the Danish ambassador Ove Giedde and the Icelander Jón Ólafsson, serving the Danes in Tanjavur, in October 1620 Raghunatha Nayaka welcomed a Danish embassy at his capital with a palanquin, an escort of courtiers and elephants, ornamented gateways, clean-swept streets, decorated palace buildings, and soldiers lining the entire route from the town walls to the audience hall. The king soon granted an audience, at which he reportedly rested on pillows on a stepped platform, with a prominent Brahmin sitting at his feet, perhaps Govinda Dikshita. Envoy Giedde initially had to stand about three metres away from the Nayaka, but was later invited to sit on one of the steps. In the following days, Raghunatha honoured Giedde and his retinue with personal attention, entertaining them with games, tours, ceremonies, and a display of the royal treasures. Yet, it took several weeks before he granted a second audience, making the ambassador complain about being forced to wait. Notwithstanding, at their departure the Nayaka accompanied the Danes out of town and presented them with gifts.

The relatively close contacts this dynasty seemingly maintained with European visitors also transpire from the work of the Portuguese chronicler António Bocarro, compiled in the 1630s. He writes that the Nayaka treated Portuguese mercenaries rather intimately, allowing them to sit down and wear their hats in his presence and just call him *Senhoria*, or Your Lordship.[63] Further, Raghunatha Nayaka's elevated seating in the audience hall is confirmed by Roland Crappe, a Dutchman in Danish service who after a naval clash with the Portuguese in 1619 was protected by the Nayaka and thus initiated Giedde's embassy. In the report of his visit to the Tanjavur court around November of that year, Crappe describes how Raghunatha had "me sit at the foot of a large stairway along which one climbs up to him."[64]

Among the earliest encounters of the Dutch East India Company with Tanjavur must have been their embassy in early 1645, dispatched to secure better trading privileges. The few remaining documents on this trip say little about protocol but state that envoy Adriaen van der Meijde presented Vijayaraghava Nayaka with valuable gifts. Yet, he spent no less than two months in the capital before he found out the Company's wishes would not be complied with, despite daily assurances of the opposite.

More detailed is a report of the magnate Chinanna Chetti, delegated to Vijayaraghava by the Dutch in September 1658, following their seizure of Nagapattinam. Chinanna was welcomed by courtiers, provided with a comfortable residence, and granted an audience the day after his arrival. Having presented the VOC's gifts, Chinanna and his entire retinue received robes of honour (*eer cleeden*). He was given more robes after he sent presents to the Nayaka's "chief concubine" (*opperste concubijn*) because she gave birth to a daughter. Although it became clear during Chinanna's mission that Tanjavur disagreed with the VOC on the jurisdiction over Nagapattinam, the concluding audience already took place a few days later, whereupon another robe of honour was sent to the Dutch.

[63] Narayana Rao, Shulman, and Subrahmanyam, *Symbols of Substance*, 59, 61, 66; Esther Fihl, "Shipwrecked on the Coromandel: The First Indian-Danish Contact, 1620," in idem and A.R. Venkatachalapathy (eds), *Beyond Tranquebar: Grappling across Cultural Borders in South India* (New Delhi, 2014), 244-8; Ólafsson, *The Life of the Icelander Jón Ólafsson*, vol. II, 15-17, 21, 25; Ramanujam, *Unheard Voices*, ch. 1; Subrahmanyam, *Improvising Empire*, 90.

[64] RA, *Tyske Kancelli, Slesvig-holsten-lauenburgske Kancelli (1618-1659), Diverse akter verdr. det ostindiske kompagni og Guinea* (German Chancellery, Schleswig-Holstein-Lauenburg Chancellery (1618-1659), Various documents concerning the East Indian Company and Guinea), no. A171, ff. 3-5: report of voyage to Tranquebar by Roland Crappe, 1621. See also: Ramanujam, *Unheard Voices*, ch. 1; Fihl, "Shipwrecked on the Coromandel," 230-1, 235-43, 248-51, 254 (n. 6).

Combining the gifts that Chinanna brought to court with those donated afterwards—together including three elephants, three horses, 10,000 *reals* (23,333 guilders) in cash, four gold necklaces, five rings with rubies and sapphires, over a hundred mirrors, twelve swords, lacquer ware, textiles, and spices—the VOC spent 36,765 guilders on this embassy.[65] Considering that the presents of a mission in 1652 amounted to just 2,584 guilders but still greatly pleased Vijayaraghava, this was a formidable sum, only justifiable by the subsequent treaty in which Tanjavur recognised the VOC's control over Nagapattinam.[66]

No further Dutch records on audience ceremonies seem to remain. There are however several documents describing protocol in other situations, such as the exchange of presents. Tanjavur's Nayakas demanded to be honoured with gifts on a regular basis, as illustrated in a letter sent in 1654 by Vijayaraghava to the VOC after a conflict about merchandise at the port of Karaikal. The Nayaka suggested here that the dispute had arisen because "your people are not waiting at the gates of my court with presents every time." Following this hint, he stated explicitly that the Dutch should send envoys with gifts over and over again. The same message was conveyed to the Danes and the English, the latter of whom complained in the 1620s that "the Naick or king [is] very covetous, expecting very great presents yearly."

Consequently, all European powers frequently dispatched gifts to the court to ensure business proceeded smoothly. Between the 1620s and 1660s, the Portuguese, the English, the Danes, and the Dutch variously presented the Nayakas with Persian carpets, Japanese objects, elephants, horses, all sorts of cloths, weapons, cash, sandalwood, and spices. In 1624, the Danes gave Raghunatha two ornamented bronze cannon and a bed of cypress or cedar wood. Whereas these gifts were accepted gratefully—the cannon reportedly being placed in the king's bedroom—in 1669 Vijayaraghava flatly rejected the presents offered by the Danes. As the Dutch wrote, the Nayaka deemed their value of about 1,000 guilders too low for his status. Insulted, he refused to let the envoys of the Danes return home and blocked all access to their settlement at Tranquebar, until they drove the besieging troops away.

There is less information about Tanjavur's counter gifts. In the early seventeenth century, Raghunatha honoured the Danes with exquisite cloths, garments, carpets, swords, daggers, and bows, while a courtier offered them a pig, goats, and other food stuffs. In 1624, the Danes were given a portrait of the Nayaka and a bed

[65] The purchasing power of 36,765 guilders in 1658 equalled that of 386,500 euros in 2018. See iisg.amsterdam/en/research/projects/hpw/calculate.php.

[66] NA, VOC, no. 1156, ff. 341-1v; no. 1231, ff. 149, 150v-1, 164, 278, 632, 720v-1: letters from Pulicat to Batavia, between Admiral Van Goens and Pulicat, from Chinanna Chetti to Van Goens, list of gifts for Tanjavur's Nayaka, Mar. 1645, Sept., Nov. 1658, Jan. 1659; Colenbrander *et al.*, *Dagh-register gehouden int Casteel Batavia ... anno 1644–1645*, 339; Coolhaas *et al.*, *Generale Missiven*, vol. II (The Hague, 1964), 599.

with ivory decorations, its estimated value a staggering 100,000 guilders. In the same year, they received two civet-cats, one of which, according to Jón Ólafsson, had sweet-smelling testicles when dead, whereas the other produced well-scented excrement while alive—the latter being sixty times as costly as the former. In marked contrast, after the Dutch sent some gifts to Vijayaraghava in 1656, he presented Governor Laurens Pit with just a robe of honour, its worth thought not to exceed 2 *reals* or 5 guilders.[67]

More is known about the way European companies treated ambassadors from the Nayaka court. Ólafsson reports that in late 1623 a prominent Tanjavur courtier visited the Danes with a retinue of seven servants, all travelling by palanquin, and twelve heavily armed soldiers displaying their martial skills and shouting. Welcomed with three volleys of the lined-up Danish garrison and three gunshots, the envoy explained he had come to purchase a large quantity of lead. The Danes replied they were happy to oblige him, but only if the Nayaka send a written specification of the exact weight and price. Greatly offended, the envoy left at once, without further ceremonial, to relate the incident to his king. Equally affronted, Raghunatha exchanged a few increasingly angry letters with the Danes, after which he declared they had broken the treaty and ordered his general to lay siege to the Danes at Tranquebar. It took Danish reinforcements to make the Tanjavur troops withdraw after several months. In March 1624 the Nayaka general visited the Danes again, now to conclude peace. Accompanied by 500 servants and nine palanquins, he was greeted with a cannonade, three volleys, blowing trumpets, and hoisted flags.[68]

While the Danes thus initially failed to pay deference to the king and his ambassador, leading to military retaliation, another Tanjavur envoy actually feared the Dutch were not given enough respect during a mission to them in 1664. This was ambassadress Vengamma, discussed in Chapter 3. She presented her Dutch hosts at Pulicat with a golden flag and a robe of honour, and, she explained, had planned to bring dancers and musicians to underscore her esteem for the Company. She had even provided them with new clothes, but they had run away fearing they would

[67] For these and other examples, see: NA, VOC, no. 1203, ff. 594-5; no. 1214, ff. 291v-2; no. 1229, f. 884v; no. 1231, f. 640; no. 1270, f. 495; no. 1277, f. 1472: correspondence between Vijayaraghava Nayaka and Pulicat, Feb., Apr. 1654, July 1656, letters from Pulicat and Nagapattinam to Batavia and Gentlemen XVII, Jan., July 1659, Sept. 1669, Feb. 1670; Foster, *The English Factories in India 1624–1629*, 19; BL/AAS, MM, no. 158: treaties of Tanjavur with the Danes and the French, ff. 5-10; Jeyaseela Stephen, *Expanding Portuguese Empire and the Tamil Economy*, 125; Prakash, *The Dutch Factories in India ... Vol. II*, 201-2, 220 (n. 22); Fihl, "Shipwrecked on the Coromandel," 240-1; Ólafsson, *The Life of the Icelander Jón Ólafsson*, vol. II, 182-3, 190; Ramanujam, *Unheard Voices*, ch. 1; Coolhaas *et al.*, *Generale Missiven*, vol. III, 98; Vriddhagirisan, *The Nayaks of Tanjore*, 103.

[68] Ólafsson, *The Life of the Icelander Jón Ólafsson*, vol. II, 173-82.

be shipped to Batavia. Although the Dutch hardly cared about this omission and honoured Vengamma with three gunshots, they did think her gifts were barely worth this salute. Nevertheless, at her departure they gave her a fine cloth and 25 *pagodas* (over 100 guilders) as "travel money," probably the same symbolic reimbursement referred to in Ikkeri as *gastos*, "betel money," and "rice money."[69]

The Dutch showed more reverence to the *kaul* (written agreement) obtained in December 1658 from Vijayaraghava to formalise their control over Nagapattinam. Engraved on a silver plate and personally blessed by the Nayaka, the document was welcomed outside the port's gates by four members of the local VOC council on horseback, accompanied by Dutch soldiers, three elephants, and an huge delegation of the town's prominent merchants and other inhabitants. Following local custom, the *kaul* was proclaimed in all the "heathen" (*gentieffse*, "Hindu") streets—no doubt to demonstrate the Company's legitimate possession of the port—and next brought "with great triumph" into the VOC's fort, while the king was honoured with three cannonades from seven guns.[70]

Such extensive ceremonial is rarely found in descriptions of Nayaka Tanjavur itself. One comparable case concerns the honour befalling Vijayaraghava's *guru* (preceptor). As a Jesuit letter from 1659 states, every December this man was paraded around town in a magnificent palanquin carried by palace women and preceded by another palanquin containing his slippers. Moreover, the Nayaka himself walked in front, swinging incense and paying homage to his *guru* continually. But Vijayaraghava also knew how to humiliate dignitaries. That is suggested by a Tamil text relating that when Madurai's King Chokkanatha Nayaka sent a delegate to ask for the hand of Vijayaraghava's daughter, the Tanjavur ruler had the Madurai envoy mounted on a donkey, branded with a red mark ("chona moodra"),[71] flogged, and sent off. As this work claims, this grave diplomatic affront was the direct cause for Chokkanatha's invasion of Tanjavur and thus led to the end of the kingdom's Nayaka dynasty.[72]

Finally, the VOC archives contain some instances of written courtesies exchanged between the Dutch and these Nayakas. A letter to Vijayaraghava of 1656 ended with the words: "May God protect Your Honourable Highness' person and wide-existing family with long years of health and all desired fortunes." In 1674,

[69] NA, VOC, no. 1246, f. 1514; no. 1248, ff. 1968-71: letters from Pulicat to Batavia, June-July 1664.

[70] NA, VOC, no. 1231, ff. 260v, 633: letters from Nagapattinam to Van Goens, from Pulicat to Batavia, Dec. 1658, Jan. 1659. For similar French-Mughal and Nayaka cases, see Raman, *Document Raj*, 147.

[71] Probably a corruption of *śoṇa mudrā* (red seal, stamp, or mark). I thank Paolo Aranha and Nikhil Bellarykar for suggesting this translation.

[72] Nelson, *The Madura Country*, vol. III, 160-1; Vriddhagirisan, *The Nayaks of Tanjore*, 159; BL/AAS, MG, no. 1, pt. 8: "The Cheritee or actions of the Vadaka-Rajahs of Tanjore, Trichinopully & Madura," f. 73. See also BL/AAS, MG, no. 1, pt. 24: "The Kyfeyat of Aachoota Bhoopal Naiq," ff. 185-6.

after the Nayakas' fall, Vijayaraghava's son Chengamaladasa—seeking support to regain his ancestral throne—began a letter to the Dutch saying he was healthy and asking about the condition of the VOC's Admiral Rijcklof van Goens. The latter replied he was most joyful at the prince's wellbeing and concluded with the wish that God would guard him and grant him victory. In the same vein, in 1620 Raghunatha wrote to the Danish king that Tanjavur was prospering and he hoped to receive similar news from Denmark.[73] Although few in number, these cases imply that this court's correspondence also called for eloquence, generally expressed by enquiring about each other's health and fortune.[74]

Although there are few sources on protocol at Tanjavur's Nayaka court, the examples above suggest it had much in common with other courts. As elsewhere, close links existed between protocol, on the one hand, and political and commercial matters, on the other. Insults—possibly reflecting smouldering tensions—easily escalated into mercantile conflicts and military clashes, and even, according to one tradition, the extinction of Tanjavur's Nayakas. Gifts appear to have been particularly valued in this kingdom. Prominently figuring in European records, presents to the court had to meet high standards before trade privileges were granted. Indeed, in one instance, the VOC's expenses on gifts exceeded any amount ever spent on presents for Vijayanagara's emperors. While the types of European gifts to these Nayakas were mostly the same as for other dynasties, the counter gifts of this court were seemingly dominated by robes of honour, presented on various occasions and to people of different ranks. On the whole, however, protocol in Nayaka-ruled Tanjavur appears to have been similar to that in Vijayanagara and Ikkeri.

Bhonsles of Tanjavur

Far more information is available on Tanjavur's protocol under the subsequent Bhonsle dynasty, especially in Dutch records. With regard to royal audiences, there are at least eight surviving reports of VOC embassies to the Bhonsles, visiting the ruler in the capital or the pilgrimage town of Tiruvarur. Dispatched between the late 1670s and mid-1760s, spanning the period from Ekoji I to Tuljaji II, these missions were usually undertaken to congratulate newly installed kings or greet them during tours of their kingdom, and so they often proceeded in a cordial manner.

[73] NA, VOC, no. 1214, f. 292v; no. 1302, ff. 614v, 617: letter from Pulicat to Vijayaraghava Nayaka, July 1756, correspondence between Chengamaladasa and Nagapattinam, June 1674; Ramanujam, *Unheard Voices*, ch. 1.

[74] See also this chapter's section on Tanjavur's Bhonsles for an example of these Nayakas addressing the Dutch.

Below we zoom in on the account of a Dutch embassy to Shahaji I, undertaken in 1688, because we also have a local portrayal of Shahaji's court, with which it can be compared. The latter is found in the laudatory Sanskrit poem *Śāhendra vilāsa*, composed by Sridhara Venkatesa (alias Ayyaval) under Shahaji's patronage. It describes how Shahaji enters his audience hall with a retinue of women and sits down on the throne, surrounded by ministers, vassals, poets, scholars, and musicians (VI 17-46). The text mentions two officials as being seated: Tryambaka Makhi, considered Tanjavur's most powerful courtier by the Dutch for some time, and his nephew Anandaraya (or Ananda Rao Peshwa), a celebrated *daḷavāy* (general). Elsewhere in the poem, the king is attended by musicians, female dancers, and carriers of his betel, spittoon, parasol, fly-whisk, and white silk cloth. Moreover, while Shahaji proceeds to his palace, town damsels cast eager looks at him (III:11-19; IV:52-8).[75]

Much less glorifying, but still quite positive, is the report of the VOC mission to Shahaji's court in 1688. The Dutch sent this embassy to convey their long overdue congratulations on his accession to the throne, but also to complain about the permission given by Tanjavur's regent of the "northern lowlands," Ragoji Pandidar, to the French to settle in the kingdom. The report includes two descriptions of Shahaji holding court in his audience hall, summarised below:

VOC ambassador Arnoldus Soolmans reached Tanjavur town on 18 November and had his first audience already the next day. Escorted by "chancellor" Koneri Pandidar, regent of the "southern lowlands" Baboji Pandidar, and musicians, he was brought from his lodging to a courtyard in the palace. Shahaji still being in his residence, Soolmans had to sit and wait some time until the king appeared, together with his younger brothers (and future successors) Sarabhoji and Tukkoji. When Shahaji sat on his throne, the envoy was ushered to the ruler's right side and graciously welcomed. Sitting on Shahaji's left side was Ragoji Pandidar, regent of the "northern lowlands." Before Soolmans sat down, he personally handed over a letter of the Dutch to the king.

After exchanging pleasantries, the envoy politely brought up the VOC's objections to the French presence in Tanjavur, running counter to the Dutch-Tanjavur treaty. Thereupon, Shahaji told the silent Ragoji Pandidar to order the French to depart. Soolmans next showed the VOC's gifts to the king, including a cockatoo with a silver chain, a lory parrot from Maluku with a golden chain, a gold necklace, silverware, two pistols, a "curiously designed" fan, cloths, spices, rosewater, sandalwood, a copper-gilded fountain crafted for the occasion, and what may have been two little dogs. Also presented were two elephants and some Persian horses, which comprised the annual "recognition" gifts the Dutch had to honour Tanjavur's rulers with. Although Shahaji complained about the small size of one elephant and the old age of

[75] Śrīdhara Venkatēśa, *Śāhendra Vilāsa*, 7-9, 11-12.

one horse, he was satisfied with the presents, particularly admiring the other horses and the fountain. When four hours had passed, the king gave Soolmans what probably were a cloth and some headgear, both made with gold thread (*gouden took, dito toepetij*),[76] and with his own hands offered the envoy betel-leaves and areca-nuts, thereby concluding the audience.

Several gifts and some pressure on the courtiers Koneri Pandidar and Baboji Pandidar were needed before Soolmans secured his second and final audience, two-and-a-half weeks later, on the evening of 5 December, at the same location. Again placed on Shahaji's right-hand side, the envoy was given some food, after which he—on Koneri's and Baboji's advice—presented the king with two more gold necklaces and silk, much to his pleasure. After a request for exotic weaponry,[77] Shahaji honoured Soolmans by putting on him, with his own hands, a kind of cloak, and giving him a silken cloth and betel. Then the king stood up, extended his hand, wished the ambassador a good trip back home, and ordered Baboji to escort Soolmans out of the palace. There, an elephant was waiting to parade him around the fort, still dressed in the king's cloak, accompanied by music and hundreds of people.[78]

Together, the *Śāhendra vilāsa* and the Dutch account of 1688 sketch a picture reminding us of ideas found in Indian political treatises. Clearly, at the Bhonsle court, too, one's position in relation to the king and permission to sit down signified one's eminence. The report of envoy Soolmans specifically states he was seated on Shahaji's right-hand side at both audiences. If the king's right side really indicated a higher status than his left side—implied by some texts from the Vijayanagara period—this means Shahaji twice bestowed a great honour on the Dutchman.[79] That was perhaps exceptional because Dutch accounts of audiences with Ekoji I and Ekoji II in 1676 and 1735 say the envoys had to sit in front of the king, in the latter case at a distance of about 18 feet.

That great reverence could be shown to some ambassadors also transpires from physical contacts with the Bhonsles. Since a king's body was deemed sacred and few could touch or get close to him, envoys usually presented letters to rulers

[76] "Took" may derive from the French *toque*, little hat or beret. I thank an anonymous reviewer for this suggestion. The Dutch seem to have used the term for a kind of turban or piece of cloth. See also H. Dunlop (ed.), *Bronnen tot de geschiedenis der Oostindische Compagnie in Perzië*, vol. I (The Hague, 1930), 811. For "toepetij," possibly referring to a hat, see Yule and Burnell, *Hobson-Jobson*, 935.

[77] Shahaji's requests comprised two "curious" shields, some "curious" swords (*houwers*), and a "calessie," perhaps a corruption and diminutive of *kuras*, breastplate or suit of armour. I thank Jos Gommans for this suggestion. See also NA, VOC, no. 1361, f. 474v: report of VOC envoy Viraraja Ayyan at Tanjavur, Aug. 1680.

[78] NA, VOC, no. 1463, ff. 185v-6v, 205-15: letter from Nagapattinam to Gentlemen XVII, Dec. 1688, report of mission to Tanjavur, Nov.-Dec. 1688.

[79] The *Bhoṃsale vaṃśa caritra* also suggests that the king's left and right were reserved for different groups of people. See Ranade, "Comparative Study of Tanjore Marathi (1750-1850 A.D.) and Modern Marathi," 50-1.

indirectly via courtiers. Yet, as Soolmans claimed, he gave his letter directly to Shahaji, he received betel straight from the king's hands, a cloak was put on him by the ruler personally, and Shahaji may even have offered him a handshake.[80] These were not isolated events. In 1676, Ekoji I himself handed over a silver *kaul* (written agreement) and betel to the Dutch ambassadors. In 1735, Ekoji II concluded an audience by presenting the VOC envoys with a bowl of fruits, saying he had laid his own hands on these. According to the Dutch, this gesture "signified the strongest proof of extraordinary affection and was regarded as a blessing [*zeegeninge*]." Indeed, Ekoji II's last words to his guests were that he hoped no other envoys than they would return to him in future because he could speak with them "mouth to mouth," probably indicating one or both of them spoke Marathi.[81] Judging from these cases, European ambassadors could be held in high esteem by the Bhonsles. However, at south Indian courts an act like taking betel from a king's hand, although honourable, was also considered a demonstration of subordination—something the VOC envoys failed to mention in their reports.[82]

The Dutch missions to the Bhonsles point to various other aspects of protocol at this court. First, these embassies comprised few audiences. Soolmans' visit was the only one by a Dutchman (rather than an Indian delegate of the VOC) that included two encounters with the king. Every other mission consisted of just one audience, at which envoys were both welcomed and dismissed, gifts presented, and negotiations—if any—conducted, all within one session. Consequently, there were no subsequent meetings that could be endlessly postponed, and even the first audience was usually granted quickly. Further, Dutch gifts were generally similar to what Soolmans brought in 1688 and to what the VOC presented at other courts. Besides the usual spices, jewels, cloths, arms, and cash, these included exotic animals and rare European devices, like binoculars, eyeglasses, and watches.[83]

Although the amounts spent on gifts during embassies fluctuated, some long-term patterns can be discerned. Recently installed monarchs, who had to

[80] Jaffer, "Diplomatic Encounters," 78. For a possible handshake and hugs between the king of Kandy and Dutch envoys in the early seventeenth century, see: Pauline Lunsingh Scheurleer, "Uitwisseling van staatsieportretten op Ceylon in 1602," in Lodewijk Wagenaar (ed.), *Aan de overkant: Ontmoetingen in dienst van de VOC en WIC (1600-1800)* (Leiden, 2015), passim, especially 165-70, 177-8; Obeyesekere, "Between the Portuguese and the Nāyakas," 163.

[81] NA, VOC, no. 1329, ff. 1172v-4; no. 2386, ff. 165-7: reports of missions to Tanjavur, Dec. 1676, Nov. 1735.

[82] Ali, "The Betel-Bag Bearer," 541-3. See also this chapter's section on Vijayanagara.

[83] For Danish gifts during an embassy in 1735 to congratulate the newly installed Ekoji II—including horses from Aceh, silver tableware, rosewater sprayers, Chinese silk, and European curiosities—see: Josefine Baark, "The *Tranquebar Palampore*: Trade, Diplomacy, and 'a Little Amusement' in an Early Modern Indo-Danish Textile," *Eighteenth-Century Studies* 52, 1 (2018), 76; Larsen, "En dansk Gesandtskabrejse i Indien," 59.

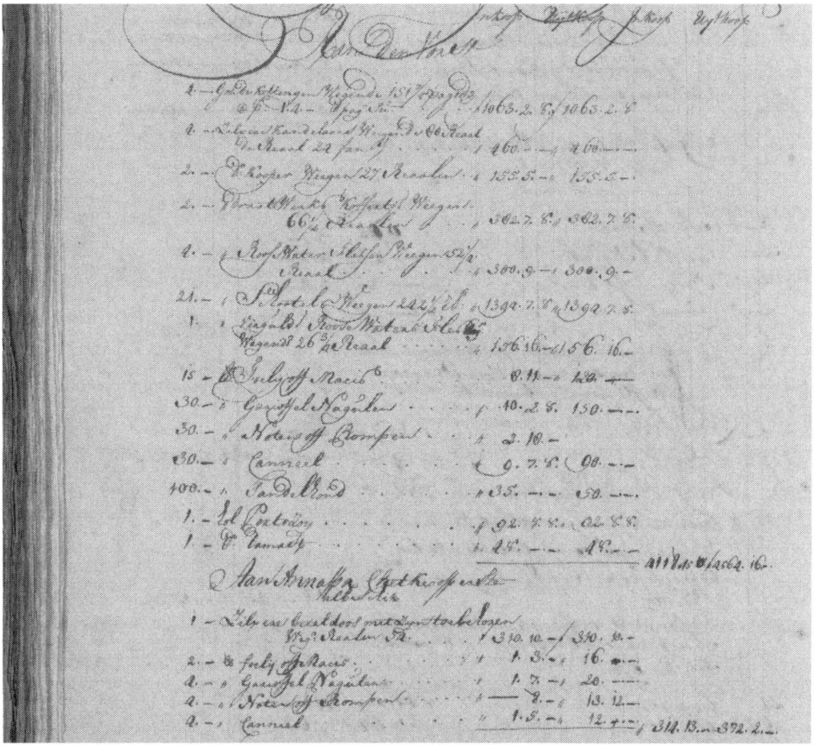

Illustration 12: List of gifts (with costs in guilders) presented to Pratapasimha Bhonsle of Tanjavur (*Aan den Vorst*) and "supreme ordain-it-all" Annappa Rao Shetke (*Aan Annappa Chetke opperste albeschik*) during their visit to the Dutch at Nagapattinam in May 1741, among other items including four gold necklaces, four silver candles, rosewater, spices, a hundred pounds of sandalwood, and cloths for the former, and a silver betel-box for the latter, *Nationaal Archief*, The Hague, archives of the *Verenigde Oost-Indische Compagnie*, no. 2539, f. 2490 (courtesy *Nationaal Archief*, source: www.nationaalarchief.nl/onderzoeken/archief/1.04.02/invnr/2539/file).

be congratulated, were given presents costing between 3,000 and 5,400 guilders, whether the Dutch met them at the capital or elsewhere. On other encounters outside the capital, usually at Tiruvarur, the value never exceeded about half of that.[84]

[84] NA, VOC, no. 1316, ff. 315, 331; no. 1329, f. 1172v; no. 1621, f. 35v; no. 1638, ff. 9-10; no. 1778, f. 95; no. 1819, ff. 38-8v; no. 2024, f. 195; no. 2031, ff. 439-41, 1299; no. 2147, ff. 4833v-4v, 4837; no. 2166, ff. 398-9; no. 2386, ff. 66-7, 70-1; no. 2538, f. 1414; no. 2539, ff. 2487-8, 2490; no. 3108, ff. 97-8: letters from Nagapattinam to Van Goens and Batavia, Nov.-Dec. 1676, Dec. 1698, Jan. 1700, May 1709, May 1712, May, Oct. 1725, July 1741, reports of missions to Tanjavur, Dec. 1676, Feb. 1764, lists of gifts for the Tanjavur king, Apr. 1725, Apr. 1730, May 1741, Nagapattinam proceedings, Mar. 1730, Nov. 1735.

A special case was Pratapasimha's visit to the Dutch at Nagapattinam in 1741, when he received gifts worth over 4,000 guilders (see illustration 12).[85] On average, these amounts were lower than what was spent for Vijayanagara's emperors, but quite a bit higher than what the few available numbers suggest for expenses in Ikkeri. The latter inequality may be related to the different reasons the Dutch generally sent embassies to Tanjavur (honouring new kings) and Ikkeri (lodging complaints), but it is also possible they held Tanjavur's Bhonsles in higher esteem than Ikkeri's Nayakas.

As under Tanjavur's Nayakas, in between embassies gifts also played an essential role in Dutch-Bhonsle relations. A VOC report from 1679 concerning the Tanjavur region states that south Indian kings had to be honoured with presents according to their status (*qualiteijt*), as they paid a great deal of attention to gifts, making sure not to give more than what they received. A Dutch letter of some years later complains about court representatives employing all possible means—including "improprieties" (*onbetamelijke middelen*)—to obtain presents from the VOC. Giving in to this had bad consequences since "their greedy mind [*hebsugtig gemoet*] is never satisfied, but always calls for more," or as the Dutch put it in 1688: "gold is their idol [*afgod*]."

Still, in 1738 Governor Elias Guillot of the Coromandel Coast wrote to his successor Jacob Mossel that regents and other courtiers should receive presents regularly, or even annually, to keep them on the VOC's side. Following local custom, Guillot explained, gifts were essential for example during visits and "remarkable incidents," yet this should not evolve into habitual events. In 1744, Mossel in turn urged his successor to limit irregular gifts since these caused expectations of yearly presents. As he concluded, the VOC could hardly abolish gifts that had grown customary without damaging its interests.[86]

Whether these men exaggerated or not, the Dutch had to honour the court with presents in all kinds of situations and courtiers frequently reminded them of this.[87] To begin with, as part of the Dutch-Tanjavur agreements, the VOC was

[85] The purchasing power of 4,000 guilders in 1741 equalled that of 40,300 euros in 2018. See iisg.amsterdam/en/research/projects/hpw/calculate.php.

[86] NA, VOC, no. 1349, f. 1405; no. 1384, f. 87; no. 2443, ff. 2676, 2772-4; no. 2631, ff. 516-17: report by Jan Sweers about the Tanjavur region, May 1679, letter from Pulicat to Batavia, Mar. 1683, final reports (*memorie van overgave*) of Coromandel Governors Elias Guillot and Jacob Mossel, Sept. 1738, Feb. 1744; ANRI, BC, no. 150e (unpaginated, entry of 30 June): Nagapattinam diary extract, June 1688. See also Martin, *India in the 17th Century*, vol. 2, pt. II (New Delhi, 1985), 1212.

[87] For some examples, see NA, VOC, no. 1361, ff. 474-4v, 480; no. 1369, f. 1531; no. 1499, ff. 75v-6; no. 2147, ff. 4833v-4v; no. 2334, ff. 182v-3; no. 2399, ff. 301-2; no. 2443, f. 2035; no. 2538, f. 265 (following f. 273); no. 2661, ff. 244v-6; no. 3108, ff. 24-5: report of VOC envoy Viraraja Ayyan at Tanjavur, Aug. 1680, letters from Nagapattinam and Pulicat to Batavia, Sept. 1680, July 1681, Aug. 1691, Oct. 1735, Oct. 1737,

to present the king annually with 4,200 *pardaos* (c. 8,400 guilders), one large or two small elephants, and, from 1688 onward, two Arab horses. Technically, these were not gifts but a "recognition" in exchange for the VOC's possession of some land around Nagapattinam.[88] Actual gifts were donated equally often, required to complement meetings and letters. Whenever courtiers, local governors, "regents of the lowlands," or their representatives called at Nagapattinam, the VOC variously presented them with elephants, weapons, jewels, and so on, sometimes totalling 700 guilders. A Tanjavur envoy named Viliyandu Khan ("Biliendoechan"), sailing in 1721 to Jaffna on Ceylon to select elephants from the VOC's stables, received the usual spices, rosewater, sandalwood, and betel, as well as 840 guilders in cash. Based on a daily amount of 15 guilders, multiplied by the fifty-six days Viliyandu Khan stayed in Jaffna, this was probably another case of the reimbursement ambassadors received from their hosts.

Other events that required gifts included marriages and births in the royal house or courtiers' families, appointments of officials, and local festivals. Between the 1720s and 1740s, for example, the Dutch sent presents for the weddings of Kings Pratapasimha and Tuljaji, the *sūbadār* of Mannargudi, and "ordain-it-all" Imam Khan Kurush Sahib, or their relatives, sometimes worth hundreds of guilders.[89] The VOC also presented gifts when Tiruvarur's *Sūbadār* Ivaji Pandidar became prime minister in 1735 and ambassador Bavadi Nayaka was appointed "state governor" (*rijksbestierder*) in 1750, in the latter case amounting to over 1,000 guilders. The arrival of a new Dutch governor in Nagapattinam could be reason for distributing presents, too. In 1698, upon the installation of Dirk Coomans, the VOC spent 1,171 guilders on a gold necklace and other items for Shahaji and his chief minister, probably to win their goodwill. With regard to festivals, in 1700 the VOC was asked to honour Shahaji with a delegation and gifts because of the so-called *spade feest*

Sept. 1738, Nov. 1746, Nagapattinam proceedings (with correspondence with the Tanjavur court), Mar. 1730, Sept. 1740, letter from Tuljaji II's uncle to Nagapattinam, Feb. 1764.

88 For a survey of elephants and horses presented to Tanjavur between 1677 and 1730, see NA, VOC, no. 2166, ff. 205-8: final report of Governor Dirk van Cloon, Mar. 1730. For the early treaties between the VOC and Tanjavur's Bhonsles, see Heeres and Stapel, *Corpus diplomaticum Neerlando-Indicum*, vol. 3 (The Hague, 1934), 34-9, 446-50.

89 For these and other examples, see: NA, VOC, no. 1835, f. 313v; no. 1957, ff. 1229, 1239-40v, 1258-60; no. 2024, f. 195; no. 2076, f. 1347; no. 2198, f. 13 (2nd numeration); no. 2243, f. 558; no. 2244, f. 766 (2nd numeration); no. 2386, ff. 943-4; no. 2412, ff. 371-3 (1st numeration), ff. 62, 273-4 (2nd numeration); no. 2427, ff. 465-5v; no. 2443, ff. 311-12, 314 (2nd numeration); no. 2471, f. 1225; no. 2506, ff. 85-6; no. 2594, f. 497; no. 2744, f. 519; no. 2764, f. 25: letters from Nagapattinam to Batavia, Aug. 1713, Oct. 1725, Sept. 1731, June 1737, Oct. 1743, Oct.-Nov. 1749, letters from Jaffna to Colombo, May, July 1721, list of gifts presented in Coromandel, 1726-7, 1730-2, 1734-9, Nagapattinam proceedings (extract), Aug. 1738, Sept. 1740; ANRI, BC, no. 150e (unpaginated, entry of 30 June): Nagapattinam diary extract, June 1688. See also Martin, *India in the 17th Century*, vol. 2, pt. II, 1399, 1434, 1459, 1527.

("shovel festival"), celebrated in September or October. This probably referred to Vishvakarma Puja, when tools were worshipped and blessed.[90] On both this occasion and what was termed "new year's day," the Dutch also gave presents to Nagapattinam's prominent residents and military chiefs.

Besides such recurrent occasions, all sorts of other opportunities were seized to claim gifts. In 1700 the VOC was requested to send presents to Baboji Pandidar because of his injuries sustained in a battle. In 1709, when *Sūbadār* Annaji Pandit intermediated in a conflict with the court, the Dutch felt compelled to present him with 2,500 guilders. And in 1713 the *Havaldār* (local commander) Ranga Pandidar obstructed Nagapattinam's water supply, forcing the VOC to give him 100 guilders to end the blockade. Indeed, it was well-nigh compulsory to present gifts and failing to do so caused offense, as illustrated by Jan Sweers' inspection tour in 1679 of weaver's towns in Tanjavur. The Dutchman deliberately bypassed Tiruvarur to avoid meeting Baboji Pandidar, who would expect expensive presents. Instead, he visited the nearby village of Vijayapuram, whose local chief was satisfied with a modest gift.[91]

The court obviously also donated gifts to the VOC. Tanjavur's presents during the Dutch embassy of 1688 were largely similar to gifts at other missions. In 1676, Ekoji honoured the envoys with robes of honour, belts, turbans, a white parasol, a palanquin, and a fan. Demonstrating south India's hybrid court culture, the first items belonged to ceremonial originating from Muslim-ruled courts, while the latter ones traditionally symbolised Indian kingship.[92] Later VOC envoys received robes, turbans, and gold-striped belts as well.[93] In fact, the court sent such items to the Dutch yearly, in exchange for their annual money and animals. Although the Dutch certainly understood this was a mark of honour, they were hardly

[90] I thank Pius Malekandathil, Sukhad Keshkamat, and Pierre Moreira for discussing the meaning of *spade feest* (at which arms may have been worshipped too). See also: Constance A. Jones, "Vishwakarma Puja," in J. Gordon Melton *et al.* (eds), *Religious Celebrations: An Encyclopedia of Holidays, Festivals, Solemn Observances, and Spiritual Commemorations* (Santa Barbara/Denver/Oxford, 2011), vol. 1, 908; Rogerius, *De open-deure tot het verborgen heydendom*, 135-6.

[91] NA, VOC, no. 1349, f. 1402; no. 1411, f. 120v; no. 1621, f. 35v; no. 1633, f. 144v; no. 1778, ff. 97-8; no. 1835, ff. 290v-1v; no. 2317, f. 192; no. 2387, ff. 322-3; no. 2764, f. 237: report by Jan Sweers about the Tanjavur region, May 1679, "news register" from Nagapattinam, Feb. 1685, letters from Nagapattinam to Pulicat and Batavia, Dec. 1698, Oct. 1700, May 1709, Aug. 1713, May 1750, list of gifts exchanged in Coromandel, 1732-3, Nagapattinam proceedings, June 1736. See also other annual lists of gifts exchanged in Coromandel.

[92] See Chapter 5 for court ceremonial deriving from Muslim-ruled polities.

[93] NA, VOC, no. 1329, f. 1174; no. 2031, f. 1122; no. 2166, f. 395; no. 2197, f. 581; no. 2386, f. 166; no. 2539, f. 2484; no. 3108, ff. 93, 105: reports of missions to Tanjavur, Tiruvarur, and Naguru, Dec. 1676, Mar.-Apr. 1725, Mar.-Apr. 1730, Nov. 1735, May 1741, Feb. 1764, list of gifts exchanged in Coromandel, 1729-30, Nagapattinam proceedings, Feb. 1764.

impressed. They registered the received garments as merchandise—their value generally estimated at 30 to 60 guilders—that could be sold and thus compensate their expenses on gifts. Marathi letters from Tuljaji II to the Danes also mention cloths (*cādara*) "with flowery work," shawls "bright as the moon" (*mahatābī*), and turbans "embroidered with gold" (*maṃdila*)—all given by the king "out of love and in agreement with the custom." Only seldom were European powers presented with other kinds of presents. One rare example concerns three falcons given to the Dutch in 1680 by the then Prince Shahaji.[94]

Gifts exchanged between the Bhonsles and other Indian parties were more diverse. The chronicle *Bhoṃsale vaṃśa caritra* relates that the kings and their ancestors received presents from the Muslim dynasties to whom they owed allegiance at different moments. Thus, the rulers of Ahmadnagar, Bijapur, and Arcot variously honoured the Bhonsles with war animals, arms, cloths, golden and silver drums, a throne, and an exotic bird. Texts like the *Śāhendra vilāsa* and *Pratāpasimhendra vijaya prabandha* state that the Bhonsles themselves presented gifts to their courtiers, poets, and messengers bringing news of victory, which besides the abovementioned items included land and, in one case, the privilege to use a palanquin, an umbrella, and three different musical instruments. According to the VOC, Shahaji I even bestowed his own palanquin and other marks of honour (*eertekenen*) on the regent of the "northern lowlands," Ragoji Pandidar, while Shahaji II sent nine elephants, fifteen horses, and jewels worth 15,000 *pardao*s to Arcot to sue for peace.[95] As all examples show, vast amounts of money were spent

94 For the Danish letters, see Strandberg, *The Moḍī Documents from Tanjore in Danish Collections*, 114-15, 136-7, 296, 305. For gifts to the Danes, see also Larsen, "En dansk Gesandtskabrejse i Indien," 66-7. For Dutch examples, see NA, VOC, no. 1329, f. 1291; no. 1355, ff. 148v-9; no. 1803, f. 303v; no. 1835, f. 314; no. 1849, f. 421v; no. 1990, f. 151v; no. 1997, f. 23; no. 2007, f. 335v; no. 2043, f. 139; no. 2065, f. 227v; no. 2076, f. 1349; no. 2092, ff. 55-5v; no. 2135, ff. 149, 152 (3rd numeration); no. 2220, ff. 262v-3; no. 2243, ff. 562, 739; no. 2244, f. 768 (2nd numeration); no. 2289, f. 112; no. 2304, ff. 323-3v; no. 2317, ff. 192-3; no. 2334, f. 185; no. 2351, ff. 3999-4000; no. 2386, f. 169; no. 2387, f. 163; no. 2412, f. 374 (1st numeration), f. 103 (2nd numeration); no. 2442, ff. 61-2; no. 2443, ff. 314, 446 (2nd numeration); no. 2538, ff. 1556, 1657; no. 3108, ff. 104-5: report on Tirumullaivasal, Mar. 1677, letters from Nagapattinam to Colombo and Batavia, Oct. 1680, Sept. 1711, Aug. 1713, Nov. 1714, May, Oct. 1723, Oct. 1726, Oct. 1727, Oct. 1728, Feb., Oct. 1732, Mar. 1733, Oct. 1734, Oct. 1735, lists of gifts exchanged in Coromandel, 1726-33, 1735-8, Nagapattinam proceedings, Oct.-Nov. 1735, Mar., Oct. 1736, Oct. 1737, Nov. 1738, Feb., June 1741, Feb. 1764.

95 BL/AAS, MT, class III, no. 87: "The historycal account of the Tonjore," ff. 33v-4, 55-5v, 120; MG, no. 10, pt. 13: "Marhatta account of the first establishment & progress of the English government at Madras," f. 226 (see Cotton, Charpentier, and Johnston, *Catalogue of Manuscripts in European Languages*, vol. I, pt. II, 80, 96); Ramakrishna Kavi Pandit, *Pratapasimhendra Vijaya Prabandha*, 33; Śrīdhara Venkatēśa, *Śāhendra Vilāsa*, 16; NA, VOC, no. 1448, f. 324; no. 2455, ff. 524-4v: letter from VOC envoy Rangappa to Nagapattinam, Feb. 1689, report by Tanjavur envoy Jaganatha Pandidar, June 1739.

on gifts in Tanjavur, both by Europeans and by the court. Presents were seemingly indispensable to maintain relations both within and without the kingdom.

Other important elements of protocol were welcome and departure ceremonies. Dutch ambassadors travelling from Nagapattinam to Tanjavur town were generally first welcomed by the governors of Mannargudi or Tiruvarur, halfway and at one-third of the route respectively. Near the capital, courtiers awaited them and accompanied them to their lodging—usually a house, sometimes a temple—provided with food and other necessities. After audiences, often still dressed in robes of honour and turbans, they were escorted by courtiers and musicians. Following a meeting with Ekoji I in 1677, envoys Thomas van Rhee and Pieter Outshoorn Sonnevelt were guided out of the palace "amid singing and as many as twenty musical instruments," placed on elephants, given fans and white umbrellas, and paraded around town amidst numerous curious onlookers. Later, they received betel and areca from Ekoji and turbans from *Qiladār* (fort-commander) Sayyid and were taken on a tour of the capital's fortifications before courtiers, drummers, and horn-blowers accompanied them out of town for half an hour.[96]

On their part, the Dutch staged their embassies as rather grandiose affairs. The expenses for a mission to Tuljaji II in 1764 included the hiring and feeding of a retinue of 555 servants—among whom seventy-eight palanquin-bearers, 200 gift-carriers, twenty-five European and 210 non-European soldiers, four drummers, seven horn-blowers, six torch-bearers, one interpreter, one Brahmin, five cooks, and one barber—costing approximately 2,200 guilders for ten days.[97] Thus, the VOC showed its reverence for the court, but no doubt also wanted to display its power.

Two events demonstrate well how the VOC in turn welcomed visitors from Tanjavur. One was a call of Baboji Pandidar, "regent of the southern lowlands," at Nagapattinam in June 1688. Quite exceptionally, an extensive Dutch description of this encounter remains, even though this was a meeting on a relatively low diplomatic level, usually not reported in detail to the Company's higher echelons. Sections of the account are summarised below:

When reaching the town of Sikkal, close to the VOC's territories, Baboji Pandidar was greeted by a middle-ranking Dutch functionary, Jan Sweers, supervisor of the lands around Nagapattinam. The settlement's highest official, commander Floris Blom, and his councillors, seated on horseback, were waiting for the regent at Puthur, on the port's outskirts, to escort him into town. But Baboji

[96] NA, VOC, no. 1329, ff. 1169v-72, 1174-6v; no. 1463, ff. 205-8; no. 2386, f. 164; no. 3108, ff. 88-90: reports of missions to Tanjavur, Dec. 1676-Jan. 1677, Nov. 1688, Nov. 1735, Feb. 1764.

[97] For this and other examples, see NA, VOC, no. 2031, ff. 1119-23; no. 2166, ff. 391-5, 400-1; no. 3108, ff. 102-4: reports of missions to Tiruvarur, Mar.-Apr. 1725, Mar.-Apr. 1730, lists of expenses for missions to Tiruvarur and Tanjavur, Apr. 1730, Feb. 1764.

sent messengers to Blom stating that the regent would not enter the Company's lands unless the commander came to meet him outside these territories. Considering Baboji's prominence, Blom complied. Finding Baboji standing amidst his entourage, the commander exchanged some courtesies with him, whereupon the regent made Blom accompany him "by the hand" to his palanquin. After the commander next sat down in his own palanquin, Baboji insisted that Blom go first. When the procession passed the Oranje Gate in the outermost wall, seven guns were fired, while the arrival at Nagapattinam proper was marked by a cannonade of thirteen guns.

At the commander's residence, Blom personally guided Baboji into the meeting room, where the VOC's officials sat on the table's left side and the regent, his brother, a brother-in-law, and a nephew on its right side, with Baboji and Blom facing each other. The regent presented the commander with a cloth and what was possibly a turban ("tooke"). The latter was also given to all other members of the VOC council. After some pleasantries, negotiations started, concerning a few debated clauses in the recently drawn-up but not yet signed Dutch-Tanjavur treaty. At the end of the meeting, Blom presented the guests with gifts (including gold necklaces and rings, a sword, cloths, and spices), honoured them with betel, sprinkled them with rosewater, and exchanged more courtesies with them. Last, the entire council escorted the regent and his retinue through the inner town walls, where they were saluted with fifteen gunshots, and beyond the Oranje Gate, marked by the firing of nine cannon.[98]

Again—now on the level of a regional official instead of a king—one notices the great value attached to protocol and the hierarchy it signified. As a prominent courtier, Baboji refused to enter the land of what was no doubt seen as a subordinate power without being received by a high-ranking person. Also, Blom had to escort the regent to his palanquin, precede him in the procession, and seat him at the meeting's room right side—all indicating the two men's different statuses. Following this ceremonial was essential to safeguard the VOC's interests.

This held especially true when in May 1741 the Dutch at Nagapattinam hosted their most distinguished guest ever: King Pratapasimha. There is no specific report of this reception, but some idea of how it proceeded transpires from other documents, especially the list of the VOC's expenses on this occasion. The king's visit was part of a trip to the pilgrimage centre of Tiruvarur and the port of Naguru, site of an important Muslim shrine. The Bhonsles called at these places regularly,[99] but Pratapasimha's stay at Nagapattinam was a one-time event.

[98] ANRI, BC, no. 150e (unpaginated, entry of 30 June): Nagapattinam diary extract, June 1688.

[99] For royal visits to Tiruvarur, see the previous paragraphs. For royal visits to Naguru, see NA, VOC, no. 1508, f. 554; no. 1621, f. 35v; no. 1778, f. 95: letter from Baboji Pandidar to Nagapattinam, Dec. 1692, letters from Nagapattinam to Batavia, Dec. 1698, May 1709. For the Bhonsles' relations with the Naguru shrine, see also S. Chinnaiyan, "Royal Patronage to Islam in Tanjore Maratha Kingdom [as Gleaned from Modi Records]," *Proceedings of the Indian History Congress* 65 (2004), 371.

When the king announced he wished to visit the town to meet Governor Jacob Mossel and worship the deity "Tiagaruasgia Swanie" (probably Tyagaraja at the Kayarohanasvami Temple),[100] the VOC council discussed how to receive him appropriately. As this meeting's notes make clear, different scenarios were considered, depending on the direction from which Pratapasimha would arrive. In any case, the king would be escorted to the governor's residence along a route guarded by soldiers between the town wall and the inner fortress' gate and lined with clerks within the fortress. He would also be requested not to enter the town with more than 200 horsemen.

A letter sent to Batavia some months later suggests that the VOC's thorough preparations worked out well. Arriving in the afternoon of 27 May, Pratapasimha was received at the town wall with a lengthy cannonade and shown around Nagapattinam's main streets. Inside the fort, Governor Mossel led him by the hand into his residence and onto a purpose-built throne. While the VOC council sat down on chairs on one side, Tanjavur's courtiers were seated on a raised platform on the other side. When after about two hours the meeting ended, Mossel presented the king with gifts and guided him, again by the hand, to the fort's bulwarks and the inner courtyard, where they said goodbye. A Dutch junior merchant (*onderkoopman*) accompanied Pratapasimha to the town's Oranje Gate where the king was honoured with a specially made horse-drawn carriage. After showing his appreciation, he departed from Nagapattinam.

The long list of expenses for this event suggests the VOC tried its best to host Pratapasimha in a befitting manner, with all due pomp and circumstance. The throne, which included a canopy and a footrest, was constructed partly of scarlet, Persian velvet, silk, forty small mirrors, four chains, and gold paper, worth nearly 670 guilders. The carriage was made of the same cloths, as well as red leather, 10,000 "leaves of Chinese gold," silver, copper, dyestuffs, and other materials, costing 1,178 guilders. Among the expenses were also a small crown with fake pearls, two horses, triumphal arches at all town gates, several shelters ("pandaals"), renovations on the king's temporary lodging, 2,608 pounds of gunpowder (for gunshots and fireworks), and three clothed rowing vessels, manned by sailors dressed up for the occasion. Combining these purchases (over 5,000 guilders) with the gifts for Pratapasimha and his retinue (about 6,000 guilders), the VOC had spent more than 11,000 guilders.[101]

[100] Jagadisa Ayyar, *South Indian Shrines*, 100-1.

[101] NA, VOC, no. 2538, ff. 1413-16, 1615-17, 1629-32; no. 2539, ff. 2483-4, 2490-4: letter from Nagapattinam to Batavia, July 1741, Nagapattinam proceedings, May 1741, report of mission to Naguru, May 1741, list of expenses on the Tanjavur king's visit to Nagapattinam, May 1741. See also *Beknopte historie*, 98. For *pandal*, see Yule and Burnell, *Hobson-Jobson*, 665-6.

Since the king appeared satisfied with his reception, the Dutch had probably followed the required protocol correctly, even though it included several unique elements. One was the extent of the cannonades, totalling no fewer than 362 gunshots.[102] In 1688, regent Baboji Pandidar was received and sent off with a total of forty-four gunshots, and when Tanjavur's ambassador Viliyandu Khan called at Jaffna in 1721, he was politely denied a cannonade, although he specifically asked for it and was highly regarded by the Dutch. However, this refusal was accepted by the envoy and did not affect the outcome of his mission.[103]

Finally, with regard to protocol in Dutch-Tanjavur correspondence, little more can be said about the Bhonsles than about the Nayakas. The former seem to have sent just a few letters to the VOC in their own name and generally let functionaries take care of this.[104] The surviving letters signed by these rulers—only some of which the Dutch fully translated, including their formal opening and concluding sections—contain few of the civilities found in the correspondence with the Nayakas of Tanjavur and Ikkeri. In 1689, the Dutch Commissioner Hendrik Adriaan van Rheede let Shahaji I know that he was in a state of good health, although without asking about the king's condition. Maybe this was a diplomatic blunder, or possibly the Company was reacting to an earlier statement by Shahaji about his wellbeing. For in correspondence with the French at Pondicherry in 1739-40, Shahaji II and Pratapasimha regularly mentioned they were healthy and enquired after the French governor's condition.

Yet, letters of the court to the Danes suggest that often only officials asked about the addressee's health, the rulers perhaps considering this below their status.[105] However, correspondence from Tanjavur's courtiers to the VOC has a rather sober tone, too, although here the Dutch also often left out standard passages in their translations. Letters from Baboji Pandidar around 1690 contain some examples, the regent enquiring after the health of VOC chiefs and saying he was fine himself. The Company's replies occasionally include similar phrases, wishing that God protect Baboji's health and fortunes.[106]

102 About seventeen shots were fired when the king arrived at and departed from the town limits, 124 while he traversed the inner town, 141 when he reached and left the central fort, and eighty at various other occasions.

103 NA, VOC, no. 1957, ff. 1221-2, 1231: correspondence between Jaffna and Colombo, May 1721.

104 Letters with royal signatures were considered special marks of honour. See Raman, *Document Raj*, 147.

105 Strandberg, *The Moḍī Documents from Tanjore in Danish Collections*, 57, 285, 287, 294. For an example of the silken letter bags, decorated with a gold-brocade lotus pattern, with which the Tanjavur court honoured the Danes when writing to them, see Louise Sebro, "You Ask Me Who Is King...," in Esther Fihl (ed.), *The Governor's Residence in Tranquebar: The House and the Daily Life of Its People, 1770–1845* (Copenhagen, 2017), 101.

106 NA, VOC, no. 1448, f. 319v; no. 1454, ff. 1017-17v; no. 1463, f. 427v; no. 1518, ff. 884-5, 887v-8v: correspondence of Shahaji I and Baboji Pandidar with Nagapattinam, Aug. 1688, Jan., July 1689, Apr.

Still, despite this relative lack of written courtesies, in the Tamil version of the Dutch-Tanjavur treaty of 1676, Ekoji I appears to have addressed the VOC's Admiral Rijcklof van Goens in an exceptionally exalted way, referring to him as "maharaja" (*maharāśa*), a title also used for the king himself in this document. This seems another illustration of how Europeans were incorporated into south India's systems of honour and protocol. Nevertheless, in the Telugu version of a treaty of 1658, Tanjavur's Vijayaraghava Nayaka had not been willing to pay homage to Van Goens' similarly named father in such terms, just calling him "admiral" (*amarāl*).[107] Possibly, Vijayaraghava was annoyed because he had to acknowledge the VOC's recent take-over of Nagapattinam from the Portuguese—which the Nayaka initially contested—while the newly established Ekoji may have wished to build up a harmonious relationship with the Company.

Not all diplomatic encounters between the Bhonsles and the Dutch proceeded as smoothly as Arnoldus Soolmans' mission to Tanjavur and Pratapasimha's visit to Nagapattinam. At this court, too, insults occurred with some regularity. Perhaps the most extreme case concerned a VOC embassy to Sarabhoji in January 1712. Sent to congratulate the king on his accession to the throne, Joan van Limburg and Hendrik Wijnhout arrived with gifts for the ruler and his courtiers worth 5,400 guilders. Notwithstanding, the envoys claimed the mission was characterised by "disdain" (*kleen agtinge*) and "continuous torments" (*gedurige quellingen*). It proved impossible to meet any courtiers, apart from one Santoji Dada Salanke. Regarded as one of the king's favourites, he was willing to meet the ambassadors only once, when he refused to discuss arrears in rice deliveries to the VOC by a court regent. Instead, he stated that the gifts for Sarabhoji were insufficient and should be added to with two elephants and four horses before an audience would be granted. This was unacceptable to the envoys, and so, without meeting Sarabhoji or achieving anything else, they were eventually forced to leave the capital, hastily and like refugees, as the account phrased it.

1692; *Lettres & conventions des gouverneurs de Pondichéry*, 74, 80, 83, 90-2, 129, 132, 138 (see also 67, 75, 81, 133-4 for Tanjavur officials writing and enquiring about health). See also NA, VOC, no. 1416, ff. 1242v-3: letter from a Tanjavur general to Kayalpatnam, May 1685. Here, the general enquires after the Dutch addressee's health too and wishes him good fortune. The general's name has been rendered as "Pavasij Pandijden," possibly a corruption of Baboji Pandidar. For a letter by Tanjavur court officials to the VOC from 1788, wishing Coromandel's Dutch governor the blessings of the goddess Lakshmi, see Nikhil Bellarykar, "Two Marathi Letters from the Arsip Nasional Republik Indonesia: A Snapshot of Dutch-Maratha Relations in the Late-Eighteenth-Century Coromandel," *Itinerario* 43, 1 (2019), 20-3.

[107] K.A. Nilakanta Sastri (ed.), "Two Negapatam Grants from the Batavia Museum," *Indian Historical Records Commission: Proceedings of Meetings*, vol. XIV (Delhi, 1937), 40-8; Menon, "Colonial Linguistics and the Spoken Language," 77-9.

Although the gifts were taken home again, the trip still cost over 1,400 guilders. Blaming the king's "malicious ministers" for this failure, the VOC felt deeply offended. When court delegates later visited the Dutch to discuss the matter, the latter flatly refused the presented robes of honour. Also, they resolved to no longer send the annual "recognition" elephants and money. Subsequently, the court doubled the toll on goods brought into Nagapattinam and rumours abounded that Sarabhoji prepared an attack on the port, both of which put considerable pressure on the VOC and its local trade associates. In the same period, however, Tanjavur had to deal with a larger crisis, as Arcot was forcing tribute from the kingdoms in the region. Probably as a consequence, an armed confrontation between Tanjavur and the Dutch did not take place, although it took years to restore relations to normalcy.[108]

While the embassy of 1712 with its aftermath was a clear case of diplomatic humiliation escalating into a fully-fledged political conflict with economic and military elements, insult was relatively rare under the Bhonsles. And in the few instances protocol was actually breached, this generally did not have far-reaching consequences. Apart from the mission in 1712, only two other embassies, in 1676-7 and 1764, caused some annoyance for the Dutch. These respectively concerned a long delay at Mannargudi, where court representatives demanded money before the envoys could proceed to the capital, and the absence of anyone welcoming them in both Tiruvarur and Tanjavur town, because all officials were attending a festival. Other than that, missions proceeded fast and smoothly under the Bhonsles.

A few minor diplomatic humiliations occurred in between embassies, mostly related to political disputes. In 1679, for instance, angered by an attack on its factory at Tirumullaivasal, the VOC did not honour Ekoji with a gift when his son Shahaji got married. Besides, the elephant it selected for that year's "recognition" presents to the king was "misshapen" (*wanschapen*) as it had only seventeen nails, considered a bad omen.[109] Ekoji was clearly offended by both actions. He refused the elephant and later complained to a VOC representative about the Company's disrespect for his son's wedding, saying that all chiefs ("Pelliagaars," Palaiyakkarars), and even the Nayaka of Madurai, his enemy, had sent ambassadors and gifts on that occasion. Perhaps as revenge, in 1683 the king declined a specially made painting depicting the Dutch Prince of Orange with a battle in the background. Excusing

[108] NA, VOC, no. 1819, ff. 38-43v; no. 1835, ff. 247, 285-92; no. 1849, ff. 316-22; no. 1863, ff. 303-5, 354; no. 1884, ff. 135-40: letters from Nagapattinam to Batavia, May 1712, Mar., Aug. 1713, Aug. 1714, Aug., Nov. 1715, final report of Coromandel Governor Daniel Bernard Guilliams, Feb. 1716.

[109] The treatise *Śukranīti* also warns against elephants with less than eighteen nails (IV:VII 33-4). See Shukracharya, *The Śukranītiḥ*, 478.

himself, Ekoji—a general who spent much of his life waging wars—claimed he did not enjoy watching brutal military scenes.[110]

A final case of insult with commercial repercussions concerns a French encounter with the Bhonsles in 1688. As both the Dutch and the English reported, the French arrived in Tanjavur hoping to set up a trading lodge and therefore sent an ambassador with leopards, birds, and other gifts for Shahaji I, regent Ragoji Pandidar, and the latter's son. Despite this gesture and a six-months' sojourn of a Brahmin representative of the French at the capital, the mission yielded mixed results. The ambassador's urgent but highly unusual request that the king receive him standing was not complied with. Instead, he was dismissed with a "very petty honour robe" (*seer gering eerkleet*) and permission to settle was granted without the special privileges enjoyed by the Dutch.[111]

The incidents discussed above demonstrate that in Bhonsle-ruled Tanjavur, too, there were close ties between court protocol and political, economic, and military developments. Protocol could both reflect and affect such events. In several respects, ceremonial at this court was similar to that at other courts. But under the Bhonsles, gifts in particular appear to have been important, figuring in VOC documents over and over again as essential tools to open doors, show appreciation, facilitate business, win over courtiers, and soften tensions.

Another aspect of protocol that stands out is the close, even physical, contact the Bhonsle rulers allowed. Seemingly unhindered by notions about the king's body being divine and unapproachable—perhaps a legacy from the family's past at Muslim-ruled courts—Ekoji I, Shahaji I, Ekoji II, and Pratapasimha all personally handed over objects to VOC ambassadors, touched the envoys, or allowed Dutchmen to guide them by the hand. Furthermore, the court's fast handling of VOC missions is striking, often involving just one audience that was usually granted quickly and dealt with all stages of embassies—welcome, negotiation, dismissal—at once.

110 NA, VOC, no. 1329, ff. 1169v-71v; no. 1351, f. 2342; no. 1361, ff. 474-4v, 480v; no. 1384, f. 259v; no. 3108, ff. 88-9: reports of missions to Tanjavur, Dec. 1676, Feb. 1764, letters from Nagapattinam and Pulicat to Batavia, Oct. 1679, Sept. 1680, Oct. 1683, report of VOC envoy Viraraja Ayyan at Tanjavur, Aug. 1680; Subramanian, *The Maratha Rajas of Tanjore*, 19-21; Srinivasan, *Maratha Rule in the Carnatic*, 137-70. For other Asian rulers disliking Dutch paintings of war scenes, see: Jos Gommans, "The Embarrassment of Political Violence in Europe and South Asia c. 1100-1800," in Jan E.M. Houben and Karel R. van Kooij (eds), *Violence Denied: Violence, Non-Violence and the Rationalization of Violence in South Asian Cultural History* (Leiden/Boston/Köln, 1999), 287-8, 310-11; Emmer and Gommans, *The Dutch Overseas Empire*, 115.

111 For this and other examples, see: NA, VOC, no. 1448, ff. 326-6v, 334-4v; no. 1454, f. 1017v; no. 1508, ff. 554-60; no. 2506, ff. 58-60: Tamil letter received at Nagapattinam, Feb. 1689, letter from Nagapattinam to Pulicat, Feb. 1689, correspondence between Baboji Pandidar and Nagapattinam, Aug. 1688, Dec. 1692, Jan. 1693, Nagapattinam proceedings, Aug. 1740; H. Dodwell (ed.), *Records of Fort St George. Letters to Fort St George for 1688* (Madras, 1915), 71.

Altogether, one gains a picture of a court that in many ways was rooted in traditional, local ideas on protocol, but in some cases adopted a more practical attitude than other courts—a difference possibly related to the Bhonsles' west Indian origins and their former service under several sultanates. This pragmatism did not mean that diplomatic humiliations did not occur. The denial of an audience during the VOC embassy of 1712 was an affront so flagrant that it never happened in the other kingdoms. By and large, however, especially compared to Dutch-Ikkeri relations, contacts between the Bhonsle court and the VOC were quite harmonious. Here, both parties used protocol chiefly to evade conflicts, rather than create them.

Nayakas of Madurai

While a fair number of both south Indian and European sources deal with protocol in Madurai, few concern royal audiences. Only some reports of Dutch missions to this court remain, and there are hardly any local accounts of such occasions that are easily accessible. The latter include the Telugu *Rāyavācakamu*, which, although it pertains to the Vijayanagara court, was probably composed at Madurai and may reflect customs prevailing under the Nayakas. This text describes the ruler holding court in the audience hall and summoning his courtiers and servants to his throne in groups. These include priests, military commanders, ministers, scholars, subordinate chiefs, musicians, and other officials. Only the priests are clearly stated to be allowed to sit because of their exalted status. Besides, they are honoured with gifts of land and seem the only people whom the monarch receives standing. The *Rāyavācakamu* mentions the military commanders in particular as having to stand, while one courtier, an inspector, prostrates himself before the ruler.[112]

These few "indirect" references are complemented by European accounts. Extensive descriptions of ceremonial in the audience hall are found in the report of a VOC embassy to Muttu Virappa Nayaka III in June-September 1689, dispatched to renew the Dutch-Madurai treaties. Envoy Nicolaes Welter reached the capital Tiruchirappalli on 6 July, accompanied by twelve palanquin-bearers, eight luggage-carriers, sixteen soldiers, one interpreter, one cook, two torch-bearers, one parasol-carrier, and nine people to collect food for and take care of the gift-animals. In abridged form, the report's sections dealing with the audiences run as follows:

Already one day after his arrival, Welter secured a meeting with the king. Escorted by a courtier, the ambassador marched from his lodging to the capital's fortress, passing six gates before reaching the palace. There, in a room with an open front, Muttu Virappa sat on a carpet placed on a platform half a metre high and covered with a dome supported by pillars, against one of

112 Wagoner, *Tidings of the King*, 77-9.

which the ruler was leaning.[113] Behind him and to his left sat some "greats of the court" (*hoffs-grooten*), whereas "assorted servants" (*verscheijde bediende*) stood on both sides. None of these men said anything unless the king told them to. The Nayaka spoke only Telugu ("Baddegas," *vaḍuga* or northern), which some courtiers translated into Tamil ("Mallabaers").[114]

Welter approached Muttu Virappa and greeted him respectfully, whereupon the Nayaka made the ambassador stand two steps away from him. Welter explained the reason for his visit and presented the VOC's letters and gifts. The latter included a tusked elephant, a Persian horse, two Bengal civet-cats, a knife, a compass, a magnifying glass, two binoculars, four Japanese fans, six mirrors, fruits, textiles, spices, sandalwood, and rosewater. The king enquired after the wellbeing of Welter's superiors in Tuticorin and Colombo and the Company as a whole. After his reply that all were in good health and a few more pleasantries, the envoy noticed that meanwhile a small silver rapier he carried on his side had been quietly unsheathed and handed over to Muttu Virappa, who had been ogling at it. Although quickly returned, it was soon taken again and not given back. Indeed, the king requested to have the sheath and accompanying belt as well, which Welter consented to. Muttu Virappa then announced this was only a welcoming audience and no business would be discussed, even though the envoy asked for this repeatedly. The Nayaka terminated the meeting by giving a coat and turban to Welter, urging him to wear these on the way to his lodging. As the king explained, this was a custom in his kingdom. Also presented with betel-leaves prepared by Muttu Virappa himself, Welter departed, dressed in what was no doubt a robe of honour and escorted by a large number of courtiers.

Two more audiences followed during Welter's mission. On 18 July, the envoy met Muttu Virappa in a room deeper inside the palace, without any courtiers but with two interpreters. Welter now honoured the king with a small cabinet and some pocket pistols. Although private possessions of the envoy, these had attracted Muttu Virappa's demanding attention. When Welter again attempted to discuss some pressing issues, the king declared that today was an inauspicious day for such matters. The Nayaka then expressed his desire to receive more "curiosities" befitting his regal status and ended the encounter by giving betel-leaves to the ambassador. Welter was granted a departure audience only five weeks later, on 22 August, after a three-hour wait at the palace. During the envoy's farewell statement, Muttu Virappa turned away to talk to a courtier. After his speech, the envoy received a gold necklace with small stones and a painted cloth and was informed that all the VOC's requests would be honoured. With the presentation of betel and areca to Welter and the exchange of some final courtesies, this last meeting was concluded.[115]

113 For literal translations of this and other passages in the report, see the section on Madurai in Chapter 5.

114 In Dutch records, the term "Mallabaers" ("Malabari") often refers to Tamil or matters Tamilian, despite its obvious associations with Malabar (Kerala) and Malayalam.

115 Vink, *Mission to Madurai*, 16, 382-3, 385-6, 408-11, 450-4, 465-7, 504-5, 536-40, 549-50, 576.

This is probably the only Dutch description of audience ceremonial in Madurai's capital that proceeded more or less properly. It is striking, however, that at none of the three meetings with the king there was room for negotiation. The Nayaka was solely interested in prestigious exotic presents—or so suggested the unhappy Welter—and left all business to be conducted by his courtiers in between audiences.

The account of a Jesuit embassy to Tiruchirappalli around 1700 provides other details on Madurai's protocol, particularly the honours that might befall visitors. The envoy, Father Bouchet, did not meet the monarch, Queen Mangammal, but was received by the powerful *Daḷavāy* (general) Narasappa Ayyan, considered the queen's favourite and called "prince-regent" by the Jesuits. Bringing gifts that included a two-foot-high globe with Tamil script, Bouchet was welcomed with great reverence. As the account goes, Narasappa rose and greeted the Jesuit as someone would salute his master: joining hands and bringing them to the forehead. Responding like a master to his subordinate, Bouchet opened his hands and extended them to the *daḷavāy*. The latter invited the envoy to sit with him on a sofa too small for two people. This was thought to be deliberate, since Narasappa's subsequent effort to make Bouchet comfortable and the physical contact between them—the *daḷavāy* even placed his knees on those of the Jesuit—were marks of honour. Later, Narasappa put an eight-foot-long piece of gold brocade on Bouchet's head and sprinkled him with sweet smelling water, regarded as signs of respect befitting ambassadors.[116]

Besides audiences at the capital, the Dutch documented encounters with the Nayakas while they toured their kingdom, visiting temples and subordinate chiefs.[117] At least eight reports of such meetings, near the VOC settlement at Tuticorin, survive, all dating from the early eighteenth century. These describe the protocol in the temporary camps where the Dutch were expected to greet the rulers. One account relates an audience with Queen Mangammal in 1705:

> On 14 July, Mangammal appeared at the village of Melur, on Tuticorin's outskirts, with her minor grandson and future successor Vijayaranga Chokkanatha and a retinue of courtiers, 300 horsemen, 1,200 foot soldiers, drummers and horn-blowers, six elephants, twenty-six camels, and four wagons carrying luggage. That afternoon, the VOC sent Huijbert Driemondt, who spoke Tamil or perhaps Telugu, to the queen with presents. Hastily put together when Mangammal's

[116] Lockman, *Travels of the Jesuits*, vol. I, 460-8 (reproduced in Sathyanatha Aiyar, *History of the Nayaks of Madura*, 308-12); Nelson, *The Madura Country*, vol. III, 230-2.

[117] For Jesuit descriptions of retinues of Tirumalai Nayaka (r. c. 1623-59) during temple visits or meetings with kings (which included his main queen, a betel-bearer, elephants, courtiers, singing girls, eunuch guards, royal arms and insignia, and military troops, see Saulière, "The Revolt of the Southern Nayaks" [pt. 1], 93, 95.

unexpected visit was announced, the gifts included Japanese lacquer ware, magnifying glasses, and two gilded mirrors apart from the usual items, together costing 1,061 guilders.[118] While the queen was honoured with fifteen gunshots from the VOC's fort, Driemondt went to the royal camp in a palanquin, accompanied by one Dutch and eleven Asian soldiers, an interpreter, and thirty-one people to carry the gifts, wearing turbans for the occasion.

At Melur, the envoy found Mangammal seated on a raised platform covered with carpets and surrounded by her principal courtiers. After some courtesies, she ordered Driemondt to sit down on another raised, carpeted platform about three steps away. Presenting the gifts, the envoy expressed the hope that the mutual friendship would never cease to flourish. Following a brief discussion in Telugu ("Tellingas") between Mangammal and *Daḷavāy* Kasturi Ranga Ayyan, the latter said that all would be fine. Driemondt then stood up, bowed before the queen, and informed her that several decorated Dutch vessels were ready to sail near the shore to entertain her, as she had requested. Next, Mangammal honoured the envoy with cloths, a turban, and betel prepared and touched by her personally.[119]

After Mangammal had thus formally ended the audience, the meeting continued with several courtiers visiting the Dutch fort at Tuticorin. Here they were welcomed with two rows of soldiers, chairs in the VOC chief's room, enquiries after the queen's health, a tour of the building, a cannonade, gifts, betel, and the sprinkling of rosewater. Mangammal herself stayed behind, however, declaring it was inappropriate for women to visit the fort.[120]

Other meetings near Tuticorin proceeded similarly. In July 1708, Vijayaranga Chokkanatha also honoured the Dutch with betel first touched by his own hands. While the Nayakas always donated robes and turbans on these occasions, the VOC often gave exotic objects in return. In June 1711, it presented Vijayaranga Chokkanatha with a self-playing organ, deemed the best gift in years by him. At

118 The purchasing power of 1,061 guilders in 1705 equalled that of 13,300 euros in 2018. See iisg.amsterdam/en/research/projects/hpw/calculate.php.

119 The importance of handling betel properly transpires from a tradition about Mangammal's incorrect conduct in this regard and its consequences. As an early English translation of one Tamil text goes: "As she [Mangammal] was one day chewing beetle, happening forgetfully to receive the beetle with her left hand, she manifested great sorrow for the deed. And in order to secure herself from the evils attending it, she ordered avenues to be established from Cassi [Benares] to Cape Comorin and along the road to Ramisverom [Rameshvaram], and moreover built additional Chittrums [*cattirams*, pilgrim rest houses], bestowed alms daily in great liberality to numerous persons and proper places for the accommodations of travellers & every article of consumption were provided for them." See BL/AAS, MT, class III, no. 25: "History of the former Gentoo Rajahs who ruled over the Pandyan Mandalom," f. 33. See also: Taylor, *Oriental Historical Manuscripts*, vol. II, 35-7, 224; BL/AAS, MG, no. 4, pt. 6a: "History of the former Rajahs of the Tellugoo nation who ruled over Paundium Mundalom"; BL/MMC, AM, no. 18021, "History of Kurtakull."

120 NA, VOC, no. 1706, ff. 1040-50v, 1054v-60: Tuticorin diary extract, July 1705, letter from Tuticorin to Colombo, July 1705.

all these audiences, the rulers sat on exquisite carpets on raised platforms under canopies and torches, surrounded by courtiers, some of them also seated. Behind the king stood young women—fanning him and providing betel—who in July 1717 were described as dressed "quite nicely [*aardig*] but very lightly [*ligtvaardig*]." The VOC envoys were usually treated with respect. In 1711, after the ambassador saluted the Nayaka with his hat off, he was allowed to put it on again and sit on a carpeted chair left of the king's platform. This was a new privilege as envoys had hitherto been seated on a carpet with crossed legs.[121]

The report of an audience with Vijayaranga Chokkanatha in June 1720 is particularly relevant. It explains how courtiers were positioned around the king literally in descending order: first the *Pradhāni* (finance minister) Sambu Ayyan and some others to the king's right and on the same carpet as him; next court merchant Sundardasu Ayyan on the carpeted stairs leading to the king's platform; and last "land regent" (local governor) Kumara Svami Mudaliyar on a carpet on the floor. This account also reveals that courtiers could disagree on the required protocol, in this case on the time envoys were made to wait before meeting the king.[122] As the VOC's local clerk Muttu Virappa Pillai reported after a preparatory visit to the royal camp:

> ... some of the courtiers being together, [court merchant] Soenderdasoe Aijen would have said to the pardanie Samboe Aijen: "why do we let those people (denoting ... the [Dutch] chief) wait so long and not make them appear before His Highness?" And thereupon the pardanie would have asked: "when the envoys of the Theuver [Tevar, Setupati of Ramnad] and Tansjour [Tanjavur] come to the king, don't they have to wait too?" And Soenderdasoe replied to that: "that is very different because these [the Dutch] are merchants," upon which Samboeaijen responded to Soenderdasoe Aijen: "you are also a merchant, now go stay with that other merchant [the Dutch chief] until an audience will be granted" ...[123]

Clearly, the different positions of *Pradhāni* Sambu Ayyan and court merchant Sundardasu Ayyan during the audience also manifested themselves in this discussion.

Turning to protocol on occasions other than royal audiences, various sources refer to gifts and marks of honour exchanged between Madurai's Nayakas and other Indian rulers, with varying aims. Some chronicles say that the emperor

121 NA, VOC, no. 1756, ff. 1194-204v; no. 1893, ff. 1048-8v: Tuticorin diary extract, July 1708, extract of letter from Tuticorin to Colombo, July 1717; DNA, DCGCC, no. 3355 (unpaginated, entry of 2 June): diary of mission to Madurai representatives at Tuticorin, Jan.-June 1711.

122 NA, VOC, no. 1941, f. 935: Tuticorin diary extract, June 1720.

123 NA, VOC, no. 1941, ff. 933v-4: Tuticorin diary extract, June 1720 (translation mine).

of Vijayanagara presented the first king, Vishvanatha, with jewellery, clothes, trophies of subjugated enemies, royal insignia, the image of the goddess Durga, and the Madurai kingdom itself to reward him for his loyalty and military feats. Recognising Vishvanatha's royal status, the Pandya king provided him with the realm's regalia.[124]

Vishvanatha himself honoured his Minister Ariyanatha Mudaliyar with jewels, garments, and privileges, and distributed animals and money to Brahmins. To secure support of the subordinate Palaiyakkarars, he gave them palanquins, titles, and permission to use fly-whisks, fans, umbrellas, torches, shells, and musical instruments, among other gifts. In return, they threw golden and silver flowers at Vishvanatha and tore off pieces of clothing in his presence. When Tirumalai Nayaka married a sister of Tanjavur's Vijayaraghava Nayaka, he received his fellow king at Tallakulam (facing Madurai across the Vaigai River) and escorted him to his capital. After the festivities, Tirumalai honoured Vijayaraghava with presents and then, says the text, formally gave him permission to leave.

Some gifts to other rulers were related to the threat they posed. Reflecting the ever growing power of Madurai's offshoot Ramnad, in the course of the seventeenth century the Nayakas donated to the Setupatis garments, land, animals, titles, permission to celebrate festivals, a golden replica of a defeated enemy's head, and even Madurai's own royal palanquin, all to thank them for military services and—unsuccessfully—keep them loyal.[125] In the 1660s Chokkanatha Nayaka was forced to give horses, jewels, and cash to Mysore after its troops had advanced as far as Tiruchirappalli. Finally, around 1700 Queen Mangammal sent jewels and cash to the Mughals to acknowledge their supremacy and win their support in a conflict with Udaiyarpalayam.[126]

124 Taylor, *Oriental Historical Manuscripts*, vol. II, 7-9, 13-15; Dirks, *The Hollow Crown*, 98-100, 103; Narayana Rao, Shulman, and Subrahmanyam, *Symbols of Substance*, 48-9, 52; BL/AAS, MT, class III, no. 25: "History of the former Gentoo Rajahs who ruled over the Pandyan Mandalom," ff. 21-1v, 24-4v.

125 BL/AAS, MG, no. 4, pt. 4: "Mootiah's chronological & historical account of the modern kings of Madura," ff. 48, 57-9; no. 4, pt. 8: "A general history of the kings of Rama Naad or the Satoo-Putty Samastanum," ff. 178, 182-3; MT, class III, no. 25: "History of the former Gentoo Rajahs who ruled over the Pandyan Mandalom," ff. 29, 31v; class III, no. 82: "Account of the Rajas who held the government of Madura," ff. 113-13v; Mahalingam, *Mackenzie Manuscripts*, vol. I, 7, 10, 35, 42, 44-6, 52-3, 62, 102-3, 110, 122, 128, 132-4, 151-2, 154, 161-2, 167, 173, 224; Taylor, *Oriental Historical Manuscripts*, vol. II, 27-9, 33; Dirks, *The Hollow Crown*, 92, 104-6. For the implications of Tirumalai Nayaka's gifts to Raghunatha Tirumalai Setupati in the 1650s, which included the Nayakas' golden lion-faced palanquin and Tirumalai's own name, see Chapter 6 and: Richard H. Davis, "Indian Art Objects as Loot," *The Journal of Asian Studies* 52, 1 (1993), 34-6; Price, *Kingship and Political Practice in Colonial India*, 30-1; Bes, "The Setupatis, the Dutch, and Other Bandits," 548.

126 Hayavadana Rao, *History of Mysore*, vol. I, 230; Manucci, *Storia do Mogor*, vol. III, 411; Sathyanatha Aiyar, *History of the Nayaks of Madura*, 205-6. For examples concerning Travancore and

The gifts Madurai's Nayakas exchanged with Indian parties were largely similar to presents to and from European powers, both at royal audiences and on other occasions. One example in the latter category concerns a meeting of the VOC official Hendrik Adriaan van Rheede with delegates of Madurai and Ramnad at Tuticorin in 1665. Mediating in a conflict between the kingdoms, Van Rheede first spoke to Madurai's General Tirumalai Kulantha Pillai, who offered the Dutchman a robe of honour and golden and white cloths. Some weeks later, other representatives presented him with gifts from King Chokkanatha, including a Persian horse and golden arm and finger rings, crest-jewels, and necklaces. Declaring that the Nayaka sent such presents only to his best friends, the envoys urged Van Rheede to wear the robe and jewels right away and then publicly announced the Dutch-Madurai friendship.[127]

The court apparently wished to treat the Dutch as close friends, but the gifts were no doubt also meant to oblige them to choose Madurai's side in the dispute. While in this case the VOC remained neutral—like in most clashes between Indian kingdoms—gifts were often employed to appease people and win them over. In 1658, after their conquest of Tuticorin from the Portuguese, the Dutch honoured Tirumalai Nayaka with two elephants and a horse, hoping these would help them secure their new possession and conclude a treaty. Around 1675, the Dutch considered offering gifts worth about 50,000 guilders, thinking this might grant them permission to build a fort at Tuticorin. Around 1688, as a token of friendship, Muttu Virappa Nayaka III sent the VOC a necklace with a monkey-shaped pearl and a jewel composed of many different gems, valued at 5,000 guilders. Pragmatic as ever, the Dutch later presented the jewellery to the king of Siam.

Although it is often unclear how much the VOC spent on presents for the court, lists of gift expenses during the Nayakas' visits to Tuticorin are still available. In the early eighteenth century these costs varied between 1,500 and 3,000 guilders, rising to over 4,300 guilders in later decades. On average, these numbers exceed those for Ikkeri and Tanjavur. The reasons for this are generally not stated in VOC documents, but in 1675 the Dutch wrote that the Nayaka of Madurai "has always been considered the greatest among his neighbours, as he also possesses a truly large and beautiful land." So Madurai's size and power, besides the considerable profits the Dutch made on its Fishery Coast, may have played a role in the Company's flattering of its rulers.[128]

Arcot, see NA, VOC, no. 1756, ff. 1216-16v; no. 1803, f. 103v: report of mission to Madurai's general, Aug.-Sept. 1708, letter from Nagapattinam to Batavia, July 1711.

127 NA, VOC, no. 1251, ff. 741-3, 756: report of mission to Travancore, Madurai, and Ramnad, Mar.-Oct. 1665; Vink, "Encounters on the Opposite Coast," 255-6.

128 NA, VOC, no. 1227, ff. 332-2v: Tuticorin proceedings, Jan. 1658; HRB, no. 542 (unpaginated, 1st document, c. halfway, after the section "Teuverslant"): description of Ceylon, Madurai, south Coromandel, Malabar, and Kanara by Rijcklof van Goens, Sept. 1675; Coolhaas *et al.*, *Generale Missiven*,

Another way of conducting diplomacy in Madurai was to maintain close relations with the kingdom's second node of power: the seat of the provincial governor or "land regent" at Tirunelveli. Soon after the Dutch captured Tuticorin, a few dozen miles away, Governor Vadamalaiyappa Pillai presented them with marks of honour ("tasserijff"), in return for which they sent cloths and spices. In March 1670, however, the VOC dispatched envoys to him, then encamped near Tuticorin, to settle a conflict. On Vadamalaiyappa's demand, the delegation was headed by Ceylon's Governor Rijkclof van Goens himself, an exceptional diplomatic gesture.[129] A summary of this mission's report, abounding with descriptions of protocol, runs thus:

Bringing cloths, spices, rosewater, sandalwood, and a gilded mirror, Van Goens was received by Vadamalaiyappa in his palanquin just outside his camp. With an entourage of elephants, oxen, horsemen, foot soldiers, horn-blowers, and drummers, he accompanied the Dutchmen to a purpose-built structure decorated with cloths and flowers, where they could rest and eat. Next, they moved to Vadamalaiyappa's nearby lodging, at the entrance of which the "land regent" again heartily welcomed Van Goens and escorted him to a platform of two feet high. There, both governors sat down, enquiring after one another's health, expressing their happiness to meet "after so many years of longing," and exchanging other courteous words (*courtoise woorden*).

Appearing to be in his fifties, sporting a grey beard and hair around a "stately face" (*stadigh van tronie*), wearing a white turban, and as a Brahmin commanding great respect, Vadamalaiyappa chose his words carefully and modestly. Thus, the conversation ended quickly. Van Goens invited Vadamalaiyappa to visit Tuticorin the following day, while the latter presented the Dutch with betel, areca, robes of honour, and ninety-nine pieces of textile—a customary number on such occasions, representing a "sacrifice." After Vadamalaiyappa had seen the Dutchmen off outside his residence and they were well on their way back, his son and some others came galloping after them, to accompany them to their destination. A bit later Van Goens urged them to return, thanking them for this honour.

The next morning Vadamalaiyappa and his retinue arrived at Tuticorin, awaited by Van Goens in his palanquin at a distance of two gunshots from the town. Saluted with a cannonade, the "land regent" was led into the VOC's meeting room and seated at the table's most prominent place. After the usual mutual compliments, the relations between Madurai and the Dutch were extensively discussed in a friendly manner. The encounter was concluded with more gifts to

vol. IV, 95, vol. V, 217, vol. VI, 169-70, 368-9, 445-6, 554, vol. VII, 369, 567, 727, vol. VIII (The Hague, 1985), 19, vol. IX, 272, 389; Vink, "Encounters on the Opposite Coast," 103-73; Bes, "The Setupatis, the Dutch, and Other Bandits," 550 (n. 17).

129 I know of only one other high-ranking VOC official travelling to meet prominent south Indians: Ceylon Governor Gustaaf Willem van Imhoff, who met the kings of Cochin and Travancore in 1739. See Wagenaar *et al.*, *Gouverneur Van Imhoff op dienstreis*, 115-16, 133-4.

Vadamalaiyappa—including a gold necklace, three mirrors, and 250 guilders—and some of his companions. Following many more pleasantries, the "land regent" was guided out of the building by Van Goens and escorted a bit further by Tuticorin's chief (*opperhoofd*) Laurens Pijl and other Dutch officials. But then Vadamalaiyappa went back and thanked Van Goens once more for the honours shown him. He was so full of praise and enthusiasm, that "the whole country seemed delighted and hoped for a better century."[130]

These two receptions suggest that Indo-Dutch diplomatic meetings mostly proceeded according to standard rules, regardless of whether they took place in a courtier's residence or a VOC settlement. The only difference seems to have concerned the seating arrangements. Whereas Vadamalaiyappa and Van Goens sat together on a raised platform in the former's camp, they sat at a table with their subordinates in Tuticorin. Other rituals, such as welcoming and departure ceremonies, gifts, and courtesies, were largely similar on both occasions. In any case, despite everyone's good intentions and expectations of a bright future, later in 1670 Vadamalaiyappa was imprisoned by the court, and although he was soon reinstalled, this started his career's decline. But subsequent Tirunelveli governors remained important figures throughout the VOC's presence in Madurai, as suggested by the regular and valuable gifts they received from the Dutch.[131]

Vadamalaiyappa also provides us with an instance of eloquence practised in Madurai. The VOC's remaining correspondence with the court contains few examples of the pleasantries that were doubtlessly exchanged. But the great importance of this element of protocol is underscored by the very first clause in the Dutch-Madurai agreement of 1690, stipulating that in their letters Dutch and Nayaka officials were to address one another courteously. The taste for eloquent language is clearly demonstrated by the wit courtiers sometimes used to convey messages, whether positive or negative.

Thus, during the Dutch embassy to Madurai in 1668 (discussed below), Vadamalaiyappa showed his disapproval of the VOC's wish for quick profit by telling ambassador Hendrik Adriaan van Rheede: "Wise men do not plant a tree in order to immediately eat its fruits, but only after the passing of time when it has reached full maturity, having been watered and allowed to grow." Accordingly, Vadamalaiyappa suggested, the VOC should cultivate its friendship with Madurai

130 NA, VOC, no. 1227, ff. 333-3v; no. 1231, f. 163; no. 1274, ff. 187-203v, 304: Tuticorin proceedings, Jan. 1658, letters from Admiral Van Goens to Pulicat, from Colombo to Gentlemen XVII, Sept. 1658, Jan. 1671, report of mission to land regent Vadamalaiyappa Pillai, Mar. 1670; Vink, "Encounters on the Opposite Coast," 294-7.

131 DNA, DCGCC, no. 38, f. 198: Colombo proceedings, July 1703; NA, VOC, no. 1762, f. 872; no. 8958, ff. 700-1: report of Kandyan mission to Madurai, Apr.-June 1708, letter from Tuticorin to Colombo, Oct. 1732.

and exercise patience before the relationship would bear fruit.[132] Undeterred and returning the eloquence, Van Rheede replied that the Dutch had already planted a tree in Madurai long ago, which the VOC's opponents had cut down, however, nearly killing its gardeners in the process. But the Company was now growing a new tree—protected with arms (a reference to the territory conquered by the Dutch from the Portuguese)—whose fruits would eventually be consumed throughout the kingdom.[133]

Like eloquence, other aspects of protocol could be used—or rather, breached—to express dissatisfaction, often causing great offence, sometimes with serious consequences. One example of humiliations meted out between Madurai and other courts concerns the visit of a Mughal ambassador to Tiruchirappalli in the late 1680s. The VOC reported that after an initial meeting with Muttu Virappa Nayaka III, the envoy waited eight months without securing another audience. Described in more detail in Chapter 5, local texts refer to Muttu Virappa's insulting of Mughal representatives, too, relating that he refused to receive a slipper sent by the Mughal with the proper respect and thus acknowledge the emperor's supremacy. Instead, in a very degrading act, the Nayaka put on the slipper himself and had the Mughal delegation beaten up and thrown out of the kingdom.[134]

A diplomatic clash between Madurai and the Kandy kingdom on Ceylon also figures in both local and VOC sources. The Dutch wrote in 1710 that the Kandyan king sent ambassadors with six elephants and eleven chests with other presents to Madurai to propose a marriage with a daughter of Chengamaladasa, the last scion of Tanjavur's Nayakas, now living in Tiruchirappalli. Kandy's envoys had already arrived in Madurai during the reign of Queen Mangammal, who agreed to the proposal on the condition she be presented with elephants and jewels. But when she was succeeded by Vijayaranga Chokkanatha in 1707, courtiers had allegedly stolen the gifts and the new king now claimed Chengamaladasa's daughter. The Kandyan ambassadors were eventually forced to flee to the VOC settlement at Nagapattinam without the requested bride, taking along another woman instead.[135]

In some contrast, a chronicle on Kandy states that its envoys asked for a relative of Vijayaranga Chokkanatha himself to marry their lord. Highly affronted because

132 The use of gardening as a metaphor for politics appears to have been common in India. See Sarangi, *A Treasure of Tāntric Ideas*, 300, 303.

133 Heeres and Stapel, *Corpus diplomaticum Neerlando-Indicum*, vol. 3, 528; Vink, *Mission to Madurai*, 5, 41-2, 192-3, 248.

134 Around 1693 a Madurai envoy at Senji was reportedly beaten with "Muslim" and "Hindu" sandals. See Martin, *India in the 17th Century*, vol. 2, pt. II, 1484.

135 Perhaps this event led to the rumour that Queen Mangammal had fled to Nagapattinam in 1707. See the section on Madurai in Chapter 2.

he regarded the Kandyan king's caste as lower than his own, the Madurai Nayaka refused the gifts and removed the ambassadors from his palace.[136] This text was probably composed in south India rather than in Kandy itself, which may explain why it portrays Vijayaranga Chokkanatha's conduct more positively than the Dutch records do.[137] But both versions show how missions between courts could end in untimely and disgraceful departures by envoys.

Such was also the fate of VOC ambassador Hendrik Adriaan van Rheede, visiting Madurai in February-July 1668 to seek permission to erect fortifications at Tuticorin. Parts of his diary are summarised below:

Van Rheede reached Tiruchirappalli's outskirts on 6 March, with gifts worth over 13,000 guilders and a retinue of some Dutch assistants, two elephant drivers, and fifty-two local soldiers. The next day, he sent a messenger to *Pradhāni* Vadamalaiyappa Pillai. Receiving a reply that today and tomorrow were inauspicious days, only in the afternoon of the 9th Van Rheede was welcomed and escorted to his temporary lodging by what he called "one of the Pillai's humblest of servants riding a cripple horse."

After this reception, the next six weeks were spent waiting for an audience with Chokkanatha Nayaka and conducting tedious negotiations with Vadamalaiyappa about the VOC's desired privileges. Not only did these encounters yield no results, Van Rheede also had to wait before meetings began, was not welcomed at Vadamalaiyappa's residence, and had to sit on an old, worn-out carpet. Further, the *pradhāni* refused to speak to the envoy's messengers, some of his soldiers were beaten up, his lodging was attacked, and the VOC flag was thrown in the mud. Van Rheede regarded these as deliberate efforts by Vadamalaiyappa to humiliate the Dutch. On 10 April, he noted about the latter incidents:

> ... everyone speaking of the event found this treatment highly curious and not customary among ambassadors of foreign rulers. These are normally greatly honoured, unless the decision had been made to wage war against them, but they are usually expelled from the

136 Indeed, a letter of 1817 by a certain Marriott at Vellore to one Macleod, both British officials, states that no marital connections had been established between Madurai and Kandy for over a century. The current head of Madurai's expelled Nayaka line (probably Bangaru Tirumalai, see the Epilogue's section on Madurai) would however be happy to provide Kandy's royal family with a wife, provided the British return the Madurai kingdom to him. But, as Marriott concluded, "this being impracticable, the business went no further." See BL/AAS, MM, no. 109, pt. 58: "Singala-Dweepum & Candy," f. 4.

137 NA, VOC, no. 8925, ff. 144-50: reports by envoys from Kandy, Feb. 1710; Coolhaas *et al.*, *Generale Missiven*, vol. VI, 623, 696; Vink, *Mission to Madurai*, 479-81 (n. 264); BL/AAS, MG, no. 4, pt. 4: "Mootiah's chronological & historical account of the modern kings of Madura," ff. 68-9; Taylor, *Oriental Historical Manuscripts*, vol. II, 205-8, Appendix, 45-7. For a slightly different version of the Dutch account, see Stein van Gollenesse, *Memoir of Julius Stein van Gollenesse*, 6-7, and also 14, 44. See also: Dewaraja, *The Kandyan Kingdom*, 33-8; Obeyesekere, "Between the Portuguese and the Nāyakas," 168.

> country unceremoniously, though not abused. Thus, the common man rumoured that the Neijk [Nayaka] sought only discord. I do not doubt that the Pulle [Vadamalaiyappa Pillai], by inciting the Company's spiteful enemies, directed this work ...[138]

Van Rheede also wrote it would be best to just depart if he wished to avoid further affronts, feeling he had every right to do so. But he feared this would be taken as an insult too and could even lead to war. He therefore stayed on and kept waiting for a royal audience. In the next days, even some of Madurai's courtiers began to question the treatment meted out to Van Rheede. When one of his assistants visited Vadamalaiyappa, he witnessed the following scene:

> ... a servant there of the lord Neijck's brother Aatsijindapa [Achyutappa] ... asked the Pulle whether it was not a shame to keep the people and ambassadors of foreign rulers for so long. The Pulle replied that these people had come uninvited, which is why they found so little time, and if they had announced their coming they would have been informed of the obstacles and told to wait for a better opportunity ... [the servant] retorted: we have always been informed and have known of their coming. If that had been inconvenient to the lord Neijk, one should have stopped them on the way and make them turn around rather than letting them run around. It could serve as a deterrent to them and other rulers to send ambassadors and honour [*vereeren*] the lord Neijk. The Pulle went that far to seek a reason for sweetening the humiliation [*versmadingh*] with some justice.[139]

Other courtiers who frowned upon the humiliations included the king's brother-in-law Tubaki Anandappa Nayaka and councillor and former General Chinna Tambi Mudaliyar. At one point, even the king asked Vadamalaiyappa why matters took so long. Thus, the envoy finally secured an audience with Chokkanatha on 21 April, a month-and-a-half after his arrival.

According to Van Rheede, his arrival for the audience lacked any dignity, Vadamalaiyappa turning his back to him and the palace's entrance being crowded with "rude" people. After some waiting, the envoy was brought before the king and made to sit on a carpet on the floor. He offered Chokkanatha the VOC's letter and gifts, comprising two elephants, two Persian horses, a bird of paradise, a diamond ring, forty-two assorted glasses, a large mirror, a featherbed, and some pistols, guns, and knives, besides the usual spices, cloths, rosewater, and sandalwood. The Nayaka, sitting on a cushion, was especially pleased with the glasses, using them to play with two young children sitting beside him. Seated behind the king were Chinna Tambi Mudaliyar and Vadamalaiyappa, the latter starting the meeting by enquiring after the well-being of Van Rheede's superiors and the Company. But the hall was so noisy and congested that the envoy could not reply or even see the Nayaka. Fearing to be crushed, he had to request for some space before he could properly address Chokkanatha. Although this was quickly arranged,

138 Vink, *Mission to Madurai*, 181-2, 239 (translation by Vink).
139 Vink, *Mission to Madurai*, 187-8, 244 (translation by Vink and myself).

the conversation lasted very briefly and ended with the king saying all negotiations would be taken care of by Vadamalaiyappa. While the commotion in the hall grew again, the Nayaka presented Van Rheede with a golden chain, two bracelets with red stones that "looked nice and cost little," a robe of honour, and betel and areca. Chokkanatha then spotted a diamond ring worn by the ambassador, asked to see it, put it on his finger, and never returned it. The king then accompanied the Dutchmen outside to inspect the VOC's donated elephants and returned inside without a further word.

The consultations with Vadamalaiyappa after this audience were delayed twice and yielded no results anyway. Van Rheede was also informed there would be no further audiences with Chokkanatha because the envoy was considered to have taken his leave when he presented his gifts. Despite repeated requests to be formally dismissed and not be forced to depart "humiliated and despised" (*met versmadingh en veraghtingh*), Van Rheede was received by neither the king nor Vadamalaiyappa again. When several courtiers sympathetic towards the VOC declared there was nothing they could do, on 5 May the ambassador returned to Tuticorin.

There is no way to tell if the offended Van Rheede exaggerated his experiences in his account, but within a year, the very thing he had tried to prevent still happened: a big military clash between Madurai and the Dutch. This was another example of political tensions manifesting themselves in diplomatic insults that subsequently contributed to a war. For the dishonourable reception of Van Rheede seemed largely orchestrated by Vadamalaiyappa, who resented the VOC's increasing power in Madurai's coastal strip, which functioned as his own power base.[140]

In turn, the humiliation of the Dutch envoy, together with the rejection of his requests, caused great indignation among his superiors. Much against the court's wishes, the Company now built fence around the Tuticorin factory. This led to a nine-month siege by Madurai's forces, ended by several Dutch sorties—one headed by Van Rheede himself—that left hundreds of the Nayaka's soldiers dead. Eventually, peace was reached under conditions not entirely favourable to the Dutch, but one reason for them to accept this was that they felt their status was restored through this victory.[141]

The subsequent decades saw other diplomatic frictions between the court and the VOC, although these usually lead to irritation rather than serious discord. When Vijayaranga Chokkanatha Nayaka passed by Tuticorin in 1720, he informed the Dutch he would receive their local chief for an audience only if he would bring

140 See also Howes, *The Courts of Pre-Colonial South India*, 46.

141 Vink, *Mission to Madurai*, 16-17, 144-8, 152-4, 167-8, 173, 179-82, 188-97, 214-17, 219-20, 228-9, 233, 237-9, 244-53; idem, "Encounters on the Opposite Coast," 258-70. While the VOC claimed it had killed over a thousand of the Nayaka's troops, the English wrote 200 men were lost by Madurai and 100 by the Dutch. See Foster, *The English Factories in India 1668–1669*, 283.

twice as many gifts as during the previous meeting. Since the Nayaka's visit was unexpected, the VOC had difficulty gathering decent presents, but still spent 2,400 guilders for the king and 1,400 guilders for his courtiers. Nevertheless, the Dutch chief had to wait more than one hour for the audience and was then seated on a bare plank, while it was complained the gifts did not include Melaka sandalwood. Although the encounter ended with the usual courtesies—such as robes of honour and enquiries after each other's health—the next year the Nayaka again asked to be honoured with proper presents this time. He even dispatched a prominent courtier to convey this message and discuss the tents and canopy to be erected for him. Vijayaranga Chokkanatha's visit was however cancelled when his only son suddenly died. When the king returned to Tuticorin in the following years, there were no more serious complaints about the VOC's gifts.[142]

All in all, protocol in Madurai had much in common with that in the other kingdoms, but also differed in some ways. The variety of the discussed audience locations underscores the importance of seating arrangements here, whether at the central court, in royal encampments near Tuticorin, or at the residence of the Tirunelveli governor. As for gifts, one striking aspect involves the regular occasions on which VOC ambassadors were urged to actually put on the received robes of honour, turbans, and jewellery.[143] It seems Madurai sought to give these events a public character, as the envoys had to return to their lodging or attend official announcements while wearing these clothes and ornaments. Perhaps, the court was keen on the *khil'at* ritual to show its superiority over the Dutch. Also noteworthy are the repeated references to donated betel first touched by the Nayakas themselves. Muttu Virappa III, Mangammal, and Vijayaranga Chokkanatha all honoured VOC ambassadors this way. That physical contact expressed deference is further suggested by the kind of seating *Daḷavāy* Narasappa Ayyan offered to the Jesuit Bouchet, making them sit very closely together.

Some aspects of protocol in Madurai really stand out. Unlike at other courts, these Nayakas were hardly or not at all involved in negotiations with VOC envoys. All kings—and one queen—just engaged in courteous conversations or else asked for gifts. Again, this dynasty may have seen itself as too illustrious to confer on political and commercial issues with Dutch merchants, although in that case it would

142 For these and other examples, see: NA, VOC, no. 1762, f. 872; no. 1941, ff. 919-21, 925-9, 933-7v, 943-5; no. 2185, ff. 998v, 1017-17v; no. 8935, ff. 716-17: report of mission to Madurai by local agents, Apr.-June 1708, letters from Tuticorin to Colombo, June 1720, June 1721, June 1731, Tuticorin diary extract, June 1720, May 1731, list of gifts presented during Nayaka's visit, June 1720, correspondence with Madurai representatives, May 1721; Coolhaas *et al.*, *Generale Missiven*, vol. VII, 727, vol. VIII, 19.

143 See, besides the examples given before, NA, VOC, no. 1941, ff. 937-7v: Tuticorin diary extract, June 1720.

seem strange that someone as eminent as Vijayanagara's Emperor Ramadeva did not mind talking about prosaic matters with VOC envoys. At any rate, in Madurai such issues were left to courtiers and nobody here performed this task with more determination than *Pradhāni* and "land regent" Vadamalaiyappa Pillai. But although he conducted the actual negotiations, contacts with him were also governed by elaborate, court-like protocol. This underlines the status of this courtier—and of the governor's seat at Tirunelveli in general—as Madurai's second political node.

The VOC's experiences with Vadamalaiyappa further show that insult was employed to express annoyance but could easily be replaced with courteousness if this better served one's purposes. Although Vadamalaiyappa sabotaged the embassy to Tiruchirappalli in 1668, declining the Company's demands and breaching the protocol, two years later—after the clash following that mission—he received Dutch envoys at his residence with all due honours, accommodating nearly all their wishes. Either the VOC's success in the war or Vadamalaiyappa's now precarious position at court made him change his behaviour with respect to both the protocol and the more prosaic issues to be discussed.

Thus, while political tensions could lead to diplomatic insults, the resultant indignation was not allowed to escalate if that proved counterproductive. Each party had to find a balance between pride and pragmatism. In this light, it is not surprising the VOC reported at least twice on disagreements between Madurai's courtiers about how to treat Dutch envoys. The question of whether protocol should be used to create harmony or discord must have been regularly debated. As Dutch-Madurai relations were relatively cordial, save for some serious but isolated clashes, both sides apparently chose to largely avoid humiliating one another.

Setupatis of Ramnad

This was not the case in Ramnad. This kingdom's contacts with the Dutch were often turbulent, both politically and diplomatically. As a consequence, VOC records deal extensively with protocol, especially the reports of the many embassies exchanged between the Setupati court and the Dutch. Because of the frequent disputes, the present section pays much attention to insult. In fact, we can consider ourselves lucky with this tumultuous relationship and the resultant mass of information, as few local sources refer to protocol.

The latter materials say little about meetings in the audience hall, for instance. One rare example is a Tamil text concerning the Setupatis' caste, the Maravars, which survived in various forms and under different names.[144] One version, titled

[144] Besides the editions mentioned below, what seems to be another version is found in Dirks, *Castes of Mind*, 74-5 (here called *Maravar cati vilakkam*).

Maṟavar jāti kaifīyat, details how Ramnad's king was supposed to be greeted by different chiefs, most of them belonging to the seventy-two Palaiyakkarars in Madurai or the eighteen Palaiyakkarars in Tanjavur. The latter, as well as the rulers of Shivagangai and Pudukkottai, acknowledged the Setupati's superior status by standing before him and joining their palms at chest height. Other chiefs—those bearing the *nāyaka* title and considered to be of lower castes—prostrated themselves and then stood with folded arms, not permitted to sit. Still other chiefs, including several Maravars, did not pay homage to the king at all. In these cases, the Setupati himself showed respect by rising up and offering seats.[145] Whether the *Maṟavar jāti kaifīyat* describes actual ceremonies or rather served to bolster the Setupatis' claim to an exalted status, the text demonstrates the importance rulers attached to honour and the protocol embodying this.

Other portrayals of audiences in Ramnad are found among the murals in the audience hall itself, the Ramalinga Vilasam. These paintings, near the hall's south-east corner, date from Muttu Vijaya Raghunatha Setupati's reign (1710-25) and depict him as he holds court, consulting with courtiers and receiving visitors.[146] It is not clear who are displayed besides the Setupati himself. One image shows him seated on a carpeted platform together with an eminent figure, perhaps also a king, surrounded by standing functionaries. Immediately below, the Setupati sits on a carpet with a prominent courtier and, probably, an infant prince, officials standing on both sides (see illustration 13). Another mural here shows the king with a queen and a young prince as he speaks with European visitors, everyone being seated (see illustration 18 in Chapter 5).

An adjacent set of murals depicts war scenes. In one of these, the Setupati sits on a platform while men with swords stand around him, probably an image of the king consulting with military commanders. A painting elsewhere in the palace also shows the seated Setupati welcoming Europeans, who are now standing, as are two courtiers behind the king (see illustration 19 in Chapter 5).[147] Together these murals show that at audiences in Ramnad, too, people's positions indicated their status. In

---

[145] Mahalingam, *Mackenzie Manuscripts*, vol. I, 238; Taylor, "Marava-Jathi-Vernanam," 357.

[146] For an extensive discussion of some of the murals in the Setupati palace, see the section on Ramnad in Chapter 5.

[147] Howes, *The Courts of Pre-Colonial South India*, 78 (fig. 37), 94, 96, 122 (fig. 63), plates 5, 12 (between 112-13); R. Nagaswamy, "Mughal Cultural Influence in the Setupati Murals of the Ramalinga Vilasam at Ramnad," in Robert Skelton *et al.* (eds), *Facets of Indian Art: A Symposium Held at the Victoria and Albert Museum* (New Delhi, 1987), 208, 210 (figs 12-13); Anila Verghese, "King and Courtly Life as Depicted in the Murals in Ramalinga Vilasam, Ramanathapuram," in idem and Anna Libera Dallapiccola (eds), *Art, Icon and Architecture in South Asia: Essays in Honour of Devangana Desai*, 2 vols (New Delhi, 2015), 476, 478-9 (fig. 34.2); and personal observation (Apr. 2012). For online images of most of the palace's murals, see: southindianpaintings.art/monuments/ramanathapuram.

Illustration 13: Mural depicting Muttu Vijaya Raghunatha Setupati of Ramnad holding court, Ramalinga Vilasam (main hall, south wall), Ramanathapuram, c. 1720 (photo by C. Ganesan, courtesy John and Fausta Eskenazi, source: southindianpaintings.art/monuments/ramanathapuram).

all paintings the king is sitting, whereas almost everyone else is standing. The few seated people were apparently bestowed a rare honour.

Reports of VOC embassies to Ramnad underscore and complement what is suggested by local sources. One example concerns the mission of Joan Richard François (van der Hooge) and Johan Hendrik Medeler in June-July 1759, dispatched to make the Setupati Sella Tevar confirm a recent treaty. In the previous few years, the Dutch-Ramnad relationship had seriously deteriorated. Accusing the court of violating agreements, the VOC had confiscated boats from Ramnad, whereupon the court had done the same with Dutch ships and overland mail. In a rapid escalation, the Dutch next refused to issue sea passes to Ramnad's vessels, the court then stationed extra soldiers near Kilakkarai's VOC factory, and the Company subsequently also sent reinforcements. This stand-off ended when in June 1658 Ramnad's troops attacked the Dutch lodge, took all merchandise, and imprisoned the VOC employees with their families in the capital.[148]

[148] NA, VOC, no. 2923, ff. 215-30v; no. 2925, ff. 841-919; no. 2957, ff. 1588-91: letter from Colombo to Batavia, Jan. 1759, correspondence between Tuticorin and Colombo, Jan.-Dec. 1758, Feb.-May 1759;

Although they were later released and a new treaty was drawn up, relations were still very sour when envoys François and Medeler reached Ramanathapuram on 26 June of the following year. To show their indignation, the Dutch did not send official gifts with this embassy, a rare and unmistakable way to make a diplomatic point. In contrast, probably to atone for its treatment of Kilakkarai's VOC staff and properties, the Ramnad court tried to host the Dutch ambassadors in the most honourable manner possible, as a summary of the embassy's diary indicates:

Already four days after their arrival, François and Medeler secured their first audience. The day before, a courtier had visited them in their lodging to ask how they wished to be received at the palace. The envoys replied that, first, they were to be escorted from their residence by two distinguished courtiers, soldiers, flying flags, and music. Next, all guards at the fort's gate and a double row of soldiers at the central square had to present arms. Finally, two other courtiers should accompany them to the audience hall, where a carpet was to be spread out for them.

The following afternoon everything largely proceeded like François and Medeler had demanded. Two courtiers—one on horseback, one in a palanquin—arrived at their lodging, bringing more than a hundred fully armed soldiers and musicians. The subsequent parade was headed by these courtiers, followed by Ramnad's troops, the VOC's Asian soldiers and the musicians, two silken flags of the Dutch prince, the envoys in their palanquins with the Company's European soldiers, and some minor gifts for the Setupati. These presents were deliberately placed at the procession's end to indicate they were personally brought by the envoys rather than formally sent by the VOC.

When François and Medeler reached the fort's gate, the guards presented arms, while the central square was filled with not one but two double rows of soldiers, the first holding banners, the other matchlock rifles worked with silver. Alighting from their palanquins, the envoys were awaited by a double line of men carrying long spears with black plumes, meant to proclaim the Setupati's status whenever he moved around. At the palace gate stood more soldiers, holding guns. In the main courtyard, François and Medeler were welcomed by two courtiers embracing them "in the land's manner."[149] Here, the envoys finally appeared before King Sella Tevar, who sat leaning against a cushion on a slightly raised, carpeted platform, inside a pavilion ("mandoe") consisting of two canopies, one worked with silver and gold, the other made of red silk, and both resting on four silver pillars of about eight feet high.[150]

Schreuder, *Memoir of Jan Schreuder*, 42-5; Coolhaas *et al.*, *Generale Missiven*, vol. XIII (The Hague, 2007), 73, 179, 298, 435-6.

149 For a modern description of the route François and Medeler probably followed, see Howes, *The Courts of Pre-Colonial South India*, 132 (fig. 65), 134 (fig. 67), 144-6, 157 (fig. 85), 160-1.

150 For literal translations of part of this passage and another short excerpt of the mission's diary, see the section on Ramnad in Chapter 5.

Next to the Setupati, on his right-hand side, sat a relative of his, named Ramasvami Tevar. Seated on carpets on the floor were, on the right, *Pradhāni* (financial minister) Damodaram Pillai with a few other courtiers, and, on the left, some "distinguished youngsters" adopted by the king to be raised at court. Other officials stood on the right, partly under the canopies sheltering the king and partly among all sorts of other people, free to gather there. François and Medeler first went under the canopies and greeted Sella "in the country's way," by bowing a little and touching their hat with their right hand. They were then made to sit on a carpet on the left, a few steps before the canopies, but had their own carpet and two pillows placed over it. Thus seated, they enquired after the health of the king, who in turn asked about the well-being of the envoys' superiors in Colombo and Tuticorin and expressed his happiness about their visit.

François and Medeler now wanted to get to business and began explaining the VOC's view on toll duties. They were soon interrupted by a courtier, saying it was not customary to negotiate during a first meeting and they had better show their presents to the Setupati. Replying they had primarily come to talk about pressing issues, they nevertheless presented a small gift worth 200 guilders. Although they emphasised this was not a present of the VOC but just a private gift, to follow local conventions, it was clearly deemed wholly insufficient. Yet, while François and Medeler once more attempted in vain to discuss tolls, they were honoured with cloths and headdresses ("tooke," "toepettij") worked with gold and probably a parasol ("talpa"),[151] which effectively ended the audience. The ambassadors were then brought to the palace gate by four courtiers and again embraced by them. With an escort and soldiers—an estimated 500 to 600 men—lining the route in the same way as before the meeting, the envoys returned by palanquin to their lodging.

The next evening, the Setupati invited François and Medeler for a display of fireworks, part of the wedding celebration of a prominent courtier's relative. Guided by a courtier, flags, and music, they arrived at a square near the town gate where thousands of people had congregated. Sella Tevar was sitting in the same double-canopied pavilion, set up under a tree. After some courtesies, the envoys were asked to sit on a carpet on the king's right. As during the welcome audience, the Setupati was surrounded by several courtiers, now differently positioned. On his lap, Sella held a "rather light-skinned and finely chiselled [*welbesneden*] naked—but decked with many gold jewels—little boy of the Waduga [*vaḍuga*, northern, Telugu][152] caste, adopted to be educated ... whom he kissed very often." Seated to the king's right was his relative Ramasvami again, and to his left, a bit backwards, sat an "important Pathan [Pattanij]" (perhaps a warrior of Afghan origin), who carried a shield and a sword. Sitting before the Setupati, still under the canopies, was a similarly armed man (referred to as "Rascha"), while closer to the king, also on his left, sat *Pradhāni* Damodaram Pillai.

151 See: Baldaeus, *Naauwkeurige beschryvinge van Malabar en Choromandel*, 2nd pt., 102; Yule and Burnell, *Hobson-Jobson*, 892.

152 See Narayana Rao, Shulman, and Subrahmanyam, *Symbols of Substance*, 33.

During the subsequent amicable conversation between Sella, François, Medeler, and François' son, who spoke Tamil, a courtier presented the Dutchmen with betel and areca on silver plates. Seeing this, the Setupati immediately offered them his own betel and areca of the finest quality. The evening proceeded with two hours of fireworks, which, despite an array of rockets (*vuurpijlen*), jumping jacks (*voetsoekers*), fire wheels (*vuurraden*), and burning paper animals, failed to impress the ambassadors. Thereupon, the bridegroom and the courtier related to him honoured the king by placing before his feet two copper bowls with betel and golden sachets (rumoured to contain 3,000 *pagodas*) and prostrating themselves, just outside the pavilion. After an exchange of pleasantries, a prominent official escorted the envoys back to their lodging.

The following days were spent sending presents to and negotiating with various courtiers, receiving food gifts from the Setupati, and attending more wedding festivities. Despite some delays and minor disagreements, François and Medeler were already granted a departure audience about a week later, in the evening of 9 July. The welcoming ceremonial was largely the same as at the first audience, but this time Sella was accompanied by fewer courtiers. Once more, Ramasvami was seated right of him, next to his cushion, while *Pradhāni* Damodaram sat in front, still under the double canopy. Sitting on the left again were a Pathan, situated slightly behind the king, another armed man, placed more to the front, and some young Brahmins, singing and playing an elongated instrument with copper strings, perhaps a *vīṇā*. The carpet on which the envoys sat was now positioned closer to the canopies.

After the usual courtesies, the changed clauses of the new treaty were read out by the VOC's interpreter in Tamil and Dutch, whereupon François and Medeler rose and presented two copies of the treaty, with the Company's seal, on a silver plate to the Setupati. Sella personally took them and signed them with a silver pen, rifles and guns being fired. Next, the *pradhāni* handed over the royal signet ring to another courtier, who stamped both papers with it. One copy was returned to the envoys, again on a silver plate, while the other was passed among the courtiers.

After both parties had congratulated one another, Sella asked if the VOC soldiers could fire some volleys, which request was executed with the court closely following the corporal's commands. François and Medeler now declared that the ratified agreement obliged all to observe the mutual friendship in perpetuity, which the king and courtiers fully agreed with. Then, headdresses, parasols, and gold necklaces were brought and, after the Setupati touched the objects, given to and put on the VOC ambassadors by the *pradhāni* and another official. Thus, after two hours and yet more courtesies—even the king bowed his head—the audience was concluded. With the same grand escort as before, but now preceded by a large tusked elephant, the envoys returned to their residence, to travel back to Kilakkarai the same night.[153]

[153] NA, VOC, no. 2956, ff. 1222, 1226v-7v, 1232v-65v: diary of mission to Ramnad, June-July 1759.

This mission doubtlessly witnessed the most splendid reception Ramnad ever honoured the Dutch with, as the latter themselves acknowledged.[154] Since it appears to have met all requirements of refined south Indian diplomacy, it may give an impression of how embassies between friendly courts proceeded. The guards of honour, the quick succession of audiences, the positioning in the audience hall, the king's personal attention, the many counter gifts—all this indicated the court wished to show full respect. This mission further demonstrates that the Dutch, too, knew how envoys should be paid homage in south India. Asked how they wanted to be welcomed, the envoys straightaway explained in detail what they expected. True enough, all demands were granted without objection.

At the same time, this embassy had much in common with other Dutch missions to Ramnad. The seating arrangements at audiences were rather similar to those during missions in 1731 and 1743. On the former occasion, the ambassador was seated on a carpet two steps away from the Setupati, Kattaya Tevar, together with the influential "regent of the lowlands" Labbai Nayinar Maraikkayar. During the latter embassy, Sivakumara Muttu Vijaya Raghunatha Setupati sat on a carpet, surrounded by bodyguards (*lijfftrawanten*) of the "royal caste" (*ragias kaste*). Below him, on both sides, were sitting "prominent princes and court notables," while his relative Kadamba Tevar and *Daḷavāy* (general) Vairavanatha Servaikkarar sat still a bit lower. The strong visible presence of armed men at audiences in 1743 and 1759 is striking, particularly during the latter mission, when they were seated close to the king. For none of the other kingdoms are there references to warriors in such prominent positions.[155]

All Dutch embassies to Ramnad comprised two or, less often, three audiences. Only in the latter cases was there room for negotiations, generally during the second meeting, because the other encounters served as welcome and departure audiences. If business was discussed, mature, ambitious rulers like Kattaya and Kilavan Tevar often actively took part in the consultations. During embassies to weak, old, or infant kings, negotiations usually took place in between audiences and involved only courtiers.[156]

The lack of official VOC gifts during the mission of 1759 was extraordinary. On all other trips, Dutch presents were considerable. Besides the standard spices, cloths, sandalwood, and rosewater, VOC envoys honoured the Setupatis and their

[154] NA, VOC, no. 2953, ff. 227-31: letter from Colombo to Batavia, Jan. 1760.

[155] For these and other examples, see NA, VOC, no. 1771, f. 1533; no. 2185, f. 1170v; no. 2599, ff. 2135v-6: diaries of missions to Ramnad, May-July 1709, Jan.-Feb. 1731, June-July 1743.

[156] NA, VOC, no. 1383, ff. 552-66v; no. 1615C, ff. 641-54v; no. 1771, ff. 1448-596; no. 2015, ff. 544-702; no. 2185, ff. 1167-87v; no. 2374, ff. 2041-76v; no. 2599, ff. 2107-62v; no. 2956, ff. 1222-69: diaries of missions to Ramnad, May-June 1683, Dec. 1698-Feb. 1699, May-July 1709, Feb.-May 1724, Jan.-Feb. 1731, Nov. 1736, June-July 1743, June-Aug. 1759.

courtiers with elephants, horses, special guns and pistols (often double- and triple-barrelled ones), and mirrors. Quite exceptionally, gifts to this court regularly included grapevines, liquor, and drinking glasses. Lists of expenses during missions from the 1720s to 1740s show that the VOC generally set aside 1,000 to 1,200 guilders for the kings,[157] and around 200 for courtiers, considerably less than for other courts.[158] Apparently, according to the Dutch, Ramnad occupied a relatively low position in south India's political constellation. That is also suggested by the extent of retinues accompanying VOC embassies to Ramnad in this period, which probably never exceeded a hundred people, considerably fewer than for Tanjavur in these decades. There are no clear figures for missions to Vijayanagara, Ikkeri, and Madurai, but it seems the sizes of entourages sent to Ramnad and Ikkeri were somewhat similar.[159]

The Dutch were expected to present gifts on occasions in between embassies, too, such as successions, all sorts of meetings, or when people had to be pleased to keep them on the VOC's side. Thus, upon their accessions to the throne, Muttu Vijaya Raghunatha and the infant Muttu Ramalinga received presents worth 830 and 164 guilders respectively. Sometimes the Dutch were reluctant to honour new Setupatis if their position seemed uncertain. Two years after Bhavani Shankara was installed, he asked the VOC to finally send gifts. The minor Sivakumara Muttu Vijaya Raghunatha, or whichever courtier acted in his name, made this request twice: upon his initial succession and after what probably was his formal inauguration when he reached some form of adulthood a few years later.[160] On the former occasion, he let the Dutch know that:

> ... after the death of my father I have succeeded in his place, which I have already informed Your Honour about. ... In such cases [successions], according to the old custom, my predecessors have been congratulated [by you] by way of delegating distinguished persons with gifts. But notwithstanding that I have stepped in the place of my father, now 7 to 8 months

157 The purchasing power of 1,000 guilders in 1685 equalled that of 10,900 euros in 2018. See iisg.amsterdam/en/research/projects/hpw/calculate.php.

158 NA, VOC, no. 1227, f. 333; no. 1625, ff. 47-8; no. 1771, ff. 1468-8v; no. 2015, ff. 689-92; no. 2185, ff. 1186-7v; no. 2374, ff. 2075-6v; no. 2599, ff. 2160-2v: Tuticorin proceedings, Jan. 1658, letter from Colombo to Kilavan Tevar, Dec. 1698, instructions for mission to Ramnad, May 1709, lists of gifts at missions to Ramnad, May 1724, Feb. 1731, Nov. 1736, July 1743; DNA, DCGCC, no. 29, f. 28v: Colombo proceedings, May 1685.

159 NA, VOC, no. 2015, ff. 693-4; no. 2185, ff. 1186-7v; no. 2374, ff. 2075-6v; no. 2599, ff. 2160-2v; no. 2956, f. 1222v: lists of expenses during missions to Ramnad, May 1724, Feb. 1731, Nov. 1736, July 1743, diary of mission to Ramnad, June 1759.

160 NA, VOC, no. 1788, ff. 1493v-5v, 1497-7v; no. 2068, f. 1382; no. 2337, ff. 1580v-1; no. 2559, ff. 1471-6; no. 3082, f. 1455: correspondence between Tuticorin and Colombo, Nov. 1710, June 1763, correspondence between Ramnad, Tuticorin, and Colombo, Nov. 1710, July 1727, Aug. 1735, Jan., May 1742.

> ago, the mentioned delegation to me—to make the friendship grow—has not been noticed. And with what ideas this is not being done, I do not know ...[161]

Further, there was pressure to give presents to the kings if they, or their envoys, visited Dutch settlements. When in 1711 the Setupati unexpectedly arrived at Kilakkarai, the VOC was obliged to honour him without delay, hastily gathering a gift of cloths, a glass jug, and two copper compasses. In 1738, Ramnad's ambassadors to Colombo were presented with a gilded carriage, a horse, a cassowary, turkeys, and geese, all for the king. Courtiers received gifts in all sorts of situations too, for example when they (or their relatives) called at VOC settlements, celebrated weddings, promised to support the Dutch, or offered presents themselves. Often, hundreds of guilders were spent on these occasions.[162]

The court offered gifts to the VOC in various situations as well. At audiences, envoys were honoured with gold-worked cloths and headdresses ("toepettij," "tocque," "chiale")[163] when welcomed, with gold necklaces when dismissed, and on some occasions with a crest-jewel or a parasol ("talpa") too. The jewels and clothes were usually put on the ambassadors, often after the Setupati had touched these items. Clearly, the *khil'at* ritual was frequently practised at this court.[164] Travelling to and from the capital, and in between audiences, ambassadors were also given garments and parasols, as well as various food stuffs, like sheep, goats, hens, vegetables, dairy products, sugar, and pastry. Ambassadors from Ramnad to the Dutch donated such items as well, once including a knife used by King Kilavan Tevar himself.

When prominent VOC officials called at Kilakkarai, they were presented with gifts, too. A special case was a brief stay of Ceylon's Governor Gustaaf Willem van

161 NA, VOC, no. 8972, ff. 2222-3: letter from Sivakumara Muttu Vijaya Raghunatha Setupati to Colombo, Mar. 1736 (translation mine).

162 For these and other examples, see: DNA, DCGCC, no. 32, ff. 164-6: Colombo proceedings, May 1692; NA, VOC, no. 1284, f. 1984; no. 1805, ff. 1048v, 1049v; no. 2224, ff. 1624v-5; no. 2245, ff. 327-8; no. 2308, ff. 2060v-1; no. 2337, ff. 1542v-3; no. 2445, ff. 1178-9; no. 2459, ff. 1629-30v; no. 2559, ff. 1487-90v, 1496, 1498v-9; no. 2621, f. 2209; no. 2666, ff. 2257, 2314v-15; no. 2757, ff. 1465v-6, 1474v-5: letter from Pulicat to Batavia, Sept. 1671, reports on receptions of Ramnad envoys, Feb.-Apr. 1711, May-July 1739, Apr. 1750, correspondence between Tuticorin and Colombo, Jan. 1711, Oct., Dec. 1731, Mar. 1734, Aug. 1735, Jan.-Mar., May-June 1742, Apr. 1744, Jan. 1750, letters from Colombo to the Setupati, from Shivagangai to the VOC, May 1738, Oct. 1746, report on meeting with Ramnad's military representatives on Rameshvaram island, Nov. 1746.

163 For "chiale" and other corruptions of *sālū*, *śāl*, or shawl, see Yule and Burnell, *Hobson-Jobson*, 706, 818-19, 824.

164 NA, VOC, no. 1383, f. 560; no. 1771, f. 1503; no. 2015, f. 676; no. 2185, f. 1184; no. 2374, ff. 2058v-9, 2070v; no. 2599, ff. 2110, 2138-8v, 2156; no. 2956, ff. 1238v, 1262v: reports and diaries of missions to Ramnad, May-June 1683, May-July 1709, Feb.-May 1724, Jan.-Feb. 1731, Nov. 1736, June-July 1743, June-July 1759; DNA, DCGCC, no. 29, f. 29: Colombo proceedings, May 1685.

Imhoff here in 1739. The court intended to honour this exceptional visitor with gold ware, textiles, cows, sheep, rice, and vessels, together worth 10,000 guilders—or so the Setupati claimed in a letter from 1742. However, due to a dispute (see below), Van Imhoff left before the gifts could be presented.[165]

The presents to and from the Dutch were partly similar to gifts the Ramnad court exchanged with Indian parties. Local texts state that on various occasions in the seventeenth century the Setupatis received gifts from Madurai's Nayakas in return for military services. First restoring order in the Ramnad area and later defeating several enemies of the Nayakas, they were presented with robes, land, emblems of subdued adversaries, titles, privileges, rice from which the Madurai king had first eaten himself, and Madurai's royal palanquin. A palanquin was also given to Kilavan by a prominent Ramnad courtier, who first recognised him as the new Setupati. Sadaika Tevar I was honoured with a red parasol by pilgrims who were grateful for his protection of the route to Rameshvaram.[166] And in 1742 the Dutch were informed that Sivakumara Muttu Vijaya Raghunatha Setupati considered the king of Kandy "a great personality of high standing." He therefore sent him a whole set of royal gifts: a gold-clasped palanquin with curved bamboo, a silver throne to ride elephants, three kinds of kettle-drums to be placed on elephants, falcons and other birds, a field tent, a canopy with four silver-worked sticks, a bow and a quiver with gold-clasped arrows, and spears ("assegaaijen").[167]

Finally, Dutch sources on Ramnad frequently mention the symbolic reimbursement given to envoys. Known in Ikkeri and Tanjavur as *gastos*, "rice money," and the like, in Ramnad it was commonly called "parrij" or "paddij." This may have been a corruption of "paddy," husked rice,[168] which would explain the term "rice money" and suggest that these remunerations traditionally consisted of rice or more generally food. Representatives of both the VOC and the court, regardless of

[165] For these and other examples, see: NA, VOC, no. 1251, ff. 747, 755; no. 1756, f. 1219v; no. 1771, ff. 1487v, 1488v, 1529; no. 2015, ff. 570, 572, 577-9, 584-5, 591-2; no. 2185, f. 1171; no. 2186, ff. 1274-4v; no. 2308, ff. 2060v-1; no. 2374, f. 2073; no. 2559, ff. 1471-1v; no. 2599, ff. 2128v, 2135, 2139; no. 2757, f. 1458; no. 2956, ff. 1224-4v, 1226, 1228, 1250v, 1253v: report of mission to Travancore, Madurai, and Ramnad, Mar.-Oct. 1665, report of trip to Ramnad by local VOC servant, Sept.-Oct. 1708, diaries of missions to Ramnad, May-July 1709, Feb.-May 1724, Jan.-Feb. 1731, Nov. 1736, June-July 1743, June-July 1759, letters from Kilakkarai and Tuticorin to Colombo, Aug. 1731, Mar. 1734, letter from the Setupati to Colombo, Jan. 1742, report on reception of Ramnad envoys, Apr. 1750; Coolhaas *et al.*, *Generale Missiven*, vol. VI, 624. For Van Imhoff's stay in Kilakkarai, see Wagenaar *et al.*, *Gouverneur Van Imhoff op dienstreis*, 168-75.

[166] For these and other examples, see: BL/AAS, MG, no. 4, pt. 8: "A general history of the kings of Rama Naad or the Satoo-Putty Samastanum," ff. 178-9, 182-4; Mahalingam, *Mackenzie Manuscripts*, vol. I, 238; Dirks, *Castes of Mind*, 74; Taylor, "Marava-Jathi-Vernanam," 357; Seshadri, "The Sētupatis of Ramnad," 38-41.

[167] NA, VOC, no. 2559, ff. 1482v-3v: report on visit of Ramnad envoy, June 1742.

[168] See Yule and Burnell, *Hobson-Jobson*, 650.

their rank, received small sums of cash from their hosts on many occasions. Dutch documents usually just speak of "the regular paddij," but in one case it amounted to 15 *fanams*, roughly 4 guilders,[169] given to a south Indian VOC servant. According to the Dutch, who sometimes called it "board wages" (*kostgeld*), the money served as a sign of goodwill.[170]

The Dutch mission report of 1759, discussed above, also provides many details on ceremonies encountered by ambassadors when travelling to and from the capital. Arriving from Tuticorin, envoys François and Medeler were first welcomed by local court representatives at Ramnad's border, next in Kilakkarai, and then on the way from there to Ramanathapuram, being offered food and greeted in the king's name. Escorted by a courtier with fifty soldiers and musicians from Kilakkarai onward, the ambassadors halted at Sakkarakottai, just south of the capital, to be received by two military commanders and over a hundred soldiers forming a double row. Under great public interest, François and Medeler were brought to their lodging in a procession headed by two bearers of the VOC flag, followed by Ramnad's troops, musicians, the envoys in their palanquins flanked by courtiers on horseback and seven Dutch soldiers, and more local troops.

The ambassadors' residence had been set up by the court in and around a rest house ("amblang," *ampalam*), where they were met by another distinguished person. After a short conversation, they offered betel and areca, cloths, and cash to those who had welcomed them. That day more courteous messages and food stuffs were received from the Setupati and his courtiers. François and Medeler were also escorted by fifty soldiers and musicians at the end of the mission, when they left for Kilakkarai, marking the end of Ramnad's diplomatic obligations.[171]

Arrivals and departures of other missions proceeded more or less similarly, although never as grandiosely as in 1759. After a welcome at the border, envoys were usually fetched in Kilakkarai by an eminent courtier, often the *rāyasam* (royal secretary), together with an escort. Another reception commonly followed when they neared the capital. On the way, they were sometimes honoured with guns, places to sleep, and sumptuous meals, for example roebuck. Once at Ramanathapuram, they were taken to their temporary residence, which could be rather pleasant and spacious. In 1743, the envoys were lodged in a compound with four earthen houses,

[169] For exchange rates between Ramnad *fanams* and other currencies in the early eighteenth century, see: Bes, "The Setupatis, the Dutch, and Other Bandits," 551 (n. 20); Barbara Mears, "Chiuli Fanams of Ramnad," *Journal of the Oriental Numismatic Society* 189 (2006), 13.

[170] NA, VOC, no. 1756, f. 1219v; no. 2337, f. 1542v; no. 2599, f. 2146; no. 2665, ff. 2005v, 2011; no. 2666, f. 2285v; no. 2925, f. 846v: reports of various missions to Ramnad, Sept.-Oct. 1708, June-July 1743, Sept. 1746, letters from Tuticorin to Colombo, Aug. 1735, May 1758, reports of meetings with Tanjavur envoys, Sept.-Oct. 1746, report of mission to Shivagangai, June 1746.

[171] NA, VOC, no. 2956, ff. 1223-8, 1265-5v: diary of mission to Ramnad, June-July 1759.

a courtyard with a canopied bench, a stone well, a "caboose" (*kombuis*), some tents, and separate sleeping quarters for the interpreters and soldiers. In return for all these marks of distinction, ambassadors generally honoured their hosts by giving them betel and areca, sprinkling them with rosewater, applying sandalwood paste on them, and donating cloths and the aforementioned "parrij."[172]

Courteous though these gestures to the Dutch were, Ramnad bestowed greater honours on envoys of Indian rulers. Characteristically, whereas a local soldier sent in 1746 by the Dutch as messenger had to wait three days before being admitted to the king, a messenger from Tanjavur with a similar rank, arriving together with the VOC representative, was received almost immediately. And, as the VOC reported, when in 1724 a fully-fledged ambassador from Tanjavur, one Baluji Pandidar, approached Ramanathapuram, Muttu Vijaya Raghunatha Setupati himself welcomed him about a mile away from the capital.[173]

The court's treatment of Dutch envoys largely resembled the reception of Ramnad's ambassadors at VOC settlements, and the protocol during the latter encounters was apparently mostly based on south Indian customs. Here, too, great value was attached to welcoming and departure rituals, gift-giving, and seating arrangements, although some details differed. Thus, Ramnad's envoys—travelling by palanquin and escorted by soldiers, musicians, and parasol-bearers—were awaited near their destination by middle-ranking VOC servants, for example interpreters, together with soldiers, musicians, flag-holders, and local merchants. In Colombo, the VOC governor often granted as many as four audiences, at the first of which the envoys were received with two rows of soldiers presenting arms. In the governor's meeting room, they were seated in chairs on the left side of the central table, with a special armchair placed on a separate carpet for the chief ambassador. Ramnad's gifts were presented at the initial or second meeting without much ceremonial. After some courtesies, such as enquiries after each other's health and that of the envoys' superiors, the Dutch would quickly come to business.

The VOC concluded audiences by offering betel, areca, and rosewater to the delegates, after which they were escorted to their lodging by interpreters and other local Company personnel. These missions generally proceeded smoothly—at least according to Dutch reports—but some minor annoyance was vented in 1739, when Ramnad's envoys requested that their two *kaṇakkuppiḷḷais* ("cannecappels," clerks) be permitted to sit on chairs. This was granted on the condition that the VOC's

[172] For these and other examples, see NA, VOC, no. 1615C, f. 641v; no. 1771, ff. 1487-8v, 1490v-1; no. 2015, ff. 570-80, 590-2; no. 2185, f. 1170; no. 2374, f. 2049v; no. 2599, ff. 2119-21, 2125v-30, 2134v-5: diaries and reports of missions to Ramnad, Feb. 1699, May 1709, Mar. 1724, Jan. 1731, Nov. 1736, June 1743.

[173] NA, VOC, no. 2015, f. 607; no. 2665, ff. 2009-10v: diaries and reports of missions to Ramnad, Apr. 1724, Sept. 1746.

kaṇakkuppiḷḷais also be allowed to sit when visiting the Ramnad court. At farewell audiences, the Company honoured the ambassadors with gifts, besides the usual betel, areca, and sprinkling of rosewater. As shown by an appreciative letter of the Setupati after the mission of 1739, embassies to the Dutch proceeding in this manner were considered appropriate by the court.[174]

As for courtesies in letters between Ramnad and the VOC, the Setupatis were much more involved in this correspondence than other rulers, whose courtiers commonly conducted such communication. As elsewhere, the Dutch often left out the original pleasantries in their copies and translations of letters, replacing them with remarks like "the usual compliments," so only a few full greetings are found in the archives. In some letters from around 1740, Ceylon's Governor Gustaaf Willem van Imhoff typically honoured the Setupati thus:

> To His Excellency the free lord [followed by royal names and titles], I [governor's names and titles] wish all the blessing and prosperity of heaven ... Let me know if there might be something of [your] service, as well as the state of [your] health ...[175]

The Setupati, in the case below Sivakumara Muttu Vijaya Raghunatha, generally returned these pleasantries as follows:

> I am in a good state of health and please let me know the state of Your Honour as well ... The good and loyal friendship that I maintain with the ... illustrious company, I hope, will last as long as heaven and earth exist. And if something of Your Honour's service might be here, please let this be known.[176]

As the example above shows, the Dutch addressed the Setupati with less exalted phrases than they used for the other rulers, whom they called "king" (usually *vorst*) rather than "free lord" (*vrijheer*), and "highness" rather than "excellency." In addition to the size of the VOC's gifts and retinues accompanying ambassadors, this

174 For these and other examples, see NA, VOC, no. 1805, ff. 1039-40, 1042v, 1044v, 1046v, 1048v; no. 2459, ff. 1617-23, 1627-30v; no. 2492, ff. 1471-2; no. 2757, ff. 1457-8v, 1466-6v: reports on receptions of Ramnad envoys, Feb.-Apr. 1711, May-July 1739, Mar.-Apr. 1750, letter from the Setupati to Colombo, Feb. 1740.

175 NA, VOC, no. 8974, ff. 1289, 1295; no. 8980, ff. 584, 1586-7: letters from Colombo to the Setupati, Apr. 1738, Sept. 1740, Jan. 1741 (translation mine).

176 NA, VOC, no. 8974, ff. 1989, 2005-6; no. 8980, ff. 1572, 1583: letters from the Setupati to Colombo, Mar. 1738, Nov. 1740 (translation mine). For other examples, see NA, VOC, no. 1274, f. 206; no. 1625, ff. 46, 48; no. 2308, f. 2076v; no. 8912, ff. 744-6: correspondence between Ramnad, Jaffna, and Colombo, Oct. 1670, Feb.-Mar. 1692, Dec. 1698, Apr. 1734. For an example in correspondence between Ramnad and the French, see *Lettres & conventions des gouverneurs de Pondichéry*, 342.

seems another indication of the lower status the Dutch attributed to the Setupatis, compared to other dynasties. However, Ramnad's house apparently accepted these designations and deemed them illustrious enough. Further, besides enquiries after each other's health in letters, the use of astronomical terms to denote infinity also derived from Indian tradition. Alongside heaven and earth, letters and agreements between Ramnad and the VOC especially mention the sun and the moon, hoping that their eternal nature would inspire everlasting friendship and observance of treaties.[177]

Despite these phrases, relations between Ramnad and the Dutch were dominated by conflicts. Largely stemming from commercial competition, these disputes frequently assumed political and military dimensions and were reflected in breaches of protocol. Below follows a range of humiliating incidents, showing that the court employed all aspects of ceremonial to express dissatisfaction: the placement of ambassadors in the audience hall, the tempo of audiences, the exchange of gifts, the welcome, dismissal, and lodging of envoys, eloquence during meetings and in correspondence, and so on. These insults usually mirrored existing discord but could also worsen and accelerate matters.

One way Ramnad demonstrated annoyance was its reception of VOC envoys. When in November 1736, while Dutch-Ramnad relations were at a low, Wouter Trek arrived at the palace for his first meeting with Sivakumara Muttu Vijaya Raghunatha Setupati, he could not pass the gate as it was obstructed by a crowd of curious onlookers. Eventually escorted inside by the club-wielding captain of the palace guard, Ravuttan Servaikkarar, Trek was brought before the king. The latter signalled that he could sit down, but no carpet had been spread out to sit on, even

[177] For examples, see: NA, VOC, no. 1302, f. 614; no. 2621, f. 2195; TNA, DR, no. 353, f. 54: letter from the Setupati to superintendent Rijcklof van Goens on Ceylon, June 1674, correspondence between Ramnad and Tuticorin, Sept.-Oct. 1742, Aug. 1744; Heeres and Stapel, *Corpus diplomaticum Neerlando-Indicum*, vol. 4, 149, vol. 5, 507. For examples under the Chalukyas, Cholas, and Hoysalas, see respectively: Eaton and Wagoner, *Power, Memory, Architecture*, 3; Stein, *Peasant State and Society*, 223; J. Duncan M. Derrett, *The Hoysaḷas: A Medieval Royal Family* (Oxford, 1957), 210-11. For Vijayanagara's dynasties, see (among many other instances): Filliozat, *l'Épigraphie de Vijayanagar*, 1-2, 6, 11-13, 15-16, and throughout the volume; Love, *Vestiges of Old Madras*, vol. I, 68; Foster, *The English Factories in India 1642–1645*, 306; Phillip B. Wagoner, "Fortuitous Convergences and Essential Ambiguities: Transcultural Political Elites in the Medieval Deccan," *International Journal of Hindu Studies* 3, 3 (1999), 250; M.S. Nagaraja Rao, "Ahmadkhān's *Dharmaśāla*," in idem (ed.), *Vijayanagara: Progress of Research 1979-1983* (Mysore, 1983), 65; Subrahmanyam, *The Political Economy of Commerce*, 87. For the period of the successor states, see: Vriddhagirisan, *The Nayaks of Tanjore*, 190; Ramakrishna Kavi Pandit, *Pratapasimhendra Vijaya Prabandha*, 33; Nilakanta Sastri and Venkataramanayya, *Further Sources of Vijayanagara History*, vol. III, 138; Wagoner, *Tidings of the King*, 160 (both concerning Madurai); Seshadri, "The Sētupatis of Ramnad', 237; Dirks, *The Hollow Crown*, 433; Ota, "Bēḍa Nāyakas and Their Historical Narratives," 183.

though this was a long-standing custom, as Trek wrote. He was forced to put down a carpet of his own, brought to place his gifts on. The court later denied him another honour since no courtier accompanied him back to his lodging.

Trek expressed his amazement during an intermediate visit by some courtiers—themselves complaining about the VOC's presents—who assured him of an appropriate treatment during the next audience. But at that meeting, again there was no carpet and once more the envoy had to use his own. Trek now became furious and let *Pradhāni* Ramalingam Pillai know that next time Ramnad would send envoys to Colombo they should bring their own chairs.[178] His indignation also clearly transpires from the derogatory opening lines of his report:

> ... at that confused and fickle court, irregularities [are] acknowledged to the highest degree. And zealously cherished by everyone are: slyness [*listigheijd*], deceit [*bedrog*], annoyance [*nijdigheid*], self-interest [*baatzugt*], distrust [*wantrouwen*], and more of such pernicious morals [*verderfelijke zeeden*], because of which all good qualities, yes, even shame [*schaamte*], honour [*eer*], and respect [*eerbiedigheijd*] for the king, are entirely banished.[179]

If the court's aim had been to disgrace the Dutch, it had certainly succeeded. During the next VOC mission, in July 1743, again in a time of disagreements, Ramnad used similar tactics to show its irritation. This time, however, envoys Johannes Krijtsman and Francois Danens had prepared themselves. When they appeared before the Setupati and were invited to sit down, yet again no carpet had been put down. Instead, another, large carpet on which most courtiers were seated, was rolled out for the envoys to sit on. Meant no doubt as a counter-humiliation, Krijtsman and Danens now placed a carpet of their own—specially brought along for this purpose—on top of the courtiers' one. Then they sat down, asked the king about his health, passed the VOC governor's regards, and presented their gifts. But nobody returned the compliments with questions about the governor's wellbeing or other pleasantries.

As the mission report has it, the rest of this meeting and the following one also proceeded without the proper protocol. The first audience was abruptly terminated and at the second and last audience, the Setupati refused to greet Krijtsman and Danens. Their standard question at the end, whether there was anything else of the king's service, remained unanswered. Moreover, *Daḷavāy* Vairavanatha Servaikkarar sneeringly said that only if Dutch ships would come from Batavia with elephants and horses and the envoys return to Ramanathapuram after three

178 NA, VOC, 2374, ff. 2043, 2055v-6, 2059, 2060v-2v, 2066v, 2071: report and diary of mission to Ramnad, Nov. 1736. For this embassy, see Bes, "Friendship as Long as the Sun and Moon Shine," 47-9.

179 NA, VOC, no. 2374, f. 2041v: report of mission to Ramnad, Nov. 1736 (translation mine).

months, the court might grant some of the VOC's wishes. The general added, almost eloquently:

> On the island of Pambe [Pamban, Rameshvaram island], much Hollanders' blood being spilled by him [the *daḷavāy*], his Swami or god at Rammanacoil [Rameshvaram] had therefore ordered to allow the Hollanders to build a stone house at Kilkare [Kilakkarai] to live there and conduct trade. And if the mentioned god would now order him to place the Hollanders on that island, that would be taken care of by him ...[180]

Vairavanatha was probably referring to the Dutch occupation of Rameshvaram island in 1690 and insinuated that more Dutch blood had to be shed before the VOC could set foot on the island again.[181] This greatly offended Krijtsman and Danens, who replied that ships from Batavia might indeed appear with gifts, hinting at Dutch reinforcements to protect the factory in Kilakkarai or even occupy the island again. The dispute went on until this audience—and the mission for that matter—was also suddenly ended.[182]

True enough, less than three years later the VOC did indeed attempt to conquer Rameshvaram island and held part of it between May 1746 and January 1747. While the embassy of 1743 was not the invasion's main cause, it had certainly contributed to the growing tensions in the subsequent years. The Dutch were highly insulted by the humiliation of their envoys and internal correspondence states they would show their resentment in due time. Their attack on the island was a failure, however. Besides a malaria outbreak among their soldiers, the presence of beef-eating infidels on the sacred island aroused the anger of several rulers, including those of Tanjavur, Shivagangai, and Travancore, and some Maratha chiefs. But most of all, the VOC army could not handle the guerrilla-like warfare of Ramnad's troops. Thus, with the military option gone, the Dutch had to fall back on diplomacy.[183]

As part of this diplomacy, the VOC itself also regularly humiliated Ramnad, intentionally and unintentionally. The Dutch only became aware of the latter if the

180 NA, VOC, no. 2599, f. 2154v: report of mission to Ramnad, June 1743 (translation mine).

181 For the Dutch occupation of the island in 1690, see: Bes and Branfoot, "'From All Quarters of the Indian World'"; Vink, "Encounters on the Opposite Coast," 364, 423-9.

182 NA, VOC, no. 2599, ff. 2109, 2136-6v, 2153, 2154-6: report and diary of mission to Ramnad, June-July 1743. For a description of this embassy, see Bes, "Friendship as Long as the Sun and Moon Shine," 64-71.

183 Bes and Branfoot, "'From All Quarters of the Indian World'"; NA, VOC, no. 2599, ff. 2174, 2199v-214; no. 2665, ff. 1987-2012; no. 2666, ff. 2053-406: correspondence between Tuticorin and Colombo, July-Dec. 1743, papers concerning the expedition against Ramnad, Dec. 1745-Dec. 1746, correspondence between Tuticorin and Tanjavur and other papers concerning Tanjavur, July-Oct. 1746; Bes, "The Setupatis, the Dutch, and Other Bandits," 565-6; idem, "Friendship as Long as the Sun and Moon Shine," 72-81.

court complained about it. These offences were usually caused by what Ramnad perceived as a lack of respect from the Company. During the VOC mission in 1724, for instance, the court was affronted because the Company's letter to the king mentioned Ceylon's Dutch governor before the Setupati. Producing VOC letters from previous decades, courtiers showed the envoys that the Setupatis had always preceded Dutch governors. The current order was a disgrace, seen as suggesting the king was not a legal successor of his ancestors, which made him hesitant to acknowledge the VOC envoys as official delegates. Although the matter was not deemed serious enough to abort the mission, the court straightaway wrote to Colombo to convey its annoyance.

A somewhat similar case concerned the Dutch embassy in 1731, when the court was displeased by the status of the envoy, Reijnier Helmondt. Whereas past ambassadors had occupied higher offices and were dispatched from the VOC governor's seat at Colombo, Helmondt held the middle-ranking position of *resident* (local chief) at the nearby Kilakkarai factory. Again, this was no reason to send him away, but the Setupati, Kattaya Tevar, immediately informed the Dutch about his irritation. As he wrote, it was only because of the mutual friendship that he received a "factor" from Kilakkarai with the honours reserved for representatives from Colombo. In future he wished not to be confronted with such disdain anymore and instead given the respect his predecessors had enjoyed.[184]

While these unintended insults proved of little consequence, other lapses had serious repercussions. In 1733, when Kattaya Tevar visited Kilakkarai, the local VOC official Wouter Trek honoured the king with gifts and a salute from a Dutch vessel, but did not give the presents himself. Although acceptable to former Setupatis, Kattaya was offended about the impersonal homage. He rejected the gifts and had them thrown down at the gate of the VOC's factory. The Dutch now felt disgraced as well and a long, bitter polemic ensued with the court. The mutual breach of protocol then acquired political and economic overtones. Ramnad closed off the strategic Pamban Channel to the Dutch and invited other European powers to the kingdom. With this, the VOC's worst fears came true and this escalation, from a ceremonial miscalculation to a commercial disaster, was certainly the last thing Trek had intended.[185]

184 NA, VOC, no. 2015, ff. 608-12, 698; no. 2185, ff. 1058, 1060, 1174v-5: reports of missions to Ramnad, Apr. 1724, Jan. 1731, letters from the Setupati to Colombo and Tuticorin, Apr. 1724, Feb. 1731. For a detailed description of the mission in 1731, see Bes, "Friendship as Long as the Sun and Moon Shine," 34-6.

185 NA, VOC, no. 2291, ff. 501-15, 519-27: correspondence between Tuticorin and Colombo, May-Sept. 1733. For more extensive descriptions of these incidents, see Bes, "The Setupatis, the Dutch, and Other Bandits," 567; and especially idem, "Friendship as Long as the Sun and Moon Shine," 41-2.

On other occasions, the VOC breached protocol deliberately. In 1709, its ambassadors refused food gifts of the "regent of the lowlands," who belonged to Kilakkarai's influential *periya tambi* family and was a long-standing opponent. The envoys' superiors disapproved of this decision and attributed the embassy's meagre results to it. Nevertheless, in 1731, during another conflict about the Pamban Channel, the governor at Colombo himself went so far as to return a letter from the Setupati unopened. Indeed, a message was sent to Kattaya Tevar telling him the governor had not even cast his eyes on the king's letter.[186]

Whereas this had little effect, at a confrontation in 1739 the Dutch managed to impress the court by breaching the protocol as much as Ramnad did. In March of that year, Ceylon's Governor Gustaaf Willem van Imhoff travelled along the Fishery Coast to inspect the VOC factories. Although this was not an embassy to the region's rulers, the Dutch still expected them to welcome the governor, albeit not personally. But upon Van Imhoff's arrival at Mukaiyur ("Mukkur"), the first village in Ramnad's territory, nobody received him. Furthermore, when he reached Kilakkarai, the court had not yet granted him permission to sail through the Pamban Channel. Normally, a request of Kilakkarai's VOC official was sufficient for that, but now Van Imhoff himself was asked to seek approval in writing. Irritated, the governor sent someone to the Setupati to make his request verbally, which was countered by a letter repeating the court's demand. Now really affronted, Van Imhoff rejected this letter and denied its messenger the usual "parrij" or reimbursement.

Although the court then gave permission to cross the Channel, the governor was not ready to forget the humiliation. When another messenger of the court arrived, Van Imhoff refused to let him sit, considering him just a courier, not an official delegate. The messenger walked out and said he could not convey his message if he was not seated. The Dutch replied they would not listen to him anymore even if he were standing and that he better not enter the building again. The messenger departed and the governor sent a furious letter to the court. Van Imhoff then sailed back to Ceylon via the Pamban Channel, despite sudden pleas by local officials and merchants to wait for court representatives now on their way with gifts and elephants to honour the governor. Thus, the Dutch won this ceremonial stand-off. The court evidently realised it had gone too far, because both a long letter and an embassy it later sent to Colombo were clearly attempts at reconciliation.[187]

[186] NA, VOC, no. 1771, ff. 1486v-7, 1581v, 1583v; no. 2245, ff. 326-7: diary of mission to Ramnad, May 1709, correspondence between Colombo and envoys in Ramnad, June 1709, letter from Colombo to Tuticorin, Oct. 1731.

[187] NA, VOC, no. 2456, ff. 556v-65v, 703-4; no. 2459, ff. 1612-14v: report of the governor's journey along the Fishery Coast, Mar. 1739, letter from the Setupati to Colombo, Apr. 1739. For an extensive description of this event, see Bes, "Friendship as Long as the Sun and Moon Shine," 57-8. The report of

Ramnad was hardly ever apologetic in other cases where it breached protocol, for example when it refused gifts. In 1692, an envoy of the Setupati at Colombo declined an elephant the Dutch presented to the king since both the animal and its tusks were deemed too small. They sent the elephant anyway, hoping the Setupati would still receive it as it was offered as a "free gift without obligation" (*vrije gifte sonder verplightingh*), unlike most presents, which compelled the recipient to give or do something in return. Further, the court frequently disgraced south Indian VOC messengers, delaying meetings and giving them very small escorts. In 1731 Kattaya Tevar was reluctant to accept a letter brought by a local VOC clerk and refused to look at or talk to him. Another such messenger was not received by the Setupati at all—considered highly unusual—and was also denied his "parrij."[188]

Insults were especially encountered during fully-fledged VOC embassies. Besides humiliations at audiences, a common dishonour was the continuous postponement of such meetings. While this happened in all kingdoms, in Ramnad it seemed a standard treatment. The reports of all six missions between 1698 and 1743 complain about endless waits. Many embassies therefore took weeks or even months. Indeed, on most trips, the envoys threatened to terminate their stay hoping this would speed up matters. In 1709 they gave this warning no fewer than three times over a period of two weeks before they secured their final audience.[189] On other occasions, nobody escorted them back to their residence after an audience, or they were told to report to the court's toll collectors to receive their "parrij," which they flatly refused to do.[190]

A last way the court humiliated Dutch ambassadors concerned their lodging. In 1709 they wrote:

> ... we were rather surprised when, having passed the town Ramanadawaram [Ramanathapuram], we had to march for another half an hour through thick thorn-bushes, [and] having finally reached our lodge, its doors were closed. Those having been opened after much knocking and shouting, inside we found a large number of faquiers and vagabonds [*landlopers*] of both sexes and strange figures [*wonderlijcke gedaentens*]. This made us lament strongly about that lodge—crawling with lice and all sorts of vermin, and

this trip has been published in Wagenaar *et al.*, *Gouverneur Van Imhoff op dienstreis*, with the Ramnad episode on 168-76.

188 DNA, DCGCC, no. 32, ff. 86-7: Colombo proceedings, Mar. 1692; NA, VOC, no. 2186, ff. 1224v-5v, 1237v; no. 2308, ff. 2057-7v; no. 2693, ff. 1262, 1264: letters from Tuticorin to Colombo, Sept. 1731, Feb. 1734, Sept. 1747.

189 NA, VOC, no. 1615C, ff. 641-54v; no. 1771, ff. 1485-543v; no. 2015, ff. 567-689; no. 2185, ff. 1167-85; no. 2374, ff. 2041-73v; no. 2599, ff. 2107-59: reports and diaries of missions to Ramnad, Dec. 1698-Feb. 1699, May-July 1709, Feb.-May 1724, Jan.-Feb. 1731, Nov. 1736, June-July 1743.

190 NA, VOC, no. 2015, f. 595; no. 2599, f. 2146: diaries of missions to Ramnad, Apr. 1724, June 1743.

> where not the least preparation or commodity had been made for our stay—and [made us] threaten to return to Kilkare right away ...[191]

Only when the fakirs and vagabonds were forced out and the place was cleaned, did the envoys decide to continue their mission. In 1724, too, the ambassadors were housed in small, dirty accommodation, forcing them to stay outside in the hot sun. They had to threaten to leave before a suitable rest house was arranged. In 1736, the lodging of the envoys seemed to reach the level of intimidation. When ambassador Wouter Trek neared Ramanathapuram—probably with the experiences of earlier delegates in mind—he sent a soldier ahead to inspect the residence prepared for him. The soldier returned saying it looked like an animal corral rather than a human dwelling. Trek then told the Ramnad courtier accompanying him that he would proceed no further until appropriate accommodation was arranged. When news came that a field tent had now been set up, the envoy continued his trip. But upon Trek's arrival, it turned out the residence was located right next to the fortress wall, from where a cannon, escorted by two soldiers, was aimed straight at his tent.[192]

Considering all these incidents, Ramnad stood out among Vijayanagara's heirs when it came to insulting the VOC. If the Company's records are to be believed, at no other court was protocol breached so blatantly, frequently, and widely. This is not surprising because Ramnad's commercial interests were often at odds with those of the Dutch, and the VOC generally only dispatched embassies to complain. Further, the Ramnad court harboured relatively many competing parties, probably easily leading to disagreements about how to treat the Dutch. Consequently, there was ample room for annoyance on both sides, ventilated through insults first before violence was considered.

Many elements of protocol in Ramnad—seating arrangements, gifts, welcome and departure ritual, eloquence—were largely the same as elsewhere. Some presents exchanged between Ramnad and the Dutch were exceptional, however. Only Ramnad's rulers regularly received alcohol-related articles such as liquor, grapevines, and drinking glasses. In turn, this court was unique in that it offered lots of food stuffs, often including meat from sheep, goats, and fowl. The regular use of alcohol and meat may be related to the low status of the Setupatis' Maravar caste, for which the consumption of such "impure" goods was perhaps less of a taboo

191 NA, VOC, no. 1771, ff. 1491-1v: diary of mission to Ramnad, May 1709 (translation mine).

192 NA, VOC, no. 2015, ff. 582-3; no. 2374, ff. 2050-1: diaries of missions to Ramnad, Mar. 1724, Nov. 1736.

than for the castes to which other rulers belonged or aspired to belong. Indeed, Maravars also offered alcohol and meat to some of their deities.[193]

All in all, protocol, and the breaching of it, was omnipresent in Ramnad—seemingly reflecting rather than shaping relations—and always called for more protocol. As ambassadors François and Medeler phrased it in their report of 1759: "sending of betel [leaves] and arreek [areca nuts] is surely a sign of homage [*eerbewijs*], but self-seeking [*eijgenbaat*] has created those ceremonies, as it always drags along a counter present [*contra present*]."[194] Thus, protocol often functioned as some kind of game everyone was supposed to take part in, as further transpires from the quarrelsome but still eloquent correspondence between the court and the VOC in 1742, concerning different interpretations of a treaty.[195] When the Dutch wrote it was "as clear as the sun shines in the afternoon" that they were in the right,[196] Sivakumara Muttu Vijaya Raghunatha Setupati replied:

> But my patience is as large as the size of a mountain. Your Honour says that what he explains to me is as clear as the sun in the afternoon, but Your Honour does not consider that after the afternoon, that sun must set behind the mountain ...[197]

Conclusions

Based on reports of VOC embassies to Vijayanagara's heirs and other Indo-Dutch diplomatic encounters, one might well be able to compile a manual on early modern south Indian protocol. Such a work would explain that honourable people must be made to sit close to the highest present authority, shall be regularly offered suitable, valuable, and extraordinary gifts, have to be welcomed and dismissed by extensive retinues headed by distinguished persons, and are to be treated with personal attention and eloquence. Also, the manual should make clear when these guidelines need to be adhered to and when they are to be ignored, depending on the sort of message one wishes to convey.

In fact, this manual would have much in common with south Indian political discourses like the twelfth-century *Mānasollāsa* compiled under Kalyana's Chalukyas and the eighteenth-century *Śivatattva ratnākara* of Ikkeri's Basavappa

193 Thurston, *Castes and Tribes of Southern India*, vol. V, 43; S. Natarajan, "Society and Culture under the Setupatis," *Proceedings of the Indian History Congress* 14 (1951), 170.

194 NA, VOC, no. 2956, f. 1224v: diary of mission to Ramnad, June 1759.

195 For disagreements between Asian courts and the VOC about treaties, see Subrahmanyam, *Courtly Encounters*, 8-9.

196 TNA, DR, no. 353, f. 65: letter from Tuticorin to Ramnad, Nov. 1742.

197 TNA, DR, no. 353, f. 85: letter from Ramnad to Tuticorin, Dec. 1742 (translation mine).

Nayaka I. Notions in these treatises greatly resemble the practices encountered by the VOC at all courts. Clearly, Indo-Dutch diplomatic ceremonial was mainly based on Indian customs, and VOC records serve as useful sources for protocol in the Vijayanagara successor states as it was performed in practice, compensating to some extent for the scarcity of relevant Indian texts. Further, the similarities between contemporary and older south Indian works (spanning a period of six centuries) and also Dutch experiences, suggest that many manifestations of court ceremonial were widespread and long-lasting. Generally speaking, no great differences existed between Vijayanagara and its heirs or among the successors themselves. The imaginary VOC manual would apply to every court.

For most aspects of protocol, just the details sometimes varied. Only in Madurai did kings never participate in negotiations with VOC envoys. It was also here that much emphasis was laid on the *khil'at* ritual, as Dutchmen repeatedly had to put on received clothes in public. Both observations imply that Madurai considered the VOC to hold a relatively low standing and that it showed this condescension through ceremonial. At the same time, Madurai's rulers and courtiers did not object to close contact with European visitors, personally giving presents or sitting next to them, thus still showing their deference.

Actual physical contact between monarchs and ambassadors chiefly occurred at Tanjavur's Bhonsle court, where kings were happy to touch or be touched by Dutchmen. Bhonsle-ruled Tanjavur also stood out for the small number of audiences deemed sufficient to conduct business and complete all ceremonies. Further, both under the Bhonsles and the preceding Nayakas, gifts appear to have been particularly important, considering the continuous requests for them by Tanjavur's rulers and courtiers.[198] Finally, Ramnad differed from other courts with regard to the kinds of exchanged presents, frequently including meat and alcohol.

Besides these minor variations, differences between the kingdoms, as experienced by the VOC, principally concerned the extent to which protocol was deliberately breached. Humiliations of the Dutch were more common in Ikkeri and Ramnad than elsewhere, no doubt related to the fact the VOC usually dispatched embassies to these courts when irritations had arisen over violations of treaties. By contrast, diplomatic meetings in the other kingdoms chiefly served to congratulate new rulers or occurred during royal tours, giving little reason to insult one another. It therefore appears that protocol and deviations from it generally did not so much affect relations as they mirrored them. There were several cases of humiliations

[198] The British also complained about the pressure in Tanjavur to present gifts constantly. See Raman, *Document Raj*, 174. For similar Portuguese experiences in south India, see Melo, "Seeking Prestige and Survival."

assuming a life of their own and worsening disputes, but insults commonly reflected underlying political or economic tensions.

It must be emphasised that breaches of protocol were rarely caused by protocolar misunderstandings. On the contrary, to effectively offend others one had to be well aware of what was considered honourable and what humiliating in south India. The often deliberate insults between courts and Europeans only show that the latter were very familiar with local protocol and usually knew when and how it was violated.[199] Indeed, it can be argued that the Dutch followed the rules even when they intentionally broke them, as this was a common way to express resentment, just as south Indian parties both adhered to and breached protocol for different purposes. Instances of mere misunderstanding were rather seldom, and even rarer were those that led to indignation and serious clashes. For example, the VOC's efforts to resell received robes of honour do not indicate that the Dutch could not appreciate their symbolic value. VOC officials obediently participated in the *khil'at* ceremony, knowing its aim was to cement a hierarchical but reciprocal relationship. Alongside this function, the clothes were considered goods that could be traded. Obviously, to the Dutch adherence to protocol and commercial pragmatism were not mutually exclusive.[200]

As in the previous chapter, the sole Dutch embassy to Mysore in 1681 provides a useful counterpoint to the other courts. While envoy Jan van Raasvelt must have had some idea of the ceremonial he was to encounter—based on experiences in adjacent kingdoms like Ikkeri and Madurai—the Wodeyar court was clearly not used to receiving European visitors. During his first night in the capital Srirangapatnam, Van Raasvelt and his assistants were paraded before *Daḷavāy* (general) Kumarayya, the king's brother-in-law Balayya, and other dignitaries who wished to have a look at these foreigners.

During the first audience, the next afternoon, King Chikkadevaraja asked his guests if they were real "Hollanders" and requested Van Raasvelt to tell him about the "state, rules, intercourse, and life" of the Dutch people. The king further wished to know how many ships, cannon, personnel, towns, and fortresses the VOC controlled. The envoy's reply greatly pleased Chikkadevaraja, who remarked that the Company, contrary to his initial belief, was also a "mighty king." At the end of

199 For discussions of intercultural understanding—often referred to as commensurability—at early modern Asian courts, see for example: Subrahmanyam, *Courtly Encounters*, 1-33; Van Meersbergen, "The Diplomatic Repertoires of the East India Companies."

200 For some debate on European perceptions of Indian court gifts in the early modern period, see: Bernard S. Cohn, *Colonialism and Its Forms of Knowledge: The British in India* (Princeton, 1996), 18-19; William R. Pinch, "Same Difference in India and Europe," *History and Theory* 38, 3 (1999), 399-405. See also Fihl, "Shipwrecked on the Coromandel," 241.

this meeting, Van Raasvelt and everyone in his retinue, including the lowest local servants, were given robes of honour, a privilege usually reserved for the highest representatives.

At the second audience, on the following day already, Chikkadevaraja first glanced over the Dutchmen from head to toe and then made Van Raasvelt recite the Dutch version of the VOC's letter to him. When the envoy began reading it aloud, the king started laughing, explaining he was not familiar with this language, although it sounded pleasant to him. He hoped Van Raasvelt was not offended, because he was only curious to hear a Dutch version of his own names and titles. Chikkadevaraja being contented with the way he was addressed, Van Raasvelt had to repeat it several times. The king then insisted the envoy also read the letter in Portuguese and the VOC's interpreter translate it into what was probably Malayalam (*Mallabaars*). Still young, the latter felt intimidated and confused, failing to produce a proper translation. Chikkadevaraja next wanted his guests to sing Dutch songs, which they tried to evade by claiming they were bad singers.[201] Undeterred, the king had some musical instruments brought in to help them, but now *Daḷavāy* Kumarayya intervened and managed to change the conversation subject.

Other incidents further illustrate the somewhat unusual and awkward but probably well-meant reception of the Dutch in Mysore. Most courtiers were reluctant to accept gifts and at the end of his stay Van Raasvelt was asked what would be an appropriate royal gift to his superiors. All in all, the court appears to have harboured good intentions—welcoming the envoy with a horse and a parasol (*sombareere*) and dismissing him with a "state parasol" and a torch (*flambauw*)—but occasionally it seemed at a loss about how to treat its guests.[202] Thus, the VOC's experiences in Mysore are a good example of what protocol looked like when there merely was some misunderstanding between a south Indian court and the Dutch. Some ceremonies in Mysore were slightly odd but certainly not insulting, as they were chiefly caused by unfamiliarity with the Dutch. Deviations from protocol at the other courts clearly happened for different, more serious reasons and, as a result, often had grimmer manifestations and consequences.

This chapter's section on Vijayanagara is largely based on south Indian sources and mainly concerns relations within the court and with adjacent sultanates. In contrast, Dutch records are the main sources for the sections on the successor states and so these parts chiefly deal with relations between the courts and the VOC. But

[201] Jesuit visitors to Chikkadevaraja were also asked questions about Europe and requested to sing. Unlike the Dutch, the Jesuits were happy to comply with the latter wish. See Ferroli, *The Jesuits in Mysore*, 95-6, 108.

[202] NA, VOC, no. 8985, ff. 104v-17: report of mission to Mysore, Jan. 1681.

the many similarities between Vijayanagara and its heirs with respect to protocol and honour imply that the findings for Indo-Dutch contacts in the successor states apply to inter-Indian contacts there, too. Thus, one can assume that between kings and courtiers, among courtiers, and between courts, protocol was also employed to initiate, affirm, or damage relationships. The few available references to such local relations—found in both south Indian and European sources—further indicate that protocol usually was either observed or intentionally breached to express respectively satisfaction and anger in the successor states.

The continuity in this regard between Vijayanagara and its heirs also suggests that the findings of this chapter are relevant for courts that preceded the empire. Thus, when the first diplomatic pleasantries and insults were exchanged between Vijayanagara and the Bahmani sultanate, protocol had probably long served as a tool to convey approval or annoyance between parties at Indian courts. It would therefore seem likely that already at the time a text like the twelfth-century *Mānasollāsa* was composed, its guidelines on court ceremonial could be followed as well as ignored. In any case, we may conclude that in early modern south India protocol played a significant role in various aspects of court politics: dynastic foundations, successions to the throne, the power of courtiers, and (as Chapter 6 demonstrates) relations between states. Protocol was also an important element of the subject of the next chapter: Islamic influences on court culture.

CHAPTER 5

Influences from Sultanate Courts[1]

Dodda Sankanna Nayaka, one of Ikkeri's early kings, one day resolved to go on a pilgrimage. As the chronicle *Keḷadi arasara vaṃśāvaḷi* relates, he appointed his brother Chikka Sankanna to reign in his absence, dressed as a poor, wandering holy man, and brought along just his royal sword and four servants. He first went south, visiting sacred towns and bathing in holy rivers. Then, he turned north and traversed the Deccan sultanates. Finally, he arrived at the ancient north Indian sultanate capital of Delhi and headed for the sultan's palace.[2] As the chronicle (in its translated version) continues, in minute detail:

> ... on entering the gate of the palace, he [Dodda Sankanna] found a sword fixed up by the king's order. On enquiring the cause, he was informed by the guards that no one being equal hitherto to engage with a Vazeer [*wazīr*, minister] named Ankoos Cawn [Ankush Khan] in single combat, this sword was hung up as defiance to all the world to take it down. When he heard these words, he said he wished to behold for once so able & great a warrior & therefore requested them to unsheathe it, which they complied with & asked him: "Who are you? Whence came you? & of what nation & caste are you?" He replied that he was a Jungum [Jangam][3] by caste, that a traveller had no country, changing his residence every night.
>
> A messenger then went & related this to the Padshah [*Bādshāh*, great king, the Delhi sultan], who was surprised & sent for him into his presence, & having enquired about his condition he assigned him a proper house for a lodging & ordered his servants to defray all his expense & to furnish him with whatever he required. The Padshah ... sent for the Vazeer Ankoos Cawn to come into his presence. On passing the gate, he [Ankush Khan] missed his sword [and] coming into the hall of audience in wrath demanded to know who had unsheathed his sword. When perceiving Sankana-Naik [Dodda Sankanna Nayaka]

[1] A slightly different version of parts of this chapter appeared in Lennart Bes, "Sultan among Dutchmen? Royal Dress at Court Audiences in South India, as Portrayed in Local Works of Art and Dutch Embassy Reports, Seventeenth–Eighteenth Centuries," *Modern Asian Studies* 50, 6 (2016).

[2] BL/AAS, MG, no. 6, pt. 11: "Historical account of Beedoonoor or Caladee Samstanum" (*Keḷadi arasara vaṃśāvaḷi*), ff. 67v-8.

[3] For Jangams, followers of the Lingayat sect or religious beggars, see Thurston, *Castes and Tribes of Southern India*, vol. II, 450-1.

with his sword in his hand, he took another sword to fight him, but the officers attending on the king requested them to suspend the combat until they had taken food.

They accordingly went to take victuals & returned to the hall richly habited. The Vazeer Ankoos Cawn, holding a highly tempered sword in his hands, stood before the Padshah, prepared to encounter his antagonist, but Sankana-Naik stood over against him without any weapons. The Padshah then called for an excellent sword & presented it to him. When he had received this sword, he drew it out & flourishing it in the manner of swordsmen the blade snapped & broke. The king was surprised & calling for another, gave it into his hand & this also in like manner was soon broken. Then the Padshah told him that he would sent for his own sword, but he [Dodda Sankanna] respectfully replied to the king that it was not proper to give his sword into any other person's hands, but that he would use his own sword. He then took his own blade, called Naugaremara [*nāgara-muri*], & examining it attentively he took it once & flourished it before his opponent, challenging him to stand out boldly & fight him.

They then engaged in a combat with swords, which lasted till a quarter part of the day was past, exhibiting their address & skill in the various modes of fencing & swordsmanship, till the fortune of the Vazeer Ankoos Cawn decreased hour by hour before the skill of Sankana-Naik. The Padshah, observing that the Vazeer Ankoos Cawn was wounded in several parts of his body tho' he had boasted that his antagonist should not escape ... & that not the least mark appeared on Sankana-Naik, he adjudged the superiority in skill & bravery to Sankana-Naik to whom no one could be esteemed equal. In this combat Sankana Naik cut his enemy's sword into two with one stroke. He wounded him in the loin & in several parts of his body with such rapidity that the spectators could not distinguish the blows, so that he was over-eyed as a dead body.

The spectators in the public hall were in doubt whether Sankana-Naik had not killed him outright, & the Padshah, observing that he was dead, in order to have the death of the Vazeer made apparent to all the people, enquired of Sankana Naik why he stood still & whether he was tired? He replied: "With whom must I fight further?" The Padshah said: "You must kill your adversary who stands before you," to which he replied: "Of what use is it to fight with a dead corpse?" & then immediately touching the body on the breast with his sword, it fell down to the great surprize of the spectators in the hall.

One of the king's officers then enquired further about him of his condition, when he gave a full & complete account of himself from beginning to end. The Padshah having attentively heard the narrative of Sankana Naik embraced him with much kindness & said: "It was not right in you to conceal your caste & rank." He then treated him with every mark of distinction & honor, presented him with betel, & requested him to signify his wishes & that whatever they were, they should be complied with. He [Dodda Sankanna] replied that if he [the sultan] solemnly promised to comply without fail with what he asked, in that case he would make his wishes known. The Padshah complied with it & took a solemn oath. Then Sankana-Naik represented to the king that he proposed to go to Benares to fulfill his vows, which were: before his return to his native country to build a handsome Mattum [*maṭha*, monastry] in all the holy places of his country & to endow them with Jagheers [*jāgīr*, land estate] for their support, that he next proposed to return to his country & he therefore requested his aid to fulfill these vows, which the Padshah immediately consented to ...[4]

The *Keḷadi arasara vaṃśāvaḷi* goes on to describe how Dodda Sankanna then travelled around north India, erecting prayer halls, setting up *liṅgams* (phallic symbols of Shiva), endowing sacred places, and worshipping in temples. Finally, he returned to Ikkeri and resumed reign over his kingdom.[5] More or less similar accounts are given in the dynasty's chronicles *Keḷadinṛpa vijayam* and *Śivatattva ratnākara*.[6] Another text states that the Delhi sultan presented Dodda Sankanna with a sword and the title of "Keladi Padshah," or "great king of Keladi," referring to Ikkeri's first capital.[7]

About a century later, another contest between a Nayaka king and the Delhi court is said to have taken place. As a summary of one version of this event goes:

During the reign of Madurai's Muttu Virappa Nayaka III (here referred to as Ranga Krishna), the *Bādshāh* (here probably the Mughal emperor) delegated one of his slippers to every subordinate ruler. When the slipper—travelling by elephant with great pomp and circumstance and accompanied by high courtiers, attendants, musicians, and thousands of troops—arrived at the border of a vassal kingdom, its king welcomed the slipper, acknowledged its supremacy, took it to his palace to put it on his own throne, and presented his tribute.

But at the border of Madurai, the *Bādshāh*'s slipper was not received by Muttu Virappa, who claimed he was unaware of the required procedures and not fit enough to come to the border anyway. He let the *Bādshāh*'s men know that if they would bring the slipper to the Kollidam (Coleroon) River, within Madurai's boundaries, he would await it there. The slipper's entourage grudgingly transferred it to the proposed spot, but Muttu Virappa again failed to show up, letting his messengers ask the *Bādshāh*'s troops to continue to the gates of the capital

[4] BL/AAS, MG, no. 6, pt. 11: "Historical account of Beedoonoor or Caladee Samstanum," ff. 68-9. This episode is still being told as a folktale in the Kannada-speaking region. In that version, the sultan of Delhi is the Mughal Emperor Akbar. He disliked vain people, including his own warrior Ankush Khan, and was happy to see him defeated. Dodda Sankanna is here said to have left Ikkeri because he became tired of being king and wished to build monasteries. See Praphulladatta Goswami (ed.), "The Monk Who Dueled," in Richard M. Dorson (ed.), *Folktales Told around the World* (Chicago/London, 1975), 193-6.

[5] BL/AAS, MG, no. 6, pt. 11: "Historical account of Beedoonoor or Caladee Samstanum," ff. 69v-70.

[6] Krishnaswami Aiyangar, *Sources of Vijayanagar History*, 337-8; Krishnamurthy, *Sivatattva Ratnākara of Keladi Basavaraja*, 107; Chitnis, *Keḷadi Polity*, 13-14; Naraharayya, "Keladi Dynasty" [pt. 1], 379-80; K.G. Vasantha Madhava, "The Mughals and the Keladi Nayakas," *Proceedings of the Indian History Congress* 37 (1976), 260.

[7] BL/AAS, MG, no. 25, pt. 27: "Memoir of Barkoor," f. 209.

Tiruchirappalli. On their arrival there, the Nayaka once more did not appear, instead inviting the slipper and its company into his fort. While the *Bādshāh*'s representatives grew more and more angry, Muttu Virappa pretended he was falling increasingly ill and thus, step by step, had the slipper moved into his palace, then alighted from the elephant, and finally brought by palanquin into his audience hall. Here, sitting on his throne in great state, the Nayaka refused to pay homage to the slipper and forced the *Bādshāh*'s courtiers to put it on the floor. Muttu Virappa then placed one of his feet in it and asked why the *Bādshāh* had not thought of sending two slippers. Next, the slipper's retinue was beaten up and driven out of Madurai. Informed of this incident, the *Bādshāh* feared other rulers might follow the Nayaka's example and never delegated his slipper again.[8]

No doubt related to tensions between Madurai and the Mughals during Muttu Virappa's reign (1682-91),[9] this story circulated in various versions. One of these claims that the Mughal emperor in fact sent his shoe to test the wisdom of his fellow rulers, the Madurai Nayaka proving to stand out among them:

> ... the king of Delhi, curious to know which of his contemporaries was the wisest & bravest, ordered cabinets to be brought & depositing in each of them an odd shoe forwarded them at once to every king or governor on the southern part of this continent. Some kings with great respect went to meet the people that brought the cabinets & paid hommages to the shoes therein contained. Some kissed these shoes; some prostrated before them; some, putting them on their heads, danced in an extacy of joy; & some received them with a concert of music and loud acclamations.
>
> But Ranga Krishna Mootoo Veerapah Naik [Muttu Virappa Nayaka], without shewing any manner of ceremony, let them bring the cabinet into his presence and seeing an odd shoe into it, he thrusted one of his feet into that shoe & asked the bearer what was become of its fellow [shoe]. Being confounded at this, the bearer stood dumb and Ranga Krishna Mootoo Veerapah Naik lashed him and sent him back with disgrace to the king of Delhi, who, admiring his wisdom and bravery, sent him valuable presents with two untameable horses. These our hero received kindly & in return loaded the Dilhean [Delhi] people with rich[es], & before their departure from his presence, he rode one of their horses & after having gallopped at full speed till that animal was out of wind, he alighted. A few minutes afterwards the horse fell down & died, and he presented [gifts to] the man that told him this news. He then caused 1,000 men of his kindred to wear the Marata fashioned robes

[8] Taylor, *Oriental Historical Manuscripts*, vol. II, 205-8. See also: Rangachari, "The History of the Naik Kingdom of Madura," *Indian Antiquary* XLVI, 122-4; Nelson, *The Madura Country*, vol. III, 210-12. These events were allegedly recorded by Jesuits as well. See S. Krishnaswami Iyengar, "Mysore and the Decline of the Vijayanagar Empire," *The Quarterly Journal of the Mythic Society* XIII, 4 (1923), 753.

[9] See also Vink, *Mission to Madurai*, 480-1 (n. 264).

> and turbans instead of long caps & cloths, giving them stile of Ravoots [*rāvuttaṉs*,[10] or (probably) "Muslim trooper"].[11]

These accounts of the visit of Ikkeri's Dodda Sankanna to Delhi and the reception of the Mughal's footwear by Madurai's Muttu Virappa suggest the Nayaka dynasties had an ambivalent perception of north India's mighty rulers. The sultans of Delhi and their Mughal successors appear to have served as a reference point against which south Indian kings measured their own power and prestige. The frequent mentioning of the *Bādshāh* seems to indicate that these rulers set a certain standard in dynastic hierarchy. At the same time, this standard apparently had to be challenged, surpassed, and denigrated. Thus, Dodda Sankanna duelled with Delhi's greatest warrior and, with the help of his unbreakable ancestral sword,[12] defeated him. This episode, described in great detail, insinuates that the Nayaka's power and standing equalled or even exceeded that of the sultan. Yet, he also seemed to seek Delhi's recognition of his status as a prominent king or indeed, in one text, as a *Bādshāh* himself.

In the same vein, Madurai's Muttu Virappa humiliated the *Bādshāh*, but, as one text adds, thereby won his admiration, apparently considered an important matter. Continuing this ambiguity, Madurai's Nayaka received two ungovernable horses from Delhi's impressed ruler, which he accepted gratefully but rode effortlessly—in the presence of Delhi's representative to be sure—after which one horse died of exhaustion. Again, this proved the Nayaka's greatness, supposedly even outdoing the *Bādshāh*.

Further, as the last quoted text goes, Muttu Virappa had his men replace their clothing of long tunics and high caps with Maratha-fashioned robes and turbans. Since the former style most likely points to attire deriving from sultanate courts,

[10] *Rāvuttaṉ* (also *irāvuttaṉ*) or "rowther," from *irauttar* (horseman, trooper), was used as a (military) title by various Tamil-speaking Muslim groups and possibly other communities. See: Bayly, *Saints, Goddesses and Kings*, 98; Thurston, *Castes and Tribes of Southern India*, vol. VI, 247; Srinivasan, *Maratha Rule in the Carnatic*, 343; Vink, *Mission to Madurai*, 314 (n. 211).

[11] BL/AAS, MG, no. 4, pt. 4: "Mootiah's chronological & historical account of the modern kings of Madura," ff. 68-9. A Persian text also deals with a slipper sent from Delhi to south India. Here, its recipient is Krishna Raya of Vijayanagara, who tells the Delhi courtier accompanying the slipper he will only pay the demanded tribute if a second slipper is presented to him. In the English manuscript translation of this work, it is unclear who emerges victorious from this showdown, but both parties deem each other's behaviour highly insulting. See BL/AAS, MT, class I, no. 18: "The Keefeyet of Panoocundah," ff. 48-9.

[12] For this magical sword, called *nāgaramuri* (or *nāgaramari*) and miraculously acquired by the dynasty's founder Chaudappa, see: Lewis Rice, *Mysore: A Gazetteer Compiled for Government*, vol. II, 458; Chitnis, *Keḷadi Polity*, 9; Shama Shastry, "Malnad Chiefs," 47; Mahalingam, *Mackenzie Manuscripts*, vol. II, 404. See also Ikkeri's foundation story in Chapter 1.

this change seems to have denoted another way of decrying Delhi's rulers. Perhaps, it represents a switch to a new reference point for Madurai, namely the west Indian Marathas, who had come to dominate large parts of south India around this time. But even though the Marathas adhered to Hinduism, Muttu Virappa's men are said now to have looked like *rāvuttaṉs*. This was a military title used by Tamil-speaking Muslims, so the dress of the Nayaka's troops was probably still associated with Muslim-style clothing. Although the author of this text—a literary man called Teruvercadu Mutiah, possibly active in intellectual circles at Madras around 1800—declared to have based his work on local written and oral accounts, its reliability has been questioned.[13] Nevertheless, this passage implies that, according to tradition, Madurai's court dress had shifted over time to combine Maratha and what may have been Islamic elements.

These references to Delhi as a standard for Vijayanagara's heirs are not isolated instances. To begin with, Vijayanagara itself looked to Delhi as an epicentre of political power. As discussed in Chapter 1, some of the empire's origin myths sought to legitimise its authority by portraying its founders Harihara and Bukka as servants of the Delhi sultan, appointed by him as governors and subsequently asserting autonomy. Another example is found in the chronicle of Tanjavur's Bhonsles, the *Bhoṃsale vaṃśa caritra*. It states that Sambhaji Bhonsle—nephew of the dynasty's founder Ekoji and son of the Maratha King Shivaji—was captured by the Mughal Emperor Aurangzeb, who wished to convert him to Islam. When Sambhaji asked for the hand of the Mughal's daughter in return, the emperor had him killed. Thereupon, Aurangzeb's daughter went into mourning, for Sambhaji would have been the ideal man and husband. Thus, he is portrayed as outshining all Muslim marital candidates but, at the same time, willing to become part of the Mughal dynasty. And indeed, Sambhaji's son Shahu was raised by the emperor's daughter as her own.[14]

Likewise, the *Śāhendra vilāsa*, praising Tanjavur's Shahaji I, challenges the Mughals by declaring: "In his forest hide-out, the cowardly king of Delhi hears the drums of our king's victory-parade."[15] Finally, various versions of Ariyalur's dynastic chronicle claim that one of its rulers gifted an elephant to Delhi's *Bādshāh*

13 TBL/AAS, MG, pt. 4, no. 4: "Mootiah's chronological & historical account of the modern kings of Madura," f. 41; Dirks, *The Hollow Crown*, 76-7 (n. 42); Teruvercadu Mutiah, "An Account of the Life of Teruvercadu Mutiah, a Learned Hindû, a Native of the Carnatic ...," in *The Asiatic Annual Register, or, a View of the History of Hindustan, and of the Politics, Commerce and Literature of Asia, for the Year 1801* (London, 1802), section "Characters," 14-15; Cotton, Charpentier, and Johnston, *Catalogue of Manuscripts in European Languages*, vol. I, pt. II, 49-50; Mantena, *The Origins of Modern Historiography in India*, 91-2.

14 BL/AAS, MT, class III, no. 87: "The historycal account of the Tonjore" (*Bhoṃsale vaṃśa caritra*), ff. 86-90v; Srinivasachari and Gopalan, *Bhonsle Vamsa Charitra*, viii.

15 Quoted in Narayana Rao, Shulman, and Subrahmanyam, *Symbols of Substance*, 318. See also: idem, 13; Wagoner, *Tidings of the King*, 60-9; Subrahmanyam, *Penumbral Visions*, 189-90, 197.

("Paudashaw of Deely"), thereby helping the *Bādshāh*'s desperate brother or brother-in-law. The latter had been forced to pawn his right-side whiskers—perhaps symbolising his masculinity—in an attempt to purchase an elephant, which he owed to the *Bādshāh* after losing a bet or chess game.[16]

The role of Delhi in Vijayanagara's foundation stories was part of a broad range of influences from sultanate courts on the empire's political culture. These affected matters like diplomacy, warfare, administration, law, architecture, art, court dress, and royal titling.[17] This chapter is concerned with the extent to which Vijayanagara's adoption of politico-cultural practices from Muslim-ruled polities continued among its heirs. Did the successor states—as the stories above suggest—take over Islamic elements from Vijayanagara, and also from contemporary sultanates? How did the heirs differ from each other in this respect? Did these adaptations develop over time? And how was all this connected to wider political developments? The references in Mutiah's chronicle to Madurai's changing court dress may have reflected a broader pattern among the successors of earlier borrowings from sultanate courts being replaced or supplemented by new adjustments.

Scholars have paid little attention to such influences on court politics in Vijayanagara's heirs, with the exception of Ramnad. Notions absorbed by the empire itself have been studied in more detail, specifically with regard to dynastic titles and royal dress. That research suggests that sultanate influences manifested themselves foremost in the public domain, whereas local customs remained dominant in the domestic sphere.[18] In order to compare Vijayanagara with its heirs, this chapter also focuses on titles and dress, to conclude that in some of the successor states these associations with the public and domestic realms gradually disappeared.[19]

[16] BL/AAS, MT, class III, no. 35: "Kyfeyeat of the Paulagars of Aureyaloor Paulaput," ff. 111v-12; Hemingway, *Trichinopoly*, vol. I, 344-5. For another Kannada Nayaka house defeating a Delhi warrior, see Ota, "Bēḍa Nāyakas and Their Historical Narratives," 177-8. For (imaginary, rejected) marital relations between south Indian dynasties and Delhi's rulers, see Richard H. Davis, "A Muslim Princess in the Temples of Viṣṇu," *International Journal of Hindu Studies* 8, 1-3 (2004), 144-5.

[17] See, for example, Wagoner, "Harihara, Bukka, and the Sultan." This process had already been going on for a long time, in both south and north India. See, for instance: Eaton, *A Social History of the Deccan*, ch. 1; idem, *India in the Persianate Age*, chs 1-2; Finbarr B. Flood, *Objects of Translation: Material Culture and Medieval "Hindu-Muslim" Encounter* (Princeton/Woodstock, 2009).

[18] See in particular Wagoner, "'Sultan among Hindu Kings'."

[19] Falling outside this study's scope, much research has been done on Islamic influences on architecture and art in Vijayanagara and its heirs. See: George Michell, *The Vijayanagara Courtly Style: Incorporation and Synthesis in the Royal Architecture of Southern India, 15th-17th Centuries* (New Delhi, 1992), 48-55, 70; idem, "Courtly Architecture at Gingee under the Nayakas," *South Asian Studies* 7 (1991), 159; idem, "Migrations and Cultural Transmissions in the Deccan: Evidence of Monuments at Vijayanagara," in Laura E. Parodi (ed.), *The Visual World of Muslim India: The Art, Culture and Society*

Below, we first consider the sources for dynastic titles and royal dress. The chapter's central sections begin with a general description of Vijayanagara's adoption of practices from sultanate courts, the reasons behind it, and the various forms it took. Then follow surveys of titles and clothing used by the succeeding dynasties. The overviews of titles not only examine Islamic terms but also designations that claim imperial status and thus suggest their bearers no longer saw themselves as subordinates of Vijayanagara. The section on Ramnad is larger than the other sections since the variety of sources on royal dress here requires an extensive discussion. The chapter ends with an overall comparison and analysis of influences from sultanate courts on the titles and dress of the successor dynasties.

Dynastic titles are found in a range of texts, most notably inscriptions issued by or on behalf of rulers, but also literary works.[20] Besides such largely public communications, addressed to Indian audiences, titles are occasionally also included in the much less public correspondence and treaties between the courts and European powers, adding to the diversity of sources. However, despite this variety, it is hardly possible to gather a representative set of titles for each royal house. Much epigraphic material of Vijayanagara's heirs has not been published or translated in full, and is available only in summaries from which titles have often been omitted. Some inscriptions have not been published at all, in whatever form.[21] Besides, epigraphic sources become scarce from the late sixteenth century onward.[22] For some dynasties, one therefore has to rely on a limited number of examples.

of the Deccan in the Early Modern Era (London/New York, 2014); John M. Fritz, George Michell, and M.S. Nagaraja Rao, *Where Kings and Gods Meet: The Royal Centre at Vijayanagara, India* (Tucson, 1985), ch. 7; Catherine B. Asher, "Islamic Influence and the Architecture of Vijayanagara," in Anna Libera Dallapiccola and Stephanie Zingel-Avé Lallemant (eds), *Vijayanagara – City and Empire: New Currents of Research* (Wiesbaden, 1985), vol. 1; B.S. Subhadra, "Impact of Indo-Islamic Art on Keladi Architecture," *Proceedings of the Indian History Congress* 59 (1998); Kanekar, "Two Temples of the Ikkeri Nayakas," 137-43, 150-7; idem, "Stylistic Origins and Change in the Temples of the Ikkeri Nayakas," 358; Anila Verghese, "Aghoreśvara Temple at Ikkeri: A Synthesis of Architectural Styles," *Journal of the Asiatic Society of Mumbai* 81 (2007), 125, 131; *Annual Report of the Mysore Archœological Department for the Year 1936* (Bangalore, 1938), 43. For a short note about Persian influence on south Indian music, see T.K. Venkatasubramanian, *Music as History in Tamilnadu* (Delhi, 2010), 48.

[20] I thank Herman Tieken, Emma Flatt, Subah Dayal, Gijs Kruijtzer, and André Wink for helping me make sense of some titles discussed in this chapter. None of them, however, is responsible for the findings presented here.

[21] See for instance: Talbot, *Precolonial India in Practice*, v, 19, 261 (n. 2); K. Gunda Jois, "Unpublished Inscriptions of Keladi Rulers," in A.V. Narasimha Murthy and K.V. Ramesh (eds), *Giridharaśrī: Essays on Indology* (Delhi, 1987); idem, "Keladi Inscriptions on Gold Sandals and Pinnacles," 64. For a discussion and overview of Ikkeri's body of inscriptions, see Bridges White, "Beyond Empire," 85-91, 237-47.

[22] Narayana Rao, Shulman, and Subrahmanyam, *Symbols of Substance*, 89, 338; Talbot, *Precolonial India in Practice*, 18, 28; Branfoot, "Royal Portrait Sculpture in the South Indian Temple," 34; Subrahmanyam, *The Political Economy of Commerce*, 2; Ludden, *Peasant History in South India*, 70-1.

Further, it has been argued that the Nayaka dynasties—at least those in the Tamil region—used comparatively few titles, and that these generally lacked claims to full sovereignty. This would have been caused by the fact that the direct successor dynasties not only originated as provincial governors but always formally remained so, being appointed by and in theory forever subjected to the emperors. Even after Vijayanagara's power waned under the Aravidu house and vanished around the mid-seventeenth century, these successors allegedly never officially asserted independence.[23] Thus, the direct heirs kept using modest titles until the end, devoid of aspirations to the supreme status of emperors and sultans, who claimed universal kingship. Therefore, below we also look for Islamic terms that denoted less exalted ranks and ambitions, possibly reflecting the specific positions of Vijayanagara's heirs.

Portrayals of royal dress are also found in various sources, although very few images survive in the palaces themselves. It has been suggested that palace locations constituted strongly "political" settings and that especially in public spaces like audience halls kings were eager to be shown in clothing styles borrowed from sultanate courts. More depictions of royal attire remain in temples, which, it has been argued, formed part of a more "sacred" environment.[24] Such representations may therefore have had different connotations from those in palaces. Temple sculpture portraying the Nayakas of Madurai, for instance, is thought to be an expression of their relationship with Hindu deities. This connection was in turn meant to be viewed by worshippers—rather than a royal display directly aimed at the general public, including the Indo-Islamic world.[25] Nonetheless, this chapter also examines depictions of royal clothing in temples to see how these relate to other sources.

In addition, reports of VOC embassies to Vijayanagara's heirs occasionally include descriptions of the attire of rulers. This dress was sometimes labelled "heathen" or "Moorish." In India, the Dutch used the term "heathen" (*heijden, jentief*) to denote Hindus (or more generally non-Muslim and non-Christian Indians) and things associated with them, as opposed to Muslims and Islamic matters, which were

23 Dirks, *The Hollow Crown*, 45-6; Francis, *Madura Gazetteer*, 41; Wagoner, *Tidings of the King*, 10; Narayana Rao, Shulman, and Subrahmanyam, *Symbols of Substance*, 43-4, 218; Robert Caldwell, *A Political and General History of the District of Tinnevelly, in the Presidency of Madras, from the Earliest Period to Its Cession to the English Government in A.D. 1801* (Madras, 1881), 61.

24 Anna Lise Seastrand, "Praise, Politics, and Language: South Indian Murals, 1500-1800" (unpublished dissertation, Columbia University, 2013), 73; Branfoot, "Royal Portrait Sculpture in the South Indian Temple," 13. I also thank Anna Dallapiccola and George Michell for discussing this distinction, although again I am responsible for the ideas presented here.

25 Branfoot, "Royal Portrait Sculpture in the South Indian Temple," passim, especially 29; idem, "In a Land of Kings: Donors, Elites, and Temple Sculpture," in Anila Verghese and Anna Libera Dallapiccola (eds), *South India under Vijayanagara: Art and Archaeology* (New Delhi, 2011), 255-6.

referred to as "Moorish" (*moors*).[26] It is hard to ascertain what these terms exactly meant in each individual case. But by the time its earliest surviving descriptions were produced, the Company had been active in south India for more than half a century and many of its employees spent years living and working in the region. The Dutch would therefore not use these labels for clothing randomly, although, as this chapter concludes, they may have missed certain nuances in royal dress styles.

Vijayanagara

From the empire's very foundation, its rulers adopted political and cultural practices from courts of sultanates. This, it has been proposed, was a strategy to participate and be understood in the Islamic world of West, Central and South Asia. In that area—which included the Delhi sultanates and the subsequent Mughal empire as well as the Bahmani sultanate with its successors in the Deccan—such customs belonged to a widely appreciated political idiom. Conforming to this idiom was an effort to increase one's legitimacy and authority. Absorbed by way of diplomacy, trade, warfare, and the like, these practices pertained to, for instance, political and social organisation, judicial conventions, art and architecture, military recruitment and technology, royal titles, and court dress and etiquette.

To differentiate such cultural and political elements of the Islamic world from its more religious aspects, the term "Islamicate" has been employed. Vijayanagara's politico-cultural borrowings from sultanate courts could thus be classified as Islamicate.[27] Another proposed term is "Persianate," indicating that these politico-cultural practices were largely absorbed from or via Persia or the Persian language, without referring to a particular religion.[28] This term is used in the present study.

The process of Persianisation in south India did not wholly replace the region's traditional local or "Indic" political and cultural notions. Rather, it has been argued,

[26] See also: Kruijtzer, *Xenophobia in Seventeenth-Century India*, 15, 285-6; Van Meersbergen, "Ethnography and Encounter," 75-7.

[27] Wagoner, "'Sultan among Hindu Kings'," 853-5. See also Richard M. Eaton, "The Articulation of Islamic Space in the Medieval Deccan," in Meenakshi Khanna (ed.), *Cultural History of Medieval India* (New Delhi, 2007), 127-30. For a rejection of the term "Islamicate," also in the context of Vijayanagara, see Shahab Ahmed, *What Is Islam? The Importance of Being Islamic* (Princeton/Oxford, 2016), 157-75, 446-7.

[28] Eaton and Wagoner, *Power, Memory, Architecture*, 4, 20-32; Eaton, *India in the Persianate Age*, passim, especially ch. 4. For recent discussions of the terms "Islamicate" and "Persianate," see: Truschke, *The Language of History*, 10-12; Flatt, *The Courts of the Deccan Sultanates*, pp. 17-24. See also Stewart Gordon, "In the Aura of the King: Trans-Asian, Trans-Regional, and Deccani Royal Symbolism," *South Asian Studies* 32, 1 (2016), passim, especially 49.

Persianate practices were chiefly employed at events with a public character, whereas Indic customs remained in use on occasions of a domestic nature. This division between domestic and public situations bears resemblance to the differentiation in south India between interior and exterior spheres, for example in literature and architecture. Both classifications refer to distinct but complementary and at times partly overlapping social domains, each connected to certain types of activities, company, representation, etc. Related to the domestic or interior realm were, for instance, close family members, leisure, and residential sections of buildings such as palaces. Linked to the public or exterior realm were, for example, one's extended family and caste, society at large, warfare, and diplomatic encounters.[29]

Various sources suggest that court dress codes in Vijayanagara and its heirs reflected this distinction between the public and domestic domains and the Persianate influences in the latter. For Vijayanagara, those sources include temple paintings and sculptures as well as travel accounts from the fifteenth and early sixteenth centuries. These often portray emperors and courtiers as wearing a long white tunic, known as *kabāyi*, worked with gold—or other attire largely covering the body—and a high conical cap, called *kuḷḷāyi*. Those two types of garment are thought to have been of Arab and Persian origin respectively. *Kabāyi*s and *kuḷḷāyi*s are for instance depicted on a mural in the sixteenth-century Virabhadra Temple at Lepakshi, where the caps moreover are decorated with what appear to be Persianate designs (see illustration 14).[30] Indeed, the Italian traveller Ludovico di Varthema, visiting Vijayanagara in 1504, wrote that prominent men here used headgear of the "Moorish" or Muslim fashion. Notably, when sources refer to rulers and courtiers wearing such dress, these men were usually involved in public activities like military processions, temple worship, and receiving ambassadors.

Additionally, a south Indian cloth painting (*kalamkārī*) from around the seventeenth century shows a Nayaka ruler—probably from Tanjavur or Madurai—in a public courtyard, heading a military procession in a *kabāyi*-like garment, although this tunic is coloured rather than white and the king wears a turban instead of a *kuḷḷāyi*. Other sections of this painting portray the Nayaka engaging in domestic activities, like musical entertainment and amorous pleasures. There, he is dressed in just a local *dhotī* (cloth wrapped around the waist and legs) and a piece of cloth over his shoulders, leaving his chest and arms exposed in a manner considered

[29] This argument is most explicitly put forward in Wagoner, "'Sultan among Hindu Kings'," 853-5, 861-71, but see also: Eaton, *A Social History of the Deccan*, chs 1-4; Subrahmanyam, *Penumbral Visions*, 227-8; Howes, *The Courts of Pre-Colonial South India*, ch. 4.

[30] For this mural, see Anna L. Dallapiccola, Brigitte Khan Majlis, George Michell, and John M. Fritz, *Lepakshi: Architecture, Sculpture, Painting* (New Delhi, 2019), 156-7, 244, 247, 265. For online images of all this temple's paintings, see: southindianpaintings.art/monuments/lepakshi-virabhadraswamy-temple.

Illustration 14: Mural showing Vijayanagara courtiers, Virabhadra Temple, Lepakshi, 16th century (photo by C. Ganesan, courtesy John and Fausta Eskenazi, source: southindianpaintings.art/monuments/lepakshi-virabhadraswamy-temple).

traditionally south Indian. Hence, it has been concluded that this kind of dress was generally reserved for domestic situations, while Persianate attire was worn on public occasions. That should not surprise us, because public events allowed rulers to demonstrate their connection with the Indo-Islamic world. Waging war, conducting diplomacy, touring the kingdom: these were instances of political exposure to other parties, requiring a broadly understood presentation.[31]

[31] Wagoner, "'Sultan among Hindu Kings'," 856-61, 868-71; Ludovico di Varthema, *The Itinerary of Ludovico di Varthema of Bologna from 1502 to 1508*, trans. John Winter Jones, ed. Richard Carnac Temple (London, 1928), 53; Sivaramamurti, *Vijayanagara Paintings*, 32-3, 69 (plate IX); Vincent Lefèvre, "À propos d'une célèbre toile peinte (kalamkari) de la collection Riboud au musée Guimet," in Henri Chambert-Loir and Bruno Dagens (eds), *Anamorphoses: Hommage à Jacques Dumarçay* (Paris, 2006). See also: Michell, *Architecture and Art of Southern India*, 250-2; Howes, *The Courts of Pre-Colonial South India*, 69, 73-4, 95; Mattiebelle Gittinger, *Master Dyers to the World: Technique and Trade in Early Dyed Cotton Textiles* (Washington, 1982), 120-7, 133. Other seventeenth-century cloth paintings (*kalamkārīs*) thought to portray the Tanjavur or Madurai court seem to point to the same association of Indic and Persianate dress with domestic and public occasions, respectively. See: Rosemary Crill, "South Indian Court Scenes," *Hali* 203 (2020), 64-7, figs 2-3; John Guy, "A Ruler and His Courtesans Celebrate Vasantotsava: Courtly and Divine Love in a Nayaka *Kalamkari*," in Navina Najat Haidar and Marika Sardar (eds), *Sultans of the South: Arts of India's Deccan Courts, 1323–1687* (New York, 2011), passim, figs 1-4. For other depictions of Indic and Persianate dress at the Vijayanagara court, see: Anila Verghese, "Court Attire of Vijayanagara (from a Study of Monuments)," *The Quarterly Journal of the Mythic Society* LXXXII, 1-2 (1991), 46-58; Anna Libera Dallapiccola, "Sculptures on the Great Platform of Vijayanagara," in Anila Verghese and Anna Libera Dallapiccola (eds), *South India under*

The adoption of Persianate dress by south Indian Hindu kings, in Vijayanagara probably from the mid-fifteenth century on, was closely linked to the use of Persianate royal titles. All of Vijayanagara's four dynasties mostly bore Indic imperial designations, like "king of great kings" (*mahārājādhirāja*), "supreme lord" (*rājaparamēśvara*), and "glory of heroes" (*vīrapratāpa*), found for instance in inscriptions and coin legends.[32]

These also occur in documents that emperors of the Aravidu house sent to European powers. VOC records contain phrases such as "the fortunate, lord of the lords, god of the lords, and famous as a very brave soldier" (*den geluckigen, heere der heeren, godt der heeren, ende vermaert voor een seer cloeckmoedich soldaet*), used by Sriranga III and probably a translation of *śrīmat rājādhirāja rājaparamēśvara vīrapratāpa*. Similar titles appear in letters by him to the English—translated as "Zree Seringo Raylo, king of kings, a god in his kingdom, in armes invincible" or "the king over all kings, the holiest, and amongst all cavalliers the greatest, Zree Renga Raya, the mighty king god"—and by Venkata I to the Portuguese, rendered as "king of the kings, great lord, great knight, King Vencatapati, very great king."[33]

In addition, Vijayanagara's first Sangama rulers already included transliterations of the Islamic term *sulṭān* in inscriptions. Except for the Saluva period, this practice continued under the subsequent dynasties until the seventeenth century. Used on its own or in composites like "sultan among Indian [or Hindu] kings" (*hindurāya suratrāṇa*) and "sultan of the world" (*gola suratrāṇa*), these titles were adopted for the same purpose as Persianate clothing. It signified the eagerness of Vijayanagara's rulers to distinguish themselves from other Hindu kings and be accepted by and participate in the Indo-Islamic political culture.

The use of these latter titles may in fact have caused the introduction of Persianate clothing. Presenting oneself as a sultan meant dressing like one and thus, on public occasions, forfeiting traditional local ideas on attire. The south Indian way of clothing, which revealed and accentuated the body, was deemed inappropriate or even dishonourable in the Islamic world, where dress should fully cover the body. The use of Persianate garments at the Vijayanagara court was probably further encouraged by the *khil'at* ritual (discussed in the previous

Vijayanagara: Art and Archaeology (New Delhi, 2011), 111-12; Nalini Rao, *Royal Imagery & Networks of Power at Vijayanagara: A Study of Kingship in South India* (Delhi, 2010), 28-34, plates 21, 23, 25-6, 34-9.

32 For examples, see two notes below.

33 For Aravidu titles in Dutch documents, see for example: Colenbrander *et al.*, *Dagh-register gehouden int Casteel Batavia ... anno 1641–1642* (The Hague, 1900), 262, 289, idem, *anno 1643–1644*, 271; Heeres and Stapel, *Corpus diplomaticum Neerlando-Indicum*, vol. 1, 230, 403-4. For English and Portuguese references, see: Foster, *The English Factories in India 1642–1645*, 285, 305; Love, *Vestiges of Old Madras*, vol. I, 67; Henry Heras, "The Jesuit Influence in the Court of Vijayanagar," *The Quarterly Journal of the Mythic Society* XIV, 2 (1924), 138.

chapter), also borrowed from the Islamic world and centred on dress gifting.[34] In sum, Vijayanagara's rulers partially adapted titles, dress, court etiquette, and other aspects of court culture to Persianate conventions in order to enhance their status in the dominant Indo-Islamic world.

Successor States

The following sections all begin with an overview of titles used by the successor dynasties and then discuss their dress. By and large, titles mentioned in local sources are dealt with first, followed by designations found in documents exchanged with European powers. With respect to royal attire, each section first discusses references in Dutch embassy reports before considering paintings and statues in palaces and temples.

[34] Wagoner, "'Sultan among Hindu Kings'," 861-7; Eaton, *A Social History of the Deccan*, 42-3, 101; Truschke, *The Language of History*, 68-70; Verghese, "Court Attire of Vijayanagara," 50-2, 57; Kulke, "Mahārājas, Mahants and Historians," 125; Venkata Raghotham, "Empire and Historiography in Late Medieval South India: A Study of the Early Vijayanagara State," in R. Champakalakshmy, Kesavan Veluthat, and T.R. Venugopalan (eds), *State and Society in Pre-Modern South India* (Thrissur, 2002), 140; Filliozat, *l'Épigraphie de Vijayanagar*, for example xvi, 23-4; Narasimhaswami, *South-Indian Inscriptions*, vol. XVI, i-ii, viii; Vijayaraghavacharya, *Inscriptions of Krishnaraya's Time*, 124-85, 270, 328-52; idem (ed.), *Inscriptions of Achyutaraya's Time from 1530 A.D. to 1542 A.D.* (Madras, 1936), passim; idem (ed.), *Inscriptions of Sadasivaraya's Time from 1541 A.D. to 1574 A.D.* (Madras, 1937), passim; idem, *Inscriptions of Venkatapatiraya's Time*, 17-145; Ritti and Gopal, *Inscriptions of the Vijayanagara Rulers*, vol. I, *Inscriptions of the Rulers of the Sangama Dynasty*, pts 1-5, passim; Y. Subbarayalu and S. Rajavelu (eds), *Inscriptions of the Vijayanagara Rulers*, vol. V, pt. I (Tamil Inscriptions) (Delhi, 2014), 65, 72, 113, 158, 164, 166-7, 192-3, 232, 459, 472, 476; S. Subrahmanya Sastry (ed.), *Early Inscriptions* (Madras, 1931), 182-3, 189-90, 193-4, 202-4, 224-5; Srinivasan and Reiniche, *Tiruvannamalai*, vol. 1.2, *Inscriptions* (Pondicherry, 1990), 436-546, 585, 615, 619; Katti, "Some Important Epigraphs of the Sangama Dynasty," 143; Butterworth and Venugopaul Chetty, *A Collection of the Inscriptions on Copper-Plates and Stones in the Nellore District*, pt. I, 15, 19, 33, 41, 76, 84, 152, 157, 196-8, 200, 203-4, 217-18, 238, 246, 255, 264, 269, 312, 315-16, 319, 363, 448, 453-4; Ramesan, "The Krāku Grant of Harihara II," 75; Venkataramanayya, "Pedda Cheppalli Plates of Dēvarāya II," 40; idem (ed.), "A Note on the Gaya Inscription of Kṛishṇadēvarāya," in idem (ed.), *Epigraphia Andhrica*, vol. I (Hyderabad, 1969), 56; A.V. Ramabrahman (ed.), "A New Copperplate Inscription of Vijayanagara King Achyuta Raya," *Proceedings of the Indian History Congress* 21 (1958); Allasani Peddana, *The Story of Manu*, 11; BL/AAS, MG, no. 3, pt. 6: "Facsimile of the seal of Ram Raja," following f. 195 (transcription in Cotton, Charpentier, and Johnston, *Catalogue of Manuscripts in European Languages*, vol. I, pt. II, 39); Patil, *Court Life under the Vijayanagar Rulers*, 54; Saletore, *Social and Political Life in the Vijayanagara Empire*, vol. II, 262; Michael Mitchiner, *The Coinage and History of Southern India*, pt. I, *Karnataka – Andhra* (London, 1998), 153-213; A.V. Narasimhamurthy, *Coins and Currency System in Vijayanagara Empire* (Varanasi, 1991), 15-16, 23, ch. 5; K. Ganesh and Girijapathy, *The Coins of the Vijayanagar Empire* (Bangalore, 1997), 29-133.

Nayakas of Ikkeri

Besides Persianate conventions that Ikkeri adopted indirectly through Vijayanagara, it was probably also directly affected by the Bijapur sultanate,[35] the Mughal empire, and Hyderabad, its successive Muslim-ruled neighbours. However, there are few unambiguous references to Persianate influences in Ikkeri. Local sources for the Nayakas' titles include a sizeable corpus of fully published inscriptions and some literary texts, both in Sanskrit and Kannada. Many designations, often combined in extensive strings, point to military feats or religious activities. An instance of the former is "disturber of forts" (*kōṭe kōlāhala*), acquired by Sadashiva Nayaka upon defeating Vijayanagara's opponents and passed on to his successors. Among the religious titles are "devoted to the faith in Shiva [and?] the guru" (*śivagurubhakti parāyaṇa*), and "establisher of the pure Vaidika Advaita doctrine" (*viśuddhavaidikādvaita siddhānta pratiṣṭhāpaka*), likely indicating the dynasty's ties with the Shaivite monastery at Sringeri. Another common designation is *eḍavamurāri*, probably honouring the voluntary death of the servants Yadava and Murari of the first Nayaka, Chaudappa, enabling him to obtain a treasure.

Less regular titles mention benevolent rule, patronage of arts, and amorous achievements. Further, references are occasionally made to conflicts with what was probably Bijapur or perhaps the Mughal empire, for instance designating the Nayakas as "a boundary mountain to stop the great ocean of the *mlēcchas* [barbarians or Muslims] ever seeking to overflow the south in victorious expeditions."[36] A rare case of a Persianate title, mentioned in this chapter's introduction, is "*bādshāh* [great king] of Keladi," supposedly received by Dodda Sankanna Nayaka from the sultan of Delhi.[37]

[35] For a recent discussion of relations between Ikkeri and Bijapur, see Subah Dayal, "Vernacular Conquest? A Persian Patron and His Image in the Seventeenth-Century Deccan," *Comparative Studies of South Asia, Africa and the Middle East* 37, 3 (2017), 558-64. See also Swaminathan, *The Nāyakas of Ikkēri*, 23-4, 37, 68, 73-5, 94-5, 104, 106-8, 110, 121.

[36] *Annual Report of the Mysore Archæological Department for the Year 1915-16*, 65, 68, idem, *for the Year 1927* (Bangalore, 1928), 135, idem, *for the Year 1928* (Bangalore, 1929), 62, idem, *for the Year 1943* (Mysore, 1944), 105-6, 108-11; *Epigraphia Carnatica*, vol. VIII, 158, 194, 290, 306, 321, and many other references; B. Lewis Rice (ed.), *Mysore Inscriptions, Translated for Government* (Bangalore, 1879), 250; M.M. Bhat (ed.), *Selected Kannada Inscriptions* (Madras, 1952), 167; Chitnis, *Keḷadi Polity*, 11, 13, 16-17; Lewis Rice, *Mysore and Coorg*, 156; Swaminathan, *The Nāyakas of Ikkēri*, 22, 24, 26-7, 33, 91; Lakshminarayan Rao, "The Nayakas of Keladi," 256-8, 267; Heras, *The Aravidu Dynasty of Vijayanagara*, vol. I, 179; K.V. Ramesh, "Notes on the Territorial History of the Keladi Kingdom," in G.S. Dikshit (ed.), *Studies in Keladi History (Seminar Papers)* (Bangalore, 1981), 82; Naraharayya, "Keladi Dynasty" [pt. 1], 373, 377; Nilakanta Sastri and Venkataramanayya, *Further Sources of Vijayanagara History*, vol. III, 191-2; BL/AAS, MG, no. 6, pt. 11: "Historical account of Beedoonoor or Caladee Samstanum," f. 66v.

[37] BL/AAS, MG, no. 25, pt. 27: "Memoir of Barkoor," f. 209.

Some inscriptions contain no or very few titles. There, the ruler's individual name is only accompanied by terms like *śrīmat* (glorious, illustrious), *keḷadi* (the dynasty's first capital), and of course *nāyaka* (originally military leader), sometimes with a pedigree, which usually goes back to Sadashiva. Legends on Ikkeri's coins are even more modest, often comprising just the honorific prefix *śrī* and Sadashiva's name or adding words like *rāja* (king) and *keḷadi* to a ruler's personal name.[38]

Only these latter, simpler terms generally appear in letters and treaties the Nayakas exchanged and concluded with the Dutch and the Portuguese. VOC records from the mid-seventeenth century on contain translations or corruptions of words the kings used to sign documents, such as: "fortunate [*geluckigen*] Sivapaneijck, born of Quelldij [*keḷadi*]" (by Shivappa I), "Srijmadoe [*śrīmat*] Quelladij Soma Sanqhera Naijqueroe," and "exalted [*verheeven*] King Queladi Somma Sanquera Naij Quero" (both Somashekara II). *Geluckigen* and *verheeven* are likely Dutch translations of *śrīmat*, while "Naijqueroe" and similar phrases are probably corruptions of *nāyaka* followed by *ayyavāru*, the latter a combination of the honorific suffixes *ayyaṉ* and *vāru*.[39] In seventeenth-century Portuguese documents, terms used by the Nayakas are equally modest and comprise the same words time and again: "I, the King [*eu el-rey*] Virapá Naique, of the house [*casa*] of Queldy" (by Virabhadra), "I, Quelady Somaxecar Naique" (Somashekara I), and "I, Quellady Bassopá Naique" (Basavappa, signing as formal ruler during the reign of his adoptive mother Chennammaji).[40]

[38] *Annual Report of the Mysore Archœological Department for the Year 1927* (Bangalore, 1928), 134-5; Lewis Rice, *Mysore Inscriptions*, 249; N. Lakshminarayan Rao (ed.), "Kap Copper-Plate of Keladi Sadasiva-Nayaka: Saka 1479," *Epigraphia Indica and Record of the Archœological Survey of India*, vol. XX (Delhi, 1929-30), 93, 95; Sundara, *The Keḷadi Nāyakas*, 35-7; Gunda Jois, "Keladi Inscriptions on Gold Sandals and Pinnacles," 65, 67-8; Pushpa Prasad (ed.), "Two Stone Slab Inscriptions of Keladi Dynasty," *Proceedings of the Indian History Congress* 35 (1974); BL/AAS, MT, class XIII (Inscriptions), no. 73: "Translation of a Neeroopam (or order) of Somaseker Naik (a king of Beedoonoore)," f. 46; Mitchiner, *The Coinage and History of Southern India*, pt. I, 217-18; and many examples in *Epigraphia Carnatica*, vol. VIII, including 73, 88, 131, 171, 247. See also Sircar, *Indian Epigraphical Glossary*, 317.

[39] Heeres and Stapel, *Corpus diplomaticum Neerlando-Indicum*, vol. 2, 109-10; NA, VOC, no. 1231, f. 515; no. 1268, f. 1117; no. 1694, ff. 54, 62, 66-7; no. 2187, f. 219; no. 2228, ff. 951-1v, 954v-5, 1055v-6, 1059; no. 2232, f. 3592; no. 2354, f. 1617; no. 2414, f. 124; no. 2435, f. 2272; no. 2446, ff. 283, 1152: documents from 1659, 1668, 1703, 1731-2, 1735-6, 1738; DNA, DCGCC, no. 3396, ff. 1-2: document from 1662; TNA, DR, no. 404, ff. 91, 155: documents from 1745, 1751.

[40] Julio Firmino Judice Biker (ed.), *Collecção de tratados e concertos de pazes que o Estado da India Portugueza fez com os Reis e Senhores com quem teve relações nas partes da Asia e Africa Oriental ...*, vol. I (Lisbon, 1881), 275-6, 302, 304, vol. IV (Lisbon, 1884), 192, 212, vol. V (Lisbon, 1884), 288-9.

With regard to royal dress in Ikkeri, there are very few references in Dutch records. The most substantial observation was made by Corijn Stevens in the account of his embassy to Somashekara Nayaka II in February 1735.[41] The following excerpt relates Stevens' appearance before the Nayaka during the welcoming audience:

> ... without shoes, I approached the king, who was sitting in a raised armchair of three steps, covered high with some Souratse [Surat] golden cloths, keeping between his legs a sword of which the sheath was gilded, being dressed in Souratse cloths, on his head a turban set with gold, wearing around his neck a few pearls and golden necklaces, and on his fingers some rings encrusted with diamonds, standing behind him a crowd of servants, and on both sides sat several state lords and highly ranked persons ...[42]

This passage is striking for the precise description of Somashekara's dress, headgear, and jewellery, although they are not classified as "heathen" (Hindu) or "Moorish" (Islamic). The word "Surat" likely refers here to textiles produced or traded at the Mughal port of that name in north-west India, rather than to a Mughal or Persianate dress style. Besides, Somashekara wore an exquisite turban and expensive jewellery, and held a sword. All these elements of royal display were apparently required at what was clearly a public audience, attended as it was by many courtiers and servants.

The other Dutch references to Ikkeri's royal dress concern Somashekara too, but are less specific. Two of these also pertain to Stevens' embassy. The envoy met the Nayaka twice in front of his lodging, when the latter happened to pass by. On both occasions, Somashekara was dressed in white garments (*in het wit gekleed* and *uitgedost in witte kleederen*).[43] Further, the report of a mission to the same ruler in October-December 1731 states that at the first audience Somashekara sat outside his palace in "his entire garment and clothing" (*sijn gantsche gewaed en cleding*), surrounded by courtiers and facing a crowd. At the final audience, he appeared in similar dress.[44]

Again, these were all public events, at which Somashekara wore attire that at least twice was white and in most cases seems to have been rather elaborate, considering the use of plural forms, repetition, and terms implying full clothing in the envoys' accounts. These descriptions resemble those of the Italian traveller Pietro Della Valle, who visited Ikkeri in the 1620s and wrote that several courtiers were dressed in long, white, coloured, and even what he termed "Persian-style" clothes.[45]

41 For documents concerning this mission, see NA, VOC, no. 2354, ff. 1491-632.

42 NA, VOC, no. 2354, ff. 1541-2: diary of mission to Ikkeri, Feb. 1735 (translation mine).

43 NA, VOC, no. 2354, ff. 1553-4, 1560-1: diary of mission to Ikkeri, Feb. 1735.

44 NA, VOC, no. 2232, ff. 3596, 3597v: diary of mission to Ikkeri, Nov.-Dec. 1731.

45 Della Valle, *The Travels of Pietro Della Valle in India*, vol. II, 248-9.

Local images of royal dress, found in temples, largely underscore Dutch observations. For example, statues at the Sadashiva Temple in Varadamula and the Rameshvara Temple in Keladi respectively portray the second and last Nayakas—Sadashiva and Somashekara III, the latter ruling under Queen Virammaji's regency—with long tunics, turbans, jewels, and, in the former case, what may be a *kamar-band* (waist belt), perhaps of Persian origin.[46] Notably, Somashekara's clothing here has been labelled as "Mughal-Maratha" fashion (see illustration 23 in the Epilogue). One of Ikkeri's most powerful rulers, Shivappa I, is presented largely in the same way in a mural at the Puttige *maṭha* (monastery) in Tirthahalli. But a statue at the Virabhadra Temple in Keladi of what is probably also one of the Nayakas, perhaps Virabhadra or Basavappa II, shows him with a bare chest and a short, ribbed, conical cap, whereas his two attendants wear long coats.[47]

Altogether, the sources on royal titles and dress in Ikkeri seem ambivalent. With one minor exception, neither local texts nor European documents suggest the Nayakas' titles included Persianate elements. As for royal attire, however, various portrayals point to influences from sultanate courts. Dutch references say that on public occasions the kings were dressed in long, often white clothes, hinting at Persianate rather than Indic garments. Further, they usually wore a turban (instead of a *kuḷḷāyi* cap) and jewellery, and kept a sword. Several temple statues also indicate that Persianate dress was in vogue at this court.

Nayakas of Tanjavur

Sources for the titles and dress of Tanjavur's Nayakas are limited. A number of Sanskrit and Tamil inscriptions of Shevappa Nayaka, Achyutappa Nayaka, and Raghunatha Nayaka published in full mention only the rulers' names with brief designations like *nāyaka*, *rājaśrī* (illustrious king), *śrīmat* (glorious), or *mānya* (chief, respectable man), and the honorific suffix *ayyaṉ*. A Telugu silver-plate grant

[46] The term *kamar-band* derives from Persian. See: Van Dam, *Beschryvinge van de Oostindische Compagnie*, vol. 2.1 (The Hague, 1931), 818; Dunlop, *Bronnen tot de geschiedenis der Oostindische Compagnie in Perzië*, vol. I, 797; Yule and Burnell, *Hobson-Jobson*, 279-80.

[47] Swaminathan, *The Nāyakas of Ikkēri*, 238; R.K.K. Rajarajan, *Art of the Vijayanagara-Nāyakas: Architecture & Iconography* (Delhi, 2006), vol. I, 147, vol. II, plate 329; Chitnis, *Keḷadi Polity*, facing title page; *Annual Report of the Mysore Archæological Department for the Year 1932* (Bangalore, 1935), 48, plate XIV, no. 2; Subhadra, "Art and Architecture of the Keḷadi Nāyakas," 455-6. See also Kanekar, "Two Temples of the Ikkeri Nayakas," 159 (n. 22). The statue thought to portray Somashekara III, together with Queen Virammaji, is regarded by some as a depiction of Rajarama, son of the Maratha King Shivaji, with Queen Chennammaji. See Keladi Gundajois, *The Glorious Keladi (History and Culture)* (Mysore, 2011), 76, 132.

Illustration 15: Detail of a gold-foil letter of April 1620 by Raghunatha Nayaka of Tanjavur to the king of Denmark, showing the Nayaka's name and titles in Tamil in the top line, *Rigsarkivet*, Copenhagen, *Udenrigsministeriet, Traktatsamling, Traktater E1, Forholdet til udlandet 1454-1699*, no. 20 (photo by P.S. Ramanujam, courtesy *Rigsarkivet*).

issued by Vijayaraghava Nayaka to the Dutch in 1658 also contains few titles, adding to the elements above little more than the name Achyuta (perhaps signifying his grandfather) and the honorific suffix *vāru*. A Tamil-Telugu gold-foil letter of Raghunatha to the king of Denmark from 1620 even contains nothing but *śrīmat* and *nāyaka* besides the king's name (see illustration 15). This modesty is found on the dynasty's coins as well, whose legends include just the rulers' names, sometimes with the honorific prefix *śrī*, or instead refer to Vijayanagara's emperors.[48]

[48] G. Venkoba Rao (ed.), "Kumbakonam Inscription of Sevvappa-Nayaka," *Epigraphia Indica*, vol. XIX (Calcutta, 1927-8), 216-17; E. Hultzsch, V. Venkayya, and H. Krishna Sastri (eds), *South-Indian Inscriptions*, vol. II, *Tamil Inscriptions in the Rajarajesvara Temple at Tanjavur and Other Miscellaneous Records of the Chola, Pallava, Pandya and Vijayanagara Dynasties* (Madras, 1916), 499; Srinivasan and Reiniche, *Tiruvannamalai*, vol. 1.2, 549-61; Nagaswamy, *Studies in Ancient Tamil Law and Society*, 116-21; Nilakanta Sastri, "Two Negapatam Grants," 40-4; RA, *Udenrigsministeriet, Traktatsamling, Traktater E1, Forholdet til udlandet 1454-1699* (Ministry of Foreign Affairs, Treaty collection, Treaties E1, Related to foreign countries 1454-1699), nos 20-1: letter from Raghunatha Nayaka to the king of Denmark, Apr. 1620, with translation; Ramanujam, *Unheard Voices*, ch. 1 (fig. 1.5); www.tharangampadi.dk/goldfoil.html (by P.S. Ramanujam); Esther Fihl, "The South Indian Setting: Kingship, Trade and Architecture" in idem (ed.), *The Governor's Residence in Tranquebar: The House and the Daily Life of Its People, 1770–1845* (Copenhagen, 2017), 32-3; Vriddhagirisan, *The Nayaks of Tanjore*, 189-90; Venkata Rao, *The Southern School in Telugu Literature*, 145-9; Mitchiner, *The Coinage and History of Southern India*, pt.

The few letters and treaties in the VOC archives authored by Tanjavur's Nayakas contain Dutch renderings of what appear to be the same terms. Examples are "Estriamata Atchijta Visia Ragoe Naijkijawarou" (*śrīmat* Achyuta Vijayaraghava Nayaka *ayyavāru*) and "Aetchieda Visia Singamale Neijck," the latter denoting the dynasty's last scion, Chengamaladasa. The only designation found in a treaty in Portuguese that Raghunatha concluded with the Danes is *nāyaka* ("Nayquo").[49] Other titles, in local literary works and inscriptions, chiefly concern governmental matters, patronage of scholars, and religious activities. As an example of the last type, a copper-plate grant of Raghunatha calls him "he who is ever delighted in listening to the nectar-like story of Rama" (*anavarata rāmakathāmṛta sevaka*).[50]

No Dutch reports or other European accounts describing these Nayakas' dress seem to have survived, except for a reference by the Jesuit Balthazar da Costa to Vijayaraghava being clothed in (probably) a white robe and a white turban. But some temple statues portray these rulers with bare chests, both caps and turbans, jewels, and arms. A statue of Raghunatha in the Ramasvami Temple at Kumbakonam, for instance, depicts him bare-chested, wearing a rounded, medium-sized cap and jewellery, and carrying a curved sword and a dagger.[51]

All in all, these few sources show no evidence of Islamic influences on this dynasty's titles, while little can be concluded about royal dress. Most notable seem the observations that turbans were used alongside rounded caps, and that the latter were not always worn together with long tunics, as happened in Vijayanagara. This is also found with some statues at the Bhu-Varaha Temple in Srimushnam portraying kings—probably the Nayakas of Senji—with bare chests and *kuḷḷāyi* caps or other tall headdress at the same time, in addition to jewels and weapons.[52]

II, *Tamilnadu – Kerala*, 204-7. See also Venkatesha, "The Kumbhakonam Plates of Vijayaraghava, Saka 1578," *Journal of the Epigraphical Society of India [Bharatiya Purabhilekha Patrika]* XI (1984), 35.

[49] NA, VOC, no. 1231, ff. 152, 259v, 771v-2; no. 1302, ff. 614, 615v: documents from 1658, 1674; Heeres and Stapel, *Corpus diplomaticum Neerlando-Indicum*, vol. 2, 138-9, 190, 334; Ramanujam, *Unheard Voices*, ch. 1 (fig. 1.3).

[50] Vriddhagirisan, *The Nayaks of Tanjore*, 111; Chithra Madhavan, *History and Culture of Tamil Nadu: As Gleaned from the Sanskrit Inscriptions*, vol. 2 (New Delhi, 2007), 79-80, 136-40; Venkatesha, "The Kumbhakonam Plates of Vijayaraghava," 35.

[51] Saulière, "The Revolt of the Southern Nayaks" [pt. 1], p. 96; Rajarajan, *Art of the Vijayanagara-Nāyakas*, vol. I, 147, vol. II, plate 22; Vivek Nanda, Anna Dallapiccola, and George Michell, "The Ramasvami Temple, Kumbakonam," *South Asian Studies* 13, 1 (1997), 8-9 (fig. 7); Aravamuthan, *Portrait Sculpture in South India*, 51-2 (figs 29-30).

[52] Branfoot, "Dynastic Genealogies," 323-30, 340-4 (figs 5-12).

Bhonsles of Tanjavur

As Tanjavur's next royal family, the Bhonsle house, was not a direct heir to Vijayanagara, the empire's Persianate practices may have influenced it only indirectly. Also, since its founder Ekoji and his ancestors served as military commanders under various Deccan sultanates, this dynasty could have adopted such customs from those kingdoms. At any rate, sources for the Bhonsles' titles and dress are more numerous than for their Nayaka predecessors. With regard to titles, inscriptions refer to various rulers from Ekoji to Tuljaji II as "king of kings" (*rājādhirāja*) and other imperial designations.[53]

Such terms are however not yet found on a Tamil silver-plate granted by Ekoji to the Dutch in 1676, immediately after he took Tanjavur. This suggests that at that time Ekoji still acknowledged the Bijapur sultan (called "Padshah Sahib") as his overlord, styling himself less ambitiously as "illustrious king" (*śrīmat rājaśrī*) and "great king" (*mahārājā*). Also seeming to point to this subordinate status, an inscription of 1679 labels Ekoji as *mahāmaṇḍalēśvaran*, a title often used for provincial governors rather than sovereign rulers. In contrast with the various Nayaka houses, the term *mahārājā* became a common legend on the Bhonsle dynasty's coins.[54]

Further, the widely used honorific title *sāheba* ("sahib," master), of Arabic origin, figures frequently in the dynasty's chronicle *Bhoṃsale vaṃśa caritra* from early on, and also appears in a grant issued by Ekoji shortly before he conquered Tanjavur. The chronicle demonstrates that *sāheba* was used by female members of the family as well, like Queen Sujana Bai (as in "Soojawnahboysaib").[55] Besides, a Persian inscription of Pratapasimha at an Islamic shrine includes the designation *'umdat al-mulk* ("pillar of the state" or "chief of dominions")—referring to himself or Ekoji—a rather generic title originally employed for high officials at Muslim-ruled courts. Additionally, two of the house's regularly occurring personal names, Sarabhoji and Shahaji, are thought to have derived from the Persian terms "Sharif" and "Shah" respectively. None of these references, nor European sources for that

53 Sewell, *List of Inscriptions*, 2; P.R. Srinivasan (ed.), *South-Indian Inscriptions*, vol. XXVI, *Inscriptions Collected during the Year 1908-09* (New Delhi, 1990), 1.

54 Nilakanta Sastri, "Two Negapatam Grants," 48; Menon, "Colonial Linguistics and the Spoken Language," 79; S. Suresh, *The Tanjavur Marathas: Art, Architecture and Culture* (New Delhi, 2015), 137, 188-9; Srinivasan, "Some Interesting Aspects of the Maratha Rule," 42; Mitchiner, *The Coinage and History of Southern India*, pt. II, 207-8. See also: Ali, *Courtly Culture and Political Life*, 33-4; Scharfe, *The State in Indian Tradition*, 79.

55 BL/AAS, MT, class III, no. 87: "The historycal account of the Tonjore," ff. 81, 94v-100, 111, 119v-20; MG, no. 19, pt. 32: "Translation of a Maratta Sunnud of Yeckojee Rajah," f. 156 (probably granted in 1670, see Cotton, Charpentier, and Johnston, *Catalogue of Manuscripts in European Languages*, vol. I, pt. II, 244, 254).

matter, contain claims by the Bhonsles to the high status of "king of kings" and the like.[56]

Titles like *rājaśrī* and *mahārājā* were regularly used in communication with Europeans. The Dutch rendered these as, for example, "Ragia Estrie Sahagie Magharagia" (Shahaji I), and "Maharaasja Rasjaasri Pratappa Singaji Raasji" (Pratapasimha). VOC documents further include corruptions of *mānya* (see above), such as "mannia." Besides, in two treaties with the Dutch, Shahaji I was referred to as "Chola king" ("Chiole Ragia"), a practice seemingly not followed by other rulers. Danish archives contain Marathi letters from the Bhonsles with largely the same words, for instance in a document signed with *mahārājā rājaśrī tuḷajā rāje* (Tuljaji II). Finally, many European sources also contain the title *sāheba*.[57]

Sources for the Bhonsles' clothing are somewhat limited in number. Reports of VOC embassies contain only two relevant passages, both concerning public occasions. In November 1735, Dutch envoys Arnoldus Oosterharen and Wouter de Jongh were dispatched to Ekoji II and soon welcomed at the palace.[58] Escorted through nine gates, they reached a courtyard where they took off their shoes, and:

> ... proceeding this way, [we] came into the hall and before the said King Ekogie Ragie, seated under a canopy on a bed hanging from four silver chains one foot above the ground, being continually and gently swung by eight fresh youngsters. The king, a well-formed man, twenty-eight years old, was dressed in a long coat [*rock*] of white fine muslin and on his head likewise a turban, on which stood a toeraaij [*turra*, turban jewel] wrought with gold, encrusted with many precious stones as a sign of his regal highness, with a staff in

[56] Ziyaud-Din A. Desai (ed.), *A Topographical List of Arabic, Persian and Urdu Inscriptions of South India* (New Delhi, 1989), 121 (no. 1250); Śrīdhara Venkatēśa, *Śāhendra Vilāsa*, ii (in notes section); Guha, "The Frontiers of Memory," 278; Moulvi Abdul Haq, "The Influence of Persian on Mahrathi," *Islamic Culture: The Hyderabad Quarterly Review* X, 4 (1936), 601. See also Ramakrishna Kavi Pandit, *Pratapasimhendra Vijaya Prabandha*, in which such exalted claims appear to be lacking as well.

[57] NA, VOC, no. 1351, f. 2255; no. 1518, ff. 884, 885; no. 2386, f. 169; no. 2427, f. 441v; no. 2539, f. 2485; no. 2665, f. 1987; no. 2764, f. 435; no. 3108, f. 25: documents from 1677, 1692, 1735, 1738, 1741, 1746, 1750, 1764; Heeres and Stapel, *Corpus diplomaticum Neerlando-Indicum*, vol. 3, 34-5, 39, 447, 560, vol. 5, 317-18, 354, 501-3, vol. 6 (The Hague, 1955), 353-60; Strandberg, *The Moḍī Documents from Tanjore in Danish Collections*, 88-9, 92-3, 112-13, 124-5, 284, 286, 295, 300. See also Yule and Burnell, *Hobson-Jobson*, 781-2. Besides the discussed titles, both Indian and European sources include (corruptions of) the words *aja rakhtakhāne*, which often precede and may seem part of the titles, but these mean "from the treasury of." See Strandberg, *The Moḍī Documents from Tanjore in Danish Collections*, 88-9, 92-3, 96-7, 204-7, 248-9, 284, 286, 288, 330-1, 345.

[58] For papers regarding this embassy, see NA, VOC, no. 2386, ff. 64-72, 163-8: Nagapattinam proceedings (*resoluties*), with mission report and correspondence inserted, Nov. 1735.

> the right hand, and a bunch of golden chains and coral strings around the neck, and rings around the arms ...[59]

The account of an earlier mission, though not mentioning royal dress, is also significant as it details the items presented to the Dutch ambassadors during a *khil'at* ceremony.[60] In December 1676 Thomas van Rhee and Pieter Outshoorn Sonnevelt were sent to Ekoji I and quickly granted an audience. They found Ekoji accompanied by his three sons and several courtiers. The meeting was concluded when the king:

> ... had the tasserijven [*tashrīf*s, marks of honour] installed, and let me [envoy Van Rhee] and the council's Secretary Sonnevelt be dressed in a cottoned silken coat and tied with a turban around the head and commerbant [*kamar-band,* waist belt] around the body, and this way we were guided outside the court ...[61]

As for local portrayals of the Bhonsles' attire, few or no temple images are known for certain to predate the nineteenth century. But some moveable paintings of a possibly earlier date portray the rulers—for instance Ekoji I and Pratapasimha—with long clothes, jewels, and elaborate turbans, or in one case a tall hat. A bronze statue thought to date from the eighteenth century that likely depicts Shahaji I shows him dressed in a similar way.[62]

The sources suggest that the Bhonsle's titles and clothing both included Persianate elements. This is clear in some of the dynasty's designations (and perhaps personal names) but is less obvious for its dress codes. As with Ikkeri, VOC envoys never labelled royal attire in Tanjavur as "Moorish" or "heathen," and it is therefore hard to classify. Even so, together the sources imply that royal dress at the Bhonsle court was rather similar to such attire in Ikkeri: long tunics and turbans. Besides, several

[59] NA, VOC, no. 2386, f. 165: report of mission to Tanjavur, Nov. 1735 (translation mine). For "toeraaij," see also NA, VOC, no. 2538, f. 251: Nagapattinam proceedings, Jan. 1741. For a somewhat similar description of Tuljaji Bhonsle II in 1769, see Ramanujam, *Unheard Voices*, ch. 9.

[60] For documents concerning this embassy, see NA, VOC, no. 1329, ff. 1164v-79: instructions and report concerning mission to Tanjavur, Dec. 1676-Jan. 1677.

[61] NA, VOC, no. 1329, f. 1174: report of mission to Tanjavur, Dec. 1676 (translation mine).

[62] Appasamy, *Tanjavur Painting of the Maratha Period*, 47-8, plate 14 (between 44-5); Peterson, "Portraiture at the Tanjore Maratha Court," 47 (fig. 2); Krishna, *Painted Manuscripts of the Sarasvati Mahal Library*, 6 (fig. 2), 11 (fig. 3); Tejpal Singh and Sanjib Kumar Singh, *Ecstasy of Classical Art: Indian Bronze: National Museum Collection* (New Delhi, 2016), 53 (fig. 11). The last work suggests the bronze statue shows Sarabhoji I, but a Tamil inscription on its base reads *cākīmākārāca* (or *sāhī māhārāja*) (personal observation, Jan. 2017), so Shahaji I seems a more probable identification.

objects used in the *khil'at* ritual were described with Arabic and Persian terms: *tashrīf* and *kamar-band*.[63] Hence, it seems that Persianate notions on titles, clothing, and etiquette were followed to some degree at this court.

Nayakas of Madurai

For royal titles and dress in Madurai there are relatively many sources, both local and external. Telugu, Tamil, and Sanskrit inscriptions and chronicles contain several designations used throughout the Nayakas' reign, including variations on "lord of the Pandya realm" and "lord of the southern throne," conferred by Vijayanagara. Other regular terms are *mahārājā*, *mānya*, *rājaśrī*, *ayyaṉ*, and the like (discussed under Tanjavur), and the name of the dynasty's founder Vishvanatha, generally used by his successors before their own names.[64] The latter also often figures in Dutch documents, together with what are likely translations of *śrīmat*, shown by renderings as "the fortunate [*wel geluckige*] Wisuanaden-Naick Renga Kistna Moutou Wirappa-Neyck" (Ranga Krishna Muttu Virappa Nayaka III).[65]

Another common title was *karttākkaḷ* (agents, executors), denoting the Nayakas' continuing formal subordination to Vijayanagara, also under later rulers.[66] In

63 *Tashrīf* (mark of honour or act of honouring) is of Arabic origin. See: Coolhaas *et al.*, *Generale Missiven*, vol. III, 100 (n. 1); Yule and Burnell, *Hobson-Jobson*, 902. For *kamar-band*, see the section on Ikkeri.

64 S.V. Viswanatha (ed.), "The Jambukesvaram Grant of Vijayaranga Chokkanatha Nayaka: Saka 1630," *Epigraphia Indica*, vol. XVI (Calcutta, 1921-2), 89, 94, 96; T.A. Gopinatha Rao and T. Raghaviah (eds), "Krishnapuram Plates of Sadasivaraya: Saka Samvat 1489," *Epigraphia Indica*, vol. IX (Calcutta, 1907-8), 330, 341; T.A. Gopinatha Rao (ed.), "Dalavay-Agraharam Plates of Venkatapatideva-Maharaya I: Saka-Samvat 1508," *Epigraphia Indica*, vol. XII (Calcutta, 1913-14), 187; V. Natesa Aiyar (ed.), "Padmaneri Grant of Venkata I: Saka-Samvat 1520," *Epigraphia Indica*, vol. XVI, 297; T.A. Gopinatha Rao (ed.), "Vellangudi Plates of Venkatapati-Deva-Maharaya I: Saka-Samvat 1520," *Epigraphia Indica*, vol. XVI, 320; H. Krishna Sastri (ed.), "Kuniyur Plates of the Time of Venkata II: Saka-Samvat 1556," *Epigraphia Indica*, vol. III (Calcutta, 1894-5), 254-5; H.K. Narasimhaswami (ed.), *South-Indian Inscriptions*, vol. XXIV, *Inscriptions of the Ranganathasvami Temple, Srirangam* (Madras, 1982), 524-5, 533-4; Burgess and Naṭēśa Śāstrī, *Tamil and Sanskrit Inscriptions*, 111; *Travancore Archæological Series*, vol. V, pt. III, 191-210, 229-35; Venkata Rao, *The Southern School in Telugu Literature*, 36, 149-57; Aseem Banu, "Polity under the Nayaks of Madurai," 26-7; Saletore, *Social and Political Life in the Vijayanagara Empire*, vol. II, 263; Sathyanatha Aiyar, *History of the Nayaks of Madura*, 350-3, 355, 357-9, 362-5; Taylor, *Oriental Historical Manuscripts*, vol. II, 13; Nelson, *The Madura Country*, vol. III, 92, 101, 121; Heras, *The Aravidu Dynasty of Vijayanagara*, vol. I, 131-2, 171; Sewell, *List of Inscriptions*, 27; Vink, *Mission to Madurai*, 184, 240. See also Sircar, *Indian Epigraphical Glossary*, 197.

65 Heeres and Stapel, *Corpus diplomaticum Neerlando-Indicum*, vol. 1, 455-6, vol. 3, 507; Vink, *Mission to Madurai*, 377, 379.

66 Caldwell, *A Political and General History of the District of Tinnevelly*, 62; A.J. Stuart, *Manual of the Tinnevelly District in the Presidency of Madras* (Madras, 1879), 42; Aseem Banu, "Polity under the Nayaks

contrast, Chokkanatha Nayaka apparently harboured loftier ambitions, calling himself "emperor of Karnataka" (*karnāṭaka cakravarti*).[67] Thereby, he seemingly appropriated the status of Madurai's former imperial overlords, "Karnataka" being the contemporary local name of Vijayanagara. However, this claim was probably not made by other kings. The overall relative modesty of the dynasty's titles also transpires from the legends on its coins. The Nayakas are here usually referred to just by their main name—often shortened—with the honorific prefix *śrī*, as in *śrī chokka* (Chokkanatha) and *śrī mangammā* (Mangammal). In addition, various titles of individual Nayakas mention religious achievements, wise rule, and support of scholars.[68]

Turning to royal dress in Madurai, both local and VOC sources provide detailed portrayals. The earliest Dutch account concerns a mission in June-September 1689 to Muttu Virappa Nayaka III,[69] already mentioned in this chapter's introduction as the ruler who ordered his men to replace their long clothes and caps with Maratha-style attire. As envoy Nicolaes Welter wrote about his first audience, a well-attended, public occasion:

> ... I was brought with all our stuff and gift animals before His Highness. I found said ruler in a room open in front, sitting on a small alcatijff [*al-katīf*, carpet], wearing a white Moorish dress [*wit Moors gewaedt*] and pearl necklace (each one of them the size of a white pea) around the neck ... To the left and behind said ruler sat several court notables, while some servants were standing on both sides ...[70]

As it turned out, not only the Nayaka was supposed to wear such clothing.

> ... His Highness gifted me with a silver linen coat made in Moorish fashion [*op zijn Moors gemaeckt*] and a gold-wrought toock [headgear or cloth].[71] The ruler stated that, since I had come to his lands as envoy of the Hon[ourable] Company ... to gift and greet him, he honoured me after their customs. In turn [as the king said], Your Honours [Welter's

of Madurai," 20; Dirks, *The Hollow Crown*, 45-6, 105; Narayana Rao, Shulman, and Subrahmanyam, *Symbols of Substance*, 33; BL/MMC, AM, no. 18021, "History of Kurtakull."

[67] Sewell, *The Historical Inscriptions of Southern India*, 286.

[68] Sai Sravan, "Coinage of Madurai Nayakas," 124-31; Mitchiner, *The Coinage and History of Southern India*, pt. II, 210-17; Heras, *The Aravidu Dynasty of Vijayanagara*, vol. I, 281-2; Madhavan, *History and Culture of Tamil Nadu*, vol. 2, 77.

[69] Vink, *Mission to Madurai*, 381-422.

[70] Vink, *Mission to Madurai*, 452, 539 (translation by Vink). For *al-katīf*, see Yule and Burnell, *Hobson-Jobson*, 11.

[71] For "toock," see the section on the Bhonsles of Tanjavur in Chapter 4.

> superiors] could treat and gift his visiting ambassadors in their [Your Honours'] manner. His Highness requested me to wear said coat and to put the toock on my head on the way to the residence, in which I obliged him ... Thus, I returned outside, having paid my reverence, and departed, rigged out in Moorish fashion [*op zijn Moors toegetaeckeld zijnde*], to our lodging ...[72]

Welter, seemingly uncomfortable with what must have been a *khil'at* ceremony, was spared this ritual during the next audience, when only some courtesies were exchanged:

> ... [I was] escorted before His Highness. He was three to four rooms deeper inside the palace, where I found him the same way as the first time, though without any jewels or gold ware and without any of his councillors ...[73]

At this quiet, more intimate event in the palace's interior, Muttu Virappa seems to have worn the same "Moorish" attire as during the first meeting, but apparently without jewellery.

In June 1711 the Dutch reported on royal clothing again. Vijayaranga Chokkanatha Nayaka was touring his kingdom and stayed in Melur on the outskirts of the VOC port Tuticorin, while a few days later he encamped at Athur, some fifteen miles south. In both places, the Dutch envoy Swen Anderson had an audience with the king. At each meeting lots of people were present, Vijayaranga Chokkanatha being surrounded by courtiers and, at some distance, many commoners. On both occasions, Anderson noted that the Nayaka was wearing "Moorish" clothing—described respectively as red damask in a "Moorish" manner and as "the Moorish garb" (*'t Moorsch habijt*)—as well as pearls and heavy gold necklaces.[74]

The last relevant observation in the VOC records dates from June 1720, when the same king travelled to the coast again. Upon Vijayaranga Chokkanatha's arrival in Melur, the local Dutch chief, Joannes Jenner, was requested to visit the king in his camp. In the VOC's diary kept at Tuticorin, Jenner's appearance before the Nayaka was recorded as follows:

> ... the chief [Jenner], alighting his palanquin, walked through the crowd to the tent of His Highness, finding just inside the tent the great land regent Coemaren Swamie Modliaar [Kumara Svami Mudaliyar], who, having welcomed the chief, conducted him before His

72 Vink, *Mission to Madurai*, 454, 540 (translation by Vink and myself).

73 Vink, *Mission to Madurai*, 466, 550 (translation by Vink and myself).

74 DNA, DCGCC, no. 3355 (unpaginated, entries of 2 and 5 June): diary of mission to Madurai representatives at Tuticorin, Jan.-June 1711.

> Highness, being dressed in a Moorish way [*op zijn Moors gekleed*], decked with costly jewels encrusted with gemstones ...[75]

At the end of the meeting, Jenner was honoured with some presents, including a "Moorish" turban with golden bands that was tied around his head. This was another public audience, with several courtiers attending and other people crowding around the Nayaka's tent.[76]

The similarities between the above accounts, dating from a period of over thirty years, indicate that "Moorish"—or some kind of Persianate—clothing was in use among Madurai's Nayakas at public audiences well into the eighteenth century, at least as VOC envoys saw it. This is underscored by the fact that both ambassador Welter and chief Jenner were made to wear such attire as well, pointing to *khilʿat* etiquette. In at least one case, this included a turban in "Moorish" fashion, suggesting that in Madurai the high conical *kuḷḷāyi* caps of the Vijayanagara court had been replaced by Persianate turbans.[77]

In addition, as in Ikkeri and Tanjavur, jewellery was an important element of royal display when the Nayakas granted public audiences to Dutchmen, but much less so (or not at all) at the one audience with a more intimate character, Welter's second meeting with Muttu Virappa. In Madurai, like elsewhere in India, jewels were associated with royalty, were used by rulers to distinguish themselves from other dynasties, and had to be worn whenever one appeared at court.[78] Welter's report seems to underline that the role of jewellery was generally similar to that of Persianate dress: to be displayed on public rather than domestic occasions. Accounts of meetings with Queen Mangammal in 1705 and Vijayaranga Chokkanatha in 1717, near Tuticorin during tours of the kingdom, further emphasise the importance of jewellery at public events. While these reports are silent about clothing, they specifically mention the large quantities of gold and jewels the monarchs were wearing.[79]

Local sources have much to add. To begin with, audiences are depicted in the Narumpunadasvami Temple at Tiruppudaimarudur, in Madurai's far south-west. Scholars disagree on the period these images were produced but mostly date them

75 NA, VOC, no. 1941, f. 935: Tuticorin diary extract, June 1720 (translation mine).

76 NA, VOC, no. 1941, ff. 919-21v, 935, 937-7v: letter from Tuticorin to Colombo, June 1720, Tuticorin diary extract, June 1720.

77 For a description of the Madurai Nayaka's clothing in the 1640s by a Jesuit, mentioning a white dress, a white turban, and elaborate jewellery, see Saulière, "The Revolt of the Southern Nayaks" [pt. 1], 95-6.

78 Jean-François Hurpré, "The Royal Jewels of Tirumala Nayaka of Madurai (1623-1659)," in Susan Stronge (ed.), *The Jewels of India* (Bombay, 1995); Ali, *Courtly Culture and Political Life*, 163-7.

79 NA, VOC, no. 1706, f. 1045; no. 1893, f. 1048v: Tuticorin diary extract, July 1705, letter from Tuticorin to Colombo, July 1717.

Illustration 16: Mural showing a south Indian king receiving a European visitor, Narumpunadasvami Temple, Tiruppudaimarudur, 16th century? (courtesy *École française d'Extrême-Orient*).

to the sixteenth century at the earliest.[80] They may therefore have been made under Madurai's Nayakas, although this has not been firmly established. Anyhow, several images show kings (perhaps the Nayakas) meeting Indian dignitaries and European visitors. In one mural, a king sits on his throne and leans on a cushion as he receives what is probably a Portuguese merchant or soldier, accompanied by horses (see illustration 16). The monarch is bare-chested and wears a medium-sized, rounded cap and profuse jewellery. A wood carving in this temple depicts a king in the same position, watching two Europeans training a horse. Now the ruler wears a body-covering garment, together with jewels, and sports a high conical cap.[81] It is not really clear what occasions are represented here, but the first scene in particular seems to be a public event. Therefore, the Indic dress in this picture might surprise us, the more so since the second image suggests that long tunics and what look like *kuḷḷāyi* caps—both considered Persianate dress—were also in fashion at this court.

[80] Seastrand, "Praise, Politics, and Language," viii-ix, 114 (n. 35). For online images of all the temple's murals, see: southindianpaintings.art/monuments/tiruppudaimarudur-narumpunatha-temple.

[81] Jean Deloche, *A Study in Nayaka-Period Social Life: Tiruppudaimarudur Paintings and Carvings* (Pondicherry, 2011), 62-4 (figs 92, 95).

Illustration 17: Mural showing a south Indian king receiving Indian officials, Narumpunadasvami Temple, Tiruppudaimarudur, 16th century? (courtesy *École française d'Extrême-Orient*).

Another painting in this temple shows a royal audience granted to Indian officials (see illustration 17). Here the king sits on the throne with a bare chest and a medium-sized rounded cap again, whereas three standing officials wear *kuḷḷāyi* caps and colourful tunics reaching their ankles.[82] The temple paintings include many other examples of bare-chested kings and courtiers with different types of caps (high and conical, curved and pointed, or short and rounded) and turbans, all worn on various kinds of occasions.[83] Thus, the associations of the public and domestic domains with Persianate and Indic clothing respectively do not seem to apply to these images. Indeed, it has been concluded that here kings generally wear *kuḷḷāyi*-like headgear at religious events, and use lower caps with rounded, curved tops when executive authority is exercised.[84] This combination of connotations implies a dress code different from or even partly contradicting earlier scholarly ideas.

These associations are not supported by other images. Several temple paintings and statues in Madurai imply that particular clothing styles were not always limited to the same occasions or social domains. For example, the Nayaka sculptures in the Putu Mandapa festival hall (see Chapter 2) present some rulers with tall headwear, including *kuḷḷāyi* caps, but others with small turbans, while all are fully

[82] Deloche, *A Study in Nayaka-Period Social Life*, 31, 33 (fig. 42).

[83] Deloche, *A Study in Nayaka-Period Social Life*, 19-36 (figs 23-51)

[84] Deloche, *A Study in Nayaka-Period Social Life*, 19-21.

or largely bare-chested, armed, and jewelled. Based on these images, it has been suggested that the turn of the seventeenth century saw a change from *kuḷḷāyi* caps to more rounded headgear, possibly signifying Madurai's striving for autonomy from Vijayanagara, where the former headdress remained in use.[85]

A south Indian cloth painting (*kalamkārī*), probably dating from the early seventeenth century but of unknown provenance, seems to underscore this assumption. It depicts meetings at several Asian courts, including what is perhaps that of Madurai's Nayakas (see cover illustration). Here, both the ruler and the courtiers sport small turbans and some of them are bare-chested.[86] Further, a mural in the Minakshi Sundareshvara Temple of Vijayaranga Chokkanatha Nayaka—whom the Dutch in 1711 and 1720 described as wearing "Moorish" clothing—shows him in dress that has been interpreted as Mughal-style, consisting of a long, coloured tunic and a white turban.[87]

Together, the sources on royal titles and attire in Madurai give an ambiguous impression. While the titles appear to contain no Persianate elements whatsoever, royal dress was repeatedly classified by Dutch envoys as "Moorish." At the same time, temple images suggest such clothing cannot be simply labelled as either Persianate or Indic, considering the varying combinations of different types of caps and turbans with both long tunics and bare chests. Apparently, dress styles that might be regarded as Persianate or Indic could blend and be shown in various kinds of scenes, a custom not reflected in the Nayakas' titles, however.

[85] Branfoot, "Dynastic Genealogies," 330-6, 353-9 (figs 22-35); Hurpré, "The Royal Jewels of Tirumala Nayaka," passim, especially 66, 68; Aravamuthan, *Portrait Sculpture in South India*, 48-51 (figs 25-8); Heras, "The Statues of the Nayaks of Madura"; Howes, *The Courts of Pre-Colonial South India*, 13; Branfoot, "Royal Portrait Sculpture in the South Indian Temple," 21-2; idem, "In a Land of Kings," 250-1, 254-9 (figs 20.5-6); idem, "Heroic Rulers and Devoted Servants," 173; Archana Venkatesan and Crispin Branfoot, *In Andal's Garden: Art, Ornament and Devotion in Srivilliputtur* (Mumbai, 2015), 116-23 (figs 5.12-16, 5.18, 5.22). See also N.S. Ramaswami, "Portrait Sculptures," *South Indian Studies* II (1979), 81.

[86] Rachel Morris, "Enter the Royal Encampment: Re-examining the Brooklyn Museum's *Kalamkari* Hanging," *Arts of Asia* 34, 6 (2004). See also: Jos Gommans, "Cosmopolitanism and Imagination in Nayaka South India: Decoding the Brooklyn *Kalamkari*," *Archives of Asian Art* 70, 1 (2020); Gittinger (with Nina Gwatkin), *Master Dyers to the World*, 89-108; Michell, *Architecture and Art of Southern India*, 255.

[87] Hurpré, "The Royal Jewels of Tirumala Nayaka," 66 (fig. 3), 68. See also R. Nagaswamy (?), "Nayak Paintings of Kailasanatha Temple at Nattam-Kovilpatti," *South Indian Studies* III (1983), 30-1, 34. For an online image of the temple mural, see: southindianpaintings.art/monuments/madurai-minakshi-sundareshvara-temple.

Setupatis of Ramnad

The Ramnad court may have adopted Persianate conventions in various ways. One theory proposes that such notions were borrowed from the Deccan sultanates and the Mughal empire, albeit indirectly via Madurai and Tanjavur, which were tributary to or received military assistance from those states. This would have led to the arrival of painters and other artists with a Persianate background.[88] It has also been argued that the growing power of nearby Arcot—an offshoot of the Mughals—stimulated the use of Persianate dress in Ramnad.[89] Another study points to influences from Muslim merchants in Ramnad itself. Their strong presence at court helped it assume certain Persianate overtones (here referred to as "sultanist"), particularly with respect to political and military organisation.[90] These different explanations do not exclude each other, nor do they contradict the idea that Vijayanagara passed its adopted Persianate conventions onto its heirs, including Ramnad.

A substantial and diverse corpus of sources deals with the titles and clothing of Ramnad's Setupatis. Many titles are found in a set of Tamil inscriptions, mostly in the Ramanathasvami Temple on Rameshvaram island, published in full.[91] Dating from the dynasty's foundation in the early 1600s until the nineteenth century, these texts contain long strings of frequently occurring titles, which make grandiose statements. Also figuring in Ramnad's origin myths,[92] some titles claim a past dominance over areas outside the kingdom. The Setupatis are labelled "establishers [*sthāpanācārya*] of the Pandya and Chola mandalams" (Madurai and Tanjavur), who "destroyed Ila and Yalpana" (Ceylon and Jaffna). Also, they "protect the dignity of Madurai" and are *aśvapati*, *gajapati*, *narapati*, and *cētupati* (Setupati) all in one. The first three of those titles—meaning lord of horses, elephants, and men—were associated with the rulers of Delhi, Orissa, and Vijayanagara respectively.[93]

That the Setupatis developed a taste for prestigious designations from early on, is suggested by a Dutch comment from 1675, when the dynasty was supposedly still subordinate to the Nayakas of Madurai:

[88] Nagaswamy, "Mughal Cultural Influence," 208-10.

[89] Michell, *Architecture and Art of Southern India*, 245.

[90] Shulman and Subrahmanyam, "Prince of Poets and Ports," passim, in particular 505.

[91] Burgess and Naṭēśa Śāstrī, *Tamil and Sanskrit Inscriptions*, 56-111. For Tamil transcriptions of all or most copper-plate inscriptions issued by the Setupatis, see S. Raju (ed.), *Cētupati Ceppēṭukaḷ* (Tanjavur, 1994).

[92] BL/AAS, MG, no. 4, pt. 8: "A general history of the kings of Rama Naad or the Satoo-Putty Samastanum," ff. 174-5, 182-3, 185. See also Seshadri, "The Sētupatis of Ramnad," 229-30, and Chapter 1.

[93] For these three titles, see for instance: Wagoner, *Tidings of the King*, 60-3, 110, 116, 122; Sinopoli, "From the Lion Throne," 380-1; Narasimhaswami, *South-Indian Inscriptions*, vol. XVI, vii-iii; and Chapter 6.

> ... [the Setupati has] arrogated the highest honorary titles [*hoogste eertitulen*] of the great Neijck of Madure, who has taken this to heart so much that the Madurese Neijck ... has laid down all the same honorary titles, resolving with sworn intentions not to accept those again before he will have forced the Teuver [Setupati] to lay those down again ...[94]

The inscriptions also demonstrate the Setupatis' ambitions in more direct terms, such as "emperor of the great world," "king of kings," "lord of the four seas," and "supreme king." Some designations reflect conflicts with Muslim-ruled states, as in "destroyer of the army of the Tulukkas [Turks]" and "putting down the pride and prosperity of the valorous and inimical Yavana [Muslim] kings." Other Setupati titles consist of standard honorific elements used by other dynasties as well—like *śrīmat*, *ayyaṉ*, and *vāru*—or denote military achievements, religious endowments, benevolent governance, patronage of artists and scholars, material possessions, sexual capacities, and so on. A particularly lyrical instance of the two latter qualities is the title "he who is of such a fair face that to his garden, which contains rich goldmines not deficient in their produce to the great and charitable mountain Meru, come young females with beautiful foreheads to write love poems."[95]

In treaties and letters exchanged with the Dutch, too, the Setupatis' designations stand out for their length, although the terms commonly found in these documents for most dynasties are lacking here, apart from *śrīmat*. An example is a letter from Kattaya Tevar, whose names and titles the Dutch rendered as "Irenia Kitpe Aresie Rawikoele Seegere Coemare Moettoe Wieseje Regoenaden Sedoepadie Katta Theuver."[96] The first three words are likely corruptions of the Tamil terms *yiraṇiya keṟpayājī*, better known in their Sanskrit form *hiraṇyagarbhayājī*, signifying the royal ceremony of symbolic rebirth through a golden cow womb. Increasingly often used by the Setupatis in both their correspondence and their inscriptions, this was

[94] NA, HRB, no. 542 (unpaginated, 1st document, c. halfway, section "Teuverslant"): description of Ceylon, Madurai, south Coromandel, Malabar, and Kanara by Rijcklof van Goens, Sept. 1675 (translation mine). See also Vink, "Encounters on the Opposite Coast," 294.

[95] For examples, see: Burgess and Naṭēśa Śāstrī, *Tamil and Sanskrit Inscriptions*, 64, 66, 70-2, 74, 77, 80, 82-3, 85, 91-2, 94, 97, 99-100, 102, 104-5; *Travancore Archæological Series*, vol. V, pt. I, ed. A.S. Ramanatha Ayyar (Trivandrum, 1924), 7-18; Seshadri, "The Sētupatis of Ramnad," 38, 40, 45, 47, 55, 71, 228-36; S.D. Nellai Nedumaran and S. Ramachandran, "Ancient Tamil Monarchy and the Sētupati Kings," *Studies in Indian Epigraphy (Bhāratīya Puṟabhilēkha Patrikā)* XXVI (2000); Heras, *The Aravidu Dynasty of Vijayanagara*, vol. I, 357; Sathyanatha Aiyar, *History of the Nayaks of Madura*, 348-9; Sewell, *List of Inscriptions*, 4. Long or ambitious titles appear to be lacking on Setupati coins, which generally just mention the dynasty's or kingdom's name. See: Mitchiner, *The Coinage and History of Southern India*, pt. II, 224-5; Tracy, "On the Coins of the Sethupatis [Sethupati Coins]," 9-10.

[96] NA, VOC, no. 2308, f. 2076: document from 1734.

apparently considered a very important title.[97] The words "Rawikoele Seegere" are no doubt a Dutch corruption of *ravikulaśēkharan*, a common Setupati designation, meaning "crest jewel of the solar race." While the next four elements are regal names used by most of Ramnad's rulers—Kumara, Muttu, Vijaya, Raghunatha—the last three terms refer to the main dynastic and caste titles, *cētupati* (Setupati), *kātta* (protector), and *tēvar* (god).[98]

The Setupatis' clothing can be relatively well studied in VOC records since three embassy reports contain relevant details. During the first of these missions, in November 1736, Wouter Trek was delegated to Sivakumara Muttu Vijaya Raghunatha Setupati.[99] Having arrived at the palace gate for his first audience, Trek was brought inside. As he wrote:

> ... [I] was guided before the young king, who sat, dressed in a Moorish way [*op zijn Moors gekleed*] and decked with some jewels, on a large outspread alcatijf [carpet], accompanied by his courtiers. As I approached, I greeted His Excellency in the Hollanders' manner, who responded to me in the Moorish way [*op de Moorse wijse*] and signalled with the hand to sit down ...[100]

At the end of this public meeting, Trek was covered with a cloak ("sadre")[101] woven of silk and gold. Considering this ritual and the king's greeting, in Ramnad etiquette

97 For a reference to the ceremony in Ramnad's palace murals, see Verghese, "King and Courtly Life," 481.

98 NA, VOC, no. 1274, f. 206; no. 1302, f. 613; no. 1865, ff. 869, 877, 882, 894; no. 2046, f. 762; no. 2185, f. 1053v; no. 2224, ff. 1629-9v; no. 2337, f. 1580; no. 2621, f. 2196: documents from 1670, 1674, 1715, 1725, 1731, 1735, 1744; Heeres and Stapel, *Corpus diplomaticum Neerlando-Indicum*, vol. 2, 161, 518, vol. 3, 370, vol. 4, 146, 149, 328, 333, vol. 5, 505, vol. 6, 239-40, 310; *Travancore Archæological Series*, vol. V, pt. I, 8. See also Nagaswamy, "Mughal Cultural Influence," 203. For the Setupatis' performance and title of *hiraṇyagarbha*, see also: Seshadri, "The Sētupatis of Ramnad," 45, 47, 72, 82, 233-4; Sathyanatha Aiyar, *History of the Nayaks of Madura*, 355-6, 358, 361, 365-7, 369; Jayanta Bhattacharya, "The Rite of Hiraṇyagarbha: Ritual Rebirth for Social Acceptance" (unpublished paper, n.d. [c. 2021?]), 13. For its celebration by the Nayakas of Tanjavur, see: Saulier, "Madurai and Tanjore," 787; Bhattacharya, "The Rite of Hiraṇyagarbha," 13, 22; Chandler, *History of the Jesuit Mission in Madura*, 6. See also the account in Niccolao Manucci's *Storia do Mogor*, vol. III, 274-5, which may concern Tanjavur—rather than Travancore, as the work's editor suggests—considering the fact the ceremony's performer is called "the victorious," possibly a translation of Vijayaraghava, the Nayaka of Tanjavur at that time. For analyses of the ceremony, see Bayly, *Saints, Goddesses and Kings*, 66-8; Bhattacharya, "The Rite of Hiraṇyagarbha."

99 For documents concerning this mission, see NA, VOC, no. 2374, ff. 2041-76v.

100 NA, VOC, no. 2374, f. 2056: diary of mission to Ramnad, Nov. 1736 (translation mine).

101 This may be a corruption of *cādor* (mantle). See Yule and Burnell, *Hobson-Jobson*, 217-18.

as well as dress was influenced by Persianate—or what was called "Moorish"—conventions in this period.[102]

In June-July 1743, the VOC sent another embassy to this ruler.[103] For their first audience, envoys Johannes Krijtsman and Francois Danens were received at the palace gates by courtiers and escorted inside the complex, where they, according to the mission's diary:

> ... were brought before the young king, who was dressed in a heathen way [*op zijn heijdens gekleet*], having a white turban on the head and further a white muslin ["bethieljes"] cloth with golden borders hanging over the shoulders, having a large sword [*houwer*] clasped with gold lying before him, being seated on an old outspread alcatijff [carpet], surrounded by some bodyguards ... [and] prominent princes and court notables ...[104]

This passage might surprise us. Only seven years after Trek's embassy to the same Setupati, then appearing in "Moorish" attire, this ruler now wore "heathen" clothes at a public audience. Although "heathen" is a somewhat ambiguous term, it seems the Dutch envoys indicated that the king was dressed in traditional local garments, apparently not following Persianate conventions. The reference to the cloth around the Setupati's shoulders further suggests he was bare-chested. At the following audience, the envoys' observations were largely similar:

> ... the king, whom we found sitting in that same appearance [*postuur*] as the first time, having a large, round, and long white cushion lying behind his back, that was certainly grubby and dirty [*morsig en vuijl*] but not in the least regal ...[105]

Whether the scene really lacked royal dignity or not, this description implies that the Setupati's dress style at the first meeting was not a one-time event. During both public audiences in 1743 Sivakumara Muttu Vijaya Raghunatha appeared in what the Dutch considered "heathen" attire, together with a large, costly sword.

Finally, in June-July 1759 Joan Richard François and Johan Hendrik Medeler were delegated to the Setupati Sella Tevar.[106] Being welcomed at the palace by courtiers, the ambassadors entered a square where in a pavilion:

102 NA, VOC, no. 2374, ff. 2058v-9, 2066-70v; diary of mission to Ramnad, Nov. 1736.

103 For papers regarding this embassy, see NA, VOC, no. 2599, ff. 2107-62v.

104 NA, VOC, no. 2599, ff. 2135v-6: diary of mission to Ramnad, June 1743 (translation mine).

105 NA, VOC, no. 2599, f. 2152v: diary of mission to Ramnad, June 1743 (translation mine).

106 For documents concerning this mission, see NA, VOC, no. 2956, ff. 1198-269.

> ... sat the Theuver [Tevar, the Setupati], leaning with the back on a round thick cushion, the head covered with a turban in the Marruasse [Maravar] way, and hanging around the shoulders a fine muslin [*neteldoek*] with golden borders, his largest jewel being two costly pendants in the ears, and just flaunting a large golden betel box [?] and similar spittoons [*quispidoors*] ...[107]

Although the term "heathen" was not used now, it seems Sella appeared in public in the same kind of dress as his predecessor sixteen years before. Again, a piece of muslin lay around his shoulders, probably leaving parts of his chest and arms exposed, while his turban was allegedly tied in "Maravar" fashion, referring to the Setupatis' caste and thus denoting a local style. Jewels and golden objects also were part of the king's display once more.

The next evening, invited to watch fireworks, the envoys met the Setupati again. His clothing style at this public event, with thousands of people, is harder to typify, since he was:

> ... graciously dressed up in a Pattanijs [Pathan] robe, the head covered with a beautiful turban of golden cloth, two singular pendants hung in the ears, being two pompous emeralds of reasonable size, and decorated around the neck and arms with broad, flat, and heavy gold necklaces. Beside lay a costly golden sword and belly-dagger [*buiksteker* (*katāra*?)], the latter encrusted with gemstones, which he, one after the other, took in his hand to show all the better a costly large ring on the little finger of his right hand, which he turned around several times ...[108]

It is uncertain what kind of turban Sella was wearing now, but his robe is described as Pathan, a term one would associate with Afghan or more generally Persianate dress.[109]

[107] NA, VOC, no. 2956, ff. 1234v-5: diary of mission to Ramnad, June 1759 (translation mine).

[108] NA, VOC, no. 2956, f. 1241v: diary of mission to Ramnad, July 1759 (translation mine).

[109] The VOC often referred to Pathans, or Afghans in general, as "Patanders," while "Pattanijs," usually indicated textiles or other matters related to the north Indian town of Patna. See Gommans, Bes, and Kruijtzer, *Dutch Sources on South Asia*, vol. 1, 398, 402. "Pattanijs" may also have denoted cloths destined for Pattani on the Malay peninsula or deriving from Patan in Gujarat (for which suggestions I thank an anonymous reviewer and Anna Seastrand). But following this mention of "Pattanijs," the diary's next page speaks of a "distinguished Pattanij armed with shield and sword," sitting close the king (see Chapter 4). This almost certainly refers to an Afghan or at least a north Indian Muslim, so I believe that here the term "Pattanijs" used for the Setupati's robe has an Islamic connotation. In many other sources, words like "Patanes" were also used to denote Afghans. See Yule and Burnell, *Hobson-Jobson*, 746-7.

These various Dutch descriptions, over a period of almost twenty-five years, suggest certain developments. On public occasions, the Setupatis initially used what seem to have been Persianate garments and etiquette, albeit sporting turbans instead of *kuḷḷāyi* caps. In the following decades, the dress style changed into what the Dutch labelled as "heathen" clothing and Maravar-style turbans. Nevertheless, it appears that Persianate dress was not entirely abandoned, the Setupatis still wearing such attire during public festivities. At the same time, other aspects of royal representation remained important, including expensive jewellery and valuable weaponry, which were prominently displayed.

Local portrayals of the Setupatis' clothing are found both in their palace and in temples. The latter depictions have much in common with temple sculptures of the Nayakas of Madurai and Tanjavur. Thus, Setupati statues, for instance in the Ramanathasvami Temple at Rameshvaram, include long tunics, bare chests, turbans, jewels, and weapons, all in various combinations. Only caps appear to be entirely non-existent in this dynasty's case.[110]

Great variety is also encountered among paintings in the palace complex at Ramanathapuram, probably constructed from the mid-seventeenth century onward.[111] The palace's building that includes the audience hall contains a remarkable collection of murals. Known as the Ramalinga Vilasam, this structure was likely built in the late seventeenth century by the Setupati Kilavan Tevar. His successor Tiru Udaya Tevar—better known under his regal name Muttu Vijaya Raghunatha—is credited with commissioning the paintings that adorn the inner walls and ceilings. Arranged in different sections, these show military and political events, Hindu deities, and court life. Murals were executed in several south-east Indian palaces, but those in Ramnad may be the only surviving paintings at such a location that predate the nineteenth century.[112]

110 Sethuraman, *Ramesvaram Temple*, 190-2; Howes, *The Courts of Pre-Colonial South India*, 76 (fig. 34), 84; T.G. Aravamuthan, *South Indian Portraits in Stone and Metal* (London, 1930), 80; Branfoot, "Royal Portrait Sculpture in the South Indian Temple," 32-3 (fig. 21); idem, "Heroic Rulers and Devoted Servants," 180-1 (fig. 7.5); R. Nagaswamy and N.S. Ramaswami, *Ramanathapuram District: An Archaeological Guide* (Ramanathapuram, 1979), between 92-3. See also Ramaswami, "Portrait Sculptures," 80.

111 For a description of the palace complex in 1772 by a Dutchman visiting it while Ramnad was occupied by Arcot and the Nawab's son stayed in the palace, see NA, VOC, no. 3349, ff. 733v-4: diary of mission to Arcot-occupied Ramnad, Dec. 1772. For a British map of Ramanathapuram and the palace complex from the same year, see BL/AAS, OOV, no. 333, pt. 34: "Plan of Ramanadaparam stormed June 2nd 1772 by the army under General Smith," f. 138.

112 Howes, *The Courts of Pre-Colonial South India*, 83, 92-3; Nagaswamy, "Mughal Cultural Influence," 203-4; Branfoot, "Heroic Rulers and Devoted Servants," 177-9; Michell, *Architecture and Art of Southern India*, 220, 244, 274. For online images of the Ramalinga Vilasam's murals, see: southindianpaintings.art/monuments/ramanathapuram. In addition, the audience hall of Tanjavur's Bhonsles

Upon entering the Ramalinga Vilasam's first and largest hall, the murals come into view. On the left-hand (south-eastern and southern) side, a group of painted battle scenes indicate when the images were made, as a Tamil text underneath declares the depicted battle was fought between the Setupati Muttu Vijaya Raghunatha and Tanjavur's King Sarabhoji Bhonsle.[113] Therefore, the paintings probably represent a war waged between Ramnad and Tanjavur in 1715. Even though the latter kingdom was supported by the Danes, the Setupati claimed to be victorious, writing to the VOC that he had slaughtered Tanjavur's commanders—a feat certainly worthy of commemoration on the palace walls.[114] If the murals indeed show this battle, they date from between 1715 and 1725, the period between the war and Muttu Vijaya Raghunatha's death.[115]

A few steps further along the Ramalinga Vilasam's south wall is another set of murals. These depict audiences granted by the Setupati, probably Muttu Vijaya Raghunatha as well, to courtiers and other dignitaries (see illustration 13 in Chapter 4).[116] In one of the paintings, the king, with a queen behind him, sits on a chair and converses with three European officers, likely envoys of a European power present in the region (see illustration 18). As in the other murals in this group,

contains several statues depicting court scenes (including Europeans), believed to date from the start of Shahaji I's reign (mid-1680s). See Josefine Baark, "Decorum: Courtly Posturing in the Visual Economy of Indo-Danish Diplomacy," in Annamaria Motrescu-Mayes and Marcus Banks (eds), *Visual Histories of South Asia* (New Delhi, 2018).

113 Howes, *The Courts of Pre-Colonial South India*, 93-5, 176, 184-5; Nagaswamy, "Mughal Cultural Influence," 204. The latter reference includes a translation of the text. For reproductions of the battle scenes, see Howes, plates 3-11 (between 112-13).

114 For Dutch documents concerning this war, see NA, VOC, no. 1865, ff. 867-97v, in particular f. 878.

115 It has earlier been concluded that the paintings depict a war around 1720 and were created shortly afterwards. See: Nagaswamy, "Mughal Cultural Influence," 204; Howes, *The Courts of Pre-Colonial South India*, 93-5. But as explained in Chapter 2, the war this conclusion refers to—which enthroned Muttu Vijaya Raghunatha's successor Bhavani Sankara after the former's passing—actually took place in 1725. Since Bhavani Sankara had already contested Muttu Vijaya Raghunatha's accession to the throne in 1710, it is unlikely he commissioned paintings showing his competitor when he had finally become king himself. Moreover, having secured the throne with the help of Tanjavur, Bhavani Sankara would not regard this assistance as a war and depict it as such in the palace. For these reasons, the suggestion that the murals mentioning Muttu Vijaya Raghunatha were painted soon after his death is improbable too. For references dating the Ramnad-Tanjavur war before Bhavani Sankara's enthronement to 1720, see: Seshadri, "The Sētupatis of Ramnad," 82, 87-8; Kadhirvel, *A History of the Maravas*, 55-9; Subramanian, *The Maratha Rajas of Tanjore*, 37.

116 Howes, *The Courts of Pre-Colonial South India*, 96, 176; Verghese, "King and Courtly Life," 478. For reproductions of some of the murals depicting audiences, see: Howes, *The Courts of Pre-Colonial South India*, 98 and plate 12 (between 112-13); Verghese, "King and Courtly Life," 478 (fig. 34.2); Nagaswamy, "Mughal Cultural Influence," 210 (fig. 13).

Illustration 18: Mural depicting Muttu Vijaya Raghunatha Setupati of Ramnad receiving European envoys, Ramalinga Vilasam (main hall, south wall), Ramanathapuram, c. 1720 (photo by the author).

the Setupati wears a long, whitish garment fully covering his body and seemingly worked with gold, an elaborate turban, some sort of shawl, and profuse jewellery. In his left hand, he probably holds a jewelled *katāra* (Indian dagger with the hilt attached crosswise to the blade). The object in his right hand may be a sceptre (*ceṅkōl*) in the form of a stylised bouquet.[117] The queen carries a small human figure (clothed in a long garment and a turban too) that likely represents an infant prince.[118]

Seated to the Setupati's right (left on the image), the Europeans are dressed in European clothes: single-colour, hip-length buttoned coats with braiding, white trousers, black hats, and black closed shoes. The middle envoy holds an object in his right hand that is not clearly visible due to the mural's weathering. All adults sit on European-style chairs, with the royal couple's feet resting on cushions.[119]

[117] See Hurpré, "The Royal Jewels of Tirumala Nayaka," 69.

[118] A small human figure depicted elsewhere in the Ramalinga Vilasam is thought to represent the crown prince. See Seastrand, "Praise, Politics, and Language," 73, 300 (fig. 45), 350 (fig. 117).

[119] I thank Pauline Lunsingh Scheurleer, Jennifer Howes, Phillip Wagoner, Jos Gommans, Marie Favereau, Liesbeth Geevers, Kim Ragetli, and Gijs Kruijtzer for helping me interpret the murals discussed here and below. Notwithstanding, I alone remain responsible for the assumptions presented here. This particular mural is also reproduced in Narayana Rao, Shulman, and Subrahmanyam, *Symbols of Substance*, fig. 16 (facing 173), where it is said to represent a negotiation over a pearl fishery (the source of which is not given). For an entirely different interpretation of this painting, see J.L.W., "Chronicles of the Marava Country," 128.

The Setupati's dress in this mural is largely similar to the Persianate attire of the Nayaka in the textile painting discussed in this chapter's Vijayanagara section. Both monarchs wear long tunics and turbans, although the Setupati's clothes are white instead of coloured, while his turban is tied in a different way, somewhat similar to a style associated with the Marathas.[120] Thus, the Setupati here adhered at least partially to a Persianate dress code, like his former overlord, the Nayaka of Madurai.[121] That is consistent with the idea that Persianate clothing was expected on public occasions, like a meeting with foreign ambassadors, even if these were Europeans.

Further into the Ramalinga Vilasam's main hall are murals depicting Hindu deities, followed by a few steps leading to a much smaller second room with more Hindu images.[122] Next, a middle-sized, again slightly raised third space—the lower floor's back room—is filled with columns joined by painted arches. These show the Setupati involved in court duties and leisure activities, and include a Tamil text that identifies him as Muttu Vijaya Raghunatha again and another figure as Madurai's contemporary ruler, Vijayaranga Chokkanatha Nayaka. Both kings wear what looks like Persianate dress.[123]

Located near the Ramalinga Vilasam's back wall, at the furthest possible distance from the building's entrance, one arch painting depicts the Setupati once more as he receives three European envoys (see illustration 19). Yet, this image is strikingly different from the mural in the first room that also shows a meeting with Europeans. Rather than sitting in a chair, the king is seated cross-legged on a small platform raised a few inches above the ground and covered with cloth. Leaning against a large cushion, with his left hand the Setupati probably greets his visitors or signals them to speak. In his right hand, he carries what is likely a jewelled *katāra* again. Behind him stand two courtiers, one of whom appears to hold a sword in its sheath, while the other keeps an object that is difficult to identify but may be a medium for text, perhaps a book, tablet, or copper plate. To the Setupati's left (right on the image), the Europeans stand rather than sit, the first two bowing slightly forward. The envoy in front has taken off his hat and salutes the king, while the second one seems to present him a gift.

120 I thank Indira Peterson for discussing this resemblance. For pictures of Maratha turbans in Bhonsle Tanjavur, see: Jaya Appasamy, *Tanjavur Painting of the Maratha Period* (New Delhi, 1980), plate 14 (between 44-5); Peterson, "Portraiture at the Tanjore Maratha Court," 47 (fig. 2); Nanditha Krishna, *Painted Manuscripts of the Sarasvati Mahal Library* (Tanjavur, 2011), 11 (fig. 3).

121 See also: Howes, *The Courts of Pre-Colonial South India*, 96; Verghese, "King and Courtly Life," 478.

122 Howes, *The Courts of Pre-Colonial South India*, 96-106.

123 Verghese, "King and Courtly Life," 480-2 (fig. 34.6); Howes, *The Courts of Pre-Colonial South India*, 106 and fig. 46 (between 100-1); Nagaswamy, "Mughal Cultural Influence," 204. The last reference gives a transliteration and translation of the Tamil text. See also Chapter 6.

Illustration 19: Mural depicting Muttu Vijaya Raghunatha Setupati of Ramnad receiving European envoys, Ramalinga Vilasam (back room, arches), Ramanathapuram, c. 1720 (photo by the author).

In terms of dress, the difference between the murals is also remarkable. Instead of long garments, the Setupati, and his courtiers, wear white *dhotīs* (cloths wrapped around the waist and legs) with ornamental bands or red borders—together with small black turbans and jewels—leaving their chests, arms, shoulders, and lower legs exposed. A multi-stranded thread is loosely wrapped around the king's torso, probably representing the *upavīta* (consecrated cord worn by adult male members of higher castes).

The clothing of the Europeans also greatly differs from their attire in the first image. They are all dressed in knee-length, multi-coloured tunics with floral patterns, coloured trousers, and coloured open shoes, and the first two wear short-sleeved clothes over long-sleeved ones. Only the black hats are similar to those in the other mural. Further, most men, Indian and European, sport beards in various stages of growth. In contrast, although hard to see, none of the men in the first painting shows any trace of a beard.

Judging from the Indic dress portrayed here, this scene depicts an occasion associated with the domestic rather than the public domain. This may surprise us, considering the idea that public events, such as diplomatic meetings, required Persianate clothing. While the first audience mural in the Ramalinga Vilasam fits that notion, this second painting, in the same building, shows the Setupati granting an audience in traditional dress. How can this disparity be explained? Were the murals executed in different periods? Do their separate locations mean they are unrelated and should not be compared? Were they created by artists with different ideas about royal representation?

These questions do not seem to provide more insight. Each mural belongs to a clearly demarcated and internally related section of images. Based on textual evidence, both these sections are linked to the reign of Muttu Vijaya Raghunatha, so it is unlikely that the murals were created more than about a decade apart. Moreover, the various groups of paintings are thought to be closely related. They have been arranged in a specific sequence so as to present a thematic progression, suggesting all murals are part of a single programme. Therefore, the dissimilarities between the two audience images were caused neither by a difference in time nor by independently operating painters.

The fact the murals are found in separate locations does not yield a wholly satisfactory explanation either. The paintings are organised in themes representing multiple facets of south Indian kingship and associated with various degrees of "interiority" or "exteriority." As explained, these two complementary social realms, observed in literature and architecture, were related to the distinction between domestic and public occasions. In the Ramalinga Vilasam, the groups of paintings depicting exterior or public events—for instance battles and audiences—are situated in the large, first room, near the entrance, obviously the structure's most exterior and public section. If one moves further into the building, the spaces become progressively more interior and domestic, as do the scenes in the murals. Eventually, one reaches the sole room on the upper floor where paintings show the Setupati engaged in erotic pleasures, clearly the Ramalinga Vilasam's most interior and domestic section.[124]

The audience hosted by the king in traditional, Indic dress is depicted near the back wall of the lower floor's third room—a relatively interior, domestic section of the building or at least a kind of transitional zone between the two social spheres. While images of Hindu deities adorn this room's walls, several paintings on the two dozen arches show domestic scenes, including courtesans, amorous encounters, the Setupati meeting his tutelary goddess Rajarajeshvari, and him listening to the *Rāmāyaṇa* epic. Some arches portray the ruler in Indic style. Hence, it makes sense that in the audience mural in this room the Setupati wears Indic clothing too. But then other arch paintings here present him in Persianate attire, making one wonder why this audience mural does not show him in such dress.[125]

The question thus remains of why a supposedly public event like the reception of foreign envoys was depicted in a comparatively interior space, with the king foregoing the Persianate dress code for diplomatic events—especially because another image depicting a similar scene was placed in a very public location, with the king appropriately dressed for the occasion. Perhaps a clue to the answer lies in the identity of the envoys in the images.

[124] Howes, *The Courts of Pre-Colonial South India*, ch. 4; Verghese, "King and Courtly Life," 481-2.

[125] Nagaswamy, "Mughal Cultural Influence," 204-7, 210; Howes, *The Courts of Pre-Colonial South India*, 102-7; Verghese, "King and Courtly Life," 482; and personal observation (Apr. 2012).

It is impossible to say whom the artists had in mind when they painted those European figures. The texts accompanying the murals are silent on this and there are no other contemporary sources on the paintings. But it seems logical that the painters modelled these foreigners on the nearest available examples. It has variously been suggested that the Europeans represent Jesuits, or perhaps Frenchmen or Dutchmen.[126] However, during the rule of Muttu Vijaya Raghunatha, when the paintings were produced, only the VOC maintained a permanent presence in Ramnad. By the time this Setupati ascended the throne in 1710, the Dutch had been the only resident Europeans in the kingdom for two decades.[127] Since 1690 they had been living in Kilakkarai, only a few hours' travel from the capital.[128] Therefore, when the murals were created, the Dutch—unlike other Europeans—had long been familiar faces, staying near the court and appearing there regularly on diplomatic missions.

The court's close links with the Dutch are also suggested by another European figure depicted in the Ramalinga Vilasam. The scenes of the battle between Ramnad and Tanjavur (see illustration 20) include a European soldier, dressed in a green-blue suit, black footwear, and a white hat, fighting on the Setupati's side and manning a cannon on wheels. It has been proposed that he is Dutch because Ramnad often asked the VOC for military assistance, although usually in vain.[129] Like Madurai, it was impressed by Dutch military skills, defence works, and

126 Nagaswamy, "Mughal Cultural Influence," 208; Michell, *Architecture and Art of Southern India*, 245; Howes, *The Courts of Pre-Colonial South India*, 96; Verghese, "King and Courtly Life," 476-8.

127 The Portuguese were expelled by the Dutch around 1658, and the French probably never settled in Ramnad, certainly not during Muttu Vijaya Raghunatha's reign. Jesuit presence seems to have been marginal in this period. In 1693, the Setupati Kilavan Tevar banished their order and had one Jesuit, John de Britto, beheaded after their mission made converts even within the royal family. Muttu Vijaya Raghunatha grew hostile towards them, too, making it unlikely he had them portrayed in his audience hall. Published Jesuit letters from the eighteenth century's early decades also suggest their activities were limited then, containing few references other than to the Setupati's oppression of Christians. The Danes, although based in neighbouring Tanjavur, never resided in Ramnad either, and the British only became active in the kingdom in the late 1750s. Further, Dutch sources from Muttu Vijaya Raghunatha's period do not mention a substantial presence of other Europeans in Ramnad, which they certainly would have done had these competitors gained a foothold here. See also: Arasaratnam, "Commercial Policies of the Sethupathis of Ramanathapuram," 251-2; Schwartzberg, *A Historical Atlas of South Asia*, 50; Seshadri, "The Sētupatis of Ramnad," 63-9, 74-5, 83-4, 106; Kadhirvel, *A History of the Maravas*, 39-44; Bayly, *Saints, Goddesses and Kings*, 398-403; *Lettres édifiantes et curieuses*, vols X-XV, *Mémoires des Indes* (Paris, 1781), vol. X, 3-35, vol. XII, 372-87.

128 Bes, "The Setupatis, the Dutch, and Other Bandits," 550-1.

129 Howes, *The Courts of Pre-Colonial South India*, 95. The soldier has also been identified as British, which seems unlikely as the British appeared in Ramnad only several decades later. See Michell, *Architecture and Art of Southern India*, 245.

Illustration 20: Mural showing a battle between Ramnad and Tanjavur, including a European soldier, Ramalinga Vilasam (main hall, south-east wall), Ramanathapuram, c. 1720 (photo by the author).

weaponry.[130] Indeed, during a VOC mission to Muttu Vijaya Raghunatha himself in 1724, he asked the envoys whether their soldiers were capable of manning cannon.[131] It is therefore likely that the European portrayed in the battle scene is a Dutchman.[132]

Considering the long-lasting, strong, and unrivalled Dutch presence in Ramnad and the probable identity of the European soldier in the battle mural, the Europeans in the audience paintings probably represent envoys of the VOC. Consequently, we

130 There are many instances of requests by Ramnad and Madurai for Dutch military support and of their admiration for Dutch military skills and equipment. See: NA, VOC, no. 1324, ff. 212-12v; no. 1491, f. 596; no. 1508, ff. 214v-15; no. 1865, ff. 869-70, 879, 883, 897v; no. 1941, ff. 941-1v; no. 2374, ff. 2056-6v; no. 2599, ff. 2137-7v; no. 2956, ff. 1261-1v: correspondence, muster rolls, mission reports, and diary extracts concerning the reception of courtiers, 1677, 1691-2, 1715, 1720, 1736, 1743, 1759; Vink, *Mission to Madurai*, 68-9, 215-16; idem, "Encounters on the Opposite Coast," 265; Arasaratnam, "The Politics of Commerce," 9-10. For such requests by Bhonsle-ruled Tanjavur, see NA, VOC, no. 1633, f. 128; no. 2387, f. 93; no. 2764, ff. 62-3: letters from Nagapattinam to Pulicat and Batavia, Oct. 1700, Sept. 1736, Nagapattinam proceedings, Oct. 1749. For a similar request by Mysore, see NA, VOC, no. 8985, f. 116: report of mission to Mysore, Feb. 1681. For Ikkeri's interest in Dutch military skills, see NA, VOC, no. 2354, ff. 1545-6: diary of mission to Ikkeri, Feb. 1735.

131 NA, VOC, no. 2015, ff. 671-2: diary of mission to Ramnad, Apr. 1724.

132 Another factor brought up to underscore the soldier's likely Dutch identity is his light hair. See Howes, *The Courts of Pre-Colonial South India*, 95. If hair colour may serve as a means of identification, this underscores the assumption that the Europeans depicted on the audience murals are Dutch too. In the first mural (illustration 18), the envoys' hair colour is nondescript or at best greyish. But the second mural (illustration 19) clearly portrays them with blond or reddish hair, which might favour a Dutch background over a Portuguese or French one.

may ask whether the Dutch themselves wrote about audiences with the Setupati of a "domestic" or private rather than public character. The VOC archives contain only one report of an embassy to Muttu Vijaya Raghunatha, the ruler responsible for the murals' execution.[133] This mission lasted from February to May 1724, when the king held court in the northern frontier town Arantangi, probably to defend himself against the imminent Tanjavur-backed invasion by his competitor Bhavani Shankara. But the following April, still or again residing at Arantangi, the Setupati passed away.[134] It is unlikely he commissioned the Ramalinga Vilasam paintings in the period of less than a year between the Dutch embassy and his death, during which he seems to have been largely absent from the capital. The murals were most probably painted before 1724 and therefore this VOC report appears to be irrelevant. Moreover, this account does not refer to any meeting with the Setupati of a private, intimate nature.

The previous Dutch embassy to Ramnad was dispatched from May to July 1709, when Muttu Vijaya Raghunatha's predecessor Kilavan Tevar still reigned.[135] While that seems too early, one of the mission's audiences was rather unusual, as a summary of the report shows:

> On 28 May, Cornelis Taaij and Barent Gast arrived in the capital Ramanathapuram, instructed to complain about recent violations of the Dutch-Ramnad treaty.[136] The following morning, consulting with courtiers about an appropriate moment for the first audience with Kilavan Tevar, the envoys received news that the seventy-year old and apparently blind and demented Setupati was more or less permanently drunk. Still, the next day Taaij and Gast were invited for an audience, and although they feared this would prove useless, they proceeded to the palace. On the way, six or seven messengers from the court, one after another, came to see the envoys, announcing the Setupati's desire and impatience to meet them. But upon their arrival, they found Kilavan outside in the hot sun, blind drunk and causing great commotion, while nothing had been prepared to receive them. Exchanging courtesies and presenting gifts was virtually impossible, leaving the ambassadors with no choice but to return to their lodging. The subsequent days were also fruitless as more reports about the Setupati's incessant drinking poured in and negotiations with Ramnad's courtiers, said to control the court, led to nothing.[137]

133 See NA, VOC, no. 2015, ff. 544-702.

134 See the Ramnad section in Chapter 2.

135 NA, VOC, no. 1771, ff. 1470-595v.

136 NA, VOC, no. 1771, ff. 1451-69: instructions for mission to Ramnad, May 1709. For examples of such violations, see Shulman and Subrahmanyam, "Prince of Poets and Ports," 501-19, 534-5.

137 NA, VOC, no. 1771, ff. 1491-500v: diary of mission to Ramnad, May-June 1709. Among the Dutch, Kilavan Tevar had a reputation for heavy drinking since at least the late 1670s. See NA, VOC, no. 1333, f. 28v: letter from Colombo to Batavia, June 1678.

In the early morning of 2 June, however, the envoys received a message from Kilavan, requesting them to come see him at that very moment. Taaij and Gast knew it was quiet in the palace at that hour, so this presented a rare opportunity to have a more private conversation with the king, without courtiers intervening. As the mission's diary goes, the envoys straightaway hurried to the court, and:

> ... having arrived there, His Excellency [Kilavan] let us [Taaij and Gast] know that we, without any retinue and only with the two of us, besides the interpreter, would stand inside, that from his side there would be nobody around either, which exceptionally good occasion we employed immediately and with just the both of us and the interpreter we went in front of His Excellency, who now sat inside a mandoetje [small "mandu," pavilion?] and was accompanied by no one but two of his children besides two, three wives ...[138]

But Taaij and Gast had hardly sat down in front of Kilavan, who was sober now, when courtiers rushed in and took over the discussion. The remainder of the audience—and of the mission for that matter—was dominated by further cumbersome, unsatisfactory negotiations with the court, and the final audience was endlessly postponed.

But amidst their frustrations, the envoys received help from an unexpected corner. The son of a courtier called "Oeria Theuver" (as the Dutch spelled it) sent them some food gifts as well as advice on how to deal with the court and speed up the negotiations. As Taaij and Gast wrote, "Oeria Theuver" was a close blood relative of Kilavan, and his son was considered the Setupati's likely successor.[139] Taking the recommendations of the son of "Oeria Theuver" to heart, the envoys finally secured a second audience on 17 June—under the watchful eyes of dozens of courtiers—and returned home the same afternoon.[140]

Kilavan died the following year and was succeeded by Muttu Vijaya Raghunatha, under whom the Ramalinga Vilasam's murals were produced. "Muttu Vijaya Raghunatha" being his regal name, before his accession to the throne he must have been known under his personal name, Tiru Udaya Tevar. Therefore, it seems that the local ally of the VOC envoys during their mission in 1709 was none other than Tiru Udaya Tevar alias Muttu Vijaya Raghunatha Setupati, the successor of Kilavan. As said, the envoys wrote that the son of "Oeria Theuver" was likely to be Kilavan's successor, since he and his father were close blood relatives of the Setupati. "Oeria

[138] NA, VOC, no. 1771, ff. 1500v-1: diary of mission to Ramnad, June 1709 (translation mine).

[139] NA, VOC, no. 1771, ff. 1480, 1529, 1531v, 1536v, 1563: report and diary of mission to Ramnad, July 1709, letter from Dutch envoys in Ramnad to Colombo, June 1709.

[140] NA, VOC, no. 1771, ff. 1500v-35: diary of mission to Ramnad, June 1709.

Theuver" is obviously a Dutch corruption of "Udaya Tevar,"[141] while *tiru* is a general honorific title in Tamil. Thus, the son of "Oeria Theuver"—who may well have borne a similar name—was most probably the same person as Tiru Udaya Tevar, the future King Muttu Vijaya Raghunatha.[142] He was indeed closely related to Kilavan, being in all probability his nephew, and, as the Dutch reported, married one of his daughters moments before the old Setupati passed away.[143]

In short, the somewhat confusing but most likely scenario is as follows. The "Oeria Theuver" mentioned by the Dutch was in fact named (Tiru) Udaya Tevar, and so was his son. Udaya junior, who supported the VOC envoys in 1709, was a nephew of Kilavan, as his father Udaya senior was Kilavan's brother-in-law. Upon Kilavan's death in 1710, Udaya junior became the new Setupati under his regal name Muttu Vijaya Raghunatha.

If this identification is correct, the king who commissioned the murals portraying the Dutch had already favoured them during their embassy in the last regnal year of his predecessor. This assumption is supported by the fact that during the mission to Muttu Vijaya Raghunatha himself in 1724, he complained to the Dutch ambassadors about their limited powers, saying the previous envoys, Taaij and Gast, had been more qualified, which suggests he clearly recalled their visit fifteen years earlier.[144] In any case, as an important courtier, Tiru Udaya Tevar alias Muttu Vijaya Raghunatha is likely to have been present when Taaij and Gast had their early morning private audience with Kilavan. Muttu Vijaya Raghunatha may well have been one of the Setupati's attending "children" mentioned in the VOC report of 1709. Alternatively, he could have been one of the courtiers who soon rushed in.

Thus, Muttu Vijaya Raghunatha would have remembered this intimate (not to say "domestic") meeting between the Setupati family and the VOC envoys, however brief. To commemorate this exceptional occasion, he may have wished to depict it in the back room in the Ramalinga Vilasam's interior. It is then not illogical that the Setupati in that image (perhaps an amalgam of Kilavan and Muttu Vijaya Raghunatha) was represented in Indic attire. After all, this mural was probably

[141] The letter combination of "oe" in Dutch sounds similar to letters transliterated as "u" in Tamil and other Indian languages.

[142] The Dutch sources are slightly confusing in this respect. They declare that the son of "Oeria Theuver" would in all probability succeed Kilavan Tevar, but also state that when the latter fell ill soon after the Dutch mission in 1709, "Oeria Theuver" was rumoured to have been summoned to the court and nominated to ascend the throne himself. This seems to imply that the son of "Oeria Theuver" bore the same name as his father, but it may also be that "Oeria Theuver" senior was selected as the new Setupati at that particular moment. See respectively NA, VOC, no. 1771, ff. 1563, 1536v: letter from envoys in Ramnad to Colombo, diary of mission to Ramnad, June 1709.

[143] See the Ramnad section in Chapter 2.

[144] NA, VOC, no. 2015, f. 639: diary of mission to Ramnad, Apr. 1724.

not meant to show a public event or be seen by people from beyond the king's domestic domain. To refer to the public audiences normally granted to the Dutch, and adhering to the convention of portraying kings in Persianate dress on such occasions, Muttu Vijaya Raghunatha may have had the other audience mural placed in a public, exterior location near the building's entrance.

Obviously, one can merely guess why an audience with the Setupati in Indic dress was included in the Ramalinga Vilasam's murals. But there might be a connection between that image, the small-scale, family-style audience granted by Kilavan to the Dutch, and the role of the future Muttu Vijaya Raghunatha during that mission. However, such a link does not easily explain all there is to see in the audience paintings. To begin with, the mural in the back room depicts the Setupati in traditional clothing while he is escorted by courtiers carrying a weapon and writing material. One would associate these objects with warfare and administration rather than close relatives, leisure, and residential areas. But these men of the sword and the pen may have signified that even though this audience started as a private occasion, political and mercantile matters would be discussed, too. Also, the audience mural in the Ramalinga Vilasam's most public area portrays the Setupati in Persianate dress while he is accompanied by a spouse and a son. This aspect of the image appears to be a family affair par excellence, which would belong to the building's interior. But in this case, depicting a queen and a prince perhaps served to convince the public of a secure continuation of the Setupati dynasty.[145]

Further, the difference between the clothing styles of the Europeans in the two murals might be explained in quite a mundane way. The garments in the second painting seem to underscore the account of envoys Taaij and Gast saying they immediately left their lodging when requested to appear without delay for a private audience with the king. The regulations of the VOC stipulated that in public its employees were not to wear what was called "Moorish" attire but should appear in European clothes.[146] Such a specific ban implies that in unofficial settings they regularly dressed in Muslim-style clothing, covering the body and still suitable to the climate. Therefore, Taaij and Gast probably wore such dress when soon after dawn the Setupati's hurried call came in and they had no time to change into European garments. The audience's impromptu character and early hour perhaps also account for the bearded appearance of all the portrayed. Finally, this mural's depiction of the Europeans wearing short-sleeved tunics over long-sleeved ones may refer to the *khil'at* ceremony, regularly practised at the Ramnad court.

145 It has also been suggested that the presence of a queen was auspicious. See Howes, *The Courts of Pre-Colonial South India*, 142-3.

146 Pauline Lunsingh Scheurleer and Gijs Kruijtzer, "Camping with the Mughal Emperor: A Golkonda Artist Portrays a Dutch Ambassador in 1689," *Arts of Asia* 35, 3 (2005), 58.

Together, the various sources—inscriptions, literary works, temple statues, palace murals, and Dutch records—suggest that in Ramnad influences from sultanate courts were limited to certain aspects. The Setupatis' titles seem to have been entirely devoid of Persianate terms. Their clothing, including turbans rather than *kuḷḷāyi* caps, could combine Persianate and Indic elements, which by the eighteenth century were apparently no longer strictly associated with public and domestic occasions respectively.

Conclusions

Comparing all courts, this section first discusses titles and next considers clothing. We start with the political or possibly even imperial ambitions titles represented. While Vijayanagara's heirs never seem to have formally asserted their independence from the empire, some titles refer to dominance over other rulers. These include rather inventive and poetic phrases like "he whose feet are illuminated by the jewels in the crowns of prostrated kings" (Ikkeri), and "champion over those who say they have such and such titles" (Mysore).[147] But it is doubtful if such expressions signified real imperial aspirations rather than competition with other houses.[148] The surveys above underscore that the Nayakas in the Tamil area (Tanjavur and Madurai) bore few titles, which were usually limited to honorary terms, designations granted by Vijayanagara, and administrative, religious, and scholarly claims. Ikkeri's Nayakas regularly used long strings of titles, but none of these point to imperial ambitions either.

Some inscriptions of Tanjavur's Bhonsles suggest they did harbour such aspirations, but literary works and their correspondence with European powers do not underline this. Ramnad's Setupatis made even more ambitious claims, even though they likely had the least exalted status among these dynasties. Not only did they use the largest number of titles, throughout their existence they were most outspoken in their imperial claims. This ties in with the image conveyed in their origin stories: a royal house that once had enjoyed a supreme status and now reclaimed its rightful place.

Only one other successor dynasty surpassed the Setupatis in this respect: the Wodeyars of Mysore. From at least the early seventeenth century onward—while Vijayanagara's power was waning—they were regularly designated as "supreme

[147] Bhat, *Selected Kannada Inscriptions*, 167; Chitnis, *Keḷadi Polity*, 17; Hayavadana Rao, *History of Mysore*, vol. I, 35, 94-5, 507; Satyanarayana, *History of the Wodeyars*, 14, 72. The latter title, *birud antembara gaṇḍa*, has also been translated as "master of title holders."

[148] For other examples, see Chapter 6.

lord of kings of great kings" (*mahārājādhirāja rājaparameśvara*), "emperor of Karnataka" (*karnāṭaka cakravarti, karnāṭaka cakreśvara*), and similar phrases.[149] Their imperial ambitions also transpire from one of the very few letters the Wodeyars sent to the VOC. Written by Chikkadevaraja in 1681, this document was signed with, as the Dutch translated, "the most illustrious and most splendid king of the kings, god of the kings, the most learned, most fortunate, and bravest king of all" (*den doorlugtigsten en alderschoonsten coninck der coningen, godt der coningen, den aldergeleersten, voorspoedigsten en dappersten coninck*).[150] Such ambitious titles are found for no other successor house in the VOC records, but as we have seen, they often appear in documents the Company received from Vijayanagara's rulers.

Given these similarities, it seems that the powerful Wodeyars, unlike Ramnad's more marginal Setupatis, really aspired to imperial rule, perhaps even trying to assume Vijayanagara's legacy. It can therefore be concluded that, with the exception of Mysore, the titles of Vijayanagara's direct successors do not reflect claims to imperial status, whereas those of the indirect successors do suggest such ambitions.

With regard to Persianate designations, apart from one reference to Ikkeri's Dodda Sankanna Nayaka as "Keladi Padshah," no such terms are found among the titles of the Nayakas of Ikkeri, Tanjavur, and Madurai. Persian ranks corresponding to the high but formally subordinate status of Vijayanagara's direct heirs—like *nawāb* or *sūbadār*—are also entirely absent.[151] The Setupatis of Ramnad regularly called themselves *aśvapati* or "lord of horses," a phrase usually associated with the sultans of Delhi, but here it was part of a wider, universalist claim involving several other titles ending with *pati*, and this Sanskrit term was not of Persian or Islamic origin anyway. Some Persianate influence is found only with Tanjavur's Bhonsles. Besides a few personal names probably of Persian origin, they used an Islamic title in a Persian inscription and regularly added *sāheba* to their names. As several sources suggest, the latter designation stemmed from the period when the Bhonsles were military commanders under the Deccan sultanates. It functioned as a common honorific title, borne by various ranks of nobility all over India.

But again, Mysore occupied a special position among Vijayanagara's successors in this respect. Just as the Wodeyars unequivocally claimed imperial rule, from the mid-seventeenth century on they also regularly used the very designation "sultan

149 Hayavadana Rao, *History of Mysore*, vol. I, 94-5, 184, 223-4, 232, 290, 507-8; Satyanarayana, *History of the Wodeyars*, 72, 99, 129; K.C. Prashanth, "Inheritance and Legitimacy: The Construction of the Vijayanagar Legacy by the Maratha and Mysore Historians," *The Quarterly Journal of the Mythic Society* XCVII, 4 (2006), 98.

150 NA, VOC, no. 1355, f. 437: letter from Mysore to Cochin, Feb. 1681.

151 Demonstrating the Persianate influence on the political organisation of Bhonsle-ruled Tanjavur, however, the term *sūbadār* was used there for provincial governors. See Chapter 3.

among Indian kings," directly adopted from Vijayanagara and thereby reinforcing their claim as the empire's sole heirs.[152] Thus, with respect to both imperial and Persianate titles, Mysore was rather exceptional.

In sum, Vijayanagara's adoption of Persianate titles was generally not or hardly continued by its successors. It is unclear why most successors did not use such designations whereas Persianate dress was certainly in vogue there. Probably deeming the title of *sulṭān* inappropriate because of its sovereign connotations, these kings may have found lower Persian rankings unattractive, and these might have suggested a status below that of the Deccan sultans or the Mughals. Also, such titles would perhaps have made the successors' wish to link themselves to sultanate court culture too explicit, while dress was possibly a more informal way of connecting with the Indo-Islamic world.[153]

Next, we turn to Persianate influences on royal attire, particularly at audiences. To start with, both Ramnad's palace murals and reports of Dutch missions to Madurai and Ramnad indicate that audiences were not always public events, but could be of a more intimate, perhaps domestic, nature. Portrayals of such private meetings in these various sources have much in common. One of the Dutch envoy's audiences with Madurai's Nayaka in 1689 took place "three to four rooms deeper inside the palace" and "without any of his councillors." The former quote brings to mind the interior location of the second audience mural in Ramnad's palace, while the latter passage could well apply to the small-scale meeting of Dutch envoys with Ramnad's Setupati in 1709. The Telugu work *Rāyavācakamu*, probably composed at the Madurai court, also suggests there were different types of audiences as it distinguishes between gatherings with the full court and meetings with only some courtiers.[154]

Furthermore, both Ramnad's murals and the report of the VOC embassy to Madurai in 1689 indicate that royal display at intimate meetings differed from that at public audiences. At the latter events, both the Madurai Nayaka and the Setupati were portrayed—in the Dutch account and the palace paintings respectively—as dressed in a kind of Persianate attire. On more private occasions, the Nayaka was reported to wear no jewellery and the Setupati was depicted in Indic clothing. Thus, the proposition that Persianate dress was connected to the public sphere, whereas the domestic domain called for a different display, holds true to some extent, at least in Madurai and Ramnad until the early eighteenth century. In brief,

152 Hayavadana Rao, *History of Mysore*, vol. I, 224, 290, 508; Satyanarayana, *History of the Wodeyars*, 72.

153 I thank Phillip Wagoner and Anna Seastrand for discussing this issue with me. The suggestions here are fully my responsibility, however.

154 Wagoner, *Tidings of the King*, 183 (n. 10).

audiences at the courts of Vijayanagara's heirs could be of various kinds, reflected in location, company, and presentation. This diversity seems to bear resemblance to the distinction between domestic and public spheres.

But the use of Persianate dress at the courts apparently changed over time, both with regard to the style's source and its associated occasions. These developments are ambiguous, however, as all sources—VOC accounts, palace murals, temple images, and Mutiah's chronicle of Madurai (discussed at this chapter's outset)—give ambivalent impressions of royal clothing. On the whole, all courts stuck to a form of Persianate dress to some degree. Dutch reports speak of "Moorish" attire until the mid-eighteenth century, palace and temple images show long tunics, and Mutiah's text seems to refer to a clothing style resembling that of Muslims. Elaborate jewellery and weaponry also remained important elements of royal display at every court.[155]

At the same time, certain elements of Persianate dress were adjusted from its initial manifestation at Vijayanagara. *Kuḷḷāyi* caps fell out of fashion, as is suggested by various sources. Madurai's Nayakas were increasingly seldom portrayed with caps, while the relatively late Setupati dynasty was never depicted with such headgear. Neither do Dutch accounts ever mention caps for any of the courts. Instead, these sources, and modern historiography, point to a wide range of turban styles, including Nayaka, Maravar, "Moorish," Mughal, and Maratha types.[156] Further, while long tunics continued to be worn,[157] their style changed. VOC records often refer to white cloths, usually worked with gold, reminding one of the *kabāyi* used in Vijayanagara. But pictorial evidence—including temple, palace, and textile paintings—shows that these garments were not invariably white. In fact, the coloured cloaks in those images resemble the Mughal *jāmā* (long coat) rather than the Arab *kabāyi*.[158]

155 As for jewellery at "private" audiences, there may have been a difference between Madurai and Ramnad. While ambassador Welter wrote in his report of 1689 that the Madurai Nayaka did not wear any jewels during their private meeting, the mural in the Ramalinga Vilasam's back room (illustration 19) depicts the Setupati with profuse jewellery (and two weapons), even though this appears to have been some sort of private audience too.

156 In addition to earlier references, see: Howes, *The Courts of Pre-Colonial South India*, 13, 96; Hurpré, "The Royal Jewels of Tirumala Nayaka," 66-9; Michell, *Architecture and Art of Southern India*, 245. It may be noted that the small black turbans of the Setupati and his courtiers in the Ramalinga Vilasam's second audience mural (illustration 19) bear some resemblance to those used in Madurai, where they have been classified as Nayaka or Madurai style. See: Howes, *The Courts of Pre-Colonial South India*, 13; Hurpré, "The Royal Jewels of Tirumala Nayaka," figs 1-2, 4-8, 12-13.

157 For references by Jesuits to largely similar clothing (and jewellery) worn by the Nayakas of Senji in 1599 and around 1645, see: Nilakanta Sastri, *A History of South India*, 315-16; Saulière, "The Revolt of the Southern Nayaks" [pt. 1], 96.

158 Nagaswamy, "Mughal Cultural Influence"; Hurpré, "The Royal Jewels of Tirumala Nayaka," 68-9. For reproductions of Ramalinga Vilasam murals and some Madurai temple paintings depicting rulers and courtiers in what is termed Mughal-style clothing, see: Nagaswamy, figs 1, 4, 7, 13; Hurpré, fig. 3.

Given the *kuḷḷāyi*'s disappearance, the *kabāyi*'s decreasing presence, and the emergence of Mughal-style tunics and turbans, it appears that the main source for Persianate dress in south India shifted from Persia and Arabia in the Vijayanagara period to the Mughal empire in the seventeenth and eighteenth centuries. That is not surprising, since the Mughals and their local representatives, for example in Arcot, dominated the region from the late seventeenth century onward. If local kings still wished to be part of the Indo-Islamic world, it would therefore pay to follow the dress style of the most powerful Indo-Islamic court, that of the Mughal empire. This focus on the Mughals also transpires from the literary works discussed at this chapter's beginning referring to Delhi and its *Bādshāh* or Mughal emperor.

But while Mughal clothing seemingly replaced earlier Persianate attire as an inspiration, its influence was not unequivocal. Sources give various examples of royal garments that appeared to be of a Maratha style—which in turn had Islamic connotations, too. In his Madurai chronicle, Mutiah stated that in the late seventeenth century the Nayakas changed from long tunics and tall caps to Maratha-fashioned robes and turbans, making them look like what probably were Tamil Muslims. Further, royal dress in late Ikkeri, as depicted in the temple statue of probably its last Nayaka, has been labelled as an amalgam of Maratha and Mughal clothing. Also, the Setupati's turban in one of Ramnad's palace murals resembles Maratha turbans, while the overall appearance of his attire seems Persianate. It thus appears that, first, by the turn of the eighteenth century Maratha dress was strongly affecting the courts of Vijayanagara's heirs, and second, this style was itself influenced by Persianate or specifically Mughal fashion. It may therefore be that what Dutch envoys called "Moorish" clothing was in fact modelled on Persianate attire worn by Marathas.

At any rate, just as the influence of Mughal dress reflected political dominance, so did the impact of Maratha clothing. The Marathas had served various Deccan sultans and been in close contact with the Mughals, thus adopting politico-cultural conventions from them. From the mid-seventeenth century onward, they campaigned in south India, subjugating or conquering most of Vijayanagara's successor states. Consequently, the same mechanism that drove Vijayanagara's eagerness to be part of the Indo-Islamic world must have operated between the empire's heirs, the Marathas, the Deccan sultanates, and the Mughals.

This was not a simple, linear process. Several dynamics were at work consecutively or simultaneously, as the successor states variously bordered the sultanates or Mughal provinces, became tributary to them, underwent Maratha invasions, and obviously maintained legacies of Vijayanagara. As a result, their court attire could include elements from all these polities, and these styles often blended and became blurred. The designations "Persianate" and "Indic" thus appear too broad and strict to encompass the diversity of royal dress here. Both categories comprised nuances, were combined, and partly overlapped. Also, clothing styles were no longer clearly associated with the public or domestic domains, as shown by various sources.

Besides this variety and intermingling of styles, Vijayanagara's heirs seem to have differed from one another. Temple sculpture and paintings as well as VOC reports suggest that Ikkeri's Nayakas and Tanjavur's Bhonsles continued to wear long tunics on public occasions, following some sort of Persianate convention, albeit possibly in a Maratha form. Dutch records indicate the same for Madurai's Nayakas, although here temple images give a somewhat different impression. But particularly Ramnad's Setupatis appear to have become less faithful to this practice. Only for this court do VOC accounts from the 1740s onward refer to attire largely devoid of Persianate elements. Indeed, employing the terms "heathen" and "Maravar," these reports suggest Indic dress was in use at public audiences, where one might expect Persianate clothing. Yet, the Setupatis wore Persianate attire at other public events. Thus, they did not forsake the latter style, but rather the associated dress code. They differed from other dynasties in that their clothing on public occasions grew more diverse.

The discrepancy between Ramnad and other states may be attributed to several factors, one of which was possibly was the close, direct connection of Ikkeri and Madurai with Vijayanagara. Both kingdoms had been founded by men installed by the "sultans among Indian kings" themselves, and their courts were directly influenced by Vijayanagara's Persianate political culture. The Setupatis, only indirectly linked to the empire, were probably less affected by this legacy and at times chose to present themselves, as it were, as "Indic king" among the "sultans" surrounding them. Tanjavur's Bhonsles formed a special case, too, being affected by their Maratha and sultanate backgrounds and thus even less connected to Vijayanagara.

The Setupatis' exceptional position was likely reinforced by more practical factors, such as the influence of Muslim- and Maratha-ruled courts in the region. While other kingdoms became tributary to Bijapur and the Mughals in the seventeenth century, and some were later subjugated by Maratha forces, Ramnad seems to have remained relatively autonomous until far into the eighteenth century—in particular after Madurai's Nayaka dynasty came to an end in the late 1730s.[159] Hence, the wish to partake in the Indo-Islamic world (now including the Marathas) and the

[159] Swaminathan, *The Nāyakas of Ikkēri*, 68; Sathyanatha Aiyar, *History of the Nayaks of Madura*, 204-5; Kadhirvel, *A History of the Maravas*, 80-1, 89, 94-5; Schwartzberg, *A Historical Atlas of South Asia*, 46, 54; *Beknopte historie*, 87-8, 94, 96-8, 101; NA, VOC, no. 1191, f. 782v; no. 1224, f. 74; no. 1464, f. 49; no. 1546, ff. 229v-30, 245: diary of Commissioner Dircq Steur's mission to Coromandel, June 1651-Mar. 1652, report on "Canara," July 1657, letters from Cochin to Gentlemen XVII, from Nagapattinam to Batavia, Jan. 1689, May 1694. See also NA, VOC, no. 2317, f. 326: final report (*memorie van overgave*) of Coromandel Governor Adriaan Pla, Feb. 1734.

adoption of Persianate practices may have become less relevant to Ramnad than to other heirs of Vijayanagara.

All in all, terms like "Persianate," "Indic," "public," and "domestic" are not specific enough to cover the varieties of royal dress in Vijayanagara's successor states and the occasions that were—or were not—associated with them. Dualistic classifications can obscure the diversity of dynastic self-fashioning, such as clothing styles. Clearly, the way dynasties presented themselves was related to political developments. Just as such processes were frequently evolving and influencing one another, so were royal dress styles. Fitting the resultant nuances and ongoing modifications within binary models could lead to simplification. Indeed, this seems to have happened when Dutch envoys described south Indian royal attire as "Moorish" or "heathen." Ambassadors who did not use these qualifications may have been more accurate, as both dress and dress codes at the courts of the successors were often blurred.

After this discussion of connections between Vijayanagara's heirs and Muslim-ruled polities, the next—and final—chapter focuses on relations among the successors themselves.

CHAPTER 6

Mutual Relations

By the empire of Vijayanagara, at the time of Narasimha's son Krishna Raya, around the year 1520, land was leased to the kings of Senji, Tanjavur, and Madurai, who at the Vijayanagara king's coronation had to perform the duty of their ancestors as spittoon, fan, and betel [leaf] box bearer.

— *Beknopte historie, van Mogolsche keyzerryk en de zuydelyke aangrensende ryken* (anonymous Dutch history of India), 1758.[1]

Beneath his [Krishna Raya of Vijayanagara] throne stood a concourse of Rajas [kings] with their hands in an obsequious manner. He allotted the tribute –
of Mysore to his chief favourite Gangiappa, a guard ["Taliar"],
of Senji to his cup-bearer Sivamadappa Nayaka,
of Tanjavur to his betel-bearer Raghunatha Nayaka,
of Madurai, to Nagama Nayaka, an overseer of his royal oxen.

— "Mootiah's chronological & historical account of the modern kings of Madura."[2]

The Raya [Krishna Raya of Vijayanagara] having divided and granted his country to his household officers, on that occasion he granted –
Senji to Virappa Nayaka, who served in the duty of carpet-spreader,
Mysore he granted to Chennadeva Raja of the treasury,
Bijapur he granted to Muhammad Sahib, who served in the office of the falconer,
Golkonda he granted to Qutb Sahib, who was dog-holder,
Tanjavur was granted to Shevappa Nayaka, who was in the office of betel-bearer.

— "The Cheritee or actions of the Vadaka-Rajahs of Tanjore, Trichinopully & Madura."[3]

[1] *Beknopte historie*, 1-2 (translation mine). This and the following quotes have been slightly rephrased.

[2] BL/AAS, MG, no. 4, pt. 4, f. 43.

[3] BL/AAS, MG, no. 1, pt. 8, f. 71.

In the reign of this king [Rama Raya of Vijayanagara], several considerable Rajas used to attend him in the duties of the following offices:
the king of Kamboja Desam presented him with the "callinjee" [possibly a plant, seed, flower, or nut],
the Pandya Raja held his bag of betel nut,
the king of Senji carried his fly-whisk ["choury"],
the Raja of Kerala district carried his water goblet,
the Raja of Anga Desam presented him betel as his servant,
the Raja of "Mucha" [Matsya?] country's office was to dress him,
the Raja of "Goul" carried the umbrella.

— "History of the kings of Beejanagur & Anagoondy."[4]

At that time, Ali Adil Shah [of Bijapur], Qutb Shah [of Golkonda], and Nizam Shah [of Ahmadnagar]—who were cousins—were personal attendants of Rama Raya. He made –
Ali Adil Shah steward of the law court,
Nizam Shah steward of the gift menagerie,
and Qutb Shah [steward] of the beverages.
They appointed deputies for their tasks and stayed constantly in attendance on the Raja.

— "Anego[n]dici kefiyat."[5]

This emperor [Rama Raya] gave his principal provinces to his servants and slaves.
Bijapur was given to one of his slaves called Yusuf,
carver at his table, a Georgian by race.
Golkonda he gave to Ibrahim Malik, of the same race,
who was the emperor's chief huntsman.
Daulatabad went to another slave of the Abyssinian race, his chamber-servant,
and Burhanpur to the head carpet-spreader, of the same race.
In this way he distributed all the provinces in his kingdom.

— *Storia do Mogor*, by Niccolao Manucci, Venetian traveller, late seventeenth–early eighteenth century.[6]

[4] BL/AAS, MG, no. 11, pt. 3b, f. 19 (see also Mackenzie, "History of the Kings of Veejanagur," 27). I thank Arjun Bali, Bhaswati Bhattacharya, Caleb Simmons, and Amol Bankar for suggesting the meaning of "callinjee."

[5] Guha, "The Frontiers of Memory," 280-1.

[6] Manucci, *Storia do Mogor*, vol. III, 98.

[Emperor Venkata at Chandragiri reigned over about fifty-six domains ("polliams," *pāḷaiyams*), including:]
Golkonda ("Cootub-Shah-Polliam"),
Ahmadnagar ("Nizam-Shah-Polliam"),
Bijapur (?) ("Hyder-Shah-Polliam"),
Maratha lands ("Maratta-Shahajee-Rajah-Polliam"),
Senji ("Chenjee-Wurdapa-Naid-Polliam"),
Tanjavur ("Tanjavoorur-Polliam"),
Madurai ("Madura-Vooror-Polliam"),
Bidar (?) ("Culbarga-War-Polliam"),
Portuguese lands (?) ("Farafs [farangi?]-War-Polliam"),
Dutch lands ("Volanda-War-Polliam"),
English lands ("Ingreze-War-Polliam"),
Ikkeri ("Ickery-War-Polliam"),
Mysore ("Mysore-War-Polliam").

— "Historical memoir of Chundrageery."[7]

The rulers [of the "Tamils"] were the following:
King Raghunatha Nayaka ruled the kingdom of Cholamandalam [Tanjavur].
The king of Tiruchirappalli [Madurai] was Muttu Virappa Nayaka.
The previous king in the kingdom of Senji was Senji Varadappa Nayaka.
The name of the king of Ikkeri was Basavappa Nayaka.
The name of the king of Mysore was Srirangadeva.
All of them were kings without a crown.

— Tamil scholars in Tanjavur, 1712.[8]

Madakari Nayaka of Chitradurga, having established a friendly connection with and received the title of "son to the Mysore Rajas," began to invade and harass Ikkeri ["Naggur country"]. Dassappa Nayaka [chief of Harapanahalli], incited by his natural arrogance and his enmity, also looked out for some support and for that purpose made proposals of amity to the king ["Polligar"] of Ikkeri, who was much pleased therewith.

[7] BL/AAS, MG, no. 25, pt. 17, ff. 127-8 (text compiled in 1808 from various accounts, provided by "Kistna-Raja Pilla, ancient Stalla Curnum of Chundrageery [Chandragiri]," translated from Telugu to Marathi, and next to English by "Sooba Row Br.," see f. 121). For a discussion of a related text, see Subrahmanyam, *Explorations in Connected History: From the Tagus to the Ganges*, 86-9.

[8] Jeyaraj and Young, *Hindu-Christian Epistolary Self-Disclosures*, 258-9.

He therefore presented Dassappa with an elephant, standards, horses, and several other valuable gifts and gave him the appellation of his son.

— "Kyfyat of Harponelly."[9]

Tirumalai Nayaka [of Madurai] was so exceedingly pleased with the bravery of [Raghunatha] Setupati [of Ramnad] in having so faithfully preserved him and the kingdom from falling into the hands of the Mysoreans, that he was at a loss as to how to reward him. He then commended him in public for the service so ably rendered to him, loaded him with valuable presents, gave him his own palanquin, elephants, camels, and horses, as well as several trophies, and having denominated him after his own name with the title of "Tirumalai Setupati," declared that he would thenceforth esteem him as his son.

— "History of the former Gentoo Rajahs who ruled over the Pandyan Mandalom."[10]

The chief ["Poligar"] of Shivagangai, named Udaya Tevar, was dog-holder to the Setupati [of Ramnad].

— "The present Maratta Rajas who are managing the country of Tanja-Nagaram."[11]

This [Setupati] appointed the eldest son of the Pandya [of Madurai] as his *daḷavāy* [general], and the second son to be superintendent; he appointed the third son to manage the political affairs of the country, and having thus appointed those three brothers under his own order or authority, he himself reigned over the kingdom of the Pandyas.

— "History of the Satoo-Putty of the Maravun Vumshum."[12]

The king [Sriranga III of Vijayanagara] received the Nayakas [of the Tamil zone] with every mark of honour, and did not allow them to throw themselves at his feet, as was their desire and duty, but gave them a seat close to himself, where each one performed his respective office: one offered him betel, the second fanned him, and the third held his spittoon. However, the king did not allow them to perform these mean duties in person, but through their favourites.

— report by the Jesuit Balthazar da Costa, 1646.[13]

[9] BL/AAS, MG, no. 11, pt. 15a, f. 126. "Naggur" or (Hyder)Nagara is the name Ikkeri's capital acquired after its conquest by Haidar Ali Khan of Mysore in 1763.

[10] BL/AAS, MT, class III, no. 25, f. 31v. For another version, see Taylor, *Oriental Historical Manuscripts*, vol. II, 33.

[11] BL/AAS, MG, no. 1, pt. 7D, f. 66.

[12] BL/AAS, MG, no. 1, pt. 7C, f. 62.

[13] Saulière, "The Revolt of the Southern Nayaks" [pt. 1], 104.

Despite the varying levels of historical accuracy in the above quotes, both these local texts and foreign observations suggest that south Indian kings placed themselves and other rulers within some dynastic hierarchy.[14] The well-known tradition that the Nayakas of Madurai, Tanjavur, and Senji served as the spittoon-, betel-, and fan-bearer of the Vijayanagara emperor, was just one of many visions on inter-dynastic relations in early modern south India.[15] According to one quote, the Nayakas of Senji and Madurai actually started as the emperor's carpet-spreader and overseer of the imperial oxen. The Wodeyars of Mysore were also labelled as descendants of an assistant of the emperor, a guard or the treasurer, although this dynasty in fact had not been dispatched from the central court but was of local origin.

One text states that Vijayanagara's Generalissimo Rama Raya regarded kings from all over India as age-old personal servants, including rulers of some of the sixteen *Mahājanapadas* ("great realms")—such as Kamboja, Anga, and maybe Matsya—north Indian states that flourished around 500 BCE.[16] Some quotes also list the Deccan sultans among the emperor's assistants, declaring they originally functioned as Krishna Raya's falconer and dog-holder or Rama Raya's personal attendants. Another text mentions even the Dutch, the English, and possibly the Portuguese as chiefs subordinated to Emperor Venkata.

The Telugu *Rāyavācakamu* presents a dynastic constellation positioning Vijayanagara in relation to both the Deccan sultans and kings in north and east India. It refers to the rulers of Vijayanagara, Orissa, and the Delhi sultanate (the last including the Mughal empire) as *narapati*, *gajapati*, and *aśvapati*, the lords of men, elephants, and horses, respectively.[17] These kings, of which the *narapati* was most prominent, each occupied a lion throne—reserved for the most exalted monarchs—and ruled over vast, prosperous realms guarded by great deities. In this arrangement, the Deccan sultans were merely denoted as "lords of the three clans," those of Bijapur, Golkonda, and Ahmadnagar. Their lands were smaller, lay in marginal areas, and

[14] See also Ali, "Royal Eulogy as World History," 184-6; Inden, "Hierarchies of Kings in Early Medieval India"; Howes, *The Courts of Pre-Colonial South India*, ch. 1.

[15] For other instances in south Indian sources, see BL/AAS, MG, no. 10, pt. 4b: "Bijanagar," f. 69; MM, no. 110, pt. 7: "The Charythy of the Vadoka Raja of Tonjore, Trinchunnapully & Madura," ff. 2-3. For more Dutch examples, see: Baldaeus, *Naauwkeurige beschryvinge van Malabar en Choromandel*, 1st pt., 160; Narayana Rao, Shulman, and Subrahmanyam, *Symbols of Substance*, 105-6; and the quotes in Chapter 1.

[16] For similar claims in inscriptions of Vijayanagara's rulers Krishna Raya, Achyuta Raya and Venkata, see: Vijayaraghavacharya, *Inscriptions of Krishnaraya's Time*, 156; Butterworth and Venugopaul Chetty, *A Collection of the Inscriptions on Copper-Plates and Stones in the Nellore District*, pt. I, 34, 41, 77, 84.

[17] The idea of three great Indian rulers, of whom Vijayanagara's emperor was the greatest, is also found in the sixteenth-century Telugu *Manucaritramu* of Allasani Peddana, court poet under Krishna Raya. See Allasani Peddana, *The Story of Manu*, 13, 37.

enjoyed no divine protection. Indeed, this view perceived the Deccan sultans not as assistants but as demons, who opposed the gods and thus were enemies.[18]

The Vijayanagara successors states not only cultivated ties of service with their superiors, but also situated other rulers in, often fictional, subordinate positions, usually as their personal servants or symbolically adopted sons. In the quotes above, the kings of Ikkeri and Mysore recognised less prominent but powerful Nayaka chiefs as their sons, as did Madurai's Nayakas with Ramnad's Setupatis. No doubt, these adoptees were supposed to acknowledge their subordinate positions and be loyal. In their turn, the Setupatis allegedly regarded the rulers of Shivagangai as their dog-holders and their foundation stories declared that the erstwhile mighty Pandyas of Madurai had once served them as well.

That such hierarchies were not always mere fancies is indicated by the last quote, of a contemporary Jesuit missionary, saying that even during the weak reign of Vijayanagara's last emperor Sriranga III, the Nayakas acted out the services their ancestors had traditionally performed for their overlords. Obviously, all sorts of symbolic hierarchies and loyalties—acknowledged or not—existed among these dynasties, besides the many wars they waged against each other.

The relations the heirs of Vijayanagara maintained among themselves and with their imperial overlords are the subject of this chapter. While Chapters 1 to 5 treat all courts separately and conclude by comparing them, the present chapter deals with the states collectively. On the basis of both literary texts and more basic accounts of political developments, it analyses connections between the courts, both perceived or imagined—as in the quotes above—and in day-to-day practice. No systematic research appears to have been conducted on relations between Vijayanagara's heirs. Without, therefore, engaging in any debate, the present study puts forward that the successors' coexistence was typified by ambivalence and fluctuations, as their mutual contacts frequently shifted between—or even merged—amity and enmity.

Indian discourses on statecraft devote much attention to relations between states, emphasising the roles of allies as well as enemies. Best-known is perhaps the concept of *rājamaṇḍala* or "circle of kings," as for instance described in the *Manusmṛti* (VII 154-8) and Kautilya's *Arthaśāstra* (VI 2:14-40; VII 5:49, 18:1-44). In brief, this notion holds that for any king the rulers of adjacent kingdoms are his rivals. In turn, the neighbours of those rulers are his rivals' rivals and therefore his friends. This pattern of alternating circles of allies and opponents may expand endlessly.

[18] Wagoner, *Tidings of the King*, 60-9, 109-10; Cynthia Talbot, "Inscribing the Other, Inscribing the Self: Hindu-Muslim Identities in Pre-Colonial India," *Comparative Studies in Society and History* 37, 4 (1995), 708-10; Narasimhaswami, *South-Indian Inscriptions*, vol. XVI, 181-2 (no. 175); Inden, "Hierarchies of Kings in Early Medieval India," 103, 105; Sinopoli, "From the Lion Throne," 380-1.

According to the *Mahābhārata*, however, there exist neither eternal friends nor eternal enemies, and surrounding polities near and far might always shift between these positions, depending on changing circumstances and interests (II 50:22; XII 136:13, 132-5). Allies (*mitra*) are deemed so important that they constitute the last of the kingdom's seven limbs or essential elements, discussed in Chapter 3. But perhaps recognising the thin line between friend and foe, a few texts mention an eighth limb: the enemy itself (*ari*, *amitra*). Apparently, some thinkers considered rival states a fundamental aspect of polities.

Not surprisingly, treatises also advise on how to deal with allies and opponents. One early modern south Indian example is the early eighteenth-century *Śivatattva ratnākara* of Ikkeri's King Basavappa Nayaka, which draws extensively on older discourses. Besides explaining the *rājamaṇḍala* theory (V 14:31-6), Basavappa presents his view on the ancient model of the six *guṇa*s (general policy actions), concerning the various methods to approach foreign states: treaties, hostile attitude, military action, neutrality, alliance, and "duplicity" or two-sided, contradictory policy (V 11:30-102, 12:2-42). To handle rival kingdoms, Basavappa further refers to four *upāya*s (political means), another classical notion, comprising conciliation, dissension, gifts, and punishment (V 12:43-122).

Showing the wide repute of such traditional concepts in early modern south India, the *guṇa*s and *upāya*s are also mentioned in the sixteenth-century Sanskrit *Acyutarāyābhyudaya* (IV 48-52) by the court poet Rajanatha Dindima III—describing the rule of Vijayanagara's Achyuta Raya—and in the Sanskrit *Sāmrājyalakṣmīpīṭhikā* (70:56-8), thought to be linked to Vijayanagara's Tuluva court as well. Other works from this period, like Krishna Raya's *Āmuktamālyada* (IV 225-70) and Shukracharya's *Śukranīti* (I 313-14; IV:I 1-40, 99-111; IV:II 7-38; IV:V 3-11; IV:VII 7, 14-15, 222-3, 229-48, 277-89, 335-400; V 1-17), consider the enemy at length, too. Like earlier texts, both advocate a careful and practical approach, moving between graciousness and animosity, based on what a particular situation requires.[19]

[19] Scharfe, *The State in Indian Tradition*, 28 (n. 18), 202-12; Doniger and Smith, *The Laws of Manu*, 143-4; Kautilya, *The Kauṭilīya Arthaśāstra*, pt. II, 368-71, 391, 439-44; Vyasa, *The Mahābhārata*, vol. 2, book 2, *The Book of the Assembly Hall* (Chicago/London, 1975), 122, vol. 7, book 12 (pt. 1), *The Book of Peace*, 513, 518-19; Wink, *Land and Sovereignty in India*, 12-17; Heesterman, *The Inner Conflict of Tradition*, 149-50; Saletore, *Ancient Indian Political Thought and Institutions*, 294-5, 474-7; Ali, *Courtly Culture and Political Life*, 33, 73-4; Krishnamurthy, *Sivatattva Ratnākara of Keladi Basavaraja*, 41-56; Chitnis, "Sivatattvaratnakara with Special Reference to Polity"; Sridhara Babu, "Kingship: State and Religion in South India," 91; Sarangi, *A Treasure of Tāntric Ideas*, 308-10; Thite, "Sāmrājyalakṣmīpīṭhikā of Ākāśabhairavakalpa," 51; Narayana Rao, Shulman, and Subrahmanyam, "A New Imperial Idiom," 94-104; Krishna(deva) Raya, *Sri Krishna Deva Raya: Āmuktamālyada*, 318-31; Shukracharya, *The Śukranītiḥ*, 86, 271-8, 291-3, 297-302, 395-7, 471, 473, 517, 519-23, 529-32, 543-57, 565-9; Nagar, *Kingship in the Śukra-Nīti*, 85-93; Mahalingam, *South Indian Polity*, 254-5, 302-3.

Nearly all these ideas were somehow put into practice among Vijayanagara's heirs. Not all aspects of their mutual relations can be discussed here in detail, but several elements stand out. To begin with, these contacts appear to have been more often than not discordant, or at least competitive. Just as courts were arenas where kings and courtiers continuously vied for power and status, so was early modern south India as a whole an arena where kingdoms endlessly struggled with each other for dominance and expansion.

To give an idea of what the region's "circle of kings" looked like in this period: Ikkeri was involved in an almost eternal conflict with its southern neighbour Mysore, which also fought many a war against Madurai, to the south-east. Madurai was at the same time part of a triangle of ever-shifting alliances and disputes with adjacent Ramnad and Tanjavur, the latter under both the Nayakas and the Bhonsles. As the English described part of this constellation in 1643: "This countrey hath byn, and still is at present, all in broyles, one Nague [Nayaka] against another, and most against the king [of Vijayanagara], which makes all trade at a stand."[20] In 1677, the Dutch portrayed the political situation as follows:

> ... [the] heathen Neycken [Nayakas] of Madure, Masoer, and others—not understanding their own interest—are at each other's throats so bitterly, without noticing that they, ruining one another in this way, let the Moors [Muslims] become masters over them and their lands, ... the lands of Tansjoer [Tanjavur] having entirely changed their lord thrice in the time of five years ...[21]

Other polities in the area—like Senji, Shivagangai, Pudukkottai, Udaiyarpalayam, Ariyalur, Arcot, Bijapur, Golkonda, and the Marathas—also participated in what appears to have been a semi-permanent state of lukewarm war. It seems no two kingdoms were ever on good terms for a long time. Allies always could, and inevitably would, turn into rivals, and sooner rather than later.[22] Dutch records abound with references to confrontations between constantly changing coalitions of south Indian states. Secondary literature based on other sources sketches a similar picture. One example concerns the VOC's registration of the region's political developments between mid-1680 and mid-1681 at Batavia, based on reports from various local Dutch settlements. Covering a period of only slightly longer than one year, an overview of these incidents is found in table 13.

20 Foster, *The English Factories in India 1642–1645*, 115.

21 Coolhaas *et al.*, *Generale Missiven*, vol. IV, 178 (translation mine).

22 See also: Narayana Rao, Shulman, and Subrahmanyam, *Symbols of Substance*, 220-1; Mukund, *The Trading World of the Tamil Merchant*, 55-7.

Table 13: Alliances and conflicts between Vijayanagara successor states from mid-1680 to mid-1681, as recorded by the Dutch.

1680, Apr.-May	Discord has arisen between Tanjavur and Madurai; the latter is supported by Ramnad.
1680, May	Mysore has invaded Madurai.
1680, Aug.	Madurai is still fighting Mysore; Madurai has been invaded by Ramnad.
1680, Oct.	Mysore, Madurai, and Ramnad have allied against Tanjavur.
1680, Nov.	Madurai and Tanjavur have concluded peace with each other.
1681, June	Mysore has invaded Madurai; the latter is supported by Ramnad.
1681, July	Tanjavur has allied with Madurai and Ramnad against Mysore.

Source: Colenbrander *et al.*, *Dagh-register gehouden int Casteel Batavia ... anno 1680* (Batavia/ The Hague, 1912), 152, 234, 281, 538, 646-7, 727-8, idem, *anno 1681*, 315, 383, 430

Additionally, in those months there were clashes between Mysore, Ikkeri, and the Marathas.[23] Even if these developments were exceptional, they demonstrate that relations could easily oscillate between friendship and enmity. Nearly all bilateral relations changed at least once during this brief period, and some even did so twice. Quite in line with the ideas in the *Mahābhārata*, shifting conditions and practical assessments rather than fixed loyalties and old resentments apparently determined which of the *Śivatattva ratnākara*'s six *guṇas* and four *upāyas* would be employed.

An important factor in the competition and hostilities between Vijayanagara's heirs was their growing autonomy from the empire, allowing them to determine their own foreign policy. This increasing independence was a slow process that in most cases would never be fully completed.[24] Among the direct successors, only the Wodeyars of Mysore openly stopped recognising the Vijayanagara rulers as their overlords, considering the imperial claims in their titles. The other houses very rarely put their autonomy in such unmistakable terms, but for all practical purposes they too, step by step, attained independence. Manifestations of this gradual secession included failure to send military assistance to the empire, refusal to pay tribute, efforts to subjugate other imperial vassals, omission of references to the emperors in inscriptions and other texts, and actual hostility towards the

[23] Swaminathan, *The Nāyakas of Ikkēri*, 119; Hayavadana Rao, *History of Mysore*, vol. I, 290-4; Satyanarayana, *History of the Wodeyars*, 89-91. For a list of the many military conflicts in the Tamil region between 1590 and 1650, see Mukund, *The Trading World of the Tamil Merchant*, 56 (n. 6).

[24] Thus, during the zenith of Vijayanagara's power, under Krishna Raya (r. c. 1509-29), and even in the subsequent decades, one can hardly already speak of actual "successor states," let alone independent ones. Consequently, the paradox discussed in Stein, *Vijayanagara*, 121, appears to be non-existent.

empire, directly or by supporting other aggressors. The following sections discuss this process in individual successor states.

Under the Nayakas of Ikkeri, an early sign of this development is found in a Portuguese letter saying that Chikka Sankanna Nayaka (r. c. 1570-80) was formerly a subject of Vijayanagara but now attempted to subdue nearby rulers himself. Other sources say that this expansionism already started under Dodda Sankanna Nayaka (r. c. 1565-70?). It is uncertain if this was related to the recent attack on Vijayanagara's capital by the Deccan sultanates in 1565 and the subsequent takeover of the imperial throne by the Aravidu dynasty. Titles and images on Ikkeri's coins from this period suggest the kingdom still strongly identified itself with Vijayanagara.

But Ikkeri's military campaigns against its neighbours intensified in the following decades. Venkatappa Nayaka (r. c. 1585-1629) is thought to have stopped acknowledging the Aravidus as his overlords in the late sixteenth century. Notably, the traveller Pietro Della Valle, visiting Ikkeri in the 1620s, described Venkatappa as a former vassal of Vijayanagara, who since its downfall had become an "absolute prince." Still, about a decade later, Virabhadra Nayaka (r. c. 1629-44) dispatched troops to assist Vijayanagara against an attack from Bijapur.

But whatever remained of the empire's authority over Ikkeri during the reign of Shivappa Nayaka (c. 1644-60) almost completely vanished when in the late 1640s the last emperor, Sriranga III, was expelled from his capital, again by the Deccan sultans. In the late 1650s Shivappa offered the fugitive Sriranga protection and assistance to regain his throne, but as much as this may have been a sign of loyalty, it also demonstrated Ikkeri's great power. No doubt, the emperor's plight also provided Shivappa with an opportunity to increase his own influence.[25] Thus, while Sadashiva Nayaka (r. c. 1530-65?) had been one of Vijayanagara's most trusted and celebrated generals, about a century later his great-grandson Shivappa embodied the nearly reversed positions of overlord and vassal.

With regard to the Nayakas of Tanjavur, epigraphic records, literary works, and coins indicate that both Shevappa Nayaka (r. c. 1530s-70s) and Achyutappa Nayaka (r. c. 1570s-97?) remained largely faithful to Vijayanagara. This apparently included the period after the Aravidus replaced the Tuluvas, to whom Shevappa was related by marriage. Achyutappa is thought to have provided military aid to the empire and defended it against assaults from the less loyal Nayakas of Madurai and Senji.

[25] Swaminathan, *The Nāyakas of Ikkēri*, 37-8, 41, 90-2; Chitnis, *Keḷadi Polity*, 14-19; Mears, "Symbols of Coins of the Vijayanagara Empire," 79-80; Della Valle, *The Travels of Pietro Della Valle in India*, vol. I, 190-1; Saletore, *Social and Political Life in the Vijayanagara Empire*, vol. I, 301-2.

But Jesuit letters and some inscriptions imply that Tanjavur sometimes declined to send tribute to Vijayanagara and at one point even rebelled against its overlord because it, together with Madurai and Senji, no longer recognised a ruler who, as it was phrased, had deposed the lawful emperor—perhaps denoting the Aravidus' overthrow of the Tuluvas.

Under Raghunatha Nayaka (r. c. 1597?-1626), Tanjavur is again said to have stood out for its loyalty. It was the only one of the three Nayaka kingdoms in the Tamil region that chose the side of the Aravidu rulers in the long, violent succession struggle following the death of Emperor Venkata in 1614. While Raghunatha thus helped the main Aravidu line keep the throne, several literary works state that this Nayaka himself installed Venkata's grandnephew Ramadeva as the new emperor. According to the poem *Sāhitya ratnākara*, this even happened on Tanjavur territory, at the town of Kumbakonam. Whether Raghunatha actually crowned Vijayanagara's ruler or not, this seems another case of the line between overlord and vassal becoming very thin, at least as Tanjavur's own texts have it.

Finally, Vijayaraghava Nayaka (r. 1631-73), although by some historians depicted as a faithful servant of the Aravidus, appears to have acted rather autonomously. First, he failed to dispatch troops to Emperor Sriranga III against the Deccan sultanates, perhaps to not risk his own position. Further, in 1643 the Dutch noted that he had not paid tribute to the empire, while two years later, both Jesuits and the VOC reported that Tanjavur had temporarily joined Senji and Madurai in their alliance against Vijayanagara. The Jesuit Antony de Proença wrote that when Sriranga, having eventually lost his empire, sought refuge in Tanjavur around 1647, the Nayaka initially received him with gifts and a daily grant. But after a year or so, possibly again fearing for his own security, Vijayaraghava started to revoke these honours, making the emperor dwell in a forest for a few months before he approached Mysore for support.[26] All in all, under the Tanjavur Nayakas a progression took place similar to that under the Nayakas of Ikkeri: increasing independence, which was however never fully asserted.

This process seems to have been a bit more pronounced in Madurai. While the first few Nayakas here may have been generally obedient to Vijayanagara, some local

[26] Vriddhagirisan, *The Nayaks of Tanjore*, 28-31, 36-43, 46-50, 67-72, 82-90, 130-40; C. Somasundara Rao, "The Loyalty of the Nāyaks of Tanjore to the Vijayanagara Empire," in A.V. Narasimha Murthy and K.V. Ramesh (eds), *Giridharaśrī: Essays on Indology* (Delhi, 1987); Krishnaswami Aiyangar, *Sources of Vijayanagar History*, 255, 274; Mears, "Symbols of Coins of the Vijayanagara Empire," 79-80; Subrahmanyam, *Penumbral Visions*, 245; Saulière, "The Revolt of the Southern Nayaks" [pt. 2], 164; Colenbrander *et al.*, *Dagh-register gehouden int Casteel Batavia ... anno 1643–1644*, 276, idem, *anno 1644–1645*, 351, 356; Mac Leod, *De Oost-Indische Compagnie*, vol. II, 188-90; Heras, *The Aravidu Dynasty of Vijayanagara*, vol. I, 308.

source material insinuates that Virappa Nayaka (r. c. 1572-95) fought a war against the Aravidu emperor, supposedly over his refusal to pay tribute. Virappa's alleged self-willed behaviour is perhaps underscored by the fact that after about 1580 he no longer referred to the Aravidus in his inscriptions. Scholars disagree about the level of loyalty under the four subsequent, short-lasting kings, but the following decades again saw confrontations between the Nayakas and their overlords, caused by Madurai's arrears in tribute and expansionist politics.

Especially during the reigns of the brothers Muttu Virappa Nayaka (c. 1606-23) and Tirumalai Nayaka (c. 1623-59), the dynasty openly strove for more independence. In the empire's succession struggle around 1614, Muttu Virappa backed the court faction that opposed the main Aravidu branch. Furthermore, mentions of the emperors in the Nayakas' inscriptions were increasingly seldom. Also, around this time the *Rāyavācakamu* was composed at Madurai's court, a work tracing the Nayakas' legitimacy back to the now extinct Tuluva emperors and the first Vijayanagara capital while entirely ignoring the Aravidus.

Tirumalai is often regarded as the ruler who achieved real autonomy from Vijayanagara. The emperors were occasionally still mentioned in inscriptions, but more to provide regnal dates than to acknowledge their overlordship. Further, the payment of tribute became rare and seems to have ended in the 1630s, when it was reportedly replaced with the occasional sending of gifts. The Dutch wrote in 1643 that the Nayaka owed two million *pardao*s to the empire. According to the Jesuit Balthazar da Costa, in the mid-1640s Emperor Sriranga III grew so offended that he let Tirumalai know he would not rest until he had flayed him alive and used his skin for a drum to be beaten as a warning against other traitors. Sriranga subsequently declared war on Madurai, Tanjavur, and Senji in a last effort to stem their separatism. But this resulted only in greater independence for Tirumalai, who allied himself with Bijapur and Golkonda—his enemy's enemies, as political treatises would phrase it.

The tables had almost completely turned when in 1646 Sriranga fled his besieged capital. As Da Costa wrote, Tirumalai honoured the fugitive emperor with gifts, fireworks, and even the performance of his ancestral duty as imperial spittoon-bearer, albeit—on Sriranga's request—not personally. But in September 1647, about a year after his arrival in Madurai, he returned to Tanjavur as no real support from Tirumalai materialised. Despite inscriptional references by later Nayakas to the last emperor and his descendants, this event marked the practical end of the hierarchical relationship between the Vijayanagara and Madurai houses.[27]

[27] Sathyanatha Aiyar, *History of the Nayaks of Madura*, 72-4, 80-1, 87, 95-6, 98-102, 115-19, 126-35, 143-4; Saulière, "The Revolt of the Southern Nayaks" [pt. 1], 90-101, 104-5, [pt. 2], 163-4; Wagoner, *Tidings of the King*, 7-12, 23-33; Dirks, *The Hollow Crown*, 45-7; Mahalingam, *Readings in South Indian History*,

Yet more explicit was the break-away of Mysore's Wodeyars from the empire. It is thought that this dynasty was basically loyal until the reign of Raja Wodeyar (1578-1617). Around the mid-1580s he started contesting the position of the imperial governor in the Kannada-speaking area, Tirumala Raja, residing at Srirangapatnam. According to the early eighteenth-century Kannada *Maisūru dhoregaḷa pūrvābhyudaya vivara* and other chronicles, Raja Wodeyar seized lands from neighbouring principalities, refused to pay tribute, fortified Mysore town and other places, and demanded exclusive honours when he visited the imperial governor.

Further, the Kannada *Chikkadēvarāya vaṃśāvaḷi* (late 1670s) has it that a dispute arose between Raja Wodeyar and Tirumala Raja over the right to use the title "champion over those who say they have such and such titles" (*birud antembara gaṇḍa*). In the 1590s these confrontations escalated into military clashes, but Tirumala Raja was unable to subdue the Mysore ruler. Eventually, in early 1610, Raja Wodeyar took Srirangapatnam from the Vijayanagara governor, who according to several texts no longer enjoyed the support of Emperor Venkata.

Raja Wodeyar now moved his capital from Mysore town to Srirangapatnam and thus in a sense took over the imperial governor's seat, referred to as the southern throne. But Mysore chronicles claim the emperor welcomed this change and even sent gifts including jewels and robes. Judging from his titles, the Wodeyar still considered himself a vassal of Vijayanagara for some more time. Yet, until his death in 1617 he kept attacking neighbouring kingdoms and expanding his realm, a policy continued by his successors Chamaraja Wodeyar V (r. 1617-37) and Kanthirava Narasaraja Wodeyar (r. 1638-59). While these rulers formally recognised Vijayanagara's overlordship in their inscriptions, they also started bearing titles that expressed imperial ambitions and sometimes were directly borrowed from the emperors, such as "supreme lord of kings of great kings" (*mahārājādhirāja rājaparameśvara*) and "emperor of Karnataka" (*karnāṭaka cakreśvara*). With the short-lasting exception of Madurai's Chokkanatha Nayaka, no other direct successors used such designations.

Notwithstanding, like the other heirs of Vijayanagara, around 1650 Kanthirava Narasaraja temporarily offered shelter and military aid to Emperor Sriranga III after the empire's fall, yet another instance of the reversed positions of vassal and overlord. With Vijayanagara more or less vanished, the titles of subsequent Mysore kings, including (Dodda) Devaraja Wodeyar (r. 1659-73) and Chikkadevaraja

170-4; K.K. Pillay, "The Pudukkottai Plates of Srivallabha and Varatungarāma," *Proceedings of the Indian History Congress* 18 (1955); Vriddhagirisan, *The Nayaks of Tanjore*, 39-46; Heras, *The Aravidu Dynasty of Vijayanagara*, vol. I, 342-3, 348-50, 358-62; Mac Leod, *De Oost-Indische Compagnie*, vol. II, 182. See also: Branfoot, "Heroic Rulers and Devoted Servants," 174-5; Mears, "Symbols of Coins of the Vijayanagara Empire," 79-80.

Wodeyar (r. 1673-1704), displayed ever stronger claims to universal reign. By this time, Mysore had also begun to use the imperial boar seal and welcomed Vijayanagara's former royal preceptors at its court.[28] All this suggests the Wodeyars attempted to appropriate the imperial position of Vijayanagara's Aravidus, even though they still occasionally referred to their formal overlords.[29]

As for the empire's indirect heirs, Tanjavur's Bhonsles never maintained formal hierarchical relations with Vijayanagara or its offshoots, but the Setupatis of Ramnad started as local chiefs under Madurai's Nayakas. After their instalment around 1605, the Setupatis behaved increasingly autonomously in the course of the following century, the process of which involved largely the same elements as described above. According to Portuguese sources, Ramnad's second ruler, Kuttan Tevar (r. c. 1622-36), revolted against Madurai as early as 1629. His successors Dalavay Setupati (r. c. 1636-40, 1640-5) and Tambi (r. c. 1640) also had conflicts with the Nayakas, revolving around Ramnad's territorial expansion, arrears in tribute, and successions to the throne.

[28] Some sources claim that Vijayanagara's lion throne was acquired by the Wodeyars as well, via the imperial governor at Srirangapatnam. See: B. Puttaiya, "A Note on the Mysore Throne," *The Quarterly Journal of the Mythic Society* XI, 3 (1921); Seshadri and Sundararaghavan, *It Happened along the Kaveri*, 58. See also Hayavadana Rao, *History of Mysore*, vol. I, 61, 321 (n. 178). The emblem of the double-headed eagle (*gaṇḍabheruṇḍa*) may have been adopted by Mysore from Vijayanagara in the same way. See R. Narasimhachar, "The Mysore Royal Insignia," *The Quarterly Journal of the Mythic Society* X, 3 (1920), 273.

[29] Hayavadana Rao, *History of Mysore*, vol. I, 36, 39, 46-67, 81, 93-6, 131-2, 144-6, 184, 223-5, 231-3, 279, 290, 507-8; Caleb Simmons, "The Goddess and Vaiṣṇavism in Search for Regional Supremacy: Woḍeyar Devotional Traditions during the Reign of Rāja Woḍeyar (1578-1617 CE)," *Indian History* 1 (2014), 33-5, 40; idem, *Devotional Sovereignty*, 5-8; idem, "The Goddess and the King," ch. 3; Satyanarayana, *History of the Wodeyars*, 14, 16-25, 35-40, 51-3, 60-4, 72, 84, 100; BL/AAS, MG, no. 3, pt. 8a: "Mysoor Aroosoogaloo Poorvaabyoodayagaloo" [1st pt.], ff. 201-7 (translated from a Kannada text found in the Srirangapatnam palace in 1799; see Cotton, Charpentier, and Johnston, *Catalogue of Manuscripts in European Languages*, vol. I, pt. II, 39-40); no. 3, pt. 8b: "Mysoor Aroosoogaloo Poorvaabyoodayagaloo" [2nd pt.], ff. 217-18; no. 3, pt. 11: "Mysore Nagurda Poorbotara," ff. 259-60 (for a note on this work, see Hayavadana Rao, *History of Mysore*, vol. I, 8, n. 11); K.C. Prashanth, "Mysore's Claim over the Vijayanagara Tradition: A Historiographical Construct," *The Quarterly Journal of the Mythic Society* XCIII, 3-4 (2002); idem, "Inheritance and Legitimacy," 95-100; Surendra Rao, "State Formation in Mysore," 174-6; Subrahmanyam, *Penumbral Visions*, 67-8; Krishnaswami Iyengar, "Mysore and the Decline of the Vijayanagar Empire," 743-4, 746-51; Rāma Sharma, *The History of the Vijayanagar Empire*, vol. II, 14-15, 81-2, 87-8; Heras, *The Aravidu Dynasty of Vijayanagara*, vol. I, 290-3, 411-16, 419-23; idem, "Venkatapatiraya I and the Portuguese," 314-15; Rubiés, "The Jesuit Discovery of Hinduism," 224. For another Mackenzie manuscript translation concerning the evolving tension between the Wodeyars and Tirumala Raja, see BL/AAS, MG, no. 3, pt. 12: "Account of the Rajahs of Mysore from the Persic," f. 264 and next folios (translated from a Persian text, itself translated from Kannada by order of Tipu Sultan; see Cotton, Charpentier, and Johnston, *Catalogue of Manuscripts in European Languages*, vol. I, pt. II, 41-2).

Raghunatha Setupati (r. c. 1645-73) is generally considered to have been loyal to Madurai, in particular because in the 1650s he prevented it from being invaded by Mysore. Besides revoking Ramnad's obligation to pay tribute, Madurai's grateful Tirumalai Nayaka presented Raghunatha with gifts and privileges that all seem to have been aimed at strengthening the bond between overlord and vassal. The Setupati was given the Nayakas' own royal palanquin, accepted into Madurai's exclusive *kumāravarkkam*—the order of the "king's sons," comprising important chiefs ritually adopted into the Nayaka family—and bestowed with Tirumalai's personal name, so that he became known as Tirumalai Setupati. These steps were certainly meant to honour the Ramnad ruler, but also served to morally bind him to the Nayaka house and incorporate him firmly into the Madurai kingdom.

If anything, however, the Setupatis' new status reinforced their striving for autonomy. In 1663 the Dutch governor of Ceylon, Rijcklof van Goens, wrote that ever since Raghunatha had concluded a treaty with the VOC in 1658, his respect for his Madurai overlord had diminished. A campaign launched by the latter around 1664 to punish the Setupati for his expansionist actions was largely a failure. As the Dutch were informed by Governor Kumara Svami Mudaliyar of Tirunelveli in 1671, Madurai's Chokkanatha Nayaka had become so frustrated with Raghunatha's behaviour that he grew his beard long enough to tie it into knots, swearing to shave it off only after he had taken revenge.

This may have happened in 1673, when Chokkanatha demonstrated his ongoing claim over Ramnad by assassinating two consecutive Setupatis. But Madurai proved incapable of controlling their successor Kilavan Tevar (r. 1673-1710). Just two years after Kilavan's accession to the throne, Van Goens remarked that the Setupati had surpassed the Nayaka in "greatness" (*grootheijt*). In 1682, he assisted Madurai one more time by helping depose the courtier Rustam Khan, who had usurped power at the Nayaka court.

But later on, when Madurai faced other threats, Kilavan refused to send troops and he even attacked the Nayakas on various occasions, confiscating parts of their territory. Madurai's subsequent punitive expeditions against Ramnad's now fortified capital were mostly fruitless and just showed that the Setupatis had become independent for all practical purposes. Fittingly, in 1702 the Dutch stated that Kilavan had originally served merely as one of Madurai's seventy-two chieftains ("visiadoor") but now reigned over his "district" by himself (*op sig selfs*).[30]

30 Seshadri, "The Sētupatis of Ramnad," 19, 23, 26-32, 37-42, 45, 50-1, 54-9, 81, 87-8; Kadhirvel, *A History of the Maravas*, 21-6, 33-50; BL/AAS, MT, class III, no. 25: "History of the former Gentoo Rajahs who ruled over the Pandyan Mandalom," ff. 31v-2v; Jeyaseela Stephen, *Expanding Portuguese Empire and the Tamil Economy*, 118; Dirks, *The Hollow Crown*, 50, 105-6; Price, *Kingship and Political Practice in Colonial India*, 29-32; Bes, "The Setupatis, the Dutch, and Other Bandits," 548-9; Howes, *The Courts*

Illustration 21: Mural depicting Muttu Vijaya Raghunatha Setupati of Ramnad being coronated by Vijayaranga Chokkanatha Nayaka of Madurai, Ramalinga Vilasam (back room, arches), Ramanathapuram, c. 1720 (courtesy Purnima Srikrishna).

Literally illustrating that Ramnad's relationship with Madurai combined formal vassalage with factual autonomy, two murals in the Setupati palace, the Ramalinga Vilasam, portray Muttu Vijaya Raghunatha (r. 1710-25) while he is installed as king. One of these depicts Madurai's Nayaka, Vijayaranga Chokkanatha, performing a coronation by adorning the Setupati with gems, suggesting that the Nayaka's official overlordship was acknowledged (see illustration 21). The other painting shows the Ramnad ruler as he receives the royal sceptre from the Setupatis' tutelary goddess Rajarajeshvari, seemingly denoting that his real authority derived from his family deity (see illustration 22).[31]

The political developments described above make clear that Vijayanagara's heirs all became practically autonomous but differed in how they expressed this.

of Pre-Colonial South India, 85-6, 106-7; Saulier, "Madurai and Tanjore," 785-7; NA, VOC, no. 1280, ff. 13v-14v; no. 1664, ff. 175-6: Colombo secret proceedings, Mar. 1671, letter from Nagapattinam to Batavia, May 1702; HRB, no. 542 (unpaginated, 1st document, c. halfway, section "Teuverslant"): description of Ceylon, Madurai, south Coromandel, Malabar, and Kanara by Rijcklof van Goens, Sept. 1675; Vink, "Encounters on the Opposite Coast," 294; Rijcklof van Goens, *Memoirs of Ryckloff van Goens, Governor of Ceylon, Delivered to His Successors Jacob Hustaart on December 26, 1663, and Ryckloff van Goens the Younger on April 12, 1675*, ed. E. Reimers (Colombo, 1932), 5; Schreuder, *Memoir of Jan Schreuder*, 35-6, 41.

31 Verghese, "King and Courtly Life," 480-2 (figs 34.4, 34.6). For online images of most of the palace's murals, see: southindianpaintings.art/monuments/ramanathapuram.

Illustration 22: Mural depicting Muttu Vijaya Raghunatha Setupati of Ramnad receiving a sceptre from the tutelary goddess Rajarajeshvari, Ramalinga Vilasam (back room, arches), Ramanathapuram, c. 1720 (photo by the author).

The Nayakas of Ikkeri and Tanjavur seem to have been relatively restrained in this regard. While they sought to extend their kingdom at the expense of other Vijayanagara vassals or stopped paying tribute, they continued to support the empire with military aid and to recognise the emperors, making no exalted claims in their titles. Madurai's Nayakas were more assertive, waging wars against Vijayanagara, backing the emperor's opponents, ignoring the Aravidu dynasty in texts, and reducing their prominence in inscriptions. The Wodeyars of Mysore were most outspoken in their pursuit of independence, formally taking over the empire's provincial governorship of the Kannada region, regularly using imperial titles and symbols, and seemingly claiming to be Vijayanagara's main or even sole heir.[32]

Ramnad's Setupatis employed nearly all these tactics to attain autonomy from Madurai—withholding tribute and assistance, expanding their territory, fighting their overlord, bearing ambitious titles—but never fully severed their ties with their parental dynasty. Thus, with the possible exception of Mysore, independence was never wholly or formally realised but rather asserted in varying degrees by the different successors.[33] Apparently, while the line between friend and enemy was thin and could be crossed swiftly and repeatedly, the path from vassalage to autonomy was long and slow for Vijayanagara's heirs and lacked a clearly demarcated end point.

[32] It is unclear to me what caused Mysore to stand out among the Vijayanagara successor states in this regard.

[33] See also Dirks, *The Hollow Crown*, 45, 47.

Returning to the relations between the successor dynasties, these could take forms other than plain warfare, although such contacts were often antagonistic or degrading, too. Several examples are found in literary works produced at the Madurai court. Besides the *Rāyavācakamu*—subtly disregarding the Aravidu emperors by not mentioning them—there are texts that seemingly aimed at humiliating other successor states and did so in a less delicate manner. Some of these describe the activities of Madurai's Muttu Virappa Nayaka III, also known as Ranga Krishna Nayaka (r. 1682-91). Chapter 5 discusses how he disgraced the Mughal emperor, refusing to treat his slipper with the proper respect. Another story indicates how he regarded neighbouring kings:

> One evening, secretly and on his own, Muttu Virappa Nayaka rode on horseback from his capital Tiruchirappalli to Tanjavur town. Not recognised in the dark, he passed the town gate and went to the bazaar. Telling a shopkeeper that he came from "Kolvakodi"—a fictitious place name meaning something like "ten million sceptres"—he borrowed one *pagoda* from him, providing his royal signet ring as security. Later that night, Muttu Virappa dressed himself as a soldier and silently entered the royal palace. Arriving at the audience hall, he sat down close to the Tanjavur king and for a while listened to the deliberations of the court. He next inspected the rest of the palace and wrote on the door between the audience hall and the domestic quarters that he, the Nayaka of Madurai, had been here and heard all the consultations.
>
> He then quietly left and the following morning returned to Tiruchirappalli. Back home, he informed Tanjavur's ambassador about his incognito visit, asking him to urge his king to take better care of his safety and pay the shopkeeper so that Madurai's signet ring could be collected. Receiving this news from his ambassador, the astonished Tanjavur king found Muttu Virappa's message on the door of his domestic quarters, quickly sent back the Nayaka's ring, and placed guards at the gates of both his palace and his capital.[34]

Although it is specifically stated that Muttu Virappa told the Tanjavur ambassador his action was not meant to be hostile, this text appears to demonstrate the perceived superiority of Madurai's ruler over the Tanjavur king—supposedly Ekoji or Shahaji of the Bhonsle house. Evidently, the powerful, fearless, and smart Nayaka, ruling from the town of ten million royal sceptres, could easily access the political and even familial headquarters of the Bhonsles. Further, he left a symbol of his dynastic might, Madurai's signet ring, in the Bhonsle capital and then had its king pay to retrieve it and return it to him. Thus, the Tanjavur king had to be reminded by Madurai's Nayaka of his most important royal duties: the protection of his realm, his court, and his family.

[34] Taylor, *Oriental Historical Manuscripts*, vol. II, 208-10. See also Rangachari, "The History of the Naik Kingdom of Madura," *Indian Antiquary* XLVI, 105.

Another text claims Muttu Virappa also visited other nearby courts in disguise, overhearing deliberations and leaving his ring in a niche. The next day he would ask for his ring back, warning the amazed kings of their carelessness, and obviously showing his supremacy over them.[35] One vassal state unmistakably shown its place in Madurai's court literature was the principality of Ariyalur:

One day, Muttu Virappa took his horse and departed from his capital without telling anyone. His destination was the court of Ariyalur because four very valuable things were kept there: a camel, a sword, an elephant, and a white horse, each of them unequalled in the world. Madurai's Nayakas had long wished to acquire these, but Ariyalur's chiefs had never voluntarily offered them. On his arrival, Muttu Virappa entered the Ariyalur palace without permission and met the surprised ruler, who honoured him with jewels.

Meanwhile, upon the discovery that the Nayaka had left his capital, Madurai's vast army came after him. As the troops neared Ariyalur, the principality's people became scared and its ruler begged Muttu Virappa to tell him what this all meant. While Madurai's forces paused, the Nayaka explained he desired to obtain the unparalleled camel, sword, elephant, and white horse. Thereupon, the Ariyalur ruler donated the items to Muttu Virappa, but said that the elephant was presently enraged and could not be transported. Having taken the other three things, the Nayaka then mounted his horse, approached the elephant, and skilfully conducted it to his capital Tiruchirappalli.[36]

Demonstrating Muttu Virappa's physical skills and Madurai's armed power, this story glorifies kingly heroism and martial prowess. Ariyalur's four valued objects—camel, sword, elephant, and white horse—also seem related to both royalty and warfare. Therefore, the text is probably meant to show the Nayakas' military superiority over Ariyalur's chiefs. The latter had never been willing to hand over their precious assets to Madurai, possibly symbolising Ariyalur's refusal to fully submit to the Nayakas. But when Muttu Virappa forced his way in and Madurai's troops were waiting nearby, the Ariyalur ruler had no choice but to yield. Even the furious elephant, which the chief was not capable of handling, proved no match for the Nayaka.

As explained in Chapter 1, in the period of Muttu Virappa's reign, Ariyalur established commercial and diplomatic ties with the Dutch, maybe a sign that around this time its rulers, traditionally one of Madurai's Palaiyakkarars,[37] aspired

35 BL/AAS, MG, no. 4, pt. 4: "Mootiah's chronological & historical account of the modern kings of Madura," f. 68.

36 Taylor, *Oriental Historical Manuscripts*, vol. II, 210-13. See also Rangachari, "The History of the Naik Kingdom of Madura," *Indian Antiquary* XLVI, 105.

37 BL/AAS, MG, no. 1, pt. 3: "An account of the Pandia Rajahs who reigned at Madurapuri," f. 18; Srinivasachari, *Ananda Ranga Pillai*, 201 (n. 22); Soundarapandian, "Palayappattu Vivaram," 14.

to greater autonomy. The story of the Nayaka's visit to Ariyalur perhaps served as a warning against those ambitions. In any case, the text clearly indicates how Madurai perceived its relationship with its vassal.

Texts downgrading neighbouring kings were also produced at other courts. The Tanjavur poem *Śāhendra vilāsa* relates that when the Setupati of Ramnad asked Shahaji Bhonsle for help against Madurai, the Tanjavur army quickly marched to Ramnad, expelled Madurai's forces, and restored the grateful Setupati (VI 47-55; VII 1-75; VIII 28-33). This episode thus effectively showed Shahaji's great power over both Ramnad and Madurai. Also, Tanjavur's chronicle *Bhoṃsale vaṃśa caritra* declares that during a pilgrimage of Pratapasimha Bhonsle to Rameshvaram in Ramnad, the Setupati honoured him by carrying his palanquin for two miles. Further, according to a tradition in Mysore, Kanthirava Narasaraja Wodeyar travelled incognito to the Nayaka court at Tiruchirappalli and in a contest killed Madurai's strongest warrior, yet another literary claim to military supremacy. Less poetically, Ikkeri's chronicle *Keḷadinṛpa vijayam* simply says that Sadashiva Nayaka was mightier than Senji's ruler Krishnappa Nayaka.[38]

Mysore's competition with Madurai was also expressed in some of the Wodeyars' titles. Kanthirava Narasaraja bore the designation "sickle to the bunch, the four-fold army of Tirumala Nayaka," showing Mysore's alleged power to cut down the forces of Madurai's Tirumalai. Other titles likened Kanthirava Narasaraja and Chikkadevaraja Wodeyar to an elephant herd, a thunderbolt, and a trident menacing the "Andhra rulers," referring to the Telugu-speaking Nayaka kings in the Tamil region. Two inscriptions of 1663 mention (Dodda) Devaraja Wodeyar as having defeated the "Pandya king," denoting the Nayakas of Madurai. An inscription of 1679 describes Chikkadevaraja as "having conquered the Pandya King Chokka in battle," claiming triumph over Madurai's Chokkanatha Nayaka.[39] These labels clearly aimed at humiliating the Nayakas of Tanjavur, Senji, and especially Madurai.

Most other successor dynasties praised themselves in their titles as slayers of enemies, but these designations include few or no references to particular royal houses. As discussed in Chapter 5, only Ramnad's Setupatis also mentioned specific dynasties in their titles. They were called "establisher" of the "Pandya throne" and the "Chola country," and labelled *narapati*, *gajapati*, and *aśvapati* (lords of men, elephants, and horses)—respectively the rulers of Vijayanagara, Orissa, and Delhi—in

[38] Śrīdhara Venkatēśa, *Śāhendra Vilāsa*, 12-15; BL/AAS, MT, class III, no. 87: "The historycal account of the Tonjore," f. 103v; Wilks, *Historical Sketches of the South of India*, vol. I, 57-8; Nilakanta Sastri and Venkataramanayya, *Further Sources of Vijayanagara History*, vol. III, 192.

[39] Hayavadana Rao, *History of Mysore*, vol. I, 184, 508; Sathyanatha Aiyar, *History of the Nayaks of Madura*, 357 (nos 161-2), 360 (no. 186).

addition to Setupati (lord of the bridge), or placed themselves on a par with these lords.[40] But these titles denote rulers distant from Ramnad's kings, in time or in space, and appear much less degrading than those used by the Wodeyars, who were seemingly exceptional in this regard.

Notably, one designation used by the Setupati Kattaya Tevar in the years 1730-1, recorded in Dutch documents, seems to actually glorify a neighbouring ruler, now to show submission instead of supremacy. When Kattaya's reign was still unstable because of his conflict with Shivagangai's Sasivarna Tevar and he depended on Tanjavur's Tukkoji Bhonsle for his survival, he started mentioning the name of his protector before his own. This possibly was a way of showing loyalty to the Tanjavur king and enlisting his support. But in the course of 1731 Kattaya stopped referring to Tukkoji and indeed, by this time, his position was growing more secure.[41]

In addition to confronting one another on battle fields and in texts, on rare occasions rulers of Vijayanagara's successor states met in person. Probably the most detailed account of such an encounter was compiled by the Jesuit Balthazar da Costa in 1646. Describing the ongoing struggle between Madurai's Tirumalai Nayaka and Vijayanagara's last ruler Sriranga III, Da Costa relates that at one point Tirumalai invited the Nayakas of Senji and Tanjavur for a personal gathering to propose an alliance against Vijayanagara. This extraordinary meeting, in August 1645, involved three kings with an equal position. Therefore, the Madurai ruler had three palaces built—each at half a mile from the others—at the spot where the boundaries of the three Nayaka kingdoms met. Tirumalai then went to the palace constructed for him, bringing 30,000 troops and elephants, which encamped at the building's side farthest from the common border. The Nayaka of Tanjavur, Vijayaraghava, arrived at his palace with an equally large army, while Senji's Nayaka, Krishnappa, came with just 10,000 men because his other forces had to guard his northern border with Vijayanagara.

At the actual meeting, all three Nayakas arrived on richly decorated elephants, wearing exquisite clothing and jewellery, accompanied by courtiers, musicians, and soldiers. Having thus come face to face, the kings spent half an hour together without dismounting their elephants, before they returned to their palaces. The following evening, Tirumalai honoured the Tanjavur and Senji Nayakas with a banquet and dance performances. Vijayaraghava intended to host a similar event

[40] Seshadri, "The Sētupatis of Ramnad," 229-30; Burgess and Naṭēśa Śāstrī, *Tamil and Sanskrit Inscriptions*, 64, 82-3, 85, 91, 94, 104-5; Sewell, *List of Inscriptions*, 4 (nos 22-3).

[41] NA, VOC, no. 2158, f. 955v; no. 2185, ff. 1053v, 1170; no. 2186, f. 1288; no. 2224, f. 1629: letter from Tuticorin to Colombo, Feb. 1730, letters from Kattaya Tevar to Colombo and to subjects indebted to the Dutch, Feb., Aug., Nov. 1731, report of mission to Ramnad, Feb. 1731. One example, corrupted by the Dutch, runs as follows: "Toekosie [Tukkoji] Maha Rasa Coemaroe Moetoewiseija Regoenade Chedoe Padij Cata Theuver." See also Bes, "The Setupatis, the Dutch, and Other Bandits," 555.

on the next day but since his palace caught fire, the three kings were forced to move to Tanjavur for further deliberations.[42]

The ceremonial of this encounter was clearly aimed at respecting the equal status of the three Nayakas. They met at the crossroads of their realms, which must have been regarded as a neutral location where none of them was a guest within the territory of one of the others and thus placed in a hierarchical or dependent relationship. They all stayed in their own purpose-built palace, each equidistant from the others. All Nayakas brought vast numbers of soldiers, who no doubt served to demonstrate military power but were kept away from the neutral area in between the palaces. And during the Nayakas' personal meeting, they all remained seated on their elephants, perhaps because none of them wanted to be the first to alight and thus submit himself before the others. Da Costa's account therefore suggests that the Nayakas of Madurai, Tanjavur, and Senji considered themselves to occupy the same rank in the region's "circle of kings," despite the many conflicts between them over time.

Apart from this Jesuit letter, there are very few descriptions of meetings between rulers of Vijayanagara's successor states. Dutch records briefly refer to two personal encounters between the houses of Madurai and Ramnad. A document of 1688 says that a son of the Setupati Kilavan Tevar had appeared before Muttu Virappa Nayaka III at Tiruchirappalli, was "stately entertained" (*deftig onthaalt*) by him, and had been provided with a residence. A report of 1708 states that Madurai's Vijayaranga Chokkanatha Nayaka would soon travel from Tiruchirappalli to Madurai town to receive the royal sceptre and thus be ceremonially installed as king. The Setupati or his son would attend this occasion to meet the Nayaka face to face.[43]

Judging from these notes, in the years around 1700 relations between the Setupatis and Madurai's Nayakas could be cordial on a personal level, even though this period saw regular military clashes between the kingdoms, Ramnad having become practically independent from Madurai. Further, the Setupati's presence at the Nayaka's inauguration recalls the attendance of the Nayakas of Senji, Tanjavur, and Madurai at the coronations of Vijayanagara's emperors. Quite possibly, even in the early 1700s, the Setupatis still participated in the installation ceremonies of their formal Nayaka overlords.

There were many other links between Vijayanagara's heirs. Marital ties between dynasties, for instance, were quite common. As explained in Chapter 1, Shevappa, founder of Tanjavur's Nayaka house, was a brother-in-law of Vijayanagara's Achyuta Raya as their wives were sisters. Even closer connections were established when

42 Saulière, "The Revolt of the Southern Nayaks" [pt. 1], 94-6.

43 NA, VOC, no. 1454, f. 1015; no. 1756, f. 1219v: reports of local VOC envoys to Tanjavur and Ramnad, Aug. 1688, Oct. 1708.

princesses married into other dynasties. The Nayakas of Madurai and Tanjavur regularly exchanged daughters and sisters. According to the *Raghunāthābhyudayamu*, composed in Tanjavur, Senji's Krishnappa Nayaka offered his daughter's hand to Tanjavur's Raghunatha Nayaka after the latter convinced Vijayanagara's emperor to release him from prison.

As between the Nayakas, marriages also were concluded among dynasties belonging to the Maravar and Kallar castes, ruling polities like Ramnad, Shivagangai, Pudukkottai, Ariyalur, and Udaiyarpalayam. In fact, Pudukkottai's very foundation in the late seventeenth century was initiated when Ramnad's Kilavan Tevar, of the Maravar caste, installed a brave subordinate Kallar as chief of the Pudukkottai region and took his sister as his second wife. A Dutch source of the late 1670s suggests that Ariyalur's ruler was a son-in-law of Udaiyarpalayam's ruler, both of them Kallars. And Sasivarna Tevar, Shivagangai's first king (r. c. 1730-9), was married to an illegitimate daughter of Ramnad's Muttu Vijaya Raghunatha Setupati, all of them Maravars.[44]

Apparently, two clusters of dynasties intermarried among themselves: the Nayakas in the Tamil region and several Maravar and Kallar houses. The kings of Ceylon's Kandy kingdom also belonged to the former group. Both before and after the establishment of Kandy's Nayaka dynasty in 1739, Kandyan rulers approached the Nayakas of Madurai and Tanjavur for brides, albeit not always successfully.[45] It seems that only seldom was a marital link forged between the two clusters, like when, as some local texts have it, a Shivagangai princess was wedded to Madurai's last Nayaka, Vijayakumara.[46] On the whole, however, inter-dynastic marriages appear to have served as bonds between specific houses sharing similar origins. This stands in contrast to Vijayanagara's dynasties, which allegedly did not object to marrying their princesses into the Deccan's sultanate houses or even the royal family of Portugal. Despite the very different backgrounds of those Islamic and Christian dynasties, Vijayanagara's rulers apparently regarded them as holding a high enough royal status.

[44] Krishnaswami Aiyangar, *Sources of Vijayanagar History*, 286; Vriddhagirisan, *The Nayaks of Tanjore*, 48; Srinivasachari, *A History of Gingee*, 93, 107; Dirks, *The Hollow Crown*, 159-61; Seshadri, "The Sētupatis of Ramnad," 59-62, 81; NA, VOC, no. 1333, f. 104: letter from Nagapattinam to Batavia, Oct. 1678.

[45] Dewaraja, *The Kandyan Kingdom*, 33-8, 40-2; Obeyesekere, "Between the Portuguese and the Nāyakas," 167-8; and see the Madurai section in Chapter 4 and the Tanjavur Nayakas section in the Epilogue.

[46] Taylor, *Oriental Historical Manuscripts*, vol. II, 47; BL/AAS, MT, class III, no. 25: "History of the former Gentoo Rajahs who ruled over the Pandyan Mandalom," f. 39; class III, no. 82: "Account of the Rajas who held the government of Madura," f. 118v.

Finally, we return to the competition between Vijayanagara's heirs. Besides regular wars, some clashes involved creating dissension at rival courts. Chapter 2 mentions various instances of kings assisting pretenders to the thrones of adjacent kingdoms or otherwise interfering in their neighbours' court politics. Between the 1630s and 1670s, Madurai's Nayakas backed or deposed no fewer than four of Ramnad's Setupatis. In the 1680s and 1690s, Mysore's Chikkadevaraja Wodeyar gave shelter to Shivappa II and his brother Sadashiva, members of the collateral branch of Ikkeri's Nayakas who opposed Queen Chennammaji. And from the 1710s to the 1730s, Tanjavur's Sarabhoji and Tukkoji Bhonsle supported a whole series of rivalling pretenders to the Ramnad throne—first Bhavani Shankara, next Kattaya Tevar and Sasivarna Tevar together, and then Bhavani Shankara again—contributing to the creation of the Shivagangai kingdom in the process.

As discussed in the Epilogue, some rulers even attempted to dethrone or reinstall other houses. The most obvious example is the extermination of Tanjavur's Nayaka dynasty by Madurai's Chokkanatha. In 1732 Tanjavur's Tukkoji, too, tried to annihilate a royal family. Both Dutch and Jesuit sources say that in May of that year, Tukkoji's son Anna Sahib and one Khan Sahib ("Canoe Saaijboe," perhaps Arcot's General Chanda Sahib) had invaded Ramnad to place the former on the Setupati throne. But an alliance of Ramnad with Shivagangai, Pudukkottai, some Palaiyakkarars, and perhaps Madurai prevented this.[47] On the whole, however, efforts to topple other dynasties were rare.

Indeed, endeavours to re-establish dethroned houses were more common. The Epilogue considers several such cases. The rulers of Ikkeri, Mysore, and Madurai each made attempts—in vain—to reinstall the fugitive last emperor of Vijayanagara, Sriranga III. Around the 1660s, Madurai allegedly launched an unsuccessful campaign to revive Senji's Nayaka dynasty.[48] Among other kingdoms, Mysore, Ikkeri, Ramnad, Ariyalur, and even Madurai were all involved in failed ventures to help Tanjavur's Nayakas regain their throne. In the end, only Ramnad and Shivagangai ever managed to re-establish a fallen house, the Nayakas of Madurai, albeit for a very short period.

All in all, it appears that Vijayanagara's heirs aspired to dominate rather than overthrow one another. In fact, they regularly tried to reinstall those dynasties that had formed the initial dynastic constellation under Vijayanagara: the imperial and Nayaka houses. No doubt, these were efforts to gain influence through such re-appointed rulers, but courts apparently felt their interests would be best served by maintaining the original *rājamaṇḍala* or "circle of kings."

[47] NA, VOC, no. 8958, ff. 746-50: letters from Tuticorin to Colombo, May-June 1732; Seshradri, "The Sētupatis of Ramnad," 94.

[48] Nelson, *The Madura Country*, vol. III, 183: Sathyanatha Aiyar, *History of the Nayaks of Madura*, 155.

All discussed aspects of the relations between the heirs of Vijayanagara suggest that these contacts were ambivalent. The thin line between ally and enemy, mentioned in the *Mahābhārata*, manifested itself among the successor states in many forms. There was permanent competition and tension between the courts, expressed in literary texts, royal titles, battles, and even dethronements. At the same time, the dynasties frequently formed alliances, exchanged princesses, recognised each other's status at personal encounters, and tried to reinstall other houses. Dynastic hierarchies were both violently contested and ceremonially acknowledged. All Vijayanagara's direct heirs sought autonomy from the empire, and Ramnad strived for practical independence from Madurai. Yet, the rulers of these kingdoms continued to refer to their overlords in inscriptions and paintings, and—if European observations are to be believed—partook in court rituals confirming their masters' formal supremacy.

Indeed, there may actually have been no line at all between friend and foe. The successor states were seemingly allies and enemies simultaneously rather than alternately. Illustrating this ambiguity, in 1627 Dutch officials wrote that "the 3 Neijcken [Nayakas], namely of Mandril [Madurai], Sensier [Senji], and Tansjour [Tanjavur], are in friendship, yet do not trust each other."[49] Phrased differently, the kingdoms' seventh and eighth limbs—ally and enemy—were one. This ambivalence appears to have been especially prevalent among Vijayanagara's heirs. Sultanates like Bijapur and Golkonda, Arcot and other Mughal authorities, Malabar polities such as Travancore and Kannur, and the Marathas were all part of south India's *rājamaṇḍala*, but in some respects the Vijayanagara successor states comprised a separate group.

Conflicts and alliances came and went among all these kingdoms, of course, and hierarchies certainly existed between Muslim-ruled polities and the successor states, as the latter became tributary to the former. Yet, Vijayanagara's heirs established no or few marital ties with those other dynasties, seem not to have participated in their coronations, seldom mentioned them in texts or titles—apart from general references like *Bādshāh* and *Tuḷukka*s ("Turks" or Muslims)—and never made efforts to reinstall dethroned sultanate, Malabar, or Maratha houses. Only Tanjavur's Bhonsles differed from the more direct heirs to some extent, given their connections with both the Deccan sultans and the Marathas in west India.

To return to one of the questions asked in the Introduction, if we consider the diverse and ambivalent relations between the Vijayanagara successor states—merging amity and enmity on both practical and symbolic levels—it seems that particularly the empire's direct heirs formed a collective of courts and dynasties seeing itself as somewhat distinct from other kingdoms. Perhaps it is no coincidence

[49] NA, VOC, no. 1094, f. 104: letter from Pulicat to Batavia, Oct. 1627.

that a text from Mysore, the *Kaṇṭhīrava narasarāja vijayam*, which describes a festival celebrated by Kanthirava Narasaraja Wodeyar in 1647, specifically refers to the presence of envoys from Ikkeri, Tanjavur, Madurai, and Senji. Apart from some of Mysore's subordinate chiefs, no other foreign power is separately mentioned.[50]

As explained in the Introduction, the five main successors were also regarded as a special cluster by some Tamil scholars in early eighteenth-century Tanjavur, who declared to German Pietist missionaries that the kings of the "Tamils" in the previous decades were the rulers of Tanjavur, Madurai, Senji, Ikkeri, and Mysore. In all likelihood implicitly emphasising their common, specific past as vassals of Vijayanagara, the scholars further stated these were all kings without crown.[51]

[50] Hayavadana Rao, *History of Mysore*, vol. I, 187-8.

[51] Jeyaraj and Young, *Hindu-Christian Epistolary Self-Disclosures*, 258-61.

Conclusion

This research has discussed and compared court politics in Vijayanagara and its heirs in six chapters, dealing with foundations and foundation myths, dynastic successions, the power of courtiers, court protocol and insult, influences from sultanate courts, and mutual relations. Combining all findings, this concluding section addresses this study's central questions, posed in the Introduction: How did court politics in Vijayanagara's heirs compare to each other and to those in the empire itself? Can the successor states really be regarded as a specific group of kingdoms? To what extent were court politics shaped by imperial legacies, local factors, and wider developments? How can court politics and the position of kings in these states generally be characterised? And how do the conclusions of this research relate to earlier studies?

While the previous chapters compare Vijayanagara and its heirs on particular topics, this section takes a different approach. First, based on the conclusions in all chapters, it considers the states one by one. Next, it discusses the differences and similarities between the kingdoms on a more general level and tries to explain them. Finally, it compares this study's conclusions with the existing historiography.

Starting with Vijayanagara, the foundation myths of the four imperial houses contain various motifs to legitimise their rule: descent from warriors and the Lunar race, martial feats, links with earlier dynasties, divine recognition, natural miracles, acquisition of wealth, migration, clearing of land, and dynastic continuity. With respect to successions, these dynasties were neither very stable nor particularly unstable compared to the successor states. On average, reigns lasted about a decade and accessions to the throne were regularly contested, sometimes violently. But emperors were mostly followed by sons or brothers and seldom by infants, women, or illegitimate relatives. With regard to Vijayanagara's courtiers, the more prominent ones were mainly Brahmins or members of the rulers' castes. They could grow very powerful but also rapidly fall from grace. They benefitted from familial and other connections, and often combined military, administrative, and mercantile functions, simultaneously or consecutively.

As for protocol, it appears that Vijayanagara's court largely adhered to ceremonial advocated in Indian political treatises. Important aspects included audiences, welcoming and departure ceremonies, gift-giving, and other moments of contact, in person or through correspondence. The required ritual was either followed—to express satisfaction and convey respect—or breached, to show resentment. Thus, protocol often reflected rather than shaped relationships, although diplomatic humiliations could have far-reaching consequences. Finally, throughout its existence influences from sultanate courts manifested themselves in Vijayanagara, as illustrated by two aspects considered here: dynastic titles and royal dress.

Moving to Ikkeri, these Nayakas' origin stories mostly contain the same elements as those of Vijayanagara. But texts here also include two other motifs—the acquisition of royal symbols and the loyalty of servants—while they do not refer to migration and chiefly mention descent from warriors only. Judging from its successions, this Nayaka house was not much more stable or unstable than the imperial dynasties, on the one hand enjoying a longer average reign, but on the other hand seeing more undesirable rulers (minors and women) and witnessing fierce competition between two family branches for a long period. Whereas there was little difference between Ikkeri and the empire when it comes to the power of courtiers, diplomatic insult seemed a more regular phenomenon in this kingdom. That was at least the impression of the Dutch, but then they mostly experienced court protocol in times of friction. Anyhow, Ikkeri's ceremonial, whether followed or violated, was mainly similar to that of Vijayanagara. As for Persianate influence, there is hardly any evidence for this in the Nayakas' titles, while references to royal clothing are somewhat ambiguous but largely point to a continuation of the Persianate imperial dress code.

For Nayaka-ruled Tanjavur there is less information than for the other heirs, but sources suggest there were several differences with them. It appears the foundation myths of this dynasty lack some motifs observed elsewhere: land clearance and the acquisition of wealth and royal symbols, perhaps related to Tanjavur's long past as a highly fertile realm. Moreover, successions under these Nayakas indicate relatively much dynastic stability. Reigns generally lasted twice as long as in the other kingdoms, the throne always passed to sons or brothers, and competition between pretenders was dealt with quickly and effectively. Tanjavur under the Nayakas appears not to have stood out with regard to the role of courtiers and protocol. This also applies to sultanate influences, at least for the one aspect that could be considered here: dynastic titles are entirely devoid of Persianate elements.

Under Tanjavur's subsequent Bhonsle rulers, court politics were also exceptional in various respects. As with its predecessors, this dynasty's origin stories contain fewer elements than those of most other heirs. There seem to be no references to natural miracles, land clearance, and wealth, while descent is claimed from celestial bodies and kings alongside warriors, unlike in Nayaka myths. Further, although not to the extent of Tanjavur's Nayakas, the Bhonsles witnessed few succession struggles, mostly passed the throne to sons or brothers, and enjoyed comparatively long reigns—apart from a brief, atypical period of violence involving some unqualified pretenders. The same relative stability is found for courtiers, whose careers generally lasted longer and who faced less aggressive competition than in other kingdoms. Also, this court included influential Muslim officials during much of its existence. Protocol appears to have been somewhat different, too, considering the few royal audiences deemed necessary to conduct business with the VOC, the regular physical contact between the kings and Dutchmen, and the relative lack of diplomatic insult. Besides, influences from Muslim-ruled courts were rather prominent, suggested both by occasional Islamic titles and names and by what seem to have been Persianate dress and ceremonial.

The foundation stories of the Nayakas of Madurai are largely similar to those of Vijayanagara and Ikkeri. Only the motif of natural miracles is not very prominent. With regard to the length of reigns, succession struggles, and the number of illegitimate rulers, Madurai had much in common with Ikkeri as well. The kingdom was different from other states, however, in that it had two important political centres—the central capital and the southernmost governor's seat—accounting for many violent clashes between powerful courtiers' families. Madurai's protocol, and the relatively limited degree to which it was breached, resembled that of most other courts. Finally, whereas sultanate influences on royal titles are not found, the continuous use of such dress is obvious here.

As for Ramnad's Setupatis, all mentioned motifs figure in their origin myths, but this house claimed descent from warriors, kings, and, uniquely, the Sun. Successions caused more instability here than anywhere else, given the frequency of short reigns, brutal struggles for the throne, and illegitimate or infant rulers. Ramnad's courtiers seem to have come from a greater variety of backgrounds than in other states, including Brahmins, Muslims, and members of the rulers' caste. With respect to protocol, too, Ramnad stood out for the regular insults meted out to the Dutch, mostly related to the conflicting commercial interests of this court and the VOC. The Setupatis were also exceptional for their partial switch from Persianate clothing to garments with traditional, Indic connotations on public occasions.

Comparing all these similarities and differences, certain broad patterns among Vijayanagara's heirs can be observed. Ikkeri and Madurai appear to have resembled both Vijayanagara and each other to a large extent. Their foundation stories, successions, role of courtiers, protocol, and Persianate influences were all rather alike. One distinction between Ikkeri and Madurai was the coexistence of two political nodes within the latter, perhaps somewhat akin to Vijayanagara with its powerful provincial governors. While Nayaka-ruled Tanjavur was similar to the other Nayaka courts with regard to the position of courtiers, protocol, and sultanate influences, its origin myths were partly different and successions caused less instability. Ramnad was still more distinct. Its foundation stories shared much with the other myths, but its dynasty was the most unstable, its courtiers most diverse, its protocol most often breached, and its Persianate elements most variable. Bhonsle-ruled Tanjavur clearly stood out the most: in none of the discussed aspects did it resemble Vijayanagara and, by extension, Ikkeri and Madurai.

These observations underscore that the empire's direct heirs indeed formed a separate group, differing in various ways and degrees from indirect heirs. Yet, there were also variations among the direct successors, with Tanjavur in particular occupying a slightly exceptional position—as did Mysore, indicated by the few, brief discussions of this court. Several factors may have caused these differences among Vijayanagara's direct and indirect heirs, perhaps most prominently geographic and demographic aspects, dynastic origins, and broader developments in south India.

Geography and demography probably influenced each element of court politics considered here. Physical features like coasts, rivers, forests, arid zones, and mountains at least partially determined levels of population, sedentarisation, and social stratification. Consequently, they affected political mobility and access to courts, and thus helped shape the size and composition of pools of courtiers and pretenders to thrones, ultimately influencing succession patterns, factionalism, and other aspects of court politics. Fertile, densely populated, and highly stratified Tanjavur was in this respect the opposite of marginal, partly nomadic, and politically fluid Ramnad. Also, Ramnad's long seashore, strategic location, and natural focus on maritime trade contributed to its many clashes with the Dutch and showed in wealthy Muslim merchants exerting power at court and furthering Persianisation. The foundation myths of each kingdom reflect geographic circumstances as well. They either speak of territories that must be cleared of jungle, or actually leave out this motif, indicating that cultivated land was already available.

The role of the different backgrounds of royal families appears harder to determine and not to have been all-pervasive anyway. Obviously, dynastic origins shaped certain motifs in foundation stories. Men establishing dynasties in regions they did not originate from, as in Tanjavur and Madurai, are generally said to have travelled vast distances to perform heroic deeds and gain recognition from kings and deities. Texts about dynastic founders of local origin do not mention such migrations or at most refer to a round trip to be acknowledged by higher powers.

In addition, a local background may have meant that royal families had stronger connections with the society they ruled, allowing for easier access to the court, more competition, and less stability, as seems to have been the case in Ikkeri and especially Ramnad. Besides, the shared Telugu milieu of the Nayakas of Tanjavur and Madurai could have facilitated both defections of courtiers and exchanges of princesses between their kingdoms, influencing internal politics at each court as well as their mutual relationship. The Maratha origins of Tanjavur's Bhonsles and their past under the Deccan sultanates also manifested themselves in various ways, ranging from motifs in origin myths—such as dynastic links, divine recognition, migration, and royal symbols—to the role of Muslim courtiers, a pragmatic attitude towards protocol, and Persianate customs.

However, the background of royal houses appears to have fundamentally affected just some aspects of court politics, or did so only for certain dynasties. The fact that the Nayakas of Tanjavur and Madurai had foreign roots whereas Ikkeri's Nayakas and Ramnad's Setupatis were of local origin, was seemingly not an important factor in the influence of courtiers, the practices of court protocol, the receptivity to Persianisation, and the nature of relations with neighbouring kingdoms. That dynastic backgrounds were insignificant for so many facets is perhaps another indication that in the Vijayanagara successor states, kings were not automatically politically dominant figures, as discussed in more detail below.

Finally, broader developments in south India greatly impacted court politics in Vijayanagara's heirs. While even origin stories may have been adjusted over time because of such changes, external influences on other political aspects are certainly evident. The interests of states outside the group of Vijayanagara's successors could be decisive, as shown by Bijapur's involvement in several successions in Ikkeri, and Arcot's increasing role in struggles for the throne in Tanjavur and Ramnad.

Further, south India's growing overseas trade and commercialisation provided both established and aspiring courtiers—ministers, military men, and merchants alike—with new opportunities to diversify their activities, extend their networks, and increase their power. Wider political processes also brought about the adoption of sultanate practices, first by Vijayanagara and later, to some extent, by its heirs, who came to look to the Mughals. In the same vein, political developments later caused Ramnad to abandon or modify Persianate customs.

All in all, several factors, each in their own way, influenced court politics, creating variety among Vijayanagara's successors. Still, there were many resemblances between the heirs, and between them and the empire. Perhaps, those shared characteristics can be regarded as the strongest legacies of Vijayanagara, being adopted by all direct and indirect heirs, regardless of geographic and demographic conditions, dynastic origins, and wider regional processes. For the aspects of court politics considered in this study, the following similarities can be observed.

All foundation myths comprised the motifs of descent from warriors, martial prowess, ties to earlier royal houses, divine acknowledgement, and dynastic continuity. Under all dynasties, successions regularly led to competition and violence between contenders for the throne. At every court, courtiers combined different ranks and portfolios, employed family relations and other networks, and acquired great or even dominating power but could also entirely lose it again. They always included Brahmins and members of the rulers' castes. The forms of protocol, the occasions that required it, and the purposes it served—following or breaching it—were all largely the same at each court. Lastly, sultanate influences seem to have been visible everywhere in royal dress, at least for some time, as well as the *khil'at* ritual.

Those similarities were of course not unique to Vijayanagara and its successors. The Introduction explains that some of these characteristics already existed in the regional kingdoms preceding the empire. The importance attached to martial feats, religious recognition, links to older royal houses, and dynastic continuation predated Vijayanagara. The same applies to the adoption of certain Persianate customs.[1] There is relatively little information, however, about the frequency and nature of succession struggles or about the backgrounds, careers, and power of courtiers before the period of regular European reports. With regard to court protocol, medieval and earlier political treatises suggest a continuity into the early modern period as far as norms are concerned. But again, not much is known about the extent to which such standards were obeyed or evaded—and for what reasons and with what effects—until European sources become available.

Therefore, returning to V.S. Naipaul's statement quoted at the beginning of the Introduction, what Vijayanagara itself contributed to the legacies passed to its heirs, was not "little" but rather must be typified as varied. For some aspects of court politics, the empire served as a catalyst, disseminating older south Indian notions and practices over the many regions it controlled. In other instances, it played a more innovative role, generating new strategies, adjusting and combining erstwhile traditions, and responding to wider Indian and international developments. These included the ongoing influence from the Indo-Islamic world and, as a new factor, the presence of European powers, both of which caused political, economic, military, and cultural changes. Thus, lasting through the vicissitudes between the fourteenth and the seventeenth centuries, Vijayanagara absorbed elements from very diverse backgrounds and dispersed these over its vast realm. In this way, the empire had a great impact on the states, courts, and dynasties that succeeded it, albeit in various manners and to different degrees.[2]

Moving to these successors, some scholars have argued that Nayaka-ruled Tanjavur exemplified the Nayaka states—at least those in the Tamil zone—in that its ideas on rulership were typical for these kingdoms. As explained in the

[1] For such customs under the Kakatiyas (reigning until the fourteenth century), see: Talbot, *Precolonial India in Practice*, 173; Eaton and Wagoner, *Power, Memory, Architecture*, 14-17; Eaton, *A Social History of the Deccan*, 11-12, 18. See also: Eaton, *India in the Persianate Age*, chs 1-2; Flood, *Objects of Translation*.

[2] For the conclusions drawn on the last few pages, see also Stein, *Vijayanagara*, 131-46.

Introduction, the ideology of Nayaka kingship is said to have comprised the following elements: personal qualities and loyalties took precedence over ascribed, high-caste affiliations and exalted ancestry; the role of Brahmins as ministers, advisors, or recipients of gifts had diminished; portable wealth (to be spent on physical pleasures) was more important than martial skills; and royalty and divinity—palace and temple—had merged. Further, those notions would have differed substantially from earlier ideas on rulership.[3]

These conclusions are no doubt valid for general concepts of kingship found in literary works composed at the Nayaka courts, the type of source mostly used for these arguments. The present research shows there is more to say about the position of kings in the Nayaka states and other heirs of Vijayanagara if one considers more practical aspects of court politics and, in addition to Indian texts, uses European sources extensively.

With regard to this study's themes, it appears Ikkeri and Madurai most closely resembled each other. Indeed, Nayaka-ruled Tanjavur was somewhat atypical among the successor states for its dynastic stability, the relative lack of violence at court, and the absence of some motifs in its foundation stories. Besides, it seems these Nayaka kingdoms actually had much in common with Vijayanagara, contradicting the abovementioned arguments. For instance, origin myths of all houses emphasise martial prowess, mentioning the founders' descent from warriors and their own physical skills. Further, while the direct heirs did not generally claim illustrious pedigrees, they did seek close ties with earlier dynasties, both imperial and local, which apparently helped legitimise their rule.[4]

Also, Brahmins still played an important part as ministers and advisers at these courts. South Indian works describe their prominent role in the foundations of some kingdoms. In each successor state, Brahmins formed a sizeable percentage of the courtiers, serving in many functions—civil, military, diplomatic, and mercantile—and often growing very powerful, as Dutch sources indicate. It therefore seems that the break between the Nayaka kingdoms and preceding polities was not that fundamental, at least not in every respect. Ramnad, too, although it differed from Vijayanagara and its direct heirs in various ways, still shared several characteristics with them, not surprisingly given its origin as an offshoot of Madurai.

As for Bhonsle-ruled Tanjavur, some scholars have stated that much remained the same here when the throne passed from the Telugu Nayakas to the Maratha Bhonsles. Studies point to the continuation of certain political institutions, royal imagery, and

[3] Narayana Rao, Shulman, and Subrahmanyam, *Symbols of Substance*, passim, for instance xii, 54-6, 169-219; Narayana Rao and Subrahmanyam, "Ideologies of State Building," 215, 225-31.

[4] For the importance of genealogies for the Nayakas, see also: Branfoot, "Dynastic Genealogies," 368, 375-6; Ota, "Bēḍa Nāyakas and Their Historical Narratives," 186-7.

religious patronage, and to the ongoing flowering of art and literature through this dynastic transition. Others have purported that the Bhonsles forsook elements of Nayaka kingship and returned to the earlier political ideology of Vijayanagara.[5]

However, the present research suggests that the Bhonsle court also differed in many ways—origin stories, successions, courtiers, protocol, Persianate practices, and relations with other courts—from both its Nayaka predecessor and the empire, as well as from other successor states. For this study, Tanjavur under the Bhonsles has thus served as a useful counterpoint, showing that Nayaka-ruled Tanjavur, Ikkeri, and Madurai—and to a lesser extent Ramnad—resembled one another and Vijayanagara rather closely, at least with regard to the aspects of court politics examined here.

More generally, this research makes clear that the day-to-day practices of court politics in the heirs of Vijayanagara were highly dynamic. As the findings in all chapters imply, power relations were constantly evolving, shaped as they were by varied competing groups and individuals. At each court, these relations could change fast and radically and were only partially determined by formal hierarchies. Although monarchs served as the kingdoms' sovereigns and symbolic centres, in several ways they were just one of the many elements in the contest for power. Like everyone else at court, rulers were vulnerable, their actual influence depending on other parties, most conspicuously courtiers. But the latter, although collectively very mighty, were also typified by diversity and rivalry. Thus, kings and courtiers all participated in the court's political dynamics and consequently shared in and contributed to the realm's power.[6]

These observations, based on both Indian and European sources, run counter to various conclusions of other scholars on the relations rulers maintained with their courts and states. As explained in the Introduction, in several studies of individual Vijayanagara successor states, historians describe courts as largely static entities, where power relations were mostly fixed and kings acted as absolute rulers or at least dominant figures, their position generally unquestioned and uncontested. That proposition appears to be untenable, given the many instances in the present study showing that monarchs were frequently challenged, outshone, or even deposed by other, often non-royal actors at these courts.[7]

[5] Narayana Rao, Shulman, and Subrahmanyam, *Symbols of Substance*, 314-18; Subrahmanyam, *Penumbral Visions*, 149, 162, 175, 231-2; Vriddhagirisan, *The Nayaks of Tanjore*, 7-8; Srinivasan, *Maratha Rule in the Carnatic*, 11; Srinivasan, "Some Interesting Aspects of the Maratha Rule"; Narayana Rao and Subrahmanyam, "Ideologies of State Building," 228-32. See also Guha, "The Frontiers of Memory," 277-8.

[6] See also Heesterman, *The Inner Conflict of Tradition*, 113-14, 143-8.

[7] Historiographic claims of absolute rulership have been questioned in revisionist studies on many pre-modern Eurasian courts. See: Duindam, "Rulers and Elites in Global History," 4; idem, "The Court as a Meeting Point," 35.

These findings also have implications for the historiography on Indian courts before the early modern age. For those earlier phases, external sources—which may complement, contextualise, and add nuance to local sources—are scarce or wholly absent. There is no reason, however, to suppose that court politics fundamentally changed when European powers appeared in India and began creating their extensive archives on the region's political developments. As suggested in several preceding chapters, the dynamics found at the courts studied here likely characterised earlier courts, too.

It is argued above that the period of Vijayanagara and its successors saw considerable change in the region, particularly caused by Persianate influences and European activities. These created wider networks and new political, military, and economic opportunities—all no doubt contributing to the dynamic nature of the courts. But it seems improbable that, for instance, heavily contested successions with undesirable outcomes, dominant and competing courtiers, and deliberate courtly insults were largely new trends in early modern south India. One may assume that these aspects of court politics had been present long before foreign sources started referring to them. Indeed, we have seen that several of these phenomena are occasionally hinted at in a variety of Indian sources, such as chronicles, proclamations, court correspondence, treatises on statecraft, and images.

Finally, the view that power and authority at Indic courts derived from the mutually dependent king and Brahmin, does not seem easily applicable to Vijayanagara's heirs. As explained in the Introduction, this notion basically holds that the king provided the Brahmin with protection and livelihood, in return for which the Brahmin sanctioned the rule of the king. However, in both the south Indian and European sources used for the present research, Brahmins predominantly appear as being heavily involved in more worldly aspects of court politics, acting as ministers, generals, diplomats, and merchants. Only some Brahmins figure in these sources as royal preceptors and family priests, playing a legitimising role.

One may wonder whether this observation can be related to the hypothesis that in the Nayaka kingdoms the king had amalgamated with the deity—or at least the deity had come to depend on the king—as a consequence of which the king no longer needed the Brahmin's sanctioning. Thus, the latter had lost his special status and, like everyone else, became merely a servant of the king,[8] with all the access to worldly power this position entailed, of course.

But some dynastic sources do actually refer to rulers seeking legitimation from Brahmins because of their special status. One striking example concerns Madurai's temple painting that depicts a Brahmin as intermediary in the presentation of the royal sceptre by the goddess Minakshi to the Nayaka Queen Mangammal

[8] Narayana Rao and Subrahmanyam, "Ideologies of State Building," 224.

(see illustration 6, left, in Chapter 2). Notably, however, no Brahmin is included in Ramnad's palace mural showing the Setupati Muttu Vijaya Raghunatha—a near contemporary of Mangammal—as he receives a sceptre from the goddess Rajarajeshvari (see illustration 22 in Chapter 6). The mediating role of a Brahmin was apparently not deemed essential here.

Whether this contrast is related to the difference between the dynasties' backgrounds, the rulers' genders, or the images' locations (temple versus palace), it implies that in Vijayanagara's successor states kings could, but not always would depend on sanctioning of Brahmins. That rulers had several options in this regard is also suggested, for instance, by the diverse roles assigned to Brahmins in dynastic foundation stories. They variously appear as world renouncer (for Vijayanagara itself), manifestation of a deity (Ikkeri), and courtier (Nayaka Tanjavur), or are even more or less absent (Madurai, Ramnad, Bhonsle Tanjavur).[9]

At any rate, as said, many Brahmins were involved in the more worldly aspects of court politics. In such cases, their relationship with kings was often characterised by political interdependence, where power was both contested and shared, rather than by ideological interdependence.[10] Furthermore, Brahmins were not exceptional in this respect. People of very different backgrounds—like members of the kings' castes, often from the low Shudra *varṇa* (caste category), and, at some courts, Muslims—maintained similar relations with rulers.

Altogether, this study indicates that in many ways neither kings nor Brahmins necessarily occupied a special place at the courts of Vijayanagara's heirs. Rather, it appears that in the dynamic court politics of these states their positions frequently resembled those of other parties striving for power. Thus, there are several gaps between these conclusions and earlier historiography, such as research considering Nayaka kingship in the Tamil zone fundamentally different from earlier political structures, works depicting the courts of the successor states as static and harmonious, and theories on the king-Brahmin nexus. This disparity may at least partly be caused by the use of different sources and a focus on different aspects of court politics. However, the bridging of these gaps must be left to the future.

[9] I thank Elaine Fisher, Dirk Kolff, Jos Gommans, Valerie Stoker, and Caleb Simmons for sharing their thoughts on relations between kings and Brahmins in Vijayanagara and its heirs. Obviously, I am solely responsible for the ideas presented here.

[10] See also Wink, *Land and Sovereignty in India*, 67.

Epilogue

Soon after the last successions to the throne discussed in Chapter 2—so from the mid-1760s onward—south India's political and dynastic constellation changed rapidly and dramatically. While Vijayanagara and some successor states had already long vanished by this time, the remaining heirs were now overthrown or gradually integrated into the British colonial system. Despite their divergent fates, however, nearly all royal houses continued to exist in some form for a considerable period, even those that lost their thrones completely. This epilogue concerns the later fortunes of these families. But first it briefly considers the last phase in south India of the other main actor in this study: the Dutch East India Company.

During the final decades of the eighteenth century, the VOC fared not much better than Vijayanagara's heirs, as it also suffered from the growing dominance of the British. By the time the latter won their rivalry with the French, the Dutch had become a marginal player, maintaining a decreasing number of factories on south India's shores and wielding less and less influence. Before Ikkeri was annexed by Mysore's Haidar Ali Khan in 1763, the VOC had already largely abandoned its trading post at Basrur because of yet another disagreement with the Nayaka court. Hoping to revive their trade at the port under the new rulers, between the 1760s and 1780s the Dutch dispatched several missions to Haidar Ali and his son Tipu Sultan, but these yielded little result.[1]

Nagapattinam, seat of Coromandel's VOC governors and the main settlement in Tanjavur, was taken by the British in 1781. Although some places in the Tamil zone were still in Dutch hands, including the factories on Madurai's and Ramnad's Fishery Coast, it seems that after the early 1760s the VOC sent no more embassies to the remaining successors. Following a temporary British seizure of its posts in 1781-4, during the Fourth Anglo-Dutch War, the VOC went bankrupt in 1795 as the Napoleonic wars in Europe signalled another British occupation of India's Dutch

[1] For Dutch activities in the Kannada-speaking region during this period, see: Van Lohuizen, *The Dutch East India Company and Mysore*; Weijerman, *Memoir of Commandeur Godefridus Weijerman*, 10, 53; Cornelius Breekpot, *Memoir of Commandeur Cornelius Breekpot Delivered to His Successor the Worshipful Titular Governor and Director-Elect Christian Lodewijk Senff* ..., ed. J. Fruijtier (Madras, 1909), 2.

settlements. A number of these, like Tuticorin and Kilakkarai, were returned to the Netherlands' government in 1818, only to be definitively transferred to the British in 1825, in exchange for territories in the South-east Asian archipelago.[2] Thus ended more than two centuries of Dutch contacts with Vijayanagara and its heirs.

Aravidus of Vijayanagara

Vijayanagara's own demise already came one and a half centuries earlier, but since this was a stretched-out and fluctuating process, its date is as uncertain as the time of the empire's foundation. Modern historiography often presents Bijapur's conquest of the capital Vellore and Emperor Sriranga III's flight around 1646 as the moment of Vijayanagara's downfall. The loss of his realm did not however mean that Sriranga, and subsequent heads of the Aravidu family, gave up all monarchical activities and ambitions. Both south Indian and European sources show how this house tried to regain its position and continued to maintain ties with the empire's heirs, albeit increasingly of a symbolic nature.

Somewhat ironically, in his effort to recover his status, the fugitive Sriranga turned to all five main successor states, visiting them one by one. Dutch records state that in May 1646 Sriranga ("Serangerijl") was rumoured to have secretly left Vellore for Senji with a few confidants as he could not possibly pay the tribute of elephants, jewels, and cash demanded by the advancing Bijapur army. The Jesuit Antony de Proença and the VOC wrote that the emperor next stayed at the courts of Madurai and Tanjavur, receiving many honours but little support. In 1649, according to the Dutch, Sriranga—paying four elephants and 60,000 *reals* to get permission to cross Bijapur's territory—was given asylum and assistance by the court of Mysore.

Finally, in the second half of the 1650s, he was welcomed at Ikkeri, as some south Indian chronicles declare. It is thought that about 1659 its King Shivappa Nayaka bestowed on the emperor the town of Belur (or Velapuram), situated in Ikkeri's south-east. Although in practice the relationship between overlord and vassal had thus clearly become reversed, these texts seem to still acknowledge the formal hierarchy, saying that in return for his military assistance Shivappa received from Sriranga titles, jewellery, the conch and discus emblems, and a royal umbrella.

Initially, in the early 1650s, various conflicts plaguing Bijapur and Golkonda allowed the emperor to win back much of his former lands, including Vellore. English sources suggest he returned to the Tamil region in 1652. But in the following

[2] Winius and Vink, *The Merchant-Warrior Pacified*, 120-4; P.H. van der Kemp, "De Nederlandsche factorijen in Vóór-Indië in den aanvang der 19e eeuw," *Bijdragen tot de taal-, land- en volkenkunde van Nederlandsch-Indië* LIII (1901), 358-407, 471-9.

years several powers invaded the area again and after some failed attempts to involve the Mughal court in his plight, Sriranga fled his capital once more in the late 1650s. During the 1660s and early 1670s, Madurai's Chokkanatha Nayaka led an effort to reinstall the emperor and Sriranga himself also made various endeavours to establish his court at the erstwhile capitals Penukonda and Chandragiri. These actions were unsuccessful or short-lived, and by the next decade all remaining Vijayanagara territory was definitively lost.[3]

Little is known of the remainder of Sriranga's career. It seems he settled at Belur in Ikkeri, where he had already been based intermittently since it was donated to him. What is certain is that all the while, inscriptions commissioned by the emperor or others acknowledging his formal overlordship continued to be produced. For instance, the Nayakas of Madurai, and to a much lesser extent the Wodeyars of Mysore, recognised Sriranga's status in several such texts in the 1660s and 1670s. Yet, he exercised no effective power whatsoever over what were technically still his subordinates. According to an English report, he passed away in 1672 and was succeeded by a brother's son. An inscription from around 1678 mentions one Venkatapati Raya staying near Vijayanagara city, the largely deserted initial imperial capital. This may have been Sriranga's nephew, now apparently leading the Aravidu house from where the empire had originated.

Sriranga's successors, no matter how limited their power, kept figuring in inscriptions of former subordinates at least into the second half of the eighteenth century.[4] They were still honoured with such imperial titles as *rājādhirāja* and *vīrapratāpa*, and were often declared to reign from Penukonda (Ghanagiri), but references to this town were perhaps mostly symbolic. All this time, the Aravidus seemingly entertained hopes of reviving the empire: according to the traveller

[3] NA, VOC, no. 1161, ff. 824v-5; no. 1215, ff. 1030-30v; no. 1227, ff. 3v-4, 18, 25, 125; no. 1233, ff. 3, 8, 20v-1, 31, 43v: letters from Pulicat to Batavia, May 1646, Jan., Mar., May, July 1658, Jan., Mar., May, July 1660, report from the army of Krishnappa Nayaka, Jan. 1657; Saulière, "The Revolt of the Southern Nayaks" [pt. 1], 100, [pt. 2], 163-6, 169; Mac Leod, *De Oost-Indische Compagnie*, vol. II, 392-403, 407-8; Coolhaas *et al.*, *Generale Missiven*, vol. II, 478; *Beknopte historie*, 25; BL/AAS, MG, no. 6, pt. 11: "Historical account of Beedoonoor or Caladee Samstanum," ff. 78v-9; Krishnaswami Aiyangar, *Sources of Vijayanagar History*, 309-10; Krishnasvami Aiyangar, "Srirangarayalu," 30-45; Krishnaswami, *The Tamil Country under Vijayanagar*, 358-67; Subrahmanyam, *Penumbral Visions*, 54; Sathianathaier, *Tamiḻaham in the 17th Century*, 43-54; Rāma Sharma, *The History of the Vijayanagar Empire*, vol. II, 281-2, 289-93, 298-301, 304-6, 310-11, 315, 319-21; Raychaudhuri, *Jan Company in Coromandel*, 46; Swaminathan, *The Nāyakas of Ikkēri*, 88-92; Sathyanatha Aiyar, *History of the Nayaks of Madura*, 128-32, 172, 264-7; Saulier, "Madurai and Tanjore," 780; Hayavadana Rao, *History of Mysore*, vol. I, 144-6, 151, 216, 219, 222-4, 227-8, 230-1, 276-7, 279; Martin, *India in the 17th Century*, vol. 1, pt. I (New Delhi, 1981), 413-15; Love, *Vestiges of Old Madras*, vol. I, 166-8; Foster, *The English Factories in India 1655–1660* (Oxford, 1921), 92, 95-9.

[4] For a list of these Aravidus, compiled by Colin Mackenzie, see Love, *Vestiges of Old Madras*, vol. I, 72.

Niccolao Manucci, one of Sriranga's descendants approached a Carmelite missionary, urging him to request European kings to send military aid.

No assistance—from either Europe or erstwhile vassals—ever materialised, however, and some scholars suggest that the family now permanently stayed on the outskirts of Vijayanagara city in the town of Anegondi, possibly donated by the Mughals around 1700 as part of a land grant (*jāgīr*). This area had passed into the hands of the Marathas by the mid-eighteenth century, to be conquered by Haidar Ali Khan of Mysore a few decades later. While most of the house's eighteenth-century history is obscure, when the British entered the region around 1790, there was a chief at Anegondi claiming descent from the Aravidu dynasty.[5]

This was the time when texts on Vijayanagara's past were collected by British functionaries like the Surveyor-General Colin Mackenzie, and a number of such sources were in fact acquired from the family ruling at Anegondi. The concluding sections of several of these works sought to bolster the chiefs' claims to an exalted past and, consequently, their requests for some kind of restoration. Included are, for example, genealogical surveys tracing their ancestry back to Sriranga III and a declaration that the family spoke Telugu rather than the local Kannada, signalling its ongoing connection with the Aravidus' background. Probably to certify the authenticity of these statements, one work says that the respective chiefs had kept "the records of all the country." We further read that the Mughal Aurangzeb ("Allum Geer Badsha") had granted the town and "fifty palaces" of Anegondi to the family, but that Tipu Sultan of Mysore had expelled the current chief from this place. It is also reported that this chief had retaken it upon Tipu's death in 1799. These remarks were no doubt intended to legitimise the family's possession of Anegondi.

Other texts clarify why these chiefs no longer wore crowns or even proper turbans. As one story goes, when Vijayanagara's sixteenth-century Tuluva emperor Achyuta Raya fled from a battle with the Deccan sultanates, he dropped his ancestral crown, which was then seized by his opponents. To remember this disgrace and because it would be inappropriate for someone used to a crown to wear a turban, all his descendants tied a handkerchief around their head. In another version it

[5] Sathyanatha Aiyar, *History of the Nayaks of Madura*, 132-4, 356-71 (nos 157, 166, 168, 183, 206, 209, 212, 214, 224, 230-1, 233, 235-6, 241, 252); *Travancore Archæological Series*, vol. V, pt. III, 231-2; Sewell, *The Historical Inscriptions of Southern India*, 280-99, 402; Viswanatha, "The Jambukesvaram Grant of Vijayaranga Chokkanatha Nayaka," 91, 94, 96; Narasimhaswami, *South-Indian Inscriptions*, vol. XVI, x, 338-40 (nos 333-4); Nelson, *The Madura Country*, vol. III, 251; Hayavadana Rao, *History of Mysore*, vol. I, 61-2, 224, 231; Krishnasvami Aiyangar, "Srirangarayalu," 40-5; Krishnaswami, *The Tamil Country under Vijayanagar*, 363-7; Sathianathaier, *Tamiḻaham in the 17th Century*, 53-4; Manucci, *Storia do Mogor*, vol. III, 235-6; Rāma Sharma, *The History of the Vijayanagar Empire*, vol. II, 301, 329, 337-8; Sewell, *List of Inscriptions*, 253; Mahalingam, *Administration and Social Life under Vijayanagar*, pt. II, 418; Krishnaswami Aiyangar, *Sources of Vijayanagar History*, 22; Guha, "The Frontiers of Memory," 274-5; Tobert, *Anegondi*, 196.

was Rama Raya, the first Aravidu ruler, who had lost both the imperial crown and his turban when he was beheaded, after which his successors decided to tie their turbans in a different manner for as long as the dynasty would last.[6]

Despite these demonstrations of the Anegondi rulers' illustrious descent, present state, and righteous claims, their situation remained marginal. In the 1790s, the principality became part of the territory of the Nizam of Hyderabad, under whom the Anegondi chief was installed as a *zamīndār* (revenue-paying landholder). About 1800, a significant portion of the family's lands was ceded to the British, in return for a monthly pension. Subsisting on this allowance and the revenues of a few villages, the chiefs maintained their reign over Anegondi during the British colonial period. As several of them passed away without leaving sons, widow-queens frequently acted as regents and adopted male relatives as heirs, fearing that the British would declare the house extinct and revoke its pension.

All the while, the family kept its regalia, including a silver mace (depicting a warrior with a rifle), a fly-whisk, seals, weaponry, and a silver throne. Also, it continued to use Vijayanagara's old imperial title *rāya*, although in 1902, in some recognition of its past, the British conferred the line with the more general royal designation *rāja* (king). Since India's independence in 1947, the chiefs' descendants have mostly been living in Anegondi, their pension finally terminated in 1984. Around 2010, on the 500th anniversary of Krishna Raya's accession to the Vijayanagara throne, the eponymous current head of the family participated in celebrations marking this occasion.[7]

Nayakas of Ikkeri

While the history of Ikkeri's Nayakas after the fall of the capital Bednur is hazy, the moment of the kingdom's end is clear. As explained in Chapter 2, in the years leading up to this event, Ikkeri was governed by Queen Virammaji (1757-63), the widow and regent of her predecessors Basavappa Nayaka II (r. c. 1739-54) and the infant

[6] BL/AAS, MG, no. 11, pt. 3b: "History of the kings of Beejanagur & Anagoondy," ff. 22-8 (see also Mackenzie, "History of the Kings of Veejanagur"); no. 10, pt. 4b: "Bijanagar," f. 70; no. 10, pt. 5: "Traditionary notices of the history of the country," f. 80; no. 11, pt. 3a: "History of the Anagoondy Rajahs," ff. 9, 11-12 (see also Mackenzie, "History of the Anagoondy Rajahs"); no. 10, pt. 1: "Notices of the present state of the Anagoondy family, ff. 37-9 (collected at Hyderabad in 1798); Sewell, *List of Inscriptions*, 253. See also: BL/AAS, MG, no. 11, pt. 18a: "Historical account of Panoo Conda," f. 174; Nilakanta Sastri and Venkataramanayya, *Further Sources of Vijayanagara History*, vol. III, 18-19.

[7] Tobert, *Anegondi*, 26-30, 77, 156-9, 196-8; Sewell, *List of Inscriptions*, 253; Rāma Sharma, *The History of the Vijayanagar Empire*, vol. II, 338; John M. Fritz, "Krishnadevaraya in Popular Imagination," in Anila Verghese (ed.), *Krishnadevaraya and His Times* (Mumbai, 2013), 377, 379. I thank Krishna Devaraya of the Anegondi royal family and John Fritz for additional information about the family.

Illustration 23: Statues thought by some scholars to depict Queen Virammaji of Ikkeri and her adopted son Somashekara III, Rameshvara Temple, Keladi (courtesy R.K.K. Rajarajan).

Chenna Basavappa Nayaka (r. c. 1754-7), respectively. Virammaji was rumoured to have been involved in the death of Chenna Basavappa—supposedly he had caught her lying with her secret lover, an enslaved man—and afterwards she adopted another boy, a son of her maternal uncle. Named Somashekara Nayaka III, he was installed as some sort of co-ruler, but his minority allowed the queen to reign more or less in her own name, with the assistance of some courtiers (see illustration 23).

Dutch and other sources tell that about a year after the Wodeyar General Haidar Ali Khan usurped the neighbouring Mysore kingdom in 1761, he was visited by a young man claiming to be Ikkeri's former King Chenna Basavappa. Supposedly, he had secretly been spared and sheltered by his assassin and now reclaimed the Ikkeri throne. Whether Haidar Ali believed this or not, he supported the pretender in exchange for 900,000 *pagoda*s—as the VOC noted—and the port of Mangalore.

A large army was dispatched to Bednur and despite Virammaji's last-minute bid to pay an even larger sum, the Ikkeri capital was taken by Mysore on (according to a Dutch letter) 16 January 1763.

Sources agree that Virammaji fled Bednur with the minor King Somashekara before Haidar Ali's troops conquered the town, but she was quickly captured. VOC documents say she had a considerable treasure with her, which was confiscated, as were the possessions of many other Ikkeri notables. A Frenchman commanding Mysore's artillery, M. Maistre de la Tour, wrote that Haidar Ali convinced the queen to accept his protégé as Ikkeri's ruler in return for a pension. The same account has it that a subsequent plot of the new king, Virammaji, and other Ikkeri dignitaries to murder Haidar Ali was discovered just in time, upon which the queen was put to death and the king incarcerated. The latter events are not mentioned in other sources, apart from a Dutch reference to the execution of eighteen prominent Ikkeri courtiers accused of performing "satanic" ceremonies to kill Haidar Ali. In any case, it is certain that the person professing to be Chenna Basavappa spent little or no time on the Ikkeri throne. The Nayaka kingdom was soon annexed by Mysore and Bednur renamed as Haidarnagara, later shortened to Nagara.[8]

Not much is known about Ikkeri's Nayaka house after its removal. Most historians state that Virammaji was spared and that she, her adopted son and co-ruler Somashekara, and the alleged Chenna Basavappa were all locked up by Haidar Ali at a place near Bangalore. It is thought that Maratha forces liberated them in 1767 and brought them to Pune but that Virammaji died on the way there. While one tradition has it that Somashekara remained unmarried, other sources suggest he married a woman from the Maratha town of Nargund (or perhaps Navalgund), where his offspring continued to live. A son called Shivappa Nayaka, based at the town of Bankapur in Maratha territory, is said to have been in contact with the Maratha Peshwa ruler about reviving the Ikkeri kingdom, but nothing came of it.

[8] NA, VOC, no. 3086, ff. 178-83v, 266-6v: letters from Cochin to Batavia, Mar., May 1763; P. Groot (ed.), *Historical Account of Nawab Hyder Ali Khan ...* (Madras, 1908), 1-2 (for the original text, see TNA, DR, no. 720); Weijerman, *Memoir of Commandeur Godefridus Weijerman*, 53-4; Moens, *Memoir Written in the Year 1781 A.D.*, 55; TNA, DR, no. 578, ff. 411-12: Cochin secret proceedings (*resoluties*), Feb. 1763; M. Maistre de la Tour, *The History of Hyder Shah, alias Hyder Ali Khan Bahadur, or, New Memoirs Concerning the East Indies with Historical Notes* (London, 1784), 53-8; Nair, "Eighteenth-Century Passages to a *History of Mysore*," 80-5; Wilks, *Historical Sketches of the South of India*, vol. I, 502-9; S. Srikantaya, "Channabasava Nāyaka (a Review)," *The Quarterly Journal of the Mythic Society* XLII, 4 (1952), 143-6; Swaminathan, *The Nāyakas of Ikkēri*, 152, 156-62; Chitnis, *Keḷadi Polity*, 23; Hayavadana Rao, *History of Mysore*, vol. II, 427-61, 470-5, 792-804; B. Sheik Ali, "Factors Responsible for Haidar's Conquest of Bidanur," in G.S. Dikshit (ed.), *Studies in Keladi History (Seminar Papers)* (Bangalore, 1981). See also: Mahalingam, *Mackenzie Manuscripts*, vol. II, 431; Galletti, Van der Burg, and Groot, *The Dutch in Malabar*, 151-2; Bes, "The Ambiguities of Female Rule in Nayaka South India."

Visiting the area in 1801, the British surveyor Francis Buchanan met a priest whose ancestors had served the Ikkeri Nayakas as *guru* (preceptor). According to him, close relatives of both Virammaji's adopted sons, Chenna Basavappa and Somashekara, were still alive and even lived together, now in Savanur. The priest considered the former's kin as the dynasty's lawful heirs, but should that branch come to an end, the latter's relatives were entitled to succeed.

The family was mentioned one more time in 1830-1, when a chieftain named Budi Basavappa Nayaka led a rebellion in the former Ikkeri region, still under Mysore rule. Calling himself Raja of Nagara—denoting the former capital Bednur—he claimed to be Virammaji's adopted son, probably referring to Chenna Basavappa. If true, he must have been about eighty years old when he headed this revolt. This was likely the last effort to re-establish the Ikkeri dynasty. Once again it proved fruitless and no secondary literature appears to mention later activities of the Nayaka line. But the house has evidently continued to exist and remember its past until today, as it is known that its current descendants live in the town of Hubli.[9]

Nayakas of Tanjavur

Compared to their Ikkeri counterparts, the Nayakas of Tanjavur initially seemed more successful in regaining their throne after they lost it. Yet, their fall was a dramatic event, recognised even by the Dutch, who, in a rare case of sympathy, referred to the dynasty's fate as "unfortunate" (*ongeluckig*), "disastrous" (*rampsalig*), and "miserable" (*ellendich*). Indeed, they almost became melancholic when, upon hearing of the kingdom's end, they pondered: "so it goes in this strange ticking [*wonderlijck geticktack*] of the world; thus people great and small play their role and all get their share."[10]

The house's demise began in 1673 with the tragic death of its last king with actual power, Vijayaraghava Nayaka—in his late fifties according to Dutch records, in his eighties as local texts have it. In September of that year, Madurai's ruler

[9] Swaminathan, *The Nāyakas of Ikkēri*, 160-1; Chitnis, *Keḷadi Polity*, 23; Hayavadana Rao, *History of Mysore*, vol. II (Bangalore, 1945), 452; Mahalingam, *Mackenzie Manuscripts*, vol. II, 418-19; Buchanan, *A Journey from Madras*, vol. III, 263-4; Wilks, *Historical Sketches of the South of India*, vol. I, 510; Simmons, *Devotional Sovereignty*, 13-14; Nair, "Eighteenth-Century Passages to a *History of Mysore*," 103 (n. 72); Lewis Rice, *Mysore and Coorg*, 160-1; Srikantaya, "Channabasava Nāyaka," 145. I thank Venkatesh Jois Keladi for information on the present members of the family.

[10] NA, VOC, no. 1291, f. 594v; no. 1295, ff. 129v, 132; no. 1298, ff. 286, 362v, 583v; no. 1302, ff. 611v, 617v; no. 1329, f. 1172: letters from Teganapatnam to St. Thomé and Rijcklof van Goens, from Colombo and Nagapattinam to Batavia, from Cochin to Gentlemen XVII, from Van Goens to Chengamaladasa and Pulicat, Oct.-Nov. 1673, June-July 1674, report of mission to Tanjavur, Jan. 1677.

Chokkanatha Nayaka besieged and starved the Tanjavur capital with his superior army, but rather than surrender, Vijayaraghava chose to fight and risk death in battle, with his son and destined successor Mannarudeva. The night before, inside Tanjavur's fort, Vijayaraghava had all his other offspring, wives and concubines, and royal treasures burnt, to prevent his enemy from laying hands on them. Perhaps illustrating his determination, a local text states that while Chokkanatha's troops approached, Vijayaraghava exclaimed:

> The celestial Rangasvami is on our side,
> what son of a whore dares to come against me?[11]

Notwithstanding the blessings of Rangasvami—possibly denoting Vishnu's form Ranganatha at the Srirangam Temple—Vijayaraghava, Mannarudeva, and 150 of their best fighters fell in combat on 29 September, near the Rajagopalasvami Temple north of the Tanjavur palace, as the VOC wrote. Marking Madurai's triumph, their heads were sent to Chokkanatha.[12] Some weeks later, the Dutch heard a rumour that the Madurai king had treated his dead opponents with utter disrespect: apparently unimpressed by their heroic deaths, he reportedly hacked Vijayaraghava's head in two and kicked Mannarudeva's head with his foot.[13]

South Indian works such as the *Tañjāvūri āndhra rājula caritra* declare that Madurai's invasion was caused by Vijayaraghava's refusal to offer his daughter as wife to Chokkanatha. The Venetian traveller Niccolao Manucci adds that the

11 BL/AAS, no. 1, pt. 7D: "The present Maratta Rajas who are managing the country of Tanja-Nagaram," f. 67. In this Mackenzie manuscript, the original Telugu is rendered as: "Nama-coo runga swamy raja-coloodoo woonnaroo / Yavoor-dâ mânâ-minda vochadee sotoo-codookâ." Maybe diminishing the plausibility that these were the Nayaka's words, in this text it was Ekoji Bhonsle's troops who killed Vijayaraghava. See f. 68.

12 Another account, recorded by Lutheran missionaries in the 1730s, states that Vijayaraghava was caught alive by Madurai's forces and wished to die honourably by being trampled by an elephant. See Utz, "Cultural Exchange, Imperialist Violence, and Pious Missions," 34. A partly similar story is found in BL/AAS, MG, no. 1, pt. 8: "The Cheritee or actions of the Vadaka-Rajahs of Tanjore, Trichinopully & Madura," f. 73. For yet another, slightly different description, given by Tanjavur scholars in 1712, see Jeyaraj and Young, *Hindu-Christian Epistolary Self-Disclosures*, 264. For Vijayaraghava's connection with the deity Ranganatha at Srirangam, see also Narayana Rao, Shulman, and Subrahmanyam, *Symbols of Substance*, 55, 69, 308.

13 NA, VOC, no. 1291, f. 594v; no. 1295, ff. 127v, 129v; no. 1329, f. 1172: letters from Nagapattinam and Teganapatnam to Batavia and St. Thomé, from Cochin to Gentlemen XVII, Oct.-Nov. 1673, report of mission to Tanjavur, Jan. 1677. For a translation of the first passage, see Narayana Rao, Shulman, and Subrahmanyam, *Symbols of Substance*, 311. According to Tanjavur scholars in 1712, Chokkanatha Nayaka treated Vijayaraghava's head respectfully and had it cremated. See Jeyaraj and Young, *Hindu-Christian Epistolary Self-Disclosures*, 264.

princess' exceptional beauty made the Madurai king propose this marriage. It is not exactly clear why Vijayaraghava would have declined Chokkanatha's request. Manucci writes that the Tanjavur Nayaka considered his own house to have a higher status than the Madurai dynasty, but some local texts and European reports say the two families had exchanged several brides since the sixteenth century.

Other sources claim Vijayaraghava regarded only Chokkanatha as inferior, as his mother was not his father's principal queen but a secondary wife, belonging to the agricultural Vellala caste. The *Tañjāvūri āndhra rājula caritra* states that Chokkanatha's grandfather Tirumalai Nayaka had married but then killed an earlier Tanjavur princess, probably an aunt of Vijayaraghava, causing Tanjavur's current rejection. Anyhow, Vijayaraghava's humiliating reception of Madurai's delegation asking for the princess' hand would have contributed to Chokkanatha's indignation, further inciting him to declare war on Tanjavur. As explained in Chapter 4, one south Indian text has it that Vijayaraghava had Madurai's ambassador beaten up, branded with a red sign, placed on an ass, and dismissed.

However, VOC records have led historians to argue that Madurai's attack resulted from wider political developments. Thus, following earlier regional disputes, Ramnad's conquest of parts of Tanjavur in 1670 had prompted Vijayaraghava to ask Madurai's Chokkanatha for military support. The latter expelled Ramnad's forces but the Tanjavur king then failed to pay the money promised to Madurai in return for its help. In a complete reversal of alliances, Chokkanatha now occupied much of Tanjavur's territory, making Vijayaraghava dispatch his circa thirteen-year old son Chengamaladasa to Ramnad to request assistance. But while on the way to back Tanjavur, Ramnad's Setupati, Surya Tevar, was captured by Madurai troops, allowing Chokkanatha to focus on the subjugation of Vijayaraghava. This, then, was the context of Madurai's siege of the Tanjavur capital.

Yet, while these events must have contributed to the animosity between Vijayaraghava and Chokkanatha, some VOC documents suggest that local texts were at least partly right about the *casus belli*. A report by the Dutch chief of Tuticorin, Marten Huijsman, from March 1674 explains that when Vijayaraghava asked Chokkanatha for support against Ramnad, he sent Tiruvenkatanatha Ayya ("Tirewengedenaderaijen," see Chapter 3) as his envoy. This Brahmin enlisted Chokkanatha's aid, but with the condition that Tanjavur indemnify the Madurai king. Greatly annoyed by this stipulation, Vijayaraghava was furious with Tiruvenkatanatha, causing the latter to defect to Madurai where he quickly gained prominence. Seeking revenge, the Tanjavur Nayaka harassed Tiruvenkatanatha's wife, children, and friends, who had stayed behind in Tanjavur. Thereupon, as the VOC chief noted, the Brahmin convinced Chokkanatha to attack Vijayaraghava, referring to the latter's refusal to let the Madurai king marry a Tanjavur princess.

Even if this insult was just a pretext for the war, it was apparently a serious enough issue to justify the assault. It therefore seems it was a combination of regional politics and inter-dynastic humiliation that led to the demise of Tanjavur's Nayaka house.[14]

The period immediately after Tanjavur's fall witnessed what may have been the closest Dutch engagement with a Vijayanagara successor dynasty. For not all of Vijayaraghava's progeny had died in the confrontation with Madurai. The *Tañjāvūri āndhra rājula caritra*, VOC records, and other sources relate that an infant son of the Nayaka, the aforementioned Chengamaladasa, escaped the massacre. The first of these sources states that the boy was a toddler who at the last moment, together with his mother's valuable jewellery, was smuggled out of the beleaguered Tanjavur palace by a nurse. Dutch documents suggest he was in his early teens and managed to flee when Madurai caught the Setupati Surya Tevar during their journey together from Ramnad to Tanjavur. Whatever saved Chengamaladasa, it was the beginning of a long quest around south India to win back his ancestral throne.[15]

[14] NA, VOC, no. 1274, ff. 13v, 206-7v; no. 1277, f. 1571; no. 1279, f. 748; no. 1282, ff. 893v-4; no. 1285, f. 395; no. 1288, ff. 178, 201, 214, 232v; no. 1291, ff. 515v, 531; no. 1304, ff. 323-3v; no. 2631, f. 421: letters from Colombo and Pulicat to Gentlemen XVII and Batavia, Sept., Nov. 1670, Sept.-Oct. 1671, Feb.-Mar., Oct.-Nov. 1672, Feb., Apr. 1673, letter from Ramnad to Jaffna, Oct. 1670, report of Tuticorin's chief (*opperhoofd*), Mar. 1674, final report (*memorie van overgave*) of Jacob Mossel, Feb. 1744; Narayana Rao, Shulman, and Subrahmanyam, *Symbols of Substance*, 305-12; Taylor, *Oriental Historical Manuscripts*, vol. II, 191-7; Krishnaswami Aiyangar, *Sources of Vijayanagar History*, 260, 324-5; BL/AAS, MG, no. 1, pt. 7D: "The present Maratta Rajas who are managing the country of Tanja-Nagaram," f. 67; no. 1, pt. 8: "The Cheritee or actions of the Vadaka-Rajahs of Tanjore, Trichinopully & Madura," f. 73; no. 1, pt. 24: "The Kyfeyat of Aachoota Bhoopal Naiq," ff. 185-6; no. 4, pt. 4: "Mootiah's chronological & historical account of the modern kings of Madura," ff. 57-8, 64; MM, no. 110, pt. 7: "The Charythy of the Vadoka Raja of Tonjore, Trinchunnapully & Madura," ff. 5-6; *Beknopte Historie*, 87; Saulier, "Madurai and Tanjore," 788; Rubiés, "The Jesuit Discovery of Hinduism," 254; Vink, *Mission to Madurai*, 262 (n. 2), 292, 296-8, 347-8; idem, "Encounters on the Opposite Coast," 288-9, 316; Manucci, *Storia do Mogor*, vol. III, 103-5; Jeyaraj and Young, *Hindu-Christian Epistolary Self-Disclosures*, 263-4; Vriddhagirisan, *The Nayaks of Tanjore*, 149-54; Sathyanatha Aiyar, *History of the Nayaks of Madura*, 101, 163-5, 279; Rangachari, "The History of the Naik Kingdom of Madura," *Indian Antiquary* XLVI, 58-62; Srinivasan, *Maratha Rule in the Carnatic*, 124-7; Sathianathaier, *Tamil̲aham in the 17th Century*, 84-8. See also: NA, VOC, no. 1246, f. 497; no. 1284, f. 1928v; no. 1295, ff. 54v, 59, 82: letters from Pulicat and Nagapattinam to Batavia, Feb. 1664, Feb. 1671, Jan.-Feb., Apr. 1673; BL/AAS, MG, no. 4, pt. 4: "Mootiah's chronological & historical account of the modern kings of Madura," f. 183.

[15] Vriddhagirisan, *The Nayaks of Tanjore*, 162-4 (ns 2-4); Krishnaswami Aiyangar, *Sources of Vijayanagar History*, 325-7; Taylor, *Oriental Historical Manuscripts*, vol. II, 197-203; Narayana Rao, Shulman, and Subrahmanyam, *Symbols of Substance*, 310-11. According to the text quoted in Taylor, Chengamaladasa was a son of Vijayaraghava's son Mannarudeva.

About two weeks after Vijayaraghava's death, VOC officials wrote that Chengamaladasa and an accompanying nurse ("amme") had appeared at Tranquebar, perhaps seeking shelter with the Danes. However, two days later the prince sailed north to stay with a former councillor at the port of Teganapatnam, at that time governed by Bijapur and also the site of a Dutch trading post. No doubt aware of the fugitive's royal status and the potential benefits of a coalition with him, the VOC for once gave up its insistence on political neutrality and approached Chengamaladasa to offer him protection and support to regain his kingdom. Although Bijapur and Mysore made similar proposals, the prince eagerly accepted the VOC's help. But soon after he was honourably welcomed at the Dutch factory, to be shipped to the Company's regional headquarters at Nagapattinam, Bijapur authorities forcibly removed him to nearby Cuddalore. They justified this by arguing that Chengamaladasa was staying in their territory, Nayaka Tanjavur had been tributary to them, and the VOC should stick to commercial activities without meddling in state affairs.[16]

It is not entirely clear what happened next to Chengamaladasa, but both the *Tañjāvūri āndhra rājula caritra* and letters by the prince himself to the Dutch from 1674 state that he—likely together with his Brahmin aide Venkanna, Tanjavur's former *rāyasam* (secretary)—now requested Bijapur's assistance. The Bijapur sultan, probably seeing an opportunity to increase his influence, then dispatched his Maratha General Ekoji Bhonsle to expel Madurai from Tanjavur and reinstate the Nayaka dynasty.[17] By January 1764, Bijapur's army had arrived at the Tanjavur border and in the following months fought together with troops of Ramnad and Mysore against Madurai's forces.

But as time passed, the Dutch started doubting the likelihood of Chengamaladasa becoming Tanjavur's new king, fearing that if Ekoji conquered the kingdom he would care more about the land's riches than the prince's ambitions. True enough, whereas in June Chengamaladasa wrote to the VOC that it was a matter of weeks before the Tanjavur capital would be captured for him, in July he asked the Dutch

16 NA, VOC, no. 1295, ff. 127-7v, 129-33v, 686-6v; no. 1298, ff. 286-7v, 569, 572, 575v; no. 1302, ff. 379-80v, 382v-3, 611v-12: correspondence between Nagapattinam, Teganapatnam, St. Thomé, Pulicat, Colombo, Batavia, Van Goens, and Bijapur authorities, Sept.-Nov. 1673, June 1674. See also Jeyaraj and Young, *Hindu-Christian Epistolary Self-Disclosures*, 265.

17 NA, VOC, no. 1302, ff. 614-14v, 615v-16v: letters from Chengamaladasa to Van Goens at Nagapattinam, June 1674; Narayana Rao, Shulman, and Subrahmanyam, *Textures of Time*, 131-2; Krishnaswami Aiyangar, *Sources of Vijayanagar History*, 325-6; Taylor, *Oriental Historical Manuscripts*, vol. II, 200-1; Mahalingam, *Mackenzie Manuscripts*, vol. II, 345-6; Vriddhagirisan, *The Nayaks of Tanjore*, 162-3; Sathyanatha Aiyar, *History of the Nayaks of Madura*, 166-7; Srinivasan, *Maratha Rule in the Carnatic*, 127-9; Sathianathaier, *Tamiḻaham in the 17th Century*, 90-1.

for protection. For in the meantime, Madurai's army had chased its opponents from Tanjavur and Ekoji was reportedly bribed to stop supporting the prince.

Following his request to the Dutch, it seems Chengamaladasa stayed with them at Nagapattinam, probably still accompanied by Venkanna. The VOC made preparations to ship the prince to Jaffna on Ceylon and grant him the revenues of some lands there. This did not materialise, however, as later in 1674 Ekoji attacked Madurai-occupied Tanjavur again and with the help of Ramnad, Ariyalur, and Udaiyarpalayam took control of the entire kingdom except the capital. This gave Chengamaladasa new hope of getting his family's throne and his companion Venkanna was even installed as regent of Tanjavur's coastal areas.

As the VOC expected, Ekoji proved to have other priorities than the continuation of the Nayaka house, and started to collect revenues and appoint his own local officials. Much of the year 1675 saw military manoeuvres between the various powers in Tanjavur that largely maintained the status quo. But in November the Dutch noted that the Bijapur sultan became increasingly annoyed with Ekoji's self-willed behaviour and moreover reached an agreement with Madurai that it could keep Tanjavur in return for a tribute. Summoned home, Ekoji however decided to stay and fight newly sent Bijapur forces.

Perhaps because of this, in December it was reported that Venkanna had convinced Ekoji and Madurai's governor in Tanjavur town, Muttu Linga alias Alakadri Nayaka, to join forces. Aspiring to rule Tanjavur autonomously, Muttu Linga had grown estranged from Madurai's King Chokkanatha, his elder brother or stepbrother, and could well use a powerful ally. But he fared badly after this alleged deal, because around January 1676 Ekoji and his troops entered the capital and gradually assumed power over the entire kingdom, forcing Muttu Linga to flee.

As the VOC wrote, Venkanna initially remained "land regent," while Chengamaladasa's accession to the throne apparently was postponed and in the end never occurred or lasted for a short time only. Indeed, by September Ekoji had arrested Venkanna, suspected of plotting with Ariyalur, Udaiyarpalayam, and other parties wishing Chengamaladasa to become king.[18] Still, as mentioned in Chapter 3, Venkanna served as a broker for the Dutch embassy to Ekoji in late 1676

[18] NA, VOC, no. 1292, ff. 390-90v, 393; no. 1298, ff. 274-4v, 276v-7v, 325, 346v-7v, 362v-3, 369-9v, 500-500v, 506, 577v, 583v; no. 1299, ff. 133v-4, 139-40v; no. 1302, ff. 614-14v, 615v-16v; no. 1304, ff. 271-1v, 327v; no. 1308, ff. 20v-1v, 160v-1, 166, 476v, 480, 483-3v, 486-6v, 489, 493v-4; no. 1313, ff. 349-50v, 361v-2; no. 1321, ff. 881v-83, 884v, 887v, 888v: correspondence between Nagapattinam, Colombo, Batavia, Van Goens, and Chengamaladasa, Jan., May-Aug. 1674, Apr., June-July, Oct.-Dec. 1675, Aug.-Sept. 1676, Nagapattinam proceedings, July, Nov.-Dec. 1674, report on the Madurai coast, Mar. 1674, report on Tanjavur mission to Nagapattinam, Aug. 1676; Vink, "Encounters on the Opposite Coast," 290. For a partial translation of one of these documents, see Subrahmanyam, *Penumbral Visions*, 145. See also Martin, *India in the 17th Century*, vol. 1, pt. II, 511.

and early 1677, but he seems to have disappeared from both the Tanjavur court and the VOC archives soon after.

These Dutch reports on the developments following Madurai's conquest of Tanjavur differ from local accounts such as the *Tañjāvūri āndhra rājula caritra*. Most notably, the latter relate that Chengamaladasa and his nurse went straight to Nagapattinam, where they were sheltered by an unnamed, wealthy Chetti merchant and later joined by Venkanna. Further, after Bijapur's General Ekoji drove Madurai out of Tanjavur, he withdrew his troops and Chengamaladasa was installed as Tanjavur's Nayaka. The young king then appointed as his prime minister and commander not his experienced aide Venkanna but the Chetti merchant from Nagapattinam, who turned out to be his nurse's lover. Dissatisfied, Venkanna invited Ekoji to return to Tanjavur and take the kingdom himself. The general was initially reluctant, but then received news that the Bijapur sultan had passed away and his land was taken by the Mughals.

The *Bhoṃsale vaṃśa caritra* adds that the deity of a nearby temple revealed to Ekoji that he was destined to rule Tanjavur. The general now accepted Venkanna's offer and dethroned Chengamaladasa, making him flee to Ariyalur or Mysore. Still, Venkanna was considered a traitor by Ekoji and forced to escape as well, spending his remaining days in obscurity in Madurai.[19]

It appears that local texts depict Ekoji's role in much more positive terms than Dutch documents. Rather than ignoring Chengamaladasa's claims, taking Tanjavur for himself, and forsaking his Bijapur overlord—as the VOC reported he did—the general would have helped the prince regain his ancestral kingdom, not accepted Tanjavur's reign until he was pressed by a local courtier or deity, and only assumed autonomy when his master died and his home kingdom was lost. These accounts may therefore have served to justify the Bhonsles' rule over Tanjavur. Admittedly, VOC records do not completely rule out some elements in the local texts, in particular Chengamaladasa's fortunes. Dutch accounts of six to eight decades later say

[19] Narayana Rao, Shulman, and Subrahmanyam, *Textures of Time*, 130-5; Krishnaswami Aiyangar, *Sources of Vijayanagar History*, 325-7; Taylor, *Oriental Historical Manuscripts*, vol. II, 200-3; Subrahmanyam, *Penumbral Visions*, 145-7; BL/AAS, MT, class III, no. 87: "The historycal account of the Tonjore," ff. 82v-3v, 91-4v; Mahalingam, *Mackenzie Manuscripts*, vol. II, 346-7; Vriddhagirisan, *The Nayaks of Tanjore*, 162-5; Sathyanatha Aiyar, *History of the Nayaks of Madura*, 168-71, 279-80; Srinivasan, *Maratha Rule in the Carnatic*, 130-5; Sathianathaier, *Tamiḻaham in the 17th Century*, 92-6. See also: Jeyaraj and Young, *Hindu-Christian Epistolary Self-Disclosures*, 265-6; BL/AAS, MG, no. 1, pt. 8: "The Cheritee or actions of the Vadaka-Rajahs of Tanjore, Trichinopully & Madura," f. 73; no. 4, pt. 4: "Mootiah's chronological & historical account of the modern kings of Madura," f. 66; MT, class III, no. 88: "Account of the Tanjore Samastanums," ff. 137-8; OOV, no. 72, pt. 17, "Brief account, by a Trichinopoly Brahman, of Tanjore, Madura, and Trichinopoly ...," ff. 129-30 (related in 1761 by a Brahmin at Tiruchirappalli to William Petrie, see f. 127).

he was in fact proclaimed king, before Ekoji's own monarchical aspirations made him flee to Mysore.[20] Yet, contemporary VOC documents seem silent on the prince's accession to the throne. Thus, if Chengamaladasa ever reigned over Tanjavur, it was a brief, insignificant affair, not even noted at that time by the Dutch in nearby Nagapattinam.

More speculatively, one might wonder if the anonymous Nagapattinam merchant who first protected Chengamaladasa and whose later influence at court was resented and terminated—as described in south Indian sources—symbolised the role of the VOC. After all, the Dutch twice willingly offered shelter to the Nayaka prince, the second time in Nagapattinam itself, and supported his ambitions to win Tanjavur back. These political activities of the Company were considered inappropriate by Bijapur's authorities and perhaps by Tanjavur's Bhonsle court too. In any case, the VOC's short but important role in Chengamaladasa's career was unique for Vijayanagara's heirs. Never before or after were the Dutch so closely involved in the court politics of these kingdoms.

After this episode, the VOC kept reporting about Chengamaladasa for another half a century. For some time, his chances of becoming king still seemed fair, since in the following decades Tanjavur's neighbours undertook several efforts to dislodge the Bhonsles and replace them with the former Nayaka line. In the late 1670s, a number of coalitions variously including Madurai, Ikkeri, Mysore, Ramnad, Ariyalur, Udaiyarpalayam, Senji (now under Maratha rule), and Bijapur allegedly prepared attacks on Ekoji, although some parties switched allegiance to him. In 1686, together with some Madurai courtiers, Ramnad, Senji, and even Bhonsle Tanjavur itself, Chengamaladasa took part in a conspiracy to remove Madurai's Muttu Virappa Nayaka III, probably hoping this would somehow further his interests. Around the same time, Mysore tried to convince the Mughals to help re-establish Tanjavur's Nayakas, and Madurai and Ramnad were thought to have similar intentions.

These endeavours continued far into the eighteenth century. About 1700, a plot by Mysore and Madurai to enthrone Chengamaladasa was rumoured to have failed only because the bribed gate-keeper of Tanjavur town was betrayed and subsequently beheaded. In 1707 Chengamaladasa, now living in Madurai's capital Tiruchirappalli, himself approached the rulers of Madurai and Ramnad for support. Finally, around 1709 the Nawab of Arcot offered to reinstall the prince in return for one million *pardaos*. None of these plans worked out, however, and the Bhonsle dynasty was to stay in Tanjavur. It appears that by the late 1720s Chengamaladasa had passed away, probably having lived into his sixties, for in 1729 Mysore, Madurai,

[20] NA, VOC, no. 2443, ff. 2685-6: final report of Elias Guillot, Sept. 1738; *Beknopte historie*, 96.

and Arcot attacked Tanjavur, again unsuccessfully, now to install a grandson of the last real Nayaka ruler, also named Vijayaraghava.[21]

But although Chengamaladasa's line never sat on the throne again, his house remained important in the region's dynastic constellation for another reason. Even after losing their kingdom, he and his relatives were apparently considered royals, as some rulers still wished to marry the family's princesses. In the early 1700s, the king of Kandy on Ceylon asked for the hand of a daughter of Chengamaladasa. In 1710, however, Madurai's Vijayaranga Chokkanatha Nayaka abducted her (or another daughter destined for Kandy) from Chengamaladasa's residence at Tiruchirappalli and kept her as what the Dutch called a concubine (*bijwijf*). After the refusal of Chengamaladasa's father Vijayaraghava to let a princess marry into Madurai's dynasty—one cause of the Tanjavur Nayakas' demise—this seizure and concubinage of Chengamaladasa's daughter must have been utterly degrading.

The *Tañjāvūri āndhra rājula caritra* ends on a somewhat similar note, stating that Chengamaladasa's grandson offered his sister as a bride to Vijayaranga Chokkanatha, an act also mentioned in VOC documents of the early 1740s. Another local text speaks of a wedding of the Kandyan king with two great-granddaughters of Chengamaladasa. Perhaps underscoring the importance of the Tanjavur family's royal blood, the Dutch wrote that Madurai's very last Nayaka ruler, Vijayakumara (reigning in the early 1750s), was a member of Chengamaladasa's "branch" (*stam*). So it seems Vijayakumara had female ancestors belonging to Tanjavur's Nayaka house, who were regarded by the Madurai court as lawful wives and whose progeny qualified as potential monarchs.[22]

Despite this status, Chengamaladasa's line faded into obscurity. It is said, however, that at various moments the rulers of Madurai, Mysore, Pudukkottai, and Kandy granted the family protection and some lands. Later, one descendant

[21] NA, VOC, no. 1316, ff. 307v-9v, 313-13v, 316, 326v, 330, 332, 336v, 340v, 408v, 414-14v, 418-18v, 585; no. 1323, f. 437; no. 1448, ff. 323-3v; no. 1454, f. 1010; no. 1633, f. 146v; no. 1638, f. 118; no. 2135, ff. 131-2, 366; no. 8595, ff. 134-5; no. 8923, ff. 315-16: correspondence between Nagapattinam, Pulicat, Colombo, Batavia, Van Goens, and VOC envoy Viraraja at Tanjavur, Nov.-Dec. 1676, Jan.-Feb. 1677, Jan. 1678, Aug. 1688, Jan. 1689, Apr., Nov. 1700, Feb. 1707, Feb. 1708, July, Sept. 1729; Vink, *Mission to Madurai*, 63, 312 (n. 196), 470 (n. 226), 480-1 (n. 264); idem, "Encounters on the Opposite Coast," 376, 379; *Beknopte historie*, 97; Coolhaas *et al.*, *Generale Missiven*, vol. VI, 497, 651; Subrahmanyam, *Penumbral Visions*, 150-1; Vriddhagirisan, *The Nayaks of Tanjore*, 167; Sathyanatha Aiyar, *History of the Nayaks of Madura*, 198.

[22] NA, VOC, no. 2457, f. 1028; no. 8595, ff. 134-5; no. 8925, ff. 145, 147-50: letter from Colombo to Batavia, Feb. 1707, letter and report of Kandy envoys received at Nagapattinam, Feb. 1710, letter from Ramnad to Tuticorin, Aug. 1739; Cornelis Joan Simons, *Memoir of Cornelis Joan Simons, Governor and Director of Ceylon, for His Successor, Hendrick Becker, 1707*, ed. Sophia Anthonisz (Colombo, 1914), 7; Coolhaas *et al.*, *Generale Missiven*, vol. X, 770; Mahalingam, *Mackenzie Manuscripts*, vol. II, 347-8; Narayana Rao, Shulman, and Subrahmanyam, *Symbols of Substance*, 308-9; idem, *Textures of Time*, 135; Vriddhagirisan, *The Nayaks of Tanjore*, 166-7. See also Dewaraja, *The Kandyan Kingdom*, 33-8, 40-2.

was reported to still dwell near Tiruchirappalli, at the town of Jambukeshvaram across the Kaveri River.[23] This may well have been the last reference to offspring of Tanjavur's Nayaka house.

Bhonsles of Tanjavur

The fate of the Nayakas' successors in Tanjavur was very different. In the course of the eighteenth century, the Bhonsles increasingly came under the influence of Arcot and the British. The last ruler discussed in Chapter 2, Tuljaji Bhonsle II, was even briefly deposed by these parties in 1773. After an interlude of Arcot rule, Tuljaji was restored in 1776 as a rather powerless king, tributary to Arcot and guarded by British troops stationed at the capital.[24] Predeceased by his children, before his death in 1787 he adopted Sarabhoji Bhonsle II from a distant collateral branch as his successor. But since Sarabhoji was only about ten years old, the throne temporarily passed to Tuljaji's elder half-brother Amarasimha Bhonsle (r. 1787-98), son of Pratapasimha Bhonsle and a so-called left-handed concubine. Amarasimha soon grew dissatisfied with his role as regent of the heir apparent and convinced the British—ever ready to strengthen their hold on the kingdom—to proclaim him a fully-fledged king. Thus, a succession struggle ensued between Amarasimha, on the one hand, and Sarabhoji and the late Tuljaji's close relatives, on the other. Around 1793 the latter faction even left Tanjavur for British territory. Finally, in 1798 the British replaced Amarasimha with the now adult Sarabhoji (r. 1798-1832).

The new ruler presided over a period of great cultural and scholarly efflorescence and the dynastic chronicle *Bhoṃsale vaṃśa caritra* was composed under his patronage. But at the same time, treaties with the British reduced the Bhonsles to mere titular monarchs, incorporated into the colonial administration. In 1799 Tanjavur was made part of the British Madras Presidency in exchange for a yearly allowance and the honours of a thirteen-gun salute and the title "His Highness" instead of "His Excellency." Yet, royal authority now did not extend much further than the capital's fort area. Upon Sarabhoji's passing in 1832, he was succeeded by his only son, Shivaji Bhonsle II (r. 1832-55).

When this ruler died without male issue in 1855, the British applied the Doctrine of Lapse, stating that in the absence of a lawful successor dynastic rule was to be

[23] Taylor, *Examination and Analysis of the Mackenzie Manuscripts*, 128; Mahalingam, *Mackenzie Manuscripts*, vol. II, 347-8; Venkasami Row, *A Manual of the District of Tanjore*, 757-8; Vriddhagirisan, *The Nayaks of Tanjore*, 166-7.

[24] For a recent discussion of these events, see Pimmanus Wibulsilp, "Nawabi Karnatak: Muhammad Ali Khan in the Making of a Mughal Successor State in Pre-Colonial South India, 1749-1795" (unpublished dissertation, Leiden University, 2019), 300-3, 313-15.

abolished. Since Shivaji's widow and daughter were not recognised as heirs, the Bhonsle house was thus pensioned off in 1857. Many of its possessions were confiscated, to be returned later apart from what were considered royal insignia: "state" jewels, swords, and other regalia. Shivaji's private estate remained in family hands, but it soon became the subject of disputes between various relatives. Although the Tanjavur palace was declared state property, the Bhonsles were allowed to stay there. After Shivaji's death, the line was continued by the adoption of his sister's grandson, Sarabhoji III. A number of the latter's offspring by two wives have continued to live in parts of the palace until today.[25]

Nayakas of Madurai

The demise of Madurai's Nayaka house was in some respects similar to that of its Tanjavur namesake: dethronement, followed by many, largely unsuccessful attempts to regain the kingdom, and eventually an increasingly marginal position. Chapter 2 has shown how Madurai's own line of secondary kings contributed to the dynasty's downfall. Descending from Kumara Rangappa, nephew of Tirumalai Nayaka (r. c. 1623-59), this collateral branch of the house seems to have long been contented with its subordinate position. Queen Minakshi's accession to the throne in 1732, however, apparently incited the then secondary ruler Bangaru Tirumalai to question the queen's legitimacy and contest her position.

Local texts say that Minakshi, perhaps to win Bangaru Tirumalai over, adopted his son Vijayakumara as her future successor. But Bangaru Tirumalai, backed by parties inside and outside Madurai, grew more and more influential, while the queen appears to have been relegated to a mostly ceremonial position. When around the mid-1730s Arcot's forces entered the region to collect tribute, Minakshi and Bangaru Tirumalai each attempted to involve the commanders of these troops in their struggle. One of them, Safdar Ali Khan, son of Arcot's Nawab, initially

[25] Subramanian, *The Maratha Rajas of Tanjore*, 61-3, 66-7, 69-70, 72-6; Srinivasan, *Maratha Rule in the Carnatic*, 301-7, 314-15, 318-25, 329-34, 338-40; Subrahmanyam, *Penumbral Visions*, 151-3, 156-78, 183; Ramanujam, *Unheard Voices*, ch. 11; Venkasami Row, *A Manual of the District of Tanjore*, 829-32; Hemingway, *Tanjore Gazetteer*, vol. I, 51-2, 192; Usha R. Vijailakshmi, "Change and Transformation in the Lives of Thanjavur Maratha Queens and the Doctrine of Lapse (1856-1862)," *Journal of Indian History and Culture* 24 (2018); Bhosale, *Rajah Serfoji – II*, 38-67, 120-30, 152-3; Bhosle, *Contributions of Thanjavur Maratha Kings*, 219-38, 298-9; Suresh, *The Tanjavur Marathas*, 27; Hickey, *The Tanjore Mahratta Principality*, 126-42, 145-59, 166-72, xvi-cxiii; Chakravarthy and Sathyanathan, *Thanjavur: A Cultural History*, 30-8; Nahla Nainar, "An Uncommon Prince," *The Hindu* (29 Aug. 2014); serfojimemorialhall.com; www.royalark.net/India4/tanjore.htm. For family affairs under Tuljaji II's reign, see BL/AAS, MG, no. 26, pt. 10 or 11: "A short account of the Maharratta reigning family at Tanjour," ff. 236-7 (probably translated from a Marathi text of 1784, see f. 231).

favoured Bangaru Tirumalai. Soon after, however, the other commander, Chanda Sahib, son-in-law of the Nawab, promised to support the queen. But even though Minakshi and Bangaru Tirumalai now allegedly reconciled and the queen paid a large sum to Chanda Sahib to safeguard her interests, the latter seized the whole kingdom and imprisoned Minakshi. Bangaru Tirumalai then fled, first to Madurai town and next to Shivagangai.[26]

VOC records add that Madurai's instability in the early 1730s was not only caused by the rivalry between Minakshi and Bangaru Tirumalai. As least as important, according to the Dutch, was the role of Naranappa Ayyan ("Naranappaijen"), referred to as Madurai's prime minister. Disgruntled because he was removed from his office, in 1733 he turned to Mysore and with its support conquered large parts of Madurai. This led several chiefs in the coastal areas to revolt against the central court too. Moreover, amidst this turmoil the governor of Tirunelveli or "great land regent of the lowlands," Alagappa Mudaliyar, was killed by a local chieftain, whereupon a violent dispute ensued between the regent's brother and his newly installed successor.

This was the state of affairs when Arcot's commanders appeared in Madurai—supposedly to support Minakshi against Bangaru Tirumalai, but probably also considering the kingdom's disorder an opportunity to extend their influence. Thus, after Safdar Ali and Chanda Sahib laid siege to Tiruchirappalli around early 1736, on 26 April Minakshi was forced to surrender the capital. The commanders confiscated her treasures, plundered the town, and detained the queen, her influential brothers, and several courtiers. While Safdar Ali seems to have reinstalled Minakshi in early 1737, Arcot reportedly more or less annexed the kingdom in September, leasing its various parts to revenue collectors and providing the queen with an annual grant.

In the meantime, as the Dutch recorded, Arcot's troops had turned south to the Nayakas' old capital, Madurai town, conquering it around June 1737 from the queen's opponent Bangaru Tirumalai. His presence there could have been part of a plan devised by Ramnad, Shivagangai, and the Palaiyakkarars (exactly seventy-two of them, as the Dutch were told) to enthrone Bangaru Tirumalai's twenty-two-year old son—in all likelihood Vijayakumara, earlier adopted by Minakshi. By tradition,

[26] Taylor, *Oriental Historical Manuscripts*, vol. I, 40, 206, vol. II, 37-43, 232-5; Sathyanatha Aiyar, *History of the Nayaks of Madura*, 232-4; K. Rajayyan, "Fall of the Nayaks of Madurai," *Journal of Indian History* XLV, III (1967), 807-12; idem, "Moghal Conquest of Trichinopoly," *Journal of Indian History* XLIX, I-III (1971), 116-21; idem, *History of Madurai*, 62-70; Kadhirvel, *A History of the Maravas*, 79-80; Mahalingam, *Readings in South Indian History*, 175-6, 182-5; Rangachari, "The History of the Naik Kingdom of Madura," *Indian Antiquary* XLVI, 213-19, 237-40; Nelson, *The Madura Country*, vol. III, 251-9; BL/AAS, MT, class III, no. 25: "History of the former Gentoo Rajahs who ruled over the Pandyan Mandalom," ff. 33v-6v.

coronations took place in Madurai town and apparently several parties had already gathered there for the occasion, considering the fact that when Arcot's forces arrived, Bangaru Tirumalai and Vijayakumara fled to Ramnad together with that kingdom's *Daḷavāy* (general) Vairavanatha Servaikkarar. Local texts say father and son escaped to Shivagangai instead, which may indeed have been their eventual destination because in 1738 the VOC wrote that various local chiefs backing Vijayakumara were headed by Shivagangai's ruler Sasivarna Udaya Tevar. The next few years saw several confrontations between this alliance and Arcot's army, none of which resulted in a decisive victory for either side.[27]

All the while, Minakshi seems to have remained Madurai's formal queen in Tiruchirappalli—or at least a Dutch document of September 1738 and a local inscription of February 1739 recording a land grant still refer to her as such. But whatever power she held under Arcot's supervision, this appears to have ended by mid-1739 because around that time it was reported Safdar Ali would make Bangaru Tirumalai king of Madurai at Tiruchirappalli.[28] According to south Indian texts, Minakshi poisoned herself, feeling betrayed by Chanda Sahib, who had not kept his promise to protect her.[29] Perhaps her demise prompted Safdar Ali to install Bangaru Tirumalai as the next puppet ruler. But if the latter actually did sit on the throne, his reign was short-lived.[30]

In 1740 a Maratha army from west India invaded the Tamil region and with the help of Mysore, Tanjavur, Ramnad, and Shivagangai captured Tiruchirappalli in March 1741. Arcot's forces were expelled and Chanda Sahib was confined. Local

[27] For a description of these clashes, see Bes, "Friendship as Long as the Sun and Moon Shine," 51-3.

[28] NA, VOC, no. 2386, ff. 35-5v, 1027-8, 1221-2; no. 2387, ff. 93-4; no. 2403, ff. 1937-7v, 1939v-43v, 1946-7, 1965-5v; no. 2412, ff. 60, 1540-1, 1982, 2137 (2nd numeration); no. 2428, f. 340v; no. 2431, ff. 1932-7, 1939-40v; no. 2443, ff. 2682, 362-3 (last ff. 2nd numeration); no. 2445, ff. 1618-19; no. 2457, ff. 1017-18, 1027v-8; no. 2459, ff. 1566v, 1599v, 1601; no. 2470, f. 71; no. 2473, ff. 99-100; no. 2492, ff. 1472v, 1475; no. 11306, ff. 48-54: (secret) letters from Nagapattinam to Batavia, from Tuticorin to Colombo, from Kilakkarai to Tuticorin, Feb.-Mar., July, Sept., Dec. 1736, Mar., May-Oct. 1737, Jan., Mar.-Apr., July, Oct.-Dec. 1738, May, July-Aug. 1739, report by Ceylon Governor Van Imhof concerning trade on Madurai's coast, 1738, final report of Elias Guillot, Sept. 1738, Colombo proceedings, Sept. 1739, letters from Ramnad to Tuticorin, Aug. 1739, Feb., Nov. 1740, description of the Nayakas of Madurai by Holst, 1762; Schreuder, *Memoir of Jan Schreuder*, 36; Coolhaas *et al.*, *Generale Missiven*, vol. X, 12, 104-5; *Beknopte historie*, 89; BL/AAS, OI, no. I, pt. 22: "Kings of Tritchanopoly from 1509," f. 240; Mahalingam, *Readings in South Indian History*, 184-5. See also Bes, "The Ambiguities of Female Rule in Nayaka South India."

[29] See: Taylor, *Oriental Historical Manuscripts*, vol. II, 235; BL/AAS, MT, class III, no. 82: "Account of the Rajas who held the government of Madura," f. 113v. A tradition recorded by the Dutch has it that Chanda Sahib imprisoned Minakshi in a Tiruchirappalli temple "built on a steep height" (probably the Rock Temple or a nearby shrine), where she died of misery. See NA, VOC, no. 11306, ff. 53-4 (note): description of the Nayakas of Madurai by Holst, 1762.

[30] My earlier conclusion that Vijayakumara reigned over Madurai for some years from 1739 onward is most probably incorrect. See Bes, "The Setupatis, the Dutch, and Other Bandits," 561-2.

sources say Bangaru Tirumalai had in fact invited the Marathas to help him get Madurai back, but the VOC noted they took their time to decide who should be the new king. The Dutch expected that this position would eventually be granted to whoever paid the Marathas the most. Meanwhile, it was said, Ramnad consulted with the Palaiyakkarars and other rulers about the same issue.[31]

All in all, from the mid-1730s onward a wide range of parties—including Arcot, Ramnad, Shivagangai, the Palaiyakkarars, and the Marathas—sought to increase their power in Madurai, supporting various rather powerless pretenders to the Nayaka throne. Exemplary was Ramnad's Sivakumara Muttu Vijaya Raghunatha Setupati (or the court faction around him), who in 1739, in a letter to the Dutch, referred to what was probably Bangaru Tirumalai as follows:

> The Naijk recently crowned at Tritchinepalij [Tiruchirappalli], with whom I maintain such a close friendship that I can say his Tritchinepalij court with the entire realm [*rijk*] of Madure is mine ...[32]

The Madurai town chronicle *Māduraittala varalāṟu* declares that in the same year—as if to bolster his claim—the Setupati, together with the Nayaka Prince Vijayakumara, removed the deity statues of Madurai's Minakshi Sundareshvara Temple and brought them to Manamadurai in his own territory, where they were kept for two years. This seems to be another case in which the roles of overlord and vassal were largely reversed. Madurai's dynasty had now become dependent on Ramnad and placing deities of the Nayakas under the Setupati's protection may have served as a confirmation of this changed relationship. Indeed, in 1740 the Dutch governor of Ceylon, Gustaaf Willem van Imhoff, literally spoke of the Nayaka family's "dependence" (*dependentie*) on Ramnad.[33]

In the end, the Marathas did not install a new Nayaka in Madurai but appointed a governor of their own. Already in August 1743, however, they were chased from the kingdom by troops of the Nizam of Hyderabad, south India's

[31] NA, VOC, no. 2523, ff. 1399-1413v; no. 11306, ff. 54-5: letters from Tuticorin to Colombo, Feb.-Aug. 1741, description of the Nayakas of Madurai by Holst, 1762; Coolhaas *et al.*, *Generale Missiven*, vol. X, 528, 886-7; Taylor, *Oriental Historical Manuscripts*, vol. I, 40, vol. II, 43-7, 245-8; Mahalingam, *Readings in South Indian History*, 176-7; Rajayyan, "Fall of the Nayaks of Madurai," 812-13; idem, *History of Madurai*, 70-81; Kadhirvel, *A History of the Maravas*, 80-1; Rangachari, "The History of the Naik Kingdom of Madura," *Indian Antiquary* XLVI, 239-43; Nelson, *The Madura Country*, vol. III, 259-64.

[32] NA, VOC, no. 2457, f. 1028: letter from Ramnad to Tuticorin, Aug. 1739 (translation mine).

[33] Sathyanatha Aiyar, *History of the Nayaks of Madura*, 378-9; NA, VOC, no. 2482, f. 1878v: final report of Gustaaf Willem van Imhoff, Mar. 1740; Gustaaf Willem van Imhoff, *Memoir Left by Gustaaf Willem Baron van Imhoff, Governor and Director of Ceylon, to His Successor, Willem Maurits Bruynink, 1740*, ed. Sophia Pieters (Colombo, 1911), 15. See also Davis, "Indian Art Objects as Loot."

increasingly autonomous Mughal governor. The VOC wrote that one of the Nizam's commanders had approached Ramnad for military assistance, purportedly to re-establish Madurai's Nayakas. Other sources say that Bangaru Tirumulai and his son Vijayakumara visited the Nizam, who promised to enthrone the family again.

In either case, matters soon turned out very differently. While waiting in Arcot to be installed as king, Bangaru Tirumalai was poisoned, supposedly by the Nawab. Thereupon Vijayakumara fled again to Shivagangai, where a marital alliance was allegedly established between his line and the local ruler. However, Bangaru Tirumalai's death did not signal the dynasty's final demise. Chanda Sahib, detained by the Marathas since their conquest of Madurai in 1741, was released about 1748. An enemy of the then Nawab of Arcot, he launched another campaign to occupy Madurai town. To win the population's support, Chanda Sahib's local representatives appointed Vijayakumara as the new Nayaka.

Now probably in his mid-thirties, the prince thus finally ascended Madurai's throne, but sensing a plot at court to get rid of him, he is said to have abdicated around 1751 and gone back to Shivagangai. He soon returned for one last time in about 1753, however, after Ramnad's and Shivagangai's troops wrested Madurai town from Mysore, which had recently taken it. Vijayakumara was again installed as king, only to be toppled after a year or so when Chanda Sahib's forces seized Madurai. Once more, the prince fled to Shivagangai, whereupon he was assigned the rule of a few villages, first around Vellikkurichi, ten miles south-west of Shivagangai town, and subsequently in Ramnad and the Palaiyakkarar chieftaincy of Gandamanayakanur.

In 1754, some Palaiyakkarars requested the British to re-establish Madurai's Nayakas, but this was obstructed by the Nawab of Arcot. In 1757 followed another unsuccessful attempt by these chiefs together with Mysore. In 1777 Vijayakumara himself made an appeal to the British but passed away in the same year, at about sixty years old. He left a son named Vishvanatha, who with an elaborate ceremony was allegedly declared Madurai's new Nayaka by a number of Palaiyakkarars. Although no other party seems to have acknowledged this, later Vishvanatha and his offspring were again granted land around Vellikkurichi, where they settled down.[34]

[34] NA, VOC, no. 2599, ff. 2316-16v, 2332-3; no. 2812, f. 230v; no. 11306, ff. 64-7: letters from Tuticorin to Colombo, from Colombo to Batavia, Apr., Aug.-Sept. 1743, Jan. 1754, description of the Nayakas of Madurai by Holst, 1762; Loten, *Memoir of Joan Gideon Loten*, 12-15; Taylor, *Oriental Historical Manuscripts*, vol. I, 41-2, vol. II, 47-9, 247-59; BL/AAS, MT, class III, no. 25: "History of the former Gentoo Rajahs who ruled over the Pandyan Mandalom," ff. 37-41v; class III, no. 82: "Account of the Rajas who held the government of Madura," ff. 114v-26v; Sathyanatha Aiyar, *History of the Nayaks of Madura*, 380-1; Rajayyan, "Fall of the Nayaks of Madurai," 813-15; idem, *History of Madurai*, 81-153; Mahalingam, *Readings in South Indian History*, 177-81; Kadhirvel, *A History of the Maravas*, 81-96; Rangachari, "The

No more Nayaka ever reigned over Madurai, although Vijayakumara's descendants initially maintained their claim to the kingdom. Several texts on the dynasty's history collected by assistants of Colin Mackenzie in the early 1800s conclude with petitions to the British. Probably mostly authored by Vishvanatha's son Bangaru Tirumalai—who took over his father's place as family head in 1800—these sections urged the colonial government to recognise his rights to the throne. Some passages specifically stress the legitimacy of the Nayaka's collateral line he belonged to, detailing his genealogy back to Kumara Rangappa (appointed Madurai's secondary ruler around 1660) in the male line and to an elder sister of Vijayaranga Chokkanatha Nayaka (r. 1707-32) in the female line.

These texts further state that since Queen Minakshi had borne no son, Prince Vijayakumara was fully entitled to become king, as the kingdom's "law" dictated and was supposedly also agreed on by Minakshi herself. Besides, the Marathas, the Nizam, the Nawab, Chanda Sahib's representatives, the kings of Ramnad and Shivagangai, and the Palaiyakkarars had all made efforts to restore the dynasty to its rightful place. Also, as Bangaru Tirumalai wrote, rulers like those of Pudukkottai, Shivagangai, and Ramnad, and several Palaiyakkarars still respected his line's status, personally welcoming him, presenting gifts such as jewellery and clothes, and erecting arches in his honour. Obviously, these pleas and arguments failed to impress the British and so the Nayaka family stayed at Vellikkurichi,[35] where they lived at least until the 1820s and probably into the twentieth century, reportedly still keeping record of their royal ancestry.[36]

Setupatis of Ramnad

Finally, the history of Ramnad's Setupatis after the 1760s is somewhat similar to that of Tanjavur's Bhonsles: a dynasty that long maintained some of its status but soon lost much of its power. As explained in Chapter 2, in June 1772 Muttu Ramalinga Setupati—like Tuljaji Bhonsle II—was dethroned by an alliance of Arcot and the British. After the Nawab of Arcot ruled Ramnad until 1780 and next

History of the Naik Kingdom of Madura," *Indian Antiquary* XLVI, 243-74; Nelson, *The Madura Country*, vol. III, 265-72. Most of these sources and literature are contradictory with respect to Vijayakumara's regnal dates, and the years given here are therefore approximate.

35 See also the footnote about this Bangaru Tirumalai in the Madurai section in Chapter 4.

36 BL/AAS, MM, no. 109, pt. 37: "The humble representation of ... Bangaroo Teeroomaly Nack," f. 1 (c. 1800); MT, class III, no. 25: "History of the former Gentoo Rajahs who ruled over the Pandyan Mandalom," ff. 41-1v (1803?); class III, no. 82: "Account of the Rajas who held the government of Madura," ff. 109-34v (1806); Rangachari, "The History of the Naik Kingdom of Madura," *Indian Antiquary* XLVI, 274-5; Francis, *Madura Gazetteer*, 59-60; Taylor, *Oriental Historical Manuscripts*, vol. II, 259-61; Seshradri, "The Sētupatis of Ramnad," 131-2.

Mysore's Haidar Ali Khan briefly occupied it, Muttu Ramalinga was reinstalled around April 1781.

While Ramnad remained tributary to Arcot, in the following decades it increasingly came under the sway of the British. Indeed, in 1792 the Nawab formally ceded the kingdom to them and in March 1795 the Setupati was deposed again, charged by his sister Mangaleshvari Nachiar with oppressive rule and accused by the British of bellicosity and arrears in tribute. Granting him a pension and transferring him to Tiruchirappalli and later Madras, the British now took over Ramnad's government. They restored it to Mangaleshvari Nachiar in February 1803, but she was to reign as a *zamīndār* (revenue-paying landholder), not as a fully-fledged monarch.

Like the rulers of neighbouring Shivagangai, the Setupatis were thus incorporated into the colonial administration and reduced to landlords of what was now called the Ramnad Estate. In this new incarnation, the dynasty survived well, although the nineteenth century witnessed a frequency of succession struggles reminiscent of the kingdom's earlier period. Several Setupatis died without leaving sons, which caused fierce, prolonged confrontations, leading to adoptions from collateral branches, minor pretenders to the throne, and three consecutive female reigns. But rather than through violent clashes, these conflicts were now solved by way of extensive litigation under Anglo-Indian law. The British also mediated in conflicts between the Setupati house and the authorities of Rameshvaram's Ramanathasvami Temple, resulting in a decreasing influence of the dynasty in temple affairs.

In the 1870s, the line was honoured with the hereditary title *rāja* (king) because of its loyalty to the colonial rulers. During the decades around India's independence, when the *zamīndār* system was abolished, the then Setupati entered regional politics, serving as a minister and member of the Madras State parliament. Until today, the family has been staying in the palace complex at Ramanathapuram, where in 1979 the current Setupati was installed.[37]

***

[37] Price, *Kingship and Political Practice in Colonial India*, chs 2-6, 190-3, 202; Seshradri, "The Sētupatis of Ramnad," 128-82 and between 182-3; Thiruvenkatachari, *The Setupatis of Ramnad*, 54-60, 71-88; Kadhirvel, *A History of the Maravas*, 159-69, 181-6, 190-3, 202-3; Rajayyan, *History of Madurai*, chs VII-XI, especially 258-62, 276-8, 329-333; Breckenridge, "From Protector to Litigant," 76-88, 94-106; Bes and Branfoot, "'From All Quarters of the Indian World'"; Sethuraman, *Ramesvaram Temple*, 233-41; Nelson, *The Madura Country*, vol. IV, ch. VII; Raja Ram Rao, *Ramnad Manual*, 242-72; J.L.W., "Chronicles of the Marava Country," 129-31.

Thus, one by one, the houses of Vijayanagara and its successors lost their kingdoms, gradually or instantly, being deposed, pensioned off, or demoted to landlords. Many aspects of court politics analysed in this study's previous chapters remained important factors during this process. Succession struggles, powerful courtiers, protocol and honour, and external polities were all instrumental in the dynasties' demises and often kept playing a role in the colonial era.

The royal families maintained their claims to their ancestral kingdoms for considerable periods, partly supporting their aspirations with references to entitlements and honours received from the erstwhile Vijayanagara emperors. In south India's dynastic constellation, the empire served as a source of authority well into the nineteenth century, although this was only sometimes recognised by the then ruling powers. It is perhaps striking that of the six royal families discussed above, precisely the three Nayaka houses—of Ikkeri, Tanjavur, and Madurai—lost their kingdoms completely. Although they continued their quests for their former thrones under colonial rule, their rights were not acknowledged by the British. It is tempting but probably far-fetched to assume this was related to the fact that these dynasties, unlike the other houses, had never claimed independent kingship but remained formally subordinate to Vijayanagara, as demonstrated by their titles.

Among the empire's heirs, the dynasties of Mysore and Ramnad's offshoot Pudukkottai, the Wodeyars and the Tondaimans, managed to keep their realms much longer. These kingdoms survived as formally autonomous princely states in British India, although both were under close supervision of the colonial government and Mysore witnessed a lengthy interlude of direct British administration between 1831 and 1881. Indicating their standing during the colonial period, the Mysore and Pudukkottai kings were honoured by the British with salutes of twenty-one and eleven guns respectively, the former signifying the highest possible rank for Indian rulers.

Only around 1950, following India's independence in 1947, did these kingdoms cease to exist when they merged with the new republic. For about two more decades, their royal families were entitled to annual grants and other privileges, finally revoked in the early 1970s.[38] This abolition signalled the formal end of the last vestiges of royalty originally derived from Vijayanagara.

Because of their pasts, however, till today most surviving royal houses occupy a somewhat exceptional position in society, for example performing religious duties, providing public services, and taking part in festivities. Even the long-vanished Nayaka dynasties have contributed to Vijayanagara's enduring legacy, with current manifestations ranging from symbols in regionalistic politics and awards named

[38] V.P. Menon, *Integration of the Indian States* (updated edition, Madras, 1985), 292-6, 307, 505-13; www.royalark.net/India/salute.htm.

after "Keladi Shivappa Nayaka" and "Keladi Chennamma"—the latter for outstanding bravery—to various art forms that include painting, architecture, literature, folk tales, music, dance, drama, cinema, and children's comics.[39]

[39] For examples, see: Fritz, "Krishnadevaraya in Popular Imagination"; Swami Sivapriyananda and Gajendra Singh Auwa, *Mysore Royal Dasara* (New Delhi, 1995), chs 3-4; Tobert, *Anegondi*, 27, 30, 44-5; Nainar, "An Uncommon Prince"; Michell, *Architecture and Art of Southern India*, 275-7; Saskia C. Kersenboom, *Nityasumaṅgalī: Devadasi Tradition in South India* (Delhi, 1987), passim, especially 31-49; Lakshmi Subramanian, *From the Tanjore Court to the Madras Music Academy: A Social History of Music in South India* (New Delhi, 2006), passim, especially 31-41; Janet O'Shea, "Dancing through History and Ethnography: Indian Classical Dance and the Performance of the Past," in Theresa Jill Buckland (ed.), *Dancing from Past to Present* (Madison, 2006); Swarnamalya Ganesh, "Notions of 'Classical' in Bharatanatyam: A Cultural Operation of the Classes – Arguments of the Cosmopolitan Margi and Indigenous Desi, Repertoires of the Nayak Period," *Kalakshetra Journal Series* I, 3 (2014); Davesh Soneji, "Living History, Performing Memory: Devadāsī Women in Telugu-Speaking South India," *Dance Research Journal* 36, 2 (2004), 34; Appasamy, *Tanjavur Painting of the Maratha Period*, 12, 73; Smita Shirole Yadav and Padma Raghavan, *The Royal Art of Tanjore Paintings* (Mumbai, 2010); Tanu Kulkarni, "State Salutes the Real Heroes," *The Hindu* (14 Nov. 2016); "Neeraj Patil to Receive Keladi Shivappa Nayaka Award," *The Hindu* (14 Aug. 2016); "Historical Novels to Be Released," *The Hindu* (5 May 2016); Velcheti Subrahmanyam, "A Pleasing Historical," *The Hindu* (24 Mar. 2017); Goswami, "The Monk Who Dueled," 193; Narayana Rao, Shulman, and Subrahmanyam, *Symbols of Substance*, 317; "Name Shimoga-Bangalore Train after Shivappa Nayaka, Says Vedike," *The Hindu* (22 Mar. 2011); "T S Nagabharana Directed Keladi Chennamma Shooting Visit," *World News* (26 Aug. 2012); and three volumes in the Amar Chitra Katha series of historical and mythical comics: Subba Rao and G.R. Naik, *Krishnadeva Raya: The Illustrious King of Vijayanagara* (Bombay, 1978); Subba Rao and K. Chandranath, *Hakka and Bukka: The Founders of the Vijayanagar Empire* (Bombay, 1981); and (in the subseries of "Bravehearts") Gayatri Madan Dutt and Souren Roy, *Chennamma of Keladi: The Queen Who Defied Aurangazeb* (Bombay, 1988).

Sources and Literature

Unpublished Sources

VRIJE UNIVERSITEIT (VU) LIBRARY, AMSTERDAM

- Special Collections

  * XW.07161.- "Waarachtig verhael van 't schrikkelijck en vrywilligh verbranden van acht vrouwen, van seker velt-oversten, van den vorst Egosia Ragie, genaemt Werra Teuver, ..." [True story of the terrible and voluntary burning of eight women, of a certain field-lord, of the King Ekoji Raja, named Vira Tevar, ...], c. 1680

TAMIL NADU ARCHIVES, CHENNAI (TNA)

- Dutch Records (DR)

  * 257, 282, 334, 353, 404, 578, 720

DEPARTMENT OF NATIONAL ARCHIVES, COLOMBO (DNA)

- Archives of the Dutch Central Government of Coastal Ceylon (DCGCC, access no. 1)

  * 29, 32, 38, 85, 2672, 2691, 2704, 2705, 3352, 3355, 3396

RIGSARKIVET (State Archives), COPENHAGEN (RA)

- *Den Ledreborgske Dokumentsamling (1466-1701)* (The Ledreborg document collection)

  * 89

- *Tyske Kancelli, Slesvig-holsten-lauenburgske Kancelli (1618-1659), Diverse akter verdr. det ostindiske kompagni og Guinea* (German Chancellery, Schleswig-Holstein-Lauenburg Chancellery (1618-1659), Various documents concerning the East Indian Company and Guinea)

  * A171

- *Udenrigsministeriet, Traktatsamling, Traktater E1, Forholdet til udlandet 1454-1699* (Ministry of Foreign Affairs, Treaty collection, Treaties E1, Related to foreign countries 1454-1699)

  * 20, 21

NATIONAAL ARCHIEF (National Archives), THE HAGUE (NA)

- Archives of the *Verenigde Oostindische Compagnie* (VOC, Dutch East India Company, access no. 1.04.02)

  Kamer Amsterdam (Amsterdam Chamber)

  Overgekomen brieven en papieren series (OBP, letters and papers received from Asia)

  From Ceylon (*years of reception*, nos)

  * *1659*: 1227
  * *1660*: 1231
  * *1666*: 1251
  * *1671*: 1274, 1277
  * *1672*: 1280
  * *1674*: 1292, 1295
  * *1675*: 1302, 1304
  * *1677*: 1316
  * *1678*: 1324
  * *1679*: 1333
  * *1683*: 1373
  * *1684*: 1383
  * *1691*: 1478
  * *1692*: 1491, 1492
  * *1700*: 1615B, 1615C, 1625
  * *1706*: 1706
  * *1709*: 1756, 1762
  * *1710*: 1771
  * *1711*: 1788
  * *1712*: 1805
  * *1716*: 1865
  * *1718*: 1893
  * *1721*: 1941
  * *1724*: 1992
  * *1725*: 2015
  * *1726*: 2026
  * *1727*: 2044, 2046
  * *1728*: 2068
  * *1731*: 2158
  * *1732*: 2185, 2186
  * *1733*: 2224, 2245
  * *1734*: 2290, 2291
  * *1735*: 2308
  * *1736*: 2337
  * *1737*: 2374, 2388
  * *1738*: 2400, 2403
  * *1739*: 2428, 2431, 2445
  * *1740*: 2456, 2457, 2459, 2473
  * *1741*: 2482, 2492
  * *1742*: 2523
  * *1743*: 2559
  * *1744*: 2599
  * *1745*: 2621
  * *1746*: 2642
  * *1747*: 2665, 2666
  * *1748*: 2693
  * *1750*: 2733, 2735
  * *1751*: 2757
  * *1752*: 2774
  * *1754*: 2812
  * *1759*: 2923, 2925
  * *1760*: 2953, 2956, 2957
  * *1763*: 3052
  * *1764*: 3082
  * *1773*: 3349

  From Coromandel (*years of reception*, nos)

  * *1607-13*: 1055
  * *1614*: 1056
  * *1629*: 1094
  * *1630*: 1098
  * *1631*: 1100
  * *1632*: 1103
  * *1645*: 1147, 1151
  * *1646*: 1156
  * *1647*: 1161
  * *1653*: 1191, 1195
  * *1694*: 1526
  * *1695*: 1546
  * *1700*: 1617, 1621
  * *1701*: 1633, 1638
  * *1702*: 1645, 1649
  * *1703*: 1657, 1664
  * *1704*: 1678
  * *1710*: 1778
  * *1711*: 1796
  * *1712*: 1803

* *1655*: 1203
* *1657*: 1214, 1215
* *1659*: 1227
* *1660*: 1229, 1231
* *1661*: 1233
* *1662*: 1234, 1236
* *1663*: 1240
* *1664*: 1243
* *1665*: 1246, 1248
* *1666*: 1252, 1253, 1254
* *1667*: 1256
* *1669*: 1268
* *1670*: 1270
* *1671*: 1277
* *1672*: 1279, 1282, 1284
* *1673*: 1285, 1288
* *1674*: 1291, 1292, 1295
* *1675*: 1298, 1299, 1302, 1304
* *1676*: 1308, 1313
* *1677*: 1316, 1321
* *1678*: 1323, 1324, 1329
* *1679*: 1333, 1340
* *1680*: 1343, 1349, 1350, 1351
* *1681*: 1355, 1361
* *1682*: 1369
* *1684*: 1384
* *1685*: 1398, 1405
* *1686*: 1411, 1416
* *1689*: 1448, 1449, 1454, 1456
* *1690*: 1463
* *1691*: 1479
* *1692*: 1494, 1499
* *1693*: 1508, 1518
* *1713*: 1819
* *1714*: 1835
* *1715*: 1849
* *1716*: 1863
* *1717*: 1884
* *1722*: 1957
* *1724*: 1990, 1997
* *1725*: 2007
* *1726*: 2024, 2031
* *1727*: 2043
* *1728*: 2065, 2076
* *1729*: 2092
* *1730*: 2135
* *1731*: 2147, 2166
* *1732*: 2197, 2198
* *1733*: 2220, 2243, 2244
* *1734*: 2289
* *1735*: 2304, 2317, 2318
* *1736*: 2334, 2350, 2351, 2352B
* *1737*: 2369, 2386, 2387
* *1738*: 2399, 2412
* *1739*: 2427, 2442, 2443
* *1740*: 2455, 2470, 2471
* *1741*: 2489, 2505, 2506
* *1742*: 2538, 2539
* *1743*: 2556, 2573, 2574, 2575
* *1744*: 2594, 2608
* *1745*: 2631
* *1747*: 2661, 2665, 2677
* *1750*: 2744
* *1751*: 2764
* *1764*: 3077
* *1765*: 3108

From Malabar, including Vengurla (*years of reception*, nos)

* *1649*: 1170
* *1658*: 1224
* *1660*: 1231
* *1661*: 1233
* *1662*: 1234, 1236
* *1663*: 1240
* *1665*: 1245, 1246
* *1669*: 1268
* *1671*: 1274
* *1673*: 1288
* *1674*: 1291, 1295
* *1675*: 1299, 1304
* *1697*: 1582
* *1698*: 1593, 1598
* *1699*: 1606, 1607
* *1705*: 1694
* *1714*: 1838
* *1715*: 1852
* *1720*: 1928
* *1721*: 1942
* *1723*: 1977
* *1730*: 2130
* *1732*: 2187, 2200, 2201
* *1733*: 2226, 2228, 2229, 2231, 2232

* *1676*: 1308
* *1677*: 1315, 1321
* *1678*: 1329
* *1681*: 1355
* *1682*: 1370
* *1683*: 1373, 1379
* *1684*: 1383, 1388
* *1685*: 1396, 1406
* *1690*: 1464
* *1691*: 1474
* *1735*: 2320
* *1736*: 2340, 2354
* *1738*: 2414
* *1739*: 2432, 2433, 2435, 2446
* *1740*: 2461, 2462
* *1744*: 2601
* *1755*: 2834
* *1756*: 2857
* *1759*: 2928, 2929
* *1764*: 3086

Kamer Zeeland (Zeeland Chamber)

Missiven en rapporten ingekomen bij gouverneur-generaal en raden series (letters and reports received by governor-general and council at Batavia)

From Ceylon (nos, *years*)

* 8595, *1707*
* 8921, *1705-7*
* 8922, *1707*
* 8923, *1708*
* 8924, *1709*
* 8925, *1710*
* 8935, *1720-1*
* 8955, *1732*
* 8958, *1733*
* 8972, *1737*
* 8974, *1738*
* 8980, *1741*

From Coromandel (nos, *years*)

* 8844, *1726*
* 8866, *1735*

From Malabar (nos, *years*)

* 8985, *1681*

Factorijen series (factories)

Ceylon

* 11306

- *Hoge Regering Batavia* collection (HRB, Batavia High Government, access no. 1.04.17)
  * 542

ARSIP NASIONAL REPUBLIK INDONESIA (National Archives Republic Indonesia), JAKARTA (ANRI)

- *Buitenland* collection (BC, "foreign countries," access no. K.48)
  * 150e

REGIONAL ARCHIVES ERNAKULAM, KOCHI

- Dutch Records
  * D 64

BRITISH LIBRARY, LONDON (BL)

Asian & African Studies department (AAS, formerly Oriental & India Office Collections, or OIOC)

- Mackenzie General collection (MG) (nos/pts)

* 1/3 (ff. 13-19)	"An account of the Pandia Rajahs who reigned at Madurapuri"
* 1/6 (ff. 25-39)	"A brief account of the ancient Rajahs in the Solah Dhesam"
* 1/7A (ff. 51-4)	"Account of the Hindoo Rajium. The Raja-Cheritram or history of the ancient Rajahs of the Dutchana-Dickum or southern country of Pandia Mundalum, Colla-Mundalum & Tonda-Mundalum"
* 1/7C (ff. 61-5)	"History of the Satoo-Putty of the Maravun Vumshum"
* 1/7D (ff. 66-70)	"The present Maratta Rajas who are managing the country of Tanja-Nagaram"
* 1/8 (ff. 71-3)	"The Cheritee or actions of the Vadaka-Rajahs of Tanjore, Trichinopully & Madura"
* 1/24 (ff. 185-6)	"The Kyfeyat of Aachoota Bhoopal Naiq"
* 1/25 (f. 187)	"The limits of the Cholla, Pandian and Charan countries"
* 3/1 (ff. 19-52)	"Sketch of the general history of the peninsula"
* 3/4c (ff. 131-4)	"Hurry-Hurra Royer Vumshum"
* 3/4d (ff. 135-43)	"Veera Narasinga Royer Vumsham"
* 3/5 (ff. 155-95)	"Ram-Rajah Cheritra"
* 3/6 (following f. 195)	"Facsimile of the seal of Ram Raja"
* 3/8a (ff. 201-16)	"Mysoor Aroosoogaloo Poorvaabyoodayagaloo" [1st pt.]
* 3/8b (ff. 217-27)	"Mysoor Aroosoogaloo Poorvaabyoodayagaloo" [2nd pt.]
* 3/11 (ff. 257-61)	"Mysore Nagurda Poorbotara"
* 3/12 (ff. 262-96)	"Account of the Rajahs of Mysore from the Persic"
* 4/4 (ff. 35-74)	"Mootiah's chronological & historical account of the modern kings of Madura"
* 4/6a (ff. 87-106)	"History of the former Rajahs of the Tellugoo nation who ruled over Paundium Mundalom"
* 4/7 (ff. 161-3)	"Memoir of the Satoo-Putty or Ramnad Polligar"
* 4/8 (ff. 171-201)	"A general history of the Kings of Rama Naad or the Satoo-Putty Samastanum"
* 4/9 (ff. 219-22)	"History of Tanjore"
* 6/11 (ff. 61-83v)	"Historical account of Beedoonoor or Caladee Samstanum"
* 9/2b (ff. 10-12)	"Historical account of Chandragerry"
* 9/13a (ff. 121-9)	"Kyfyat of Gingee"
* 9/13e (ff. 138-59)	"Historical account of Gingee"
* 10/1 (ff. 37-9)	"Notices of the present state of the Anagoondy family"
* 10/2 (ff. 41-6)	"The Vaamashavally of Cristna-Deva-Rayaloo"
* 10/4a (ff. 64-5)	"Account of Bisnagur"
* 10/4b (ff. 69-70)	"Bijanagar"
* 10/5 (ff. 77-80)	"Traditionary notices of the history of the country"
* 10/11 (ff. 211-18)	"Kaalaganum"
* 10/13 (ff. 225-8)	"Marhatta account of the first establishment & progress of the English government at Madras"

* 10/15 (ff. 237-41)	"Danaputram at Chitteldroog"
* 11/2 (ff. 5-8)	"Preliminary note to the historical account of the kings of Beejanagur"
* 11/3a (ff. 9-12)	"History of the Anagoondy Rajahs"
* 11/3b (ff. 13-29)	"History of the kings of Beejanagur & Anagoondy"
* 11/12 (ff. 84-99)	"Kyfyat of Bellary"
* 11/15a (ff. 125-32)	"Kyfyat of Harponelly"
* 11/17 (f. 160)	"Genealogy or Vanshavallee of Kistna Rayeel"
* 11/18a (ff. 163-76)	"Historical account of Panoo Conda"
* 19/32 (ff. 156-7)	"Translation of a Maratta Sunnud of Yeckojee Rajah"
* 25/17 (ff. 121-9)	"Historical memoir of Chundrageery"
* 25/27 (ff. 207-9)	"Memoir of Barkur"
* 26/10 or 11 (ff. 231-40)	"A short account of the Maharratta reigning family at Tanjour"
* 40/last pt. (ff. 353-93)	"History of the kings of Beejayanagurr"
* 49/2 (ff. 27-30)	"Abstract history of the Marawar"

- Mackenzie Miscellaneous collection (MM) (nos/pts)

* 77/23 (ff. 1-39)	"Tanjour report"
* 109/37 (ff. 1-4)	"The humble representation of ... Bangaroo Teeroomaly Nack"
* 109/43 (ff. 1-4)	[untitled, similar to Mackenzie Translations, class III, no. 25]
* 109/44 (ff. 1-4)	"Historical memoir of the Satoo-Samstaan"
* 109/58 (ff. 1-4)	"Singala-Dweepum & Candy"
* 110/7 (ff. 1-8)	"The Charythy of the Vadoka Raja of Tonjore, Trinchunnapully & Madura"
* 118/1st pt. (ff. 1-41)	"Kypheat of Gingee"
* 118/74 (ff. 1-6)	"Names of the Rayers who have reigned Techanautterady"
* 158 (ff. 1-23)	Treaties of Tanjavur with the Danes and the French, 1620-1788

- Mackenzie Private collection (nos/pts)

* 47/1 (ff. 4-9)	Final report (*memorie van overgave*) of the Dutch governor of Coromandel, Maerten IJsbrantsz, 1632 (copy from c. 1740)

- Mackenzie Translations collection (MT)

Class I (Persian)

* 18 (ff. 1-63)	"The Keefeyet of Panoocundah"

Class II (Tamil: Tonda Mandalam)

* 12 (ff. 1-28)	"Kyfieth of Roya Vellore"

Class III (Tamil: Southern Provinces)

* 25 (ff. 18-41v)	"History of the former Gentoo Rajahs who ruled over the Pandyan Mandalom"
* 32 (ff. 88-104)	"The history of the Tonjore Rajas"
* 35 (ff. 110-15)	"Kyfeyeat of the Paulagars of Aureyaloor Paulaput"
* 77 (ff. 72-7)	"Regarding the Zemindars of Ramnad"
* 82 (ff. 109-34)	"Account of the Rajahs who held the government of Madura"

* 87 (ff. 31-136)	"The historycal account of the Tonjore"
* 88 (ff. 137-49v)	"Account of the Tanjore Samastanums"
* 90 (ff. 162-5v)	"The genelogical account of the Madura Vadoka Rajahs"

Class VII (Telugu: Northern Circars)

* 23 (ff. 130-41v)	"Chronological account of Bijayanagar"

Class XII (Letters and reports, from local agents collecting texts, traditions, etc.)

* 9 (ff. 39-99v)	"Monthly memorendum & report of C.V. Lutchmia to Major C. Makinzee S.M.S. of the progress made in collection of historical materials," 1804
* 11 (ff. 103-11v)	"Report of the Soobarow Marratta writer to Major C. Mackenzie," 1805

Class XIII (Inscriptions)

* 73 (ff. 46-7)	"Translation of a Neeroopam (or order) of Somaseker Naik (a king of Beedoonoore)"

- Orme Collection: India (OI) (nos/pts)

* I/17 (ff. 219-25)	"Devi Cotah, Lord Clive" (description of attacks on Devikottai in 1749 in favour of the pretender to the Tanjavur throne)
* I/22 (ff. 239-40)	"Kings of Tritchanopoly from 1509"
* I/24 (f. 242)	"Morratoe kings of Tanjore" [2nd pt.]
* I/27 (ff. 244-5)	"Morratoe kings of Tanjore" [3rd pt.]
* II/33 (ff. 451-2)	"Account of the pretender to Tanjore & the expedition to Devi Cotah in 1749..."

- Orme Collection: O.V. (OOV) (nos/pts)

* 10/19 (ff. 221-8)	Letter from General Joseph Smith at Madras to Brigadier-General Richard Smith concerning Tanjavur's expedition against Ramnad, 1771
* 33/11 (1) (ff. 155-66)	Extract diary and proceedings, Fort St. George, 1771, "concerning the state of affairs and quarrel between the Nawab and the king of Tanjore"
* 33/11 (2) (ff. 167-76)	Extract consultations, Fort St. George, 1771, "concerning the origin and state of the Maravars ..."
* 72/17 (ff. 123-30)	"Brief account, by a Trichinopoly Brahman, of Tanjore, Madura, and Trichinopoly ..."
* 247/1 (ff. 1-4)	"Application to Fort St. David by Sahajee ... for assistance to recover his rights at Tanjore," 1749
* 333/6	"Promontory of India for the intelligence of Hyder Ally's war, copied from Captain Kapper, reduced," map of south India, c. 1760s-70s
* 333/34 (f. 138)	"Plan of Ramanadaparam stormed June 2nd 1772 by the army under General Smith"

Manuscript and Map Collections (MMC)

- Additional Manuscripts (AM)

* 18021 (ff. 1-49)	"History of Kurtakull"

Published Sources

SOURCES IN SOUTH ASIAN LANGUAGES (including Persian)

Allasani Peddana, *The Story of Manu* (Murty Classical Library of India 4), trans. Velcheru Narayana Rao and David Shulman (Cambridge (MA)/London: Harvard University Press, 2015).

Ananda Ranga Pillai, *The Private Diary of Ananda Ranga Pillai, Dubash to Joseph François Dupleix, Knight of the Order of St. Michael, and Governor of Pondichery ...*, 12 vols, ed. J. Frederick Price, K. Rangachari, and Henry Dodwell (Madras: Government Press, 1904-28).

Annual Report of the Mysore Archæological Department [Archaeological Survey of Mysore] for the Year ... (Bangalore/Mysore: University of Mysore, 1887-1964).

Annual Report[s] on South-Indian Epigraphy for the Year Ending ... (Madras/New Delhi: Department of Archaeology, Government of India, 1921-55).

Basavappa Nayaka (Basavaraja), *Śivatattva Ratnākara of Basavarāja of Keḷadi*, 2 vols (Oriental Research Institute Publications, Sanskrit Series 108, 112), ed. S. Narayanaswamy Sastry and R. Rama Shastry (Mysore: Oriental Research Institute, University of Mysore, 1964, 1969).

Bhat, M.M. (ed.), *Selected Kannada Inscriptions* (Madras: University of Madras, 1952).

Burgess, Jas. (ed.), and S.M. Naṭēśa Śāstrī (trans.), *Tamil and Sanskrit Inscriptions with Some Notes on Village Antiquities Collected Chiefly in the South of the Madras Presidency* (Archaeological Survey of Southern India, vol. IV) (Madras: Government Press, 1886).

Butterworth, Alan, and V. Venugopaul Chetty (eds), *A Collection of the Inscriptions on Copper-Plates and Stones in the Nellore District*, 3 pts (Madras: Government Press, 1905).

Dallapiccola, Anna Libera (ed.), and C.T.M. Kotraiah (trans.), *King, Court and Capital: An Anthology of Kannada Literary Sources from the Vijayanagara Period* (Vijayanagara Research Project Monograph Series 9) (New Delhi: Manohar/American Institute of Indian Studies, 2003).

Desai, Ziyaud-Din A. (ed.), *A Topographical List of Arabic, Persian and Urdu Inscriptions of South India* (New Delhi: Indian Council of Historical Research, 1989).

Doniger, Wendy, and Brian K. Smith (eds), *The Laws of Manu* (New Delhi: Penguin Books, 1991).

"The Dynasty of Kaḷale," *Annual Report of the Mysore Archæological Department for the Year 1942* (Mysore: University of Mysore, 1943).

Edwardes, S.M., "A Manuscript History of the Rulers of Jinji," *The Indian Antiquary: A Journal of Oriental Research* LV (1926).

Epigraphia Carnatica [Mysore Archæological Series], 18 & 13 vols (Bangalore: Mysore Government Central Press, 1886-1970; Mysore: Institute of Kannada Studies, 1972-90; Mysore: Directorate of Archaeology and Museums, 1987).

Epigraphia Indica [and Record of the Archæological Survey of India], 43 vols (Calcutta/Delhi: Department of Archaeology/Archaeological Survey of India, 1892-2012).

Filliozat, Vasundhara (ed.), *l'Épigraphie de Vijayanagar du début à 1377* (Publications de l'École française d'Extrême-Orient 91) (Paris: École française d'Extrême Orient, 1973).

Gopinatha Rao, T.A. (ed.), Dalavay-Agraharam Plates of Venkatapatideva-Maharaya I: Saka-Samvat 1508," *Epigraphia Indica and Record of the Archæological Survey of India*, vol. XII (Calcutta: Government of India, 1913-14).

——, "Vellangudi Plates of Venkatapati-Deva-Maharaya I: Saka-Samvat 1520," *Epigraphia Indica and Record of the Archæological Survey of India*, vol. XVI (Calcutta: Government of India Press, 1921-2).

Gopinatha Rao, T.A., and T. Raghaviah (eds), "Krishnapuram Plates of Sadasivaraya: Saka Samvat 1489," *Epigraphia Indica*, vol. IX (Calcutta: Government of India, 1907-8).

Gunda Jois, K. (ed.), "Keladi Inscriptions on Gold Sandals and Pinnacles," *The Quarterly Journal of the Mythic Society* LXXXII, 1-2 (1991).

Hultzsch, E., V. Venkayya, and H. Krishna Sastri (eds), *South-Indian Inscriptions*, vol. II, *Tamil Inscriptions in the Rajarajesvara Temple at Tanjavur and Other Miscellaneous Records of the Chola, Pallava, Pandya and Vijayanagara Dynasties* (Madras: Archæological Survey of India, 1916).

Jeyaraj, Daniel, and Richard Fox Young (eds), *Hindu-Christian Epistolary Self-Disclosures: "Malabarian Correspondence" between German Pietist Missionaries and South Indian Hindus (1712–1714)* (Dokumente zur Außereuropäischen Christentumsgeschichte (Asien, Afrika, Lateinamerika) 3) (Wiesbaden: Harrassowitz Verlag, 2013).

Kautilya, *The Kauṭilīya Arthaśāstra*, 3 pts (University of Bombay Studies, Sanskrit, Prakrit and Pali 3), ed. R.P. Kangle (Bombay: University of Bombay, 1960-5).

Krishna(deva) Raya, *Sri Krishna Deva Raya: Āmuktamālyada*, ed. Srinivas Sistla (Visakhapatnam: Drusya Kala Deepika, 2010).

Krishna Sastri, H. (ed.), "Kuniyur Plates of the Time of Venkata II: Saka-Samvat 1556," *Epigraphia Indica and Record of the Archæological Survey of India*, vol. III (Calcutta: Government of India, 1894-5).

Krishnaswami Aiyangar, S. (ed.), *Sources of Vijayanagar History* (Madras: University of Madras, 1919; reprint New Delhi: Aryan Books International, 2003).

Lakshminarayan Rao, N. (ed.), "Kap Copper-Plate of Keladi Sadasiva-Nayaka: Saka 1479," *Epigraphia Indica and Record of the Archæological Survey of India*, vol. XX (Delhi, 1929-30).

Lewis Rice, B. (ed.), *Mysore Inscriptions, Translated for Government* (Bangalore, 1879; reprint New Delhi: Navrang, 1983).

Mackenzie, Colin (ed.), "History of the Anagoondy Rajahs, Taken from the Verbal Account of Timmapah, the Present Representative of that Family, at Camlapore ...," in Lawrence Dundas Campbell (ed.), *The Asiatic Annual Register, or, View of the History of Hindustan, and of the Politics, Commerce, and Literature of Asia, for the Year 1804* (London, 1806).

——, "History of the Kings of Veejanagur, or Beejanagur, and Anagoondy, from Enquiries Made at Alputtun and Anagoondy ...," in Lawrence Dundas Campbell (ed.), *The Asiatic Annual Register, or, View of the History of Hindustan, and of the Politics, Commerce, and Literature of Asia, for the Year 1804* (London, 1806).

Mahalingam, T.V. (ed.), *Mackenzie Manuscripts: Summaries of the Historical Manuscripts in the Mackenzie Collection*, vol. I (Tamil and Malayalam), vol. II (Telugu, Kannada, and Marathi) (Madras: University of Madras, 1972, 1976).

Major, R.H. (ed.), *India in the Fifteenth Century: Being a Collection of Narratives of Voyages to India, in the Century Preceding the Portuguese Discovery of the Cape of Good Hope* ... (London: Hakluyt Society, 1857; reprint New Delhi/Chennai: Asian Educational Services, 1992).

Muhammad Qasim Firishta, *Ferishta's History of the Dekkan from the First Mahummedan Conquests* ..., 2 vols, ed. Jonathan Scott (Shrewsbury: John Stockdale, 1794).

Narasimhaswami, H.K. (ed.), *South-Indian Inscriptions*, vol. XVI, *Telugu Inscriptions of the Vijayanagara Dynasty* (New Delhi: Archæological Survey of India, 1972).

——, *South-Indian Inscriptions*, vol. XXIV, *Inscriptions of the Ranganathasvami Temple, Srirangam* (Madras: Archæological Survey of India, 1982).

Narayana Rao, Velcheru, and David Shulman (eds), *A Poem at the Right Moment: Remembered Verses from Premodern South India* (Delhi: Oxford University Press, 1999).

——, *Classical Telugu Poetry: An Anthology* (New Delhi: Oxford University Press, 2002).

Natesa Aiyar, V. (ed.), "Padmaneri Grant of Venkata I: Saka-Samvat 1520," *Epigraphia Indica and Record of the Archæological Survey of India*, vol. XVI (Calcutta: Government of India Press, 1921-2).

Nilakanta Sastri, K.A. (ed.), "Two Negapatam Grants from the Batavia Museum," *Indian Historical Records Commission: Proceedings of Meetings*, vol. XIV (Delhi, 1937).

Nilakanta Sastri, K.A., and N. Venkataramanayya (eds), *Further Sources of Vijayanagara History*, 3 vols (Madras: University of Madras, 1946).

Parabrahma Sastry, P.V. (ed.), "Polepalli Grant of Achyutarāya," in idem (ed.), *Epigraphia Āndhrica*, vol. IV (Hyderabad: Government of Andhra Pradesh, 1975).

Prasad, Pushpa (ed.), "Two Stone Slab Inscriptions of Keladi Dynasty," *Proceedings of the Indian History Congress* 35 (1974).

Rafi al-Din Ibrahim Shirazi, "A Portrayal of Vijayanagar by Rafiuddin Shirazi in Tadhkirattul Muluk," ed. Parveen Rukhsana, in P. Shanmugam and Srinivasan Srinivasan (eds), *Recent Advances in Vijayanagara Studies* (Chennai: New Era Publications, 2006).

——, "History of Vijayanagara in *Tazkiratul Muluk* of Rafiuddin Shirazi," ed. Abdul Gani Imaratwale, in Shrinivas Ritti and Y. Subbarayalu (eds), *Vijayanagara and Kṛṣṇadēvarāya* (New Delhi/Bangalore: Indian Council of Historical Research, 2010).

Raju, S. (ed.), *Tañcai Marāṭṭiyar Ceppēṭukaḷ-50* (Tanjavur: Tamil University, 1983).

——, *Tañcai Marāṭṭiyar Kalveṭṭukkaḷ / Inscriptions of the Marathas of Thanjavur* (Tanjavur: Tamil University, 1987).

——, *Cētupati Ceppēṭukaḷ* (Tanjavur: Tamil University, 1994).

Ramabrahman, A.V. (ed.), "A New Copperplate Inscription of Vijayanagara King Achyuta Raya," *Proceedings of the Indian History Congress* 21 (1958).

Ramakrishna Kavi Pandit, *Pratapasimhendra Vijaya Prabandha* (Madras Government Oriental Series LIII; Saraswathi Mahal Series 5), ed. A. Krishnaswamy Mahadick Rao Sahib (Tanjore: T.M.S.S.M. Library, 1950).

Ramesan, N. (ed.), "The Krāku Grant of Harihara II," in N. Venkataramanayya and P.V. Parabrahma Sastry (eds), *Epigraphia Āndhrica*, vol. II (Hyderabad: Government of Andhra Pradesh, 1974).

Ritti, Shrinivas, and B.R. Gopal (eds), *Inscriptions of the Vijayanagara Rulers*, vol. I, *Inscriptions of the Rulers of the Sangama Dynasty (1336 A.D. – 1485 A.D.)*, 5 pts (New Delhi: Indian Council of Historical Research & Northern Book Centre, 2004).

Sen, Surendranath (ed.), *Śiva Chhatrapati: Being a Translation of Sabhāsad Bakhar with Extracts from Chiṭṇīs and Śivadigvijaya, with Notes* (Extracts and Documents Relating to Mārāṭhā History I) (Calcutta: University of Calcutta, 1920).

Sewell, Robert (ed.), *Lists of Inscriptions, and Sketch of the Dynasties of Southern India* (Archaeological Survey of Southern India II) (Madras, 1884; reprint New Delhi: Archaeological Survey of India, 1998).

——, *The Historical Inscriptions of Southern India (Collected till 1923) and Outlines of Political History* (Madras: University of Madras, 1932; reprint New Delhi: Asian Educational Services, 1983).

Shama Shastry, R. (trans.), "Malnad Chiefs (Extract from Chronicles Compiled around 1820 A.D.)," *The Quarterly Journal of the Mythic Society* XII, I (1921).

Shukracharya, *The Śukranītiḥ (Original Sanskrit Text with Translation into English)*, ed. Krishna Lal, trans. Benoy Kumar Sarkar (Delhi: J.P. Publishing House, 2005).

Sohoni, Pushkar (ed.), *The Great Inscription at Tanjore: Bhoṃsalevaṃśacaritra* (forthcoming).

Soundarapandian, S. (ed.), "Palayappattu Vivaram / Estates of Polegars," *Bulletin of the Government Oriental Manuscripts Library* 28 (2001).

Śrīdhara Venkatēśa (Ayyaval), *Śāhendra Vilāsa (A Poem on the Life of King Śāhaji of Tanjore) (1684-1710)* (Tanjore Saraswati Mahal Series 54), ed. V. Raghavan (Tanjore: T.M.S.S.M. Library, 1952).

Srinivasachari, V., and S. Gopalan (eds), *Bhonsle Vamsa Charitra: Being the Marathi Historical Inscription in the Big Temple, Tanjore, on the History of the Mahratta Rajas of Tanjore* (Tanjore Sarasvati Mahal Series 46) (3rd edition, Tanjavur, 1990).

Srinivasan, P.R. (ed.), *South-Indian Inscriptions*, vol. XXVI, *Inscriptions Collected during the Year 1908-09* (New Delhi: Archæological Survey of India, 1990).

Srinivasan, P.R., and Marie-Louise Reiniche (eds), *Tiruvannamalai: A Śaiva Sacred Complex of South India*, vols 1.1-1.2, *Inscriptions* (Pondicherry: Institut Français de Pondichéry, 1990).

Strandberg, Elisabeth (ed.), *The Moḍī Documents from Tanjore in Danish Collections* (Beiträge zur Südasienforschung, Südasien-Institut, Universität Heidelberg 81) (Wiesbaden: Franz Steiner Verlag, 1983).

Subbarayalu, Y., and S. Rajavelu (eds), *Inscriptions of the Vijayanagara Rulers*, vol. V, pt. I (Tamil Inscriptions) (Delhi: Primus Books & Indian Council of Historical Research, 2014).

Subrahmanya Sastry, S. (ed.), *Early Inscriptions* (Tirumalai-Tirupati Devasthanam Epigraphical Series I) (Madras, 1931; reprint Delhi: Sri Satguru Publications, 1984 [Sri Garib Dass Oriental Series 17]).

Sumabala, P. (ed.), "Perundevi Samudram, Devaraja Samudram and Accharavakkam Grants of Srirangaraya III (or VI) of Aravidu Dynasty," *Journal of Indian History and Culture* 13 (2006).

Taylor, William (ed.), *Oriental Historical Manuscripts in the Tamil Language, Translated with Annotations*, 2 vols (Madras: Charles Josiah Taylor, 1835).

——, "Marava-Jathi-Vernanam," *Madras Journal of Literature and Science* IV (1836).

Thackston, W.M. (ed.), *A Century of Princes: Sources on Timurid History and Art* (Cambridge (MA): The Aga Khan Program for Islamic Architecture, 1989).

Tieken, Herman (ed.), *Between Colombo and the Cape: Letters in Tamil, Dutch and Sinhala, Sent to Nicolaas Ondaatje from Ceylon, Exile at the Cape of Good Hope (1728-1737)* (Dutch Sources on South Asia c. 1600-1825, 6) (New Delhi: Manohar, 2015).

Travancore Archæological Series, 9 vols (Trivandrum: Government Press/Madras: Methodist Publishing House, 1910-41).

Tryambakayajvan, *The Perfect Wife (Strīdharmapaddhati)*, ed. I. Julia Leslie (New Delhi: Penguin Books, 1995); first published as *The Perfect Wife: The Orthodox Hindu Woman According to the Strīdharmapaddhati of Tryambakayajvan* (Delhi/Oxford: Oxford University Press, 1989).

Venkataramanayya, N. (ed.), "Pedda Cheppalli Plates of Dēvarāya II," in idem (ed.), *Epigraphia Andhrica*, vol. I (Hyderabad: Director of Archaeology and Museums, Government of Andhra Pradesh, 1969).

——, "A Note on the Gaya Inscription of Kṛishṇadēvarāya," in idem (ed.), *Epigraphia Andhrica*, vol. I (Hyderabad: Director of Archaeology and Museums, Government of Andhra Pradesh, 1969).

Venkataramiah, K.M. (ed.), *Tañcai Marāṭṭiya Maṉṉar Varalāṟu (History of the Maratha Rulers of Thanjavur, Mackenzie manuscript D 3180)* (Tanjavur: Tamil University, 1987).

Venkoba Rao, G. (ed.), "Kumbakonam Inscription of Sevvappa-Nayaka," *Epigraphia Indica and Record of the Archæological Survey of India*, vol. XIX (Calcutta: Government of India Central Publication Branch, 1927-8).

Vijayaraghavacharya, V. (ed.), *Inscriptions of Krishnaraya's Time from 1509 A.D. to 1531 A.D.* (Tirumalai-Tirupati Devasthanam Epigraphical Series III) (Madras, 1935; reprint Delhi: Sri Satguru Publications, 1984 [Sri Garib Dass Oriental Series 19]).

——, *Inscriptions of Achyutaraya's Time from 1530 A.D. to 1542 A.D.* (Tirumalai-Tirupati Devasthanam Epigraphical Series IV) (Madras, 1936; reprint Delhi: Sri Satguru Publications, 1984 [Sri Garib Dass Oriental Series 20]).

——, *Inscriptions of Sadasivaraya's Time from 1541 A.D. to 1574 A.D.* (Tirumalai-Tirupati Devasthanam Epigraphical Series V) (Madras, 1937; reprint Delhi: Sri Satguru Publications, 1984 [Sri Garib Dass Oriental Series 21]).

——, *Inscriptions of Venkatapatiraya's Time* (Tirumalai-Tirupati Devasthanam Epigraphical Series VI, pt. I) (Madras, 1937; reprint Delhi: Sri Satguru Publications, 1984 [Sri Garib Dass Oriental Series 22]).

Virupaksha Pandita, "Channa-Basava Puráṇa of the Lingaits," ed. G. Würth, *Journal of the Bombay Branch of the Royal Asiatic Society* XXIV, VIII (1865).

Viswanatha, S.V. (ed.), "The Jambukesvaram Grant of Vijayaranga Chokkanatha Nayaka: Saka 1630," *Epigraphia Indica and Record of the Archæological Survey of India*, vol. XVI (Calcutta: Government of India Press, 1921-2).

Vyasa, *The Mahābhārata*, 12 books in 7 vols, ed. J.A.B. van Buitenen and James L. Fitzgerald (Chicago/London: The University of Chicago Press, 1973-2004).

Wagoner, Phillip B. (ed.), *Tidings of the King: A Translation and Ethnohistorical Analysis of the* Rāyavācakamu (Honolulu: University of Hawaii Press, 1993).

SOURCES IN EUROPEAN LANGUAGES

Baldaeus, Philippus, *Naauwkeurige beschryvinge van Malabar en Choromandel, der zelver aangrenzende ryken, en het machtige eyland Ceylon: Nevens een omstandige en grondigh doorzochte ontdekking en wederlegginge van de afgoderye der Oost-Indische heydenen* ... (Amsterdam: Johannes Janssonius van Waasberge en Johannes van Someren, 1672).

Barbosa, Duarte, *A Description of the Coasts of East Africa and Malabar in the Beginning of the Sixteenth Century*, ed. H.E.J. Stanley (London: Hakluyt Society, 1866; reprint New Delhi/Madras: Asian Educational Services, 1995).

Becker, Hendrick, *Memoir of Hendrick Becker, Governor and Director of Ceylon, for His Successor, Isaac Augustyn Rumpf, 1716*, ed. Sophia Anthonisz (Colombo: H.C. Cottle, 1914).

Beknopte historie, van het Mogolsche keyzerryk en de zuydelyke aangrensende ryken (Batavia: C.C. Renhard, 1758).

Biker, Julio Firmino Judice (ed.), *Collecção de tratados e concertos de pazes que o Estado da India Portugueza fez com os Reis e Senhores com quem teve relações nas partes da Asia e Africa Oriental* ..., 14 vols (Lisbon: Imprensa Nacional, 1881-7).

Breekpot, Cornelius, *Memoir of Commandeur Cornelius Breekpot Delivered to His Successor the Worshipful Titular Governor and Director-Elect Christian Lodewijk Senff* ... (Selections from the Records of the Madras Government. Dutch Records 7), ed. J. Fruijtier (Madras: Government Press, 1909).

Buchanan, Francis, *A Journey from Madras through the Countries of Mysore, Canara, and Malabar*, 3 vols (London: East India Company, 1807; reprint New Delhi: Asian Educational Services, 1999).

Canter Visscher, Jacobus, *Mallabaarse brieven, behelzende eene naukeurige beschryving van de kust van Mallabaar* ... (Leeuwarden: Abraham Ferwerda, 1743).

Colenbrander, H.T., *et al.* (eds), *Dagh-register gehouden int Casteel Batavia vant passerende daer ter plaetse als over geheel Nederlandts-India anno ... [1624-82]*, 31 vols (Batavia/The Hague: Martinus Nijhoff, 1887-1931).

Coolhaas, W.Ph., J. van Goor, J.E. Schooneveld-Oosterling, and H.K. s'Jacob (eds), *Generale Missiven van Gouverneurs-Generaal en Raden aan Heren XVII der VOC*, 13 vols (Rijks Geschiedkundige Publicatiën, Grote Serie 104, 112, 125, 134, 150, 159, 164, 193, 205, 232, 250, 257-8) (The Hague: Martinus Nijhoff, 1960-2007).

Coutre, Jaques de, *Aziatische omzwervingen: Het levensverhaal van Jaques de Coutre, een Brugs diamanthandelaar 1591-1627*, ed. Johan Verberckmoes and Eddy Stols (Berchem: EPO, 1988).

Dam, Pieter van, *Beschryvinge van de Oostindische Compagnie*, 4 vols, 7 pts (Rijks Geschiedkundige Publicatiën, Grote Serie 63, 68, 74, 76, 83, 87, 96), ed. F.W. Stapel and C.W.Th. van Boetzelaer (The Hague: Martinus Nijhoff, 1927-54).

Danvers, Frederick Charles, and William Foster (eds), *Letters Received by the East India Company from its Servants in the East ... [1602-17]*, 6 vols (London: Sampson Low, Marston & Company, 1896-1902).

Della Valle, Pietro, *The Travels of Pietro Della Valle in India: From the Old English Translation of 1644 by G. Havers*, 2 vols, ed. Edward Grey (London: Hakluyt Society, 1892; reprint New Delhi/Madras: Asian Educational Services, 1991).

Dodwell, H. (ed.), *Records of Fort St George: Letters to Fort St George for 1688* (Madras: Government Press, 1915).

Dunlop, H. (ed.), *Bronnen tot de geschiedenis der Oostindische Compagnie in Perzië*, vol. I (Rijks Geschiedkundige Publicatiën, Grote Serie 72) (The Hague: Martinus Nijhoff, 1930).

Fawcett, Charles (ed.), *The English Factories in India*, 4 vols (New Series, 1670-7, 1678-84) (Oxford: Clarendon Press, 1936-55).

Foster, William (ed.), *The English Factories in India ... [1618-69]: A Calendar of Documents in ...*, 13 vols (Oxford: Clarendon Press, 1906-27).

Frederici, Cesare, "The Voyage of Master Cesar Frederick into the East India, and beyonde the Indies, Anno 1563," in Richard Hakluyt (ed.), *The Principal Navigations Voyages Traffiques & Discoveries of the English Nation ...*, 8 vols, ed. John Masefield (London: J.M. Dent and sons, 1927).

Fryer, John, *A New Account of East-India and Persia in Eight Letters Being Nine Years Travels, Begun 1672, and Finished 1681* (London: Ri. Chiswell, 1698).

Galletti, A., A.J. van der Burg, and P. Groot (eds), *The Dutch in Malabar: Being a Translation of Selections Nos. 1 and 2 with Introduction and Notes* (Selections from the Records of the Madras Government. Dutch Records 13) (Madras: Government Press, 1911; reprint New Delhi: Usha Publications, 1984).

Goens, Rijcklof van, *Memoirs of Ryckloff van Goens, Governor of Ceylon, Delivered to His Successors Jacob Hustaart on December 26, 1663, and Ryckloff van Goens the Younger on April 12, 1675* (Selections from the Dutch Records of the Ceylon Government 3), ed. E. Reimers (Colombo: Ceylon Government Press, 1932).

Gommans, Jos, Jeroen Bos, Gijs Kruijtzer, *et al.* (eds), *Grote Atlas van de Verenigde Oost-Indische Compagnie / Comprehensive Atlas of the Dutch United East India Company*, vol. VI, *Voor-Indië, Perzië, Arabisch Schiereiland / India, Persia, Arabian Peninsula* (Voorburg: Asia Maior/Atlas Maior, 2010).

Groot, P. (ed.), *Historical Account of Nawab Hyder Ali Khan ...* (Selections from the Records of the Madras Government. Dutch Records 5) (Madras: Government Press, 1908).

Heeres, J.E., and F.W. Stapel (eds), *Corpus diplomaticum Neerlando-Indicum: Verzameling van politieke contracten en verdere verdragen door de Nederlanders in het oosten gesloten, van privilegebrieven aan hen verleend, enz.*, 6 vols (The Hague: Martinus Nijhoff, 1907-55).

Imhoff, Gustaaf Willem van, *Memoir Left by Gustaaf Willem Baron van Imhoff, Governor and Director of Ceylon, to His Successor, Willem Maurits Bruynink, 1740*, ed. Sophia Pieters (Colombo: H.C. Cottle, 1911).

Jacob, Hugo K. s' (ed.), *De Nederlanders in Kerala 1663-1701: De memories en instructies betreffende het commandement Malabar van de Verenigde Oost-Indische Compagnie* (Rijks Geschiedkundige Publicatiën, Kleine Serie 43) (The Hague: Martinus Nijhoff, 1976).

Lettres édifiantes et curieuses, écrites des missions étrangères, nouvelle edition, vols X-XV, *Mémoires des Indes* (Paris: J.G. Merigot, 1781).

Lettres & conventions des gouverneurs de Pondichéry avec differents princes hindous 1666 à 1793 (Archives de l'Inde française) (Pondicherry: Société de l'histoire de l'Inde française, 1911-14).

Lockman, J. (ed.), *Travels of the Jesuits into Various Parts of the World ...*, 2 vols (London: John Noon, 1743; reprint New Delhi/Madras: Asian Educational Services, 1995).

Lopes, David (ed.), *Chronica dos Reis de Bisnaga: Manuscripto inedito do seculo XVI* (Lisbon: Imprensa Nacional, 1897).

Loten, Joan Gideon, *Memoir of Joan Gideon Loten 1752–1757* (Selections from the Dutch Records of the Ceylon Government 4), ed. E. Reimers (Colombo: Ceylon Government Press, 1935).

Love, Henry Davison (ed.), *Vestiges of Old Madras 1640–1800, Traced from the East India Company's Records Preserved at Fort St. George and the India Office, and from Other Sources*, 4 vols (London: John Murray/Government of India, 1913).

Maistre de la Tour, M., *The History of Hyder Shah, alias Hyder Ali Khan Bahadur, or, New Memoirs Concerning the East Indies with Historical Notes* (London: J. Johnson, 1784).

Manucci, Niccolao, *Storia do Mogor or Mogul India 1653–1708*, 4 vols (Indian Texts Series 1), ed. William Irvine (London: John Murray/Government of India, 1907-8).

Martin, François, *India in the 17th Century (Social, Economic and Political): Memoirs of François Martin (1670-1694)*, ed. Lotika Varadarajan, 2 vols (New Delhi: Manohar, 1981-5).

Moens, Adriaan, *Memoir Written in the Year 1781 A.D., by Adriaan Moens ...* (Selections from the Records of the Madras Government. Dutch Records 2), ed. P. Groot (Madras: Government Press, 1908).

Mundy, Peter, *The Travels of Peter Mundy in Europe and Asia, 1608-1667*, 5 pts in 6 vols (Works Issued by the Hakluyt Society, 2nd series 17, 35, 45-6, 55, 78), ed. Richard Carnac Temple and Lavinia Mary Anstey (London: Hakluyt Society, 1907-36).

Ólafsson, Jón, *The Life of the Icelander Jón Ólafsson: Traveller to India*, 2 vols (Works Issued by the Hakluyt Society, 2nd series LIII, LXVIII), ed. Bertha S. Phillpotts, Richard Temple, and Lavinia Mary Anstrey (London: Hakluyt Society, 1923, 1932).

Orme, Robert, *A History of the Military Transactions of the British Nation in Indostan, from the Year MDCCXLV ...*, 2 vols (London: John Nourse, 1763-78).

Overbeek, Daniel, *Memoir of Daniel Overbeek, Governor of Ceylon, 1742 – 1743, for His Successor Julius Stein van Gollenesse, 22 April 1743*, ed. K.D. Paranavitana (Colombo: Department of National Archives, 2009).

Pires, Tomé, *The Suma Oriental of Tomé Pires: An Account of the East, from the Red Sea to China, Written in Malacca and India in 1512-1515 ...*, 2 vols, ed. Armando Cortesão (London: Hakluyt Society, 1944; reprint New Delhi/Madras: Asian Educational Services, 1990).

Prakash, Om (ed.), *The Dutch Factories in India 1617-1623: A Collection of Dutch East India Company Documents Pertaining to India* (New Delhi: Munshiram Manoharlal Publishers, 1984).

——, *The Dutch Factories in India: A Collection of Dutch East India Company Documents Pertaining to India, Vol. II (1624-1627)* (New Delhi: Manohar, 2007).

Rogerius, Abraham, *De open-deure tot het verborgen heydendom* (Werken uitgegeven door de Linschoten-Vereeniging X), ed. W. Caland (The Hague: Martinus Nijhoff, 1915).

Saulier, A. (ed.), "Madurai and Tanjore, 1659-1666," *Journal of Indian History* XLIV, III (1966).

Saulière, A. (ed.), "The Revolt of the Southern Nayaks" [2 pts], *Journal of Indian History* XLII, I (1964), XLIV:I (1966).

Schlegel, Johann Heinrich, *Samlung zur Dänischen Geschichte, Münzkenntniß, Oekonomie und Sprache*, 8 pts in 2 vols (Copenhagen: H.C. Sander and J.F. Morthorst, 1771-6).

Schreuder, Jan, *Memoir of Jan Schreuder 1757-1762* (Selections from the Dutch Records of the Ceylon Government 5), ed. E. Reimers (Colombo: Ceylon Government Press, 1946).

Simons, Cornelis Joan, *Memoir of Cornelis Joan Simons, Governor and Director of Ceylon, for His Successor, Hendrick Becker, 1707*, ed. Sophia Anthonisz (Colombo: H.C. Cottle, 1914).

Stein van Gollenesse, Julius Valentijn, *Memoir on the Malabar Coast by J. V. Stein van Gollenesse ...* (Selections from the Records of the Madras Government. Dutch Records 1), ed. A.J. van der Burg (Madras: Government Press, 1908).

——, *Memoir of Julius Stein van Gollenesse, Governor of Ceylon 1743-1751, for His Successor Gerrit Joan Vreeland, 28th February, 1751* (Selections from the Dutch Records of the Government of Sri Lanka), ed. Sinnappah Arasaratnam (Colombo: Department of National Archives, 1974).

Valentijn, François, *Oud en Nieuw Oost-Indiën*, 8 books in 5 vols (Dordrecht: Joannes van Braam, 1724-6).

Varthema, Ludovico di, *The Itinerary of Ludovico di Varthema of Bologna from 1502 to 1508*, trans. John Winter Jones, ed. Richard Carnac Temple (London: The Argonaut Press, 1928; reprint New Delhi/ Madras: Asian Educational Services, 1997).

Vink, Markus (ed.), *Mission to Madurai: Dutch Embassies to the Nayaka Court of Madurai in the Seventeenth Century* (Dutch Sources on South Asia c. 1600-1825, 4) (New Delhi: Manohar, 2012).

Wagenaar, Lodewijk, *et al.* (eds), *Gouverneur Van Imhoff op dienstreis in 1739 naar Cochin, Travancore en Tuticorin, en terug over Jaffna en Mannar naar Colombo (zondag 25 januari tot zaterdag 18 april)* (Werken uitgegeven door de Linschoten-Vereeniging CVI) (Zutphen: Walburg Pers, 2007).

Weijerman, Godefridus, *Memoir of Commandeur Godefridus Weijerman Delivered to His Successor Cornelis Breekpot ...* (Selections from the Records of the Madras Government. Dutch Records 12), ed. P. Groot (Madras: Government Press, 1910).

Secondary Literature

Abdul Haq, Moulvi, "The Influence of Persian on Mahrathi," *Islamic Culture: The Hyderabad Quarterly Review* X, 4 (1936).

"Account of the Province of Rámnád, Southern Peninsula of India," *Journal of the Royal Asiatic Society* 3, 5 (1836).

Ahmed, Shahab, *What Is Islam? The Importance of Being Islamic* (Princeton/Oxford: Princeton University Press, 2016).

Alam, Ishrat, "The Dutch East-India Company Trade at Vengurla in the Seventeenth Century," *Proceedings of the Indian History Congress* 64 (2003).

Ali, Daud, "Tanjavur: Capital of the Delta," in George Michell (ed.), *Eternal Kaveri: Historical Sites along South India's Greatest River* (Mumbai: Marg Publications, 1999).

——, "Royal Eulogy as World History: Rethinking Copper-Plate Inscriptions in Cōḻa India," in Ronald Inden, Jonathan Walters, and Daud Ali (eds), *Querying the Medieval: Texts and the History of Practices in South Asia* (Oxford: Oxford University Press, 2000).

——, *Courtly Culture and Political Life in Early Medieval India* (Cambridge: Cambridge University Press, 2004).

——, "Between Market and Court: The Careers of Two Courtier-Merchants in the Twelfth-Century Deccan," *Journal of the Economic and Social History of the Orient* 52, 4-5 (2009).

——, "The Idea of the Medieval in the Writing of South Asian History: Contexts, Methods and Politics," *Social History* 39, 3 (2014).

——, "The Betel-Bag Bearer in Medieval South Indian History: A Study from Inscriptions," in Manu Devadevan (ed.), *Clio and Her Descendants: Essays for Kesavan Veluthat* (Delhi: Primus Books, 2018).

Altekar, A.S., "The Yādavas of Seuṇadeśa," in G. Yazdani (ed.), *The Early History of the Deccan*, pts VII-XI (London: Oxford University Press, 1960).

Anjaiah, G., "Saluva Usurpation and Its Historical Importance in the History of Vijayanagar Empire," *Itihas: Journal of the Andhra Pradesh State Archives & Research Institute* XXVII, 1-2 (2001).

Appasamy, Jaya, *Tanjavur Painting of the Maratha Period* (New Delhi: Abhinav Publications, 1980).

Arasaratnam, Sinnappah, "The Dutch East India Company and the Kingdom of Madura, 1650-1700," *Tamil Culture* X, 1 (1963).

——, "Commercial Policies of the Sethupathis of Ramanathapuram 1660-1690," in R.E. Asher (ed.), *Proceedings of the Second International Conference Seminar of Tamil Studies*, vol. 2 (Madras: International Association of Tamil Research, 1968).

——, "The Politics of Commerce in the Coastal Kingdoms of Tamil Nad, 1650-1700," *South Asia: Journal of South Asian Studies* 1 (1971).

——, *Merchants, Companies and Commerce on the Coromandel Coast 1650-1740* (Delhi: Oxford University Press, 1986).

Aravamuthan, T.G., *South Indian Portraits in Stone and Metal* (London: Luzac & Co, 1930).

——, *Portrait Sculpture in South India* (London: The India Society, 1931).

Aseem Banu, M., "Polity under the Nayaks of Madurai (1529-1736)" (unpublished dissertation, Madurai Kamaraj University, 1981).

Asher, Catherine B., "Islamic Influence and the Architecture of Vijayanagara," in Anna Libera Dallapiccola and Stephanie Zingel-Avé Lallemant (eds), *Vijayanagara – City and Empire: New Currents of Research*, vol. 1 (Beiträge zur Südasienforschung, Südasien-Institut, Universität Heidelberg 100) (Wiesbaden: Franz Steiner Verlag, 1985).

Asher, Catherine B., and Cynthia Talbot, *India before Europe* (Cambridge: Cambridge University Press, 2006).

Asif, Manan Ahmed, *The Loss of Hindustan: The Invention of India* (Cambridge (MA)/London: Harvard University Press, 2020).

Augusta Lima Cruz, Maria, "Notes on Portuguese Relations with Vijayanagara, 1500-1565," in Sanjay Subrahmanyam (ed.), *Sinners and Saints: The Successors of Vasco da Gama* (Delhi: Oxford University Press, 1998).

Baark, Josefine, "Decorum: Courtly Posturing in the Visual Economy of Indo-Danish Diplomacy," in Annamaria Motrescu-Mayes and Marcus Banks (eds), *Visual Histories of South Asia* (New Delhi: Primus Books, 2018).

——, "The *Tranquebar Palampore*: Trade, Diplomacy, and 'a Little Amusement' in an Early Modern Indo-Danish Textile," *Eighteenth-Century Studies* 52, 1 (2018).

Balambal, V., "The Saptanga Theory and the State in the Sangam Age" [summary], *Proceedings of the Indian History Congress* 52 (1991).

Balasubrahmanyan, Suchitra, *The Myth of the Hare and Hounds: Making Sense of a Recurring City-Foundation Story* (NMML Occasional Paper, History and Society, New Series 44) (New Delhi: Nehru Memorial Museum and Library, 2014).

Barendse, R.J., *The Arabian Seas: The Indian Ocean World of the Seventeenth Century* (New Delhi: Vision Books, 2002).

Barnett, L.D., "The Keladi Rajas of Ikkeri and Bednur," *Journal of the Royal Asiatic Society* (New Series) 42, 1 (1910).

Basava Raja, K.R., "Qualifications of Ministers under Hoysaḷas," in B. Sheik Ali (ed.), *The Hoysaḷa Dynasty* (Mysore: Prasaranga, University of Mysore, 1972).

——, "The Central Government under the Chālukyas of Kalyāṇa," in M.S. Nagaraja Rao (ed.), *The Chālukyas of Kalyāṇa (Seminar Papers)* (Bangalore: The Mythic Society, 1983).

——, "Sources of the History of Minor Principalities," in S.P. Sen (ed.), *Sources of the History of India*, vol. I (Calcutta: Institute of Historical Studies, 1988).

Bawa, V.K. (ed.), "Rama Raya and the Fall of the Vijayanagara Empire: V.S. Naipaul versus William Dalrymple," *Deccan Studies* II, 2 (2004).

Bayly, Susan, *Saints, Goddesses and Kings: Muslims and Christians in South Indian Society, 1700-1900* (Cambridge: Cambridge University Press, 1989).

Bellarykar, Nikhil, "Conflict and Co-operation: Preliminary Explorations in VOC – Tanjavur (Maratha) Relations during 1676-1691," *Prag Samiksha* 5, 9 (2017).

——, "Two Marathi Letters from the Arsip Nasional Republik Indonesia: A Snapshot of Dutch-Maratha Relations in the Late-Eighteenth-Century Coromandel," *Itinerario* 43, 1 (2019).

Bes, Lennart, "Friendship as Long as the Sun and Moon Shine: Ramnad and Its Perception of the Dutch East India Company, 1725-1750" (unpublished MA thesis, Leiden University, 1997).

——, "The Setupatis, the Dutch, and Other Bandits in Eighteenth-Century Ramnad (South India)," *Journal of the Economic and Social History of the Orient* 44, 4 (2001).

——, "Toddlers, Widows, and Bastards Enthroned: Dynastic Successions in Early-Modern South India as Observed by the Dutch," *Leidschrift: Historisch Tijdschrift* 27, 1 (2012).

——, "Gold-Leaf Flattery, Calcuttan Dust, and a Brand New Flagpole: Five Little-Known VOC Collections in Asia on India and Ceylon," *Itinerario: International Journal on the History of European Expansion and Global Interaction* 36, 1 (2012).

——, "Thalassophobia, Women's Power, and Diplomatic Insult at Karnataka Courts: Two Dutch Embassies to Mysore and Ikkeri in the 1680s" (unpublished paper, 2014).

——, "Sultan among Dutchmen? Royal Dress at Court Audiences in South India, as Portrayed in Local Works of Art and Dutch Embassy Reports, Seventeenth–Eighteenth Centuries," *Modern Asian Studies* 50, 6 (2016).

——, "The Ambiguities of Female Rule in Nayaka South India, Seventeenth to Eighteenth Centuries," in Elena Woodacre (ed.), *A Companion to Global Queenship* (Kalamazoo/Bradford: Arc Humanities Press, 2018).

Bes, Lennart, and Crispin Branfoot, "'From All Quarters of the Indian World': Hindu Kings, Dutch Merchants and the Temple at Rameshvaram" (forthcoming).

Bes, Lennart, and Gijs Kruijtzer, *Dutch Sources on South Asia c. 1600-1825*, vol. 3, *Archival Guide to Repositories outside The Netherlands* (New Delhi: Manohar, 2015).

Bhandarkar, V.K., "Kampili Raya and the Founders of Vijayanagara," *Proceedings of the Indian History Congress* 5 (1941).

Bhattacharya, Jayanta, "The Rite of Hiraṇyagarbha: Ritual Rebirth for Social Acceptance" (unpublished paper, n.d. [c. 2021?]).

Bhattacherje, S.B., *Encyclopaedia of Indian Events and Dates* (New Delhi: Sterling Publishers, 1995).

Bhosale, Tulajendra Rajah P., *Rajah Serfoji – II (With a Short History of Thanjavur Mahrattas)* (2nd edition, Tanjavur: Shivaji Rajah T. Bhosale, 1999).

Bhosle, Pratap Sinh Serfoji Raje, *Contributions of Thanjavur Maratha Kings* (2nd edition, Chennai: Notion Press, 2017).

"A Biographical Account of the Ancestors of the Present Rajah of Coorga," in *The Asiatic Annual Register, or, a View of the History of Hindustan, and of the Politics, Commerce and Literature of Asia, for the Year 1800* (London, 1801).

Blake, David M., "Introduction," in J.S. Cotton, J.H.R.T. Charpentier, and E.H. Johnston, *Catalogue of Manuscripts in European Languages Belonging to the Library of the India Office*, vol. I, pt. II, *The Mackenzie General and Miscellaneous Collections* (London: British Library, 1992).

Boyle, James, "Chronicles of Southern India: Part II.–The Marava Country," *Calcutta Review* 59, 117 (1874).

Branfoot, Crispin, "Royal Portrait Sculpture in the South Indian Temple," *South Asian Studies* 16, 1 (2000).

——, "Mangammal of Madurai and South Indian Portraiture," *East and West* 51, 3-4 (2001).

——, "In a Land of Kings: Donors, Elites, and Temple Sculpture," in Anila Verghese and Anna Libera Dallapiccola (eds), *South India under Vijayanagara: Art and Archaeology* (New Delhi: Oxford University Press, 2011).

——, "Dynastic Genealogies, Portraiture, and the Place of the Past in Early Modern South India," *Artibus Asiae* LXXII, 2 (2012).

——, "Imperial Memory: The Vijayanagara Legacy in the Art of the Tamil Nayakas," in Anila Verghese (ed.), *Krishnadevaraya and His Times* (Mumbai: K R Cama Oriental Institute, 2013).

——, "Heroic Rulers and Devoted Servants: Performing Kingship in the Tamil Temple," in idem (ed.), *Portraiture in South Asia since the Mughals: Art, Representation and History* (London/New York: I.B. Tauris, 2018).

Breckenridge, Carol Appadurai, "From Protector to Litigant—Changing Relations between Hindu Temples and the Rājā of Ramnad," *The Indian Economic and Social History Review* 14, 1 (1977).

Brennig, Joseph J., "Chief Merchants and the European Enclaves of Seventeenth-Century Coromandel," *Modern Asian Studies* 11, 3 (1977).

Bridges White, Elizabeth Jane, "Beyond Empire: Vijayanagara Imperialism and the Emergence of the Keladi-Ikkeri Nayaka State, 1499-1763 C.E." (unpublished dissertation, University of Michigan, 2015).

Burgess, Jas., "The Ritual of Râmêśvaram," *The Indian Antiquary: A Journal of Oriental Research* XII (1883).

Burling, Robbins, *The Passage of Power: Studies in Political Succession* (New York/London: Academic Press, 1974).

Caldwell, Robert, *A Political and General History of the District of Tinnevelly, in the Presidency of Madras, from the Earliest Period to Its Cession to the English Government in A.D. 1801* (Madras: Government Press, 1881); reprinted as *A History of Tinnevelly* (New Delhi: Asian Educational Services, 1982).

Casparis, J.G. de, "Inscriptions and South Asian Dynastic Traditions," in R.J. Moore (ed.), *Traditions and Politics in South Asia* (New Delhi: Vikas Publishing House, 1979).

Chakravarthy, Pradeep, and Vikram Sathyanathan, *Thanjavur: A Cultural History* (New Delhi: Niyogi Books, 2010).

Chandler, J.S., *History of the Jesuit Mission in Madura, South India, in the Seveneenth and Eighteenth Centuries* (Madras: M.E. Publishing House, 1909).

Chandra, C., "The Cultural History of the Nayaks of Madurai" (unpublished dissertation, Madurai Kamaraj University, 2006).

Chandrashekar, S., "Robert Sewell's Vijayanagara – A Critique," in Shrinivas Ritti and Y. Subbarayalu (eds), *Vijayanagara and Kṛṣṇadēvarāya* (New Delhi/Bangalore: Indian Council of Historical Research, 2010).

Chekuri, Christopher, "Between Family and Empire: Nayaka Strategies of Rule in Vijayanagara South India, 1400-1700" (unpublished dissertation, University of Wisconsin-Madison, 2005).

——, "'Fathers' and 'Sons': Inscribing Self and Empire at Vijayanagara, Fifteenth and Sixteenth Centuries," *The Medieval History Journal* 15, 1 (2012).

Chidananda Murthy, M., "*Keḷadinṛipa Vijayam* – A Historical Poem," in G.S. Dikshit (ed.), *Studies in Keladi History (Seminar Papers)* (Bangalore: Mythic Society, 1981).

Chinnaiyan, S., "Royal Patronage to Islam in Tanjore Maratha Kingdom [as Gleaned from Modi Records]," *Proceedings of the Indian History Congress* 65 (2004).

Chitnis, K.N., "Sivatattvaratnakara with Special Reference to Polity," *Proceedings of the Indian History Congress* 28 (1966).

——, *Keḷadi Polity* (Research Publications 17) (Dharwar: Karnatak University, 1974).

Clulow, Adam, and Tristan Mostert (eds), *The Dutch and English East India Companies: Diplomacy, Trade and Violence in Early Modern Asia* (Amsterdam: Amsterdam University Press, 2018).

Coelho, William, *The Hoysaḷa Vaṁśa* (Studies in Indian History … 11) (Bombay: Indian Historical Research Institute, St. Xavier's College, 1950).

Cohn, Bernard S., *Colonialism and Its Forms of Knowledge: The British in India* (Princeton: Princeton University Press, 1996).

Colebrooke, Mr., "A Disquisition on Regal Succession, by Jaganatha Tercapanchanana: From the Digest of Hindu Law, Translated from the Original Sanscrit," in *The Asiatic Annual Register, or, a View of the History of Hindustan, and of the Politics, Commerce and Literature of Asia, for the Year 1800* (London, 1801).

Cotton, J.S., J.H.R.T. Charpentier, and E.H. Johnston, *Catalogue of Manuscripts in European Languages Belonging to the Library of the India Office*, vol. I, pt. II, *The Mackenzie General and Miscellaneous Collections* (London: British Library, 1992).

Cox, Whitney, *Politics, Kingship, and Poetry in Medieval South India: Moonset on Sunrise Mountain* (Cambridge: Cambridge University Press, 2016).

Crill, Rosemary, "South Indian Court Scenes," *Hali* 203 (2020).

Dallapiccola, Anna Libera, "Sculptures on the Great Platform of Vijayanagara," in Anila Verghese and Anna Libera Dallapiccola (eds), *South India under Vijayanagara: Art and Archaeology* (New Delhi: Oxford University Press, 2011).

——, "Ramayana in Southern Indian Art: Themes and Variations," in Anila Verghese and Anna Libera Dallapiccola (eds), *South India under Vijayanagara: Art and Archaeology* (New Delhi: Oxford University Press, 2011).

Dallapiccola, Anna Libera, Brigitte Khan Majlis, George Michell, and John M. Fritz, *Lepakshi: Architecture, Sculpture, Painting* (New Delhi: Niyogi Books, 2019).

Dalrymple, William, "'Sir Vidia Gets It Badly Wrong'," *Outlook* (15 Mar. 2004).

Davis, Donald R., Jr, *The Spirit of Hindu Law* (Cambridge: Cambridge University Press, 2010).

Davis, Richard H., "Indian Art Objects as Loot," *The Journal of Asian Studies* 52, 1 (1993).

——, "A Muslim Princess in the Temples of Viṣṇu," *International Journal of Hindu Studies* 8, 1-3 (2004).

Dayal, Subah, "Vernacular Conquest? A Persian Patron and His Image in the Seventeenth-Century Deccan," *Comparative Studies of South Asia, Africa and the Middle East* 37, 3 (2017).

Dębicka-Borek, Ewa, "The Bravery of Sāḷuva Narasiṃha and the Grace of Narasiṃha Deity," in Tiziana Pontillo (ed.), *Indologica Taurinensia: The Journal of the International Association of Sanskrit Studies*, vol. XL (Turin: Comitato AIT, 2014).

Deloche, Jean, *A Study in Nayaka-Period Social Life: Tiruppudaimarudur Paintings and Carvings* (Collection Indologie 116) (Pondicherry: Institut Français de Pondichéry, 2011).

Derrett, J. Duncan M., *The Hoysaḷas: A Medieval Royal Family* (Oxford: Oxford University Press, 1957).

Devadevan, Manu V., *A Prehistory of Hinduism* (Warsaw/Berlin: De Gruyter Open, 2016).

Devaraj, D.V., "Date of Krishnadevaraya's Coronation," *The Quarterly Journal of the Mythic Society* XCIX, 1 (2008).

Dewaraja, Lorna S., *The Kandyan Kingdom of Sri Lanka 1707-1782* (2nd edition, Colombo: Lake House Investments, 1988).

Dijk, L.C.D. van, *Zes jaren uit het leven van Wemmer van Berchem, gevolgd door iets over onze vroegste betrekkingen met Japan, twee geschiedkundige bijdragen* (Amsterdam: J.H. Scheltema, 1858).

Dikshit, G.S. (ed.), *Early Vijayanagara: Studies in Its History & Culture (Proceedings of S. Srikantaya Centenary Seminar)* (Bangalore: B.M.S. Memorial Foundation, n.d. [1988]).

——, "The Foundation of Vijayanagar," *The Karnataka Historical Review* XXVI (1992).

Dinnell, Darry, "*Sāmrājyalakṣmīpīṭhikā*: An Imperial Tantric Manual from Vijayanagara" (unpublished MA thesis, McGill University, 2011).

Dirks, Nicholas B., *The Hollow Crown: Ethnohistory of an Indian Kingdom* (Cambridge: Cambridge University Press, 1987).

——, *Castes of Mind: Colonialism and the Making of Modern India* (Princeton/Oxford: Princeton University Press, 2001).

——, "Colin Mackenzie: Autobiography of an Archive," in Thomas R. Trautman (ed.), *The Madras School of Orientalism: Producing Knowledge in Colonial South India* (Oxford: Oxford University Press, 2009).

Dodamani, B.A., *Gaṅgādevī's Madhurāvijayaṁ: A Literary Study* (Delhi: Sharada Publishing House, 2008).

Dua, J.C., *Palegars of South India: Forms and Contents of Their Resistance in Ceded Districts* (New Delhi: Reliance Publishing House, 1996).

Duindam, Jeroen, *Dynasties: A Global History of Power, 1300–1800* (Cambridge: Cambridge University Press, 2016).

——, "Rulers and Elites in Global History: Introductory Observations," in Maaike van Berkel and Jeroen Duindam (eds), *Prince, Pen, and Sword: Eurasian Perspectives* (Rulers & Elites 15) (Leiden/Boston: Brill, 2018).

——, "The Court as a Meeting Point: Cohesion, Competition, Control," in Maaike van Berkel and Jeroen Duindam (eds), *Prince, Pen, and Sword: Eurasian Perspectives* (Rulers & Elites 15) (Leiden/Boston: Brill, 2018).

Dumont, Louis, *Religion/Politics and History in India: Collected Papers in Indian Sociology* (Paris/The Hague: Mouton Publishers, 1970).

Dutt, Gayatri Madan, and Souren Roy, *Chennamma of Keladi: The Queen Who Defied Aurangazeb* (Bombay: Amar Chitra Katha, 1988).

Eaton, Richard M., *A Social History of the Deccan, 1300-1761: Eight Indian Lives* (The New Cambridge History of India I, 8) (Cambridge: Cambridge University Press, 2005).

——, "The Articulation of Islamic Space in the Medieval Deccan," in Meenakshi Khanna (ed.), *Cultural History of Medieval India* (New Delhi: Social Science Press, 2007); first published in Irene A. Bierman (ed.), *The Experience of Islamic Art on the Margins of Islam* (Reading: Ithaca Press, 2005).

——, "'Kiss My Foot,' Said the King: Firearms, Diplomacy, and the Battle for Raichur, 1520," *Modern Asian Studies* 43, 1 (2009).

——, *India in the Persianate Age 1000-1765* (London: Allen Lane/Penguin Books, 2019).

Eaton, Richard M., and Phillip B. Wagoner, *Power, Memory, Architecture: Contested Sites on India's Deccan Plateau, 1300-1600* (New Delhi: Oxford University Press, 2014).

Ebeling, Sascha, *Colonizing the Realm of Words: The Transformation of Tamil Literature in Nineteenth-Century South India* (Albany: State University of New York Press, 2010).

Emmer, Pieter C., and Jos J.L. Gommans, *The Dutch Overseas Empire, 1600–1800* (Cambridge: Cambridge University Press, 2021).

Ferroli, D., *The Jesuits in Mysore* (Kozhikode: Xavier Press, 1955).

Fihl, Esther, "Shipwrecked on the Coromandel: The First Indian-Danish Contact, 1620," in idem and A.R. Venkatachalapathy (eds), *Beyond Tranquebar: Grappling across Cultural Borders in South India* (New Delhi: Orient Blackswan, 2014).

——, "The South Indian Setting: Kingship, Trade and Architecture" in idem (ed.), *The Governor's Residence in Tranquebar: The House and the Daily Life of Its People, 1770–1845* (Copenhagen: Museum Tusculanum Press, 2017).

Filliozat, Vasundhara, "Relatives and Officers of Ballala III and IV Who Accepted Service under the Kings of Vijayanagara," *Itihas: Journal of the Andhra Pradesh Archives* I, 2 (1973).

——, "Hampi – Vijayanagar," in G.S. Dikshit (ed.), *Early Vijayanagara: Studies in Its History & Culture (Proceedings of S. Srikantaya Centenary Seminar)* (Bangalore: B.M.S. Memorial Foundation, n.d. [1988]).

Fischel, Roy S., *Local States in an Imperial World: Identity, Society and Politics in the Early Modern Deccan* (Edinburgh: Edinburgh University Press, 2020).

Fisher, Elaine M., *Hindu Pluralism: Religion and the Public Sphere in Early Modern South India* (South Asia across the Disciplines) (Oakland: University of California Press, 2017).

Flatt, Emma J., *The Courts of the Deccan Sultanates: Living Well in the Persian Cosmopolis* (Cambridge: Cambridge University Press, 2019).

Flood, Finbarr B., *Objects of Translation: Material Culture and Medieval "Hindu-Muslim" Encounter* (Princeton/Woodstock: Princeton University Press, 2009).

Flores, Jorge, "'I Will Do as My Father Did': On Portuguese and Other European Views of Mughal Succession Crises," *e-Journal of Portuguese History* 3, 2 (2005).

Francis, Emmanuel, "Imperial Languages and Public Writings in Tamil South India: A Bird's-Eye View in the Very *Longue Durée*," in Peter C. Bisschop and Elizabeth A. Cecil (eds), *Primary Sources and Asian Pasts* (Religion, Region, Language and the State 8) (Berlin/Boston: De Gruyter, 2021)

Francis, W., *Madura Gazetteer* (Madras: Government Press, 1906; reprint New Delhi: Cosmo Publications, 2000).

Fritz, John M., "Was Vijayanagara a 'Cosmic City'?," in Anna Libera Dallapiccola and Stephanie Zingel-Avé Lallemant (eds), *Vijayanagara – City and Empire: New Currents of Research*, vol. 1 (Beiträge zur Südasienforschung, Südasien-Institut, Universität Heidelberg 100) (Wiesbaden: Franz Steiner Verlag, 1985).

——, "Vijayanagara: Authority and Meaning of a South Indian Imperial Capital," *American Anthropologist* 88, 1 (1986).

——, "Krishnadevaraya in Popular Imagination," in Anila Verghese (ed.), *Krishnadevaraya and His Times* (Mumbai: K R Cama Oriental Institute, 2013).

Fritz, John M., George Michell, and M.S. Nagaraja Rao, *Where Kings and Gods Meet: The Royal Centre at Vijayanagara, India* (Tucson: The University of Arizona Press, 1985).

Gadgil, Vidya, "The Bṛhadīśvara Temple Inscription of the Bhosales of Tanjore: A Critical Study," in R.K. Sharma and Devendra Handa (eds), *Revealing India's Past (Recent Trends in Art and Archaeology): Prof. Ajay Mitra Shastri Commemoration Volume*, vol. II (New Delhi: Aryan Books International, 2005).

Ganesh, K., and Girijapathy, *The Coins of the Vijayanagar Empire* (Bangalore: K. Ganesh, 1997).

Ganesh, Swarnamalya, "Notions of 'Classical' in Bharatanatyam: A Cultural Operation of the Classes – Arguments of the Cosmopolitan Margi and Indigenous Desi, Repertoires of the Nayak Period," *Kalakshetra Journal Series* I, 3 (2014).

Gittinger, Mattiebelle, *Master Dyers to the World: Technique and Trade in Early Dyed Cotton Textiles* (Washington: Textile Museum, 1982).

Gode, P.K., "Ākāśabhairava-Kalpa, an Unknown Source of the History of Vijayanagara," in idem, *Studies in Indian Literary History*, vol. II (Shri Bahadur Singh Singhi Memoirs 5) (Bombay: Singhi Jain Śāstra Śikshāpīth, 1954).

——, "Raghunātha, a Protégé of Queen Dīpābāi of Tanjore, and His Works – Between A. D. 1675-1712," in idem, *Studies in Indian Literary History*, vol. II (Shri Bahadur Singh Singhi Memoirs 5) (Bombay: Singhi Jain Śāstra Śikshāpīth, 1954).

——, "The Identification of Raghunātha, the Protégé of Queen Dīpābāi of Tanjore and His Contact with Saint Rāmadāsa – Between A. D. 1648 and 1682," in idem, *Studies in Indian Literary History*, vol. II (Shri Bahadur Singh Singhi Memoirs 5) (Bombay: Singhi Jain Śāstra Śikshāpīth, 1954).

——, "The Contact of Bhaṭṭoji Dīkṣita and Some Members of His Family with the Keḷadi Rulers of Ikkeri – Between c. A. D. 1592 and 1645," in idem, *Studies in Indian Literary History*, vol. III (Pune: Prof. P. K. Gode Collected Works Publication Committee, 1956).

Goldstone, Jack A., and John F. Haldon, "Ancient States, Empires, and Exploitation: Problems and Perspectives," in Ian Morris and Walter Scheidel (eds), *The Dynamics of Ancient Empires: State Power from Assyria to Byzantium* (New York: Oxford University Press, 2009).

Gommans, Jos, "The Silent Frontier in South Asia, c. A.D. 1100-1800," *Journal of World History* 9, 1 (1998).

——, "The Embarrassment of Political Violence in Europe and South Asia c. 1100-1800," in Jan E.M. Houben and Karel R. van Kooij (eds), *Violence Denied: Violence, Non-Violence and the Rationalization of Violence in South Asian Cultural History* (Brill's Indological Library 16) (Leiden/Boston/Köln: Brill, 1999).

——, *The Unseen World: The Netherlands and India from 1550* (Amsterdam: Rijksmuseum/Vantilt, 2018).

——, "Rethinking the VOC: Two Cheers for Progress," *BMGN – Low Countries Historical Review* 134, 2 (2019).

——, "Cosmopolitanism and Imagination in Nayaka South India: Decoding the Brooklyn *Kalamkari*," *Archives of Asian Art* 70, 1 (2020).

Gommans, Jos, Lennart Bes, and Gijs Kruijtzer, *Dutch Sources on South Asia c. 1600-1825*, vol. 1, *Bibliography and Archival Guide to the National Archives at The Hague (The Netherlands)* (New Delhi: Manohar, 2001).

Gommans, Jos, and Jitske Kuiper, "The Surat Castle Revolutions: Myth of an Anglo-Bania Order and Dutch Neutrality, c. 1740-60," *Journal of Early Modern History* 10, 4 (2006).

Gonda, J., *Ancient Indian Kingship from the Religious Point of View* (Leiden: E.J. Brill, 1966).

Goor, Jurrien van (ed.), *Trading Companies in Asia 1600-1830* (HES Studies in Colonial and Non-European History 3) (Utrecht: HES Uitgevers, 1986).

——, "Merchants as Diplomats: Embassies as an Illustration of European-Asian Relations," in idem (ed.), *Preclude to Colonialism: The Dutch in Asia* (Hilversum: Verloren, 2004).

Gopal, B.R., "A Note on the Genealogy of the Early Chiefs of Keḷadi," in G.S. Dikshit (ed.), *Studies in Keladi History (Seminar Papers)* (Bangalore: Mythic Society, 1981).

Gopal, Lallanji, "The *Śukranīti*—A Nineteenth-Century Text," *Bulletin of the School of Oriental and African Studies* 25, 1/3 (1962).

Gopala Krishna Rao, K.G., "Krishnaraya as a Great King in Politics and Warfare," in Anila Verghese (ed.), *Krishnadevaraya and His Times* (Mumbai: K R Cama Oriental Institute, 2013).

Gordon, Stewart, "Robes of Honour: A 'Transactional' Kingly Ceremony," *The Indian Economic and Social History Review* 33, 3 (1996).

——, "A World of Investiture," in idem (ed.), *Robes and Honor: The Medieval World of Investiture* (New York: Palgrave Macmillan, 2001).

——, "In the Aura of the King: Trans-Asian, Trans-Regional, and Deccani Royal Symbolism," *South Asian Studies* 32, 1 (2016).

Goswami, Praphulladatta (ed.), "The Monk Who Dueled," in Richard M. Dorson (ed.), *Folktales Told around the World* (Chicago/London: University of Chicago Press, 1975).

Guha, Sumit, "Transitions and Translations: Regional Power Vernacular Identity in the Dakhan, 1500-1800," *Comparative Studies of South Asia, Africa and the Middle East* 24, 2 (2004).

——, "Literary Tropes and Historical Settings: A Study from Southern India," in Rajat Datta (ed.), *Rethinking a Millennium: Perspectives on Indian History from the Eighth to the Eighteenth Century: Essays for Harbans Mukhia* (Delhi: Aakar Books, 2008).

——, "The Frontiers of Memory: What the Marathas Remembered of Vijayanagara," *Modern Asian Studies* 43, 1 (2009).

——, *History and Collective Memory in South Asia, 1200–2000* (Seattle: University of Washington Press, 2019).

Gunda Jois, K., "Unpublished Inscriptions of Keladi Rulers," in A.V. Narasimha Murthy and K.V. Ramesh (eds), *Giridharaśrī: Essays on Indology (Dr. G.S. Dikshit Felicitation Volume)* (Delhi: Agam Kala Prakashan, 1987).

Gundajois, Keladi, *The Glorious Keladi (History and Culture)* (Mysore: Directorate of Archaeology and Museums, 2011).

Guy, John, "A Ruler and His Courtesans Celebrate Vasantotsava: Courtly and Divine Love in a Nayaka *Kalamkari*," in Navina Najat Haidar and Marika Sardar (eds), *Sultans of the South: Arts of India's Deccan Courts, 1323–1687* (New York: The Metropolitan Museum of Art, 2011).

Hatalkar, V.G., *Relations between the French and the Marathas (1668-1815)* (Bombay: University of Bombay, 1958).

Hayavadana Rao, C., *History of Mysore (1399-1799 A.D.)*, 3 vols (Bangalore: Government Press, 1943-8).

Heesterman, J.C., *The Inner Conflict of Tradition: Essays in Indian Ritual, Kingship, and Society* (Chicago/London: The University of Chicago Press, 1985).

——, "Warrior, Peasant and Brahmin," *Modern Asian Studies* 29, 3 (1995).

Hemingway, F.R., *Tanjore Gazetteer*, vol. I (Madras, 1906; reprint New Delhi: Cosmo Publications, 2000).

——, *Trichinopoly* (Madras District Gazatteers), vol. I (Madras: Government Press, 1907).

Henige, David, *Princely States of India: A Guide to Chronology and Rulers* (Bangkok: Orchid Press, 2004).

Heras, Henry, "The Jesuit Influence in the Court of Vijayanagar," *The Quarterly Journal of the Mythic Society* XIV, 2 (1924).

——, "Venkatapatiraya I and the Portuguese," *The Quarterly Journal of the Mythic Society* XIV, 4 (1924).

——, "The Statues of the Nayaks of Madura in the Pudu Mantapam," *The Quarterly Journal of the Mythic Society* XV, 3 (1925).

——, "Early Relations between Vijayanagara and Portugal," *The Quarterly Journal of the Mythic Society* XVI, 2 (1925).

——, *The Aravidu Dynasty of Vijayanagara*, vol. 1 (Madras: B.G. Paul & Co. Publishers, 1927).

——, *Beginnings of Vijayanagara History* (Bombay: Indian Historical Institute, 1929).

Hickey, William, *The Tanjore Mahratta Principality in Southern India: The Land of the Chola, the Eden of the South* (Madras: Caleb Foster, 1873; reprint New Delhi/Madras: Asian Educational Services, 1988).

Hiltebeitel, Alf C., *The Cult of Draupadī*, vol. 1, *Mythologies: From Gingee to Kurukṣetra* (Chicago: University of Chicago Press, 1988).

"Historical Novels to Be Released," *The Hindu* (5 May 2016).

Howes, Jennifer, *The Courts of Pre-Colonial South India: Material Culture and Kingship* (London/New York: RoutledgeCurzon, 2003).

Hurpré, Jean-François, "The Royal Jewels of Tirumala Nayaka of Madurai (1623-1659)," in Susan Stronge (ed.), *The Jewels of India* (Bombay: Marg Publications, 1995).

Inden, Ronald, "Hierarchies of Kings in Early Medieval India," *Contributions to Indian Sociology* 15, 1-2 (1981).

"The Indo-Danish Connect," *The Hindu* (3 May 2015).

J.L.W., "The Chronicles of the Marava Country in Southern India," *Calcutta Review* 66, 133 (1878).

——, "Chronicles of the Marava Country," *Calcutta Review* 75, 149 (1882).

Jackson, William J., *Vijayanagara Voices: Exploring South Indian History and Hindu Literature* (Aldershot/Burlington: Ashgate, 2005).

Jaffer, Amin, "Diplomatic Encounters: Europe and South Asia," in Anna Jackson and Amin Jaffer, *Encounters: The Meeting of Asia and Europe 1500–1800* (London: V&A Publications, 2004).

Jagadisa Ayyar, P.V., *South Indian Shrines* (Madras: Madras Times Printing and Publishing Co., 1920).

Jeyaseela Stephen, S., "Rise and Decline of Pulicat under the Dutch East India Company (AD.1612-1690)," *The Historical Review: A Bi-Annual Journal of History and Archaeology* (New Series) X, 1-2 (2002).

——, *Expanding Portuguese Empire and the Tamil Economy (Sixteenth-Eighteenth Centuries)* (New Delhi: Manohar, 2009).

Jones, Constance A., "Vishwakarma Puja," in J. Gordon Melton *et al.* (eds), *Religious Celebrations: An Encyclopedia of Holidays, Festivals, Solemn Observances, and Spiritual Commemorations* (Santa Barbara/Denver/Oxford: ABC-Clio, 2011).

Kadhirvel, S., *A History of the Maravas, 1700-1802* (Madurai: Madurai Publishing House, 1977).

Kamaliah, K.C., "Anatomy of *Rāmappaiyaṉ Ammāṉai*," *Journal of Tamil Studies* 7 (1975).

Kamath, Suryanath U., "Keladi Nayakas and Marathas," *The Quarterly Journal of the Mythic Society* LXI, 1-4 (1970).

—— (ed.), "Special Number on Karnataka Historiography," *The Quarterly Journal of the Mythic Society* LXXX, 1-4 (1989).

——, *Krishnadevaraya of Vijayanagara and His Times* (Bangalore: IBH Prakashana, 2009).

Kanekar, Amita, "Two Temples of the Ikkeri Nayakas," *South Asian Studies* 26, 2 (2010).

——, "Stylistic Origins and Change in the Temples of the Ikkeri Nayakas," in Anila Verghese (ed.), *Krishnadevaraya and His Times* (Mumbai: K R Cama Oriental Institute, 2013).

Karashima, Noburu, *Towards a New Formation: South Indian Society under Vijayanagar Rule* (New Delhi: Oxford University Press, 1992).

—— (ed.), *A Concise History of South India: Issues and Interpretations* (New Delhi: Oxford University Press, 2014).

Katti, Madhav N., "Some Important Epigraphs of the Sangama Dynasty," in G.S. Dikshit (ed.), *Early Vijayanagara: Studies in Its History & Culture (Proceedings of S. Srikantaya Centenary Seminar)* (Bangalore: B.M.S. Memorial Foundation, n.d. [1988]).

Kemp, P.H. van der, "De Nederlandsche factorijen in Vóór-Indië in den aanvang der 19e eeuw," *Bijdragen tot de taal-, land- en volkenkunde van Nederlandsch-Indië* LIII (1901).

Kersenboom, Saskia C., *Nityasumaṅgalī: Devadasi Tradition in South India* (Delhi: Motilal Banarsidass Publishers, 1987).

Knaap, Gerrit, and Ger Teitler (eds), *De Verenigde Oost-Indische Compagnie tussen oorlog en diplomatie* (Verhandelingen van het Koninklijk Instituut voor Taal-, Land- en Volkenkunde 197) (Leiden: KITLV Uitgeverij, 2002).

Kodandaramaiah, Timmavajjhala, *The Telugu Poets of Madura and Tanjore* (Hyderabad: Andhra Pradesh Sahitya Akademi, n.d. [c. 1975]).

Krishna, M.H., "The Dalavāi Family of Mysore," in N.K. Sidhanta *et al.* (ed.), *Bhārata-Kaumudī: Studies in Indology in Honour of Dr. Radha Kumud Mookerji*, pt. I (Allahabad: The Indian Press, 1945).

Krishna, Nanditha, *Painted Manuscripts of the Sarasvati Mahal Library* (T.M.S.S.M. Library Series 347) (Tanjavur: Thanjavur Maharaja Serfoji's Saravati Mahal Library, 2011).

Krishna Sastri, H., "The First Vijayanagara Dynasty: Its Viceroys and Ministers," *Annual Report 1907-8: Archæological Survey of India* (Calcutta: Superintendent Government Printing, 1911).

——, "The Second Vijayanagara Dynasty: Its Viceroys and Ministers," *Annual Report 1908-9: Archæological Survey of India* (Calcutta: Superintendent Government Printing, n.d.).

——, "The Third Vijayanagara Dynasty: Its Viceroys and Ministers," *Annual Report 1911-12: Archæological Survey of India*, ed. John Marshall (Calcutta: Superintendent Government Printing, 1915).

Krishnamachariar, M., *History of Classical Sanskrit Literature* ... (Madras: Tirumalai-Tirupati Devasthanams Press, 1937).

Krishnamurthy, Radha, *Sivatattva Ratnākara of Keladi Basavaraja: A Cultural Study* (Keladi: Keladi Museum and Historical Research Bureau, 1995).

Krishnasvami Aiyangar, S., "Srirangarayalu: The Last Emperor of Vijayanagar," *Journal of Indian History* XVIII, 1 (1939).

Krishnaswami, A., *The Tamil Country under Vijayanagar* (Annamalai University Historical Series 20) (Annamalainagar: Annamalai University, 1964).

Krishnaswami Aiyangar, S., *South India and Her Muhammadan Invaders* (Oxford: Milford, 1921; reprint New Delhi/Madras: Asian Educational Services, 1991).

Krishnaswami Aiyangar, S., *et al.* (eds), *Vijayanagara Sexcentenary Commemoration Volume* (Dharwar: Vijayanagara Empire Sexcentenary Association, 1936); reprinted as *Vijayanagara: History and Legacy* (New Delhi: Aryan Books International, 2000).

Krishnaswami Iyengar, S., "Mysore and the Decline of the Vijayanagar Empire," *The Quarterly Journal of the Mythic Society* XIII, 4 (1923).

Kruijtzer, Gijs, *Xenophobia in Seventeenth-Century India* (Leiden: Leiden University Press, 2009).

Kulkarni, A.R., "The Chiefs of Sonda (Swādi) and the Marathas in the Seventeenth Century," in G.S. Dikshit (ed.), *Studies in Keladi History (Seminar Papers)* (Bangalore: Mythic Society, 1981).

Kulkarni, Tanu, "State Salutes the Real Heroes," *The Hindu* (14 Nov. 2016).

Kulke, Hermann, "Mahārājas, Mahants and Historians: Reflections on the Historiography of Early Vijayanagara and Sringeri," in Anna Libera Dallapiccola and Stephanie Zingel-Avé Lallemant (eds), *Vijayanagara – City and Empire: New Currents of Research*, vol. 1 (Beiträge zur Südasienforschung, Südasien-Institut, Universität Heidelberg 100) (Wiesbaden: Franz Steiner Verlag, 1985).

—— (ed.), *The State in India 1000-1700* (Delhi: Oxford University Press, 1995).

——, *History of Precolonial India: Issues and Debates*, ed. Bhairabi Prasad Sahu, trans. Parnal Chirmuley (New Delhi: Oxford University Press, 2018).

Kuppuram, G., "The Genealogy and Chronology of Keḷadi Rulers: A Review," *The Quarterly Journal of the Mythic Society* LXIX, 1-2 (1978).

——, "Principles of Succession under Keladi Rule," *Bulletin of the Institute of Traditional Cultures* 71 (1979).

Kuruppath, Manjusha, *Staging Asia: The Dutch East India Company and the Amsterdam Theatre, c. 1650 to 1780* (Colonial and Global History through Dutch Sources) (Leiden: Leiden University Press, 2016).

Lakshmi, Kumari Jhansi, "The Chronology of the Sangama Dynasty," *Proceedings of the Indian History Congress* 21 (1958).

Lakshminarayan Rao, N., "The Nayakas of Keladi," in S. Krishnaswami Aiyangar *et al.* (eds), *Vijayanagara Sexcentenary Commemoration Volume* (Dharwar: Vijayanagara Empire Sexcentenary Association, 1936), reprinted as *Vijayanagara: History and Legacy* (New Delhi: Aryan Books International, 2000).

Lalitha, P.M., *Palayagars as Feudatories under the Nayaks of Madurai* (Chennai: P.M. Lalitha, 2009).

Larsen, Kay, "En dansk Gesandtskabrejse i Indien (1735)," *Historisk Tidsskrift* 8, 3 (1910-12).

Lefèvre, Vincent, "À propos d'une célèbre toile peinte (kalamkari) de la collection Riboud au musée Guimet," in Henri Chambert-Loir and Bruno Dagens (eds), *Anamorphoses: Hommage à Jacques Dumarçay* (Paris: Les Indes Savantes, 2006).

Lewis Rice, B., *Mysore: A Gazetteer Compiled for Government*, 2 vols (revised edition, Westminster: Archibald Constable and Company, 1897; reprint New Delhi/Chennai: Asian Educational Services, 2001).

——, *Mysore and Coorg: From the Inscriptions* (London: Constable, 1909; reprint New Delhi: Asian Educational Services, 1986).

Linderman, Michael Christian, "Charity's Venue: Representing Indian Kingship in the Monumental Pilgrim Rest Houses of the Maratha Rajas of Tanjavur, 1761-1832" (unpublished dissertation, University of Pennsylvania, 2009).

Locher-Scholten, Elsbeth, and Peter Rietbergen (eds), *Hof en handel: Aziatische vorsten en de VOC 1620-1720* (Verhandelingen van het Koninklijk Instituut voor Taal-, Land- en Volkenkunde 223) (Leiden: KITLV Uitgeverij, 2004).

Loewy Shacham, Ilanit, "Expanding Domains and the Personal, Imperial Style of Kṛṣṇadevarāya," *The Indian Economic and Social History Review* 56, 3 (2019).

Lohuizen, J. van, *The Dutch East India Company and Mysore* (Verhandelingen van het Koninklijk Instituut voor Taal-, Land- en Volkenkunde 31) (The Hague: Martinus Nijhoff, 1961).

Ludden, David, *Peasant History in South India* (Princeton/Guildford: Princeton University Press, 1985).

——, "Spectres of Agrarian Territory in Southern India," *The Indian Economic and Social History Review* 39, 2-3 (2002).

Lunsingh Scheurleer, Pauline, "Uitwisseling van staatsieportretten op Ceylon in 1602," in Lodewijk Wagenaar (ed.), *Aan de overkant: Ontmoetingen in dienst van de VOC en WIC (1600-1800)* (Leiden: Sidestone Press, 2015).

Lunsingh Scheurleer, Pauline, and Gijs Kruijtzer, "Camping with the Mughal Emperor: A Golkonda Artist Portrays a Dutch Ambassador in 1689," *Arts of Asia* 35, 3 (2005).

Lycett, Mark T., and Kathleen D. Morrison, "The 'Fall' of Vijayanagara Reconsidered: Political Destruction and Historical Construction in South Indian History," *Journal of the Economic and Social History of the Orient* 56, 3 (2013).

Mac Leod, N., *De Oost-Indische Compagnie als zeemogendheid in Azië*, 2 vols (Rijswijk: Blankwaardt & Schoonhoven, 1927).

Madhavan, Chithra, *History and Culture of Tamil Nadu: As Gleaned from the Sanskrit Inscriptions*, vol. 2 (Reconstructing Indian History and Culture 31) (New Delhi: D.K. Printworld, 2007).

Mahalingam, T.V., "Tirumalaideva Maharaya," *Journal of Indian History* XVII, 1 (1938).

——, *Administration and Social Life under Vijayanagar*, 2 pts (Madras: University of Madras, 1940).

——, "Historical Material in the Ramappayyan Ammanai," *Proceedings of the Indian History Congress* 10 (1947).

——, *South Indian Polity* (Madras: University of Madras, 1967).

——, *Readings in South Indian History*, ed. K.S. Ramachandran (Delhi: B.R. Publishing Corporation, 1977).

Mailaparambil, Binu John, "The VOC and the Prospects of Trade between Cannanore and Mysore in the Late Seventeenth Century," in K.S. Mathew and J. Varkey (eds), *Winds of Spices: Essays on Portuguese Establishments in Medieval India with Special Reference to Cannanore* (Tellicherry: Irish, 2006).

Manamalar, K., "Administration and Social Life under the Mahrathas of Thanjavur" (unpublished dissertation, Bharathidasan University, 1995).

Manian, T.C.S., "Keladi Chiefs: Their Contribution to the History of Mysore," *The Asiatic Review* (New Series) XXXIV, 120 (1938).

Mantena, Rama Sundari, "The Kavali Brothers: Intellectual Life in Early Colonial Madras," in Thomas R. Trautman (ed.), *The Madras School of Orientalism: Producing Knowledge in Colonial South India* (Oxford: Oxford University Press, 2009).

——, *The Origins of Modern Historiography in India: Antiquarianism and Philology, 1780-1880* (New York: Palgrave Macmillan, 2012).

Maruthumohan, K.V.S., "Sasivarna Thevar and Formation of Sivagangai Seemai," *The Quarterly Journal of the Mythic Society* XCVII, 3 (2006).

McKim Malville, John, and John M. Fritz, "Cosmos and Kings at Vijayanagara," in Clive L.N. Ruggles and Nicholas J. Saunders (eds), *Astronomies and Cultures* (Niwot: University Press of Colorado, 1993).

Mears, Barbara, "Chiuli Fanams of Ramnad," *Journal of the Oriental Numismatic Society* 189 (2006).

——, "Symbols of Coins of the Vijayanagara Empire," *South Asian Studies* 24, 1 (2008).

——, "Propaganda and Power: The Coinage of Vijayanagara," in Anila Verghese and Anna Libera Dallapiccola (eds), *South India under Vijayanagara: Art and Archaeology* (New Delhi: Oxford University Press, 2011).

Meersbergen, Guido van, "Ethnography and Encounter: Dutch and English Approaches to Cross-Cultural Contact in Seventeenth-Century South Asia" (unpublished dissertation, University College London, 2015).

——, "Kijken en bekeken worden: Een Nederlandse gezant in Delhi, 1677-1678," in Lodewijk Wagenaar (ed.), *Aan de overkant: Ontmoetingen in dienst van de VOC en WIC (1600-1800)* (Leiden: Sidestone Press, 2015).

——, "Writing East India Company History after the Cultural Turn: Interdisciplinary Perspectives on the Seventeenth-Century East India Company and Verenigde Oostindische Compagnie," *Journal for Early Modern Cultural Studies* 17, 3 (2017).

——, "The Diplomatic Repertoires of the East India Companies in Mughal South Asia, 1608-1717," *The Historical Journal* 62, 4 (2019).

Melo, João, "Seeking Prestige and Survival: Gift-Exchange Practices between the Portuguese Estado da Índia and Asian Rulers," *Journal of the Economic and Social History of the Orient* 56, 4/5 (2013).

Menon, A.G., "Colonial Linguistics and the Spoken Language," *International Journal of Dravidian Linguistics* 32, 1 (2003).

Menon, V.P., *Integration of the Indian States* (updated edition, Madras: Orient Longman, 1985).

Michell, George, "Courtly Architecture at Gingee under the Nayakas," *South Asian Studies*, 7 (1991).

——, *The Vijayanagara Courtly Style: Incorporation and Synthesis in the Royal Architecture of Southern India, 15th-17th Centuries* (Vijayanagara Research Project Monograph Series 3) (New Delhi: Manohar/American Institute of Indian Studies, 1992).

——, *Architecture and Art of Southern India: Vijayanagara and the Successor States* (The New Cambridge History of India I, 6) (Cambridge: Cambridge University Press, 1995).

——, "Migrations and Cultural Transmissions in the Deccan: Evidence of Monuments at Vijayanagara," in Laura E. Parodi (ed.), *The Visual World of Muslim India: The Art, Culture and Society of the Deccan in the Early Modern Era* (London/New York: I.B. Tauris & Co, 2014).

Michell, George, and Indira Viswanathan Peterson, *The Great Temple at Thanjavur: One Thousand Years, 1010-2010* (Mumbai, Marg Publications, 2010).

Mitchiner, Michael, *The Coinage and History of Southern India*, 2 pts (London: Hawkins Publications, 1998).

Moore, Lewis, *A Manual of the Trichinopoly District in the Presidency of Madras* (Madras: Government Press, 1878; reprint Chennai: Tamilnadu Archives, 1998).

Morris, Rachel, "Enter the Royal Encampment: Re-examining the Brooklyn Museum's *Kalamkari* Hanging," *Arts of Asia* 34, 6 (2004).

Morrison, Kathleen D., *Fields of Victory: Vijayanagara and the Course of Intensification* (Berkeley: University of California, 1995).

——, "Coercion, Resistance, and Hierarchy: Local Processes and Imperial Strategies in the Vijayanagara Empire," in Susan E. Alcock *et al.* (eds), *Empires: Perspectives from Archaeology and History* (Cambridge: Cambridge University Press, 2001).

Mukund, Kanakalatha, *The Trading World of the Tamil Merchant: Evolution of Merchant Capitalism in the Coromandel* (London: Sangam Books, 1999).

Mutiah, Teruvercadu, "An Account of the Life of Teruvercadu Mutiah, a Learned Hindû, a Native of the Carnatic ...," in *The Asiatic Annual Register, or, a View of the History of Hindustan, and of the Politics, Commerce and Literature of Asia, for the Year 1801* (London, 1802).

Nagar, Vandana, *Kingship in the Śukra-Nīti* (Delhi: Parimal Publications, 1992).

Nagaraja Rao, M.S., "Ahmadkhān's *Dharmaśāla*," in idem (ed.), *Vijayanagara: Progress of Research 1979-1983* (Vijayanagara Research Centre Series 1) (Mysore: Directorate of Archaeology & Museums, 1983).

Nagaraju, H.M., *Devaraya II and His Times (History of Vijayanagara)* (Mysore: University of Mysore, 1991).

Nagaswamy, R., *Studies in Ancient Tamil Law and Society* (n.p.: Tamilnadu State Department of Archaeology, 1978).

—— (?), "Nayak Paintings of Kailasanatha Temple at Nattam-Kovilpatti," *South Indian Studies* III (1983).

——, "Mughal Cultural Influence in the Setupati Murals of the Ramalinga Vilasam at Ramnad," in Robert Skelton *et al.* (eds), *Facets of Indian Art: A Symposium Held at the Victoria and Albert Museum* (New Delhi: Heritage Publishers, 1987).

Nagaswamy, R., and N.S. Ramaswami, *Ramanathapuram District: An Archaeological Guide* (Ramanathapuram: Collector of Ramanathapuram, 1979).

Nainar, Nahla, "An Uncommon Prince," *The Hindu* (29 Aug. 2014).

Naipaul, V.S., *An Area of Darkness* (London: André Deutsch, 1964).

——, *India: A Wounded Civilization* (London: André Deutsch, 1977).

Nair, Janaki, "Beyond Exceptionalism: South India and the Modern Historical Imagination," *The Indian Economic and Social History Review* 43, 3 (2006).

——, "Eighteenth-Century Passages to a *History of Mysore*," in Raziuddin Aquil and Partha Chatterjee (eds), *History in the Vernacular* (Ranikhet: Permanent Black, 2008).

"Name Shimoga-Bangalore Train after Shivappa Nayaka, Says Vedike," *The Hindu* (22 Mar. 2011).

Nanda, Vivek, Anna Dallapiccola, and George Michell, "The Ramasvami Temple, Kumbakonam," *South Asian Studies* 13, 1 (1997).

Naraharayya, S.N., "Keladi Dynasty" [2 pts], *The Quarterly Journal of the Mythic Society* XXI, 4 (1931), XXII, 1 (1931).

Narasimha Murthy, A.V., *The Sevunas of Devagiri* (Mysore: Rao and Raghavan, 1971).

Narasimhamurthy, A.V., *Coins and Currency System in Vijayanagara Empire* (Numismatic Notes and Monographs 21) (Varanasi: The Numismatic Society of India, 1991).

Narasimhachar, R., "The Keladi Rajas of Ikkeri and Bednur," *Journal of the Royal Asiatic Society* (New Series) 43, 1 (1911).

——, "The Mysore Royal Insignia," *The Quarterly Journal of the Mythic Society* X, 3 (1920).

Narayana Rao, Velcheru, "Coconut and Honey: Sanskrit and Telugu in Medieval Andhra," in idem (ed.), *Text and Tradition in South India* (Ranikhet: Permanent Black, 2016); first published in *Social Scientist* 23, 10/12 (1995).

——, "Multiple Literary Cultures in Telugu: Court, Temple, and Public," in idem (ed.), *Text and Tradition in South India* (Ranikhet: Permanent Black, 2016); first published in Sheldon Pollock (ed.), *Literary Cultures in History: Reconstructions from South Asia* (Berkeley: University of California Press, 2003).

Narayana Rao, Velcheru, and David Shulman, "History, Biography and Poetry at the Tanjavur Nāyaka Court," *Social Analysis* 25 (1989).

——, "The Powers of Parody in Nāyaka-Period Tanjavur," in Arjun Appadurai, Frank J. Korom, and Margaret A. Mills (eds), *Gender, Genre, and Power in South Asian Expressive Traditions* (Philadelphia: University of Pennsylvania Press, 1991).

Narayana Rao, Velcheru, David Shulman, and Sanjay Subrahmanyam, *Symbols of Substance: Court and State in Nāyaka Period Tamilnadu* (Delhi: Oxford University Press, 1992).

——, *Textures of Time: Writing History in South India 1600-1800* (Delhi: Permanent Black, 2001).

——, "A New Imperial Idiom in the Sixteenth Century: Krishnadevaraya and His Political Theory of Vijayanagara," in Sheldon Pollock (ed.), *Forms of Knowledge in Early Modern Asia: Explorations in the Intellectual History of India and Tibet, 1500-1800* (Durham/London: Duke University Press, 2011).

Narayana Rao, Velcheru, and Sanjay Subrahmanyam, "History and Politics in the Vernacular: Reflections on Medieval and Early Modern South India," in Raziuddin Aquil and Partha Chatterjee (eds), *History in the Vernacular* (Ranikhet: Permanent Black, 2008).

——, "Notes on Political Thought in Medieval and Early Modern India," *Modern Asian Studies* 43, 1 (2009).

——, "Ideologies of State Building in Vijayanagara and Post-Vijayanagara South India: Some Reflections," in Peter Fibiger Bang and Dariusz Kołodziejczyk (eds), *Universal Empire: A Comparative Approach to Imperial Culture and Representation in Eurasian History* (Cambridge: Cambridge University Press, 2012).

Natarajan, S., "Society and Culture under the Setupatis," *Proceedings of the Indian History Congress* 14 (1951).

"Neeraj Patil to Receive Keladi Shivappa Nayaka Award," *The Hindu* (14 Aug. 2016).

Nellai Nedumaran, S.D., and S. Ramachandran, "Ancient Tamil Monarchy and the Sētupati Kings," *Studies in Indian Epigraphy (Bhāratīya Purabhilēkha Patrikā)* XXVI (2000).

Nelson, J.H., *The Madura Country: A Manual* (Madras: Lawrence Asylum Press, 1868; reprint New Delhi: Asian Educational Services, 1994).

Nilakanta Sastri, K.A., *The Pāṇḍyan Kingdom: From the Earliest Times to the Sixteenth Century* (London: Luzac & Co., 1929).

——, *The Cōḷas*, 2 vols (Madras: University of Madras, 1935-7).

——, "Tirumala Naik, the Portuguese and the Dutch," *Indian Historical Records Commission: Proceedings of Meetings*, vol. XVI (Delhi, 1939).

——, "The Chāḷukyas of Kalyāṇi," in G. Yazdani (ed.), *The Early History of the Deccan*, pts I-VI (London: Oxford University Press, 1960).

——, *A History of South India: From Prehistoric Times to the Fall of Vijayanagar* (4th edition, Madras: Oxford University Press, 1975).

Obeyesekere, Gananath, "Between the Portuguese and the Nāyakas: The Many Faces of the Kandyan Kingdom, 1591-1765," in Zoltán Biedermann and Alan Strathern (eds), *Sri Lanka at the Crossroads of History* (London: UCL Press, 2017).

Olivelle, Patrick, *The* Āśrama *System: The History and Hermeneutics of a Religious Institution* (New York/ Oxford: Oxford University Press, 1993).

O'Shea, Janet, "Dancing through History and Ethnography: Indian Classical Dance and the Performance of the Past," in Theresa Jill Buckland (ed.), *Dancing from Past to Present* (Madison: The University of Wisconsin Press, 2006).

Ota, Nobuhiro, "Bēḍa Nāyakas and Their Historical Narratives in Karnataka during the Post-Vijayanagara Period," in Noboru Karashima (ed.), *Kingship in Indian History* (Japanese Studies on South Asia 2) (New Delhi: Manohar, 2004).

——, "A Study of Two *Nāyaka* Families in the Vijayanagara Kingdom in the Sixteenth Century," *Memoirs of the Research Department of the Toyo Bunko* 66 (2008).

——, "A Reappraisal of Studies on *Nāyakas*," *Journal of Karnataka Studies* 5, 2 (2008).

——, "Who Built 'the City of Victory'? Representation of a 'Hindu' Capital in an 'Islamicate' World," in Crispin Bates and Minoru Mio (eds), *Cities in South Asia* (London/New York: Routledge, 2015).

Padigar, Shrinivas V., "Inscriptions of the Vijayanagara Rulers: Volumes: I to III (Kannada Inscriptions)," in Shrinivas Ritti and Y. Subbarayalu (eds), *Vijayanagara and Kṛṣṇadēvarāya* (New Delhi/ Bangalore: Indian Council of Historical Research, 2010).

Pai, Gita V., "From Warrior Queen to Shiva's Consort to Political Pawn: The Genesis and Development of a Local Goddess in Madurai," in Diana Dimitrova and Tatiana Oranskaia (eds), *Divinizing in South Asian Traditions* (London/New York: Routledge, 2018).

Patil, Madhao P., *Court Life under the Vijayanagar Rulers* (Delhi: B.R. Publishing Corporation, 1999).

Peterson, Indira Viswanathan, "Portraiture at the Tanjore Maratha Court: Toward Modernity in the Early 19th Century," in Rosie Llewellyn-Jones (ed.), *Portraits in Princely India 1700-1947* (Mumbai: Marg Publications, 2008).

——, "Multilingual Dramas at the Tanjavur Maratha Court and Literary Cultures in Early Modern South India," *The Medieval History Journal* 14, 2 (2011).

Philips, C.H. (ed.), *Handbook of Oriental History* (London: Royal Historical Society, 1963).

Pillay, K.K., "The Pudukkottai Plates of Srivallabha and Varatungarāma," *Proceedings of the Indian History Congress* 18 (1955).

Pinch, William R., "Same Difference in India and Europe," *History and Theory* 38, 3 (1999).

Pinto, Pius Fidelis, *History of Christians in Coastal Karnataka (1500 – 1763 A.D.)* (Mangalore: Samanvaya, 1999).

Pol, Bauke van der, *The Dutch East India Company in India: A Heritage Tour through Gujarat, Malabar, Coromandel and Bengal* (Bath: Parragon Books Ltd, 2004).

Pollock, Sheldon, "Playing by the Rules: Śāstra and Sanskrit Literature," in Anna Libera Dallapiccola, Christine Walter-Mendy, and Stephanie Zingel-Avé Lallement (eds), *Shastric Traditions in Indian Arts*, vol. 1 (Beiträge zur Südasienforschung, Südasien-Institut, Universität Heidelberg 125) (Stuttgart: Steiner Verlag Wiesbaden GMBH, 1989).

Prakash, Om, "The Dutch Factory at Vengurla in the Seventeenth Century," in A.R. Kulkarni, M.A. Nayeem, and T.R. de Souza (eds), *Medieval Deccan History: Commemoration Volume in Honour of P.M. Joshi* (Bombay: Popular Prakashan, 1996).

——, *European Commercial Enterprise in Pre-Colonial India* (The New Cambridge History of India II, 5) (Cambridge: Cambridge University Press, 1998).

Prashanth, K.C., "Mysore's Claim over the Vijayanagara Tradition: A Historiographical Construct," *The Quarterly Journal of the Mythic Society* XCIII, 3-4 (2002).

——, "The Dalavai Project in Trichinopoly: The Evaluation of a Mysore Historian," *The Quarterly Journal of the Mythic Society* XCVI, 1-2 (2005).

——, "Inheritance and Legitimacy: The Construction of the Vijayanagar Legacy by the Maratha and Mysore Historians," *The Quarterly Journal of the Mythic Society* XCVII, 4 (2006).

Price, Pamela G., *Kingship and Political Practice in Colonial India* (Oriental Publications 51) (Cambridge: Cambridge University Press, 1996).

Puttaiya, B., "A Note on the Mysore Throne," *The Quarterly Journal of the Mythic Society* XI, 3 (1921).

Raghotham, Venkata, "Empire and Historiography in Late Medieval South India: A Study of the Early Vijayanagara State," in R. Champakalakshmy, Kesavan Veluthat, and T.R. Venugopalan (eds), *State and Society in Pre-Modern South India* (Thrissur: Cosmobooks, 2002).

Raja Ram Rao, T., *Ramnad Manual* (Madras: Government Press, 1889).

Rajarajan, R.K.K., *Art of the Vijayanagara-Nāyakas: Architecture & Iconography*, 2 vols (Delhi: Sharada Publishing House, 2006).

Rajaram, K., *History of Thirumalai Nayak* (Madurai: Ennes Publications, 1982).

Rajayyan, K., "Fall of the Nayaks of Madurai," *Journal of Indian History* XLV, III (1967).

——, *A History of British Diplomacy in Tanjore* (Mysore: Rao and Raghavan, 1969).

——, "Moghal Conquest of Trichinopoly," *Journal of Indian History* XLIX, I-III (1971).

——, *History of Madurai (1736-1801)* (Madurai: Madurai University, 1974).

——, *Rise and Fall of the Poligars of Tamilnadu* (Madras: University of Madras, 1974).

Rama Sarma, P., *Saluva Dynasty of Vijayanagar* (Hyderabad: Prabhakar Publications, 1979).

Rama Sarma, P. Sree, "Rāma Rāya's Policy," *Proceedings of the Indian History Congress* 36 (1975).

Rāma Sharma, M.H., *The History of the Vijayanagar Empire*, 2 vols, ed. M.H. Gopal (Bombay: Popular Prakashan, 1978, 1980).

Ramachandra Chettiar, C.M., "Rule of Vijayanagara over Kongu Country," in S. Krishnaswami Aiyangar *et al.* (eds), *Vijayanagara Sexcentenary Commemoration Volume* (Dharwar: Vijayanagara Empire Sexcentenary Association, 1936), reprinted as *Vijayanagara: History and Legacy* (New Delhi: Aryan Books International, 2000).

Raman, Bhavani, *Document Raj: Writing and Scribes in Early Colonial India* (Ranikhet: Permanent Black, 2012).

Ramanujam, P.S., *Unheard Voices: A Tranquebarian Stroll* (Odense: University Press of Southern Denmark, 2021).

Ramaswami, N.S., "Portrait Sculptures," *South Indian Studies* II (1979).

Ramesh, K.V., "Notes on the Territorial History of the Keladi Kingdom," in G.S. Dikshit (ed.), *Studies in Keladi History (Seminar Papers)* (Bangalore: Mythic Society, 1981).

Ranade, Usha Ramakrishna, "Comparative Study of Tanjore Marathi (1750-1850 A.D.) and Modern Marathi" (unpublished dissertation, Savitribai Phule Pune University, 1988).

Rangachari, V., "The History of the Naik Kingdom of Madura," *The Indian Antiquary: A Journal of Oriental Research* XLIII-VI (1914-17).

Ranganatha Rao, S., "The Beḷagutti Kaifiyats," *The Quarterly Journal of the Mythic Society* XXXV, 2 (1944).

Rangasvami Sarasvati, A., "Political Maxims of the Emperor-Poet, Krishnadeva Raya," *Journal of Indian History* IV, III (1926).

Rangaswami Ayyangar, T.R., "The Setupatis of Ramnad," *The Calcutta Review* (New Series) 32 (1920).

Rao, Ajay K., "A New Perspective on the Royal Rāma Cult at Vijayanagara," in Yigal Bronner, Whitney Cox, and Lawrence J. McCrea (eds), *South Asian Texts in History: Critical Engagements with Sheldon Pollock* (Ann Arbor: University of Michigan Press, 2011).

——, "From Fear to Hostility: Responses to the Conquests of Madurai," *South Asian Studies* 32, 1 (2016).

Rao, Nagendra E., *Craft Production and Trade in South Kanara A.D. 1000-1763* (New Delhi: Gyan Publishing House, 2006).

Rao, Nalini, *Royal Imagery & Networks of Power at Vijayanagara: A Study of Kingship in South India* (Delhi: Originals, 2010).

Rao, Subba, and K. Chandranath, *Hakka and Bukka: The Founders of the Vijayanagara Empire* (Bombay: Amar Chitra Katha, 1981).

Rao, Subba, and G.R. Naik, *Krishnadeva Raya: The Illustrious King of Vijayanagara* (Bombay: Amar Chitra Katha, 1978).

Ray, Aniruddha, "French Establishment at Karikkal: Early Efforts," *Proceedings of the Indian History Congress* 62 (2001).

——, "The Rise and Fall of Vijayanagar – An Alternative Hypothesis to 'Hindu Nationalism' Thesis," *Proceedings of the Indian History Congress* 64 (2003).

Raychaudhuri, Tapan, *Jan Company in Coromandel 1605-1690: A Study in the Interrelations of European Commerce and Traditional Economies* (Verhandelingen van het Koninklijk Instituut voor Taal-, Land- en Volkenkunde 38) (The Hague: Martinus Nijhoff, 1962).

Reddy, Srinivas, *Raya: Krishnadevaraya of Vijayanagara* (New Delhi: Juggernaut, 2020).

Revathy, G., *History of Tamil Nadu: The Palayams* (New Delhi: Dominant, 2005).

Rietbergen, Peter, *Europa's India: Fascinatie en cultureel imperialisme, circa 1750-circa 2000* (Nijmegen: Uitgeverij Vantilt, 2007).

Roberts, Michael, *Sinhala Consciousness in the Kandyan Period 1590s to 1815* (Colombo: Vijitha Yapa Publications, 2003).

Ross, Robert, and George D. Winius (eds), *All of One Company: The VOC in Biographical Perspective* (Utrecht: HES Uitgevers, 1986).

Rubiés, Joan-Pau, *Travel and Ethnology in the Renaissance: South India through European Eyes, 1250-1625* (Past & Present Publications) (Cambridge: Cambridge University Press, 2000).

——, "The Jesuit Discovery of Hinduism: Antonio Rubino's Account of the History and Religion of Vijayanagara (1608)," *Archiv für Religionsgeschichte* 3, 1 (2001).

——, "Late Medieval Ambassadors and the Practice of Cross-Cultural Encounters, 1250–1450," in Palmira Brummett (ed.), *The "Book" of Travels: Genre, Ethnology, and Pilgrimage, 1250-1700* (Studies in Medieval and Reformation Traditions 140) (Leiden: Brill, 2009).

Sabapathy, P., "Muslims under the Setupatis of Ramnad: A Study in the Socio-Cultural History of Tamilnadu (17th and 18th Centuries)," *Proceedings of the Indian History Congress* 60 (1999).

Sai Sravan, R.V.R., "Coinage of Madurai Nayakas – A Reappraisal," *Numismatic Digest* 42 (2018).

Saletore, B.A., *Social and Political Life in the Vijayanagara Empire (A.D. 1346–A.D. 1646)*, 2 vols (Madras: B.G. Paul & Co., 1934).

——, *Ancient Indian Political Thought and Institutions* (Bombay: Asia Publishing House, 1963).

Sampath, Vikram, *Splendours of Royal Mysore: The Untold Story of the Wodeyars* (New Delhi: Rupa & Co, 2008).

Sarangi, Artatrana, *A Treasure of Tāntric Ideas: A Study of the Sāmrājyalakṣmīpīṭhikā* (Calcutta: Punthi Pustak, 1993).

Sarkar, Jadunath, *House of Shivaji (Studies and Documents on Maratha History: Royal Period)* (3rd edition, Calcutta: M.C. Sarkar & Sons, 1955).

Sathianathaier, R., *Tamiḻaham in the 17th Century* (Madras: University of Madras, 1956).

Sathyanatha Aiyar, R., *History of the Nayaks of Madura* (Madras: Oxford University Press, 1924; reprint New Delhi: Asian Educational Services, 1991).

Satyanarayana, A., *History of the Wodeyars of Mysore (1610-1748)* (Mysore: Directorate of Archaeology and Museums, 1996).

Saulière, A., "The Date of Accession of Muttu Vīrappa Nāyaka I of Madurai Settled by Letters of His Contemporary Fr. Robert de Nobili," *Journal of Indian History* XXXII, I (1954).

Scharfe, Hartmut, *The State in Indian Tradition* (Handbuch der Orientalistik, Zweite Abteilung: Indien, Dritter Band: Geschichte 2) (Leiden: E.J. Brill, 1989).

Schwartzberg, Joseph E., *et al.*, *A Historical Atlas of South Asia* (2nd edition, New York: Oxford University Press, 1992).

Seastrand, Anna Lise, "Praise, Politics, and Language: South Indian Murals, 1500-1800" (unpublished dissertation, Columbia University, 2013).

Sebro, Louise, "You Ask Me Who Is King...," in Esther Fihl (ed.), *The Governor's Residence in Tranquebar: The House and the Daily Life of Its People, 1770–1845* (Copenhagen: Museum Tusculanum Press, 2017).

Seshadri, K., "The Origin and Restoration of the Setupatis," in Somalay (ed.), *The Saga of Rameswaram Temple: Kumbabishekam Souvenir* (Rameshvaram: Arulmigu Ramanathaswami Thirukkoil, 1975) (?).

——, "The Sētupatis of Ramnad" (unpublished dissertation, University of Madurai, 1976).

Seshadri, Padma, and Padma Malini Sundararaghavan, *It Happened along the Kaveri: A Journey through Space and Time* (New Delhi: Niyogi Books, 2012).

Seshan, Radhika, "From Folk Culture to Court Culture: The *Kuravanji* in the Tanjore Court," *Proceedings of the Indian History Congress* 65 (2004).

——, *Trade and Politics on the Coromandel Coast: Seventeenth and Early Eighteenth Centuries* (Delhi: Primus Books, 2012).

Sethuraman, G., *Ramesvaram Temple (History, Art and Architecture)* (Madurai: J.J. Publications, 1998).

Sewell, Robert, *A Forgotten Empire (Vijayanagar): A Contribution to the History of India* (London, 1900; reprint New Delhi: Asian Educational Services, 1980).

Shastry, B.S., "The Portuguese and Immadi Sadashiva Raya of Swadi (Sonda), 1745-1764," *South Indian History Congress: Proceedings of Fifth Annual Conference* (Tirupati: South Indian History Congress, 1987).

——, *Goa-Kanara Portuguese Relations 1498-1763*, ed. Charles J. Borges (Xavier Centre of Historical Research Studies Series 8) (New Delhi: Concept Publishing Company, 2000).

Sheik Ali, B., "Factors Responsible for Haidar's Conquest of Bidanur," in G.S. Dikshit (ed.), *Studies in Keladi History (Seminar Papers)* (Bangalore: Mythic Society, 1981).

Shreedhara Naik, B., "European Trade and Politics in Medieval South Canara," *Proceedings of the Indian History Congress* 69 (2008).

Shrivastavya, Vidayanand Swami, "Are Maratha-Rajput Marriages Morganatic?," in Usha Sharma (ed.), *Marriage in Indian Society: From Tradition to Modernity*, 2 vols (New Delhi: Mittal Publications, 2005; article first published in 1952).

Shulman, David, "On South Indian Bandits and Kings," *The Indian Economic and Social History Review* 17, 3 (1980).

——, *The King and the Clown in South Indian Myth and Poetry* (Princeton: Princeton University Press, 1985).

Shulman, David, and Velcheru Narayana Rao, "Marriage-Broker for the God: The Tanjavur Nāyakas and the Maṉṉārkuṭi Temple," in Hans Bakker (ed.), *The Sacred Centre as the Focus of Political Interest* (Groningen Oriental Studies VI) (Groningen: Egbert Forsten, 1992).

Shulman, David, and Sanjay Subrahmanyam, "Prince of Poets and Ports: Cītakkāti, the Maraikkāyars and Ramnad, ca. 1690-1710," in Anna Libera Dallapiccola and Stephanie Zingel-Avé Lallement (eds), *Islam and Indian Regions*, vol. 1 (Beiträge zur Südasienforschung, Südasien-Institut, Universität Heidelberg 145) (Stuttgart: Franz Steiner Verlag, 1993).

Silva, Severine, "The Nayaks of Soonda," *The Quarterly Journal of the Mythic Society* LXV, 2 (1974).

Simmons, Caleb, "The Goddess and Vaiṣṇavism in Search for Regional Supremacy: Woḍeyar Devotional Traditions during the Reign of Rāja Woḍeyar (1578-1617 CE)," *Indian History* 1 (2014).

——, "The Goddess and the King: Cāmuṇḍēśvari and the Fashioning of the Woḍeyar Court of Mysore" (unpublished dissertation, University of Florida, 2014).

——, *Devotional Sovereignty: Kingship and Religion in India* (New York: Oxford University Press, 2020).

Singh, Tejpal, and Sanjib Kumar Singh, *Ecstasy of Classical Art: Indian Bronze: National Museum Collection* (New Delhi: National Museum, 2016).

Sinopoli, Carla M., "From the Lion Throne: Political and Social Dynamics of the Vijayanagara Empire," *Journal of the Economic and Social History of the Orient* 43, 3 (2000).

Sinopoli, Carla M., and Kathleen D. Morrison, "Dimensions of Imperial Control: The Vijayanagara Capital," *American Anthropologist* (New Series) 97, 1 (1995).

Sircar, D.C., *Indian Epigraphical Glossary* (Delhi/Varanasi/Patna: Motilal Banarsidass, 1966).

Sistla, Srinivas, "Allegory in Telugu Poetry during the Time of Krishnadevaraya," in Anila Verghese (ed.), *Krishnadevaraya and His Times* (Mumbai: K R Cama Oriental Institute, 2013).

Siva Ganesha Murthy, R.S., "Sanskrit Literature under Keḷadi Rule," in G.S. Dikshit (ed.), *Studies in Keladi History (Seminar Papers)* (Bangalore: Mythic Society, 1981).

Sivapriyananda, Swami, and Gajendra Singh Auwa, *Mysore Royal Dasara* (New Delhi: Abhinav Publications, 1995).

Sivaramamurti, Calambur, *Vijayanagara Paintings* (New Delhi: Ministry of Information and Broadcasting, 1985).

Sohoni, Pushkar, "The Hunt for a Location: Narratives on the Foundation of Cities in South and Southeast Asia," *Asian Ethnology* 77, 1-2 (2018).

Somasundara Rao, C., "The Loyalty of the Nāyaks of Tanjore to the Vijayanagara Empire," in A.V. Narasimha Murthy and K.V. Ramesh (eds), *Giridharaśrī: Essays on Indology (Dr. G.S. Dikshit Felicitation Volume)* (Delhi: Agam Kala Prakashan, 1987).

Somasundra Desikar, S., "Tiruvēṅkaṭanātha of Mātai," *Journal of Indian History* XVI, 2 (1937).

——, "Venkatesa, Viceroy of Rangakrishna Muttuvirappa III," *Journal of Indian History* XVI, 3 (1937).

——, "Viceroys of the Nayaks of Madura," *Journal of Indian History* XVII, 2 (1938).

Soneji, Davesh, "Living History, Performing Memory: Devadāsī Women in Telugu-Speaking South India," *Dance Research Journal* 36, 2 (2004).

Souza, Teotonio R. de, *Medieval Goa: A Socio-Economic History* (New Delhi: Concept Publishing Company, 1979).

Spate, O.H.K., and A.T.A. Learmonth, *India and Pakistan: A General and Regional Geography* (3rd edition, Suffolk: Methuen & Co, 1967).

Sri Sri Sri Raja Saheb, "The Origin of Vizayanagar in Kalinga," *Deccan History Conference (First Session)* (Hyderabad, 1945).

Sridhara Babu, D., "Kingship: State and Religion in South India According to South Indian Historical Biographies of Kings (Madhurāvijaya, Acyutarāyābhyudaya and Vemabhūpālacarita)" (unpublished dissertation, Georg-August-Universität Göttingen, 1975).

Srikantaya, S., *Founders of Vijayanagara* (Bangalore: Mythic Society, 1938).

——, "Channabasava Nāyaka (a Review)," *The Quarterly Journal of the Mythic Society* XLII, 4 (1952).

Srikantha Sastri, S., "Deva Raya II," *The Indian Antiquary: A Journal of Oriental Research* LVII (1928).

——, "Development of Sanskrit Literature under Vijayanagara," in S. Krishnaswami Aiyangar *et al.* (eds), *Vijayanagara Sexcentenary Commemoration Volume* (Dharwar: Vijayanagara Empire Sexcentenary Association, 1936), reprinted as *Vijayanagara: History and Legacy* (New Delhi: Aryan Books International, 2000).

Srinivasachari, C.S., *Ananda Ranga Pillai: The "Pepys" of French India* (Madras; P. Varadachary & Co., 1940; reprint New Delhi/Madras: Asian Educational Services, 1991).

——, *A History of Gingee and Its Rulers* (Annamalainagar: Annamalai University, 1943).

——, "The Southern Poligars and Their Place in the Political System," in D.R. Bhandarkar *et al.* (eds), *B. C. Law Volume*, pt. I (Calcutta: The Indian Research Institute, 1945).

Srinivasachariar, C.S., "Muslim Adventurers in the Kingdoms of Tanjore and Madura," in S.M. Katre and P.K. Gode (eds), *A Volume of Indian and Iranian Studies: Presented to Sir E. Denison Ross ...* (Bombay: Karnatak Publishing House, 1939).

Srinivasan, C.K., *Maratha Rule in the Carnatic* (Annamalainagar: Annamalai University, 1944).

Srinivasan, C.R., "Some Interesting Aspects of the Maratha Rule as Gleaned from the Tamil Copper-Plates of the Thanjavur Marathas," *Journal of the Epigraphical Society of India [Bharatiya Purabhilekha Patrika]* XI (1984).

Srinivasan, V., "Disputed Succession after Achyutharaya," *The Quarterly Journal of the Mythic Society* LXIII, 1-4 (1972).

Stein, Burton, "Agrarian Integration in South India," in Robert Eric Frykenberg (ed.), *Land Control and Social Structure in Indian History* (Madison: University of Wisconsin Press, 1969).

——, "Circulation and the Historical Geography of Tamil Country," *The Journal of Asian Studies* XXXVII, 1 (1977).

——, *Peasant State and Society in Medieval South India* (New Delhi: Oxford University Press, 1980).

——, *Vijayanagara* (The New Cambridge History of India I, 2) (Cambridge: Cambridge University Press, 1989).

——, *A History of India* (Oxford: Blackwell Publishers, 1998).

Stoker, Valerie, *Polemics and Patronage in the City of Victory: Vyāsatīrtha, Hindu Sectarianism, and the Sixteenth-Century Vijayanagara Court* (South Asia across the Disciplines) (Oakland: University of California Press, 2016).

Stolte, Carolien, "Onbekend en onbemind: Over de 'anonimiteit' van lokale medewerkers in zeventiende-eeuws India," in Lodewijk Wagenaar (ed.), *Aan de overkant: Ontmoetingen in dienst van de VOC en WIC (1600-1800)* (Leiden: Sidestone Press, 2015).

Stuart, A.J., *Manual of the Tinnevelly District in the Presidency of Madras* (Madras: Government Press, 1879; reprint Chennai: Tamilnadu Archives, 1998).

Subbarayalu, Y., "Administrative Divisions of the Vijayanagara State," in P. Shanmugam and Srinivasan Srinivasan (eds), *Recent Advances in Vijayanagara Studies* (Chennai: New Era Publications, 2006).

——, *South India under the Cholas* (New Delhi: Oxford University Press, 2012).

Subhadra, B.S., "Art and Architecture of the Keḷadi Nāyakas" (unpublished dissertation, Karnatak University, 1991).

——, "Impact of Indo-Islamic Art on Keladi Architecture," *Proceedings of the Indian History Congress* 59 (1998).

Subrahmaniam, N., "The Question of Succession to the Throne in the History of Tamilnad," *Proceedings of the Indian History Congress* 37 (1976).

Subrahmanian, N., *Tamilian Historiography* (Madurai: Ennes Publications, 1988).

Subrahmanyam, Sanjay, "Aspects of State Formation in South India and Southeast Asia, 1500-1650," *The Indian Economic and Social History Review* 23, 4 (1986).

——, "The Portuguese, the Port of Basrur, and the Rice Trade, 1600-50," in idem (ed.), *Merchants, Markets and the State in Early Modern India* (Delhi: Oxford University Press, 1990).

——, *The Political Economy of Commerce: Southern India 1500-1650* (Cambridge: Cambridge University Press, 1990).

——, *Improvising Empire: Portuguese Trade and Settlement in the Bay of Bengal 1500-1700* (Delhi: Oxford University Press, 1990).

——, "The Politics of Fiscal Decline: A Reconsideration of Maratha Tanjavur, 1676-1799," *The Indian Economic and Social History Review* 32, 2 (1995).

——, "Agreeing to Disagree: Burton Stein on Vijayanagara," *South Asia Research* 17, 2 (1997).

——, "Reflections on State-Making and History-Making in South India," *Journal of the Economic and Social History of the Orient* XLI, 3 (1998).

——, "Recovering Babel: Polyglot Histories from the Eighteenth-Century Tamil Country," in Daud Ali (ed.), *Invoking the Past: The Uses of History in South Asia* (New Delhi: Oxford University Press, 1999).

——, *Penumbral Visions: Making Polities in Early Modern South India* (New Delhi: Oxford University Press, 2001).

——, *Explorations in Connected History: From the Tagus to the Ganges* (New Delhi: Oxford University Press, 2005).

——, "Forcing the Doors of Heathendom: Ethnography, Violence, and the Dutch East India Company," in Charles H. Parker and Jerry H. Bentley (eds), *Between the Middle Ages and Modernity: Individual and Community in the Early Modern World* (Lanham/Plymouth: Rowman & Littlefield Publishers, 2007).

——, *Courtly Encounters: Translating Courtliness and Violence in Early Modern Eurasia* (Cambridge (MA)/London: Harvard University Press, 2012).

——, *Is "Indian Civilization" a Myth? Fictions and Histories* (Ranikhet: Permanent Black, 2013).

——, *Europe's India: Words, People, Empires, 1500–1800* (Cambridge (MA)/London: Harvard University Press, 2017).

Subrahmanyam, Sanjay, and C.A. Bayly, "Portfolio Capitalists and the Political Economy of Early Modern India," *The Indian Economic and Social History Review* 25, 4 (1988).

Subrahmanyam, Sanjay, and David Shulman, "The Men Who Would Be King? The Politics of Expansion in Early Seventeenth-Century Northern Tamilnadu," *Modern Asian Studies* 24, 2 (1990).

Subrahmanyam, Velcheti, "A Pleasing Historical," *The Hindu* (24 Mar. 2017).

Subramanian, K.R., *The Maratha Rajas of Tanjore* (Madras, 1928; reprint New Delhi: Asian Educational Services, 1995).

Subramanian, Lakshmi, *From the Tanjore Court to the Madras Music Academy: A Social History of Music in South India* (New Delhi: Oxford University Press, 2006).

Sudyka, Lidia, "A War Expedition or a Pilgrimage? Acyutarāya's Southern Campaign as Depicted in the *Acyutarāyābhyudaya*," in idem and Anna Nitecka (eds), *Cracow Indological Studies*, vol. XV, *History and Society as Depicted in Indian Literature and Art*, pt. II, *ŚRĀVYA: Poetry & Prose* (Cracow: Jagiellonian University, Institute of Oriental Studies, 2013).

Suebsantiwongse, Saran, "Dating and Locating the *Sāmrājyalakṣmīpīṭhikā*: A Hybrid Manual on Kingship and Tantric Practices," *Thai Prajñā: International Journal of Indology and Culture* I (2017).

Sundara, A., *The Keḷadi Nāyakas: Architecture and Art*, vol. V, pt. 2, *The Shivappa Nayaka Palace in Shimoga* (Centenary Publication 7, Karnataka Cultural Heritage Series: Art) (Mysore: Directorate of Archaeology and Museums, Government of Karnataka, 1987).

Surendra Rao, B., "State Formation in Mysore: The Wodeyars," in R. Champakalakshmy, Kesavan Veluthat, and T.R. Venugopalan (eds), *State and Society in Pre-Modern South India* (Thrissur: Cosmobooks, 2002).

Suresh, S., *The Tanjavur Marathas: Art, Architecture and Culture* (New Delhi: Intach/Aryan Books International, 2015).

Suryanarain Row, B., *A History of Vijayanagar: The Never to Be Forgotten Empire* (Madras: Addison & Co., 1905; reprint New Delhi: Asian Educational Services, 1993).

Swaminathan, K.D., *The Nāyakas of Ikkēri* (Madras: P. Varadachary & Co., 1957).

"T S Nagabharana Directed Keladi Chennamma Shooting Visit," *World News* (26 Aug. 2012).

Talbot, Cynthia, "Inscribing the Other, Inscribing the Self: Hindu-Muslim Identities in Pre-Colonial India," *Comparative Studies in Society and History* 37, 4 (1995).

——, "The Story of Prataparudra: Hindu Historiography on the Deccan Frontier," in David Gilmartin and Bruce B. Lawrence (eds), *Beyond Turk and Hindu: Rethinking Religious Identities in Islamic South Asia* (Gainesville: University Press of Florida, 2000).

——, *Precolonial India in Practice: Society, Region, and Identity in Medieval Andhra* (New Delhi: Oxford University Press, 2001).

Taylor, William (ed.), *Examination and Analysis of the Mackenzie Manuscripts Deposited in the Madras College Library* (Calcutta, 1838).

——, *Catalogue Raisonné[e] of Oriental Manuscripts in the Library of the (Late) College, Fort Saint George, Now in Charge of the Board of Examiners / in the Government Library*, 3 vols (Madras, 1857-62).

Terpstra, Heert, *De vestiging van de Nederlanders aan de kust van Koromandel* (Groningen: De Waal, 1911).

——, *De Nederlanders in Voor-Indië* (Patria vaderlandsche cultuurgeschiedenis in monografieën XXXIX) (Amsterdam: P.N. van Kampen & Zoon N.V., 1947).

Thapar, Romila, "Origin Myths and the Early Indian Historical Tradition," in idem (ed.), *Ancient Indian Social History: Some Interpretations* (London: Sangam Books, 1978).

Thiruvenkatachari, S., *The Setupatis of Ramnad* (Karaikudi: Dr. Alagappa Chettiar Training College, 1959).

Thite, Ganesh, "Sāmrājyalakṣmīpīṭhikā of Ākāśabhairavakalpa: A Tāntric Encyclopaedia of Magicoreligion," *Sambodhi* 7, 1-4 (1978-9).

Thurston, Edgar, *Castes and Tribes of Southern India*, 7 vols (Madras: Government Press, 1909).

Tobert, Natalie, *Anegondi: Architectural Ethnography of a Royal Village* (Vijayanagara Research Project Monograph Series 7) (New Delhi: Manohar/American Institute of Indian Studies, 2000).

Tracy, J.E., "On the Coins of the Sethupatis [Sethupati Coins]," *The Madras Journal of Literature and Science* 32 (1889-94).

Tracy, James D., "Asian Despotism? Mughal Government as Seen from the Dutch East India Company Factory in Surat," *Journal of Early Modern History* 3, 3 (1999).

Trautmann, Thomas R., "Length of Generation and Reign in Ancient India," *Journal of the American Oriental Society* 89, 3 (1969).

Truschke, Audrey, *The Language of History: Sanskrit Narratives of Indo-Muslim Rule* (New York: Columbia University Press, 2021).

Tschacher, Torsten, "Challenging Orders: *Ṭarīqas* and Muslim Society in Southeastern India and Laṅkā, ca. 1400–1950," in R. Michael Feener and Anne M. Blackburn (eds), *Buddhist and Islamic Orders in Southern Asia: Comparative Perspectives* (Honolulu: University of Hawai'i Press, 2019).

Utz, Axel, "Cultural Exchange, Imperialist Violence, and Pious Missions: Local Perspectives from Tanjavur and Lenape Country, 1720-1760" (unpublished dissertation, Pennsylvania State University, 2011).

Vadivelu, A., *The Aristocracy of Southern India*, 2 vols (Madras: Vest and Co., 1903).

Vanamamalai Pillai, N., *Temples of the Setu and Rameswaram* (Delhi: Kunj Publishing House, 1982; first published 1929).

Vasantha Madhava, K.G., "The Mughals and the Keladi Nayakas," *Proceedings of the Indian History Congress* 37 (1976).

——, "The Dutch in Coastal Karnataka 1602-1763," *The Quarterly Journal of the Mythic Society* LXXIII, 3-4 (1982).

Veerendra, P.M., "Royal Farmhouse of Keladi Rulers is a Shambles," *The Hindu* (16 Dec. 2019).

Veeresha, K., "Saluva-Timmarasu the Crafty Prime-Minister of Krsnadeva Raya," *Itihas: Journal of the Andhra Pradesh State Archives & Research Institute* XXI, 1-2 (1995).

Veluthat, Kesavan, *The Political Structure of Early Medieval South India* (2nd edition, Hyderabad: Orient BlackSwan, 2012).

Venkasami Row, T., *A Manual of the District of Tanjore, in the Madras Presidency* (Madras: Lawrence Asylum Press, 1883).

Venkata Ramanayya, N., *Kampili and Vijayanagara* (Madras: Christian Literature Society's Press, 1929).

——, *Vijayanagara: Origin of the City and the Empire* (Madras: University of Madras, 1933; reprint New Delhi/Chennai: Asian Educational Services, 2007).

——, *Studies in the History of the Third Dynasty of Vijayanagara* (Madras: University of Madras, 1935).

Venkataramanayya, N., and M. Somasekhara Sarma, "The Kākatīyas of Warangal," in G. Yazdani (ed.), *The Early History of the Deccan*, pts VII-XI (London: Oxford University Press, 1960).

Venkata Rao, N., *The Southern School in Telugu Literature* (Madras: University of Madras, 1978).

Venkatasubramanian, T.K., *Music as History in Tamilnadu* (Delhi: Primus Books, 2010).

Venkatesam, N.K., "Govinda Deekshita: The Minister of the Tanjore Nayak Kings," *The Quarterly Journal of the Andhra Historical Research Society* II, 3-4 (1928).

Venkatesan, Archana, and Crispin Branfoot, *In Andal's Garden: Art, Ornament and Devotion in Srivilliputtur* (Mumbai: Marg Publications, 2015).

Venkatesha, "The Kumbhakonam Plates of Vijayaraghava, Saka 1578," *Journal of the Epigraphical Society of India [Bharatiya Purabhilekha Patrika]* XI (1984).

Verghese, Anila, "Court Attire of Vijayanagara (from a Study of Monuments)," *The Quarterly Journal of the Mythic Society* LXXXII, 1-2 (1991).

——, *Religious Traditions at Vijayanagara: As Revealed through Its Monuments* (Vijayanagara Research Project Monograph Series 4) (New Delhi: Manohar/American Institute of Indian Studies, 1995).

——, *Archaeology, Art and Religion: New Perspectives on Vijayanagara* (New Delhi: Oxford University Press, 2000).

——, "Deities, Cults and Kings at Vijayanagara," *World Archaeology* 36, 3 (2004).

——, "Aghoreśvara Temple at Ikkeri: A Synthesis of Architectural Styles," *Journal of the Asiatic Society of Mumbai* 81 (2007).

——, "Introduction," in idem and Anna Libera Dallapiccola (eds), *South India under Vijayanagara: Art and Archaeology* (New Delhi: Oxford University Press, 2011).

——, "The Sacred Topography of Hampi-Vijayanagara," in idem and Anna Libera Dallapiccola (eds), *South India under Vijayanagara: Art and Archaeology* (New Delhi: Oxford University Press, 2011).

——, "King and Courtly Life as Depicted in the Murals in Ramalinga Vilasam, Ramanathapuram," in idem and Anna Libera Dallapiccola (eds), *Art, Icon and Architecture in South Asia: Essays in Honour of Devangana Desai*, 2 vols (New Delhi: Aryan Books International, 2015).

Vijailakshmi, Usha R., "Change and Transformation in the Lives of Thanjavur Maratha Queens and the Doctrine of Lapse (1856-1862)," *Journal of Indian History and Culture* 24 (2018).

Vijayaraghavacharya, V. (ed.), *Epigraphical Glossary on Inscriptions* (Tirumalai-Tirupati Devasthanam Epigraphical Series VI, pt. II) (Madras, 1938; reprint Delhi: Sri Satguru Publications, 1984 [Sri Garib Dass Oriental Series 23]).

Vink, Markus, "Encounters on the Opposite Coast: Cross-Cultural Contacts between the Dutch East India Company and the Nayaka State of Madurai in the Seventeenth Century" (unpublished dissertation, University of Minnesota, 1999); revised version published as *Encounters on the Opposite Coast: The Dutch East India Company and the Nayaka State of Madurai in the Seventeenth Century* (Leiden: Brill, 2015).

Vriddhagirisan, V., *The Nayaks of Tanjore* (Annamalainagar: Annamalai University, 1942; reprint New Delhi: Asian Educational Services, 1995).

Wagenaar, Lodewijk, *Galle, VOC-vestiging in Ceylon: Beschrijving van een koloniale samenleving aan de vooravond van de Singalese opstand tegen het Nederlandse gezag, 1760* (Amsterdam: De Bataafsche Leeuw, 1994).

Waghorne, Joanne Punzo, *The Raja's Magic Clothes: Re-visioning Kingship and Divinity in England's India* (University Park: Pennsylvania State University Press, 1994).

Wagoner, Phillip B., "'Sultan among Hindu Kings': Dress, Titles, and the Islamicization of Hindu Culture at Vijayanagara," *The Journal of Asian Studies* 55, 4 (1996).

——, "Fortuitous Convergences and Essential Ambiguities: Transcultural Political Elites in the Medieval Deccan," *International Journal of Hindu Studies* 3, 3 (1999).

——, "Harihara, Bukka, and the Sultan: The Delhi Sultanate in the Political Imagination of Vijayanagara," in David Gilmartin and Bruce B. Lawrence (eds), *Beyond Turk and Hindu: Rethinking Religious Identities in Islamic South Asia* (Gainesville: University Press of Florida, 2000).

——, "From Manuscript to Archive to Print: The Mackenzie Collection and Later Telugu Literary Historiography," in Thomas R. Trautman (ed.), *The Madras School of Orientalism: Producing Knowledge in Colonial South India* (Oxford: Oxford University Press, 2009).

——, "Retrieving the Chalukyan Past: The Stepped Tank in the Royal Centre," in Anila Verghese and Anna Libera Dallapiccola (eds), *South India under Vijayanagara: Art and Archaeology* (New Delhi: Oxford University Press, 2011).

Walaardt, Tycho, "Peper of Portugezen: Een geschiedenis van de Hollandse factorij Vengurla in de nabijheid van Goa in de zeventiende eeuw" (unpublished MA thesis, Leiden University, 1999).

Wibulsilp, Pimmanus, "Nawabi Karnatak: Muhammad Ali Khan in the Making of a Mughal Successor State in Pre-Colonial South India, 1749-1795" (unpublished dissertation, Leiden University, 2019).

Wilks, Mark, *Historical Sketches of the South of India in an Attempt to Trace the History of Mysore from the Origin of the Hindu Government of that State, to the Extinction of the Mohammedan Dynasty in 1799*, 2 vols, ed. Murray Hammick (n.p., 1810; reprint New Delhi/Madras: Asian Educational Services, 1989).

Wilson, H.H., *The Mackenzie Collection: A Descriptive Catalogue of the Oriental Manuscripts and Other Articles Illustrative of the Literature, History, Statistics and Antiquities of the South of India; Collected by the Late Lieut. Col. Colin Mackenzie* (Calcutta, 1828; 2nd edition, Madras, 1882).

Winius, George, and Markus Vink, *The Merchant-Warrior Pacified: The VOC (The Dutch East India Co.) and Its Changing Political Economy in India* (Delhi: Oxford University Press, 1991).

Wink, André, *Land and Sovereignty in India: Agrarian Society and Politics under the Eighteenth-Century Maratha Svarājya* (University of Cambridge Oriental Publications 36) (Cambridge: Cambridge University Press, 1986).

Yadav, Smita Shirole, and Padma Raghavan, *The Royal Art of Tanjore Paintings* (Mumbai: English Edition, 2010).

Yule, Henry, and A.C. Burnell, *Hobson-Jobson: The Anglo-Indian Dictionary* (London: John Murray, 1886).

Works Not Referred to (selection)

Anthonisz, R.G., *Digest of Resolutions of the Dutch Political Council, Colombo 1644 – 1796*, ed. K.D. Paranavitana (Colombo: The Department of National Archives, 2012).

Bes, Lennart, "Hundreds of Rosetta Stones and Other Patient Papers: The Dutch Records at the Tamil Nadu Archives," *Itinerario: European Journal of Overseas History* XXVII, 1 (2003).

——, "Provisional Inventory of the Archives of the VOC Establishments Malabar, Coromandel, Surat and Bengal and Legal Successors (so-called 'Dutch Records') (1647-) 1664-1825 (-1852)" (unpublished inventory, The Hague: Nationaal Archief, 2003).

——, *Dutch Sources on South Asia c. 1600-1825*, vol. 2, *Archival Guide to Repositories in The Netherlands Other than the National Archives* (New Delhi: Manohar, 2007).

——, "Records in a Rival's Repository: Archives of the Dutch East India Company and Related Materials in the India Office Records (British Library), London (and the National Archives of Malaysia, Kuala Lumpur)," *Itinerario: International Journal on the History of European Expansion and Global Interaction* XXXI, 3 (2007).

Blagden, C.O., *Catalogue of Manuscripts in European Languages Belonging to the Library of the India Office*, vol. I, pt. I, *The Mackenzie Collections: The 1822 Collection & the Private Collection* (Oxford: Oxford University Press, 1916).

Heyligers, A.J.M., *Press List of Ancient Dutch Records, from 1657 to 1825* (Madras, c. 1900?).

Hill, S.C., *Catalogue of Manuscripts in European Languages Belonging to the Library of the India Office*, vol. II, pt. I, *The Orme Collection* (Oxford: Oxford University Press, 1916).

Jurriaanse, M.W., *Catalogue of the Archives of the Dutch Central Government of Coastal Ceylon 1640-1796* (Colombo: Ceylon Government Press, 1943).

Mangkudilaga, M., "Inventaris Arsip Buitenland" (unpublished inventory, Jakarta: Arsip Nasional Republik Indonesia, 1977).

Meilink-Roelofsz, M.A.P., R. Raben, and H. Spijkerman, *De archieven van de Verenigde Oostindische Compagnie / The Archives of the Dutch East India Company (1602-1795)* (The Hague: Algemeen Rijksarchief/Sdu Uitgeverij, 1992).

Meilink-Roelofsz, M.A.P., M. de Lannoy, and J.H. de Vries, *Inventaris van het archief van de Hoge Regering van Batavia, 1602-1827* (unpublished inventory, The Hague: Nationaal Archief, 2002).

Murphy, Wayne (ed.), *India & Bangladesh: Road Atlas* (Footscray: Lonely Planet Publications, 2001).

Rao, Madhumita Mund (ed.), *India: Road Atlas* (New Delhi: Eicher Goodearth Limited, 2006).

Websites (selection, last consulted in December 2021)

* gtb.ivdnt.org
* iisg.amsterdam/en/research/projects/hpw/calculate.php
* resources.huygens.knaw.nl
* serfojimemorialhall.com
* southindianpaintings.art
* tiruchendur.org/dutch_gallery.htm
* www.google.com/maps
* www.nationaalarchief.nl
* www.royalark.net/India/India.htm
* www.sejarah-nusantara.anri.go.id
* www.tanap.net
* www.tharangampadi.dk
* www.whatisindia.com/inscriptions.html

Index

Footnotes are not separately marked; references to page numbers may include footnotes on those pages. Entries with personal names do not necessarily refer to one single person but may cover various people with similar names. Europeans are found under their surname (without prefixes).

Colonial and Global History through Dutch Sources

The series *Colonial and Global History through Dutch Sources* stimulates historical research on the basis of Dutch archival and primary sources. These sources are imperative for understanding Dutch overseas history from the time of the earliest explorations to the latest phase of decolonization. At the same time, Dutch sources provide a fascinating contemporary window on the regional histories of Africa, the Americas and Asia and the various ways in which these areas were linked through global networks of migration, trade and empire. Hence the series effectively combines the use of Dutch sources with materials of other European powers and/or that of their local African, American and Asian counterparts. The result is a peer-refereed series of dissertations, monographs, edited volumes and edited translations of key texts that not only builds on the rich Dutch colonial archive but also integrates the Dutch case into a much wider global framework of comparisons and connections.

Editor-in-Chief
Jos Gommans (Leiden University)

Editors
Cátia Antunes (Leiden University)
Lennart Bes (Leiden University)
Jan-Bart Gewald (Leiden University)
Michiel van Groesen (Leiden University)
Gert Oostindie (KITLV: Royal Netherlands Institute of Southeast Asian and Caribbean Studies)

Advisory Board
Tonio Andrade (Emory University)
Gita Dharampal-Frick (Heidelberg University)
Chris Ebert (Brooklyn College, New York)
Jorge Flores (European University Institute, Florence)
Anne McGinness (John Carroll University)
Filipa Ribeiro da Silva (IISG: International Institute of Social History, Amsterdam)
Marcus Vink (State University of New York at Fredonia)

Other titles in this series:

Manjusha Kuruppath, *Staging Asia. The Dutch East India Company and the Amsterdam Theatre*, 2016

Mikko Toivanen, *The Travels of Pieter Albert Bik. Writings from the Dutch Colonial World of the Early Nineteenth Century*, 2017

Michael J. Douma, *The Colonization of Freed African Americans in Suriname. Archival Sources relating to the U.S.-Dutch Negotiations, 1860-1866*, 2019

Erik Odegard, *The Company Fortress. Military Engineering and the Dutch East India Company in South Asia, 1638-1795*, 2020

23W25204/ T1/ 9789087283711